AA002021

Fifth Workshop on NLP for Similar Languages, Varieties and Dialects (VarDial 2018)

Santa Fe, New Mexico, USA
20 August 2018

ISBN: 978-1-5108-6916-5

Printed from e-media with permission by:

Curran Associates, Inc.
57 Morehouse Lane
Red Hook, NY 12571

Some format issues inherent in the e-media version may also appear in this print version.

Copyright© (2018) by the Association for Computational Linguistics
All rights reserved.

Printed by Curran Associates, Inc. (2018)

For permission requests, please contact the Association for Computational Linguistics
at the address below.

Association for Computational Linguistics
209 N. Eighth Street
Stroudsburg, Pennsylvania 18360

Phone: 1-570-476-8006
Fax: 1-570-476-0860

acl@aclweb.org

Additional copies of this publication are available from:

Curran Associates, Inc.
57 Morehouse Lane
Red Hook, NY 12571 USA
Phone: 845-758-0400
Fax: 845-758-2633
Email: curran@proceedings.com
Web: www.proceedings.com

COLING 2018

**The 27th International Conference
on Computational Linguistics**

**Proceedings of the Fifth Workshop
on NLP for Similar Languages, Varieties and Dialects
(VarDial'2018)**

August 20, 2018
Santa Fe, New Mexico, USA

Copyright of each paper stays with the respective authors (or their employers).

Introduction

VarDial is now a well-established workshop series that has been attracting researchers working on a wide range of topics related to (diatopic) linguistic variation. VarDial is currently in its 5th edition and since its very first edition it has been co-located with international NLP conferences such as COLING, EACL, and RANLP. This year, VarDial is co-located with COLING in Santa Fe, United States.

In five years we have seen VarDial become the main venue dedicated to research on similar languages, varieties, and dialects within the NLP community and 2018 was a particularly important year for VarDial. For the first time we organized five shared tasks, an all-time record, as part of the second VarDial Evaluation Campaign. The tasks organized this year were: Arabic Dialect Identification (ADI), German Dialect Identification (GDI), Morphosyntactic Tagging of Tweets (MTT), Discriminating between Dutch and Flemish in Subtitles (DSF) and Indo-Aryan Language Identification (ILI). The second edition of the campaign received a very positive response from the community with a total of 54 teams subscribed to participate in the five shared tasks, another all-time record for VarDial. 24 teams submitted official runs to one or more of the five shared tasks, and 22 system description papers appear in this volume along with a shared task report by the task organizers.

We further received 15 regular VarDial workshop papers, and we selected 9 of them to be presented at the workshop. The papers that appear in this volume reflect the wide range of interests related to language variation. This volume includes papers applying NLP methods to perform text normalization, identify false friends in closely-related languages, measure language distance between historical varieties of a pluricentric language, and translate between language varieties.

We take the opportunity to thank the VarDial program committee for their thorough reviews. We further thank the VarDial Evaluation Campaign shared task organizers and the participants, Finally, we also thank participants who presented regular research papers, for the valuable feedback and discussions.

The organizers: Marcos Zampieri, Preslav Nakov, Nikola Ljubešić, Jörg Tiedemann, Shervin Malmasi, and Ahmed Ali

Workshop Organisers

Marcos Zampieri (University of Wolverhampton, United Kingdom)
Preslav Nakov (Qatar Computing Research Institute, HBKU, Qatar)
Nikola Ljubešić (Jožef Stefan Institute, Slovenia, and University of Zagreb, Croatia)
Jörg Tiedemann (University of Helsinki, Finland)
Shervin Malmasi (Harvard Medical School, USA)
Ahmed Ali (Qatar Computing Research Institute, HBKU, Qatar)

VarDial Evaluation Campaign Organisers

(ADI) Arabic Dialect Identification

Ahmed Ali (Qatar Computing Research Institute, HBKU, Qatar)
Preslav Nakov (Qatar Computing Research Institute, HBKU, Qatar)
Suwon Shon (Massachusetts Institute of Technology, United States)
James Glass (Massachusetts Institute of Technology, United States)

(GDI) German Dialect Identification

Yves Scherrer (University of Helsinki, Finland)
Tanja Samardžić (University of Zurich, Switzerland)

(MTT) Morphosyntactic Tagging of Tweets

Nikola Ljubešić (Jožef Stefan Institute, Slovenia and University of Zagreb, Croatia)
Jörg Tiedemann (University of Helsinki, Finland)

(DFS) Discriminating between Dutch and Flemish in Subtitles

Chris van der Lee (Tilburg University, The Netherlands)
Stef Grondelaers (Radboud University, The Netherlands)
Nelleke Oostdijk (Radboud University, The Netherlands)
Dirk Speelman (University of Leuven, Belgium)
Antal van den Bosch (Meertens Institute and Radboud University, The Netherlands)

(ILI) Indo-Aryan Language Identification

Ritesh Kumar (Bhim Rao Ambedkar University, India)
Bornini Lahiri (Jadavpur University, India)
Mayank Jain (Jawaharlal Nehru University, India)

General Organization

Marcos Zampieri (University of Wolverhampton, United Kingdom)
Shervin Malmasi (Harvard Medical School, USA)

Programme Committee

Željko Agić (IT University of Copenhagen, Denmark)

Cesar Aguilar (Pontifical Catholic University of Chile, Chile)
Laura Alonso y Alemany (University of Cordoba, Argentina)
Jorge Baptista (University of Algarve and INESC-ID, Portugal)
Eckhard Bick (University of Southern Denmark, Denmark)
Johannes Bjerva (University of Copenhagen, Denmark)
Francis Bond (Nanyang Technological University, Singapore)
Aoife Cahill (Educational Testing Service, United States)
David Chiang (University of Notre Dame, United States)
Paul Cook (University of New Brunswick, Canada)
Marta Costa-Jussà (Universitat Politècnica de Catalunya, Spain)
Jon Dehdari (Think Big Analytics, United States)
Liviu Dinu (University of Bucharest, Romania)
Stefanie Dipper (Ruhr University Bochum, Germany)
Sascha Diwersy (University of Montpellier, France)
Mark Dras (Macquarie University, Australia)
Tomaž Erjavec (Jožef Stefan Institute, Slovenia)
Mikel L. Forcada (Universitat d'Alacant, Spain)
Pablo Gamallo (University of Santiago de Compostela, Spain)
Binyam Gebrekidan Gebre (Phillips Research, The Netherlands)
Cyril Goutte (National Research Council, Canada)
Nizar Habash (New York University Abu Dhabi, UAE)
Chu-Ren Huang (Hong Kong Polytechnic University, Hong Kong)
Radu Ionescu (University of Bucharest, Romania)
Jeremy Jancsary (Nuance Communications, Austria)
Lung-Hao Lee (National Taiwan Normal University, Taiwan)
John Nerbonne (University of Groningen, Netherlands and University of Freiburg, Germany)
Kemal Oflazer (Carnegie-Mellon University in Qatar, Qatar)
Maciej Ogrodniczuk (IPAN, Polish Academy of Sciences, Poland)
Petya Osenova (Bulgarian Academy of Sciences, Bulgaria)
Santanu Pal (Saarland University, Germany)
Barbara Plank (IT University of Copenhagen, Denmark)
Francisco Rangel (Autoritas Consulting, Spain)
Taraka Rama (University of Oslo, Norway)
Reinhard Rapp (University of Mainz, Germany and University of Aix-Marsaille, France)
Paolo Rosso (Technical University of Valencia, Spain)
Fatiha Sadat (Université du Québec à Montréal (UQAM), Canada)
Tanja Samardžić (University of Zurich, Switzerland)
Felipe Sánchez Martínez (Universitat d'Alacant, Spain)
Kevin Scannell (Saint Louis University, United States)
Yves Scherrer (University of Helsinki, Finland)
Serge Sharoff (University of Leeds, United Kingdom)
Kiril Simov (Bulgarian Academy of Sciences, Bulgaria)
Milena Slavcheva (Bulgarian Academy of Sciences, Bulgaria)
Marco Tadić (University of Zagreb, Croatia)
Liling Tan (Rakuten Institute of Technology, Singapore)
Joel Tetreault (Grammarly, United States)
Francis Tyers (Higher School of Economics, Russia)
Duško Vitas (University of Belgrade, Serbia)
Taro Watanabe (Google Inc., Japan)
Pidong Wang (Machine Zone Inc., United States)

Table of Contents

Conference Program

Monday, August 20, 2018

9:00–9:10   ***Opening***

9:10-9:30   *Language Identification and Morphosyntactic Tagging: The Second VarDial Evaluation Campaign*
Marcos Zampieri, Shervin Malmasi, Preslav Nakov, Ahmed Ali, Suwon Shon, James Glass, Yves Scherrer, Tanja Samardžić, Nikola Ljubešić, Jörg Tiedemann, Chris van der Lee, Stefan Grondelaers, Nelleke Oostdijk, Dirk Speelman, Antal van den Bosch, Ritesh Kumar, Bornini Lahiri and Mayank Jain

9:30–10:00   *Encoder-Decoder Methods for Text Normalization*
Massimo Lusetti, Tatyana Ruzsics, Anne Göhring, Tanja Samardžić and Elisabeth Stark

10:00–10:30   *A High Coverage Method for Automatic False Friends Detection for Spanish and Portuguese*
Santiago Castro, Jairo Bonanata and Aiala Rosá

10:30–11:00   ***Coffee break***

11:00–11:30   *Sub-label dependencies for Neural Morphological Tagging – The Joint Submission of University of Colorado and University of Helsinki for VarDial 2018*
Miikka Silfverberg and Senka Drobac

11:30–12:00   *Part of Speech Tagging in Luyia: A Bantu Macrolanguage*
Kenneth Steimel

12:00–12:30   *Tübingen-Oslo Team at the VarDial 2018 Evaluation Campaign: An Analysis of N-gram Features in Language Variety Identification*
Çağrı Çöltekin, Taraka Rama and Verena Blaschke

12:30–14:00   ***Lunch***

14:00–14:30   *Iterative Language Model Adaptation for Indo-Aryan Language Identification*
Tommi Jauhiainen, Heidi Jauhiainen and Krister Lindén

14:30–15:40   **Invited talk - Timothy Baldwin (University of Melbourne)**

Language and the Shifting Sands of Domain, Space and Time (Invited Talk)
Timothy Baldwin

15:40–15:50   **Closing Remarks**

15:50–16:20   **Coffee break**

16:20–18:00   **Poster Session**

UnibucKernel Reloaded: First Place in Arabic Dialect Identification for the Second Year in a Row
Andrei Butnaru and Radu Tudor Ionescu

Varying image description tasks: spoken versus written descriptions
Emiel van Miltenburg, Ruud Koolen and Emiel Krahmer

Transfer Learning for British Sign Language Modelling
Boris Mocialov, Helen Hastie and Graham Turner

Paraphrastic Variance between European and Brazilian Portuguese
Anabela Barreiro and Cristina Mota

Character Level Convolutional Neural Network for Arabic Dialect Identification
Mohamed Ali

Neural Network Architectures for Arabic Dialect Identification
Elise Michon, Minh Quang Pham, Josep Crego and Jean Senellart

HeLI-based Experiments in Discriminating Between Dutch and Flemish Subtitles
Tommi Jauhiainen, Heidi Jauhiainen and Krister Lindén

Language Identification and Morphosyntactic Tagging:
The Second VarDial Evaluation Campaign

Marcos Zampieri[1], Shervin Malmasi[2], Preslav Nakov[3], Ahmed Ali[3], Suwon Shon[4]
James Glass[4], Yves Scherrer[5], Tanja Samardžić[6], Nikola Ljubešić[7,8], Jörg Tiedemann[5]
Chris van der Lee[9], Stefan Grondelaers[10], Nelleke Oostdijk[10], Dirk Speelman[11]
Antal van den Bosch[10,12], Ritesh Kumar[13], Bornini Lahiri[14], Mayank Jain[15]

[1]University of Wolverhampton, [2]Harvard Medical School
[3]Qatar Computing Research Institute, HBKU, [4]Massachusetts Institute of Technology (MIT)
[5]University of Helsinki, [6]University of Zurich, [7]Jožef Stefan Institute, [8]University of Zagreb
[9]Tilburg University, [10]Radboud University, [11]University of Leuven, [12]Meertens Institute
[13]Bhim Rao Ambedkar University, [14]Jadavpur University, [15]Jawaharlal Nehru University

Abstract

We present the results and the findings of the Second VarDial Evaluation Campaign on Natural Language Processing (NLP) for Similar Languages, Varieties and Dialects. The campaign was organized as part of the fifth edition of the VarDial workshop, collocated with COLING'2018. This year, the campaign included five shared tasks, including two task re-runs – Arabic Dialect Identification (ADI) and German Dialect Identification (GDI) –, and three new tasks – Morphosyntactic Tagging of Tweets (MTT), Discriminating between Dutch and Flemish in Subtitles (DFS), and Indo-Aryan Language Identification (ILI). A total of 24 teams submitted runs across the five shared tasks, and contributed 22 system description papers, which were included in the VarDial workshop proceedings and are referred to in this report.

1 Introduction

The interest in applying Natural Language Processing (NLP) methods to similar languages, varieties, and dialects has been growing in recent years. This is evidenced by the growing number of publications and the organization of well-attended workshops co-located with the major NLP conferences such as LT4CloseLang at EMNLP'2014 and the now well-established VarDial workshop series, which is currently in its fifth edition and has been co-located with conferences such as COLING and EACL.

Since its first edition, shared tasks have been organized as part of VarDial. The Discriminating Between Similar Languages (DSL) shared task (Zampieri et al., 2014) was run continuously from 2014 to 2018. In 2016, the DSL task was split into two sub-tasks: a second iteration of the DSL task and the first iteration of the Arabic Dialect Identification (ADI) shared task (Malmasi et al., 2016). In the following year, the organizers decided to broaden the scope of the workshop and to organize an evaluation campaign with four shared tasks (Zampieri et al., 2017): along with iterations of the ADI and the DSL shared tasks, new tasks were started such as the first German Dialect Identification (GDI) and the shared task on Cross-lingual Dependency Parsing (CLP). This year, we continue with a similar setup, covering five shared tasks as part of the Second VarDial Evaluation Campaign.

The remainder of this paper is organized as follows: Section 2 describes this year's shared tasks, Section 3 presents the teams who participated in each task including references to their system descriptions, Section 4 briefly summarizes the related work on the topics of the campaign and on the previous iterations of the ADI and GDI shared tasks. Sections 5, 6, 7, 8, and 9, present the data, the task setup, and the results for each of the shared tasks. Finally, Section 10 concludes this report and points to possible directions for future work.

This work is licensed under a Creative Commons Attribution 4.0 International License:
`http://creativecommons.org/licenses/by/4.0/`

1

Proceedings of the Fifth Workshop on NLP for Similar Languages, Varieties and Dialects, pages 1–17
Santa Fe, New Mexico, USA, August 20, 2018.

2 Shared Tasks at VarDial 2018

The VarDial Evaluation Campaign 2018 featured five shared tasks including two task re-runs and three new shared tasks. The two task re-runs were the following:

Third Arabic Dialect Identification (ADI): This year's third edition of the ADI task addressed the multi-dialectal challenge in spoken Arabic in the broadcast domain. Previously, we shared acoustic features and lexical word sequences extracted from large-vocabulary speech recognition (LVCSR). This year, we added phonetic features, aiming at enabling the use of both prosodic and phonetic features, which are helpful for distinguishing between different dialects. We have seen many researchers combine acoustic with linguistic features in previous years (Malmasi et al., 2016; Zampieri et al., 2017), and thus we thought it would be interesting to explore the contribution of phonetic features in overall dialect identification systems.

Second German Dialect Identification (GDI): Following a successful first edition of the (Swiss) German Dialect Identification task in 2017, a second iteration of the GDI task has been organized. We provided updated data on the same Swiss German dialect areas as last year (Basel, Bern, Lucerne, Zurich), and added a fifth "surprise dialect", for which no training data was made available. The participants could take part in two sub-tracks: one on the traditional four-way classification (without the surprise dialect), and another one on five-way classification (with the surprise dialect).

Along with the two task re-runs, the VarDial evaluation campaign included three new shared tasks:

Morphosyntactic Tagging of Tweets (MTT): This task focused on morphosyntactic annotation (900+ labels) of non-canonical Twitter varieties for three South-Slavic languages: Slovene, Croatian, and Serbian. Task participants obtained large manually annotated and raw canonical datasets, as well as small manually annotated Twitter datasets. The task allowed participants to exploit the varieties on two dimensions: (*i*) a comparison of canonical vs. non-canonical language, and (*ii*) the overall proximity of the three languages.

Discriminating between Dutch and Flemish in Subtitles (DFS): The task focused on determining whether a text is written in the Netherlandic vs. the Flemish variant of the Dutch language. For this task, participants were provided with a dataset consisting of over 50,000 subtitle phrases. Since there is a lack of automatic classification studies on the Netherlandic and the Flemish Dutch varieties, and no Netherlandic/Flemish corpus of this size existed, we believe the task was a scientifically interesting step towards developing and comparing language variety classification models using subtitles, and thereby analyzing the proximity of the language varieties in a new way. The latter is not only of interest for improving computational linguistics applications, but it also adds to insights in variational linguistics in general.

Indo-Aryan Language Identification (ILI): This task focused on identifying five closely-related languages from the Indo-Aryan language family – Hindi (also known as Khari Boli), Braj Bhasha, Awadhi, Bhojpuri and Magahi. These languages are part of a continuum starting from Western Uttar Pradesh (Hindi and Braj Bhasha) to Eastern Uttar Pradesh (Awadhi and Bhojpuri) and the neighbouring Eastern state of Bihar (Bhojpuri and Magahi). For this task, the participants were provided with a dataset of approximately 15,000 sentences in each language, mainly from the literature domain, which were published either on the web or in print. This is the first dataset made available for these languages (except for Hindi). We believe that it will not only be useful for the automatic identification of these languages and for developing NLP applications, but it will also enable insights into the proximity level of these languages, which are often mistakenly considered as varieties of Hindi, especially outside the scholarly linguistic circles.

3 Participating Teams

The VarDial Evaluation Campaign received a very positive response from the NLP community. A total of 54 teams registered to participate in the five shared tasks, which is an absolute record for VarDial. Eventually, 24 teams submitted runs and 22 of them also contributed system description papers. The participants were free to participate in one or more tasks, and the number of submissions varied widely across the tasks, ranging from 6 entries for ADI and MTT to 12 entries for DFS. Table 1 lists the participating teams, the shared tasks they took part in, and a reference to the system description paper.

Team	ADI	DFS	GDI	ILI	MTT	System Description Papers
Arabic_Identification	✓					
benf		✓				
BZU	✓					(Naser and Hanani, 2018)
CLiPS		✓				(Kreutz and Daelemans, 2018)
CEA List DeepLIMA					✓	(Meftah and Semmar, 2018)
CoAStaL					✓	
DFSlangid		✓				
dkosmajac		✓	✓	✓		
GDI_classification			✓			(Ciobanu et al., 2018a)
ILIdentification				✓		(Ciobanu et al., 2018b)
JANES					✓	(Ljubešić, 2018)
JSI					✓	(Ljubešić, 2018)
LaMa		✓	✓	✓		
LTL-UDE					✓	
mmb_lct		✓				(Kroon et al., 2018)
safina	✓	✓	✓		✓	(Ali, 2018a; Ali, 2018b; Ali, 2018c)
STEVENDU2018		✓				(Du and Wang, 2018)
SUKI		✓	✓	✓		(Jauhiainen et al., 2018a; Jauhiainen et al., 2018b; Jauhiainen et al., 2018c)
SYSTRAN	✓					(Michon et al., 2018)
Taurus		✓				(van Halteren and Oostdijk, 2018)
Tübingen-Oslo	✓	✓	✓	✓		(Çöltekin et al., 2018)
Twist Bytes Meta			✓			(Benites et al., 2018)
UH&CU					✓	(Silfverberg and Drobac, 2018)
UnibucKernel	✓					(Butnaru and Ionescu, 2018)
we_are_indian				✓		(Gupta et al., 2018)
XAC		✓	✓	✓		(Barbaresi, 2018)
Total	**6**	**12**	**8**	**8**	**6**	**22**

Table 1: The teams that participated in the VarDial'2018 evaluation campaign.

4 Previous Shared Tasks

Since the first DSL challenge, the shared tasks organized within the scope of the VarDial workshop have enjoyed substantial increase in the number of participants and in the overall interest from the NLP community. This motivated the organizers to turn the shared tasks at VarDial into a more comprehensive evaluation exercise with four shared tasks in 2017. This year, the VarDial workshop featured the second edition of the VarDial evaluation campaign with five shared tasks.

This year's second edition of the VarDial Evaluation Campaign was preceded by the first edition of the campaign in 2017 with four shared tasks (Zampieri et al., 2017). Earlier editions of the VarDial workshop featured the DSL shared task, and the ADI shared tasks, which focused on discriminating between similar languages and language varieties in a multilingual dataset and for Arabic dialects, respectively (Zampieri et al., 2014; Zampieri et al., 2015; Malmasi et al., 2016).

4.1 Previous ADI tasks

The first ADI task was introduced in 2016 (Malmasi et al., 2016). It offered as input only lexical information extracted from Arabic LVCSR. The second iteration of the ADI task (Zampieri et al., 2017) introduced multi-modality for dialect identification, using i-vectors for the acoustic representation in addition to lexical features.

The Arabic Multi-Genre Broadcast MGB-3 challenge (Ali et al., 2017) built on the success of the previous two VarDial ADI tasks and introduced the challenge to the speech community, where more attention was paid to the raw audio data using various acoustic representations as well as unsupervised techniques. It is worth noting that all previous challenges used data from the broadcast news domain, with ten hours per dialect for training and two hours per dialect for development and two hours for testing. In contrast, we had fifty hours for training, ten hours testing, and ten hours for development.

4.2 Previous GDI task

The previous GDI task was part of the first VarDial evaluation campaign (Zampieri et al., 2017). It provided manual transcriptions of recorded interviews from four dialect areas of the German-speaking Switzerland, namely Bern, Basel, Lucerne, and Zurich. The training and the test data was extracted from the ArchiMob corpus (Samardžić et al., 2016). The training data consisted in 3,000–4,000 utterances from 3–5 different speakers per dialect; the test data consisted of about 900 utterances by a single speaker per dialect. A total of ten teams participated in the 2017 GDI task and the two best-performing systems (Bestgen, 2017; Malmasi and Zampieri, 2017b) achieved weighted F1-measure of up to 0.66. Transcribers were shown to affect the performance of the systems, e.g., for the Lucerne dialect, whose test set was transcribed by a different person than the training set, recall figures were only around 0.3.

5 Third Arabic Dialect Identification (ADI)

This year's third edition of the ADI task addressed the multi-dialectal challenge in spoken Arabic in the broadcast domain. Last year, in the second edition of the ADI task (Zampieri et al., 2017), we offered the input represented as (*i*) automatic text transcriptions generated using large-vocabulary speech recognition (LVCSR), and (*ii*) acoustic features. This year, we further added phonetic input, which enabled researchers to use both prosodic and phonetic features, which have been shown to be helpful for distinguishing between different dialects (Najafian et al., 2018). We have seen many researchers combine acoustic and lexical features, and thus it was interesting to explore the potential contribution of phonetic features in an overall dialect identification system.

5.1 Dataset

For training and development, we released the same data as for last year's VarDial evaluation campaign (Zampieri et al., 2017). For testing, we prepared two new datasets: (*i*) an in-domain one as in 2017, and (*ii*) an out-of-domain one from YouTube. The duration of the utterances in the YouTube dataset was uniformly distributed between 5 and 30 seconds. We did not inform the participants that there would be an out-of-domain test dataset; we just merged (*i*) and (*ii*) to make a combined test set, but we then evaluated the two parts separately. Each dataset consisted of five Arabic dialects: Egyptian (EGY), Levantine (LEV), Gulf (GLF), North African (NOR), and Modern Standard Arabic (MSA). Detailed statistics about all ADI datasets are shown in Table 2.

For all datasets, we provided to the participants already extracted acoustic features, ASR output, and phonetic features. For acoustic features, we extracted dialect embeddings using an end-to-end dialect identification system, as studies have shown that embeddings from end-to-end models outperform the conventional i-vectors. We used four convolutional layers and two fully connected layers. The parameters for the DNN structure and the training setup were as described in (Shon et al., 2018). We extracted embeddings from the last fully connected layer which was 600-dimensional.

We generated the ASR output using a multi-dialect LVCSR system trained on 1,200 hours for acoustic modeling and on 110 million words for language modeling. More detail about the system, which is the winning system in the MGB-2 challenge, can be found in (Khurana and Ali, 2016).

For the phoneme features, we used the BUT phoneme recognizer (Matejka et al., 2005), which supports languages such as Czech, Russian, Hungarian and English. Despite the language mismatch, the recognizer made predictions for each phoneme label. This is consistent with a previous study that has shown that the Hungarian phoneme recognizer can be useful for Arabic dialect identification (Shon et al., 2017).

	Training		Development		Testing (Broadcast)		Testing (YouTube)	
Dialect	Ex.	Dur.	Ex.	Dur.	Ex.	Dur.	Ex.	Dur.
EGY	3,093	12.4	298	2.0	302	2.0	1,143	5.5
GLF	2,744	10.0	264	2.0	250	2.1	1,147	5.6
LAV	2,851	10.3	330	2.0	334	2.0	1,131	5.5
MSA	2,183	10.4	281	2.0	262	1.9	944	4.6
NOR	2,954	10.5	351	2.0	344	2.1	980	4.8
Total	13,825	53.6	1,524	10.0	1,492	10.1	5,345	26.0

Table 2: The ADI data: examples (Ex.) in utterances, duration (Dur.), in number of hours.

5.2 Participants and Approaches

In this section, we present a short description of the systems that competed in the ADI shared task:

- **UnibucKernel** system (Butnaru and Ionescu, 2018) combines three kernel matrices: one calculated using just the lexical features, another one computed on embeddings, and a combined kernel computed on the phonetic features. The final matrix is the mean of these three matrices. As a classifier, they used Kernel Ridge Regression. The approach is similar to the systems that ranked second and first in the previous two ADI tasks (Ionescu and Popescu, 2016; Ionescu and Butnaru, 2017).

- **Safina** system (Ali, 2018a) accepts a sequence of 256 characters as input in addition to the acoustic embedding vectors. First, the sequence of characters is one-hot encoded, then it is passed to a GRU layer, which is followed by a convolutional layer with different filter sizes ranging from 2 to 7. The convolutional layer is followed by batch normalizations, max-pooling, and dropout layers, and finally a softmax layer. In contrast, the acoustic embedding vectors go directly to another softmax layer. The final output is the average between these two softmax layers, which represents the probability distribution over the labels.

- **BZU** system (Naser and Hanani, 2018) fuses four models, two feed-forward neural networks and two multiclass support vector machines. All models use embedding of size 600 as features, and the training is conducted on the union of the development and of the training data.

- **SYSTRAN** system (Michon et al., 2018) uses a multi-input convolutional neural network. The system first learns character-based embeddings of sentences and phoneme-based embeddings of phoneme representations by running one-dimension convolutions and max-pooling with various filter sizes. Subsequently, it concatenates the output and the given acoustic embeddings for the sentences. Then, it adds several fully-connected layers, and finally makes a prediction.

- **Tübingen-Oslo** system (Çöltekin et al., 2018) is trained on word and character n-grams using a single SVM classifier, which is fine-tuned using cross-validation. It is similar to the submissions by the same authors to previous VarDial shared tasks (Çöltekin and Rama, 2017; Çöltekin and Rama, 2016). They also tried an approach based on RNN, which worked worse.

- **Arabic_Identification** system is based on an ensemble of SVM classifiers trained on character and word n-grams. The approach is similar to the systems ranked second and first in the previous two ADI tasks (Malmasi and Zampieri, 2017a; Malmasi and Zampieri, 2016).

5.3 Results

Six teams submitted runs for the ADI shared task and the results are shown in Table 3. The best result, an F1 score of 0.589, was achieved by *UnibucKernel*,[1] followed by *safina*, with an F1 score of 0.575. The following three teams are tied for the third place as they are not statistically different.

Rank	Team	F1 (Macro)
1	UnibucKernel	0.589
2	safina	0.576
3	BZU	0.534
3	SYSTRAN	0.529
3	Tübingen-Oslo	0.514
4	Arabic_Identification	0.500

Table 3: ADI results: ranked taking statistical significance into account.

5.4 Summary

We introduced multi-phoneme representation for the dialectal data, thus enriching the multi-modal aspect of the dialectal challenge. For the acoustic data, we introduced new dialectal embedding features from an end-to-end dialect identification system. For the evaluation, we used a new surprise test set collected from YouTube, with the aim to test whether the participating systems are robust with respect to new domains, different from broadcast news. The results show that participants did benefit both from the linguistic and from the acoustic features. In the future, we plan to add more data from different domains.

6 Second German Dialect Identification (GDI)

Following the first edition of the (Swiss) German Dialect Identification task in 2017, we organized a second iteration this year. We provided cleaned and updated data on the same Swiss German dialect areas as last year (Basel, Bern, Lucerne, Zurich), and we also added a fifth "surprise dialect" for which no training data was made available. The participants could take part in the traditional four-way classification (without the surprise dialect) or in the five-way classification (with it). We received eight submissions for the four-way classification task, and one submission for the five-way classification task.

6.1 Dataset

As in 2017, we extracted the training and the test datasets from the ArchiMob corpus of Spoken Swiss German. The last publicly available release of the corpus (Samardžić et al., 2016) contains 34 oral history interviews with informants speaking different Swiss German dialects, with nine additional transcriptions currently available, some of which were included in this year's GDI task.

Each interview was transcribed by one of four transcribers, using the writing system "Schwyzertütschi Dialäktschrift" proposed by Dieth (1986). The transcription is expected to show the phonetic properties of the variety, but in a way that is legible for everybody who is familiar with the standard German orthography. Although its objective is to keep track of the pronunciation, Dieth's transcription method is orthographic and partially adapted to the spelling habits in standard German. Therefore, it does not provide the same precision and explicitness as phonetic transcription methods do. Moreover, the transcription choices are dependent on the dialect, the accentuation of the syllables and – to a substantial degree – also the dialectal background of the transcriber. Following the findings of last year's GDI task, we identified several transcriber-specific idiosyncrasies and unified them wherever possible, so that transcriber effects could be reduced.[2] The transcriptions exclusively used lowercase. Also note that Dieth's system is hardly known to laymen, and thus Swiss German data extracted from social media would look fairly different from our transcripts.

---

[1] The *UnibucKernel* team had the best system for the ADI task in 2017 as well (Ionescu and Butnaru, 2017).

[2] In 2017, the Lucerne dialect achieved recall values of around 30%, and now we increased it to around 45%.

Dialect	Set	Document IDs	Utterances	Tokens	Transcribers
BE	Train	1142, 1170, 1215	3,889	28,558	P, M
	Dev	1121	1,067	7,404	M
	Test	1203	1,191	12,013	A
BS	Train	1044, 1073, 1075	3,349	27,421	A, P
	Dev	1263	1,572	9,544	A
	Test	1224	1,200	9,802	A
LU	Train	1007, 1261, 1008	3,514	29,441	A, P
	Dev	1195	1,079	8,887	P
	Test	1138, 1235	1,186	11,372	A
ZH	Train	1082, 1087, 1143, 1244, 1270, 1055	3,894	28,820	A, P, M
	Dev	1225	940	8,099	M
	Test	1188, 1083	1,175	9,610	A, M
XY	Test	1212	790	8,938	P

Table 4: ArchiMob interviews used for the GDI task. The surprise dialect is labeled XY.

We provided the updated versions of the GDI 2017 training data for training, the updated GDI 2017 test data for development, and yet unseen data for testing (see Table 4).[3] The training set contains utterances from at least three interviews per dialect, and the development and the test sets each contain utterances from at least one other interview per dialect (see Table 4). For the surprise dialect, we provided a slightly smaller test set. We encouraged the participants to include the development data as additional training data in their final systems.

As surprise dialect, we chose a text from the Valais region. The Valais Swiss German dialect is known to be very distinct from the other Swiss German dialects in terms of pronunciation and lexicon (Scherrer and Stoeckle, 2016). The Valais dialect is geographically closest to Bern and Lucerne; linguistically, it is most closely related to the Bern dialect, although it also shares some linguistic features with the Basel and the Lucerne dialects.

6.2 Participants and Approaches

- The **SUKI** submissions are generated using the HeLI method with language models containing only character 4-grams. The HeLI method is based on a product of relative frequencies with a backoff function between different language models, but the backoff function was not used in the submissions for the GDI task. The winning submission used adaptive language models, which were updated while recursively analyzing the test data.

- The **Twist Bytes Meta** system is trained on multiple features such as words and character n-grams (1-7 words and character bigrams). A linear SVM is trained on each feature set and on top of that, a linear SVM meta classifier using cross-validation was trained to gather the predictions.

- **safina** is based on character-level convolutional neural networks. This model accepts a sequence of 256 characters as input. The sequence of characters are one-hot encoded then go to a recurrent GRU layer (which works as an embedding layer), followed by a convolutional layer with different filter sizes ranging from 2 to 7. The convolutional layer is followed by batch normalization, max-pooling, dropout, and finally a softmax layer. The output of the softmax layer represents the probability distribution over the labels.

- **Tübingen-Oslo** submitted one system based on a linear SVM classifier and another one based on an RNN as previously described in Section 5.

---

[3] For Lucerne, we exchanged parts of the development and of the training data to reduce the transcriber effects seen last year.

- The **LaMa** system is a blend (weighted vote) of eight classifiers being stochastic gradient descent (hinge and modified Huber), multinomial Naïve Bayes, both counts and tf-idf, FastText, and modified Kneser-Ney smoothing. The classifiers were trained using word n-grams (1-6) and character n-grams (1-8). The hyperparameters were determined with cross-validation and searching on the development set.

- **XAC** system is a refined version of the n-gram-based Bayesline system described in last year's XAC submission to the VarDial shared tasks (Barbaresi, 2017), and previously used as a baseline for the DSL shared task (Tan et al., 2014). The XAC team achieved their best results using a Naïve Bayes classifier.

- The **GDI_classification** system is based on an ensemble of multiple SVM classifiers. The system was trained on various word- and character-level features.

- The **dkosmajac** system is based on a normalized Euclidean distance measure. The distances are calculated between a sample and each class profile. The class profiles are generated by selecting the most frequent features for each class, which results in profiles that are of the same length for all the classes.

6.3 Results

For the standard 4-way classification, we received a total of eight submissions presented in Table 5.

Rank	Team	F1 (Macro)
1	SUKI	0.686
2	Twist Bytes Meta	0.646
2	safina	0.645
2	Tübingen-Oslo	0.640
2	LaMa	0.637
3	XAC	0.634
3	GDI_classification	0.620
4	dkosmajac	0.591
	Twist Bytes Meta (5-way)	0.512

Table 5: GDI results: ranked taking statistical significance into account.

This year, the *SUKI* system is the clear winner, achieving significantly higher results than the other seven teams, with an F1 score of 0.686. Four teams ended the competition tied in the second place: *Twist Bytes Meta, safina, Tübingen-Oslo* and *LaMa*. This year's results are in the same range as last year's, even though the test data is different. With 5 out of 8 teams in an F1 bracket of 0.012, one could argue that a plateau has been reached for this type of transcription data, but the clear win of the *SUKI* system suggests that further improvements can be achieved.

For the extended 5-way classification, we received one submission, which achieved an F1 score of 0.512. It was able to identify the surprise dialect with 22.8% precision and 11.6% recall, suggesting that identifying unseen dialects is still a hard task. The surprise dialect utterances were most often identified as BE or LU, which are the two dialect areas that are geographically closest.

6.4 Summary

In this second iteration of the GDI task, we provided cleaned and updated data from the same source as in 2017. This allowed us to obtain more stable results across dialects. We also launched a surprise dialect task, whose success was limited; a post-submission survey indicated that (prospective) participants mostly lacked time and resources to adapt their systems to such a semi-supervised scenario. Participants also indicated that acoustic data as well as a larger set of dialects would be welcome additions for future iterations of the GDI task.

7 Morphosyntactic Tagging of Tweets (MTT)

The task on morphosyntactic tagging of tweets focused on annotating each token of utterances in non-canonical Twitter varieties of three South-Slavic languages (Slovene, Croatian, and Serbian) with the correct morphosyntactic label out of more than 900 possible ones. The task participants were provided both with large manually annotated and raw canonical datasets, as well as small manually annotated Twitter datasets. Two dimensions of variety could be exploited in the task: (*i*) the dimension of canonical vs. non-canonical language, and (*ii*) the overall proximity of the three languages.

7.1 Datasets

The provided datasets consisted of three types of data: (*i*) standard manually annotated data (`standard.train`), (*ii*) automatically annotated web data (`web.auto`), and (*iii*) Twitter variety manually annotated data (`twitter.*`). The latter were split into train, dev and test sets, with the test data being withheld for the final evaluation. We give an overview of the different datasets (in number of tokens) in Table 6.

The `twitter.*` datasets come from the Janes-Tag manually annotated dataset of Slovene computer-mediated communication (Erjavec et al., 2017) and the ReLDI-NormTagNER-* manually annotated datasets of Croatian (Ljubešić et al., 2017a) and Serbian (Ljubešić et al., 2017b) tweets. These datasets are all similar in size, with around 40 thousand tokens available for training, 8 thousand for development and 20 thousand for testing.

The `standard.train` datasets mostly cover the general domain. While the Slovene and Croatian datasets are similar in size with around 500 thousand tokens, the Serbian dataset is significantly smaller, with just 87 thousand tokens.

The `web.auto` datasets are large web-based datasets: slWac for Slovene (Erjavec et al., 2015), hrWaC for Croatian, and srWaC for Serbian (Ljubešić and Klubička, 2014). They are automatically annotated with state-of-the-art taggers for standard Slovene (Ljubešić and Erjavec, 2016), Croatian, and Serbian (Ljubešić et al., 2016), respectively.

	twitter.train	twitter.dev	twitter.test	standard.train	web.auto
Slovene	37,756	7,056	19,296	586,248	895,875,492
Croatian	45,609	8,886	21,412	506,460	1,397,757,548
Serbian	45,708	9,581	23,327	86,765	554,627,647

Table 6: MTT task: size of the datasets (in number of tokens).

7.2 Participants and Approaches

The following teams handed in their system descriptions:

- The **UH&CU** system uses a bidirectional LSTM system for sequence modeling, representing words via word embeddings and character embeddings encoding the character-level word representation with a separate BiLSTM. They use an intriguing approach to emitting tags: they generate tags as character sequences using an LSTM generator in order to handle unknown tags and complex tags (combinations of several tags for one token as a result of conflating tokens in the non-standard varieties).

- The **JSI** system also applies a bidirectional BiLSTM to model the sequence, representing each word via a combination of word embeddings and character-level word representations obtained via character embeddings from a separate BiLSTM. They train the network first on a concatenation of all manually annotated data, and then they tune it only on non-standard (in-domain) data. They also pretrain the character-level BiLSTM word encoder on automatically generated inflectional lexicons from the available automatically annotated web data.

- The **JANES** system uses a conditional random field for sequence labeling, with carefully engineered context-level, word-level, and character-level features. The authors further enrich the representation of each word with Brown clusters that were calculated on the available web data. They train their system on a combination of standard and non-standard data, in which they overrepresent non-standard data by repeating the non-standard instances. They also heavily borrow data between Croatian and Serbian.

- The **DeepLIMA** system uses a BiGRU modeling technique, representing words as a combination of word-level and character-level embeddings. The latter generate a word representation from character-level embeddings with a separate BiGRU. They exploit both the non-standard (in-domain) and the standard (out-of-domain) training data by training the network first on the standard data, and then on the non-standard data.

7.3 Results

The MTT shared task received seven submissions by six teams, each of the teams submitting results for all the three languages of the shared task.

We used token-level accuracy as an evaluation measure, and we ranked the systems, taking statistical significance into account, based on the McNemar test whether the results of two neighbouring submissions are statistically significantly different at the $p < 0.05$ level.

The results are shown in Table 7. We can see that the three best-performing teams, *UH&CU*, *JSI* and *JANES* share the first position in all languages except for Slovene, where the *JANES* team achieved statistically significantly worse results than the two other teams. All other teams performed below the *HunPos* baseline system, which was trained on a concatenation of all the available manually annotated data per language.

Given that the results for three teams are very close to each other, it is reasonable to assume that these results represent the state of the art in morphosyntactic annotation.

The high ranking of the *JANES* system, which is not neural but CRF-based, has shown that the improvements yielded by using neural networks are rather small. Ljubešić (2018) has also noted that his *JANES* system comes closer to the neural approaches as the level of non-standardness of the test data drops off. Namely, the most similar results between *JANES* and the neural approaches were obtained on Serbian and Croatian, for which 10% and 13% of the tokens, respectively, are non-standard, while significantly lower results were obtained for Slovene, where the percentage of non-standard tokens is about 17%.[4]

Team	Slovenian		Croatian		Serbian	
	Acc	Rank	Acc	Rank	Acc	Rank
UH&CU	0.884	1	0.887	1	0.900	1
JSI	0.883	1	0.890	1	0.900	1
JANES	0.871	4	0.893	1	0.900	1
CEA List DeepLIMA	0.826	6	0.829	6	0.821	6
LTL-UDE	0.627	7	0.752	7	0.773	7
CoAStaL	0.626	8	0.632	8	0.524	8
HunPos baseline	0.832	5	0.834	5	0.832	5

Table 7: MTT results: ranked taking statistical significance into account.

---

[4]The author also reports results that he obtained after the system submission deadline, with statistically significant improvements over *JANES* being obtained for all languages, and the improvements strongly correlating with the percentage of non-standard tokens in the test sets.

7.4 Summary

The experimental results have shown that by combining standard (out-of-domain) and non-standard (in-domain) training data, as well as training data from closely related languages by using neural approaches or conditional random fields, the traditional *HunPos* baseline can be beaten by a wide margin, with the error reduction lying somewhere around 45%.

Moreover, the improvements when replacing traditional sequence labeling approaches such as CRFs with corresponding neural ones are quite small. However, conditional random fields need the features to be manually engineered, which requires a good knowledge of the target languages. The results also demonstrate that improvements can be achieved with neural approaches on datasets where the level of non-standardness is highest, showing that, as expected, the more complex modeling approaches start to pay off as the problems get harder.

8   Discriminating between Dutch and Flemish in Subtitles (DFS)

The DSF shared task focused on determining whether a text is written in the Netherlandic or in the Flemish variant of the Dutch language. The participants were provided with professionally produced subtitles written for either a Northern Dutch or a Flemish audience. Since there is a lack of automatic classification studies on Netherlandic and Flemish Dutch varieties, and no Netherlandic/Flemish corpus of this size exists, we believe it is a scientifically interesting step forward to develop and to compare language variety classification using subtitles, and thereby analyze the proximity of the language varieties in a new way. The latter is not only of interest for improving computational linguistics applications, but also for finding insights in variational linguistics in general.

8.1   Dataset

As stated above, the dataset consisted of subtitles from an international media localization company that produces, among others, subtitles for television channels in The Netherlands and Belgium. These subtitles range from documentaries, television shows, and movies. These raw subtitles were originally converted into linguistically annotated text in the original SUBTIEL corpus (van der Lee and van den Bosch, 2017). The dataset used for the current shared task was based on this corpus. A total of 320,500 lines were provided to the participants (300,000 for training, 20,000 for testing, and 500 for development). These lines were randomly taken from the SUBTIEL corpus, while keeping a 50/50 split of Netherlandic and Flemish Dutch lines. Each line consisted of about two to three sentences or parts of a sentence: about the length of a tweet. This resulted in a total of 11,102,274 word tokens for all three sets.

8.2   Participants and Approaches

- **Tübingen-Oslo** team used one system based on a linear SVM classifier and another one based on RNN as previously described in Section 5.

- **Taurus** team used a voting-based system that used character n-grams and n-grams containing syntactical information derived from Frog, Alpino and a custom surfacing procedure.

- **CLiPS** team used an ensemble of two Linear SVMs, one trained on word n-grams and another one trained on part-of-speech n-grams. The prediction for a document was made by the classification method that outputs the highest probability for a label.

- **LaMa** team had a system that is a weighted vote blending 8 classifiers: stochastic gradient descent (hinge and modified huber), multinomial Naïve Bayes, both counts and TF.IDF, FastText, and modified Kneser-Ney smoothing, as previously described in Section 6

- **XAC** team used the "Bayesline" system as described in Section 6. In the DFS shared task, *XAC*'s best result was obtained using a Ridge classifier.

- **safina** team used a one-hot encoded character-level convolutional neural network, based on character-level convolutional neural networks, as previously described in Section 5.

- **STEVENDU2018** team used a Linear SVM trained on word n-grams and a Convolutional Neural Network with pre-trained word embeddings built for Netherlandic and Flemish Dutch each, which were subsequently concatenated.

- **mmb_lct** team used a Naïve Bayes classifier using word unigrams and bigrams.

- **SUKI** team submitted identification results from an identifier using the basic HeLI method with words and character n-grams from 1 to 8. Note that using adaptive language models with the DFS dataset did not improve the results as it did for the GDI and the ILI tasks.

- **DFSlangid** team used n-grams, skip-grams, and clustering-based word representations.

- **dkosmajac** team used normalised Eucledian distance measure using Adaptive Gradient Descent to optimize weights. The features used were character n-grams, as previously described in Section 6.

- **benf** team submitted a system trained on a separate Linear SVM on word and on character n-grams. Then they trained a Linear SVM on the output for the two feature sets.

8.3 Results

The DFS shared task received the highest number of submissions across the five tasks, and it was also the most competitive shared task this year with nine out of twelve teams achieving an F1 score between 0.61 and 0.66. The results are presented in Table 8.

Rank	Team	F1 (Macro)
1	Tübingen-Oslo	0.660
2	Taurus	0.646
3	CLiPS	0.636
3	LaMa	0.633
3	XAC	0.632
3	safina	0.631
4	STEVENDU2018	0.623
4	mmb_lct	0.620
5	SUKI	0.613
6	DFSlangid	0.596
7	dkosmajac	0.567
7	benf	0.558

Table 8: DFS results: ranked taking statistical significance into account.

The best-performing system was the one by *Tübingen-Oslo*, and it achieved an F1 score of 0.66, followed by *Taurus* with 0.646. Four teams: *CLiPS*, *LaMa*, *XAC*, and *safina* ended up tied in the third position. Even though the task proved to be very challenging, all teams achieved scores over 0.5, which is the expected baseline for this task.

8.4 Summary

This year's first DFS Shared Task has shown that discriminating between Dutch and Flemish is a challenging but feasible task: all submissions performed better than a 0.5 baseline. No large differences in performance were found between the groups, but the methods to achieve the best performance were quite different. Supervised methods achieved similar scores with different features, and unsupervised methods were competitive as well. We also received some suggestions from participants to further improve the corpus. It would be interesting to see if and how the performance would differ if the data is updated and cleaned based on this feedback.

9   Indo-Aryan Language Identification (ILI)

Organized for the first time in VarDial 2018, the ILI shared task focused on identifying five closely-related languages from the Indo-Aryan language family: Hindi (also known as Khari Boli), Braj Bhasha, Awadhi, Bhojpuri, and Magahi. These languages form part of a continuum starting from Western Uttar Pradesh (Hindi and Braj Bhasha) to Eastern Uttar Pradesh (Awadhi and Bhojpuri) and the neighbouring Eastern state of Bihar (Bhojpuri and Magahi).

For this task, participants were provided with a dataset of approximately 15,000 sentences in each language, mainly from the literature domain, published on the web or in print. It is the first dataset that is made available for these languages (except for Hindi), and we believe it would be useful not only for automatic identification of languages and for developing NLP applications, but it could also help in gaining insights into the proximity level of these languages, which are hypothesised to form a continuum and are often wrongly considered to be varieties of Hindi, especially outside scholarly linguistic circles.

9.1   Dataset

The data for this task was collected from both hard printed and digital sources. Printed materials were obtained from different institutions that promote these languages. We also gathered data from libraries, as well as from local literary and cultural groups. We collected printed stories, novels and essays in books, magazines, and newspapers. We scanned the printed materials, then we performed OCR, and finally we asked native speakers of the respective languages to correct the OCR output. Since there are no specific OCR models available for these languages, we used the Google OCR for Hindi, part of the Drive API. Since all the languages used the Devanagari script, we expected the OCR to work reasonably well, and overall it did. We further managed to get some blogs in Magahi and Bhojpuri.

There are several corpora already available for Modern Standard Hindi (Kumar, 2012; Kumar, 2014a; Kumar, 2014b; Choudhary and Jha, 2011). However, in order to keep the domain the same as for the other languages, we collected data from blogs that mainly contain stories and novels. Thus, the Modern Standard Hindi data collected for this study is also from the literature domain.[5]

9.2   Participants and Approaches

- The **SUKI** team used HeLI with adaptive language models based on character n-grams from 1 to 6, as previously described in Section 5. The also used an iterative version of the language model adaptation technique, with three additional adaptation epochs.

- **Tübingen-Oslo** team submitted a system using a linear SVM and another one based on an RNN, as previously described in Section 5.

- **XAC** team used the "Bayesline" system, as described in Section 6. In the ILI shared task, XAC's best result was obtained using a Ridge classifier.

- **ILIdentification** team used features such as n-grams, skip-grams, and clustering-based word representations. They tried both single classifiers as well as ensembles and stacked generalization.

- **safina** team used one-hot encoded character-level convolutional neural network, as previously described in Section 6.

- **dkosmajac** used character n-grams with a normalized Eucledian distance measure and Adaptive Gradient Descent to optimize weights, as previously described in Section 6.

- **we_are_indian** team combined an RNN-sequence model with bidirectional LSTMs. They created word embedding for all the languages present in the dataset.

- The **LaMa** team used a Multinomial Naïve Bayes classifier with both word and character n-grams, of size 1-8 and 1-6 respectively, for which the raw counts are the feature values.

---

[5]For more detail about the dataset, please see (Kumar et al., 2018).

9.3 Results

The ILI shared task received eight submissions, and the results are shown in Table 9.

Rank	Team	F1 (Macro)
1	SUKI	0.958
2	Tübingen-Oslo	0.902
2	XAC	0.898
3	ILIdentification	0.889
4	safina	0.863
5	dkosmajac	0.847
5	we_are_indian	0.836
6	LaMa	0.819

Table 9: ILI results: ranked taking statistical significance into account.

The highest ranked team was *SUKI*, which achieved an F1 score of 0.958, while the *LaMa* team had the lowest F1 score of 0.819. Two teams were tied for the second place: *Tübingen-Oslo* and *XAC*. There was a tie between two teams for the fifth place as well.

9.4 Summary

The first ILI shared task was successful in terms of participation with eight submissions. In terms of performance, all submissions achieved an F1 score of more than 0.81, which is a high score for a 5-class classification set-up, and higher than the results achieved in the other VarDial shared tasks. One of the interesting aspects of the task was the wide variety of approaches used by the participants.

In future work, we plan to increase the dataset of these less-resourced languages: Braj Bhasha, Awadhi, Bhojpuri and Magahi.

10 Conclusion and Future Work

We have presented the results and the findings for the five shared tasks that were organized as part of the VarDial Evaluation Campaign in 2018. Two tasks were re-runs from previous years (ADI and GDI), and there were also three new tasks (DFS, ILI, and MTT).

We included a short description for each participant's systems. For a complete description, we included references to the system description papers, which were presented in the VarDial workshop and published in the workshop proceedings.

The VarDial evaluation campaign was introduced in 2017, following the organization of successful shared tasks that have been co-located with VarDial since 2004. In its second edition, the campaign featured a record number of shared tasks and attracted a record number of participants. Participation in each individual task ranged from six teams competing in the ADI and MTT tasks to 12 teams for the DFS task.

In a potential third edition of the VarDial evaluation campaign, we aim to bring more diversity by organizing competitions on other relevant NLP tasks such as lexical variation or machine translation, to name a few. With the exception of MTT, the shared tasks this year dealt mostly with the problem of discriminating between similar languages, varieties, and dialects. Even though this topic has been attracting a lot of attention from the research community (Jauhiainen et al., 2018d), we believe that there is room for shared tasks on other relevant topics in future iterations of the VarDial evaluation campaign.

Acknowledgements

We would like to thank the participants of the VarDial Evaluation Campaign for their hard work, support, and feedback. We further thank the VarDial workshop program committee members for thoroughly reviewing the shared task system papers as well as this report.

References

Ahmed Ali, Stephan Vogel, and Steve Renals. 2017. Speech recognition challenge in the wild: Arabic MGB-3. In *Proceedings of the IEEE Automatic Speech Recognition and Understanding Workshop (ASRU)*.

Mohamed Ali. 2018a. Character level convolutional neural network for Arabic dialect identification. In *Proceedings of the Fifth Workshop on NLP for Similar Languages, Varieties and Dialects (VarDial)*.

Mohamed Ali. 2018b. Character level convolutional neural network for German dialect identification. In *Proceedings of the Fifth Workshop on NLP for Similar Languages, Varieties and Dialects (VarDial)*.

Mohamed Ali. 2018c. Character level convolutional neural network for Indo-Aryan language identification. In *Proceedings of the Fifth Workshop on NLP for Similar Languages, Varieties and Dialects (VarDial)*.

Adrien Barbaresi. 2017. Discriminating between similar languages using weighted subword features. In *Proceedings of the VarDial Workshop (VarDial)*.

Adrien Barbaresi. 2018. Computationally efficient discrimination between language varieties with large feature vectors and regularized classifiers. In *Proceedings of the Fifth Workshop on NLP for Similar Languages, Varieties and Dialects (VarDial)*.

Fernando Benites, Ralf Grubenmann, Pius von Däniken, Dirk von Grünigen, Jan Deriu, and Mark Cieliebak. 2018. Twist Bytes – German dialect identification with data mining optimization. In *Proceedings of the Fifth Workshop on NLP for Similar Languages, Varieties and Dialects (VarDial)*.

Yves Bestgen. 2017. Improving the character ngram model for the DSL task with BM25 weighting and less frequently used feature sets. In *Proceedings of the VarDial Workshop (VarDial)*.

Andrei M. Butnaru and Radu Ionescu. 2018. UnibucKernel Reloaded: First place in Arabic dialect identification for the second year in a row. In *Proceedings of the Fifth Workshop on NLP for Similar Languages, Varieties and Dialects (VarDial)*.

Çağrı Çöltekin and Taraka Rama. 2016. Discriminating similar languages with linear SVMs and neural networks. In *Proceedings of the VarDial Workshop (VarDial)*.

Çağrı Çöltekin and Taraka Rama. 2017. Tübingen system in VarDial 2017 shared task: Experiments with language identification and cross-lingual parsing. In *Proceedings of the VarDial Workshop (VarDial)*.

Çağrı Çöltekin, Taraka Rama, and Verena Blaschke. 2018. Tübingen-Oslo team at the VarDial 2018 evaluation campaign: An analysis of n-gram features in language variety identification. In *Proceedings of the Fifth Workshop on NLP for Similar Languages, Varieties and Dialects (VarDial)*.

Narayan Choudhary and Girish Nath Jha. 2011. Creating multilingual parallel corpora in Indian languages. In *Proceedings of LTC*.

Alina Maria Ciobanu, Shervin Malmasi, and Liviu P. Dinu. 2018a. German dialect identification using classifier ensembles. In *Proceedings of the Fifth Workshop on NLP for Similar Languages, Varieties and Dialects (VarDial)*.

Alina Maria Ciobanu, Marcos Zampieri, Shervin Malmasi, Santanu Pal, and Liviu P. Dinu. 2018b. Discriminating between Indo-Aryan languages using SVM ensembles. In *Proceedings of the Fifth Workshop on NLP for Similar Languages, Varieties and Dialects (VarDial)*.

Eugen Dieth. 1986. *Schwyzertütschi Dialäktschrift*. 2 edition.

Steven Du and Yuan Yuan Wang. 2018. STEVENDU2018's system in VarDial 2018: Discriminating between Dutch and Flemish in subtitles. In *Proceedings of the Fifth Workshop on NLP for Similar Languages, Varieties and Dialects (VarDial)*.

Tomaž Erjavec, Nikola Ljubešić, and Nataša Logar. 2015. The slWaC corpus of the Slovene web. *Informatica*, 39(1):35–42.

Tomaž Erjavec, Darja Fišer, Jaka Čibej, Špela Arhar Holdt, Nikola Ljubešić, and Katja Zupan. 2017. CMC training corpus Janes-Tag 2.0. Slovenian language resource repository CLARIN.SI.

Divyanshu Gupta, Gourav Dhakad, Jayprakash Gupta, and Anil Kumar Singh. 2018. IIT (BHU) System for Indo-Aryan language identification (ILI) at VarDial 2018. In *Proceedings of the Fifth Workshop on NLP for Similar Languages, Varieties and Dialects (VarDial)*.

Radu Tudor Ionescu and Andrei Butnaru. 2017. Learning to identify Arabic and German dialects using multiple kernels. In *Proceedings of the VarDial Workshop (VarDial)*.

Radu Tudor Ionescu and Marius Popescu. 2016. UnibucKernel: An approach for Arabic dialect identification based on multiple string kernels. In *Proceedings of the VarDial Workshop (VarDial)*.

Tommi Jauhiainen, Heidi Jauhiainen, and Krister Lindén. 2018a. HeLI-based experiments in discriminating between Dutch and Flemish subtitles. In *Proceedings of the Fifth Workshop on NLP for Similar Languages, Varieties and Dialects (VarDial)*.

Tommi Jauhiainen, Heidi Jauhiainen, and Krister Lindén. 2018b. HeLI-based experiments in Swiss German dialect identification. In *Proceedings of the Fifth Workshop on NLP for Similar Languages, Varieties and Dialects (VarDial)*.

Tommi Jauhiainen, Heidi Jauhiainen, and Krister Lindén. 2018c. Iterative language model adaptation for Indo-Aryan language identification. In *Proceedings of the Fifth Workshop on NLP for Similar Languages, Varieties and Dialects (VarDial)*.

Tommi Jauhiainen, Marco Lui, Marcos Zampieri, Timothy Baldwin, and Krister Lindén. 2018d. Automatic language identification in texts: A survey. *arXiv preprint arXiv:1804.08186*.

Sameer Khurana and Ahmed Ali. 2016. QCRI advanced transcription system (QATS) for the Arabic Multi-Dialect Broadcast Media Recognition: MGB-2 Challenge. In *Proceedings of SLT*.

Tim Kreutz and Walter Daelemans. 2018. Exploring classifier combinations for language variety identification. In *Proceedings of the Fifth Workshop on NLP for Similar Languages, Varieties and Dialects (VarDial)*.

Martin Kroon, Maria Medvedeva, and Barbara Plank. 2018. When simple n-gram models outperform syntactic approaches: Discriminating between Dutch and Flemish. In *Proceedings of the Fifth Workshop on NLP for Similar Languages, Varieties and Dialects (VarDial)*.

Ritesh Kumar, Bornini Lahiri, Deepak Alok, Atul Kr. Ojha, Mayank Jain, Abdul Basit, and Yogesh Dawar. 2018. Automatic identification of closely-related Indian languages: Resources and experiments. In *Proceedings of the Eleventh International Conference on Language Resources and Evaluation (LREC)*.

Ritesh Kumar. 2012. Challenges in the development of annotated corpora of computer-mediated communication in Indian languages: A case of Hindi. In *Proceedings of the Eight International Conference on Language Resources and Evaluation (LREC)*.

Ritesh Kumar. 2014a. Developing politeness annotated corpus of Hindi blogs. In *Proceedings of the Ninth International Conference on Language Resources and Evaluation (LREC)*.

Ritesh Kumar. 2014b. *Politeness in Online Hindi Texts: Pragmatic and Computational Aspects*. Ph.D. thesis, Jawaharlal Nehru University.

Nikola Ljubešić and Filip Klubička. 2014. {bs,hr,sr}wac - web corpora of Bosnian, Croatian and Serbian. In *Proceedings of the 9th Web as Corpus Workshop (WaC-9)*, pages 29–35.

Nikola Ljubešić, Tomaž Erjavec, Maja Miličević, and Tanja Samardžić. 2017a. Croatian Twitter training corpus ReLDI-NormTagNER-hr 2.0. Slovenian language resource repository CLARIN.SI.

Nikola Ljubešić, Tomaž Erjavec, Maja Miličević, and Tanja Samardžić. 2017b. Serbian Twitter training corpus ReLDI-NormTagNER-sr 2.0. Slovenian language resource repository CLARIN.SI.

Nikola Ljubešić. 2018. Comparing CRF and LSTM performance on the task of morphosyntactic tagging of non-standard varieties of South Slavic languages. In *Proceedings of the Fifth Workshop on NLP for Similar Languages, Varieties and Dialects (VarDial)*.

Nikola Ljubešić and Tomaž Erjavec. 2016. Corpus vs. lexicon supervision in morphosyntactic tagging: the case of Slovene. In *Proceedings of the Tenth International Conference on Language Resources and Evaluation (LREC)*.

Nikola Ljubešić, Filip Klubička, Željko Agić, and Ivo-Pavao Jazbec. 2016. New inflectional lexicons and training corpora for improved morphosyntactic annotation of Croatian and Serbian. In *Proceedings of the Tenth International Conference on Language Resources and Evaluation (LREC)*.

Shervin Malmasi and Marcos Zampieri. 2016. Arabic dialect identification in speech transcripts. In *Proceedings of the VarDial Workshop (VarDial)*.

Shervin Malmasi and Marcos Zampieri. 2017a. Arabic dialect identification using iVectors and ASR transcripts. In *Proceedings of the VarDial Workshop (VarDial)*.

Shervin Malmasi and Marcos Zampieri. 2017b. German dialect identification in interview transcriptions. In *Proceedings of the VarDial Workshop (VarDial)*.

Shervin Malmasi, Marcos Zampieri, Nikola Ljubešić, Preslav Nakov, Ahmed Ali, and Jörg Tiedemann. 2016. Discriminating between similar languages and Arabic dialect identification: A report on the third DSL shared task.

Pavel Matejka, Petr Schwarz, Jan Cernockỳ, and Pavel Chytil. 2005. Phonotactic language identification using high quality phoneme recognition. In *Proc. Interspeech*.

Sara Meftah and Nasredine Semmar. 2018. Using neural transfer learning for morpho-syntactic tagging of South-Slavic languages tweets. In *Proceedings of the Fifth Workshop on NLP for Similar Languages, Varieties and Dialects (VarDial)*.

Elise Michon, Minh Quang Pham, Josep Crego, and Jean Senellart. 2018. Neural network architectures for Arabic dialect identification. In *Proceedings of the Fifth Workshop on NLP for Similar Languages, Varieties and Dialects (VarDial)*.

Maryam Najafian, Sameer Khurana, Suwon Shon, Ahmed Ali, and James Glass. 2018. Exploiting convolutional neural networks for phonotactic based dialect identification. In *IEEE ICASSP*, pages 5174–5178.

Rabee Naser and Abualsoud Hanani. 2018. Birzeit Arabic dialect identication system for the 2018 VarDial challenge. In *Proceedings of the Fifth Workshop on NLP for Similar Languages, Varieties and Dialects (VarDial)*.

Tanja Samardžić, Yves Scherrer, and Elvira Glaser. 2016. ArchiMob – a corpus of spoken Swiss German. In *Proceedings of LREC*.

Yves Scherrer and Philipp Stoeckle. 2016. A quantitative approach to Swiss German – dialectometric analyses and comparisons of linguistic levels. *Dialectologia et Geolinguistica*, 24(1):92–125.

Suwon Shon, Ahmed Ali, and James Glass. 2017. MIT-QCRI Arabic dialect identification system for the 2017 multi-genre broadcast challenge. In *IEEE Workshop on Automatic Speech Recognition and Understanding (ASRU)*, pages 374–380.

Suwon Shon, Ahmed Ali, and James Glass. 2018. Convolutional neural network and language embeddings for end-to-end dialect recognition. In *Proceedings of the Speaker and Language Recognition Workshop (Odyssey)*.

Miikka Silfverberg and Senka Drobac. 2018. Sub-label dependencies for neural morphological tagging – the joint submission of University of Colorado and University of Helsinki for VarDial 2018. In *Proceedings of the Fifth Workshop on NLP for Similar Languages, Varieties and Dialects (VarDial)*.

Liling Tan, Marcos Zampieri, Nikola Ljubešic, and Jörg Tiedemann. 2014. Merging comparable data sources for the discrimination of similar languages: The DSL corpus collection. In *Proceedings of the BUCC Workshop*.

Chris van der Lee and Antal van den Bosch. 2017. Exploring lexical and syntactic features for language variety identification. In *Proceedings of the Fourth Workshop on NLP for Similar Languages, Varieties and Dialects (VarDial)*.

Hans van Halteren and Nelleke Oostdijk. 2018. Identification of differences between Dutch language varieties with the VarDial2018 Dutch-Flemish subtitle data. In *Proceedings of the Fifth Workshop on NLP for Similar Languages, Varieties and Dialects (VarDial)*.

Marcos Zampieri, Liling Tan, Nikola Ljubešić, and Jörg Tiedemann. 2014. A report on the DSL shared task 2014. In *Proceedings of the VarDial Workshop (VarDial)*.

Marcos Zampieri, Liling Tan, Nikola Ljubešić, Jörg Tiedemann, and Preslav Nakov. 2015. Overview of the DSL shared task 2015. In *Proceedings of the LT4VarDial Workshop (LT4VarDial)*.

Marcos Zampieri, Shervin Malmasi, Nikola Ljubešić, Preslav Nakov, Ahmed Ali, Jörg Tiedemann, Yves Scherrer, and Noëmi Aepli. 2017. Findings of the VarDial evaluation campaign 2017. In *Proceedings of the Fourth Workshop on NLP for Similar Languages, Varieties and Dialects (VarDial)*.

Encoder-Decoder Methods for Text Normalization

Massimo Lusetti[*‡]
massimo.lusetti@uzh.ch

Tatyana Ruzsics[†]
tatiana.ruzsics@uzh.ch

Anne Göhring[*‡]
goehring@cl.uzh.ch

Tanja Samardžić[†]
tanja.samardzic@uzh.ch

Elisabeth Stark[‡]
estark@rom.uzh.ch

[*]Institute of Computational Linguistics, University of Zurich, Switzerland
[†]URPP Language and Space, University of Zurich, Switzerland
[‡]Institute of Romance Studies, University of Zurich, Switzerland

Abstract

Text normalization is the task of mapping non-canonical language, typical of speech transcription and computer-mediated communication, to a standardized writing. It is an up-stream task necessary to enable the subsequent direct employment of standard natural language processing tools and indispensable for languages such as Swiss German, with strong regional variation and no written standard. Text normalization has been addressed with a variety of methods, most successfully with character-level statistical machine translation (CSMT). In the meantime, machine translation has changed and the new methods, known as neural encoder-decoder (ED) models, resulted in remarkable improvements. Text normalization, however, has not yet followed. A number of neural methods have been tried, but CSMT remains the state-of-the-art. In this work, we normalize Swiss German WhatsApp messages using the ED framework. We exploit the flexibility of this framework, which allows us to learn from the same training data in different ways. In particular, we modify the decoding stage of a plain ED model to include target-side language models operating at different levels of granularity: characters and words. Our systematic comparison shows that our approach results in an improvement over the CSMT state-of-the-art.

1 Introduction

Largely influenced by the work on English and other languages with a strong orthographic tradition (e.g. German, Spanish, French), the natural language processing (NLP) pipeline typically requires standardized text as input. Recently, however, text processing has extended to non-standard varieties, including historical texts, transcribed spoken language and user-generated content (blogs, comments, social media posts, messaging). Modern NLP is also increasingly multilingual, starting to address languages that have no writing standard at all.

What is characteristic of non-standard text is a non-uniform way of writing the same word types (e.g. *u* instead of *you* in English). While this might appear as a marginal stylistic variation in English, it is a substantial feature of less standardized varieties. This is the case, for instance, with Swiss German. The German-speaking part of Switzerland is characterized by a phenomenon known as diglossia, i.e. two different varieties of the same language are used within a community in different social situations. One variety is known as standard Swiss German, that is the variety of standard German that is accepted as the norm in Switzerland. It is used in most written contexts (literature, newspapers, private correspondence, official documents), in formal and official spoken contexts (education, parliament speeches) and in interactions with foreigners. The second variety, that is the dialect, is known as Swiss German and is used in everyday life, within the family as well as in most radio and television programs.[1] Since Swiss

---

This work is licensed under a Creative Commons Attribution 4.0 International License. License details: http://creativecommons.org/licenses/by/4.0/

[1]See Rash (1998), among other sources, for a comprehensive survey of Swiss German.

Proceedings of the Fifth Workshop on NLP for Similar Languages, Varieties and Dialects, pages 18–28
Santa Fe, New Mexico, USA, August 20, 2018.

German does not have a standardized orthography, it is rarely used in written contexts. However, nowadays we observe an increasing use of the dialect in written computer-mediated communication (CMC). This phenomenon has multiple and interesting repercussions, as it makes valuable material available for NLP tasks, thus granting Swiss German a stronger position among the languages studied in the NLP community. However, given the high degree of variation, the need for text normalization, i.e. mapping different variants of the same word type to a single string, becomes immediately evident. The aim of this work is to normalize WhatsApp messages written in Swiss German. Several factors contribute to the high degree of variation of the source text. Firstly, the lack of a standardized spelling is further complicated by the strong regional variation and the numerous local variants of the same word. As a result, the word *viel* ('much') can appear as *viel, viil, vill, viu,* and many other potential variations. Secondly, CMC is characterized by various peculiarities, such as vowel reduplication and unconventional abbreviations, which increase variation.

A major breakthrough in performing text normalization was achieved when this task was approached as a case of character-level statistical machine translation (CSMT) (Sánchez-Martínez et al., 2013; De Clercq et al., 2013). With a small modification of the input, so that the models are estimated over characters rather than over words, well-known off-the-shelf SMT tools like Moses (Koehn et al., 2007) could be used to obtain significant improvements in comparison to previous solutions.

Currently widely used for text normalization, SMT is slowly abandoned in proper machine translation. New neural methods achieve much better performance, providing at the same time a more flexible framework for designing and testing different models. They, however, require large training sets, which makes them unsuitable for text normalization, where training sets, unlike in machine translation, are small and created by experts specifically for the task. Several attempts have been made to train neural normalization models, but the resulting systems could not reach the performance of CSMT.[2]

In this paper, we tackle the issue of introducing neural methods to text normalization. We work with the neural framework that proved most successful in machine translation: a combination of two recurrent neural networks known as the encoder-decoder (ED) architecture. Inspired by similar approaches to other tasks (Gulcehre et al., 2016; Ruzsics and Samardžić, 2017), we enrich the basic ED architecture with a mechanism that allows us to overcome the limitation of having a small training set. This modification concerns including two kinds of language models at the decoding stage: word-level and character-level. We compare our approach to a strong baseline and the current state-of-the-art CSMT methods.

2   Related Work

Text normalization is primarily performed in processing historical texts, where several automatic approaches have been developed, including a rule-based method that learns rules from training data (Bollmann, 2012), edit distance methods (Baron and Rayson, 2008; Pettersson et al., 2013) and CSMT. Sánchez-Martínez et al. (2013) use CSMT to normalize old Spanish; Pettersson et al. (2014) apply it to old English, German, Hungarian, Icelandic, Swedish; and Scherrer and Erjavec (2016) to historical Slovene.

Outside of historical texts, normalization is mostly performed with CSMT, which has been applied to Dutch user-generated content (De Clercq et al., 2013), Slovene tweets (Ljubešić et al., 2014) and Swiss German dialects (Samardžić et al., 2015; Scherrer and Ljubešić, 2016). CSMT proves particularly suitable for text normalization because it captures well intra-word transformations. One further advantage of CSMT is that it can be highly effective when little training data is available, thanks to a small vocabulary (the set of characters). Once a transformation pattern has been learned for a string of characters, it can be applied to translate unknown words that would be considered out of vocabulary (OOV) in the usual word-level formulation of the task.

CSMT was initially applied to translating between closely related languages, such as Spanish and Catalan (Vilar et al., 2007). Although it did not produce better results compared to word-level SMT, it did help improve overall translation quality when the two levels were combined, taking the output of

---

[2] See Koehn and Knowles (2017), among other sources, for an analysis of the poor performance of neural systems when training data is limited.

CSMT only for unknown words. Tiedemann (2009) used CSMT for Norwegian and Swedish, concluding that, although it makes more errors than word-level SMT, many errors are of small entity in that the translated word is very similar to the reference. Moreover, he found that CSMT can also learn mappings between words that are not formally similar. Applied to the task of normalization, however, CSMT barely outperforms a simple baseline that consists in selecting, for each source word in the test set, its most common normalization in the training set and copying the source word if it is not found in the training set (Samardžić et al., 2015). The improvement, here too, comes from the relatively good performance on unknown words.

Since the introduction of neural methods to machine translation (Kalchbrenner and Blunsom, 2013; Cho et al., 2014; Sutskever et al., 2014), some attempts have been made to apply the new framework to the task of normalization. A recent shared task (Tjong Kim Sang et al., 2017) allowed a direct comparison of CSMT with some neural methods, with CSMT still outperforming neural systems. Honnet et al. (2017) apply a neural method embedded in other techniques, but without direct comparison to CSMT. Bollmann and Søgaard (2016) report experiments with deep, long short-term memory (LSTM) networks, but again without a direct comparison to CSMT.

The neural methods applied to text normalization so far employ mostly convolutional neural networks (with the exception of Bollmann and Søgaard (2016)), whereas our approach draws on the line of work known as the encoder-decoder framework. In this framework, one recurrent neural network (RNN) encodes a sequence of symbols into a fixed-length vector representation, and the other decodes the representation into an output sequence of symbols. We extend this with the soft attention mechanism introduced by Bahdanau et al. (2014), that allows a model to search for parts of a source sequence that are relevant to predicting a target symbol.

Our work is closely related to those which implement a modification of the ED framework that allows to incorporate additional language model scores at the decoding stage. Gulcehre et al. (2016) integrated a language model into an ED framework to augment the parallel training data with additional monolingual corpora on the target side. Adapting this framework to the task of morphological segmentation, Ruzsics and Samardžić (2017) introduced a "synchronization mechanism" that allows to integrate language model scores at different levels: the basic ED component is trained on character sequences and the target-side language model component is trained on the sequences of morphemes. We adapt this approach by integrating word-level scores of a language model on top of the character-level neural normalization framework. We compare our method to both the simple memory baseline of Samardžić et al. (2015) and to the standard CSMT, which still represents the state-of-the-art on this task.

3 Data

The data for our experiments comes from manually normalized Swiss German corpora:[3]

- **WUS** set is a corpus of WhatsApp messages (Stark et al., 2014; Ueberwasser and Stark, 2017). The entire collection contains 763,650 messages in different languages spoken in Switzerland. A portion of the data, 5,345 messages in Swiss German, was selected for manual normalization in order to provide a gold standard for automatic normalization. We use this manually annotated portion (a total of 54,229 alignment units) as our main dataset. Table 1 shows examples of alignment units in the corpus.

- **SMS** set is a corpus of SMS messages, again in different languages spoken in Switzerland (Stark et al., 2009 2015). This is a smaller corpus entirely manually normalized. The Swiss German portion contains 10,674 messages. We use this set (a total of 262,494 alignment units) as additional training data, as described in more detail below.

All the messages in our dataset are manually normalized using the same web annotation tool and following the same guidelines (Ruef and Ueberwasser, 2013). This normalization process implies a monotonic alignment between the source tokens and the normalized ones. Table 1 shows the different

---

[3]The data set used in our experiments can be provided on request. Please contact the authors.

alignment type	source form	normalized form	English gloss
one-to-one	viu	viel	much
one-to-many	hämmers	haben wir es	have we it
many-to-one	ü ber	über	on; above
	aweg riise	wegreissen	tear away; rip off
	morge sport	Morgensport	morning gym
many-to-many	über chunts	überkommt es	receives it

Table 1: Examples of aligned token sequences.

types of aligned token sequences. Most of the alignments are pairs of single tokens (one-to-one alignments). There are also many contracted forms corresponding to multiple normalized words (one-to-many alignments). These are typically verb forms merged with subject and object clitics, as shown in the second example in Table 1. The few cases of many-to-one alignments are due to typos (a space instead of a character) and the lack of spelling conventions for Swiss German, most noticeable in arbitrarily split compounds and separable verb particles. Finally, different combinations of the factors listed above can result in many-to-many mappings.

One peculiarity of the WUS corpus is, unsurprisingly given the source of the texts, the frequent use of emojis, which, if untreated, increase significantly the size of the vocabulary. We address this issue by processing two versions of the corpus.

- **Original** is the version of the corpus as provided by its authors, where emojis are replaced with a sequence of characters describing the symbol. For example, the emoji 😃 is rendered as *emojiQsmilingFaceWithOpenMouth*. While they rely on the same vocabulary as the text (i.e. the alphabet), such long sequences may pose a problem to a character-level normalization system and have a negative impact on training time. Moreover, they might produce normalization errors which could be avoided if the sequence were simply copied from source to target.

- **Modified** is the version of the corpus that we created by representing emojis with their Unicode hexadecimal character codes (U+1F603 for the example above). Also, we have removed hyperlinks found in the original corpus, which are often represented by long character strings and might create confusion for the models we use.

In order to assess the impact of the manipulation of the input data, we perform our experiments on both versions of the corpus.

4 Methods

In the following sections, we describe the details of our adaptation of the ED framework to the task of normalizing Swiss German WhatsApp messages. We also give a short description of the standard CSMT framework implemented in the off-the-shelf software Moses, that we use for the purpose of comparison with the current state-of-the-art. Each source sequence is automatically normalized in isolation and compared with the manually normalized form (reference) for evaluation. Most source and target sequences consist of one-to-one word alignments (see Table 1).[4]

4.1 Encoder-Decoder Model (ED)

We define two discrete alphabets, Σ consisting of the character symbols that form the source sequences (second column in Table 1) and Σ_n of the character symbols that form the normalized sequences (third column in Table 1). Our task is to learn a mapping from an original character sequence $x \in \Sigma^*$ to its normalized form $y \in \Sigma_n^*$. To learn this transformation we apply an encoder-decoder model with soft

---

[4]Scherrer and Ljubešić (2016) showed that using longer segments can improve performance by capturing a larger context, which can help resolve ambiguity. We decided to focus on the sequences as shown in Table 1 and to leave the use of longer segments for future work.

attention (Bahdanau et al., 2014). Next, we review the architecture of this model presented by Luong et al. (2015). The model transforms the input sequence into a sequence of hidden states, i.e. a fixed-dimensional vector representation, with a bidirectional encoder which consists of forward and backward RNN. The forward RNN reads the input sequence of embedding vectors $\mathbf{x}_1, \ldots, \mathbf{x}_{n_x}$, in forward direction and encodes them into a sequence of vectors representing forward hidden states:

$$\overrightarrow{\mathbf{h}}_t = f(\overrightarrow{\mathbf{h}}_{t-1}, \mathbf{x}_t), \quad t = 1, \ldots, n_x \tag{1}$$

while the backward RNN reads the sequence in the opposite direction and produces backward hidden states:

$$\overleftarrow{\mathbf{h}}_t = f(\overleftarrow{\mathbf{h}}_{t-1}, \mathbf{x}_t), \quad t = n_x, \ldots, 1 \tag{2}$$

where f stands for LSTM (Hochreiter and Schmidhuber, 1997). The hidden state $\mathbf{h}_t$ for each time step is obtained by concatenating a forward and backward state, so that $\mathbf{h}_t = [\overrightarrow{\mathbf{h}}_t; \overleftarrow{\mathbf{h}}_t]$.

The decoder RNN transforms the internal fixed-length input representation into a variable length output sequence $y = (y_1, \ldots, y_{n_y})$. At each prediction step t, the decoder reads the previous output $\mathbf{y}_{t-1}$ and outputs a hidden state representation $\mathbf{s}_t$:

$$\mathbf{s}_t = f(\mathbf{s}_{t-1}, \mathbf{y}_{t-1}), \quad t = 1, \ldots, n_y \tag{3}$$

The conditional probability over output characters is modeled at each prediction step t as a function of the current decoder hidden state $\mathbf{s}_t$ and the current context vector $\mathbf{c}_t$:

$$p(y_t | y_1, \ldots, y_{t-1}, x) = g(\mathbf{s}_t, \mathbf{c}_t) \tag{4}$$

where g is a concatenation layer followed by a softmax layer (Luong et al., 2015). The context vector $\mathbf{c}_t$ is computed at each step from the encoded input as a weighted sum of the hidden states:

$$\mathbf{c}_t = \sum_{k=1}^{n_x} \alpha_{tk} \mathbf{h}_k \tag{5}$$

The weights are calculated by an alignment model which scores how much attention should be given to the inputs around position k to generate the output at position t:

$$\alpha_{tk} = \phi(\mathbf{s}_t, \mathbf{h}_k) \tag{6}$$

where ϕ is a feed-forward neural network (Bahdanau et al., 2014; Luong et al., 2015). Therefore, the model learns the alignment between input and output jointly with transduction using a deterministic function, whereas the alignment is modeled as latent variable in SMT.

The training objective is to maximize the conditional log-likelihood of the training corpus:

$$L = \frac{1}{N} \sum_{(x,y)} \sum_{t=1}^{n_y} \log p(y_t | y_1, \ldots, y_{t-1}, x) \tag{7}$$

where N is the number of training pairs (x, y).

4.1.1   Integrating Language Models

Before the integration, we assume that a plain ED and a language model (LM) are trained separately. The ED model is trained on character sequences in a parallel corpus consisting of aligned source words and their normalized forms (as shown in Table 1). The ED model learns a conditional probability distribution over the normalized character sequences given the source sequences, as shown in Eq. (4). This probability captures context-sensitive individual character mappings, therefore already including the information provided by a usual LM. We augment this model with an additional LM, separately trained only over the target side of the corpus. We propose two ways of augmenting the initial ED. First, following Ruzsics and Samardžić (2017), we train a word-level LM and fuse it with the character-level ED using the "synchronization mechanism". Second, following Gulcehre et al. (2016), we augment the training set with additional target-side data. In the following, we describe how this mechanism allows us to fuse the scores of different models at the decoding stage in a log-linear fashion.

The "synchronized" decoding approach relies on a beam search to find the prediction steps where different scores are combined. The beam search is run at two levels of granularity. First, it produces the output sequence hypotheses (candidates) at the character level using ED scores until the time step s_1, where K best hypotheses $\{(y_1 y_2 \ldots y_{s1})^i\}$, $y_t \in \Omega$, $i = 1, \ldots, K$ end with a boundary symbol.[5] We consider two boundary symbol types: space, which marks the end of a word in a partial predicted sequence, and a special eow symbol, which marks the end of a completed predicted sequence. The step s_1 is the first synchronization step where we re-score the normalization hypotheses with a weighted sum of the ED score and the LM score:

$$\log p(y_{s1}|y_1, \ldots, y_{s1-1}, x) \quad = \quad \log p_{ED}(y_{s1}|y_1, \ldots, y_{s1-1}, x) \; + \; \alpha_{LM} \log p_{LM}(y_1, \ldots, y_{s1}) \quad (8)$$

At this step, $y_1, \ldots, y_{s1}$ is considered a sequence of $s1$ characters by the ED system, and one word by the LM. After the first synchronization point we continue to produce the re-scored hypotheses using ED scores until the next synchronization point. The search process ends at the synchronization point where the last symbol of the best scored hypotheses (using the combined ED and LM score) is the end of complete prediction symbol eow.

The decoding process scores the hypotheses at two levels: normally working at the character level with ED scores and adding the LM scores only when it hits a boundary symbol. In this way, the LM score helps to evaluate how probable the last generated word is based on the predicted word history, that is the sequence of words generated at the previous synchronization time steps. The described synchronization mechanism is extended in our study to integrate both character-level LM and higher word-level LM.[6] However, in principle, it can be used to add any kind of potentially useful predictors or scores obtained separately from different data sources.

4.2 Character-level Statistical Machine Translation (CSMT)

The core idea behind traditional SMT systems relies on the noisy-channel model, where two basic components are combined: the *translation model* $p(f|e)$,[7] responsible for the adequacy of the translation from source to target sentence, and the *language model* $p(e)$, responsible for the fluency of a sentence in the target language, as shown in Eq. (9), where E is the set of all target sentences.

$$\underset{e \in E}{\operatorname{argmax}} \, p(e|f) = \underset{e \in E}{\operatorname{argmax}} \, p(e)p(f|e) \tag{9}$$

To achieve better context-sensitive source-target mappings, obtained through encoding and memory in the neural approaches, traditional SMT systems rely on phrase-level translation models. These models allow to build a phrase table to store aligned phrase pairs, in the source and target language, that are consistent with the single word alignments established by the IBM models (Brown et al., 1993) with the Expectation-Maximization (EM) algorithm.[8] In phrase-based models, the translation model in Eq. (9) is decomposed as follows:

$$p(\bar{f}_1^I|\bar{e}_1^I) = \prod_{i=1}^{I} \phi(\bar{f}_i|\bar{e}_i) d(\text{start}_i - \text{end}_{i-1} - 1) \tag{10}$$

---

[5] Some of the best hypotheses can have length shorter than s_1, but we assume they are of the same length for the ease of notation.

[6] Although it is possible to fuse a character-level LM with the ED system at each prediction step, as in the "shallow fusion" of Gulcehre et al. (2016), in our initial experiments the performance of such model was inferior to our synchronized approach, where we combine the scores for the whole segments at word boundaries.

[7] While, in section 4.1, x refers to the input sequence and y to the output sequence, here we follow SMT conventions and use e to refer to the target sequence and f to the source sequence.

[8] Koehn et al. (2003) improved the mono-directional IBM alignments, which only allow at most one target word to be aligned with a source word, with a heuristic method based on a bidirectional alignment.

In Eq. (10), $\bar{f}_1^I$ and $\bar{e}_1^I$ are sequences of phrases, $\phi(\bar{f}_i|\bar{e}_i)$ is the probability distribution that models phrase translation and $d(\text{start}_i - \text{end}_{i-1} - 1)$ the probability distribution that models the reordering of the target phrases. The various model components (translation, reordering and language model) are weighted in a log-linear model to scale their contribution to the final translation. The reordering model is ignored when reordering is disabled under the assumption of a monotonic translation, which is the case in our experiments.

In CSMT, we simply replace words with characters as the symbols that make up a phrase. CSMT is a suitable approach for those tasks in which many word pairs in the source and target languages are formally similar, such as the Swiss German word *Sunne* normalized as *Sonne* ('sun'), or are characterized by regular transformation patterns that are not captured by word-level systems, such as the pattern *ii* → *ei*, which is responsible for the transformations *Ziit* → *Zeit* ('time'), *wiiter* → *weiter* ('further'), *Priis* → *Preis* ('price').

This setting requires to pre-process the parallel corpus by replacing spaces between words with underscores and adding spaces between characters. This converts the corpus alignment unit *hani* ↔ *habe ich* into *h a n i* ↔ *h a b e _ i c h* ('I have'). As a result, the characters are now the tokens of the alignment units, phrases are sequences of characters and the language model is based on character n-grams. After running Moses, the predictions made by the system are post-processed, by removing spaces and underscores, before evaluation with a reference.

5 Experiments and Tools

To assess whether our approach provides an improvement over CSMT, we perform a systematic comparison, training and testing both systems on our datasets. In this section we describe the details of the experiments. We run the ED experiments using an extended version of the code from Ruzsics and Samardžić (2017), which offers the possibility to integrate several LM predictors trained on different levels.[9] In a character-level framework, where most alignment units consist of single words, evaluation metrics such as precision, recall and BLEU may provide information on the extent to which a unit normalized by the model, viewed as a sequence of characters, differs from its reference. They thus express the magnitude of the intra-word error. However, we chose to simply assess whether a source sequence has been correctly normalized or not by the system. For this reason, the accuracy score is used to evaluate the baseline and the various models implemented.

5.1 Parameter Settings

ED Hyperparameters and Settings. The character embeddings are shared between input (source) and output (target) vocabulary and set to 100 for the original corpus and 200 for the modified one. The forward and backward RNN of the bidirectional encoder have $H_e = 200$ hidden units each. The decoder also has $H_d = 200$ hidden units. We apply an ensemble of 5 ED models where each model is trained with random start using SGD optimization. The models are trained for a maximum of 30 epochs, possibly stopping earlier if the performance measured on the development set stagnates. The training examples are shuffled before each epoch. We use n-gram order of 7 for the character-level language models. Additionally, the word-level language models used in some of the ED experiments are built on 3-grams.[10] Beam size 3 is used for the final predictions on the test set in all the settings. The weights of the different components of the model are tuned with MERT by maximizing the accuracy score on the development set.

CSMT Settings. We used the Moses toolkit with the following adjustments to the standard settings: i) assuming monotonic character alignment, distortion (reordering) was disabled; ii) in tuning, we used WER[11] instead of BLEU for MERT optimization. We used the KenLM language model toolkit (Heafield,

---

[9] https://github.com/tatyana-ruzsics/uzh-corpuslab-normalization
[10] Kneser-Ney smoothing is used on the modified corpus and modified Kneser-Ney is used on the original one.
[11] WER: Word Error Rate. This metric becomes Character Error Rate in CSMT.

2011) with character 7-grams.[12]

5.2 Baseline and Comparison

The baseline for our task is the one defined by Samardžić et al. (2015), where each original word in the test set is normalized as follows: if the word is found in the training set, use the most frequent normalization, otherwise, copy the source word as its normalization (leave unchanged).

To assess how our modifications influence the performance, we run different versions of our ED system on different datasets. Our plain ED is a soft-attention model described in Section 4.1, with the selected hyperparameters set as described above. In further ED experiments, we integrate language models trained at different levels, character and word, and combine their scores over words in a synchronized decoding approach. The word-level language models are built on the target sides of the two datasets: the train part of the WUS corpus only and its concatenation with the SMS corpus (WUS+SMS). The character-level language model is only trained using the WUS+SMS corpus, since the decoder of the ED system already acts as a (neural) character-level language model over the target side of WUS. In addition, we try a combination of the ED system with both types of language models.

For the purpose of a systematic comparison, we consider two settings for CSMT. First, we train the model on the WUS corpus only. Second, we add an additional language model trained over the target side of the SMS corpus. Note that the CSMT language models operate only at the character level.[13]

5.3 Train/Test Split

We compute the accuracy of the normalized test set word tokens (token sequences in the case of many-to-one or many-to-many alignments), by comparison with the manual normalization. We split the randomly shuffled WUS corpus in 80% training, 10% development and 10% test set, and use these same splits for all our experiments. The original training set contains 43,385 parallel items; the modified training set is slightly smaller with 43,370 parallel items, since we removed hyperlinks from the original. Both test sets contain 5,422 items, the original development set also has 5,422 items, and the modified development set 5,418. For the experiments where we use additional target data, we add 262,494 target token sequences of the SMS corpus. This results in a total of 305,864 items for the extended target WUS+SMS data.

6 Results

The results of our experiments are shown in Table 2. Both the CSMT and the ED models outperform the baseline in all settings. With respect to the ED models, the integration of the additional word-level language model, the first trained on the WUS corpus, the second on the WUS+SMS corpus, results in better performance. Adding a character-level language model trained on the WUS+SMS corpus produces a higher accuracy too, when applied in isolation. Further improvements are observed from combining language models trained on different levels only for the modified corpus. The CSMT method benefits more than the ED method from the additional character-level LM trained on the SMS corpus. However, the capability of ED models to overcome certain limitations of the CSMT approach becomes evident when we exploit the possibility of augmenting them with word-level language models. These produce, for example, improvements in the normalization of foreign words (e.g. source *cream*, where CSMT erroneously forces normalization and gives *kream*), single source words that are normalized as two or more target words (e.g. source *söuis* → reference *soll ich es* ('should I [...] it')), and source words whose reference normalization is formally very different (e.g. source *wg* → reference *wohngemeinschaft* 'shared apartment'). The best accuracy overall (87.61% for the original corpus) is obtained by the ED model augmented with the word-level LM trained over the extended target data. We observe a slight drop in the performance for the modified corpus which is due to choices of the systems on the ambiguous source items.

---

[12] We have observed improvements with order 12, but we chose to use a general setting for normalization and to leave this investigation for future work.

[13] It is not a trivial task to incorporate a synchronized LM over words into the CSMT framework and to the best of our knowledge such work has not been done before.

System	Corpus	
	Original	**Modified**
ED + LMwus+sms:char + LMwus+sms:word	87.57	87.22
ED + LMwus+sms:char + LMwus:word	87.38	87.09
ED + LMwus+sms:word	**87.61**	87.05
ED + LMwus+sms:char	87.38	87.07
ED + LMwus:words	87.15	86.55
ED ensemble 5	87.03	86.50
ED average 5	85.03	84.70
CSMT LMwus+sms:char	86.35	86.43
CSMT LMwus:char	85.30	85.85
Baseline	84.45	84.45

Table 2: Text normalization accuracy scores. Original: corpus with hyperlinks and emojis as description of the symbol. Modified: corpus without hyperlinks and with emojis as symbols. ED: character based encoder-decoder model. CSMT: character-level statistical machine translation. LM: language models on words or characters. ED average 5: average over five encoder-decoder models. ED ensemble 5: ensemble of five encoder-decoder models (all other ED models, except the average, are extensions of this ensemble). wus: corpus of WhatsApp messages. sms: corpus of sms messages.

We carried out a comparison of the predictions made by the best model of each approach with the reference (5,422 test set normalization units), when the original corpus is used. The analysis reveals 229 cases in which only CSMT is wrong, and 161 in which only ED is wrong. A wrong prediction is made by both models in 511 cases. In particular, in 354 cases they make the same error, whereas in 157 cases they make different errors. Many errors common to both models are related to ambiguity in the source text, that arises when one source word has more than one normalization form in the training set. For example, the source word *di* is manually normalized 83 times as *dich* ('you' as object), and 68 times as *die* (feminine definite article). Moreover, both systems have difficulty normalizing source words characterized by irregularities such as vowel reduplication, e.g. *bitteeeee* instead of the more plausible *bitte* ('please'), and by spelling which is not due to an arbitrary choice of the writer, but rather to a typo (e.g., *ado* instead of the more plausible *aso* ('so')).

Of a total of 166 emojis, all of them are correctly normalized by both models in the original version of the corpus. This means that the models are able to effectively process them, thus avoiding the need for solutions that could be cumbersome in terms of framework engineering, such as copying emojis at decoding time.

7   Conclusion

We have shown in this paper that integrating different-level language models into a neural encoder-decoder framework allows a neural method to reach and even improve the performance of character-level statistical machine translation methods, previously considered superior to neural methods in the task of text normalization. The method that we propose is an adaptation of mechanisms introduced in machine translation and morphological segmentation. While the experiments conducted in this paper show the advantage of integrating different-level language models, the adaptation that we propose can be extended to integrating other potential scores into a single encoder-decoder framework. This possibility can be exploited for further improvements of text normalization methods.

Acknowledgements

This research is funded by the Swiss National Science Foundation, project "What's Up, Switzerland? Language, Individuals and Ideologies in mobile messaging" (Sinergia: CRSII1_160714).

References

Dzmitry Bahdanau, Kyunghyun Cho, and Yoshua Bengio. 2014. Neural machine translation by jointly learning to align and translate. *CoRR*, abs/1409.0473.

Alistair Baron and Paul Rayson. 2008. VARD 2: A tool for dealing with spelling variation in historical corpora. In *Proceedings of the Postgraduate Conference in Corpus Linguistics*, Aston University.

Marcel Bollmann and Anders Søgaard. 2016. Improving historical spelling normalization with bi-directional LSTMs and multi-task learning. In *Proceedings of COLING 2016, the 26th International Conference on Computational Linguistics: Technical Papers*, pages 131–139. The COLING 2016 Organizing Committee.

Marcel Bollmann. 2012. (Semi-)automatic normalization of historical texts using distance measures and the Norma tool. In *Proceedings of the Second Workshop on Annotation of Corpora for Research in the Humanities (ACRH-2)*, pages 3–14, Lisbon, Portugal.

Peter F. Brown, Vincent J. Della Pietra, Stephen A. Della Pietra, and Robert L. Mercer. 1993. The mathematics of statistical machine translation: Parameter estimation. *Computational Linguistics*, 19(2):263–311.

Kyunghyun Cho, Bart van Merrienboer, Caglar Gulcehre, Dzmitry Bahdanau, Fethi Bougares, Holger Schwenk, and Yoshua Bengio. 2014. Learning Phrase Representations using RNN Encoder–Decoder for Statistical Machine Translation. In *Proceedings of the 2014 Conference on Empirical Methods in Natural Language Processing (EMNLP)*, pages 1724–1734, Doha, Qatar, October. Association for Computational Linguistics.

Orphée De Clercq, Bart Desmet, Sarah Schulz, Els Lefever, and Véronique Hoste. 2013. Normalization of Dutch user-generated content. In *Proceedings of RANLP 2013*, pages 179–188, Hissar, Bulgaria.

Caglar Gulcehre, Orhan Firat, Kelvin Xu, Kyunghyun Cho, and Yoshua Bengio. 2016. On integrating a language model into neural machine translation. *Computer Speech and Language*, 5.

Kenneth Heafield. 2011. KenLM: faster and smaller language model queries. In *Proceedings of the EMNLP 2011 Sixth Workshop on Statistical Machine Translation*, pages 187–197, Edinburgh, Scotland, United Kingdom, July.

Sepp Hochreiter and Jürgen Schmidhuber. 1997. Long short-term memory. *Neural Comput.*, 9(8):1735–1780, November.

Pierre-Edouard Honnet, Andrei Popescu-Belis, Claudiu Musat, and Michael Baeriswyl. 2017. Machine Translation of Low-Resource Spoken Dialects: Strategies for Normalizing Swiss German. *ArXiv e-prints*, 1710.11035, October.

Nal Kalchbrenner and Phil Blunsom. 2013. Recurrent continuous translation models. In *Proceedings of the 2013 Conference on Empirical Methods in Natural Language Processing*, pages 1700–1709, Seattle, Washington, USA, October. Association for Computational Linguistics.

Philipp Koehn and Rebecca Knowles. 2017. Six challenges for neural machine translation. *CoRR*, abs/1706.03872.

Philipp Koehn, Franz Josef Och, and Daniel Marcu. 2003. Statistical phrase-based translation. In *Proceedings of the 2003 Human Language Technology Conference of the North American Chapter of the Association for Computational Linguistics (Volume 1)*, pages 48–54, Edmonton, Canada.

Philipp Koehn, Hieu Hoang, Alexandra Birch, Chris Callison-Burch, Marcello Federico, Nicola Bertoldi, Brooke Cowan, Wade Shen, Christine Moran, Richard Zens, Chris Dyer, Ondrej Bojar, Alexandra Constantin, and Evan Herbst. 2007. Moses: Open source toolkit for statistical machine translation. In *Proceedings of the ACL 2007 demonstration session*, pages 177–180, Prague, Czech Republic.

Nikola Ljubešić, Tomaž Erjavec, and Darja Fišer. 2014. Standardizing tweets with character-level machine translation. In *Proceedings of CICLing 2014*, Lecture notes in computer science, pages 164–175, Kathmandu, Nepal. Springer.

Minh-Thang Luong, Hieu Pham, and Christopher D. Manning. 2015. Effective approaches to attention-based neural machine translation. In *Empirical Methods in Natural Language Processing (EMNLP)*, pages 1412–1421, Lisbon, Portugal, September. Association for Computational Linguistics.

Eva Pettersson, Beáta B. Megyesi, and Joakim Nivre. 2013. Normalisation of historical text using context-sensitive weighted Levenshtein distance and compound splitting. In *Proceedings of the 19th Nordic Conference of Computational Linguistics (Nodalida 2013)*, pages 163–79, Oslo, Norway.

Eva Pettersson, Beáta B. Megyesi, and Joakim Nivre. 2014. A multilingual evaluation of three spelling normalisation methods for historical text. In *Proceedings of the 8th Workshop on Language Technology for Cultural Heritage, Social Sciences, and Humanities (LaTeCH)*, pages 32–41, Gothenburg, Sweden.

Felicity Rash. 1998. *The German language in Switzerland: multilingualism, diglossia and variation.* Lang, Bern.

Beni Ruef and Simone Ueberwasser. 2013. The taming of a dialect: Interlinear glossing of Swiss German text messages. In Marcos Zampieri and Sascha Diwersy, editors, *Non-standard Data Sources in Corpus-based Research*, pages 61–68, Aachen.

Tatyana Ruzsics and Tanja Samardžić. 2017. Neural sequence-to-sequence learning of internal word structure. In *Proceedings of the 21st Conference on Computational Natural Language Learning (CoNLL 2017)*, pages 184–194, Vancouver, Canada. Association for Computational Linguistics.

Tanja Samardžić, Yves Scherrer, and Elvira Glaser. 2015. Normalising orthographic and dialectal variants for the automatic processing of Swiss German. In *Proceedings of The 4th Biennial Workshop on Less-Resourced Languages*. ELRA.

Felipe Sánchez-Martínez, Isabel Martínez-Sempere, Xavier Ivars-Ribes, and Rafael C. Carrasco. 2013. An open diachronic corpus of historical Spanish: annotation criteria and automatic modernisation of spelling. Research report, Departament de Llenguatges i Sistemes Informàtics, Universitat d'Alacant, Alicante.

Yves Scherrer and Tomaž Erjavec. 2016. Modernising historical Slovene words. *Natural Language Engineering*, 22(6):881–905.

Yves Scherrer and Nikola Ljubešić. 2016. Automatic normalisation of the Swiss German ArchiMob corpus using character-level machine translation. In *Proceedings of the 13th Conference on Natural Language Processing (KONVENS 2016)*, pages 248–255.

Elisabeth Stark, Simone Ueberwasser, and Beni Ruef. 2009-2015. Swiss SMS corpus, University of Zurich. https://sms.linguistik.uzh.ch.

Elisabeth Stark, Simone Ueberwasser, and Anne Göhring. 2014. Corpus "What's up, Switzerland?". Technical report, University of Zurich.

Ilya Sutskever, Oriol Vinyals, and Quoc V. Le. 2014. Sequence to sequence learning with neural networks. In *Advances in Neural Information Processing Systems 27: Annual Conference on Neural Information Processing Systems 2014, December 8-13 2014, Montreal, Quebec, Canada*, pages 3104–3112.

Jörg Tiedemann. 2009. Character-based PSMT for closely related languages. In *Proceedings of 13th Annual Conference of the European Association for Machine Translation*, pages 12–19, Barcelona, Spain.

Erik Tjong Kim Sang, Marcel Bollmann, Remko Boschker, Francisco Casacuberta, Feike Dietz, Stefanie Dipper, Miguel Domingo, Rob van der Goot, Marjo van Koppen, Nikola Ljubešić, Robert Östling, Florian Petran, Eva Pettersson, Yves Scherrer, Marijn Schraagen, Leen Sevens, Jörg Tiedemann, Tom Vanallemeersch, and Kalliopi Zervanou. 2017. The CLIN27 shared task: Translating historical text to contemporary language for improving automatic linguistic annotation. *Computational Linguistics in the Netherlands Journal*, 7:53–64, 12/2017.

Simone Ueberwasser and Elisabeth Stark. 2017. What's up, Switzerland? A corpus-based research project in a multilingual country. *Linguistik Online*, 84(5).

David Vilar, Jan-Thorsten Peter, and Hermann Ney. 2007. Can we translate letters? In *Proceedings of the Second Workshop on Statistical Machine Translation*, pages 33–39, Prague, Czech Republic.

A High Coverage Method for Automatic False Friends Detection for Spanish and Portuguese

Santiago Castro   **Jairo Bonanata**   **Aiala Rosá**

Grupo de Procesamiento de Lenguaje Natural
Universidad de la República — Uruguay
`{sacastro,jbonanata,aialar}@fing.edu.uy`

Abstract

False friends are words in two languages that look or sound similar, but have different meanings. They are a common source of confusion among language learners. Methods to detect them automatically do exist, however they make use of large aligned bilingual corpora, which are hard to find and expensive to build, or encounter problems dealing with infrequent words. In this work we propose a high coverage method that uses word vector representations to build a false friends classifier for any pair of languages, which we apply to the particular case of Spanish and Portuguese. The required resources are a large corpus for each language and a small bilingual lexicon for the pair.

1 Introduction

Closely related languages often share a significant number of similar words which may have different meanings in each language. Similar words with different meanings are called *false friends*, while similar words sharing meaning are called *cognates*. For instance, between Spanish and Portuguese, the amount of cognates reaches the 85% of the total vocabulary (Ulsh, 1971). This fact represents a clear advantage for language learners, but it may also lead to an important number of interferences, since similar words will be interpreted as in the native language, which is not correct in the case of false friends.

Generally, the expression false friends refers not only to pairs of identical words, but also to pairs of similar words, differing in a few characters. Thus, the Spanish verb *halagar* ("to flatten") and the similar Portuguese verb *alagar* ("to flood") are usually considered false friends.

Besides traditional false friends, that are similar words with different meanings, Humblé (2006) analyses three more types. First, he mentions words with similar meanings but used in different contexts, as *esclarecer*, which is used in a few contexts in Spanish (*esclarecer un crimen*, "clarify a crime"), but not in other contexts where *aclarar* is used (*aclarar una duda*, "clarify a doubt"), while in Portuguese *esclarecer* is used in all these contexts. Secondly, there are similar words with partial meaning differences, as *abrigo*, which in Spanish means "shelter" and "coat", but in Portuguese has just the first meaning. Finally, Humblé (2006) also considers false friends as similar words with the same meaning but used in different syntactic structures in each language, as the Spanish verb *hablar* ("to speak"), which does not accept a sentential direct object, and its Portuguese equivalent *falar*, which does (**yo hablé que …/ eu falei que …*, **"I spoke that …"*). These non-traditional false friends are more difficult to detect by language learners than traditional ones, because of their subtle differences.

Having a list of false friends can help native speakers of one language to avoid confusion when speaking and writing in the other language. Such a list could be integrated into a writing assistant to prevent the writer when using these words. For Spanish/Portuguese, in particular, while there are printed dictionaries that compile false friends (Otero Brabo Cruz, 2004), we did not find a complete digital false friends list, therefore, an automatic method for false friends detection would be useful. Furthermore, it

---

This work is licensed under a Creative Commons Attribution 4.0 International License. License details: `https://creativecommons.org/licenses/by/4.0/`.

Proceedings of the Fifth Workshop on NLP for Similar Languages, Varieties and Dialects, pages 29–36
Santa Fe, New Mexico, USA, August 20, 2018.

is interesting to study methods which could generate false friends lists for any pair of similar languages, particularly, languages for which this phenomenon has not been studied.

In this work we present an automatic method for false friends detection. We focus on the traditional false friends definition (similar words with different meanings) because of the dataset we count with and also to present our method in a simple context. We describe a supervised classifier we constructed to distinguish false friends from cognates based on word embeddings. Although for the method development and evaluation we used Spanish and Portuguese, the method could be applied to other language pairs, provided that the resources needed for the method building are available. We do not deal with the problem of determining if two words are similar or not, which is prior to the issue we tackle.

The paper is organized as follows: in Section 2 we describe some related work, in Section 3 we introduce the word embeddings used in this work, in Section 4 we describe our method, in Section 5 we present and analyze the experiments carried out. Finally, in Section 6, we present our conclusions and sketch some future work.

2   Related Work

Previous work use a combination of orthographic, syntactic, semantic and frequency-based features. Frunza (2006) worked with French and English, focusing only on orthographic features via a supervised machine learning algorithm. While this method can work in some cases — e.g. to detect true cognates with a common root, such as *inaccesible* in Spanish and *inacessível* in Portuguese ("inaccessible"), that come from the Latin word *inaccessibilis* — it does not take into account the meanings of the words.

Mitkov et al. (2007) used both a distributional and taxonomy-based approach to multiple language pairs: English–French, English–German, English–Spanish and French–Spanish. For the former approach, they build vectors based on the words that appear in a window in the corpus, computing the co-occurrence probability. Then they defined two methods for classification: one that considers the N nearest neighbors for each word in the pair and computes the Dice coefficient to determine the similarity between both[1], and another one that is similar but using syntactically related words instead of the adjacent words. Additionally, they evaluated a method which uses a taxonomy to classify false friends, and fails back to the distributional similarity for words not included in the taxonomy. They achieved better results under this experiment than only using the distributional similarity. Based on the former technique, Ljubešic et al. (2013) focused on detecting false friends in closely related languages: Slovene and Croatian. Likewise, they exploited a distributional technique but also propose the use of Pointwise Mutual Information (PMI) as an effective way to classify false friends via the frequencies in the corpora.

Sepúlveda and Aluísio (2011) tackled this task for Portuguese and Spanish, taking the same orthographic approach as Frunza (2006). Nonetheless, they carried out an additional experiment in which they added a new feature whose value is the likelihood of one of the words of the pair to be a translation of the other one. This number was obtained from a probabilistic Spanish-Portuguese dictionary, previously generated taking a large sentence-aligned bilingual corpus.

3   Word Vector Representations

As seen in the previous section, some authors (Mitkov et al., 2007; Ljubešic et al., 2013) represented words as vectors by counting occurrences or by building tf–idf vectors, among other techniques. Similarly, Mikolov et al. (2013a) proposed an unsupervised technique, known as *word2vec*, to efficiently represent words as vectors from a large unlabeled corpus, which has proven to outperform several other representations in tasks involving text as input (LeCun et al., 2015). As it is a vector-based distributional representation technique, it is based on computing a vector space in which vectors are close if their corresponding words appear frequently in the same contexts in the corpus used to train it. Interesting relationships and patterns are learned in particular with this method, e.g. the result of the vector calculation $vector(``Madrid")-vector(``Spain")+vector(``France")$ is closer to $vector(``Paris")$ than to any other word vector (Mikolov et al., 2013a). Additionally, Mikolov et al. (2013c) has shown a technique

---

[1]Note that for this approach a bilingual dictionary is needed.

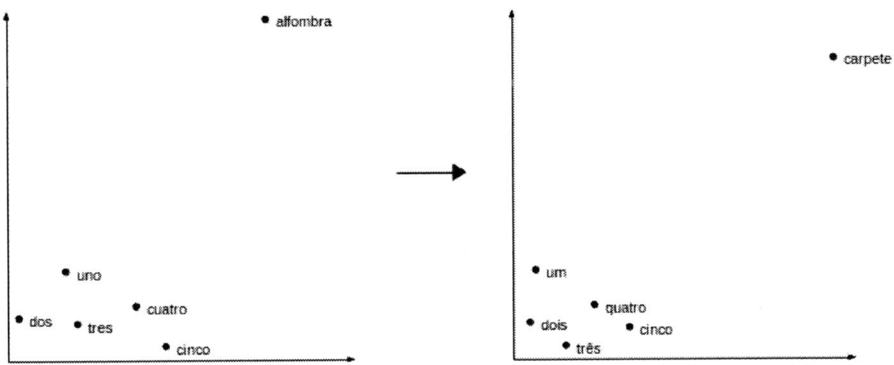

Figure 1: Example showing word2vec properties. The 2D graphs represent Spanish and Portuguese word spaces after applying PCA, scaling and rotating to exaggerate the similarities and emphasize the differences. The left graph is the source language vector space (in this case Spanish) and the right one is the target language vector space (Portuguese).

to detect common phrases such as "New York" to be part of the vector space, being able to detect more entities and at the same time enhancing the context of others.

To exploit multi-language capabilities, Mikolov et al. (2013b) developed a method to automatically generate dictionaries and phrase tables from small bilingual data (translation word pairs), based on the calculation of a linear transformation between the vector spaces built with word2vec. This is presented as an optimization problem that tries to minimize the sum of the Euclidean distances between the translated source word vectors and the target vectors of each pair, and the translation matrix is obtained by means of stochastic gradient descent. We chose this distributional representation technique because of this translation property, which is what our method is mainly based on.

These concepts around word2vec are shown in Fig. 1. In the example, the five word vectors corresponding to the numbers from "one" to "five" are shown, and also the word vector "carpet" for each language. More related words have closer vectors, while unrelated word vectors are at a greater distance. At the same time, groups of words are arranged in a similar way, allowing to build translation candidates.

4 Method Description

As false friends are word pairs in which one seems to be a translation of the other one, our idea is to compare their vectors using Mikolov et al. (2013b) technique. Our hypothesis is that a word vector in one language should be close to the cognate word vector in another language when it is transformed using this technique, but far when they are false friends, as described hereafter.

First, we exploited the Spanish and Portuguese Wikipedia's (containing several hundreds of thousands of words) to build the vector spaces we needed, using Gensim's skip-gram based word2vec implementation (Řehůřek and Sojka, 2010). The preprocessing of the Wikipedia's involved the following steps. The text was tokenized based on the alphabet of each language, removing words that contain other characters. Numbers were converted to their equivalent words. Wikipedia non-article pages were removed (e.g. disambiguation pages) and punctuation marks were discarded as well. Portuguese was harder to tokenize provided that the hyphen is widely used as part of the words in the language. For example, *bem-vindo* ("welcome") is a single word whereas *Uruguai-Japão* ("Uruguay-Japan") in *jogo Uruguai-Japão* ("Uruguay-Japan match") are two different words, used with an hyphen only in some contexts. The right option is to treat them as separate tokens in order to avoid spurious words in the model and to provide more information to existing words (*Uruguai* and *Japão*). As the word embedding method exploits the text at the level of sentences (and to avoid splitting ambiguous sentences), paragraphs were used as sentences, which still keep semantic relationships. A word had to appear at least five times in the corresponding Wikipedia to be considered for construction of the vector space.

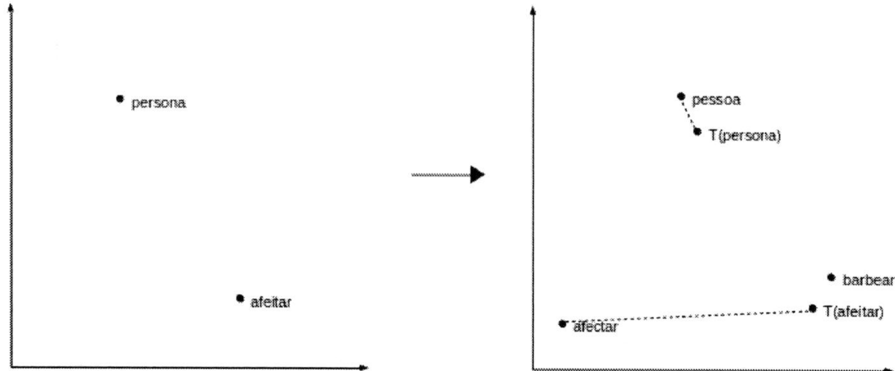

Figure 2: Example showing our method's main idea. The 2D graphs represent the word spaces after applying PCA, scaling and rotating to emphasize the differences. The left graph is the source language vector space (in this case Spanish) and the right one is the target language vector space (Portuguese).

Secondly, WordNet (Fellbaum, 1998) was used as the bilingual lexicon to build the linear transformation between the vector spaces by applying the same technique described in (Mikolov et al., 2013b), taking advantage of the multi-language synset alignment available in NLTK (Bird et al., 2009) between Spanish (Gonzalez-Agirre et al., 2012) and Portuguese (de Paiva and Rademaker, 2012), based on Open Multilingual WordNet (Bond and Paik, 2012). We generated this lexicon by iterating through each of the 40,000 WordNet synsets and forming pairs taking their most common Spanish word and Portuguese word. Note that this is a small figure compared with the corpus sizes, and we show in the next section that it could be considerably lower. We also show that the transformation source needs not to be WordNet (we used it just for convenience), which is an expensive and carefully handcrafted resource; it could be just a bilingual dictionary.

Finally, we defined a method to distinguish false friends from cognates. We defined a binary classifier for determining the class, *false friends* or *cognates*, for each pair of similar words.

Given a candidate pair $(source\_word, target\_word)$, and the corresponding vectors $(source\_vector, target\_vector)$, the first step consists of transforming $source\_vector$ to the space computed for the target language, using the transformation described above. Let $T(source\_vector)$ be the result of this transformation.

Then, to determine if $source\_word$ and $target\_word$ are cognates (if one of them is a possible translation of the other one), we analyzed the relationship between $T(source\_vector)$ and $target\_vector$. According to Mikolov et al. (2013b), the transformation we compute between the vector spaces keeps semantic relations between words from the source space to the target space. So, if $(source\_word, target\_word)$ is a pair of cognates, then $T(source\_vector)$ should be close to $target\_vector$. Otherwise, $source\_word$ and $target\_word$ are false friends.

The method is illustrated in Fig. 2. In the example, the pair $(persona, pessoa)$ are cognates (meaning "person" in English) while the pair $(afeitar, afectar)$ are false friends (meaning "to shave" and "that affects", respectively). If we transform the source word vectors ($persona$ and $afeitar$) and thus obtain vectors in the target vector space, $T(persona)$ and $pessoa$ are close while $T(afeitar)$ and $afectar$ are far from each other (while a valid translation of $afeitar$, $barbear$, is close to $T(afeitar)$).

Following this idea, a threshold needs to be established by which two words are considered cognates. In addition to this, we wanted to see if similar properties help to constitute an acceptable division. Hence, we trained and tested by means of cross-validation a supervised binary Support Vector Machines classifier, based on three features:

- Feature 1: the cosine distance between $T(source\_vector)$ and $target\_vector$.

- Feature 2: the number of word vectors in the target vector space closer to $target\_vector$ than

$T(source\_vector)$, using the cosine distance. We believe that in some cases the distance for cognates may be larger but what it counts is if the transformed vector lays within the closest ones to the target vector.

- Feature 3: the sum of the distances between $target\_vector$ and $T(source\_vector_i)$ for the five word vectors $source\_vector_i$ nearest to $source\_vector$, using the cosine distance. The idea here is that the first feature may be error prone since it only considers one vector, so considering more vectors (by taking both the context from the source vector and the one from its transformed vector) should reduce the variance, as neighbor word vectors from the source word should be neighbors of the target word.

We carried out different experiments alternating the language we used as the source and the language we used as the target, and also other parameters, which we show in the next section.

The source code is public and available to use.[2]

5 Experimental Analysis

Unfortunately, we are not able to compare our method to several others presented by other authors as they are not only based on non-public code, but also on non-public datasets which are not directly comparable with the one used here. Nevertheless, we compare our technique against several methods, for the particular case of Spanish and Portuguese and show it is solid. First, we set a simple baseline that does the following: it checks if there exist a WordNet synset which contains both pair words within the Spanish and Portuguese words of it, and if it is does, then they are considered cognates. Then, we compare to the Machine Translation software Apertium[3]: we take one of the pair words, translate it and check if the translation matches the other word. We chose this software since it can be accessed offline and it is freely available. Apart from this, we compare with Sepúlveda and Aluísio (2011, experiment 2 and 3.2) method and also with a variant of our method that adds a word frequency feature (the relative number of times each word appeared in the corpus). Word frequencies are used by other authors and we believe they are a different data source from what the word2vec vectors can provide.

For these experiments we use the same data set as in (Sepúlveda and Aluísio, 2011).[4] This resource is composed by 710 Spanish-Portuguese word pairs: 338 cognates and 372 false friends. The word pairs were selected from the following resources: an online Spanish-Brazilian Portuguese dictionary, an online Spanish-Portuguese dictionary, a list of the most frequent words in Portuguese and Spanish and an online list of different words in Portuguese and Spanish. There are not multi-word expressions and roughly half of the pairs are composed of identically spelled words. It was annotated by two people.

It is important to consider that the word coverage is a concern in this task since every method can only works when the pair words are present in their resources (in other words, they are not out of a method's vocabulary). The accuracy thus only takes into account the covered pairs. The coverage for the simple baseline can be measured by counting the pairs were both words are present in WordNet. Sepúlveda and Aluísio (2011, experiment 2) only considers orthographic and phonetic differences, so always covers all pairs. Sepúlveda and Aluísio (2011, experiment 3.2) uses a dictionary, then the pairs that are in it count towards the coverage. The words that could not be translated by Apertium are counted against the coverage of its related method. Finally, the pairs that cannot be translated into vectors are counted as not covered by our methods.

Results are shown in Table 1. It can be appreciated that our method provides both high accuracy and coverage, and that word embedding information can be further improved if additional information, such as the word frequencies, is included. We also tested a version of our method that only uses Feature 1 via logistic regression, which reduced the accuracy by 3% roughly, showing that the other two features add some missing information to improve the accuracy. As an additional experiment, we tried exploiting

---

[2]`https://github.com/pln-fing-udelar/false-friends`
[3]`https://www.apertium.org`
[4]This data set is available at `http://ec.europa.eu/translation/portuguese/magazine/documents/folha47_lista_pt.pdf`

Method	Accuracy	Coverage
WN Baseline	68.18	55.38
Sepúlveda 2	63.52	100.00
Sepúlveda 3.2	76.37	59.44
Apertium	77.75	66.01
Our method	77.28	97.91
With frequencies	79.42	97.91

Table 1: Results (%) obtained by the different methods. *WN Baseline* and *Apertium* methods were measured using the whole dataset, whereas our method's evaluation was carried out with a five-fold cross-validation.

Method	Accuracy
es-400-100-1	**77.28**
es-800-100-1	76.99
es-100-100-1	76.98
es-200-100-1	76.84
es-200-200-1	76.55
pt-200-200-1	76.13
es-200-800-1	75.99
pt-400-100-1	75.99
pt-100-100-1	75.84
es-100-200-1	75.83
es-100-100-2	74.98

Table 2: Results obtained under different configurations. The method name complies with the format: `[source language]-[Spanish vectors dimension]-[Portuguese vectors dimension]-[phrases max size]`. All configurations present the same coverage as before.

WordNet to compute taxonomy-based distances as features in the same manner as Mitkov et al. (2007) did, but we did not obtain a significant difference, thus we conclude that it does not add information to what already lays in the features built upon the embeddings.

As Mikolov et al. (2013b) did, we wondered how our method works under different vector configurations, hence we carried out several experiments, varying vector space dimensions. We also experimented with vectors for phrases up to two words. Finally, we evaluated how the election of the source language, Spanish or Portuguese, affects the results. Accuracy obtained for the ten best configurations, and for the experiment with two word vectors are presented in Table 2. For the experiment we used the vector dimensions 100, 200, 400 and 800; source vector space Spanish and Portuguese; and we also tried with a single run with two-word phrases (with Spanish as source and 100 as the vector dimension), summing up 33 configurations in total. As it can be noted, there are no significant differences in the accuracy of our method when varying the vector sizes. Higher dimensions do not provide better results and they even worsen when the target language dimension is greater than or equal to the source language dimension, as Mikolov et al. (2013b) claimed. Taking Spanish as the source language seems to be better, maybe this is due to the corpus sizes: the corpus used to generate the Spanish vector space is 1.4 times larger than the one used for Portuguese. Finally, we can observe that including vectors for two-word phrases does not improve results.

5.1 Linear Transformation Analysis

We were intrigued in knowing how different qualities and quantities of bilingual lexicon entries would affect our method performance. We show how the accuracy varies according to the bilingual lexicon size and its source in the Fig. 3. *WN* seems to be slightly better than using *Apertium* as source, albeit they both perform well. Also, both rapidly achieve acceptable results, with less than a thousand entries, and

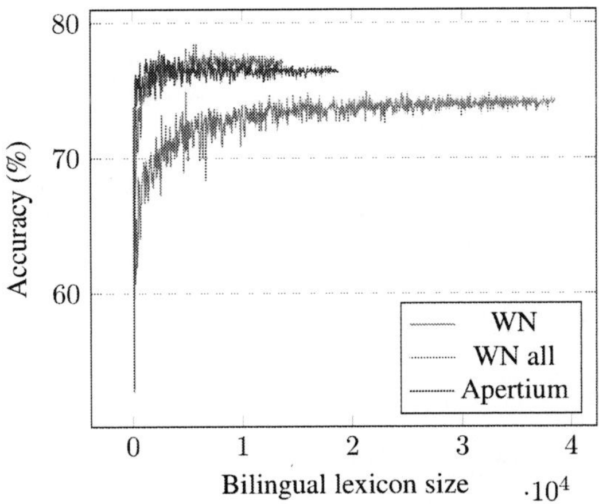

Figure 3: Accuracy of our method with respect to different bilingual lexicon sizes and sources. *WN* is the original approach we take to build the bilingual lexicon, *WN all* is a method that takes every pair of lemmas from both languages in every WordNet synset and *Apertium* uses the translations of the top 50,000 Spanish words in frequencies from the Wikipedia (and that could be translated to Portuguese). Note that the usage of Apertium here has nothing to do with *Apertium* baseline.

yield stable results when the number of entries is larger. This is not the case for the method *WN all*, which needs more word pairs to achieve reasonable results (around 5,000) and it is less stable with larger number of entries.

Even though we use WordNet to build the lexicon, which is a rich and expensive resource, it could also be built with less quality entries, such as those that come from the output of a Machine Translation software or just by having a list of known word translations. Furthermore, our method proved to work with a small number of word pairs, it can be applied to language pairs with scarce bilingual resources.

Additionally, it is interesting to observe that despite the fact that some test set pairs may appear in the bilingual lexicon in which our method is based on, when having changed it (by reducing its size or using Apertium), it still shows great performance. This suggest the results are not biased towards the test set used in this work.

6 Conclusions and Future Work

We have provided an approach to classify false friends and cognates which showed to have both high accuracy and coverage, studying it for the particular case of Spanish and Portuguese and providing state-of-the-art results for this pair of languages. Here we use up-to-date word embedding techniques, which have shown to excel in other tasks, and which can be enriched with other information such as the words frequencies to enhance the classifier. In the future we want to experiment with other word vector representations and state-of-the-art vector space linear transformation such as (Artetxe et al., 2017; Artetxe et al., 2018). Also, we would like to work on fine-grained classifications, as we mentioned before there are some word pairs that behave like cognates in some cases but like false friends in others.

Our method can be applied to any pair of languages, without requiring a large bilingual corpus or taxonomy, which can be hard to find or expensive to build. In contrast, large untagged monolingual corpora are easily obtained on the Internet. Similar languages, that commonly have a high number of false friends, can benefit from the technique we present in this document, for example by generating a list of false friends pairs automatically based on words that are written in both languages in the same way.

References

Mikel Artetxe, Gorka Labaka, and Eneko Agirre. 2017. Learning bilingual word embeddings with (almost) no bilingual data. In *Proceedings of the 55th Annual Meeting of the Association for Computational Linguistics (Volume 1: Long Papers)*, volume 1, pages 451–462.

Mikel Artetxe, Gorka Labaka, and Eneko Agirre. 2018. Generalizing and improving bilingual word embedding mappings with a multi-step framework of linear transformations. In *Proceedings of the Thirty-Second AAAI Conference on Artificial Intelligence (AAAI-18)*.

Steven Bird, Ewan Klein, and Edward Loper. 2009. *Natural language processing with Python: analyzing text with the natural language toolkit*. " O'Reilly Media, Inc.".

Francis Bond and Kyonghee Paik. 2012. A survey of wordnets and their licenses. In *Proceedings of the 6th Global WordNet Conference (GWC 2012)*, Matsue. 64–71.

Valeria de Paiva and Alexandre Rademaker. 2012. Revisiting a Brazilian wordnet. In *Proceedings of the 6th Global WordNet Conference (GWC 2012)*, Matsue.

Christiane Fellbaum, editor. 1998. *WordNet: An Electronic Lexical Database*. MIT Press, Cambridge, MA.

Oana Magdalena Frunza. 2006. *Automatic identification of cognates, false friends, and partial cognates*. Ph.D. thesis, University of Ottawa (Canada).

Aitor Gonzalez-Agirre, Egoitz Laparra, and German Rigau. 2012. Multilingual central repository version 3.0: upgrading a very large lexical knowledge base. In *Proceedings of the 6th Global WordNet Conference (GWC 2012)*, Matsue.

Philippe Humblé. 2006. Falsos cognados. falsos problemas. un aspecto de la enseñanza del español en brasil. *Revista de Lexicografía*, 12:197–207.

Yann LeCun, Yoshua Bengio, and Geoffrey Hinton. 2015. Deep learning. *Nature*, 521(7553):436–444.

Nikola Ljubešic, Ivana Lucica, and Darja Fišer. 2013. Identifying false friends between closely related languages. *ACL 2013*, page 69.

Tomas Mikolov, Kai Chen, Greg Corrado, and Jeffrey Dean. 2013a. Efficient estimation of word representations in vector space. In *Workshop at International Conference on Learning Representations*.

Tomas Mikolov, Quoc V Le, and Ilya Sutskever. 2013b. Exploiting similarities among languages for machine translation. *CoRR*, abs/1309.4168.

Tomas Mikolov, Ilya Sutskever, Kai Chen, Greg S Corrado, and Jeff Dean. 2013c. Distributed representations of words and phrases and their compositionality. In *Advances in neural information processing systems*, pages 3111–3119.

Ruslan Mitkov, Viktor Pekar, Dimitar Blagoev, and Andrea Mulloni. 2007. Methods for extracting and classifying pairs of cognates and false friends. *Machine translation*, 21(1):29.

María de Lourdes Otero Brabo Cruz. 2004. Diccionario de falsos amigos (español-portugués / portugués-español): Propuesta de utilización en la enseñanza del español a luso hablantes. In *Actas del XV Congreso Internacional de Asele, Sevilla*, pages 632–637. Universidad de Sevilla.

Radim Řehůřek and Petr Sojka. 2010. Software Framework for Topic Modelling with Large Corpora. In *Proceedings of the LREC 2010 Workshop on New Challenges for NLP Frameworks*, pages 45–50, Valletta, Malta, May. ELRA. http://is.muni.cz/publication/884893/en.

Lianet Sepúlveda and Sandra María Aluísio. 2011. Using machine learning methods to avoid the pitfall of cognates and false friends in spanish-portuguese word pairs. In *8th Brazilian Symposium in Information and Human Language Technology*, pages 67–76.

Jack L Ulsh. 1971. From spanish to portuguese. Washington DC: Foreign Service Institute.

Sub-label dependencies for Neural Morphological Tagging – The Joint Submission of University of Colorado and University of Helsinki for VarDial 2018

Miikka Silfverberg
Department of Linguistics
University of Colorado Boulder
`mpsilfve@iki.fi`

Senka Drobac
Department of Modern Languages
University of Helsinki
`senka.drobac@helsinki.fi`

Abstract

This paper presents the submission of the UH&CU team (Joint University of Colorado and University of Helsinki team) for the VarDial 2018 shared task on morphosyntactic tagging of Croatian, Slovenian and Serbian tweets. Our system is a bidirectional LSTM tagger which emits tags as character sequences using an LSTM generator in order to be able to handle unknown tags and combinations of several tags for one token which occur in the shared task data sets. To the best of our knowledge, using an LSTM generator is a novel approach. The system delivers sizable improvements of more than 6%-points over a baseline trigram tagger. Overall, the performance of our system is quite even for all three languages.

1 Introduction

This paper[1] presents the joint submission of University of Colorado and University of Helsinki for the 2018 VarDial shared task on morphosyntactic tagging of Croatian, Serbian and Slovenian tweets (Zampieri et al., 2018). Morphosyntactic tagging is a useful preprocessing task when parsing morphologically complex languages since these typically encode syntactic information as inflectional material in word forms. For example, both of the following Croatian words forms are inflected forms of 'dog': **pas** and **psa**. However, the first one is far more likely to encode a grammatical subject since it displays nominative case. This demonstrates that coarse POS tags are not sufficient for capturing all syntactically relevant aspects of words in morphologically complex languages. Instead, rich morphological tags are needed.

It is not sufficient to train one morphosyntactic tagger and expect it to perform well in all domains. The reason for this is that the performance of data-driven models typically suffers when they are applied to domains which considerably differ from their training domain. Consequently, NLP models often deliver poor results when applied to the social media domain since most models are trained on newswire or related, more formal, domains. This is a problem because text analysis for social media has become increasingly important both from an economical and research perspective in recent years.

Social media differs from newswire in many respects. As explained in Section 3, Croatian, Serbian and Slovenian text in the social media domain often lacks diacritics, which ordinarily are a prominent feature in the orthographies of these languages. Moreover, orthographic rules concerning capitalization are frequently ignored. Furthermore, our error analysis in Section 5 shows that Twitter text contains a large amount of foreign, mainly English, loan words. These are some of the reasons why NLP systems can fail to deliver good performance on social media text.

The VarDial shared task specifically targets the social media domain. Our system is trained on collections of morphosyntactically annotated Tweets (Ljubešić et al., 2017a; Ljubešić et al., 2017b; Erjavec et al., 2015). It is an LSTM (Hochreiter and Schmidhuber, 1997) morphosyntactic tagger which utilizes pretrained subword-aware word embeddings and character-based word embeddings. The setup is shown in Figure 1. This basic setup for an LSTM tagger is not new. However, our system does have novel aspects, especially in the output layer.

---

[1]This work is licensed under a Creative Commons Attribution 4.0 International License. License details: `http://creativecommons.org/licenses/by/4.0/`.

Proceedings of the Fifth Workshop on NLP for Similar Languages, Varieties and Dialects, pages 37–45
Santa Fe, New Mexico, USA, August 20, 2018.

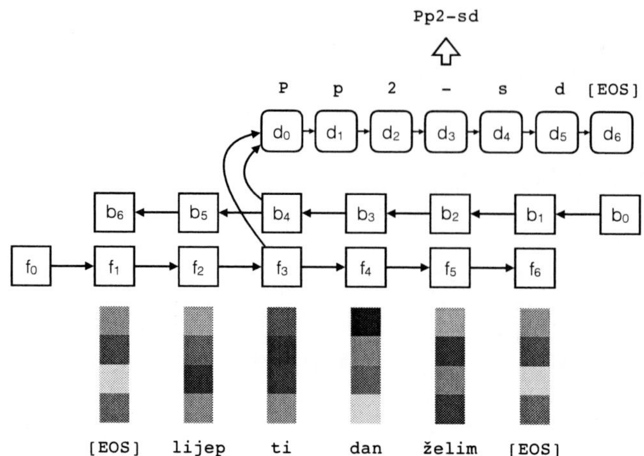

Figure 1: Our system starts by padding the input sentence $x_1, ..., x_T$ with end-of-sequence symbols [EOS]. It then embeds all tokens in the sentence (see Figure 3 for details). Embeddings are fed into a bidirectional LSTM encoder which outputs forward and backward representation vectors f_t and b_{T-t} at each position t. To predict the morphosyntactic tag at position t, the concatenated representation $[f_t; b_{T-t}]$ is then fed into an LSTM generator which emits the MULTEXT-East tag for token x_t one character at a time.

Previous approaches to neural morphosyntactic tagging have either treated complex morphological tags like Npmsn (the singular nominative of a masculine noun) as atomic units or predicted each feature (for example N, p, m, s, n) separately. Both of these approaches are insufficient for our needs. The first approach is suboptimal because the system will treat MULTEXT-East tags (Erjavec, 2012) Npmsn and Npmsl as completely separate entities even though both are in fact proper noun tags which share number and gender. Indeed, Müller et al. (2013) and Silfverberg et al. (2014) show that sub-tag dependencies improve the performance of linear taggers. It is conceivable that the same applies to deeper neural architectures.

```
i           Cc
jel         Var3s Qq
izljubio    Vmp-sm
punicu      Ncfsa
?           Z
```

Figure 2: In this sentence 'and did he kiss mother in law?', the token **jel** receives two separate tags because it is a contraction of the verb **je** ('to be' in 3rd person singular) and the interrogative particle **li**.

The second approach, namely individually predicting each feature of the tag, does take into account individual sub-tags. However, this approach does not model their dependencies or the complete tag in any way which also seems problematic. In the case of morphosyntactic tagging in the MULTEXT-East schema, there is also a more serious problem with predicting each sub-label in isolation. Namely, tokens can sometimes receive multiple tags, for example in the case of contractions (Ljubešić et al., 2017a). An example of this is shown in Figure 2. A straightforward approach to predicting sub-tags cannot handle this situation. Therefore, we opt for using an LSTM generator for emitting tags. It can model both individual sub-tags and dependencies between sub-tags. Because LSTM networks excel at long range dependencies, there is reason to believe that our approach also captures information about complete MULTEXT-East tags.

The paper is structured in the following way: In Section 2 we present related approaches neural to morphosyntactic tagging and tagging in the social media domain. In Section 3, we present our LSTM tagger. Section 4 presents the data sets used in the VarDial task and Section 5 presents our experiments and results. Finally, we present discussion and directions for future work in Section 6 and conclude the paper in Section 7.

2 Related Work

Our system is inspired by the neural POS tagger introduced by Dozat et al. (2017), however, we have extended their approach to handle morphological tagging. In the past two years, POS tagging for morphologically complex languages has received a fair amount of attention. Starting with the work by Plank et al. (2016a), neural approaches, particularly bidirectional LSTM taggers, have dominated the field. This is exemplified by the entry of Dozat et al. (2017) for the 2017 CoNLL shared task on multilingual parsing, where their neural POS tagger delivered the best results by far for nearly all languages (Zeman et al., 2017).

Even though work on neural POS tagging has received more attention, there are a number of papers on neural morphosyntactic tagging. Heigold et al. (2016a) evaluate several architectures for morphosyntactic tagging[2] of German and Czech. They find that pretrained word embeddings bring large gains in presence of small training sets and that character-based architectures deliver the best performance. Heigold et al. (2016b) extend these experiments to 12 additional languages.

Most existing systems for morphosyntactic tagging treat complex morphosyntactic tags in the same way as POS tags, that is, they do not model the internal structure of tags. As an exception to this, Krasnowska-Kieraś (2017) predict each sub-tag in complex morphosyntactic tags separately. As mentioned above, this is not a sufficient solution in our case since it does not address the problem of multiple morphosyntactic possible tags for one token. Therefore, we opt for using an LSTM generator for emitting tags. To the best of our knowledge, this approach is novel.

We utilize automatically tagged data from the web domain (Ljubešić and Klubička, 2014) to improve the performance of our system. Plank and Nissim (2016b) use a similar approach for POS tagging of Italian tweets. They use automatically tagged data from the social media domain and find that it can deliver sizable improvements. Our results point in the same direction.

3 Methods

This section describes our bidirectional LSTM tagger. It also describes how automatically tagged web data is used for improving tagger accuracy and the data transformations that we perform on the web data in order improve performance in the Twitter domain.

3.1 A Neural Morphological tagger

Our system is an unstructured morphosyntactic LSTM tagger[3]. We utilize character-based embeddings and pretrained embeddings and the system emits morphological tags using an LSTM generator. This allows us to both emit tags, which we have not seen in the training data, and emit combinations of several tags for one token. This is necessary for handling contractions present in the shared task datasets, as explained above.

Embedding layer Our word embedding layer combines three types of word embeddings: pretrained word embeddings, randomly initialized word embeddings and character-based embeddings. See Figure 3 for a visualization.

Pretrained embeddings are initialized using FastText (Bojanowski et al., 2017) which treats word forms as a bags of character n-grams. We use FastText because it can provide an embedding vector both for tokens that were observed during training and for other tokens. This is important when dealing with morphologically complex languages, where out-of-vocabulary (OOV) rates are typically high. We train pretrained FastText embeddings using large quantities of plain text. In addition to pretrained embeddings, we use regular randomly initialized token based embeddings. It is common practice to include both types of embeddings in a tagger.

---

[2]Many authors including (Heigold et al., 2016b) refer to morphosyntactic tagging as morphological tagging.

[3]The term unstructured refers to the fact that the tag for each token in the sentence is predicted in isolation. This is common practice in the field of neural morphological tagging.

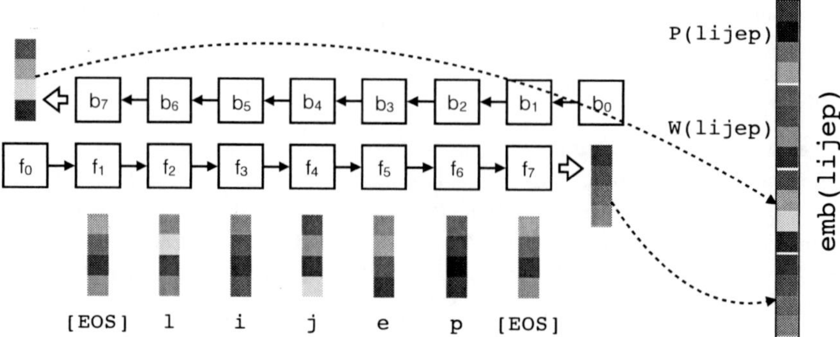

Figure 3: Word embeddings in our system are a concatenation of four vectors: a pretrained word embedding $P(w)$, a randomly initialized whole word embedding $W(w)$ as well as forward and backward character based embeddings $\mathbf{f_C}(w)$ and $\mathbf{b_C}(w)$ computed by a bidirectional LSTM encoder.

Finally we use character-based embeddings based on a bidirectional character-level LSTM encoder. To compute character-level embeddings, we treat the input word as a sequence of characters $c_1, ..., c_N$ and pad it with end-of-sequence symbols resulting in a sequence $c_0, ..., c_{N+1}$. We then compute character embeddings $E(c_i)$ for each character in the sequence $c_0, ..., c_{N+1}$. Subsequently, we use the forward component of the LSTM encoder for encoding the sequence $E(c_0), ..., E(c_{N+1})$ into a representation vector. Similarly, we use the backward component of the encoder for encoding the reverse sequence $E(c_{N+1}), ..., E(c_0)$ into a representation vector. We use the final cell-state $[\mathbf{f_C}; \mathbf{b_C}]$ of the bidirectional LSTM encoder as the representation of the sequence.

As a final step, we concatenate all vectors into a unified token representation. As stated above, any word form, whether seen during training or not, will receive a pretrained embedding vector. Therefore, we do not need to treat OOV tokens differently with regard to the pretrained embedding. In contrast, the random initialized token embedding may encounter unknown tokens during test time. Therefore, we use a special unknown word token [UNK], whose embedding is initialized randomly. During training, we then replace input token embeddings with the embedding for [UNK] with probability p_{WORDUNK}. In order to simulate the distribution of OOV tokens, [UNK] embeddings are trained exclusively on input tokens which occur once in the training data.

It may also happen that we encounter unknown characters in the test data. Therefore, we also use an unknown character symbol and train it analogously to the unknown word symbol, that is, we randomly replace character with [UNK] during training with probability p_{CHARUNK}.

Sentence-level LSTM encoder   We use a bidirectional encoder LSTM for deriving a sequence of state vectors $[\mathbf{f_t}; \mathbf{b_{T-t}}]$ from token representation vectors. The state vector $\mathbf{s_t} = [\mathbf{f_t}; \mathbf{b_{T-t}}]$ is the concatenation of the cell states of the forward and backward components of the bidirectional LSTM.

Tag generator   The sentence-level representation at position t is fed into an LSTM generator, which generates MULTEXT-East tags, for example Npmsn, as character sequences. Formally, the generator is a recursive function $G(E_{\text{TAG}}(c_{k-1}), \mathbf{h_k}, \mathbf{s_t})$ conditioned on the embedding $E_{\text{TAG}}(c_{k-1})$ of the previously generated character c_{k-1}, the current hidden state of the generator $\mathbf{h_k}$, and the hidden state of the sentence-level encoder LSTM $\mathbf{s_t}$. The function value $G(E_{\text{TAG}}(c_{k-1}), \mathbf{h_k}, \mathbf{s_t})$ is a distribution over possible characters occurring in MULTEXT-East tags and the output character c_k is determined as the mode of that distribution. The process is initialized by setting c_0 to an end-of-sequence symbol [EOS]. We apply teacher forcing (Goldberg, 2017) when training the generator.

3.2   Data transformation

There are a number of differences between the language use in Croatian, Serbian and Slovenian Tweets and language use in more formal domains. Capitalization and diacritics are often omitted in Tweets and there are far more English and foreign language words in Tweets. Additionally, there are English words whose orthography has been adapted to Croatian, Serbian or Slovenian spelling. Although, addressing all of these points is likely to improve tagging accuracy, we decided to focus on capitalization and diacritics.

Before training pretrained embeddings, we remove all diacritics from words in the embedding training data. For example, **korištenjem** $\rightarrow$ **koristenjem**. When indexing the word embedding, we remove diacritics from the query word. In addition, we make embeddings case insensitive so **grijanje, Grijanje** and **GRIJANJE** all receive the same embedding vector.

3.3 Improving Performance using Web Data

As further explained in Section 5, we use automatically tagged Croatian, Serbian and Slovenian web data (Ljubešić and Klubička, 2014) for improving the performance of the tagger. This is done simply by combining web data and Twitter data into one training corpus. We train several taggers combining different parts of the web data with the Twitter data and perform majority voting to get the final result.

3.4 Implementation Details

We use 300 dimensional randomly initialized word embeddings, pretrained word embeddings, character embeddings and sub-tag embeddings. We use 2-layer bidirectional LSTM encoders for computing character representations, sentence-level representations and for generating output tags.

Due to the small size of the Twitter training corpora and the well known tendency of deep learning models to overfit, we add Gaussian noise with standard deviation 0.2% to randomly initialized word embeddings and pretrained embeddings during training. We also apply 50% dropout to the parameters of all LSTM networks. Additionally, we replace characters with an [UNK] symbol with probability 0.1 during training. We also replace the randomly initialized word embedding for words that occur once in the training corpus with an [UNK] embedding with probability 30%. During training, we use minibatches of size 50 and train for 100 epochs using Adam (Kingma and Ba, 2014). The tagger is implemented using DyNet (Neubig et al., 2017).

4 Data

P	Attribute (en)	Value (en)	Code (en)
0	CATEGORY	Noun	N
1	Type	common	c
		proper	p
2	Gender	masculine	m
		feminine	f
		neuter	n
3	Number	singular	s
		plural	p
4	Case	nominative	n
		genitive	g
		dative	d
		accusative	a
		vocative	v
		locative	l
		instrumental	i
5	Animate	no	n
		yes	y

Table 1: Croatian and Serbian Specifications for Noun

For training we use the following data sets: Twitter data for Croatian (Ljubešić et al., 2017a), Serbian (Ljubešić et al., 2017b) and Slovenian (Erjavec et al., 2015). Additionally, we use automatically tagged web data for all thee languages (Ljubešić and Klubička, 2014). All data sets were tagged according to MULTEXT-East Morphosyntactic Specifications[4]. For all three languages the specification recognizes 12 parts of speech (Noun, Verb, Adjective, Pronoun, Adverb, Adposition, Conjunction, Numeral, Particle, Interjection, Abbreviation, Residual) and each category has different numbers of language specific attributes and values. For example, in all three languages, nouns have 5 attributes (Type, Gender, Number, Case and Animate) and each attribute has language-specific values. Table 1 shows attributes and corresponding values for the Croatian and Serbian Noun category. Slovenian has the same attributes, but different values for the category Number (singular, plural and dual) and Case (there is no vocative in Slovenian). Two examples for noun tags are shown in figure 4.

```
Uskrs    Npmsn (Noun, proper, masculine, singular, nominative)
sudbinu  Ncfsa (Noun, common, feminine, singular, accusative)
```

Figure 4: Tag explanation for two nouns: "**Uskrs**" (eng. *Easter*) and "**sudbinu**" (eng. *destiny*)

As mentioned above, the MULTEXT-East specification allows for several tags for one token. This happens for contractions like **jel** which are in fact combinations of two ore more distinct word form **je** "to be" and **li**, which is an interrogative particle, in this case.

5 Experiments and Results

We perform experiments on morphosyntactic tagging of Croatian, Serbian and Slovenian Twitter data. Additionally, we use automatically tagged web data for each language to improve performance.[5] For each language, we create pretrained FastText embeddings using the first 10M sentences from the web data.[6] We then form ten tagger training sets using Twitter training data and the tagged web data. These training sets are used for training ten models, in total. Each training set contains the entire original Twitter data but all of them contain disjoint segments of the web data. We use 500K tokens of web data for each training set (more than this degraded results in preliminary experiments). The web data segments are consecutive 500K token chunks data starting at the top of the data set.

	CROATIAN			SERBIAN			SLOVENIAN		
	POS	MOR	TAG	POS	MOR	TAG	POS	MOR	TAG
BASELINE	-	-	0.834	-	-	0.832	-	-	0.832
OUR SYSTEM	0.943	0.886	0.887	0.957	0.900	0.900	0.946	0.884	0.884

Table 2: Accuracy for part-of-speech (POS), morphological features (MOR) and the complete morphosyntactic tag (TAG).

We apply the ten different systems for tagging the test set and perform majority voting to get the final test set tag for each word. We compare the system against a baseline HunPos trigram tagger (Halácsy et al., 2007) which is described in Zampieri et al. (2018). The results are shown in Table 2. Our system substantially outperforms the baseline on all three languages.

Table 3 shows the most common tagging errors that our system makes. As can be seen, confusions between noun tags like Npmsn and the foreign word tag Xf are frequent for all three languages. Most of these concern English words which the tagger incorrectly identifies as Croatian, Serbian or Slovenian words and labels accordingly. Another common error type is that nominatives are tagged as accusatives or vice versa. For example, many Croatian and Slovenian singular masculine nominatives Ncmsn are incorrectly tagged as inanimate accusatives Ncmsan. This is an understandable error since Croatian and Slovenian do not overtly mark singular accusatives of inanimate nouns (Barić et al., 1995; Pauliny et al., 1968).

In Serbian, a common error type is the confusion of conjunctions Cs and adverbs Rgp. This happens because adverbs can be used for combining sentences into one. If one of the sentences is subordinate

---

[4] http://nl.ijs.si/ME/V4/msd/html/
[5] We do not use the manually tagged out-of-domain data provided in the shared task.
[6] We do not use the morphosyntactic tags for pretrained embeddings. We use default settings for FastText.

Croatian			Serbian			Slovenian		
No	GT	Result	No	GT	Result	No	GT	Result
69	Npmsn	Xf	56	Rgp	Cs	44	Xf	Npmsn
45	Ncmsn	Ncmsan	43	Cs	Rgp	36	Ncmsn	Ncmsan
38	Qo	Cc	42	Ncmsn	Ncmsan	28	Sl	Sa
30	Xf	Npmsn	35	Qo	Cc	28	Ncmsan	Ncmsn
29	Ncmsan	Ncmsn	35	Ncmsan	Ncmsn	27	Q	Px------y
28	Npmsn	Ncmsn	30	Vmm2s	Vmr3s	27	Npmsn	Ncmsn
23	Ncmsn	Xf	27	Npmsn	Xf	25	Ncmsn	Npmsn
22	Sl	Sa	26	Agpnsny Rgp	Xf	24	Agpnsn	Rgp
20	Xf	Ncmsn	22	Cc	Qo	23	Xf	Ncmsn
20	Sa	Sl	19	Sl	Sa	22	Npfsn	Ncfsn

Table 3: Most common mistakes per line (total error lines: HR 2428, SR 2325, SL 2246)

to the other one, the word is analyzed as an adverb. However, when neither sentence is subordinate, the word is analyzed as a conjunction.This, of course, requires rather elaborate analysis of the sentences involved. Therefore, it is not surprising that the distinction results in tagging-errors. The same confusion happens in the Croatian test set, however it is less common. The reason for this is that tokens that are causing this error (**kad(a)** 'when', **kako** 'how' and **gde** 'where', cro. 'gdje') are almost two times more often present in the Serbian test set than in Croatian as shown in Table 4.

	sr	hr
kad (when)	112	72
kada (when)	53	13
kako (how)	66	40
gde/gdje (where)	24	13
TOTAL	255	138

Table 4: Occurrences of words *kad*, *kada*, *kako* and *gde* (Croatian *gdje*) in Serbian and Croatian test data

6 Discussion and Future Work

Our results show that neural methods deliver large improvements in accuracy compared to a traditional trigram tagger. This is a nice result because our neural tagger is unstructured whereas the HunPos baseline is a second order structured model. However, it is not as easy to beat a well engineered discriminative model as the shared task results show (Zampieri et al., 2018).

Our error analysis uncovers a number of directions for future work. It would clearly be beneficial to be able to better model foreign words. Also better contextual modeling is required in order to be able to distinguish nominatives and accusatives in cases where there is no overt morphological marking. It will probably be quite challenging to model the distinction between conjunctions and adverbs in Serbian since this may require rather deep analysis of the embedded sentences.

It is possible that the errors related to the confusion between noun forms as well as conjunctions and adverbs are related to data sparsity, on one hand, and tagging errors in the web data, on the other hand. This requires further analysis.

7 Conclusions

In this paper, we presented an LSTM tagger for morphosyntactic tagging of Croatian, Serbian and Slovenian tweets. The tagger employs pretrained FastText embeddings and an LSTM generator for emitting tags. Our experiments show that a neural approach results in large improvements compared to a traditional trigram tagger. However, our error analysis still uncovers a number of directions for future work.

Especially better modeling of foreign words could help to further improve results.

Acknowledgements

We wish to thank the anonymous reviewers for their valuable feedback. The first author is supported by the Society of Swedish Literature in Finland.

References

Eugenija Barić, Mijo Lončarić, Dragica Malić, Slavko Pavešić, Mirko Peti, Vesna Zečević, Marija Znika, et al. 1995. *Hrvatska gramatika*. Školska knjiga.

Piotr Bojanowski, Edouard Grave, Armand Joulin, and Tomas Mikolov. 2017. Enriching word vectors with subword information. *Transactions of the Association for Computational Linguistics*, 5:135–146.

Timothy Dozat, Peng Qi, and Christopher D Manning. 2017. Stanford's graph-based neural dependency parser at the conll 2017 shared task. *Proceedings of the CoNLL 2017 Shared Task: Multilingual Parsing from Raw Text to Universal Dependencies*, pages 20–30.

Tomaž Erjavec, Nikola Ljubešić, and Nataša Logar. 2015. The slWaC Corpus of the Slovene Web. *Informatica*, 39(1):35–42.

Tomaž Erjavec. 2012. Multext-east: Morphosyntactic resources for central and eastern european languages. *Lang. Resour. Eval.*, 46(1):131–142, March.

Yoav Goldberg. 2017. *Neural Network Methods in Natural Language Processing*. Morgan & Claypool Publishers.

Péter Halácsy, András Kornai, and Csaba Oravecz. 2007. Hunpos: An open source trigram tagger. In *Proceedings of the 45th Annual Meeting of the ACL on Interactive Poster and Demonstration Sessions*, ACL '07, pages 209–212, Stroudsburg, PA, USA. Association for Computational Linguistics.

Georg Heigold, Guenter Neumann, and Josef van Genabith. 2016a. Neural morphological tagging from characters for morphologically rich languages. *CoRR*, abs/1606.06640.

G. Heigold, J. van Genabith, and G. Neumann. 2016b. Scaling character-based morphological tagging to fourteen languages. In *2016 IEEE International Conference on Big Data (Big Data)*, pages 3895–3902, Dec.

Sepp Hochreiter and Jürgen Schmidhuber. 1997. Long short-term memory. *Neural Comput.*, 9(8):1735–1780, November.

Diederik P. Kingma and Jimmy Ba. 2014. Adam: A method for stochastic optimization. *CoRR*, abs/1412.6980.

Katarzyna Krasnowska-Kieraś. 2017. Morphosyntactic disambiguation for Polish with bi-LSTM neural networks. In Zygmunt Vetulani and Patrick Paroubek, editors, *Proceedings of the 8th Language & Technology Conference: Human Language Technologies as a Challenge for Computer Science and Linguistics*, pages 367–371, Poznań, Poland. Fundacja Uniwersytetu im. Adama Mickiewicza w Poznaniu.

Nikola Ljubešić and Filip Klubička. 2014. {bs,hr,sr}wac - web corpora of bosnian, croatian and serbian. In *Proceedings of the 9th Web as Corpus Workshop (WaC-9)*, pages 29–35. Association for Computational Linguistics.

Nikola Ljubešić, Tomaž Erjavec, Maja Miličević, and Tanja Samardžić. 2017a. Croatian twitter training corpus ReLDI-NormTagNER-hr 2.0. Slovenian language resource repository CLARIN.SI.

Nikola Ljubešić, Tomaž Erjavec, Maja Miličević, and Tanja Samardžić. 2017b. Serbian twitter training corpus ReLDI-NormTagNER-sr 2.0. Slovenian language resource repository CLARIN.SI.

Thomas Müller, Helmut Schmid, and Hinrich Schütze. 2013. Efficient higher-order crfs for morphological tagging. In *Proceedings of the 2013 Conference on Empirical Methods in Natural Language Processing*, pages 322–332.

Graham Neubig, Chris Dyer, Yoav Goldberg, Austin Matthews, Waleed Ammar, Antonios Anastasopoulos, Miguel Ballesteros, David Chiang, Daniel Clothiaux, Trevor Cohn, Kevin Duh, Manaal Faruqui, Cynthia Gan, Dan Garrette, Yangfeng Ji, Lingpeng Kong, Adhiguna Kuncoro, Gaurav Kumar, Chaitanya Malaviya, Paul Michel, Yusuke Oda, Matthew Richardson, Naomi Saphra, Swabha Swayamdipta, and Pengcheng Yin. 2017. Dynet: The dynamic neural network toolkit. *arXiv preprint arXiv:1701.03980*.

Eugen Pauliny, Jozef Ružička, and Jozef Štolc. 1968. *Slovenská gramatika*. SPN.

Barbara Plank and Malvina Nissim. 2016b. When silver glitters more than gold: Bootstrapping an italian part-of-speech tagger for twitter. *CoRR*, abs/1611.03057.

Barbara Plank, Anders Søgaard, and Yoav Goldberg. 2016a. Multilingual part-of-speech tagging with bidirectional long short-term memory models and auxiliary loss. In *Proceedings of the 54th Annual Meeting of the Association for Computational Linguistics, ACL 2016, August 7-12, 2016, Berlin, Germany, Volume 2: Short Papers*.

Miikka Silfverberg, Teemu Ruokolainen, Krister Lindén, and Mikko Kurimo. 2014. Part-of-speech tagging using conditional random fields: Exploiting sub-label dependencies for improved accuracy. Proceedings of the 52nd Annual Meeting of the Association for Computational Linguistics (Volume 2: Short Papers), pages 259–264. Association for Computational Linguistics.

Marcos Zampieri, Shervin Malmasi, Preslav Nakov, Ahmed Ali, Suwon Shuon, James Glass, Yves Scherrer, Tanja Samardžić, Nikola Ljubešić, Jörg Tiedemann, Chris van der Lee, Stefan Grondelaers, Nelleke Oostdijk, Antal van den Bosch, Ritesh Kumar, Bornini Lahiri, and Mayank Jain. 2018. Language Identification and Morphosyntactic Tagging: The Second VarDial Evaluation Campaign. In *Proceedings of the Fifth Workshop on NLP for Similar Languages, Varieties and Dialects (VarDial)*, Santa Fe, USA.

Daniel Zeman, Martin Popel, Milan Straka, Jan Hajic, Joakim Nivre, Filip Ginter, Juhani Luotolahti, Sampo Pyysalo, Slav Petrov, Martin Potthast, Francis Tyers, Elena Badmaeva, Memduh Gokirmak, Anna Nedoluzhko, Silvie Cinkova, Jan Hajic jr., Jaroslava Hlavacova, Václava Kettnerová, Zdenka Uresova, Jenna Kanerva, Stina Ojala, Anna Missilä, Christopher D. Manning, Sebastian Schuster, Siva Reddy, Dima Taji, Nizar Habash, Herman Leung, Marie-Catherine de Marneffe, Manuela Sanguinetti, Maria Simi, Hiroshi Kanayama, Valeria de-Paiva, Kira Droganova, Héctor Martínez Alonso, Çağrı Çöltekin, Umut Sulubacak, Hans Uszkoreit, Vivien Macketanz, Aljoscha Burchardt, Kim Harris, Katrin Marheinecke, Georg Rehm, Tolga Kayadelen, Mohammed Attia, Ali Elkahky, Zhuoran Yu, Emily Pitler, Saran Lertpradit, Michael Mandl, Jesse Kirchner, Hector Fernandez Alcalde, Jana Strnadová, Esha Banerjee, Ruli Manurung, Antonio Stella, Atsuko Shimada, Sookyoung Kwak, Gustavo Mendonca, Tatiana Lando, Rattima Nitisaroj, and Josie Li. 2017. Conll 2017 shared task: Multilingual parsing from raw text to universal dependencies. In *Proceedings of the CoNLL 2017 Shared Task: Multilingual Parsing from Raw Text to Universal Dependencies*, pages 1–19, Vancouver, Canada, August. Association for Computational Linguistics.

Part of Speech Tagging in Luyia: A Bantu Macrolanguage

Kenneth Steimel
Indiana University
Bloomington, Indiana
`ksteimel@iu.edu`

Abstract

Luyia is a macrolanguage in central Kenya. The Luyia languages, like other Bantu languages, have a complex morphological system. This system can be leveraged to aid in part of speech tagging. Bag-of-characters taggers trained on a source Luyia language can be applied directly to another Luyia language with some degree of success. In addition, mixing data from the target language with data from the source language does produce more accurate predictive models compared to models trained on just the target language data when the training set size is small. However, for both of these tagging tasks, models involving the more distantly related language, Tiriki, are better at predicting part of speech tags for Wanga data. The models incorporating Bukusu data are not as successful despite the closer relationship between Bukusu and Wanga. Overlapping vocabulary between the Wanga and Tiriki corpora as well as a bias towards open class words help Tiriki outperform Bukusu.

1 Introduction

Luyia is a macrolanguage comprised of over 20 individual languages that form a dialect continuum. These languages have a very high degree of cognates. This provides a unique opportunity to examine the performance of Natural Language Processing tools on a cluster of very closely related Bantu languages. The structure of this paper is as follows: first, I provide some background on the Luyia languages, then, I evaluate the relative performance of different languages on two types of predictive part of speech tagging tasks. The first task involves direct training of an SVM part of speech tagging model on one language and then evaluation of this model on another language. The second task involves augmenting an SVM part of speech tagging model by training on a mixture of data from the target language and another variety of Luyia.

2 The Luyia languages

Oluluyia or Luyia[1] is a macro-language spoken in Kenya by approximately 5.3 million people (Simons and Fennig, 2017). The varieties of Luyia belong to JE30 and JE40 in the revised Guthrie Bantu classification scheme (Maho, 2009, 61-62). This macrolanguage consists of over 20 sub groupings. As a macrolanguage, Luyia consists of a number of linguistic groupings that are individual languages but that are treated as a single language in some contexts (Simons and Fennig, 2017). Older works like (Williams, 1973) refer to the linguistic groups that compose Luyia as dialects instead of unique languages. However, newer works on Luyia like Ebarb (2014) refer to Luyia as a dialect continuum with "geographically close varieties enjoy[ing] higher rates of mutual intelligibility" Ebarb (2014, 7). The map shown in figure 1 displays the geographic distribution of the Luyia languages.

The generalization that geographically closer languages have more in common is largely supported by the cognate probability table shown in 1. The Luyia languages are italicized in the table. The non-Luyia languages (Soga, Ganda, and Gusii) are closely related to the Luyia languages but are outside of

This work is licensed under a Creative Commons Attribution 4.0 International License. License details: `http://creativecommons.org/licenses/by/4.0/`

[1] Also spelled Luhya

Proceedings of the Fifth Workshop on NLP for Similar Languages, Varieties and Dialects, pages 46–54
Santa Fe, New Mexico, USA, August 20, 2018.

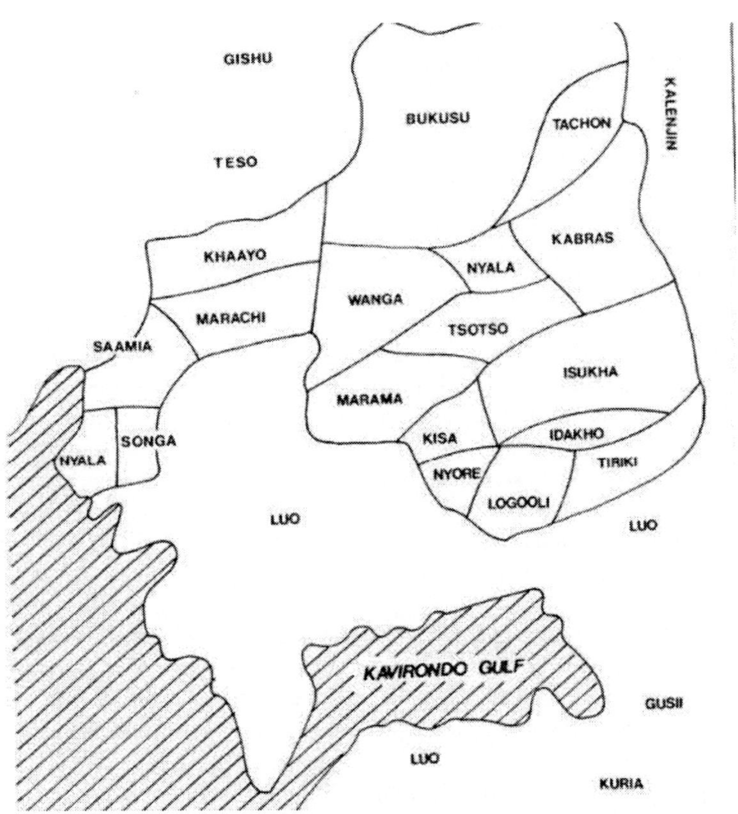

Figure 1: A map of the Luyia languages (Hinnebusch et al., 1981)

	Ganda	Soga	Saamia	Wanga	Bukusu	Idakho	Logooli
Soga	83.0						
Saamia	54.0	59.0					
Wanga	54.0	59.0	88.0				
Bukusu	52.0	60.0	77.0	81.0			
Idakho[3]	48.0	51.0	71.0	71.0	68.0		
Logooli	51.0	55.0	75.0	78.0	70.0	80.0	
Gusii	40.0	42.5	48.5	47.5	42.5	44.0	47.0

Table 1: Cognate percentages using 200-word lists (Hinnebusch et al., 1981, 184)

the macro-language[2]. The language pairs with cognate probabilities higher than 75% are geographically adjacent. This threshold of 75% is estimated to indicate sufficient mutual intelligibility to consider languages sharing such percentages to be dialects of a single language (Ladefoged et al., 1972) as cited in (Hinnebusch et al., 1981, 184).

The languages being examined in this study are Wanga (lwg), Bukusu (bxk), and Tiriki (ida). Bukusu is classified as JE31c while Wanga is JE32a in the New Guthrie Classification (Maho, 2009, 61). However, both belong to the Masaba-Luhya group (Maho, 2009). Tiriki (JE413), is part of a more distant branch of Luhya, the Logooli-Kuria group (Maho, 2009, 62).

3   Related Work

Most previous approaches to Bantu part of speech tagging have been based upon two-level finite state morphologies (Hurskainen, 1992; Pretorius and Bosch, 2009). However, these methods are expensive in terms of person hours and monetary cost because they rely on highly trained grammar writers. While Pretorius and Bosch (2009) use an existing morphology to expedite morphology creation in a related language, there are other disadvantages to finite-state morphologies for POS labels; systems like these are also difficult to expand. Most significantly for this particular setting, these require fairly extensive knowledge about the language being modeled. As documentation of the Luyia languages is still in progress, development of a finite state grammar with sufficient coverage does not seem to be feasible at this time. An alternative course is to develop a corpus and then use probabilistic methods to do the analysis.

Corpus creation is also a laborious process, however, there have been attempts to mitigate the expense. For example, (Yarowsky and Ngai, 2001) used cross-linguistic projection to apply existing resources for English to bilingual text corpora and project the analysis of the English text onto the second language using statistically derived word alignments. While this method is successful, what if reliable parallel texts are not available?

Hana et al. (2004) uses a morphological analyzer for their target language (Russian) and then used transition probabilities from a related language (Czech) using a Hidden Markov Model (HMM). This approach is similar in that I am using information from a related language to bolster taggers without doing projection. However, I propose the possibility of using robust machine learning techniques, rather than relying on an expensive morphological analyzer. Morphologically rich languages can have a large number of morphological variants for a single word resulting in high rates of Out of Vocabulary (OOV) terms. Statistical taggers perform worse on tokens that are not found in the training data. A common way to make taggers more robust to OOV terms is to use components of words as features during training rather than whole words. Such methods include using induced and hand labeled suffixes as features (Hasan and Ng, 2009), initial and final characters of words combined with the tags of surrounding words (Màrquez et al., 2000) and morphologically segmented words (Tachbelie et al., 2011). However, unlike these approaches, I use a simple character n-gram model instead of building a segmenter. This is similar

---

[2]These languages are not the subject of this paper. They are only included as a point of reference for these probabilities

[3]While Hinnebusch et al. (1981) does not include figures for Tiriki, Idakho is a good reference for what the expected values would be for Tiriki. Both languages share the same ISO-639-3 code (ida) and are considered by some to be part of a single Idakho-Isukha-Tiriki variety (Simons and Fennig, 2017).

Language	Number of Sentences	Number of Words
Wanga	1,294	7,337
Bukusu	1,107	7,940
Tiriki	1,393	9,319

Table 2: Total corpus size for the Luyia corpora

to the MaxEnt tagger in Gambäck et al. (2009) but with all possible character n-grams rather than n-grams anchored to the beginning or end of the word and with fewer contextual features. This is not unfounded as De Pauw et al. (2012) found that contextual information was not necessary to achieve good tagging accuracy for machine learning in Bantu languages.

In this light I, like Tachbelie et al. (2011), am interested in how much data is required to obtain satisfactory prediction accuracies (85%). I experiment with using a corpus from one language directly to tag the target language as well as mixing data from both a source and target language to tag the target language.

4   Corpora

The Luyia corpora used for this analysis are extracted from a Fieldworks database (International, 2018) manually annotated by language documentation researchers (Green et al., 2018). For this analysis, the corpus was filtered to include only sentences where all words were labeled with POS tags. The size of the filtered Luyia corpora are displayed in table 4. All three corpora are roughly the same size with Tiriki being slightly larger than the other two by about 1,000 words.

The Swahili corpus used for comparison with the Luyia corpora differs significantly in terms of annotation methods, composition and size. The Helsinki Corpus of Swahili is a large, automatically annotated corpus using a two-level finite state morphology. This corpus consists of parliamentary proceedings and newspaper articles in contrast to the personal narratives that comprise the Wanga corpus. In addition, the full Helsinki Corpus consists of 25 million words and is much larger than the Wanga corpus. Due to my limited access to the Helsinki Corpus, in this study I use a much smaller sampling taken from 70 files consisting of 1,000 sentences each. These files were collected by searching for the top 10 most common words in the corpus[4] and collecting a number of JSON files[5] for each using the web interface to the annotated corpus.

5   Methods

The following sections describe methods for tagging Wanga data using a modified version of the Helsinki Corpus of Swahili tagset (Hurskainen and Department of World Cultures, University of Helsinki, 2016)[6]. All experiments used Wanga as the target language. The test set was kept the same for all experiments. The training dataset was slightly over half of the filtered Wanga corpus at 591 sentences and 3274 words. In this study, I seek to determine how well one variety of Luyia can be used to tag another variety of Luyia directly and how effectively one variety can augment a small training corpus from the target language. In essence, how much data in the target language is required? The first set of experiments uses no data from the target language while the other experiments use various amounts of target language data mixed with data from another variety of Luyia. Table 3 displays the size of the datasets at different training splits. A Support Vector Machine (SVM) is a geometric supervised learning method that takes labeled data and

---

[4]Determined using the unannotated version of the Helsinki corpus which can be downloaded in its entirety.

[5]The number of JSON files downloaded for each seed word differed based upon how independent the words are. For example, one of the most common words was Mhesimiwa which means 'honorable', a title that precedes many names in the parliamentary proceedings portion of the corpus. The files from this search term contain a sampling of the corpus heavily biased towards proper nouns. A small number of files were used for **Mhesimiwa** while a larger number were used for more grammatically neutral terms like **na**, meaning 'and'.

[6]All punctuation was reduced to a single 'PUNCT' tag instead of having separate parts of speech for each punctuation mark

Training Proportion	Wanga Words	Tiriki Words	Bukusu Words	Swahili Words	Sentences
0.05	378	379	545	1404	59
0.1	758	785	1054	2973	118
0.2	1431	1648	2057	5779	236
0.5	3686	4247	4800	14914	590

Table 3: Number of words and sentences for various training dataset sizes

learns a hyperplane to separate one class from another [7].

The features extracted for each word were the following:

- Character unigrams, bigrams, trigrams and 4-grams internal to the word

- The first 3 characters of the preceeding word or the whole word if less than 3 characters [8]

- The first 3 characters of the following word or the whole word if less than 3 characters [9]

The set of all attested features were collected from the training data for each experiment and then filled in the counts of each feature for each word in a kind of "count-hot" encoding. Only features found in the training set were used to extract features from the test set. Two sets of SVM models were employed in this study. First a Luyia language by itself is used to train a model and then evaluate on the test portion of the Wanga dataset. Next, a combination of the source Luyia language and the Wanga training set are used to train a model and then evaluate on that same Wanga test dataset.

5.1 Direct Source to Wanga

For this set of experiments features were extracted and then those features were used to train on the different training dataset sizes described in table 3 The model created was then used to predict part of speech labels for the Wanga training set.

5.2 Wanga and Source Mixture to Wanga

After establishing the baseline of using Wanga character n-grams alone to tag Wanga, the Wanga data was combined in a 2 to 1 ratio with the source language data. Thus, four training sets were created which were composed of 5, 10, 20 and 50% of the Wanga Corpus. Half the number of sentences used in the Wanga Corpus were extracted from the source language corpus and mixed in with the Wanga data. For example, with the Wanga dataset containing 59 sentences, 30 randomly sampled Tiriki sentences were mixed in. This was done because I wanted to ensure that the Wanga data was not overwhelmed by the source language data[10]. The features discussed in section 5 were extracted from these combined training sets and the SVM models were trained. The resulting models were used to tag the test set.

6 Results

First, I discuss results for training a model one of the source languages and then directly applying this model to predict parts of speech for the Wanga test data. Then, language mixture models are discussed.

---

[7]The particular implementation used for this work (Pedregosa et al., 2011) employed 1 versus 1 for multiclass-classification. One versus rest classification is also common

[8]These character sequences were appended to "BEG_" making these features distinct. The three initial characters of the preceding word are used because Bantu languages (including Luyia) make heavy use of prefixes for inflectional markers. By using initial characters, I aim to make use of these inflectional markers without adding significantly to the dimensionality of the training vectors.

[9]These character sequences were appended to "AFT_" making these features distinct.

[10]However, some trials with larger and smaller mixing ratios were also conducted. These yielded worse results.

Training Set Size	Swahili	Tiriki	Bukusu	Wanga
0.05	26.91	**57.76**	54.51	76.36
0.1	27.46	**60.84**	58.67	81.89
0.2	29.61	**62.47**	56.22	86.10
0.5	25.56	**63.07**	62.49	91.06

Table 4: Accuracy of training on one language

Training Set Size	Swahili	Tiriki	Bukusu	Wanga
0.05	76.45	**78.40**	**77.30**	76.36
0.1	80.58	**82.66**	79.94	81.89
0.2	86.76	86.49	85.88	86.10
0.5	90.34	90.04	90.20	91.06

Table 5: Accuracy of language mixture models

6.1 Direct Source to Target Tagging

Table 4 displays the accuracies obtained by applying the models trained on data from one language to label parts of speech for the Wanga test set. Swahili is provided as a baseline while Wanga itself is provided as an upper bound. The training set size proportion is with reference to the Wanga corpus.

Surprisingly, Tiriki, the more distantly related variety, is more effective at tagging Wanga than Bukusu. The accuracy of the taggers trained on Tiriki are higher across the board. In addition, the accuracy of the tagger trained on Tiriki consistently rises as the amount of training data increases. For training on Bukusu, the tagger benefits from having access to more data overall. However, the drop at 0.2 may indicate that the machine learner is overfitting on Bukusu data and is not able to generalize to predicting on the Wanga test data.

Though the tagger trained on Tiriki performs much worse than the upper bound, the highest dataset size for Tiriki is approaching the accuracy obtained for the smallest Wanga training set. A new corpus for a Luyia language could get preliminary POS tags by training on a large portion of another Luyia language. Future research will have to investigate if the trends observed here, where the more distantly related of two varieties is most effective, generalizes to other source-target pairs.

6.2 Language Mixture Tagging

Now we turn to results obtained by training on a mixture of the Wanga training dataset and the source language dataset. Table 5 displays the accuracies of predictions using combination models of different sizes. The Wanga values listed are the prediction accuracies from training on Wanga alone. They repeat the Wanga data in table 4. The entries in bold represent cases where the accuracy was considerably higher than the accuracy of training on Wanga alone.

Once again, Tiriki performs better than Bukusu despite the fact that Bukusu is more closely related to Wanga. The combination model that uses Bukusu is only considerably higher than the baseline for the lowest training set size. In addition, the combination model that incorporates Tiriki data outperforms the baseline by a wider margin in this case. The Tiriki combination model also performs much better than the baseline for the 0.1 training set size.

Overall, augmenting Wanga taggers with data from another variety of Luyia is beneficial at smaller training set sizes. However, this augmentation has no effect or even a slightly negative effect on performance for larger training set sizes.

7 Analysis

Tiriki outperforming Bukusu on the combination tagging task is somewhat unsurprising: if Bukusu and Wanga are extremely similar varieties, the Bukusu data may contribute nothing new. However, if Bukusu and Wanga are so similar, Bukusu would be expected to perform better on the direct tagging task. The fact that Tiriki is still performing better on this task is very surprising.

Training Set Size	Swahili	Tiriki	Bukusu	Wanga
0.05	25.33	47.75	41.62	58.17
0.1	25.85	49.77	46.54	64.24
0.2	28.47	51.31	43.21	68.12
0.5	22.74	49.75	51.08	72.68

Table 6: Out of Vocabulary accuracy for source-Wanga

Training Set Size	Swahili	Tiriki	Bukusu	Wanga
0.05	58.84	63.47	62.38	58.17
0.1	63.31	66.51	62.60	64.24
0.2	70.13	70.66	70.78	68.12
0.5	70.73	74.66	72.72	72.68

Table 7: Out of Vocabulary accuracy for language mixture tagger

Performance on out of vocabulary (OOV) terms is higher for Tiriki than Bukusu. In tables 6 and 7 the accuracy of the Tiriki tagger is higher than or approximately the same as the Bukusu accuracies[11].

One possibility is that the Wanga and Tiriki corpora themselves have more in common, even if the varieties themselves do not. This does seem to be the case. Table 8 displays the percentage of words in each of the source corpora that are within the specified Levenshtein distance of a word in the Wanga corpus.

The Tiriki corpus has a three percent higher rate of absolute matches compared to Bukusu. While Bukusu has a higher percentage of words within a distance of 2, the large number of exact matches between Tiriki and Wanga is likely to blame for the increased performance of Tiriki relative to Bukusu[12].

Upon further analysis of the words that Tiriki gets correct but Bukusu does not (using the 0.05 training set size), it appears that the Tiriki classifier has a beneficial bias towards nouns and verbs. The Bukusu tagger tends to incorrectly predict closed classes like pronouns and conjunctions when the Tiriki classifier correctly predicted noun and verb tags. Most mistaken conjunction tags in Bukusu are for short words: all of these mistaken conjunctions and pronouns are less than the median word length of 9. The Tiriki classifier is more heavily biased towards predicting open class parts of speech than the Bukusu classifier.

Some of the Tiriki corpus's advantages originate from sources of ambiguity. Infinitive verbs like **okhushina** share some aspects of both verbs and nouns: they are part of the noun class system (class 15) and can trigger agreement with nominal modifiers like demonstratives, numerals and adjectives. However, they are semantically verbal and can take verbal morphemes like passive markers and causative markers. The Bukusu tagger consistently labels these as verbs while the Tiriki tagger tends to label them as nouns. The Wanga corpus uses the noun label more often for these infinitives resulting in higher performance for Tiriki.

Only a small handful of the cases where Tiriki outperforms Wanga appear to be due to errors in the gold standard labels. However, a more thorough investigation of the errors should be conducted using judgements from a native speaker of Wanga.

---

[11] An exception to this is in the application of the largest non-mixed models. Bukusu outperforms Tiriki by 1.33% for this scenario

[12] Though how this should be interpreted in light of the higher out of vocabulary scores for Tiriki is still unclear

Levenshtein Distance Threshold	Tiriki	Bukusu
0	31.82%	28.46%
1	55.67%	57.15%
2	78.89%	78.19%

Table 8: Percentage of source corpus within specified distance of any word in Wanga corpus

One last source of Tiriki's higher performance relative to Bukusu is due to borrowed words. The words that Tiriki predicts correctly but Bukusu misses are frequently loan words from English or Swahili. Words like **i-proverb** and **i-nursery** are borrowed from English with the addition of an augment prefix from Wanga. Swahili borrowed words are pervasive including coordinating conjunctions like **lakini**, meaning 'but' and numerals like **saba**[13]. The character n-gram model used in this work can rely on morphological clues to determine parts of speech for Luyia words. However, for borrowed words, these morphological queues are likely not strong enough. The Tiriki tagger's training data likely had tokens similar to or identical to these borrowed words.

8   Future Work

I intend to implement this research for the other two other pairings given the three Luyia languages for which data is available at the moment. The findings discussed herein are for using Tiriki and Bukusu to tag Wanga. What differences emerge when using Bukusu and Wanga to tag Tiriki or Wanga and Tiriki to tag Bukusu? In addition, certain parts of speech benefit more with the mixed language models described in section 5.2. What kind of accuracy can be obtained by combining finite-state and machine learning approaches using machine learning for open class parts of speech and

9   Conclusion

Wanga, a Luyia language can be tagged more effectively by using data from other varieties of Luyia. However, this effectiveness has a few stipulations. The variety that is effective is not necessarily the variety that is closest to Wanga. In these experiments, Tiriki, the more distantly related language fared better than Bukusu in both the direct tagging tasks and the combination tasks. A number of factors led to this advantage including vocabulary overlap between the Wanga and Tiriki corpora and a bias towards predicting open class parts of speech using the Tiriki tagger. In addition, while the introduction of data in the combination models can help, this effect is limited to cases where the training set size is small. As there are no annotated corpora at all for the 20 Luyia languages not used in this document, these findings could be used to create annotated corpora. This could be done either by using all available annotated data from another Luyia variety11 to annotate the new variety or by annotating a very small corpus from the new variety and then creating a mixture model.

References

Guy De Pauw, Gilles-Maurice de Schryver, and Janneke van de Loo. 2012. Resource-light Bantu part-of-speech tagging. In *Workshop on Language Technology for Normalisation of Less-Resourced Languages (SALTMIL 8-AFLAT 2012)*, pages 85–92. European Language Resources Association.

Kristopher J Ebarb. 2014. *Tone and variation in Idakho and other Luhya varieties*. Ph.D. thesis, Indiana University.

Björn Gambäck, Fredrik Olsson, Atelach Alemu Argaw, and Lars Asker. 2009. Methods for Amharic part-of-speech tagging. In *Proceedings of the First Workshop on Language Technologies for African Languages*, pages 104–111. Association for Computational Linguistics.

Christopher R. Green, Michael J. K. Diercks, and Michael R. Marlo. 2018. A grammar sketch of Wanga.

Jiri Hana, Anna Feldman, and Chris Brew. 2004. A resource-light approach to russian morphology: Tagging Russian using Czech resources. In *Proceedings of the 2004 Conference on Empirical Methods in Natural Language Processing*.

Kazi Saidul Hasan and Vincent Ng. 2009. Weakly supervised part-of-speech tagging for morphologically-rich, resource-scarce languages. In *Proceedings of the 12th Conference of the European Chapter of the Association for Computational Linguistics*, EACL '09, pages 363–371, Stroudsburg, PA, USA. Association for Computational Linguistics.

---

[13]Both of these terms were actually originally borrowed from Arabic

Thomas J Hinnebusch, Derek Nurse, and Martin Joel Mould. 1981. *Studies in the classification of Eastern Bantu languages*, volume 3. Buske.

Arvi Hurskainen and Department of World Cultures, University of Helsinki. 2016. Helsinki Corpus of Swahili 2.0 Annotated Version.

Arvi Hurskainen. 1992. A two-level computer formalism for the analysis of Bantu morphology: an application to Swahili. *Nordic Journal of African Studies*, 1(1):87–122.

SIL International. 2018. Fieldworks language explorer. `https://software.sil.org/fieldworks/`, March. Release 8.3.12.

Peter Ladefoged, Ruth Glick, and Clive Criper. 1972. *Language in Uganda*. Oxford University Press.

Jouni Filip Maho. 2009. Nugl online: The online version of the new updated Guthrie list, a referential classification of the Bantu languages. *Online file: http://goto. glocalnet. net/mahopapers/nuglonline. pdf.*

Lluís Màrquez, Lluis Padro, and Horacio Rodriguez. 2000. A machine learning approach to POS tagging. *Machine Learning*, 39(1):59–91.

F. Pedregosa, G. Varoquaux, A. Gramfort, V. Michel, B. Thirion, O. Grisel, M. Blondel, P. Prettenhofer, R. Weiss, V. Dubourg, J. Vanderplas, A. Passos, D. Cournapeau, M. Brucher, M. Perrot, and E. Duchesnay. 2011. Scikit-learn: Machine learning in Python. *Journal of Machine Learning Research*, 12:2825–2830.

Laurette Pretorius and Sonja Bosch. 2009. Exploiting cross-linguistic similarities in Zulu and Xhosa computational morphology. In *Proceedings of the EACL 2009 Workshop on Language Technologies for African Languages – AfLaT 2009*, pages 96–103, Athens, Greece, March. Association for Computational Linguistics.

Gary Simons and Charles Fennig. 2017. Ethnologue: Langauges of the world, twentieth edition.

Martha Yifiru Tachbelie, Solomon Teferra Abate, and Laurent Besacier. 2011. Part-of-speech tagging for under-resourced and morphologically rich languages–the case of Amharic. *HLTD (2011)*, pages 50–55.

Ralph Williams. 1973. A lexico-statistical look at Oluluyia. In *Fourth Annual Conference on African Linguistics*.

David Yarowsky and Grace Ngai. 2001. Inducing multilingual pos taggers and np bracketers via robust projection across aligned corpora. In *Proceedings of the Second Meeting of the North American Chapter of the Association for Computational Linguistics on Language Technologies*, NAACL '01, pages 1–8, Stroudsburg, PA, USA. Association for Computational Linguistics.

Tübingen-Oslo Team at the VarDial 2018 Evaluation Campaign: An Analysis of N-gram Features in Language Variety Identification

Çağrı Çöltekin[♠]   Taraka Rama[♡]   Verena Blaschke[♠]
[♠]Department of Linguistics, University of Tübingen, Germany
[♡]Department of Informatics, University of Oslo, Norway
tarakark@ifi.uio.no, ccoltekin@sfs.uni-tuebingen.de, verena.blaschke@student.uni-tuebingen.de

Abstract

This paper describes our systems for the VarDial 2018 evaluation campaign. We participated in all language identification tasks, namely, Arabic dialect identification (ADI), German dialect identification (GDI), Discriminating between Dutch and Flemish in Subtitles (DFS), and Indo-Aryan Language Identification (ILI). In all of the tasks, we only used textual transcripts (not using audio features for ADI). We submitted system runs based on support vector machine classifiers (SVMs) with bag of character and word n-grams as features, and gated bidirectional recurrent neural networks (RNNs) using units of characters and words. Our SVM models outperformed our RNN models in all tasks, obtaining the first place on the DFS task, third place on the ADI task, and second place on others according to the official rankings. As well as describing the models we used in the shared task participation, we present an analysis of the n-gram features used by the SVM models in each task, and also report additional results (that were run after the official competition deadline) on the GDI surprise dialect track.

1   Introduction

Identifying the language of a text or speech is an important step for many (multi-lingual) natural language processing applications. At least for written text, the language identification is a 'mostly-solved' problem. High accuracy values can be obtained with relatively simple machine learning models. One challenging issue, however, is identifying closely related languages or dialects, which is an interesting research question as well as being relevant to practical NLP applications. The series of VarDial evaluation campaigns (Malmasi et al., 2016; Zampieri et al., 2017; Zampieri et al., 2018) included tasks of identifying closely related languages and dialects from written or spoken language data. This paper is a description of our efforts in the VarDial 2018 shared task, which featured four dialect/language identification tasks, as well as one morphosyntactic tagging task. We only participated in the language identification tasks.

The aim of the ADI task, which was also part of the earlier two VarDial evaluation campaigns, is to recognize the five varieties of Arabic (Egyptian, Gulf, Levantine, North-African, and Modern Standard Arabic) from spoken language samples. The task provides transcribed text as well as pre-extracted audio features and raw audio recordings. The DFS task, introduced this year, is on discriminating Dutch and Flemish subtitles. The GDI is another task that was present in earlier VarDial shared tasks, where the aim is to identify four Swiss German Dialects (Basel, Bern, Lucerne, Zurich). This year's edition also included a surprise dialect. Finally, the ILI task, another newcomer, is about identifying five closely related Indo-Aryan languages (Hindi, Braj Bhasha, Awadhi, Bhojpuri, and Magah).

A simple approach to language/dialect identification is to treat it as a text (or document) classification task. Two well-known methods for solving this task are linear classifiers with bag-of-n-gram representations, and, recently popularized, recurrent neural networks. As in our participation at earlier VarDial evaluation campaigns (Çöltekin and Rama, 2016; Çöltekin and Rama, 2017), we experiment with both

This work is licensed under a Creative Commons Attribution 4.0 International License. License details: http://creativecommons.org/licenses/by/4.0/.

Proceedings of the Fifth Workshop on NLP for Similar Languages, Varieties and Dialects, pages 55–65
Santa Fe, New Mexico, USA, August 20, 2018.

the methods. Although our main participation is based on the SVM models, we also report the performance of the RNN models for comparison, and provide further analyses regarding the feature sets used in the SVM models.

We outline our approach in the next section, describing the models used briefly and explaining the strategies we used for the GDI surprise dialect track. Section 3 introduces the data, explains the experimental procedure used, and presents the analyses and results from the experiments run during and after the shared task. After a general discussion in Section 4, Section 5 concludes with pointers to potential future improvements.

2 Approach

2.1 SVMs with bag-of-n-gram features

Our SVM model is practically the same as the one used in Çöltekin and Rama (2016) and Çöltekin and Rama (2017), which in turn was similar to Zampieri et al. (2014). Similar to last year's participation, we used a combination of character and word n-grams as features.[1] All features are concatenated as a single feature vector per text instance and weighted by sub-linear tf-idf scaling. For the multi-class classification tasks (all except the DFS task which is binary), we used one-vs-rest SVM classifiers. All SVM models were implemented with scikit-learn (Pedregosa et al., 2011) and trained and tested using the Liblinear backend (Fan et al., 2008).

2.2 Bidirectional gated RNNs

Our neural model, for this task, again based on our previous models (Çöltekin and Rama, 2016; Çöltekin and Rama, 2017), includes two bidirectional gated RNN components: one taking a sequence of words as input and another taking a sequence of characters as input. The recurrent components of the network build two representations for the text (one based on characters and the other based on words), the representations are concatenated and passed to a fully connected softmax layer that assigns a language label to the document based on the RNN representations. Both sequence representations are trained jointly within a single model. We experimented with two well-known gated recurrent network variants, GRU (Cho et al., 2014) and LSTM (Hochreiter and Schmidhuber, 1997). For both character and word inputs, we used embedding layers before the RNN layers. Character sequences longer than 250 characters and word sequences longer than 100 tokens are truncated. All neural network experiments were implemented with Tensorflow (Abadi et al., 2015) using the Keras API (Chollet and others, 2015).

2.3 GDI surprise dialect

After the submission deadline, we experimented with the surprise dialect track of the GDI task, wherein the test set contains the surprise dialect 'XY' in addition to the four dialects for which training and development sets had been provided. We used the tuned SVM model for the classification of the four known dialects, but changed its decision rule such that it allows the classifier to predict a fifth class as well. Our initial SVM system consists of one one-versus-rest (OvR) SVM classifier per dialect in the training data; and, the dialect predicted for a given sample is the one whose corresponding OvR classifier yields the highest decision function value for the sample.

We experimented with this decision rule by altering it in the following ways:

- **Rejected by all**: When a sample is rejected (i.e. classified as 'rest') by all OvR classifiers, it is predicted as XY.
- **Accepted by several**: When a sample is accepted by several OvR classifiers, it is predicted as XY.
- **Rejected or multi-accepted**: When either of the two previous rules applies, the label is predicted as XY.
- **Standard deviation**: The fifth of the test set where the OvR classifiers' decision function values exhibit the smallest standard deviations is predicted as XY.

---

[1] 'Word' refers to the strings produced by a simple regular-expression tokenizer that splits documents into consecutive alphanumeric characters or consecutive non-space, non-alphanumeric characters.

- **Difference**: The fifth of the test set where the differences between the two highest decision function values are smallest is predicted as XY.

The last two rules naïvely assume a balanced label distribution, which is actually not the case for the gold-standard test set. The four known dialects each constitute 21–22% of the gold-standard labels whereas the surprise dialect only contributed 14%.

3 Experiments and results

3.1 Data

The ILI and DFS tasks are new tasks that featured for the first time, whereas ADI and GDI are tasks that were present over the past years. The Arabic data set is based on Ali et al. (2016). This year's shared task data included additional audio features and access to the audio recordings. However, in this study our focus is text classification, hence we did not use of any of the audio features, nor did we use the transcripts created by automatic speech recognition systems. A new aspect of the current GDI data set (Samardžić et al., 2016) was a surprise dialect that was not part of the four dialect labels that were present in the training set. We did not try to guess the 'unknown' dialect for our submission, but experimented with it afterwards. The new DFS data set (van der Lee and van den Bosch, 2017) is the largest of the data sets and contains only two labels. Finally, the ILI data set (Kumar et al., 2018) contains written texts from five closely-related Indo-Aryan languages. Some statistics about the data sets are presented in Table 1. The DFS data set has a perfectly balanced label distribution, while the other data sets show slight label imbalance. The reader is referred to the shared task description paper (Zampieri et al., 2018) for further details.

	Number of instances			Text size			
	train	dev	test	mean	st. dev.	min	max
ADI	14 591	1 566	6 837	124.32	185.78	0	6 830
DFS	300 000	500	20 000	39.90	22.73	1	267
GDI	14 646	4 658	4 752	181.24	25.00	118	953
ILI	70 263	10 329	9 692	76.60	64.65	3	2 910

Table 1: The number of instances in the training (train), development (dev), and test sets followed by the length of texts in each data set. The text-length statistics are calculated on combined training and development sets.

We did not perform any preprocessing, except for truncating the longer documents (and padding the shorter ones) to 250 characters and 100 tokens for the RNN models. We treated frequency cut-off and case normalization (where it made sense) as hyperparameters.

3.2 Experimental procedure

For all results submitted, we combined the training and development sets, and tuned the hyperparameters of the models with 5-fold cross validation. For the bag-of-n-grams models, we used an exhaustive grid search over the range of hyperparameter settings. For the RNN models, we used random search, since the RNN models required higher run times, and a full grid search was not feasible.[2] The ranges of parameter values used during random or grid search are listed in Table 2. The bag-of-n-gram features always include all n-gram sizes from unigrams to the n-grams of the specified order for the systems used in the shared participation. We use the same set of parameters for the backward and forward RNNs in our bidirectional RNN models. The random search is run for approximately 40 different parameter settings for each data set (task).

---

[2] As a rough indication, we note that the full grid search using SVMs (5-fold training/testing over 560 hyperparameter configurations) on a modern multi-core CPU took approximately the same amount of time as it took for 40 random RNN

Parameter	SVM	RNN
Minimum document frequency (`min_df`)	1–5	1–5
Case normalization (`lowercase`)	word, character, both, none	word, character, both, none
Maximum word n-gram size (`c_ngmax`)	2–6	–
Maximum character n-gram size (`w_ngmax`)	4–10	–
SVM margin (`C`)	0.01–1.20	–
Character embedding dimension (`c_embdim`)	–	16, 32, 64
Word embedding dimension (`w_embdim`)	–	32, 64, 128
RNN architecture (`rnn`)	–	GRU, LSTM
Char RNN hidden state dimension (`c_featdim`)	–	32, 64, 128
Word RNN hidden state dimension (`w_featdim`)	–	64, 128, 256
Dropout rate for character/word embedding/RNN layers (`c_embdrop, w_embdrop, c_featdrop, w_featdrop`)	–	0.10–0.50

Table 2: The range of values used for hyper-parameter search for the SVM and the RNN models. Case normalization only applies to the DFS data set. The last row corresponds to 4 separate parameters (used both for forward- and backward-RNNs).

Table 3 presents the parameter settings that yielded best average macro-averaged F_1 score based on 5-fold cross validation on the combined training and development sets. Although we report these values for the purpose of reproducibility, a rather large range of values result in similar performance scores. The distributions of F_1 scores for both models are presented in Figure 1. The central tendency in box plots presented in Figure 1 indicate that the F_1 score for many parameter settings for the SVM models are close to the top score. Hence, a large range of 'reasonable' hyperparameter settings yield the scores similar to the top performing setting. The scores of the RNNs distributed more evenly (symmetrically), since they include a smaller number of randomly selected hyperparameter configurations.

We tune the hyperparameters which interact, for instance, both decreasing C and increasing `min_df` may reduce overfitting. As a result, it is difficult to observe global trends of hyperparameter settings that yields better performance in a particular task. However, in general, frequency thresholds seems to hurt systems' performances. The best performing hyperparameter settings used all features regardless of their frequencies (hence, frequency thresholds are not shown in Table 3).

3.3 Shared task results

During the evaluation campaign, we submitted predictions from the SVM and RNN models described above. In all the tasks, our SVM models were the best models among the ones for which we submitted predictions. Table 4 presents the macro-averaged precision, recall, and F_1 scores of our SVM and RNN models, as well as the official ranks obtained by the SVM model, and a rough indication of the rank of the RNN models assuming they were the only additional models to be included in the official rankings. For the ADI task, we only used the manually transcribed data, not making use of automatic transcriptions or audio features. The data presented in Table 4 also excludes the surprise dialect of the GDI task. We present results of the experiments on the surprise dialect conducted after the end of the shared task below. In general, our SVM system got the first rank on the DFS task, as well as ranking second or third on the other tasks. The scores of the RNN models are always behind the score of the SVMs, and the gap is particularly large for the ADI and ILI tasks.

The results on the test set presented in Table 4 are also drastically lower than the ones we obtained during development for some of the tasks, particularly for GDI and ADI, and to some extent for ILI. As presented in Table 5, the results on tests set is lower than the k-fold cross validation results on combined

---

hyperparameter settings on an NVIDIA Titan Xp GPU. However, we did not measure the training/tuning times of both models precisely and systematically, and our implementations does not pay attention to computational efficiency or parallelization.

	SVM				RNN			
	ADI	DFS	GDI	ILI	ADI	DFS	GDI	ILI
lowercase	–	word	–	–	–	word	–	–
C	1.00	0.40	0.70	1.00	–	–	–	–
c_ngmax	9	4	6	6	–	–	–	–
c_wgmax	3	2	3	3	–	–	–	–
c_embdim	–	–	–	–	64	16	64	64
w_embdim	–	–	–	–	128	128	128	32
rnn	–	–	–	–	GRU	LSTM	LSTM	GRU
c_featdim	–	–	–	–	32	128	64	32
w_featdim	–	–	–	–	128	256	64	256
c_embdrop	–	–	–	–	0.10	0.20	0.20	0.10
w_embdrop	–	–	–	–	0.50	0.50	0.10	0.20
c_featdrop	–	–	–	–	0.10	0.10	0.10	0.20
w_featdrop	–	–	–	–	0.50	0.50	0.50	0.50
Best epoch	–	–	–	–	17	4	10	27

Table 3: Best parameters for both SVM and RNN models tuned with 5-fold cross validation on the combined training and development data. The abbreviations for the parameters are explained in Table 2.

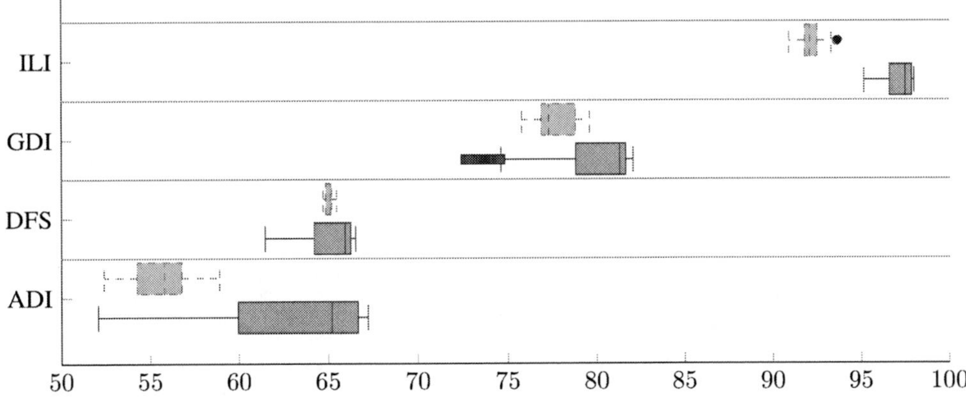

Figure 1: Box plots showing the distribution of F_1 scores obtained during the tuning process for the SVM (blue, solid) and the RNN (dashed, red) models. The SVM scores include all hyperparameter values listed in Table 2, while the RNN scores only include approximately 40 random choices among indicated list of hyperparameters. Note that the RNN models have much lower number of data points and does not necessarily include the settings within the hyperparameter ranges that result in worst or best performance which may explain low variance in the RNN score distributions.

training and development sets with 15.97 %, 18.07 %, and 7.27 %, for ADI, GDI, and ILI respectively, indicating a difference in distributions of training and the test sets. To check whether the designated development sets are closer to training or test sets, we also tuned the SVM models on the development set, whose results are also presented in Table 5. Indeed, for most data sets, the development sets seems to be closer to the test set. This may suggest that tuning the parameter values on the development sets rather than using k-fold cross validation may be better for obtaining better results in the shared task, despite its inferior performance to k-fold cross validation in an i.i.d. setting.

The differences between training/development/test distributions aside, the results on ADI and GDI data sets are similar to the last year's results. Our scores for these tasks are approximately 7 % and 4 %

Task	SVM				RNN			
	Precision	Recall	F1-score	Rank	Precision	Recall	F1-score	Rank
ADI	51.44	51.69	51.26	3 (5/ 6)	46.17	44.84	44.57	7
DFS	66.01	66.01	66.00	1 (1/11)	64.19	63.61	63.24	4
GDI	64.28	64.37	63.99	2 (4/ 8)	62.13	61.76	61.62	8
ILI	91.28	90.86	90.72	2 (2/ 8)	77.96	75.21	75.29	9

Table 4: Macro-averaged Precision, Recall, and F_1-score of our SVM and RNN models. The scores of the SVM models are the official results calculated by the organizers. The scores of the RNN models are calculated by us on the provided gold-standard test set. The 'Rank' column for the SVM lists the official rank based on statistically-significant differences, followed by the absolute rank and the number of participants for each task. The 'Rank' column of the RNN model is provided for a rough comparison and lists the absolute rank that would be obtained if the model were the only additional/unlisted model during the competition.

	K-fold	Dev-set	Official
ADI	67.23	52.14	51.26
DFS	66.54	73.60	66.00
GDI	82.06	67.63	63.99
ILI	97.99	96.26	90.72

Table 5: The best F1-scores obtained during tuning with k-fold CV and using development set, as well as the official score. Clearly, there is a discrepancy between the full training set (k-fold results) and the test set for ADI and GDI. In the case of DFS, the development set seems to be closer to the training set. For ILI, the extent of the discrepancy seems to be smaller, but also development set is not necessarily closer to the test set than the training set.

5 % below the winning systems in ADI, GDI and ILI tasks respectively. The low performance of the system for the ADI is, however, expected since we did not make use of all the information. In general, the ILI task seems to be relatively easy, allowing over 90 % F_1 score on 5-way classification task. The DFS task, on the other hand, seems more difficult. Although the classifiers certainly does much better than a random baseline, about 66 % F_1 score is hardly impressive on a binary classification task.

3.4 Contribution of n-gram features

Our SVM models combine the word and character n-grams of various sizes. To investigate the usefulness of the individual n-gram features, we run a set of additional experiments, using only a limited set of features at a time. The results of these experiments are shown in Figure 2. The figure present the results of individual features (character or n-gram sizes) and combined features up to the indicated character or word n-gram order (e.g., the performance score corresponding to 'combined' trigrams include unigrams and bigrams of the indicated feature type). Across the datasets, we find that higher order features do not improve the results. In fact, we find that the F_1 scores drop rapidly when only higher-order n-grams are used for both with character and word features.

For most data sets, performance of the systems peak for individual character ngrams of order 4 or 5, after which usefulness of the higher order character n-grams start to degrade. It is also worth noting that even character unigrams are useful features across all data sets. The combined character n-gram features seem to yield slightly better scores than best-performing single n-gram order across the data sets, and with proper tuning, the additional, relatively useless features does not seem to hurt.

The point where higher order n-grams becomes less useful is much earlier for word n-grams. Except for the ILI task, even word bigrams are not as useful as word unigrams. However, again, combining 'less-

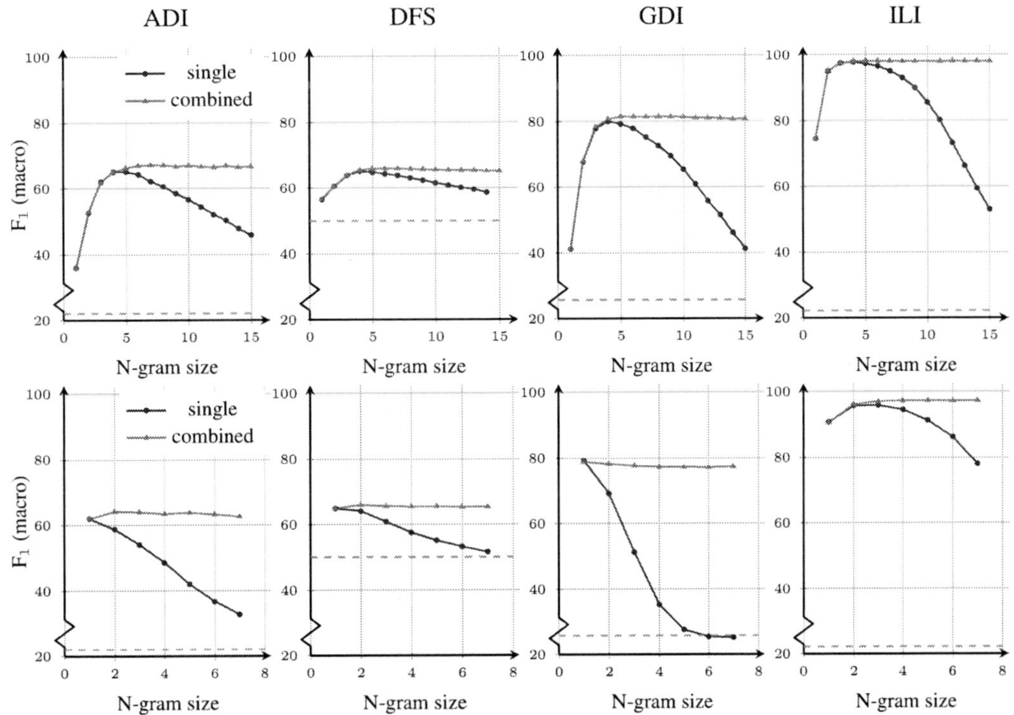

Figure 2: The macro averaged F1-scores for the SVM models using character (top) or word (bottom) n-gram of only the indicated n-gram size (blue lines with round markers) and up to the indicated n-gram size (red lines with triangle markers). The scores are the best macro-averaged F_1 scores obtained on the combined training and development sets using 5-fold cross validation (averaged over 5 folds). Dashed horizontal lines indicate the expected scores of majority class baselines for each data set.

useful' bigrams (or trigrams in case of ILI) seems to have a positive effect on the combined models. The GDI dataset presents an exception here. As well as slight performance drop when bigrams are combined with unigrams, higher-order word n-grams becomes less-informative, and degrades to majority baseline very quickly.

Figure 2 also indicates that character n-grams yield slightly better scores. This is also evident in the best F_1 scores obtained by the character and word n-gram combinations presented in Table 6. We also present the best setting that combines character and word n-grams for each dataset in Table 6. Although the character n-grams yield better results across all data sets, combining word n-grams is useful for DFS and GDI. Interestingly, despite the word n-grams seem least useful in the GDI task, the combination of character and word n-ngrams bring a noteworthy gain. In the ADI and the ILI tasks, we observe small performance loss when character and word n-grams are combined, compared to only using character n-grams.

3.5 GDI surprise dialect

Our submitted predictions and all the results related to the GDI task presented so far are based on four non-surprise dialects. Table 3.5 shows the performance scores of the SVM models with the different decision rules described in Section 2.3 for predicting the surprise dialect. The first row presents the scores for the 4-way classifier evaluated on gold-standard label set with five classes. Although all of the results are (naturally) lower than the non-surprise 4-way classification, all strategies do substantially better than not predicting the surprise dialect. Particularly, the 'rejected by all' rule yields the best macro-averaged F1-score, and the proportion of samples it classifies as the surprise dialect is also closest to the actual proportion of XY labels within the entire test set.

	ADI			DFS			GDI			ILI		
	F_1	c	w	F_1	c	w	F_1	c	w	F_1	c	w
Characters	67.28	7	0	65.98	6	0	81.42	8	0	98.05	7	0
Words	64.12	0	2	65.92	0	2	78.86	0	1	97.25	0	7
Characters and words	67.23	9	3	66.54	4	2	82.06	6	3	97.99	6	3

Table 6: Best macro-averaged F_1 scores obtained on the combined training/development set with 5-fold cross validation with the SVM model. The column 'c' indicates the maximum character n-gram size and the column 'w' indicates maximum word n-gram size that yielded the corresponding score.

Decision rule	No. of samples predicted as XY	Precision	Recall	F1-score
– (only four dialects)	0	44.02	51.48	47.39
Rejected by all	985	52.57	51.80	51.96
Accepted by several	413	46.80	49.36	47.74
Rejected or multi-accepted	1 398	52.91	49.62	50.51
Standard deviation	1 108	51.55	49.69	50.32
Difference	1 108	52.08	50.38	50.90

Table 7: Number of predictions for the surprise dialect 'XY' and macro-averaged precision, recall and F1-score of the SVM model for different decision criteria for predicting XY. We calculated the scores on the full gold-standard test set including the surprise dialect. The test set contains 790 XY samples out of 5542 samples total.

4   General discussion

As in earlier years, our participation in the VarDial 2018 shared task was based on two well-known classification methods, namely linear SVMs with bag-of-n-gram features, and recurrent ANN classifiers. Besides describing the systems, and presenting the official results, we also present a number of additional experiments and analysis of features used in our SVM models.

A common theme in our participation to VarDial has been the comparison between SVM and RNN classifiers. We and others have found SVMs to outperform RNNs in dialect / language identification tasks (Çöltekin and Rama, 2016; Çöltekin and Rama, 2017; Clematide and Makarov, 2017; Medvedeva et al., 2017), as well a few other text classification tasks (Rama and Çöltekin, 2017; Çöltekin and Rama, 2018; Malmasi and Dras, 2018). Similar to the results of the previous years, we found SVM models to work better than RNNs across all dialect identification tasks. Although in-line with earlier findings, the DFS task provided a possible advantage for RNNs, since the DFS data set is larger when compared to the other data sets, and large data is often considered one of the strengths of the deep learning methods. Our SVM model not only outperformed our RNN model, but also obtained the first place with an F_1-score difference of 1.50 % above the systems sharing the second place. Although RNNs are clearly behind SVMs also at the DFS task, the gap between RNNs and SVMs are smaller for DFS compared to ILI and ADI. One potential explanation, indeed, is the large data size. However, the GDI task, which has one of the smallest data sets, also exhibits a small performance difference similar to DFS task. A common trait of both the DFS and the GDI data sets is a more balanced text-length distribution (see Table 1), which may also be responsible for relatively better performance of the RNN models. However, more systematic experiments are required for identifying the conditions that affect the performances of the models.

Although we tuned both models through hyperparameter search, our models, and training methods are relatively simple. Both models can be improved in various ways. For example ensemble of n-grams (Malmasi and Zampieri, 2017b; Malmasi and Zampieri, 2017a), or simple extensions to feature weighting (Bestgen, 2017) are shown to improve the SVM classifiers considerably. Besides many possible architectural improvements, performance of RNNs may be improved through data augmentation (Clematide and Makarov, 2017). Nevertheless, with their 'baseline' forms our present results support the earlier findings that in similar text classification tasks, SVMs with bag-of-n-gram features outperform the ANN classifiers based on gated RNN architectures.

With the SVM classifiers, it has been found earlier that character n-gram features perform well in language / dialect identification tasks (Çöltekin and Rama, 2016; Bestgen, 2017). Our best submissions in this VarDial evaluation campaign were based on a combination of both character and word n-gram features which is supported through our analysis presented in Section 3.4. Moreover, the analysis also shows that depending on the task at hand, combining character n-gram features with word n-gram features may be helpful. The analysis in this section also shows that most of the gain in classification performance is based on rather low order features, character n-grams of order 4–5 and word uni- or bigrams seem to contain most valuable information while the higher order n-grams do not contribute much. This trend seems to persist with data sets with different size and properties, only with slight variation.

One of the interesting aspects of the present VarDial evaluation campaign has been the 'surprise dialect' track of the GDI task. Although we did not submit results during the shared task due to time restrictions, we did a number of experiments with this task. Our results show that simple strategies based on assigning test instances where one-vs-rest multi-class classifiers are uncertain to the surprise dialect yields reasonable improvements. Particularly, assigning the test instances which were rejected by all of the one-vs-rest classifiers seems to perform the best in the present task.

5   Conclusions and outlook

In this paper we described our participation in the VarDial 2018 shared task. Our systems based on SVMs with bag-of-n-grams features ranked first in the DFS task, while obtaining second or third place in other language/dialect identification tasks. We reported scores of the alternative RNN classifier, presented analysis of usefulness of n-gram features in the SVM models, and also discussed possible strategies for predicting the surprise dialect in the GDI task.

Our results and analysis supports the earlier results that SVMs work better than RNNs in the tasks presented, and character (n-gram) features are seem to be most useful in SVM classifiers, while there may be small gains using both character and word n-gram features. Although we do not have a baseline to compare to at the time of this writing, our strategies for the surprise dialect also seem to bring reasonable improvements compared to not predicting the surprise dialect at all.

Although our models were successful during the shared task, they are 'baseline' models based on our participations in the earlier VarDial evaluation campaigns. There are a few straightforward points of improvements that can increase the performances of both the SVM and RNN models. For SVMs, one point of improvement is using a better feature weighting method than the sub-linear tf-idf used in this study. Another potentially useful direction for both SVMs and RNNs is the use of ensemble methods. This has been shown to work well with SVMs in earlier VarDial tasks. However, it is clearly not limited to the SVMs, it can be applied to RNNs too. Furthermore, since most ensemble methods work best when underlying classifiers are diverse, hybrid SVM-RNN ensembles are likely to perform even better. Last, but not the least, data augmentation methods are often shown to improve performance of deep learning methods such as RNNs. Although it is common to apply data augmentation for deep learning systems, investigating their effects on more 'traditional' models such as SVMs is another interesting possibility for improving results obtained with these models.

Acknowledgements

The authors thank the organizers for all the support during the process of paper writing. The second author is supported BIGMED project, a NRC Lighthouse grant which is gratefully acknowledged. Part of the experiments reported on this paper is run on a Titan Xp donated by the NVIDIA Corporation.

References

Martín Abadi, Ashish Agarwal, Paul Barham, Eugene Brevdo, Zhifeng Chen, Craig Citro, Greg S. Corrado, Andy Davis, Jeffrey Dean, Matthieu Devin, Sanjay Ghemawat, Ian Goodfellow, Andrew Harp, Geoffrey Irving, Michael Isard, Yangqing Jia, Rafal Jozefowicz, Lukasz Kaiser, Manjunath Kudlur, Josh Levenberg, Dan Mané, Rajat Monga, Sherry Moore, Derek Murray, Chris Olah, Mike Schuster, Jonathon Shlens, Benoit Steiner, Ilya Sutskever, Kunal Talwar, Paul Tucker, Vincent Vanhoucke, Vijay Vasudevan, Fernanda Viégas, Oriol Vinyals, Pete Warden, Martin Wattenberg, Martin Wicke, Yuan Yu, and Xiaoqiang Zheng. 2015. TensorFlow: Large-scale machine learning on heterogeneous systems. Software available from tensorflow.org.

Ahmed Ali, Najim Dehak, Patrick Cardinal, Sameer Khurana, Sree Harsha Yella, James Glass, Peter Bell, and Steve Renals. 2016. Automatic dialect detection in Arabic broadcast speech. In *Proceedings of INTER-SPEECH*, pages 2934–2938.

Yves Bestgen. 2017. Improving the character ngram model for the DSL task with BM25 weighting and less frequently used feature sets. In *Proceedings of the Fourth Workshop on NLP for Similar Languages, Varieties and Dialects (VarDial)*, pages 115–123, Valencia, Spain, April.

Çağrı Çöltekin and Taraka Rama. 2016. Discriminating similar languages with linear SVMs and neural networks. In *Proceedings of the Third Workshop on NLP for Similar Languages, Varieties and Dialects (VarDial3)*, pages 15–24, Osaka, Japan.

Çağrı Çöltekin and Taraka Rama. 2017. Tübingen system in VarDial 2017 shared task: experiments with language identification and cross-lingual parsing. In *Proceedings of the Fourth Workshop on NLP for Similar Languages, Varieties and Dialects (VarDial)*, pages 146–155, Valencia, Spain.

Kyunghyun Cho, Bart van Merrienboer, Dzmitry Bahdanau, and Yoshua Bengio. 2014. On the properties of neural machine translation: Encoder–decoder approaches. In *Proceedings of SSST-8, Eighth Workshop on Syntax, Semantics and Structure in Statistical Translation*, pages 103–111.

François Chollet et al. 2015. Keras. `https://github.com/keras-team/keras`.

Simon Clematide and Peter Makarov. 2017. CLUZH at VarDial GDI 2017: Testing a variety of machine learning tools for the classification of swiss German dialects. In *Proceedings of the Fourth Workshop on NLP for Similar Languages, Varieties and Dialects (VarDial)*, pages 170–177, Valencia, Spain, April.

Rong-En Fan, Kai-Wei Chang, Cho-Jui Hsieh, Xiang-Rui Wang, and Chih-Jen Lin. 2008. LIBLINEAR: A library for large linear classification. *Journal of Machine Learning Research*, 9:1871–1874.

Sepp Hochreiter and Jürgen Schmidhuber. 1997. Long short-term memory. *Neural computation*, 9(8):1735–1780.

Ritesh Kumar, Bornini Lahiri, Deepak Alok, Atul Kr. Ojha, Mayank Jain, Abdul Basit, and Yogesh Dawar. 2018. Automatic Identification of Closely-related Indian Languages: Resources and Experiments. In *Proceedings of the Eleventh International Conference on Language Resources and Evaluation (LREC)*.

Shervin Malmasi and Mark Dras. 2018. Native language identification with classifier stacking and ensembles. *Computational Linguistics*, (in press).

Shervin Malmasi and Marcos Zampieri. 2017a. Arabic dialect identification using iVectors and ASR transcripts. In *Proceedings of the Fourth Workshop on NLP for Similar Languages, Varieties and Dialects (VarDial)*, pages 178–183, Valencia, Spain, April.

Shervin Malmasi and Marcos Zampieri. 2017b. German dialect identification in interview transcriptions. In *Proceedings of the Fourth Workshop on NLP for Similar Languages, Varieties and Dialects (VarDial)*, pages 164–169, Valencia, Spain, April.

Shervin Malmasi, Marcos Zampieri, Nikola Ljubešić, Preslav Nakov, Ahmed Ali, and Jörg Tiedemann. 2016. Discriminating between similar languages and Arabic dialect identification: A report on the third DSL shared task. In *Proceedings of the 3rd Workshop on Language Technology for Closely Related Languages, Varieties and Dialects (VarDial)*, Osaka, Japan.

Maria Medvedeva, Martin Kroon, and Barbara Plank. 2017. When sparse traditional models outperform dense neural networks: the curious case of discriminating between similar languages. In *Proceedings of the Fourth Workshop on NLP for Similar Languages, Varieties and Dialects (VarDial)*, pages 156–163, Valencia, Spain, April.

F. Pedregosa, G. Varoquaux, A. Gramfort, V. Michel, B. Thirion, O. Grisel, M. Blondel, P. Prettenhofer, R. Weiss, V. Dubourg, J. Vanderplas, A. Passos, D. Cournapeau, M. Brucher, M. Perrot, and E. Duchesnay. 2011. Scikit-learn: Machine learning in Python. *Journal of Machine Learning Research*, 12:2825–2830.

Taraka Rama and Çağrı Çöltekin. 2017. Fewer features perform well at native language identification task. In *Proceedings of the 12th Workshop on Innovative Use of NLP for Building Educational Applications*, pages 255–260, Copenhagen, Denmark.

Tanja Samardžić, Yves Scherrer, and Elvira Glaser. 2016. ArchiMob–A corpus of spoken Swiss German. In *Proceedings of the Language Resources and Evaluation (LREC)*, pages 4061–4066, Portoroz, Slovenia).

Chris van der Lee and Antal van den Bosch. 2017. Exploring Lexical and Syntactic Features for Language Variety Identification. In *Proceedings of the Fourth Workshop on NLP for Similar Languages, Varieties and Dialects (VarDial)*, pages 190–199, Valencia, Spain.

Marcos Zampieri, Liling Tan, Nikola Ljubešić, and Jörg Tiedemann. 2014. A report on the dsl shared task 2014. In *Proceedings of the First Workshop on Applying NLP Tools to Similar Languages, Varieties and Dialects (VarDial)*, pages 58–67, Dublin, Ireland.

Marcos Zampieri, Shervin Malmasi, Nikola Ljubešić, Preslav Nakov, Ahmed Ali, Jörg Tiedemann, Yves Scherrer, and Noëmi Aepli. 2017. Findings of the VarDial Evaluation Campaign 2017. In *Proceedings of the Fourth Workshop on NLP for Similar Languages, Varieties and Dialects (VarDial)*, Valencia, Spain.

Marcos Zampieri, Shervin Malmasi, Preslav Nakov, Ahmed Ali, Suwon Shuon, James Glass, Yves Scherrer, Tanja Samardžić, Nikola Ljubešić, Jörg Tiedemann, Chris van der Lee, Stefan Grondelaers, Nelleke Oostdijk, Antal van den Bosch, Ritesh Kumar, Bornini Lahiri, and Mayank Jain. 2018. Language Identification and Morphosyntactic Tagging: The Second VarDial Evaluation Campaign. In *Proceedings of the Fifth Workshop on NLP for Similar Languages, Varieties and Dialects (VarDial)*, Santa Fe, USA.

Çağrı Çöltekin and Taraka Rama. 2018. Tübingen-Oslo at SemEval-2018 task 2: SVMs perform better than RNNs at emoji prediction. In *Proceedings of the 12th International Workshop on Semantic Evaluation (SemEval-2018)*, pages 34–38, New Orleans, LA, United States.

Iterative Language Model Adaptation for Indo-Aryan Language Identification

Tommi Jauhiainen
University of Helsinki
@helsinki.fi

Heidi Jauhiainen
University of Helsinki
@helsinki.fi

Krister Lindén
University of Helsinki
@helsinki.fi

Abstract

This paper presents the experiments and results obtained by the SUKI team in the Indo-Aryan Language Identification shared task of the VarDial 2018 Evaluation Campaign. The shared task was an open one, but we did not use any corpora other than what was distributed by the organizers. A total of eight teams provided results for this shared task. Our submission using a HeLI-method based language identifier with iterative language model adaptation obtained the best results in the shared task with a macro F1-score of 0.958.

1 Introduction

In the past, the VarDial workshops have hosted several different shared tasks related to language identification and especially the identification of close languages, language varieties, and dialects (Zampieri et al., 2014; Zampieri et al., 2015; Malmasi et al., 2016; Zampieri et al., 2017). The fifth VarDial workshop included for the first time a shared task for Indo-Aryan language identification (ILI) (Zampieri et al., 2018). The goal of the shared task was to identify the language used in unlabeled texts written in Hindi and four related languages using the Devanagari script: Bhojpuri, Awadhi, Magahi, and Braj.

We have participated in the shared tasks of three previous VarDial workshops using systems based on different variations of the HeLI method (Jauhiainen et al., 2015b; Jauhiainen et al., 2016; Jauhiainen et al., 2017a). The HeLI method has turned out to be robust and competitive with other state-of-the-art language identification methods, gaining shared first place in the VarDial 2016 Discriminating between Similar Languages (DSL) shared task. The HeLI method is not especially tailored to be a dialect identification method, but it is a general purpose language identification method capable of distinguishing between hundreds of languages, some of which might be very close to each other (Jauhiainen et al., 2017b). In the Kone foundation funded Finno-Ugric Languages and the Internet project, a language identifier implementing the HeLI method has been used together with the Heritrix web-crawler to collect text in Uralic languages from the internet (Jauhiainen et al., 2015a). The language identifier using the HeLI method is available for download in GitHub[1]. In the current workshop, we wanted to try out some new variations and possible improvements to the original method. For the ILI task, we used the basic HeLI method, HeLI with adaptive language models, as well as an iterative version of the language model adaptation method.

2 Related work

The first automatic language identifier for digital text was described by Mustonen (1965). During more than 50 years, hundreds of conference and journal articles describing language identification experiments and methods have been published. For a recent survey on language identification and the methods used in the literature, see Jauhiainen et al. (2018). The HeLI method was first presented by Jauhiainen (2010)

This work is licensed under a Creative Commons Attribution 4.0 International Licence. Licence details: http://creativecommons.org/licenses/by/4.0/.

[1]https://github.com/tosaja/HeLI

Proceedings of the Fifth Workshop on NLP for Similar Languages, Varieties and Dialects, pages 66–75
Santa Fe, New Mexico, USA, August 20, 2018.

and later more formally by Jauhiainen et al. (2016), but we also provide a full description of the exact variation of the method used to submit the best results on the ILI shared task.

2.1 Language identification for Devanagari script

The language identification between languages using the Devanagari script has been considered earlier. Kruengkrai et al. (2006) presented language identification results between ten Indian languages, including four languages written in Devanagari: Sanskrit, Marathi, Magahi, and Hindi. For the ten Indian languages they obtained over 90% accuracy with mystery texts 70 bytes in length. As language identification method, they used support vector machines (SVM) with string kernels. Murthy and Kumar (2006) compared the use of language models based on bytes and aksharas. Aksharas are the syllables or orthographic units of the Brahmi scripts (Vaid and Gupta, 2002). After evaluating the language identification between different pairs of languages, they concluded that the akshara-based models perform better than byte-based. They used multiple linear regression as the classification method.

Sreejith et al. (2013) tested language identification with Markovian character and word n-grams from one to three with Hindi and Sanskrit. A character bigram-based language identifier fared the best and managed to gain the accuracy of 99.75% for sentence-sized mystery texts. Indhuja et al. (2014) continued the work of Sreejith et al. (2013) investigating the language identification between Hindi, Sanskrit, Marathi, Nepali, and Bhojpuri. They also evaluated the use of Markovian character and word n-grams from one to three. For this set of languages word unigrams performed the best, obtaining 88% accuracy with the sentence-sized mystery texts.

Bergsma et al. (2012) collected tweets in three languages written with the Devanagari script: Hindi, Marathi, and Nepali. They managed to identify the language of the tweets with 96.2% accuracy using a logistic regression (LR) classifier (Hosmer et al., 2013) with up to 4-grams of characters. Using an additional training corpus, they reached 97.9% accuracy with the A-variant of prediction by partial matching (PPM). Later, Pla and Hurtado (2017) experimented with the corpus of Bergsma et al. (2012). Their approach using words weighted with TF-IDF (product of term frequency and inverse document frequency) and SVMs reached 97.7% accuracy on the tweets when using only the provided tweet training corpora. Hasimu and Silamu (2018) included the same three languages in their test setting. They used a two-stage language identification system, where the languages were first identified as a group using Unicode code ranges. In the second stage, the languages written with the Devanagari script were individually identified using SVMs with character bigrams. Their tests resulted in an F1-score of 0.993 within the group of languages using Devanagari with 700 best distinguishing bigrams. Indhuja et al. (2014) provided test results for several different combinations of the five languages and for the set of languages used by Hasimu and Silamu (2018) they reached 96% accuracy with word unigrams.

Rani et al. (2018) described a language identification system, which they used for discriminating between Hindi and Magahi. Their language identifier using lexicons and three character suffixes obtained an accuracy of 86.34%. Kumar et al. (2018) provided an overview of experiments on an earlier version of the dataset used in this shared task. They managed to obtain the accuracy of 96.48% and a macro F1-score of 0.96 on the dataset they used. For sentence level identification these results are quite good, and as such they indicate that the languages, at least in their written form as evidenced by the corpus, are not as closely related as for example the Balkan languages Croatian, Serbian, and Bosnian.

2.2 Unsupervised language model adaptation

In unsupervised language model adaptation, the language models are modified while identifying the language of previously unseen and unlabeled text. The goal is to adapt the models to better suit the language or languages used in the texts to be identified in order to reach higher identification accuracy.

The use of on-line language model adaptation for language identification of digital text has been very limited. Blodgett et al. (2017) experimented with a method where they first identified the language of tweets using standard *langid-py* (Lui and Baldwin, 2012), and then collected the tweets with high posterior probability for English. From the collected tweets they generated a second language model for English to be used by the language identifier. Language identifiers can have several language models for one language, all of them providing the same classification if chosen. Their experiments produced a small increase in recall.

Chen and Liu (2005) use language model adaptation with language identification of speech similarly as we are using it in the language identification of text. The language identification system used by Chen and Liu (2005) first runs the speech through Hidden Markov Model-based phone recognizers (one for each language), which tokenize the speech into sequences of phones. The probabilities of these phone sequences for corresponding languages are calculated using language models and the most probable language is selected. An adaptation routine is then used so that each of the phonetic transcriptions of the individual speech utterances is used to calculate probabilities for words t, given a word n-gram history of h as in Equation 1.

$$P_a(t|h) = \lambda P_o(t|h) + (1 - \lambda)P_n(t|h), \tag{1}$$

where P_o is the original probability calculated from the training material, P_n the probability calculated from the data being identified, and P_a the new adapted probability. λ is the weight given to original probabilities. Using this adaptation method resulted in decreasing the language identification error rate in a three-way identification between Chinese, English, and Russian by 2.88% and 3.84% on an out-of-domain (different channels) data, and by 0.44% on in-domain (same channel) data.

Zhong et al. (2007) describe a confidence measure which they use with language identification of speech and define as follows:

$$C(g_i, M) = \frac{1}{n}[\log(P(M|g_i)) - \log(P(M|g_j))], \tag{2}$$

where M is the sequence to be identified, n the number of frames in the utterance, g_i the best identified language, and g_j the second best identified language. In the evaluations of Zhong et al. (2007), this confidence measure performed clearly better than two other ones they experimented with. They also evaluated an ensemble of all three confidence measures which managed to slightly improve the results. They then use the same language adaptation method as Chen and Liu (2005), using the confidence measures to set the λ for each utterance.

Bacchiani and Roark (2003) used unsupervised language model adaptation in a speech recognition task. They experimented with iterative adaptation on their language models. One additional adaptation iteration raised the accuracy gain of the language model adaptation from 3.4% to 3.9%, but subsequent iterations made the accuracy worse.

3   Task setup and data

For the preparation of the shared task, the participants were provided with training and development datasets. An early version of the dataset used, as well as its creation, was described by Kumar et al. (2018). The dataset used for the shared task included text in five languages, Bhojpuri, Hindi, Awadhi, Magahi, and Braj as shown in Table 1. The size of the training material was considerably smaller for the Awadhi language at slightly over 9,000 lines compared with the others which were around 15,000 long. The difference in size of the training material might produce problems for some methods that have been used for language identification. The HeLI method has turned out to be very robust in this respect, so we did not need to take this into any special consideration.

Language name	Code used	Training data (lines)	Development data (lines)
Bhojpuri	BHO	14,897	2,003
Hindi	HIN	15,642	2,253
Awadhi	AWA	9,307	1,480
Magahi	MAG	15,306	2,285
Braj	BRA	15,111	2,308

Table 1: List of languages with the sizes of their training and development sets.

The task was an open one, allowing the use of any additional data or means. However, we did not try to use any external means and our results would have been exactly the same in a closed version of the task. Participants were allowed to submit three runs for the ILI task and the best out of those submissions would be ranked. We submitted one with the original HeLI method, one using language model adaptation, and one using an iterative version of language model adaptation.

4   The HeLI method, run 1

To make this article more self-contained, we present the full description of the method as used in the submitted runs. This description differs from the original by Jauhiainen et al. (2016) mostly in that we leave out the cut-off value c for the size of the language models. In this year's shared tasks we found, and have already noticed it earlier, that if the corpora used as the training corpus is of good quality it is generally advisable to use all the available material. Furthermore, the penalty value compensates for some of the possible impurities in the language models. The final submissions were done with a system not using words at all, so we leave them out of the description as well.

Description of the HeLI method   The goal is to correctly guess the language $g \in G$ for each of the lines in the test set. In the HeLI method, each language g is represented by several different language models only one of which is used for every word t in the line M. The language models in this version are based on character n-grams from one to n_{max}. When none of the n-grams of the size n_{max} generated from the word under scrutiny are found in any of the language models, we back off to using the n-grams of the size $n_{max} - 1$. If needed, we continue backing off until character unigrams.

The training data is tokenized into words using non-alphabetic and non-ideographic characters as delimiters. The data is lowercased, even though the actual Devanagari script does not use capital letters, but there is some material in the data in other scripts as well. The relative frequencies of character n-grams from 1 to n_{max} are calculated inside the words, so that the preceding and the following space-characters are included. The n-grams are overlapping, so that for example a word with three characters includes three character trigrams. Then we transform the relative frequencies into scores using 10-based logarithms. Among the language models generated from the ILI training corpus, the largest model, Hindi 5-grams, included 80,539 different n-grams.

The corpus containing only the n-grams of the length n in the language models is called C^n. The domain $dom(O(C^n))$ is the set of all character n-grams of length n found in the models of any language $g \in G$. The values $v_{C_g^n}(u)$ are calculated similarly for all n-grams $u \in dom(O(C^n))$ for each language g, as shown in Equation 3.

$$v_{C_g^n}(u) = \begin{cases} -\log_{10}\left(\frac{c(C_g^n, u)}{l_{C_g^n}}\right) & \text{, if } c(C_g^n, u) > 0 \\ p & \text{, if } c(C_g^n, u) = 0, \end{cases} \tag{3}$$

where $c(C_g^n, u)$ is the number of n-grams u found in the corpus of the language g and $l_{C_g^n}$ is the total number of the n-grams of length n in the corpus of language g. These values are used when scoring the words while identifying the language of a text. When using n-grams, the word t is split into overlapping n-grams of characters u_i^n, where $i = 1, ..., l_t - n$, of the length n. Each of the n-grams u_i^n is then scored separately for each language g.

If the n-gram u_i^n is found in $dom(O(C_g^n))$, the values in the models are used. If the n-gram u_i^n is not found in any of the models, it is simply discarded. We define the function $d_g(t, n)$ for counting n-grams in t found in a model in Equation 4.

$$d_g(t, n) = \sum_{i=1}^{l_t - n} \begin{cases} 1 & \text{, if } u_i^n \in dom(O(C^n)) \\ 0 & \text{, otherwise.} \end{cases} \tag{4}$$

When all the n-grams of the size n in the word t have been processed, the word gets the value of the average of the scored n-grams u_i^n for each language, as in Equation 5.

$$v_g(t,n) = \begin{cases} \frac{1}{d_g(t,n)} \sum_{i=1}^{l_t-n} v_{C_g^n}(u_i^n) & \text{, if } d_g(t,n) > 0 \\ v_g(t, n-1) & \text{, otherwise,} \end{cases} \tag{5}$$

where $d_g(t,n)$ is the number of n-grams u_i^n found in the domain $dom(O(C_g^m))$. If all of the n-grams of the size n were discarded, $d_g(t,n) = 0$, the language identifier backs off to using n-grams of the size $n-1$. If no values are found even for unigrams, a word gets the penalty value p for every language, as in Equation 6.

$$v_g(t,0) = p \tag{6}$$

The mystery text is tokenized into words using the non-alphabetic and non-ideographic characters as delimiters. The words are lowercased when lowercased models are being used. After this, a score $v_g(t)$ is calculated for each word t in the mystery text for each language g, as shown in Equation 7.

$$v_g(t) = v_g(t, min(n_{max}, l_t + 2)) \tag{7}$$

If the length of the word l_t is at least $n_{max} - 2$, the language identifier backs off to using character n-grams of the length n_{max}. In case the word t is shorter than $n_{max} - 2$ characters, $n = l_t + 2$.

The whole line M gets the score $R_g(M)$ equal to the average of the scores of the words $v_g(t)$ for each language g, as in Equation 8.

$$R_g(M) = \frac{\sum_{i=1}^{l_{T(M)}} v_g(t_i)}{l_{T(M)}}, \tag{8}$$

where $T(M)$ is the sequence of words and $l_{T(M)}$ is the number of words in the line M. Since we are using negative logarithms of probabilities, the language having the lowest score is returned as the language with the maximum probability for the mystery text.

Results of the run1 on the development and the test sets The development set was used for finding the best values for the parameter p and to decide which language models to use. We experimented with several different combinations of language models and the resulting recall-values of these trials can be seen in Table 2. "Original n_{max}" refers to the maximum size used with the original n-grams and "Lowercased n_{max}" to the size used with the lowercased n-grams. The differences in recall between the combinations are not very high.

Original words	Original n_{max}	Lowercased words	Lowercased n_{max}	Penalty p	Recall
no	-	no	6	5.9	95.26%
no	-	no	5	6.4	95.11%
no	-	no	7	6.0	95.08%
no	8	no	8	5.7	95.01%
no	7	no	8	5.7	95.01%
no	6	no	8	5.7	95.01%
no	-	no	8	5.7	95.01%
no	-	no	4	6.7	95.00%
yes	8	yes	8	6.0	94.81%
yes	8	no	8	6.0	94.81%
no	8	yes	8	6.0	94.81%
no	-	yes	8	6.0	94.81%

Table 2: Baseline HeLI recall in development data with different combinations of parameters.

We decided to use lowercased character n-grams from one to six with the penalty value of 5.9 for the first run. We included the development set in the training material to generate the final language models. The recall for the test set was 89.28% and the macro F1-score, which is used for ranking in the ILI shared task, was 0.8873.

5 Unsupervised language model adaptation, run 2

The idea behind language model adaptation is to incorporate new language material into the language models while previously unseen and untagged text is processed. Most language identifiers that can indicate how well they perform could be used with language model adaptation. The system also benefits if adding new information to the language models is reasonably easy. Our method is recursive and it builds on the fact that we can process the same batch of previously unseen texts several times before providing the final labels. In our method, the information from the sentences in the unseen text is added to the language models one sentence at a time. The sentence to be processed next is always the one that the language identifier deems to be the one that is most probably correctly identified using the current language models. In order to determine which of the sentences is most identifiable, we could use the probabilities given to the sentence by the language models. However, this probability can be almost equally high for several languages if they are very close to each other. What we want to find is a sentence that gains high probability in one of the languages, but low probability in others. We achieve this by maximizing the difference between the probabilities of the first and the second identified languages.

Description of the unsupervised language model adaptation method All the lines M are first identified using the HeLI method. Then the best identified line, as ranked by the confidence score CM, is set as identified. In order to rank the identified lines to use for language model adaptation, we must be able to tell how confident the language identifier is in its decision. As confidence measure CM, we used the difference between the scores of the best $R_g(M)$ and the second best $R_h(M)$ identified language for each line. This is basically the same as the confidence measure proposed by Zhong et al. (2007). We did not test the other two methods presented by Zhong et al. (2007), or their Bayesian classifier-based ensemble. In our case, the confidence measure is calculated using Equation 9:

$$CM(C_g, M) = R_h(M) - R_g(M), \tag{9}$$

where M is the line containing the mystery text. The character n-grams up to the length of six are created from the line with the best confidence and they are added to the language models of the winning language. After this, the rest of the lines are re-identified with the adapted models and the line with the best confidence is again added to the models of the language it was identified to be written with. This process is repeated until all the lines have been added to the language models. Each time the lines are re-identified there is one less line to process. Nevertheless, the number of identifications is exponential relative to the number of lines to be identified when compared with only identifying them once.

Results of run2 on the development and the test sets In preparation for the second run, we used the same language models and penalty value as for the first run. The language identifier with language model adaptation achieved 96.22% recall on the development set. It was an increase of 0.96% on top of the recall of the basic HeLI method. For the submission run, we used both the development and the training sets to generate the initial language models. The submitted second run reached a recall of 95.66% on the test set, a formidable increase of 6.38% when compared with the first run. In other words, using the language model adaptation reduced the error rate by 59.5%. The fact that the percentage gain using language model adaptation was clearly more considerable on the test set than on the development set indicates that the test set is more out-of-domain from the combined development and trainings sets than the development set was from the training set. The macro F1-score obtained on our second run was 0.9553.

6 Iterative language model adaptation, run 3

While we were experimenting with language model adaptation, we noticed that if the initial language models are good enough, the adaptation process can be repeated. The additional accuracy gained was usually very small, but the repeated adaptation only very rarely affected the results in any negative manner. This is in contrast to the findings of Bacchiani and Roark (2003), who found that performing subsequent adaptations made the results worse.

Iterative language model adaptation basically means that the process for language model adaptation is restarted after one learning epoch. We noted the time it took to produce the results on the second run and decided to use four epochs for our third run on the basis of time left before the submissions were due. We used iterative adaptation with four epochs on the test set, gaining a small additional increase of 0.22% to recall, reaching 95.88% with the F1 score of 0.9576. The final results of all our runs and the best runs of the other teams are listed in Table 3.

Method (or team)	F1 (macro)
HeLI with iterative language model adaptation (run3)	**0.9576**
HeLI with language model adaptation (run2)	**0.9553**
taraka_rama	0.9022
XAC	0.8933
ILIdentification	0.8895
HeLI (run1)	**0.8873**
safina	0.8627
dkosmajac	0.8472
we_are_indian	0.8360
LaMa	0.8195
Random Baseline	0.2024

Table 3: Macro F1 scores obtained by different runs submitted by the SUKI-team (bolded) and the best runs of the other teams.

Figure 1 shows the confusion matrix for the Indo-Aryan languages in our third and final run. From the figure it seems that the largest misclassified group was 146 sentences in Bhojpuri, which were identified as Hindi. We randomly selected some Bhojpuri sentences to try with Google translator and it detected them all as Hindi and was also able to produce seemingly intelligible English translations for them. Unfortunately, our limited understanding of the languages in question prevents us from doing any deeper error analysis.

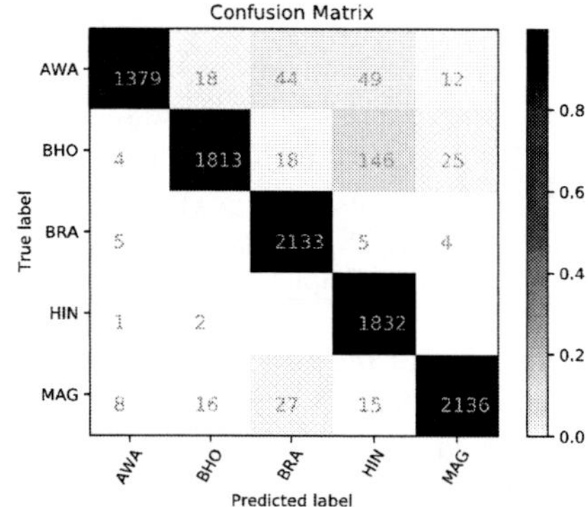

Figure 1: Confusion matrix for final submitted run.

7   Other experiments

We experimented with leaving out shorter lowercased n-grams with $n_{max} = 6$. Leaving out character unigrams and bigrams did not affect the recall, but leaving out trigrams dropped the recall to 94.53% indicating that the HeLI back-off function is also needed for these languages. With the German dialect identification task we ended up using only 4-grams of characters.

We also experimented with an unsupervised language set adaptation method. In unsupervised language set adaptation, the mystery text is first identified using all the available languages. The language with the worst score is left out and the text re-identified with the remaining languages. The process is continued until only one language is left. In a non-discriminative language identification method, the effect of leaving out languages with the worst scores does not affect the order of the top scoring languages.

However, if the back-off function of the HeLI method is used, it gives equal penalty values to those languages in which a word is not found. If the word was found in an otherwise poorly scoring language, which was subsequently left out, the following run might use the back-off function with the word in question and find a difference between the better candidates using character n-grams. We expected the effect to be small, and it turned out to be slightly negative reducing the recall from 95.26% to 95.22%.

We, furthermore, evaluated the same non-linear mappings, the gamma and the loglike functions, we used in the DSL shared task at VarDial 2017 (Jauhiainen et al., 2017a). The experiments with the gamma function ended up with the same recall of 95.26% as the original method. Several different trials with loglike functions fell short of the recall of the original method at 95.25%.

8 Conclusions

The language model adaptation scheme works very well on the ILI test set. With the German dialect identification task, we noticed that the language adaptation method works especially well when the test set is out-of-domain compared with the training set. The very good results in the ILI task might indicate that there is a clear domain difference between the training/development sets and the test set. The iterative use of the adaptation method with 4 epochs also turned to be beneficial, reducing the remaining errors by 5.1%.

Acknowledgments

This research was partly conducted with funding from the Kone Foundation Language Programme (Kone Foundation, 2012).

References

Michiel Bacchiani and Brian Roark. 2003. Unsupervised language model adaptation. In *Proceedings of the International Conference on Acoustics, Speech and Signal Processing (ICASSP 2003)*, pages 224–227.

Shane Bergsma, Paul McNamee, Mossaab Bagdouri, Clayton Fink, and Theresa Wilson. 2012. Language Identification for Creating Language-specific Twitter Collections. In *Proceedings of the Second Workshop on Language in Social Media (LSM2012)*, pages 65–74, Montréal, Canada.

Su Lin Blodgett, Johnny Tian-Zheng Wei, and Brendan O'Connor. 2017. A Dataset and Classifier for Recognizing Social Media English. In *Proceedings of the 3rd Workshop on Noisy User-generated Text*, pages 56–61, Copenhagen, Denmark.

Yingna Chen and Jia Liu. 2005. Language Model Adaptation and Confidence Measure for Robust Language Identification. In *Proceedings of International Symposium on Communications and Information Technologies 2005 (ISCIT 2005)*, volume 1, pages 270–273, Beijing, China.

Maimaitiyiming Hasimu and Wushour Silamu. 2018. On Hierarchical Text Language-Identification Algorithms. *Algorithms*, 11(39).

David W. Hosmer, Stanley Lemeshow, and Rodney X. Sturdivant. 2013. *Applied logistic regression*. Wiley Series in Probability and Statistics. Wiley, Hoboken, N.J., USA, 3rd ed edition.

K. Indhuja, M. Indu, C. Sreejith, and P. C. Reghu Raj. 2014. Text Based Language Identification System for Indian Languages Following Devanagiri Script. *International Journal of Engineering Reseach and Technology*, 3(4):327–331.

Heidi Jauhiainen, Tommi Jauhiainen, and Krister Lindén. 2015a. The Finno-Ugric Languages and The Internet Project. *Septentrio Conference Series*, 0(2):87–98.

Tommi Jauhiainen, Heidi Jauhiainen, and Krister Lindén. 2015b. Discriminating Similar Languages with Token-Based Backoff. In *Proceedings of the Joint Workshop on Language Technology for Closely Related Languages, Varieties and Dialects (LT4VarDial)*, pages 44–51, Hissar, Bulgaria.

Tommi Jauhiainen, Krister Lindén, and Heidi Jauhiainen. 2016. HeLI, a Word-Based Backoff Method for Language Identification. In *Proceedings of the Third Workshop on NLP for Similar Languages, Varieties and Dialects (VarDial3)*, pages 153–162, Osaka, Japan.

Tommi Jauhiainen, Krister Lindén, and Heidi Jauhiainen. 2017a. Evaluating HeLI with Non-Linear Mappings. In *Proceedings of the Fourth Workshop on NLP for Similar Languages, Varieties and Dialects (VarDial)*, pages 102–108, Valencia, Spain.

Tommi Jauhiainen, Krister Lindén, and Heidi Jauhiainen. 2017b. Evaluation of Language Identification Methods Using 285 Languages. In *Proceedings of the 21st Nordic Conference on Computational Linguistics (NoDaLiDa 2017)*, pages 183–191, Gothenburg, Sweden. Linköping University Electronic Press.

Tommi Jauhiainen, Marco Lui, Marcos Zampieri, Timothy Baldwin, and Krister Lindén. 2018. Automatic Language Identification in Texts: A Survey. *arXiv preprint arXiv:1804.08186*.

Tommi Jauhiainen. 2010. Tekstin kielen automaattinen tunnistaminen. Master's thesis, University of Helsinki, Helsinki.

Kone Foundation. 2012. The language programme 2012-2016. http://www.koneensaatio.fi/en.

Canasai Kruengkrai, Virach Sornlertlamvanich, and Hitoshi Isahara. 2006. Language, Script, and Encoding Identification with String Kernel Classifiers. In *Proceedings of the 1st International Conference on Knowledge, Information and Creativity Support Systems (KICSS 2006)*, Ayutthaya, Thailand.

Ritesh Kumar, Bornini Lahiri, Deepak Alok, Atul Kr. Ojha, Mayank Jain, Abdul Basit, and Yogesh Dawar. 2018. Automatic Identification of Closely-related Indian Languages: Resources and Experiments. In *Proceedings of the Eleventh International Conference on Language Resources and Evaluation (LREC)*, Miyazaki, Japan.

Marco Lui and Timothy Baldwin. 2012. langid.py: An Off-the-shelf Language Identification Tool. In *Proceedings of the 50th Annual Meeting of the Association for Computational Linguistics (ACL 2012) Demo Session*, pages 25–30, Jeju, Republic of Korea.

Shervin Malmasi, Marcos Zampieri, Nikola Ljubešić, Preslav Nakov, Ahmed Ali, and Jörg Tiedemann. 2016. Discriminating between Similar Languages and Arabic Dialect Identification: A Report on the Third DSL Shared Task. In *Proceedings of the 3rd Workshop on Language Technology for Closely Related Languages, Varieties and Dialects (VarDial)*, Osaka, Japan.

Kavi Narayana Murthy and G. Bharadwaja Kumar. 2006. Language Identification from Small Text Samples. *Journal of Quantitative Linguistics*, 13(1):57–80.

Seppo Mustonen. 1965. Multiple Discriminant Analysis in Linguistic Problems. *Statistical Methods in Linguistics*, 4:37–44.

Ferran Pla and Lluís-F. Hurtado. 2017. Language Identification of Multilingual Posts from Twitter: A Case Study. *Knowledge and Information Systems*, 51(3):965–989.

Priya Rani, Atul Kr. Ojha, and Girish Nath Jha. 2018. Automatic language identification system for hindi and magahi. In *Proceedings of the Eleventh International Conference on Language Resources and Evaluation (LREC 2018)*, Miyazaki, Japan.

C. Sreejith, M. Indu, and P. C. Reghu Raj. 2013. N-gram based Algorithm for Distinguishing Between Hindi and Sanskrit Texts. In *Proceedings of the Fourth IEEE International Conference on Computing, Communication and Networking Technologies*, Tiruchengode, India.

Jyotsna Vaid and Ashum Gupta. 2002. Exploring Word Recognition in a Semi-Alphabetic Script: The Case of Devanagari. *Brain and Language*, 81:679–690.

Marcos Zampieri, Liling Tan, Nikola Ljubešić, and Jörg Tiedemann. 2014. A Report on the DSL Shared Task 2014. In *Proceedings of the First Workshop on Applying NLP Tools to Similar Languages, Varieties and Dialects (VarDial)*, pages 58–67, Dublin, Ireland.

Marcos Zampieri, Liling Tan, Nikola Ljubešić, Jörg Tiedemann, and Preslav Nakov. 2015. Overview of the DSL Shared Task 2015. In *Proceedings of the Joint Workshop on Language Technology for Closely Related Languages, Varieties and Dialects (LT4VarDial)*, pages 1–9, Hissar, Bulgaria.

Marcos Zampieri, Shervin Malmasi, Nikola Ljubešić, Preslav Nakov, Ahmed Ali, Jörg Tiedemann, Yves Scherrer, and Noëmi Aepli. 2017. Findings of the VarDial Evaluation Campaign 2017. In *Proceedings of the Fourth Workshop on NLP for Similar Languages, Varieties and Dialects (VarDial)*, Valencia, Spain.

Marcos Zampieri, Shervin Malmasi, Preslav Nakov, Ahmed Ali, Suwon Shon, James Glass, Yves Scherrer, Tanja Samardžić, Nikola Ljubešić, Jörg Tiedemann, Chris van der Lee, Stefan Grondelaers, Nelleke Oostdijk, Antal van den Bosch, Ritesh Kumar, Bornini Lahiri, and Mayank Jain. 2018. Language Identification and Morphosyntactic Tagging: The Second VarDial Evaluation Campaign. In *Proceedings of the Fifth Workshop on NLP for Similar Languages, Varieties and Dialects (VarDial)*, Santa Fe, USA.

Shan Zhong, Yingna Chen, Chunyi Zhu, and Jia Liu. 2007. Confidence measure based incremental adaptation for online language identification. In *Proceedings of International Conference on Human-Computer Interaction (HCI 2007)*, pages 535–543, Beijing, China.

Language and the Shifting Sands of Domain, Space and Time
(Invited Talk)

Tim Baldwin
School of Computing and Information Systems
The University of Melbourne, Australia
`tb@ldwin.net`

Abstract

In this talk, I will first present recent work on domain debiasing in the context of language identification, then discuss a new line of work on language variety analysis in the form of dialect map generation. Finally, I will reflect on the interplay between time and space on language variation, and speculate on how these can be captured in a single model.

1 Bio

Tim Baldwin is a Professor in the School of Computing and Information Systems, The University of Melbourne, and Associate Dean (Research Training) within the Melbourne School of Engineering. He is also Director of the ARC Centre for Cognitive Computing in Medical Technologies, in partnership with IBM Research. He has previously held visiting positions at Cambridge University, University of Washington, University of Tokyo, Saarland University, NTT Communication Science Laboratories, and National Institute of Informatics. His primary research focus is on natural language processing (NLP), including social media analytics, computational lexical semantics, deep learning, and topic modelling.

Tim completed a BSc(CS/Maths) and BA(Linguistics/Japanese) at The University of Melbourne in 1995, and an MEng(CS) and PhD(CS) at the Tokyo Institute of Technology in 1998 and 2001, respectively. Prior to joining The University of Melbourne in 2004, he was a Senior Research Engineer at the Center for the Study of Language and Information, Stanford University (2001-2004). He is the author of around 350 peer-reviewed publications across diverse topics in natural language processing.

This work is licensed under a Creative Commons Attribution 4.0 International License. License details: `http://creativecommons.org/licenses/by/4.0/`

Proceedings of the Fifth Workshop on NLP for Similar Languages, Varieties and Dialects, page 76
Santa Fe, New Mexico, USA, August 20, 2018.

UnibucKernel Reloaded: First Place in Arabic Dialect Identification for the Second Year in a Row

Andrei M. Butnaru and **Radu Tudor Ionescu**
Department of Computer Science, University of Bucharest
14 Academiei, Bucharest, Romania
`butnaruandreimadalin@gmail.com, raducu.ionescu@gmail.com`

Abstract

We present a machine learning approach that ranked on the first place in the Arabic Dialect Identification (ADI) Closed Shared Tasks of the 2018 VarDial Evaluation Campaign. The proposed approach combines several kernels using multiple kernel learning. While most of our kernels are based on character p-grams (also known as n-grams) extracted from speech or phonetic transcripts, we also use a kernel based on dialectal embeddings generated from audio recordings by the organizers. In the learning stage, we independently employ Kernel Discriminant Analysis (KDA) and Kernel Ridge Regression (KRR). Preliminary experiments indicate that KRR provides better classification results. Our approach is shallow and simple, but the empirical results obtained in the 2018 ADI Closed Shared Task prove that it achieves the best performance. Furthermore, our top macro-F_1 score (58.92%) is significantly better than the second best score (57.59%) in the 2018 ADI Shared Task, according to the statistical significance test performed by the organizers. Nevertheless, we obtain even better post-competition results (a macro-F_1 score of 62.28%) using the audio embeddings released by the organizers after the competition. With a very similar approach (that did not include phonetic features), we also ranked first in the ADI Closed Shared Tasks of the 2017 VarDial Evaluation Campaign, surpassing the second best method by 4.62%. We therefore conclude that our multiple kernel learning method is the best approach to date for Arabic dialect identification.

1 Introduction

The 2016 and 2017 VarDial Evaluation Campaigns (Malmasi et al., 2016; Zampieri et al., 2017) indicate that dialect identification is a challenging NLP task, actively studied by researchers in nowadays. Based solely on speech transcripts, the top two Arabic dialect identification (ADI) systems (Ionescu and Popescu, 2016b; Malmasi and Zampieri, 2016) that participated in the 2016 ADI Shared Task (Malmasi et al., 2016) attained weighted F_1 scores just over 50%, in a 5-way classification setting. For the 2017 ADI Shared Task (Zampieri et al., 2017), the organizers provided audio features along with speech transcripts. The top two systems (Ionescu and Butnaru, 2017; Malmasi and Zampieri, 2017) were able to reach weighted F_1 scores above 70% by using audio features and by including the samples from the development set into the training set. For the 2018 ADI Shared Task (Zampieri et al., 2018), the organizers have added phonetic features along with audio features and speech transcripts. To this end, we present our approach to the 2018 ADI Shared Task, which is based on adding string kernels computed on phonetic transcripts to the multiple kernel learning model (Ionescu and Butnaru, 2017) that we previously designed for the 2017 ADI Shared Task. In the 2018 ADI Shared Task, the participants had to discriminate between Modern Standard Arabic (MSA) and four Arabic dialects, in a 5-way classification setting. A number of 6 teams have submitted their results on the test set, and our team (UnibucKernel) ranked on the first place with an accuracy of 58.65% and a macro-F_1 score of 58.92%.

Our best scoring system in the ADI Shared Task combines several kernels using multiple kernel learning. The first kernel that we considered is the p-grams presence bits kernel[1], which takes into account

---

This work is licensed under a Creative Commons Attribution 4.0 International License. License details: `http://creativecommons.org/licenses/by/4.0/`.

[1]We computed the p-grams presence bits kernel using the code available at http://string-kernels.herokuapp.com.

Proceedings of the Fifth Workshop on NLP for Similar Languages, Varieties and Dialects, pages 77–87
Santa Fe, New Mexico, USA, August 20, 2018.

only the presence of p-grams instead of their frequency. The second kernel is the (histogram) intersection string kernel[2], which was first used in a text mining task by Ionescu et al. (2014). The third kernel is derived from Local Rank Distance (LRD)[3], a distance measure that was first introduced in computational biology (Ionescu, 2013; Dinu et al., 2014), but it has also shown its application in NLP (Popescu and Ionescu, 2013; Ionescu, 2015). These string kernels have been previously used for Arabic dialect identification from speech transcripts by Ionescu and Popescu (2016b), and they obtained very good results, taking the second place in the 2016 ADI Shared Task (Malmasi et al., 2016). In this paper, we apply string kernels on speech transcripts as well as phonetic transcripts, obtaining better results. While most of our kernels are based on character p-grams from speech or phonetic transcripts, we also use an RBF kernel (Shawe-Taylor and Cristianini, 2004) based on dialectal embeddings automatically generated from audio recordings using the approach described in (Shon et al., 2018). In our previous work (Ionescu and Butnaru, 2017), we have successfully combined string kernels computed on speech transcripts with an RBF kernel computed on audio features and we ranked on the first place in the 2017 ADI Shared Task (Zampieri et al., 2017). For the 2018 ADI Shared Task, our multiple kernel learning method includes string kernels computed on phonetic transcripts along with the other kernels.

We considered two kernel classifiers (Shawe-Taylor and Cristianini, 2004) for the learning task, namely Kernel Ridge Regression (KRR) and Kernel Discriminant Analysis (KDA). In a set of preliminary experiments performed on the ADI development set, we found that KRR gives slightly better results than KDA. In the end, we decided to submit results using only KRR. Before submitting our results, we have also tuned our string kernels for the task. First of all, we tried out p-grams of various lengths, including blended variants of string kernels as well. Second of all, we evaluated the individual kernels and various kernel combinations. The empirical results indicate that string kernels computed on speech transcripts attain significantly better performance than string kernels computed on phonetic transcripts. When we combined the string kernels computed on speech transcripts with the kernel base on audio embeddings, we found that the performance improves by nearly 5%. We obtained another improvement of almost 1% when we included the string kernels computed on phonetic transcripts. All these choices played an important role in obtaining the first place in the final ranking of the 2018 ADI Shared Task.

The paper is organized as follows. Work related to Arabic dialect identification and to methods based on string kernels is presented in Section 2. Section 3 presents the kernels that we used in our approach. The learning methods employed in the experiments are described in Section 4. Details about the Arabic dialect identification experiments are provided in Sections 5. Finally, we draw our conclusion in Section 6.

2 Related Work

2.1 Arabic Dialect Identification

Arabic dialect identification is a relatively new NLP task with only a handful of works (Biadsy et al., 2009; Zaidan and Callison-Burch, 2011; Elfardy and Diab, 2013; Darwish et al., 2014; Zaidan and Callison-Burch, 2014; Malmasi et al., 2015) to address it before the 2016 VarDial Evaluation Campaign (Malmasi et al., 2016). Although it did not received too much attention before 2016, the task is very important for Arabic NLP tools, as most of these tools have only been design for Modern Standard Arabic. Biadsy et al. (2009) describe a phonotactic approach that automatically identifies the Arabic dialect of a speaker given a sample of speech. While Biadsy et al. (2009) focus on spoken Arabic dialect identification, others have tried to identify the Arabic dialect of given texts (Zaidan and Callison-Burch, 2011; Elfardy and Diab, 2013; Darwish et al., 2014; Malmasi et al., 2015). Zaidan and Callison-Burch (2011) introduce the Arabic Online Commentary (AOC) data set of 108K labeled sentences, 41% of them having dialectal content. They employ a language model for automatic dialect identification on their collected data. A supervised approach for sentence-level dialect identification between Egyptian and MSA is proposed by Elfardy and Diab (2013). Their system outperforms the approach presented by Zaidan and Callison-Burch (2011) on the same data set. Zaidan and Callison-Burch (2014) extend their previous

---

[2]We computed the intersection string kernel using the code available at http://string-kernels.herokuapp.com.
[3]We computed the Local Rank Distance using the code available at http://lrd.herokuapp.com.

work (Zaidan and Callison-Burch, 2011) and conduct several ADI experiments using word and character p-grams. Different from most of the previous work, Darwish et al. (2014) have found that word unigram models do not generalize well to unseen topics. They suggest that lexical, morphological and phonological features can capture more relevant information for discriminating dialects. As the AOC corpus is not controlled for topical bias, Malmasi et al. (2015) also state that the models trained on this corpus may not generalize to other data as they implicitly capture topical cues. They perform ADI experiments on the Multidialectal Parallel Corpus of Arabic (MPCA) (Bouamor et al., 2014) using various word and character p-grams models in order to assess the influence of topical bias. Interestingly, Malmasi et al. (2015) find that character p-grams are "in most scenarios the best single feature for this task", even in a cross-corpus setting. Their findings are consistent with the results of Ionescu and Popescu (2016b) in the 2016 ADI Shared Task (Malmasi et al., 2016), as Ionescu and Popescu (2016b) ranked on the second place using solely character p-grams from Automatic Speech Recognition (ASR) transcripts. The 2017 ADI Shared Task data set (Ali et al., 2016) contains the original audio files and some low-level audio features, called i-vectors, along with the ASR transcripts of Arabic speech collected from the Broadcast News domain. The results of the top systems (Ionescu and Butnaru, 2017; Malmasi and Zampieri, 2017) in the 2017 ADI Shared Task (Zampieri et al., 2017) indicate that the audio features produce a much better performance, probably because there are many ASR errors (perhaps more in the dialectal speech segments) that make Arabic dialect identification from ASR transcripts much more difficult. In 2017, ADI has attracted a higher attention in the scientific community, since researchers have organized three independent shared tasks (Ali et al., 2017; Rangel et al., 2017; Zampieri et al., 2017), with 32 participants in total. For a comprehensive and complete survey on ADI, we refer the reader to the work of (Jauhiainen et al., 2018).

2.2 String Kernels

From the beginning of the 21st century to the present days, methods of handling text at the character level have demonstrated impressive performance levels in various text analysis tasks (Lodhi et al., 2002; Sanderson and Guenter, 2006; Kate and Mooney, 2006; Escalante et al., 2011; Popescu and Grozea, 2012; Ionescu et al., 2014; Ionescu et al., 2016; Giménez-Pérez et al., 2017; Popescu et al., 2017; Cozma et al., 2018). String kernels are a common form of using information at the character level. They are a particular case of the more general convolution kernels (Haussler, 1999). Lodhi et al. (2002) used string kernels for document categorization with very good results. String kernels were also successfully used in authorship identification (Sanderson and Guenter, 2006; Popescu and Grozea, 2012). For example, the system described by Popescu and Grozea (2012) ranked first in most problems and overall in the PAN 2012 Traditional Authorship Attribution tasks. More recently, various blended string kernels reached state-of-the-art accuracy rates for native language identification (Ionescu et al., 2016; Ionescu and Popescu, 2017), Arabic dialect identification (Ionescu and Popescu, 2016b; Ionescu and Butnaru, 2017), polarity classification (Giménez-Pérez et al., 2017; Popescu et al., 2017) and automatic essay scoring (Cozma et al., 2018).

3 Kernels for Arabic Dialect Identification

3.1 String Kernels

Kernel functions (Shawe-Taylor and Cristianini, 2004) capture the intuitive notion of similarity between objects in a specific domain. For strings, many such kernel functions exist with various applications in computational biology and computational linguistics. String kernels embed the texts in a very large feature space, given by all the substrings of length p, and leave the job of selecting important (discriminative) features for the specific classification task to the learning algorithm, which assigns higher weights to the important features (character p-grams). Perhaps one of the most natural ways to measure the similarity of two strings is to count how many substrings of length p the two strings have in common. This gives rise to the p-spectrum kernel. Formally, for two strings over an alphabet Σ, $s, t \in \Sigma^*$, the p-spectrum kernel is defined as:

$$k_p(s, t) = \sum_{v \in \Sigma^p} \text{num}_v(s) \cdot \text{num}_v(t),$$

where $\text{num}_v(s)$ is the number of occurrences of string v as a substring in s.[4] The feature map defined by this kernel associates to each string a vector of dimension $|\Sigma|^p$ containing the histogram of frequencies of all its substrings of length p (p-grams). A variant of this kernel can be obtained if the embedding feature map is modified to associate to each string a vector of dimension $|\Sigma|^p$ containing the presence bits (instead of frequencies) of all its substrings of length p. Thus, the character p-grams presence bits kernel is obtained:

$$k_p^{0/1}(s,t) = \sum_{v \in \Sigma^p} \text{in}_v(s) \cdot \text{in}_v(t),$$

where $\text{in}_v(s)$ is 1 if string v occurs as a substring in s, and 0 otherwise.

In computer vision, the (histogram) intersection kernel has successfully been used for object class recognition from images (Maji et al., 2008; Vedaldi and Zisserman, 2010). Ionescu et al. (2014) have used the intersection kernel as a kernel for strings, in the context of native language identification. The intersection string kernel is defined as follows:

$$k_p^{\cap}(s,t) = \sum_{v \in \Sigma^p} \min\{\text{num}_v(s), \text{num}_v(t)\}.$$

For the p-spectrum kernel, the frequency of a p-gram has a very significant contribution to the kernel, since it considers the product of such frequencies. On the other hand, the frequency of a p-gram is completely disregarded in the p-grams presence bits kernel. The intersection kernel lies somewhere in the middle between the p-grams presence bits kernel and the p-spectrum kernel, in the sense that the frequency of a p-gram has a moderate contribution to the intersection kernel. In other words, the intersection kernel assigns a high score to a p-gram only if it has a high frequency in both strings, since it considers the minimum of the two frequencies. The p-spectrum kernel assigns a high score even when the p-gram has a high frequency in only one of the two strings. Thus, the intersection kernel captures something more about the correlation between the p-gram frequencies in the two strings. Based on these comments, we decided to use only the p-grams presence bits kernel and the intersection string kernel in the ADI experiments.

Data normalization helps to improve machine learning performance for various applications. Since the value range of raw data can have large variations, classifier objective functions will not work properly without normalization. After normalization, each feature has an approximately equal contribution to the similarity between two samples. To obtain a normalized kernel matrix of pairwise similarities between samples, each component is divided by the square root of the product of the two corresponding diagonal components:

$$\hat{K}_{ij} = \frac{K_{ij}}{\sqrt{K_{ii} \cdot K_{jj}}}.$$

To ensure a fair comparison among strings of different lengths, we use normalized versions of the p-grams presence bits kernel and the intersection kernel in our experiments. Taking into account p-grams of different lengths and summing up the corresponding kernels, new kernels, termed *blended spectrum kernels*, can be obtained. We have used various blended spectrum kernels in the ADI experiments in order to find the best combination. It is important to mention that we applied the blended p-grams presence bits kernel and the blended intersection kernel on both speech transcripts and phonetic transcripts.

3.2   Kernel based on Local Rank Distance

Local Rank Distance (Ionescu, 2013) is a recently introduced distance that measures the non-alignment score between two strings. It has already shown promising results in computational biology (Ionescu, 2013; Dinu et al., 2014) and native language identification (Popescu and Ionescu, 2013; Ionescu, 2015).

In order to describe LRD, we use the following notations. Given a string x over an alphabet Σ, the length of x is denoted by $|x|$. Strings are considered to be indexed starting from position 1, that is $x = x[1]x[2] \cdots x[|x|]$. Moreover, $x[i:j]$ denotes its substring $x[i]x[i+1] \cdots x[j-1]$. Given a fixed integer $p \geq 1$, a threshold $m \geq 1$, and two strings x and y over Σ, the *Local Rank Distance* between x

---

[4]The notion of substring requires contiguity. Shawe-Taylor and Cristianini (2004) discuss the ambiguity between the terms *substring* and *subsequence* across different domains: biology, computer science.

and y, denoted by $\Delta_{LRD}(x, y)$, is defined through the following algorithmic process. For each position i in x ($1 \leq i \leq |x| - p + 1$), the algorithm searches for that position j in y ($1 \leq j \leq |y| - p + 1$) such that $x[i : i + p] = y[j : j + p]$ and $|i - j|$ is minimized. If j exists and $|i - j| < m$, then the offset $|i - j|$ is added to the Local Rank Distance. Otherwise, the maximal offset m is added to the Local Rank Distance. LRD is focused on the local phenomenon, and tries to pair identical p-grams at a minimum offset. To ensure that LRD is a (symmetric) distance function, the algorithm also has to sum up the offsets obtained from the above process by exchanging x and y. LRD is formally defined in (Ionescu, 2013; Dinu et al., 2014; Ionescu and Popescu, 2016a).

The search for matching p-grams is limited within a window of fixed size. The size of this window is determined by the maximum offset parameter m. We set $m = 300$ in our experiments, which is larger than the maximum length of the ASR transcripts provided in the training set. In the experiments, the efficient algorithm of Ionescu (2015) is used to compute LRD. However, LRD needs to be used as a kernel function. We use the RBF kernel (Shawe-Taylor and Cristianini, 2004) to transform LRD into a similarity measure:

$$\hat{k}_p^{LRD}(s, t) = exp\left(-\frac{\Delta_{LRD}(s, t)}{2\sigma^2}\right),$$

where s and t are two strings and p is the p-grams length. The parameter σ is usually chosen so that values of $\hat{k}(s, t)$ are well scaled. We have tuned σ in a set of preliminary experiments. In the above equation, Δ_{LRD} is already normalized to a value in the $[0, 1]$ interval to ensure a fair comparison of strings of different length. The resulted similarity matrix is then squared, i.e. $K = K \cdot K'$, to ensure that it becomes a symmetric and positive definite kernel matrix. Due to time constraints, we applied the kernel based on Local Rank Distance only on speech transcripts.

3.3 Kernel based on Audio Features

Along with the string kernels, we also build a kernel from the audio embeddings provided with the data set (Shon et al., 2018). The dialectal embeddings are generated by training convolutional neural networks on audio recordings, as described in (Shon et al., 2018; Najafian et al., 2018). The provided embeddings have 600 dimensions. In order to build a kernel from the audio embeddings, we first compute the Euclidean distance between each pair of embedding vectors. We then employ the RBF kernel to transform the distance into a similarity measure:

$$\hat{k}_{audio}(x, y) = exp\left(-\frac{\sqrt{\sum_{j=1}^{m}(x_j - y_j)^2}}{2\sigma^2}\right),$$

where x and y are two audio embedding vectors and m represents the size of the two embedding vectors, 600 in our case. For optimal results, we have tuned the parameter σ in a set of preliminary experiments. As for the LRD kernel, we square the kernel matrix of the kernel based on audio embeddings.

4 Learning Methods

Kernel-based learning algorithms work by embedding the data into a Hilbert feature space and by searching for linear relations in that space. The embedding is performed implicitly, by specifying the inner product between each pair of points rather than by giving their coordinates explicitly. More precisely, a kernel matrix that contains the pairwise similarities between every pair of training samples is used in the learning stage to assign a vector of weights to the training samples. Let α denote this weight vector. In the test stage, the pairwise similarities between a test sample x and all the training samples are computed. Then, the following binary classification function assigns a positive or a negative label to the test sample:

$$g(x) = \sum_{i=1}^{n} \alpha_i \cdot k(x, x_i),$$

where x is the test sample, n is the number of training samples, $X = \{x_1, x_2, ..., x_n\}$ is the set of training samples, k is a kernel function, and α_i is the weight assigned to the training sample x_i.

The advantage of using the dual representation induced by the kernel function becomes clear if the dimension of the feature space m is taken into consideration. Since string kernels are based on character p-grams, the feature space is indeed very high. For instance, using 5-grams based only on the 28 letters of the basic Arabic alphabet will result in a feature space of $28^5 = 17,210,368$ features. However, our best kernels are based on a feature space that includes 3-grams, 4-grams, 5-grams and 6-grams. As long as the number of samples n is much lower than the number of features m, it can be more efficient to use the dual representation given by the kernel matrix. This fact is also known as the *kernel trick* (Shawe-Taylor and Cristianini, 2004).

Various kernel methods differ in the way they learn to separate the samples. In the case of binary classification problems, kernel-based learning algorithms look for a discriminant function, a function that assigns $+1$ to examples belonging to one class and -1 to examples belonging to the other class. In the ADI experiments, we used the Kernel Ridge Regression (KRR) binary classifier. Kernel Ridge Regression selects the vector of weights that simultaneously has small empirical error and small norm in the Reproducing Kernel Hilbert Space generated by the kernel function. KRR is a binary classifier, but Arabic dialect identification is a multi-class classification problem. There are many approaches for combining binary classifiers to solve multi-class problems. Typically, the multi-class problem is broken down into multiple binary classification problems using common decomposition schemes such as: one-versus-all and one-versus-one. We considered the one-versus-all scheme for our Arabic dialect classification task. There are also kernel methods that take the multi-class nature of the problem directly into account, for instance Kernel Discriminant Analysis. The KDA classifier is sometimes able to improve accuracy by avoiding the masking problem (Hastie and Tibshirani, 2003). More details about KRR and KDA are given in (Shawe-Taylor and Cristianini, 2004).

5 Experiments on Arabic Dialects

5.1 Data Set

The 2018 ADI Shared Task data set (Ali et al., 2016) contains audio recordings, ASR transcripts and phonetic transcripts of Arabic speech collected from the Broadcast News domain. The task is to discriminate between Modern Standard Arabic (MSA) and four Arabic dialects, namely Egyptian (EGY), Gulf (GLF), Levantine (LAV), and North-African or Maghrebi (NOR). Although the data set is similar to those used in the 2016 and the 2017 ADI Shared Tasks (Malmasi et al., 2016; Zampieri et al., 2017), this year the organizers provided phonetic transcripts produced by four non-Arabic automatic phoneme recognizers (Czech, English, Hungarian and Russian), which perform long temporal phoneme recognition and have been previously shown to be useful for discriminating between the dialects of various languages.

5.2 Parameter and System Choices

In our approach, we treat both ASR transcripts and phonetic transcripts as strings. Because the approach works at the character level, there is no need to split the texts into tokens, or to do any NLP-specific processing before computing the string kernels. The only editing done to the transcripts was the replacing of sequences of consecutive space characters (space, tab, and so on) with a single space character. This normalization was needed in order to prevent the artificial increase or decrease of the similarity between texts, as a result of different spacing.

In order to tune the parameters and find the best system choices, we used the development set. We first carried out a set of preliminary experiments to determine the optimal range of p-grams for each string kernel and each type of input, i.e. speech transcripts or phonetic transcripts in four languages. We fixed the learning method to KRR and we evaluated all the p-grams in the range 2-12. The optimal range of p-grams and the associated accuracy and macro-F_1 score for each kernel and each input is presented in Table 1. In most cases, it seems that the optimal range of p-grams is 3-5 or 3-6. An exception is the range of p-grams that provides the best results on English phonetic transcripts. Regarding the input type, it is clear that string kernels provide better results when they are applied on speech transcripts. With an accuracy of 54.85% and a macro-F_1 score of 53.94%, the best individual kernel on the development set is the blended presence bits kernel ($\hat{k}^{0/1}$) computed on speech transcripts. On the other hand, the

Kernel	Input	Range of p-grams	Accuracy	Macro-F_1
$\hat{k}^{0/1}$	Speech transcripts	3-6	54.85%	53.94%
$\hat{k}^{\cap}$	Speech transcripts	3-6	54.53%	53.77%
$\hat{k}^{LRD}$	Speech transcripts	3-6	51.09%	50.15%
$\hat{k}^{0/1}$	Czech phonetic transcripts	3-6	39.14%	39.43%
$\hat{k}^{\cap}$	Czech phonetic transcripts	3-4	39.08%	38.52%
$\hat{k}^{0/1}$	English phonetic transcripts	9-10	31.42%	30.49%
$\hat{k}^{\cap}$	English phonetic transcripts	9-11	31.36%	30.47%
$\hat{k}^{0/1}$	Hungarian phonetic transcripts	3-5	39.78%	39.40%
$\hat{k}^{\cap}$	Hungarian phonetic transcripts	3-5	40.36%	40.39%
$\hat{k}^{0/1}$	Russian phonetic transcripts	3-5	36.08%	36.28%
$\hat{k}^{\cap}$	Russian phonetic transcripts	3-4	38.19%	38.04%

Table 1: Optimal ranges of p-grams and corresponding results for each string kernel and each input type on the development set of the ADI Shared Task. All results are obtained using KRR as classifier.

Kernels	Input	Accuracy	Macro-F_1
$\hat{k}_{speech} = \hat{k}^{0/1}_{3-6} + \hat{k}^{\cap}_{3-6} + \hat{k}^{LRD}_{3-6}$	Speech transcripts	55.17%	54.72%
$\hat{k}_{CZ} = \hat{k}^{0/1}_{3-6} + \hat{k}^{\cap}_{3-4}$	Czech phonetic transcripts	39.72%	39.71%
$\hat{k}_{EN} = \hat{k}^{0/1}_{9-10} + \hat{k}^{\cap}_{9-11}$	English phonetic transcripts	31.42%	30.54%
$\hat{k}_{HU} = \hat{k}^{0/1}_{3-5} + \hat{k}^{\cap}_{3-5}$	Hungarian phonetic transcripts	41.06%	40.85%
$\hat{k}_{RU} = \hat{k}^{0/1}_{3-5} + \hat{k}^{\cap}_{3-4}$	Russian phonetic transcripts	38.38%	37.75%
$\hat{k}_{phonetic} = \hat{k}_{CZ} + \hat{k}_{EN} + \hat{k}_{HU} + \hat{k}_{RU}$	All phonetic transcripts	45.02%	45.06%
$\hat{k}_{audio}$	Audio embeddings	52.87%	52.72%

Table 2: Results of best kernel combinations for each input type on the development set of the ADI Shared Task. All results are obtained using KRR as classifier.

best kernel computed on (Hungarian) phonetic transcripts is the blended intersection kernel ($\hat{k}^{\cap}$), which obtains an accuracy of 40.36% and a macro-F_1 score of 40.39%.

After determining the optimal range of p-grams for each kernel and input pair, we conducted further experiments by combining the kernels for each type of input. When multiple kernels are combined, the features are actually embedded in a higher-dimensional space. As a consequence, the search space of linear patterns grows, which helps the classifier to select a better discriminant function. We adopt the most natural way of combining two or more kernels, namely we simply sum up the corresponding kernels. The process of summing up kernels or kernel matrices is equivalent to feature vector concatenation. The results of kernel combinations for each input type are presented in Table 2. For the phonetic transcripts, we tried out kernel combinations for each non-Arabic phoneme recognizer, as well as a kernel combination on all phonetic transcripts. Compared to the individual components, we observed the highest improvement when we combined all string kernels based on phonetic transcripts. Indeed, the best combination (presented in Table 2) using only phonetic transcripts as input reaches an accuracy of 45.02% and a macro-F_1 score of 45.06%, while the best individual kernel (presented in Table 1) applied over phonetic transcripts reaches an accuracy of 40.36% and a macro-F_1 score of 40.39%. For the speech transcripts, the kernel combination is better than each individual component, but the performance gain is not as high as in the case of phonetic transcripts. For the audio recordings, we used only a single kernel based on audio embeddings ($\hat{k}_{audio}$). We tuned the parameter σ of the RBF kernel based on audio embeddings, and the best option seems to be $\sigma = 1$, which produces an accuracy of 52.87% and a macro-F_1 score of 52.72%.

Since we obtained different kernel representations from speech transcripts, phonetic transcripts and audio recordings, a good approach for improving the performance is to further combine the best kernel

Kernels	KRR		KDA	
	Accuracy	**Macro-F$_1$**	**Accuracy**	**Macro-F$_1$**
$\hat{k}_{speech} + \hat{k}_{audio}$ (Ionescu and Butnaru, 2017)	59.52%	59.12%	58.05%	58.13%
$\hat{k}_{speech} + \hat{k}_{audio} + \hat{k}_{phonetic}$	60.66%	60.46%	58.94%	59.20%

Table 3: Accuracy rates and macro-F_1 scores of various kernels combined across different input types: audio recordings, speech transcripts and phonetic transcripts. Both KRR and KDA are alternatively employ for the learning task. The results are obtained on the ADI development set.

System	Accuracy	Macro-F$_1$
Random Baseline	-	19.95%
Run 1	**58.65%**	**58.92%**
Run 2	54.50%	54.91%
Run 3	58.36%	58.55%
Run 4 (post-competition)	62.15%	62.02%
Run 5 (post-competition)	**62.22%**	**62.28%**

Table 4: Results on the test set of the 2018 ADI Shared Task (closed training) of our multiple kernel learning method based on KRR versus a random baseline. The best results during and after the competition are highlighted in bold.

combinations in order to obtain a multiple kernel learning approach that benefits from all three types of input formats (audio embeddings, speech transcripts and phonetic transcripts). The results of our multiple kernel learning method on the development set are reported in Table 3. It is important to note that, in Table 3, we included the results of the multiple kernel learning approach (Ionescu and Butnaru, 2017) that ranked first the 2017 ADI Shared Task, as reference. We notice that the string kernels computed on phonetic features help to improve the performance over the last year's winning approach by almost 1%. We also note that the combination of string kernels computed on speech transcripts ($\hat{k}_{speech}$) and the kernel based on audio embeddings ($\hat{k}_{audio}$) improves the accuracy of the individual components by more than 4%. Indeed, the kernel combination that includes $\hat{k}_{speech}$ and $\hat{k}_{audio}$ attains an accuracy of 59.52% and a macro-F_1 score of 59.12% when KRR is employed for the learning task, while the better kernel component ($\hat{k}_{speech}$) reaches an accuracy of 55.17% and a macro-F_1 score of 54.72%. Among the two kernel classifiers, it seems that KRR attains slightly better results than KDA. In fact, KRR is the only classifier that surpasses the 60% performance threshold on the development set. This happens when the string kernels computed on phonetic features ($\hat{k}_{phonetic}$) are included in the multiple kernel learning framework. We note that, in all the experiments performed on the development set, KRR yields the best results when we use a regularization parameter of 10^{-3}. In the end, we decided to submit three runs for final evaluation on the test set. All submissions are based on the KRR classifier. The first submission (run 1) is based on the sum of $\hat{k}_{speech}$, $\hat{k}_{audio}$ and $\hat{k}_{phonetic}$. The second submission (run 2) is almost identical to the first submission, except that we replaced the squared versions of $\hat{k}_{3-6}^{LRD}$ and $\hat{k}_{audio}$ with non-squared versions. Since all the submitted models are trained on both the provided training and development sets, we considered that KRR might provide better results if we choose a lower regularization parameter. Hence, the third submission (run 3) is also similar to the first submission, the only difference being that we changed the regularization parameter of KRR from 10^{-3} to 10^{-4}.

5.3   Results on the 2018 ADI Test Set

Table 4 presents our results for the Arabic Dialect Identification Closed Shared Task of the 2018 VarDial Evaluation Campaign. Among the submitted systems, the best performance is obtained when the KRR regularization parameter is set to 10^{-3} and the kernel combination includes squared versions of $\hat{k}_{3-6}^{LRD}$ and $\hat{k}_{audio}$. The submitted systems were ranked by their macro-F_1 scores, and among the 6 participants, our best model obtained the first place with a macro-F_1 score of 58.92%. Remarkably, the statistical significance tests performed by the organizers indicate that our best system is significantly better than

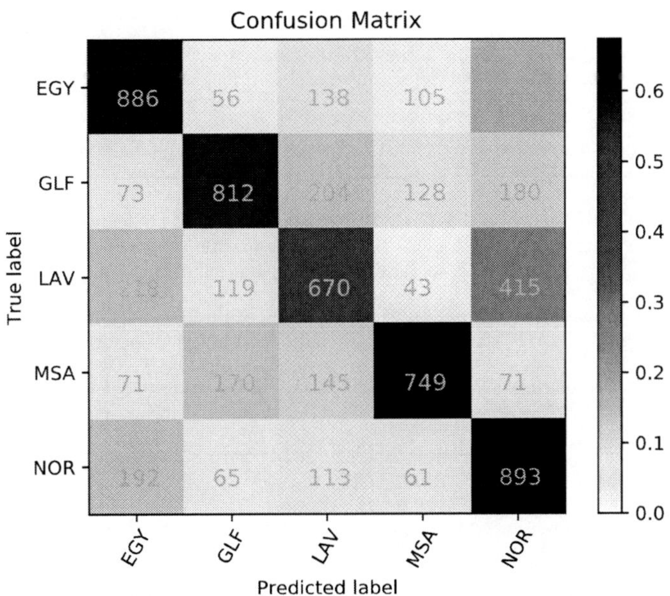

Figure 1: Confusion matrix (on the test set) of KRR based on the sum of $\hat{k}_{speech}$, $\hat{k}_{audio}$ and $\hat{k}_{phonetic}$ (run 1). Best viewed in color.

the system that ranked on the second place with a macro-F_1 score of 57.59%.

The confusion matrix for our best model is presented in Figure 1. The confusion matrix reveals that our system wrongly predicted more than 400 examples of the Levantine dialect as part of the Maghrebi dialect. Furthermore, it has some difficulties in distinguishing the Levantine dialect from the Egyptian dialect on one hand, and the Egyptian dialect from the Maghrebi dialect on the other hand. Overall, the results look good, as the main diagonal scores dominate the other matrix components.

After the competition ended, the organizers released a new set of audio embeddings that are computed on both the training and the development sets. By replacing the audio embeddings released during the competition with the new embeddings (run 4), we obtained results that are more than 3% better than out top system (run 1) during the competition. We also tried to include both embeddings based on audio features (run 5) into our multiple kernel learning approach, resulting in a slight improvement. The results of our post-competition runs 4 and 5 are reported in Table 4. Our best post-competition results are an accuracy of 62.22% and a macro-F_1 score of 62.28%, obtained by run 5.

6   Conclusion

In this paper, we presented an approach based on learning with multiple kernels for the ADI Shared Tasks of the 2018 VarDial Evaluation Campaign (Zampieri et al., 2018). Our approach attained very good results, as our team (UnibucKernel) ranked on the first place in the 2018 ADI Shared Task. The fact that we obtained the first place for the second year in a row indicates that our multiple kernel learning method did not reach the top performance simply by chance. We therefore conclude that the approach of combining multiple kernels based on different kinds of input, i.e. audio recordings, speech transcripts and phonetic transcripts, provides state-of-the-art performance in Arabic dialect identification. Since most of our kernels are based on character p-grams, we can also conclude that character p-grams represent the best feature set for the ADI task.

References

Ahmed Ali, Najim Dehak, Patrick Cardinal, Sameer Khurana, Sree Harsha Yella, James Glass, Peter Bell, and Steve Renals. 2016. Automatic dialect detection in arabic broadcast speech. In *Proceedings of Interspeech*, pages 2934–2938.

Ahmed Ali, Stephan Vogel, and Steve Renals. 2017. Speech Recognition Challenge in the Wild: Arabic MGB-3. *arXiv preprint arXiv:1709.07276*.

Fadi Biadsy, Julia Hirschberg, and Nizar Habash. 2009. Spoken Arabic Dialect Identification Using Phonotactic Modeling. In *Proceedings of the EACL 2009 Workshop on Computational Approaches to Semitic Languages*, pages 53–61, Stroudsburg, PA, USA. Association for Computational Linguistics.

Houda Bouamor, Nizar Habash, and Kemal Oflazer. 2014. A Multidialectal Parallel Corpus of Arabic. In *Proceedings of LREC*, pages 1240–1245. European Language Resources Association (ELRA), May.

Mădălina Cozma, Andrei Butnaru, and Radu Tudor Ionescu. 2018. Automated essay scoring with string kernels and word embeddings. In *Proceedings of ACL*.

Kareem Darwish, Hassan Sajjad, and Hamdy Mubarak. 2014. Verifiably Effective Arabic Dialect Identification. In *Proceedings of EMNLP*, pages 1465–1468. ACL.

Liviu P. Dinu, Radu Tudor Ionescu, and Alexandru I. Tomescu. 2014. A rank-based sequence aligner with applications in phylogenetic analysis. *PLoS ONE*, 9(8):e104006, 08.

Heba Elfardy and Mona T. Diab. 2013. Sentence Level Dialect Identification in Arabic. In *Proceedings of ACL*, pages 456–461. Association for Computer Linguistics.

Hugo Jair Escalante, Thamar Solorio, and Manuel Montes-y-Gómez. 2011. Local Histograms of Character N-grams for Authorship Attribution. In *Proceedings of ACL: HLT*, volume 1, pages 288–298.

Rosa M. Giménez-Pérez, Marc Franco-Salvador, and Paolo Rosso. 2017. Single and Cross-domain Polarity Classification using String Kernels. In *Proceedings of EACL*, pages 558–563, April.

Trevor Hastie and Robert Tibshirani. 2003. *The Elements of Statistical Learning*. Springer, corrected edition, July.

David Haussler. 1999. Convolution Kernels on Discrete Structures. Technical Report UCS-CRL-99-10, University of California at Santa Cruz, Santa Cruz, CA, USA.

Radu Tudor Ionescu and Andrei Butnaru. 2017. Learning to Identify Arabic and German Dialects using Multiple Kernels. In *Proceedings of VarDial Workshop of EACL*, pages 200–209.

Radu Tudor Ionescu and Marius Popescu. 2016a. *Knowledge Transfer between Computer Vision and Text Mining*. Advances in Computer Vision and Pattern Recognition. Springer International Publishing.

Radu Tudor Ionescu and Marius Popescu. 2016b. UnibucKernel: An Approach for Arabic Dialect Identification based on Multiple String Kernels. In *Proceedings of VarDial Workshop of COLING*, pages 135–144.

Radu Tudor Ionescu and Marius Popescu. 2017. Can string kernels pass the test of time in native language identification? In *Proceedings of BEA-12 Workshop of EMNLP*, pages 224–234.

Radu Tudor Ionescu, Marius Popescu, and Aoife Cahill. 2014. Can characters reveal your native language? A language-independent approach to native language identification. In *Proceedings of EMNLP*, pages 1363–1373. Association for Computational Linguistics, October.

Radu Tudor Ionescu, Marius Popescu, and Aoife Cahill. 2016. String kernels for native language identification: Insights from behind the curtains. *Computational Linguistics*, 42(3):491–525.

Radu Tudor Ionescu. 2013. Local Rank Distance. In *Proceedings of SYNASC*, pages 221–228, Timisoara, Romania. IEEE Computer Society.

Radu Tudor Ionescu. 2015. A Fast Algorithm for Local Rank Distance: Application to Arabic Native Language Identification. In *Proceedings of ICONIP*, volume 9490, pages 390–400. Springer LNCS.

Tommi Jauhiainen, Marco Lui, Marcos Zampieri, Timothy Baldwin, and Krister Lindén. 2018. Automatic language identification in texts: A survey. *arXiv preprint arXiv:1804.08186*.

Rohit J. Kate and Raymond J. Mooney. 2006. Using String-kernels for Learning Semantic Parsers. In *Proceedings of ACL*, pages 913–920, Stroudsburg, PA, USA. Association for Computational Linguistics.

Huma Lodhi, Craig Saunders, John Shawe-Taylor, Nello Cristianini, and Christopher J. C. H. Watkins. 2002. Text Classification using String Kernels. *Journal of Machine Learning Research*, 2:419–444.

Subhransu Maji, Alexander C. Berg, and Jitendra Malik. 2008. Classification using intersection kernel support vector machines is efficient. In *Proceedings of CVPR*, pages 1–8. IEEE Computer Society.

Shervin Malmasi and Marcos Zampieri. 2016. Arabic Dialect Identification in Speech Transcripts. In *Proceedings of VarDial Workshop of COLING*, pages 106–113. ACL Anthology.

Shervin Malmasi and Marcos Zampieri. 2017. Arabic Dialect Identification Using iVectors and ASR Transcripts. In *Proceedings of VarDial Workshop of EACL*, pages 178–183, Valencia, Spain, April.

Shervin Malmasi, Eshrag Refaee, and Mark Dras. 2015. Arabic Dialect Identification using a Parallel Multidialectal Corpus. In *Proceedings of PACLING*, pages 209–217, Bali, Indonesia, May.

Shervin Malmasi, Marcos Zampieri, Nikola Ljubešić, Preslav Nakov, Ahmed Ali, and Jörg Tiedemann. 2016. Discriminating between Similar Languages and Arabic Dialect Identification: A Report on the Third DSL Shared Task. In *Proceedings of VarDial Workshop of COLING*, Osaka, Japan.

Maryam Najafian, Sameer Khurana, Suwon Shon, Ahmed Ali, and James Glass. 2018. Exploiting convolutional neural networks for phonotactic based dialect identification. In *Proceedings of ICASSP*, pages 5174–5175.

Marius Popescu and Cristian Grozea. 2012. Kernel methods and string kernels for authorship analysis. In Pamela Forner, Jussi Karlgren, and Christa Womser-Hacker, editors, *CLEF (Online Working Notes/Labs/Workshop)*, Rome, Italy, September.

Marius Popescu and Radu Tudor Ionescu. 2013. The Story of the Characters, the DNA and the Native Language. In *Proceedings of BEA-8 Workshop of NAACL*, pages 270–278, Atlanta, Georgia, June. Association for Computational Linguistics.

Marius Popescu, Cristian Grozea, and Radu Tudor Ionescu. 2017. HASKER: An efficient algorithm for string kernels. Application to polarity classification in various languages. In *Proceedings of KES*, pages 1755–1763.

Francisco Rangel, Paolo Rosso, Martin Potthast, and Benno Stein. 2017. Overview of the 5th author profiling task at pan 2017: Gender and language variety identification in twitter. *Working Notes Papers of the CLEF*.

Conrad Sanderson and Simon Guenter. 2006. Short text authorship attribution via sequence kernels, markov chains and author unmasking: An investigation. In *Proceedings of EMNLP*, pages 482–491, Sydney, Australia, July. Association for Computational Linguistics.

John Shawe-Taylor and Nello Cristianini. 2004. *Kernel Methods for Pattern Analysis*. Cambridge University Press.

Suwon Shon, Ahmed Ali, and James Glass. 2018. Convolutional Neural Networks and Language Embeddings for End-to-End Dialect Recognition. In *Proceedings of Odyssey*.

Andrea Vedaldi and Andrew Zisserman. 2010. Efficient additive kernels via explicit feature maps. In *Proceedings of CVPR*, pages 3539–3546, San Francisco, CA, USA. IEEE Computer Society.

Omar F. Zaidan and Chris Callison-Burch. 2011. The Arabic Online Commentary Dataset: An Annotated Dataset of Informal Arabic with High Dialectal Content. In *Proceedings of ACL: HLT*, volume 2, pages 37–41, Stroudsburg, PA, USA. Association for Computational Linguistics.

Omar F. Zaidan and Chris Callison-Burch. 2014. Arabic dialect identification. *Computational Linguistics*, 40(1):171–202.

Marcos Zampieri, Shervin Malmasi, Nikola Ljubešić, Preslav Nakov, Ahmed Ali, Jörg Tiedemann, Yves Scherrer, and Noëmi Aepli. 2017. Findings of the VarDial Evaluation Campaign 2017. In *Proceedings of VarDial Workshop of EACL*, Valencia, Spain.

Marcos Zampieri, Shervin Malmasi, Preslav Nakov, Ahmed Ali, Suwon Shon, James Glass, Yves Scherrer, Tanja Samardžić, Nikola Ljubešić, Jörg Tiedemann, Chris van der Lee, Stefan Grondelaers, Nelleke Oostdijk, Antal van den Bosch, Ritesh Kumar, Bornini Lahiri, and Mayank Jain. 2018. Language Identification and Morphosyntactic Tagging: The Second VarDial Evaluation Campaign. In *Proceedings of VarDial Workshop of COLING*, Santa Fe, USA.

Varying image description tasks: spoken versus written descriptions

Emiel van Miltenburg
Vrije Universiteit Amsterdam
Emiel.van.Miltenburg@vu.nl

Ruud Koolen
Tilburg University
R.M.F.Koolen@tilburguniversity.edu

Emiel Krahmer
Tilburg University
E.J.Krahmer@tilburguniversity.edu

Abstract

Automatic image description systems are commonly trained and evaluated on *written* image descriptions. At the same time, these systems are often used to provide *spoken* descriptions (e.g. for visually impaired users) through apps like *TapTapSee* or *Seeing AI*. This is not a problem, as long as spoken and written descriptions are very similar. However, linguistic research suggests that spoken language often differs from written language. These differences are not regular, and vary from context to context. Therefore, this paper investigates whether there are differences between written and spoken image descriptions, even if they are elicited through similar tasks. We compare descriptions produced in two languages (English and Dutch), and in both languages observe substantial differences between spoken and written descriptions. Future research should see if users prefer the spoken over the written style and, if so, aim to emulate spoken descriptions.

1 Introduction

Automatic image description systems (Bernardi et al., 2016) are commonly trained and evaluated on datasets of described images, such as Flickr30K and MS COCO (Young et al., 2014; Lin et al., 2014). These datasets have been collected by asking workers on Mechanical Turk to write English descriptions that capture the contents of the images that are presented to them. But how much are these descriptions influenced by the modality of the task? This paper explores the differences between spoken and written image descriptions. While many papers at VarDial aim to distinguish similar *dialects* using machine learning (e.g. in shared tasks such as those in Malmasi et al., 2016; Zampieri et al., 2017), we aim to identify the features distinguishing two similar *varieties* (spoken and written language) of the same language (either English or Dutch) in a particular domain (image descriptions).

One of the motivations behind automatic image description research is to support blind or visually impaired people (e.g. Gella and Mitchell, 2016), and indeed *apps* are starting to appear which describe visual content for blind users (e.g. *TapTapSee* or Microsoft's *Seeing AI*[1]). These apps are commonly used together with screen readers, which convert on-screen text to speech. Given this presentation through speech, it is worth asking: should we not also collect *spoken* rather than *written* training data? That might give us more natural-sounding descriptions. But a big downside of collecting spoken training data is that it also requires a costly transcription procedure (unless we go for an *end-to-end* approach, see Chrupała et al., 2017). An alternative is to try to understand what the differences are between written and spoken image descriptions. Once we know those differences, and we know what kind of descriptions users prefer, we may be able to direct image description systems to produce more human-like descriptions, similar to the way we can modify the style of the descriptions, for example with positive/negative sentiment (Mathews et al., 2016), or humorous descriptions (Gan et al., 2017).

This paper presents an exploratory study of the differences between spoken and written image descriptions, for two languages: English and Dutch. We provide an overview of the variables that have been found to differ between spoken and written language, and see whether these differences also hold

---

This work is licensed under a Creative Commons Attribution 4.0 International License. License details: http://creativecommons.org/licenses/by/4.0/

[1]TapTapSee: https://taptapseeapp.com/; Seeing AI: https://www.microsoft.com/en-us/seeing-ai/

Proceedings of the Fifth Workshop on NLP for Similar Languages, Varieties and Dialects, pages 88–100
Santa Fe, New Mexico, USA, August 20, 2018.

between English spoken and written image descriptions. Following this, we repeat the same experiment for Dutch. Our main findings are that spoken descriptions (1) tend to be longer than written descriptions, (2) contain more adverbs than written descriptions, (3) contain more pseudo-quantifiers and allness terms (DeVito, 1966), and (4) tend to reflect the certainty of the speaker's beliefs more-so than written descriptions. Our work paves the way for a future controlled replication study, and follow-up studies to assess what kind of descriptions users prefer. All of our code and data is available online.[2]

2   Technical background: Manipulating the image description task

Recently, researchers have started to manipulate the image description task to obtain a better understanding of how this influences the resulting descriptions. This section presents a brief list of variables that have been considered in the literature.

Language. The most common modification is the *language* in which the task is carried out (e.g. Elliott et al., 2016; Li et al., 2016; Miyazaki and Shimizu, 2016). This is typically done to be able to train an image description system in a different language, but van Miltenburg et al. (2017) use this manipulation to show that speakers of different languages may also provide different descriptions. For example, speakers of American English described sports fans barbecuing on a parking lot as *tailgating*, a concept unknown to Dutch and German speakers.

Style. Another possible manipulation is the requested *style* of the descriptions. Gan et al. (2017) asked crowd workers to provide 'humorous' and 'romantic' descriptions, but found that it is impossible to control the quality of the resulting descriptions. So they, like Mathews et al. (2016), further changed the description task to a *description editing* task.

Content. Gella and Mitchell (2016) emphasize the importance of *emotional or descriptive content* and *humor* in the image, and explicitly ask for these to be annotated. This makes the elicited descriptions useful for training an assistive image description system which can provide descriptions for blind people.

Other. Baltaretu and Castro Ferreira (2016) present variations on an *object description* task (the *ReferIt* task, by Kazemzadeh et al. (2014)). The authors show that asking participants to work very fast, or produce thorough or creative descriptions, results in very different kinds of descriptions.

While the studies listed above cover a wide range of variables, there are many more possibilities that are still unexplored. Van Miltenburg et al. (2017) provide a (non-exhaustive) list of other factors that may influence the image description process. This paper aims to identify the role of modality.

3   Theoretical background: Spoken versus written language

The differences between spoken and written language have been thoroughly studied in the linguistics literature since the 1960s. Extensive overviews are provided by Akinnaso (1982), Chafe and Danielewicz (1987), Chafe and Tannen (1987), Biber (1988), and Miller and Fernandez-Vest (2006). Why should we study differences between spoken and written image descriptions, when so many linguists before us have studied differences between spoken and written language? Because spoken and written language are not monoliths. Biber (1988) notes that there is often as much variation within each modality, as there is between the two modalities. Biber attributes this variation to situational, functional, and processing considerations (p. 24-25). So while there may be general tendencies for particular linguistic phenomena to occur more in written than in spoken language (or vice versa), the only way to know for sure how speech differs from writing in a particular domain is to investigate that particular domain. For image description, the seminal study by Drieman (1962a; 1962b) is of particular interest to us. Drieman asked eight participants to describe two realistic paintings (one by Renoir and one by Weissenbruch), providing either spoken or written descriptions. He found that written texts (1) are shorter; but (2) have longer words (fewer words of one syllable, more words of more than one syllable); (3) have more attributive adjectives[3]; and (4) a more varied vocabulary. The drawback of this study is its limited size. Moreover, it is unclear if Drieman's conclusions about descriptions of paintings extend to one-sentence image

---

[2]Our code and data is available at https://github.com/cltl/Spoken-versus-Written

[3]In English, this means that the adjective is used in the prenominal position (*the **good** book*) rather than postnominal (*the book is **good***). The same holds for Dutch.

MS COCO instructions	Flickr30K instructions
1. Describe all the important parts of the scene. 2. Do not start the sentences with "There is." 3. Do not describe unimportant details. 4. Do not describe things that might have happened in the future or past. 5. Do not describe what a person might say. 6. Do not give people proper names. 7. The sentences should contain at least 8 words.	1. Describe the image in one complete but simple sentence. 2. Provide an explicit description of prominent entities. 3. Do not make unfounded assumptions about what is occurring. 4. Only talk about entities that appear in the image. 5. Provide an accurate description of the activities, people, animals and objects you see depicted in the image. 6. Each description must be a single sentence under 100 characters.

Figure 1: Instructions for the written English data. MS COCO instructions are from Chen et al. (2015). Flickr30K instructions are from the appendix of Hodosh et al. (2013), edited for brevity.

descriptions like those in MS COCO and Flickr30K. This is what we intend to study.

Following Drieman's study, researchers have proposed many other variables that seem to correlate with the speech/writing distinction. After surveying the literature on spoken versus written language, Biber (1988) presents an extensive list of linguistic features. The features used in this paper are based on Biber's list, see Section 4.3 for an overview. Noted in almost all surveys is the *ephemeral nature* of speech; whereas writing samples can be edited and reworded, speech cannot be edited the same way. Hence, spoken language also contains false starts, speech errors, and subsequent repairs. But despite those flaws, we must not think of spoken language as somehow *inferior* to written language. Halliday (1989) notes that the two are simply different media that serve different functions, which may require different forms of language. It is our task, as language users, to pick the right form (and medium) for the right job. If we find significant differences between spoken and written language, we should ask ourselves: now that we know about these differences in the way people describe images, which form is the most suitable for an image description system?

4 Data and methods for analyzing image descriptions

We present an analysis for both Dutch and English image descriptions. For each language, we took existing sets of spoken and written image descriptions, and automatically computed their differences in terms of the literature discussed above. The rationale here is that, even if these corpora are not perfectly comparable, they do provide an indication of the extent to which spoken and written image descriptions may differ. If we find structural differences between spoken and written image descriptions, it may be worth it to explore these differences further in a more controlled environment. If we fail to find any differences, we should conclude that there is no evidence for the effect of modality on the image description task. But, as we will see later, there do seem to be structural differences between spoken and written descriptions in both Dutch and English.

4.1 English data

For the written sample, we use the Flickr30K and the MS COCO datasets. Both were collected through Mechanical Turk, and have 5 written descriptions per image. We only use the training splits from both datasets, so that we remain ignorant of the properties of the validation and test splits. Figure 1 provides the instructions for both datasets. One of the main differences between the two is that the MS COCO instructions explicitly forbid the use of *there is* at the start of a sentence, which leads to the use of different syntactic constructions. Otherwise the instructions are very similar.

For the spoken sample, we use the Places Audio Caption Corpus, Part 1 (Harwath et al., 2016; Harwath and Glass, 2017), which contains about 230,000 spoken descriptions for a selection of images that were equally sampled from the 205 scene categories in the Places205 dataset (Zhou et al., 2014). The spoken descriptions were collected through Mechanical Turk using the Spoke framework (Saylor, 2015). These were then automatically transcribed by Harwath et al. (2016) using the Google Speech API. Because the transcriptions were not manually corrected, they have a word error rate of about 20%. It is unclear how participants were instructed to describe the image. The authors only mention that the descriptions are free-form, and that they should describe the salient objects in the scene.[4]

Image selection. The images from Flickr30K, MS COCO, and Places205 were all collected from online sources. Flickr30K and MS COCO exclusively use images from Flickr,[5] while Places also contains images found through general image search engines (Google and Bing). The main difference between the datasets is in the kind of images that are included. For the Flickr30K dataset, the authors downloaded images from six different user groups on the Flickr website.[6] The MS COCO authors compiled a list of 91 object categories, and searched for different object+object combinations of different categories on Flickr. They also selected 60 scene categories from the SUN database (Xiao et al., 2010), and searched for different object+scene combinations to diversify their data. Finally, the Places205 dataset is built by querying different search engines for adjective+scene combinations. The 205 scenes come from the SUN database, and the adjectives come from a manually curated list. Examples are: *messy, spare, sunny.*

Comparability. To what extent can we compare the descriptions in these datasets? Ideally, we would have one set of images that is provided with both spoken and written descriptions. But if the tasks are similar enough, and we compare the image descriptions on a large scale, we may still be able to confirm general tendencies of spoken versus written data, e.g. that spoken descriptions tend to be longer than written ones (Drieman, 1962a), or use more self-reference terms (DeVito, 1966). What we *cannot* do, is compare how often particular properties or kinds of entities are mentioned, because the distribution of those properties or entities might be dramatically different. Generally speaking, using different sets of images also means that we can never exclude the possibility that the underlying cause of the differences between the descriptions lies with the images rather than the modality. However, as the sets of images become more similar, chances of the images being a major source of the differences between the written and spoken descriptions become smaller. So how big *are* the differences between existing datasets?

To answer this question, we tagged the descriptions in all three datasets using the SpaCy part-of-speech tagger.[7] Table 1 shows the top-10 most frequent nouns in all three datasets. These correspond to the most frequent entities. We observe that while the Flickr30K and MS COCO datasets are fairly similar (sharing 5 words in their top-10), the Places dataset stands out from the other two (sharing only 2 words). Thus, the only spoken English descriptions that are available, describe images that are fairly different from the other datasets. Luckily we have more comparable data for Dutch.

#	Flickr30K Word	Count	MS COCO Word	Count	Places Word	Count
1	man	42595	man	48847	picture	36020
2	woman	22197	people	25723	people	26094
3	people	17338	woman	22992	building	25735
4	shirt	14341	table	21104	trees	22449
5	girl	9656	street	20527	water	20324
6	men	9499	person	16857	man	18609
7	boy	9399	top	14755	front	16584
8	dog	9093	field	14597	background	15484
9	street	8012	group	14450	side	15254
10	group	7852	tennis	13411	room	12985

Table 1: Top-10 most frequent nouns for all three datasets. Flickr30K and MS COCO are fairly similar (they have a larger overlap), but Places differs from the other two.

4.2 Dutch Data

For the written sample, we use the data collected by van Miltenburg et al. (2017). The authors crowdsourced Dutch descriptions for the Flickr30K validation and test sets (1014 + 1000 images, with 5 descriptions per image). The annotation task was translated from the Flickr30K and Multi30K templates (Elliott et al., 2016), to stay as close to these datasets as possible. We only use the validation split for our comparison, so that we remain ignorant of the properties of the test set.

For our spoken sample, we use data from a task that we carried out for another purpose, and that will be published separately (van Miltenburg et al., 2018). 45 Dutch students participated in a lab experiment

---

[4] We contacted the authors for more information about the crowd-sourcing task, but have not received any response.

[5] A social image sharing platform, see: www.flickr.com.

[6] These user groups are: *strangers!; Wild-Child (Kids in Action); Dogs in Action (Read the Rules); Outdoor Activities; Action Photography; Flickr-Social (two or more people in the photo).* See (Hodosh et al., 2013) for the full methodology.

[7] We use version 2.0.4. See: http://spacy.io/

where they were asked to describe a series of images, while we also measured their eye movements. We used the 307 images from MS COCO that both appear in SALICON and the Visual Genome dataset (Jiang et al., 2015; Krishna et al., 2016). We transcribed and annotated the recorded descriptions, so that we ended up with three layers: (1) a raw layer; (2) an annotated layer indicating (filled) pauses, corrections and repetitions; and (3) a normalized layer, with the 'intended' description. In total, we collected 14-16 descriptions per image, resulting in a grand total of 4604 descriptions for the entire dataset. This study uses the normalized descriptions, so that our metrics are unaffected by corrections and repetitions, and we can focus more on the content of the descriptions.

4.3 Preprocessing, metrics, and hypotheses

We tokenize, tag, and parse the descriptions using SpaCy. Then, we compute the following metrics:

1. **Average token length** Drieman (1962a) and others have found that the tokens in spoken language are shorter than those in written language. We measure token length in terms of syllables (following e.g. Drieman 1962a) and characters (following e.g. Biber 1988), using Hunspell to obtain the syllables.[8]

2. **Average description length** Drieman (1962a) and others have shown that spoken language has a higher sentence length than written language. We measure description length in tokens and syllables.

3. **Mean-segmental type-token ratio** (MSTTR) corresponds to the average number of types per 1000 tokens (Johnson, 1944). It is used as a measure of lexical variation. Because it is computed for a fixed number of tokens, it is unaffected by corpus size or sentence length. Drieman (1962a) shows that written language is more diverse than spoken language. One issue is that the Places Audio Caption Corpus has only one description per image, versus five descriptions per image for MS COCO and Flickr30K. This means that for every description in Flickr30K or MS COCO, there are four very similar descriptions, which makes these corpora less diverse overall. For a fair comparison, we treat Flickr30K and MS COCO as collections of five similar corpora, compute MSTTR for each of these, and report the average.

4. **Attributive adjectives** Drieman shows that spoken language contains fewer attributive adjectives than written language. We use SpaCy's tagger and parser to determine if an adjective is attributive or not. We consider a token to be an attributive adjective if its part-of-speech tag is ADJ, and it has an *amod* dependency relation with a head that is either tagged as NOUN or PROPN. In other words: if it's an adjective modifying a noun.

5. **Adverbs** We count all tokens with the ADV part-of-speech tag. The literature shows mixed results for the use of adverbs: Harrell (1957) studied children's production of stories, and found *fewer* adverbs in spoken than in written language, while Chafe and Danielewicz (1987) show that adverbs are used *more* in conversation and letters, and less in lectures and academic writing. They explain this pattern by arguing that the key variable is not *modality* but *involvement*. Whenever people are more involved with their audience or their environment, they also tend to use more locative or temporal adverbials. And whenever they are more *detached* (talking about more abstract ideas), they tend to use fewer adverbs.

6. **Prepositions** Chafe and Danielewicz (1987) show that prepositions are used more in (academic) written language. We count all tokens with the ADP part-of-speech tag.

The metrics below are computed by matching the tokenized descriptions with different sets of words.

7. **Consciousness-of-projection terms** DeVito (1966) defines these as: "words which indicate that the observed is in part a function of the observer." He shows that these words are more frequently used in speech than in writing. Since DeVito does not provide a list of the terms used in his work, we compiled our own list containing the following words: *apparently, appear, appears, certainly, clearly, definitely, likely, may, maybe, might, obviously, perhaps, possibly, presumably, probably, seem, seemed, seemingly, seems, surely*. The consciousness-of-projection terms contain Biber's (1988) set of *possibility modals* and *seem and appear*.

8. **Self-reference terms** DeVito (1966) also shows that self-reference terms (first-person pronouns and phrases like *the author*) are used more in spoken than in written language. We only use *I, me, my* as self-reference terms, since phrases like *the author* are not relevant in this domain.

---

[8]Hunspell is the spell checker from LibreOffice, which has a powerful hyphenation function. See: https://hunspell.github.io for more details. We use the Pyphen library (https:/github.com/Kozea/Pyphen) as an interface.

Feature	Terms
Consciousness-of-projection	*Lijkt, lijken, waarschijnlijk, misschien, duidelijk, mogelijk, zeker*
Self-reference	*Ik, me, mij*
Positive allness	*Alle, elke, iedere, iedereen*
Negations	*Geen, niet, niemand, nergens, noch, nooit, niets*
Pseudo-quantifiers	*Veel, vele, weinig, enkele, een paar, een hoop, grote hoeveelheid, kleine hoeveelheid*

Table 2: Dutch terms that were used for each feature.

9. **Positive allness terms** DeVito (1966) shows that spoken language contains more 'allness terms' than written language. For DeVito, these include both positive (*all, every, always*) and negative (*none, never*) terms. Following more recent work, which also focuses explicitly on negations, we decided to distinguish between the two. As *positive* allness terms, we use the words *all, each* and *every*.

10. **Negations** Biber et al. (1999, Chapter 3) show that spoken language contains more negations than written language. For the *negative* allness terms, we focus on explicit, non-affixal negations: *n't, neither, never, no, nobody, none, nor, not, nothing, nowhere*. (Using the terminology from Tottie (1980).)

11. **Pseudo-quantifiers** While DeVito (1966) did not find any significant differences in the use of exact numerals, between spoken and written language, he did find such differences in the usage of terms like *many*, that are "loosely indicative of amount or size." We use the following terms: *few, lots, many, much, plenty, some* and *a lot*.

Table 2 shows the Dutch terms used for each feature. For all features except average token length, average description length, and MSTTR, we report the average number of occurrences per description, and per 1000 tokens. We also compute the Propositional Idea Density (PID) for the spoken and written descriptions. PID corresponds to the average number of propositional ideas per word in a text (Turner and Greene, 1977). According to Turner and Greene's annotation scheme, sentence (1a) breaks down into the five ideas expressed in (1b).[9] Because the nine words in (1a) express five ideas, the PID for this sentence is $5/9 = 0.56$.

(1)   a.   The old gray mare has a very large nose

    b.   HAS(MARE, NOSE), OLD(MARE), GRAY(MARE), LARGE(NOSE), VERY(LARGE)(NOSE)

We expect that written language has a higher PID than spoken language. In other words: that spoken language uses more words to convey the same amount of information. This hypothesis is based on the idea that written language is edited or condensed to convey as much information as possible. For example, Chafe and Danielewicz (1987) show that nominalizations (e.g. *categorization, development*) occur more often in written language. They argue that the spoken alternatives for nominalizations are often much longer: several clauses instead of one. Another example comes from Ravid and Berman (2006), who show that written narratives contain relatively more *propositional* content ("events, descriptions, and interpretations") and less *ancillary* content ("nonnovel, nonreferential, or nonnarrative"). Spoken narratives are said contain more ancillary content for communicative purposes. We use existing tools to measure idea density. For English, we use the Computerized Propositional Idea Density Rater (Brown et al., 2008).[10] For Dutch, we use the tool developed by Marckx (2017).

Because this is an exploratory study, we will only report descriptive statistics. These allow us to formulate hypotheses about the differences between spoken versus written image descriptions. We can test these hypotheses in a future study with spoken and written descriptions for the same images, collected in the same controlled setting.

5   Results

This section presents an overview of the different metrics for the Dutch and the English data. We first present the English results, followed by the Dutch results, and end with a summary of our main findings.

Name	#Desc	#Tok	TokLen		DescLen		Attributives		Adverbs		Prepositions	
			Syll	Char	Syll	Tok	Desc	‰	Desc	‰	Desc	‰
MS COCO	414,113	4,348,698	1.29	4.01	13.53	10.50	0.64	60.97	0.16	14.99	1.75	166.37
Flickr30K	145,000	1,787,693	1.30	4.11	16.05	12.33	0.97	78.81	0.15	12.20	1.91	154.78
Places	229,388	4,765,891	1.26	4.08	26.27	20.78	1.39	66.77	0.97	46.67	3.06	147.14

Name	MSTTR	Consciousness		Self-reference		Allness		Negations		PseudoQuant	
		Desc	‰	Desc	‰	Desc	‰	Desc	‰	Desc	‰
MS COCO	0.32	0.00	0.22	0.00	0.09	0.02	1.56	0.00	0.42	0.06	6.01
Flickr30K	0.38	0.01	0.63	0.00	0.09	0.02	1.30	0.00	0.35	0.04	2.88
Places	0.34	0.08	4.07	0.05	2.49	0.07	3.22	0.06	2.88	0.24	11.66

Table 3: Results for our analysis of MS COCO, Flickr30K (both written), and the Places Audio Caption Corpus (spoken). For the top table, columns correspond to: number of descriptions, number of tokens, average token length (in syllables), average description length (in syllables, in tokens), features 4-6 (per description, per 1000 tokens). For the bottom table, columns correspond to the mean-segmental type-token ratio, followed by features 7-11 (per description, per 1000 tokens).

5.1 English results

Table 3 shows the results for the English descriptions. We immediately see that, in line with the literature, spoken image descriptions are almost twice as long as their written counterparts. With almost half the number of descriptions of MS COCO, the Places dataset has significantly more tokens. Based on the literature, we might also expect spoken descriptions to use shorter words than written descriptions. This is indeed the case when we look at syllable length, but when we look at the number of characters, tokens in the MS COCO dataset have a shorter average length. We conclude there is no clear difference in token length between spoken and written image descriptions.

MSTTR. We next look at the richness of the vocabulary used by the crowd workers. Following Drieman's work, we expected that written descriptions would have a higher type-token ratio than spoken descriptions. This expectation is not borne out by the data. The MSTTR score for the Places data falls between the scores for MS COCO and Flickr30K. A possible explanation for this result is that spoken language is typically produced without any preparation, which leads speakers to 'fall back' on a more basic vocabulary. But with the Places dataset, participants could think of a description before they pressed the 'record' button, alleviating cognitive constraints on language production.

Adjectives and prepositions. For the remaining features, we report the average number of occurrences per description, as well as per 1000 tokens. Based on Drieman's work, we thought that attributive adjectives might occur more in written descriptions, but when we look at Table 3, we find a mixed result: spoken descriptions contain *more* attributive adjectives per description, but *fewer* attributive adjectives per 1000 tokens than the written descriptions in the Flickr30K dataset. This is possible because the spoken descriptions are longer than the written ones. We conclude that there is no clear difference between written and spoken descriptions in the use of attributive adjectives. We draw the same conclusion for the use of prepositions.

Adverbs and other features. We observe that spoken descriptions contain more adverbs than written ones; three times more adverb tokens than MS COCO, and almost four

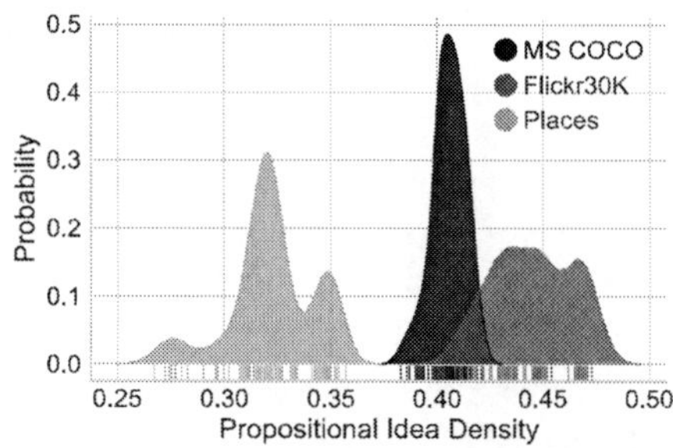

Figure 2: Distribution of the Propositional Idea Density scores for each of the three datasets, computed over $3 \cdot 100$ sets of 1000 descriptions. The lines on the x-axis show individual scores.

---

[9]This example was taken from (Brown et al., 2008).

[10]We use CPIDR version 3.2.3738.41169 on OS X 10.13.2, using Wine version 1.8-rc4.

Name	#Desc	#Tok	TokLen		DescLen		Attributives		Adverbs		Prepositions	
			Syll	Char	Syll	Tok	Desc	‰	Desc	‰	Desc	‰
Written	5,070	52,548	1.47	4.60	15.22	10.36	0.52	50.37	0.22	21.56	1.91	184.03
Spoken	4,604	57,805	1.49	4.58	18.70	12.56	0.50	39.51	0.67	52.76	1.83	144.69

Name	MSTTR	Consciousness		Self-reference		Allness		Negations		PseudoQuant	
		Desc	‰	Desc	‰	Desc	‰	Desc	‰	Desc	‰
Written	0.39	0.01	0.84	0.00	0.04	0	0.04	0.00	0.21	0.02	1.69
Spoken	0.37	0.03	2.22	0.02	1.53	0	0.33	0.01	0.79	0.06	4.78

Table 4: Results for our analysis of the Dutch spoken and written descriptions.

times more than Flickr30K. The same holds for consciousness-of-projection terms, self-reference terms, positive allness terms, negations, and pseudo-quantifiers: all these kinds of terms are used more often in spoken than in written image descriptions.

Propositional idea density. Figure 2 shows the distribution of Propositional Idea Density scores for each of the three datasets, visualized using Kernel Density Estimation. We computed the PID scores over 100 samples of 1000 descriptions for each dataset. We observe that the spoken descriptions have a lower PID than both written datasets, confirming the hypothesis that spoken descriptions use more words to convey the same amount of propositional information. Of course, the extra-propositional information may be useful as well, e.g. to convey pragmatic messages. Future research should look into whether users prefer the spoken or the written variant.

5.2 Dutch results

Table 4 shows the results for the Dutch descriptions. As with the English descriptions, we observe that the spoken descriptions are longer than their written counterparts, albeit to a lesser extent. Whereas the English spoken descriptions were almost twice as long as the written descriptions, the Dutch spoken descriptions are only two tokens longer on average.

Token length and MSTTR. We do not find any major differences in terms of token length or mean-segmental type-token ratios. The spoken descriptions *are* slightly less diverse, but not by a large margin. Unlike the English spoken data, the participants for the Dutch spoken data did not have any time to prepare, since the experiment immediately started recording as the picture was presented. We hypothesize that the differences that Drieman found might have been due to the length of the spoken and written samples, and that with a description spanning multiple sentences, speakers are perhaps more likely to repeat themselves, leading to less diversity in their descriptions.[11]

Adjectives and prepositions. In contrast to the English descriptions, we do observe a difference in the use of attributive adjectives between spoken and written descriptions. Written description contain slightly more attributive adjectives per description (even though written descriptions are shorter on average), and significantly more attributive adjectives per 1000 tokens. We also find that written descriptions contain more prepositions than spoken descriptions. These findings are in line with Drieman's original results.

Adverbs and other features. We find that spoken descriptions contain more than twice as many adverbs than written descriptions, mirroring the results for English. And, just like in English, we find that spoken descriptions also contain more negations, pseudo-quantifiers, and consciousness-of-projection, self-reference, and allness terms.

Propositional idea density. We also computed the Propositional Idea Density for both written and spoken descriptions, but we found little difference between the two: 0.44 for written descriptions versus 0.46 for their spoken counterparts. This is a far cry from the highly contrastive results we found for English. We conclude that there is no clear difference for Dutch spoken and written descriptions, though we should note that Marckx (2017) translated the rules to compute propositional idea density

---

[11]We did use normalized rather than raw spoken descriptions in our analysis, but the entire corpus of spoken Dutch descriptions contains only 139 repetitions/false starts, which is unlikely to have a strong effect over 57K+ tokens.

from English to Dutch. It may be the case that the Dutch PID rater overlooked linguistic constructions for communicating propositional ideas that only exist in Dutch.

5.3 Summary and discussion of our findings

Looking at the results for both Dutch and English, we have found that: (1) Spoken descriptions are likely to be longer than written descriptions and, in English, seem to have a lower propositional information density than written descriptions. (2) Spoken descriptions contain more adverbs than written descriptions. (3) Spoken descriptions contain more pseudo-quantifiers and allness terms. (4) Speakers have a bigger tendency to "show themselves" in their descriptions than writers, who are less *involved* (in the sense of Chafe and Danielewicz 1987). We can see this in the use of more consciousness-of-projection and self-reference terms. Akinnaso (1982) calls this *egocentric language*, indicating "that the observed is in part a function of the observer" (p. 102). It has been shown that negations in image descriptions often reflect the author's expectations about the image they are describing (van Miltenburg et al., 2016).

Negative findings. Some of the 'negative' findings (where, unlike earlier work, we find no difference between spoken and written language) may be explained in functionalist terms. For example, token length may not be a function of spoken versus written language, but rather of *register*; abstract or formal language tends to use longer words than concrete or informal language (Feng et al., 2011). Another explanation comes from the fact that Drieman (1962a) used *paintings* as a stimuli, which also come with a particular vocabulary, whereas MS COCO, Flickr30K, and the Places Audio Caption corpus use real-life, everyday photographs, which may not elicit the same kind of expert language.[12]

Limitations. There are two main threats to the validity of this study. First, the English descriptions from the Places Audio Caption Corpus have been automatically transcribed, with a 20% word error rate. This means that there may be biases in which words are recognized from the audio and which are not. McKoskey and Boley (2000) show that short words and function words are often confused by Automatic Speech Recognition (ASR) systems with other function words, brief periods of silence, background noise, or filled pauses. Fosler-Lussier and Morgan (1999) also show that infrequent words are less likely to be recognized correctly. See Goldwater et al. (2010) for a survey and further analysis of ASR errors.

Second, for both comparisons (Dutch and English), the images differ between the spoken and the written descriptions. The use of different images may have an effect on the length of the descriptions, for example if one set of images is more complex, or contains more objects per image than another. The length difference in English between spoken and written descriptions is much larger than in Dutch, making the impressive average of 21 tokens per description looking more like a peculiarity of the Places dataset, than a general property of spoken descriptions. Using different sets of images may also influence the word distribution, though perhaps more in terms of content words, than in the way participants report their observations. It seems to us that the use of self-reference terms, for example, should be relatively independent from the contents of the images. Finally, this study is limited in scope. We have only focused on descriptions in Dutch and English, two Germanic languages. It is an open question whether the differences we have found also hold up in other languages.

6 Conclusion and future research

We performed an exploratory study to find differences between spoken and written image descriptions in both Dutch and English. We found four main differences, summarized in the previous section. Where should we go from here? We offer three directions to consider.

---

[12]Here is a written sample from Drieman's study:

"A landscape with rushes —could be the Biesbos. The subject sounds charming, rural: fisherman near the edge of the rushes, — open water, in the background trees and a churchtower. Yet, the impression made by the actual painting is much less charming. There is a suggestion of movement among the rushes in the foreground and also in the clouds — a movement from left to right — investing the calm subject with something ominous and troubled. The bright patches in the sky, too, enhance this impression. Especially the bright horizon, on the right and beyond the churchtower, recalls, by contrast with the dark patches, elsewhere, an atmosphere of thunder."

Controlled replication. As Akinnaso (1982) notes, Drieman's study carefully controlled for (1) the topic of the descriptions; (2) the circumstances in which participants were asked to provide the descriptions; and (3) participants' background and level of linguistic knowledge. Changing any of these factors between the written and spoken condition makes the resulting data less comparable. Because we used existing datasets, we were not able to control for these. Although we believe that our main findings *should* hold up, the only way to know for sure is to carry out a follow-up study. The benefit of this exploratory study is that we have compiled a freely available set of tools to analyze spoken versus written language, and we have narrowed down the potential differences between spoken and written descriptions to four main differences. We can now also begin to study how potential users feel about these differences.

Qualitative analysis. We have limited ourselves to a quantitative analysis of the differences between spoken and written language. The key reason for this is that we do not have any parallel sets of spoken and written descriptions for the same images. However, we would still like to emphasize the importance of looking at individual images and individual descriptions in more detail, as manual inspection may reveal interesting examples and phenomena that are glossed over by automated metrics.

What do users want? Having found differences between spoken and written language, we should now ask ourselves: what kind of descriptions would users of image description technology prefer? Research on this topic goes back to user studies of ALT-text on the internet. For example, Petrie et al. (2005) asked a group of blind people about the type of content they would like to be described. They found that there is no single answer to this question, because descriptions are context dependent. But generally speaking, blind users like to know about objects, buildings, and people; activities; the use of color; the purpose of the image; the emotion and atmosphere; and the location where the picture was taken. Gella and Mitchell (2016) asked a panel of visually impaired users about automatic image captioning, and also found that users want to hear about humor and emotional content (besides concrete, literal content). While these studies are important for our understanding of the needs of blind users, they only focus on *what* should be described, and not so much on *how* images should be described, which is still an open question. Possibly the most interesting feature to explore in the context of this paper is the use of subjective language. Furthermore, the datasets discussed in this paper all use pictures from Flickr, or unspecified images from the web. But Gella and Mitchell found that blind users would also like to have image description technology for personal, news, and social media images. It is unclear how these should be described, and whether these kinds of images would elicit similar differences between spoken and written descriptions.

There are many ways to describe an image. As Vedantam et al. (2015) show, we can collect 50 descriptions for an image and still find meaningful variation. But this variation is not random. By manipulating the image description task, we can identify the different factors influencing the description process. With this paper, we hope to have shown that modality is one of the factors causing descriptions to diverge.

7 Acknowledgements

We thank four anonymous reviewers for their comments and suggestions. Emiel van Miltenburg is supported via the 2013 NWO Spinoza grant awarded to Piek Vossen.

References

F Niyi Akinnaso. 1982. On the differences between spoken and written language. *Language and speech*, 25(2):97–125.

Adriana Baltaretu and Thiago Castro Ferreira. 2016. Task demands and individual variation in referring expressions. In *Proceedings of the 9th International Natural Language Generation conference*, pages 89–93, Edinburgh, UK, September 5-8. Association for Computational Linguistics.

Raffaella Bernardi, Ruket Cakici, Desmond Elliott, Aykut Erdem, Erkut Erdem, Nazli Ikizler-Cinbis, Frank Keller, Adrian Muscat, and Barbara Plank. 2016. Automatic description generation from images: A survey of models, datasets, and evaluation measures. *Journal of Artificial Intelligence Research*, 55:409–442.

Douglas Biber, Stig Johansson, Geoffrey Leech, Susan Conrad, and Edward Finegan. 1999. *Longman grammar of spoken and written English*. London: Longman.

Douglas Biber. 1988. *Variation across speech and writing*. Cambridge University Press.

Cati Brown, Tony Snodgrass, Susan J Kemper, Ruth Herman, and Michael A Covington. 2008. Automatic measurement of propositional idea density from part-of-speech tagging. *Behavior research methods*, 40(2):540–545.

Wallace Chafe and Jane Danielewicz. 1987. Properties of spoken and written language. In R. Horowitz and F.J. Samuels, editors, *Comprehending oral and written language*. New York: Academic Press.

Wallace Chafe and Deborah Tannen. 1987. The relation between written and spoken language. *Annual Review of Anthropology*, 16(1):383–407.

Xinlei Chen, Hao Fang, Tsung-Yi Lin, Ramakrishna Vedantam, Saurabh Gupta, Piotr Dollár, and C Lawrence Zitnick. 2015. Microsoft coco captions: Data collection and evaluation server. *arXiv preprint arXiv:1504.00325*.

Grzegorz Chrupała, Lieke Gelderloos, and Afra Alishahi. 2017. Representations of language in a model of visually grounded speech signal. In *Proceedings of the 55th Annual Meeting of the Association for Computational Linguistics (Volume 1: Long Papers)*, pages 613–622. Association for Computational Linguistics.

Joseph A. DeVito. 1966. Psychogrammatical factors in oral and written discourse by skilled communicators. *Speech Monographs*, 33(1):73–76.

Gerard HJ Drieman. 1962a. Differences between written and spoken language: An exploratory study, I. quantitative approach. *Acta Psychologica*, 20:36–57.

Gerard HJ Drieman. 1962b. Differences between written and spoken language: An exploratory study, II. qualitative approach. *Acta Psychologica*, 20:78–100.

Desmond Elliott, Stella Frank, Khalil Sima'an, and Lucia Specia. 2016. Multi30k: Multilingual english-german image descriptions. In *Proceedings of the 5th Workshop on Vision and Language*, pages 70–74. Association for Computational Linguistics.

Shi Feng, Zhiqiang Cai, Scott A Crossley, and Danielle S McNamara. 2011. Simulating human ratings on word concreteness. In *FLAIRS Conference*.

Eric Fosler-Lussier and Nelson Morgan. 1999. Effects of speaking rate and word frequency on pronunciations in convertional speech. *Speech Communication*, 29(2-4):137–158.

Chuang Gan, Zhe Gan, Xiaodong He, Jianfeng Gao, and Li Deng. 2017. Stylenet: Generating attractive visual captions with styles. In *The IEEE Conference on Computer Vision and Pattern Recognition (CVPR)*, July.

Spandana Gella and Margaret Mitchell. 2016. Residual multiple instance learning for visually impaired image descriptions. In *11th Women in Machine Learning Workshop, in conjunction with NIPS*.

Sharon Goldwater, Dan Jurafsky, and Christopher D. Manning. 2010. Which words are hard to recognize? prosodic, lexical, and disfluency factors that increase speech recognition error rates. *Speech Communication*, 52(3):181 – 200.

Michael Alexander Kirkwood Halliday. 1989. *Spoken and written language*. Language Education. Oxford University Press. Second edition.

Lester E Harrell. 1957. *A comparison of the development of oral and written language in school-age children*, volume 22 of *Monographs of the Society for Research in Child Development*. Wiley.

David Harwath and James Glass. 2017. Learning word-like units from joint audio-visual analysis. In *Proceedings of the 55th Annual Meeting of the Association for Computational Linguistics (Volume 1: Long Papers)*, pages 506–517, Vancouver, Canada, July. Association for Computational Linguistics.

David Harwath, Antonio Torralba, and James Glass. 2016. Unsupervised learning of spoken language with visual context. In D. D. Lee, M. Sugiyama, U. V. Luxburg, I. Guyon, and R. Garnett, editors, *Advances in Neural Information Processing Systems 29*, pages 1858–1866. Curran Associates, Inc.

Micah Hodosh, Peter Young, and Julia Hockenmaier. 2013. Framing image description as a ranking task: Data, models and evaluation metrics. *J. Artif. Int. Res.*, 47(1):853–899, May.

Ming Jiang, Shengsheng Huang, Juanyong Duan, and Qi Zhao. 2015. Salicon: Saliency in context. In *The IEEE Conference on Computer Vision and Pattern Recognition (CVPR)*, June.

Wendell Johnson. 1944. I. a program of research. *Psychological Monographs*, 56(2):1.

Sahar Kazemzadeh, Vicente Ordonez, Mark Matten, and Tamara Berg. 2014. Referitgame: Referring to objects in photographs of natural scenes. In *Proceedings of the 2014 Conference on Empirical Methods in Natural Language Processing (EMNLP)*, pages 787–798, Doha, Qatar, October. Association for Computational Linguistics.

Ranjay Krishna, Yuke Zhu, Oliver Groth, Justin Johnson, Kenji Hata, Joshua Kravitz, Stephanie Chen, Yannis Kalantidis, Li-Jia Li, David A Shamma, Michael Bernstein, and Li Fei-Fei. 2016. Visual genome: Connecting language and vision using crowdsourced dense image annotations.

Xirong Li, Weiyu Lan, Jianfeng Dong, and Hailong Liu. 2016. Adding chinese captions to images. In *Proceedings of the 2016 ACM on International Conference on Multimedia Retrieval*, pages 271–275. ACM.

Tsung-Yi Lin, Michael Maire, Serge Belongie, James Hays, Pietro Perona, Deva Ramanan, Piotr Dollár, and C Lawrence Zitnick. 2014. Microsoft coco: Common objects in context. In *ECCV*, pages 740–755. Springer.

Shervin Malmasi, Marcos Zampieri, Nikola Ljubešić, Preslav Nakov, Ahmed Ali, and Jörg Tiedemann. 2016. Discriminating between similar languages and arabic dialect identification: A report on the third dsl shared task. In *Proceedings of the Third Workshop on NLP for Similar Languages, Varieties and Dialects (VarDial3)*, pages 1–14, Osaka, Japan, December. The COLING 2016 Organizing Committee.

Silke Marckx. 2017. Propositional idea density in patients with alzheimer's disease: An exploratory study. Master's thesis, Universiteit Antwerpen.

Alexander Patrick Mathews, Lexing Xie, and Xuming He. 2016. Senticap: Generating image descriptions with sentiments. In *AAAI*, pages 3574–3580.

David McKoskey and Daniel Boley. 2000. Error analysis of automatic speech recognition using principal direction divisive partitioning. In Ramon López de Mántaras and Enric Plaza, editors, *Machine Learning: ECML 2000*, pages 263–270, Berlin, Heidelberg. Springer Berlin Heidelberg.

Jim Miller and M. M. Jocelyne Fernandez-Vest. 2006. Spoken and written language. In Giuliano Bernini and Marcia L. Schwartz, editors, *Pragmatic organization of discourse in the languages of Europe*, Empirical approaches to language typology. EUROTYP. Berlin ; New York : Mouton de Gruyter.

Takashi Miyazaki and Nobuyuki Shimizu. 2016. Cross-lingual image caption generation. In *Proceedings of the 54th Annual Meeting of the Association for Computational Linguistics (Volume 1: Long Papers)*, pages 1780–1790, Berlin, Germany, August. Association for Computational Linguistics.

Helen Petrie, Chandra Harrison, and Sundeep Dev. 2005. Describing images on the web: a survey of current practice and prospects for the future. *Proceedings of Human Computer Interaction International (HCII)*, 71.

Dorit Ravid and Ruth A. Berman. 2006. Information density in the development of spoken and written narratives in english and hebrew. *Discourse Processes*, 41(2):117–149.

Patricia Saylor. 2015. Spoke: A framework for building speech-enabled websites. Master's thesis, Massachusetts Institute of Technology.

Gunnel Tottie. 1980. Affixal and non-affixal negation in English: Two systems in (almost) complementary distribution. *Studia linguistica*, 34(2):101–123.

Althea Turner and Edith Greene. 1977. *The construction and use of a propositional text base*. Institute for the Study of Intellectual Behavior, University of Colorado Boulder.

Emiel van Miltenburg, Roser Morante, and Desmond Elliott. 2016. Pragmatic factors in image description: The case of negations. In *Proceedings of the 5th Workshop on Vision and Language*, pages 54–59, Berlin, Germany, August. Association for Computational Linguistics.

Emiel van Miltenburg, Desmond Elliott, and Piek Vossen. 2017. Cross-linguistic differences and similarities in image descriptions. In *Proceedings of the 10th International Conference on Natural Language Generation*, pages 21–30, Santiago de Compostela, Spain, September. Association for Computational Linguistics.

Emiel van Miltenburg, Ákos Kádar, Ruud Koolen, and Emiel Krahmer. 2018. DIDEC: The Dutch Image Description and Eye-tracking Corpus. In *Proceedings of COLING 2018, the 27th International Conference on Computational Linguistics*. Resource available at https://didec.uvt.nl.

Ramakrishna Vedantam, C. Lawrence Zitnick, and Devi Parikh. 2015. Cider: Consensus-based image description evaluation. In *The IEEE Conference on Computer Vision and Pattern Recognition (CVPR)*, June.

Jianxiong Xiao, James Hays, Krista A Ehinger, Aude Oliva, and Antonio Torralba. 2010. Sun database: Large-scale scene recognition from abbey to zoo. In *Computer vision and pattern recognition (CVPR), 2010 IEEE conference on*, pages 3485–3492. IEEE.

Peter Young, Alice Lai, Micah Hodosh, and Julia Hockenmaier. 2014. From image descriptions to visual denotations: New similarity metrics for semantic inference over event descriptions. *Transactions of the Association for Computational Linguistics*, 2:67–78.

Marcos Zampieri, Shervin Malmasi, Nikola Ljubešić, Preslav Nakov, Ahmed Ali, Jörg Tiedemann, Yves Scherrer, and Noëmi Aepli. 2017. Findings of the vardial evaluation campaign 2017. In *Proceedings of the Fourth Workshop on NLP for Similar Languages, Varieties and Dialects (VarDial)*, pages 1–15, Valencia, Spain, April. Association for Computational Linguistics.

Bolei Zhou, Agata Lapedriza, Jianxiong Xiao, Antonio Torralba, and Aude Oliva. 2014. Learning deep features for scene recognition using places database. In Z. Ghahramani, M. Welling, C. Cortes, N. D. Lawrence, and K. Q. Weinberger, editors, *Advances in Neural Information Processing Systems 27*, pages 487–495. Curran Associates, Inc.

Transfer Learning for British Sign Language Modelling

Boris Mocialov
School of Mathematical
and Computer Sciences and
Edinburgh Centre for Robotics
Heriot-Watt University
Edinburgh, UK
bm4@hw.ac.uk

Graham Turner
School of Social Sciences and
Centre for Translation &
Interpreting Studies in Scotland
Heriot-Watt University
Edinburgh, UK
g.h.turner@hw.ac.uk

Helen Hastie
School of Mathematical
and Computer Sciences and
Edinburgh Centre for Robotics
Heriot-Watt University
Edinburgh, UK
h.hastie@hw.ac.uk

Abstract

Automatic speech recognition and spoken dialogue systems have made great advances through
the use of deep machine learning methods. This is partly due to greater computing power but also
through the large amount of data available in common languages, such as English. Conversely,
research in minority languages, including sign languages, is hampered by the severe lack of data.
This has led to work on transfer learning methods, whereby a model developed for one language
is reused as the starting point for a model on a second language, which is less resourced. In
this paper, we examine two transfer learning techniques of fine-tuning and layer substitution for
language modelling of British Sign Language. Our results show improvement in perplexity when
using transfer learning with standard stacked LSTM models, trained initially using a large corpus
for standard English from the Penn Treebank corpus.

1 Introduction

Spoken dialogue systems and voice assistants have been developed to facilitate natural conversation
between machines and humans. They provide services through devices such as Amazon Echo Show
and smartphones to help the user do tasks (McTear, 2004) and, more recently, for open domain chitchat
(Serban et al., 2016), all through voice. Recent advances have been facilitated by the huge amounts of
data collected through such devices and have resulted in the recent success of deep machine methods,
providing significant improvements in performance. However, not all languages are able to benefit from
these advances, particularly those that are under-resourced. These include sign languages and it means
that those who sign are not able to leverage such interactive systems nor the benefits that automatic
transcription and translating of signing would afford.

Here, we advance the state of the art with respect to transcribing British Sign Language (BSL). Our aim
is for automated transcription of the BSL into English leveraging video recognition technologies. BSL
enables communication of meaning through parameters such as hand shape, position, hand orientation,
motion, and non-manual signals (Sutton-Spence and Woll, 1999). BSL has no standard notation for
writing the signs, as with letters and words in English. Analogous to the International Phonetic Alphabet
(IPA), highly detailed mapping of visual indicators to written form are available, such as HamNoSys
(Hanke, 2004). Despite the expressiveness of the HamNoSys writing system, its practical uses are limited
and only a handful of experts know how to use it. Recent methods for automatic speech recognition
(ASR) use deep neural models to bypass the need for phoneme dictionaries (Hannun et al., 2014), which
are then combined with language models. Previous work (Mocialov et al., 2016; Mocialov et al., 2017)
has shown that we can use visual features to automatically predict individual signs. This work follows
on in that these individual signs are to be used with a language model to take into account context and
therefore increase accuracy of the transcriber, which outputs a string of word-like tokens. These tokens
are called glosses (Sutton-Spence and Woll, 1999; Cormier et al., 2015). Although glosses are translated
BSL signs, they also convey some grammatical information about BSL. This makes glosses useful in

This work is licenced under a Creative Commons Attribution 4.0 International Licence. Licence details: http://
creativecommons.org/licenses/by/4.0/

Proceedings of the Fifth Workshop on NLP for Similar Languages, Varieties and Dialects, pages 101–110
Santa Fe, New Mexico, USA, August 20, 2018.

their own right without the videos of the BSL signs and sheds some light into the syntax and semantics of the BSL.

This paper focuses on language modelling, a common technique in the field of ASR and Natural Language Processing to model the likelihood of certain words following each other in a sequence. We improve modelling of the BSL glosses by proposing to use transfer learning approaches, such as fine-tuning and layer substitution. The use of transfer learning technique can overcome the data sparsity issue in statistical modelling for scarce resource languages by using similar resources that can be found in large quantities and then further training the models on a specific low resource data.

We show that a model, pre-trained on the Penn Treebank (PTB) dataset[1] and fine-tuned on the BSL monolingual corpus[2] can yield better results. This is in contrast to the same architecture that is trained directly on the BSL dataset without pre-training. This is a somewhat surprising result as there are marked differences between the two languages, particularly with the respect to the syntax (Sutton-Spence and Woll, 1999).

The paper begins with presenting methods for modelling languages and how they can be utilised in the BSL modelling. Section 2.2 gives an overview of how transfer learning can be achieved as well as the use of transfer learning in sign languages. Section 3 gives an overview of the datasets that are used in this paper, their statistics, and pre-processing steps to create two monolingual corpora for statistical model training. Section 4 describes in detail the setup for the experiments in this paper. Section 5 presents the results of the models employed for this research and discusses these results and the limitations of the approach taken in terms of the data used in Section 5.3. The paper is then concluded and future work is proposed.

2 Related Work

2.1 Sign Language Modelling

Despite the availability of many alternatives for language modelling, such as count-based n-grams and their variations (Chen and Goodman, 1999; Rosenfeld, 2000; MacCartney, 2005; Bulyko et al., 2007; Guthrie et al., 2006), hidden Markov models (Dreuw and Ney, 2008; Dreuw et al., 2008), decision trees and decision forests (Filimonov, 2011), and neural networks (Deena et al., 2016; Mikolov et al., 2010), research in sign language modelling predominantly employs simple n-gram models, such as in Cate and Hussain (2017), Forster et al. (2012), and Massó and Badia (2010).

The reason for the wide-spread use of n-grams in sign language modelling is the simplicity of the method. However, there is a disconnect between n-grams and sign language in that signing is embodied and perceived visually, while the n-grams are commonly applied to text sequence modelling. For this reason, the authors in Stein et al. (2007), Zhao et al. (2000), Dreuw et al. (2008), Massó and Badia (2010), and Forster et al. (2013) model glosses, such as the ones shown on Figure 2, which are obtained from the transcribed sign languages, in a similar way to how language modelling is applied to automatic transcribed words from speech.

Glosses model the meaning of a sign in a written language, but not the execution (i.e. facial expressions, hand movement). Therefore, the more detailed meaning of what was signed may get lost when working with the higher-level glosses. To overcome this issue and to incorporate valuable information into sign language modelling, additional features are added in similar research, such as non-manual features (e.g facial expressions) (San-Segundo et al., 2009; Massó and Badia, 2010; Zhao et al., 2000; Stein et al., 2007).

In this work we use glosses because we want to model BSL purely at the gloss level without any additional information (e.g. facial expressions).

2.2 Transfer Learning

While transfer learning is a more general machine learning term, cross-domain adaptation of language models is used in the language modelling literature (Deena et al., 2016; Ma et al., 2017). Models are

---

[1] https://catalog.ldc.upenn.edu/ldc99t42

[2] http://www.bslcorpusproject.org/

usually trained on some specific domain that consists of a specific topic, genre, and similar features that can be identified by an expert. For example, a restaurant domain when a new type of a restaurant is created then the system needs to be able to adapt and be able to understand and discuss this new type of the restaurant. Unfortunately, it is nearly impossible to train a model for all possible configuration of current or future features. Commonly, a set of features are extracted from the raw data. When features change, re-training is required. Useful features can also be extracted without expert knowledge with such techniques as Latent Dirichlet Allocation (LDA). These features usually take the form of words that represent topics in the data (Deena et al., 2016). Best practice tries to avoid re-training the models every time one of the features changes as the domain changes due to the overhead involved.

Model-based adaptation to the new domains, on the other hand, is achieved by either fine-tuning or the introduction of adaptation layer(s) (Yosinski et al., 2014). Fine-tuning involves further training the already pre-trained model using the data from the new domain. The intuition behind the fine-tuning is that it is much quicker to learn new information with related knowledge. The adaptation layer approach incorporates new knowledge by re-training only the adaptation layer, whereas the rest of the model remains exactly the same as if it was used in the original domain and acts as a feature extractor for the new domain (Deena et al., 2016).

Transfer learning has been applied to sign languages in computing for various purposes to demonstrate that the method is suitable for the task due to the lack of substantial domain-specific sign language data. Transfer learning has been successfully applied to static pose estimation, transferring the knowledge from pose estimation to the sign language pose estimation (Gattupalli et al., 2016) and classification of fingerspelled letters in American Sign Language (Garcia and Viesca, 2016; Karthick Arya, 2017; Chaudhary, 2017; Muskan Dhiman, 2017). In particular, most of the transfer learning in sign language has been applied to static image recognition to recognise the hand shape in an image using convolutional neural networks.

We apply transfer learning to the language modelling task as this is a key challenge in successfully transcribing BSL.

3 Corpora

The BSL corpus and the preprocessed Penn Treebank (PTB) corpus were chosen for this research. The monolingual PTB dataset consists of telephone speech, newswire, microphone speech, and transcribed speech. The dataset is preprocessed to eliminate letters, numbers, or punctuation and was used by Mikolov (2010). The BSL corpus contains video conversations among deaf native, near-native and fluent signers across the United Kingdom. Almost all of the approximately one hundred recorded conversations are annotated for thirty seconds each at the gloss level using ELAN[3] annotation tool (Schembri et al., 2013).

Figure 1: The BSL Corpus Project Sample Video Snippets[4]

---

[3]https://tla.mpi.nl/tools/tla-tools/elan/

All recordings of the signers were made using up to four standard video cameras with a plain backdrop to provide full body view of the individuals, as well as, views from above of their use of signing space. The conversations between the signers included signing personal experience anecdotes, spontaneous conversations (Schembri et al., 2013).

The BSL data that we focused on was narratives between two participants, where one person had to think of a topic to sign about to another participant during the elicitation.

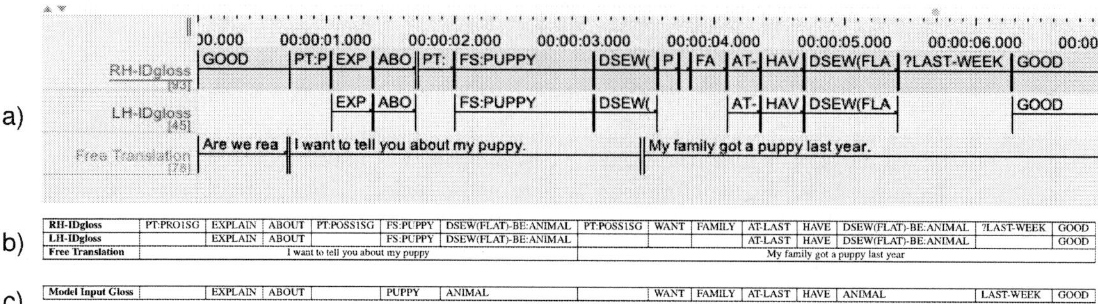

Figure 2: a) The BSL Corpus Annotation in ELAN; b) Table shows full text of the annotated glosses for the two first sentences from the ELAN annotation; c) Glosses that are used for the BSL modelling

The corpus is annotated with glosses, taken from the BSL SignBank in ELAN as shown in Figure 2a. Figure 2b shows all the glosses of the first sentence. As mentioned above, gloss is an identifier of a unique sign, written in English and should represent its phonological and morphological meaning (Schembri et al., 2013). In the corpus, the glosses are identified throughout the videos for both left and right hands as sometimes different signs can be signed at the same time. Apart from the glossing, the annotations include the corresponding free English written translation of the meaning of the signing split into sentences (see the Free Translation in the Figure 2). Figure 2c shows which glosses are considered for the BSL modelling and which are ignored. This is done to match the vocabulary of the PTB corpus for the transfer learning purposes.

3.1 Data Pre-processing

For the BSL corpus, we ignore the free translation and extract English text from the glosses, preserving the order of the signs executed. For example, in Figure 2, right-hand glosses identify the following order of the signs: good, explain, about, puppy, etc. excluding glosses, such as PT:PRO for pointing signs or PT:POSS for possessives and others (Figure 2c), which are explained in more detail in Fenlon et al. (2014). Since the gloss annotation does not include explicit punctuation, it is impossible to tell where a signed sentence begins and where it stops. To overcome this limitation of the gloss annotation, we use the Free Translation annotation, which gives the boundaries of sentences in videos. Later, we split the extracted glosses into sentences using these sentence boundaries. By the end of the pre-processing stage, we have glosses (excluding special glosses for pointing signs, posessives or other non-lexical glosses) in the order that the corresponding signs were executed in the video, split into sentences. As a result, we extracted 810 nominal sentences from the BSL corpus with an average length of the sentence being 4.31 glossed signs, minimum and maximum lengths of 1 and 13 glossed signs respectively. A monolingual dataset has been created with the extracted sentences. As obtained from the PTB dataset (Merity et al., 2017), the English language corpus has 23.09 words on average per sentence with minimum being 3 and maximum 84 words per sentence. The pre-processed BSL corpus has a vocabulary of 666 words, while the PTB dataset has a vocabulary of 10,002 words. From this point on in this paper, we will use the term 'words' to refer to both glosses in the BSL and words in the PTB datasets because we aim to use a common vocabulary for training our models.

---

[4] http://www.bslcorpusproject.org/cava/

Both monolingual datasets were split into training, validation, and testing sets as required for training and evaluation of the statistical models. Both datasets were split using ratio 85:15. The smaller subset, in turn, was split 50:50 for validation and testing for the two datasets.

4 Language Modelling Methodology

4.1 Statistical Language Models

Perplexity measure has been used for evaluation and comparison purposes of different models. We used the following formula to calculate the perplexity values: $e^{Cross-Entropy}$ as used in Bengio et al. (2003), which approximates geometric average of the predicted words probabilities on the test set. We have explicitly modelled out-of-vocabulary (OOV), such as $< unk >$ placeholder in all the experiments.

4.1.1 Neural Models

For comparison, we use two methods: 1) stacked LSTM and 2) Feed-Forward (FFNN) architectures to create the BSL language models. All models are implemented in PyTorch[5] with weight-drop recurrent regularisation scheme for the LSTMs, which is important for overcoming commonly known LSTM model generalisation issues (Merity et al., 2017; Merity et al., 2018). The feed-forward model, on the other hand, had no regularisations as it is less susceptible to overfitting due to the much smaller number of parameters.

The parameters that were modified to achieve the lowest perplexity were input size of the overall input sequence for the recurrent neural network (back-propagation through time, BPTT), batch size, learning rate, and the optimizer. The parameters were selected using the grid search approach using perplexity metric. As a result, for the stacked LSTMs, bptt was set to 5, batch size was set to 16, discounted learning rate was set to 30, and the optimizer was set to stochastic gradient descent. In case of the feed-forward network, input was set to 5 words, batch size was set to 16, discounted learning rate was set to 30, and the optimizer was set to stochastic gradient descent. All the neural models were trained for 100 epochs.

In the case of the neural networks, the sequences of words were tokenised (i.e. turned into integers) and the tokenisation was stored to ensure the same tokenisation during the transfer learning phase. The input, therefore, consisted of a set of tokens, while the outputs (i.e. predicted words) were turned into a one-hot vectors.

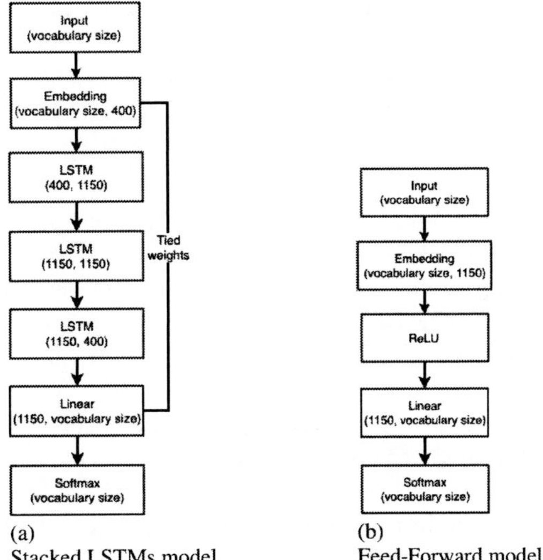

Figure 3: The two types of neural models used to test transfer methods for sign language modelling

---

[5]http://pytorch.org/

4.1.1.1 Stacked LSTMs

Figure 3a shows the architecture of the stacked LSTM model. The model consists of an embedding layer of 400 nodes, which, together with the tokenisation, turns string of words into a vector of real numbers. Secondly, three LSTM layers with 1150 nodes each are stacked vertically for deeper feature extraction. Thirdly, the linear layer downsizes the stacked LSTMs output to the vocabulary size and applies linear transformation with softmax normalisation. The weights of the embedding and the linear layers are tied. This means that the two layers share the same weights, which reduces the number of parameters of the network and makes the convergence during training faster. The same architecture was used in Merity et al. (2017) to model PTB dataset, reporting 57.3 perplexity, utilising cache in the model from recent predictions.

4.1.1.2 FFNN

Figure 3b shows the Feed-forward model architecture. The model does not have the stacked LSTMs layers. Instead, the stacked LSTMs are substituted with one hidden fully-connected rectifier layer, which is known to overcome the vanishing gradient problem. The weights of the embedding and the outputs layers are not tied together. Similar architectures have been used for language modelling in Le et al. (2013), Mikolov et al. (2009), and de Brébisson et al. (2015) with the hidden layer having different activation functions with the PTB dataset being used in Audhkhasi et al. (2014), reporting 137.32 perplexity.

4.1.2 Training the Models

Transfer learning was achieved with both fine-tuning and substitution. Both FFNN and LSTM were trained on the PTB dataset and then either fine-tuned or the last layer was substituted with the new adaptation layer, freezing the rest of the weights, and further training on the BSL dataset.

To achieve fine-tuning, first the best model is saved after the training of both the FFNN and the stacked LSTMs on the PTB dataset. Then the training is restarted on the BSL corpus, having initialised the model with the weights, trained on the PTB dataset.

To perform layer substitution as a transfer learning approach, the same first step as with the fine-tuning is repeated and the model, trained on the PTB, is saved. When the training is restarted on the BSL dataset, the saved model is loaded and the last linear layer is substituted with a layer that has as many nodes as the BSL vocabulary. Later, all the weights of the network are locked and will not be modified during the optimisation. Only the weights of the last substituted layer will be modified. This method uses the pretrained network as a feature extractor and only modifies the last layer weights to train the model for the BSL dataset.

5 Results

This section is split into two subsections. We firstly present results without transfer learning, namely both the FFNN and the stacked LSTMs models trained and tested on the PTB dataset or trained and tested on the BSL. Later we present results with the transfer learning, with both FFNN and the stacked LSTMs models trained on the PTB dataset and then fine-tuned and tested on the BSL.

To show that the two languages are different, as discussed in Section 3.1, we applied the model trained on one language to the other language and vice versa. As a result, the model trained on English language and applied to the BSL scored 1051.91 in perplexity using SRILM toolkit (Stolcke, 2002). Conversely, a model trained on the BSL has been applied to the English language and scored 1447.23 in perplexity. As expected, the perplexity is high in both cases, which means that the probability distribution over the next word in one language is far from the true distribution of words in the other language.

5.1 Without Transfer Learning

Table 1 shows perplexities on the two datasets with two statistical models. From the table, we can infer that the trained models on the PTB dataset have lower perplexity than the same architectures trained on the BSL dataset. This can be explained by the fact that the PTB dataset has more data than the BSL

Method	Penn Treebank (PTB)	The BSL Corpus Project
FFNN	190.46	**258.1**
Stacked LSTMs	65.91	274.03
OOV	6.09%	25.18%

Table 1: Perplexities on either the PTB or the BSL test sets using models trained and tested on the same corpus (i.e. PTB and BSL)

dataset and, therefore, statistical models can generalise better. Furthermore, the amount of data is further reduced in the BSL case as the OOV covers a quarter of the overall dataset.

5.2   With Transfer Learning

Table 2 shows perplexities on the two datasets with two statistical models, applying transfer learning. From this table, it can be seen that the substitution approach gives very similar results independent of the whether FFNN or stacked LSTMs model is used (123.92 versus 125.32). The best result is achieved with the fine-tuning approach on the stacked LSTMs model, while the higher perplexity result is on the FFNN model with the fine-tuning approach. Similar results have been reported in Irie et al. (2016), where fine-tuned GRU performed worse than fine-tuned LSTM model. In addition, the OOV count differs from that of the Table 1 due to the fact that a subset of the vocabulary, observed in the PTB dataset during training is then identified in the BSL dataset during testing.

Method	Fine-tuning	Substitution
FFNN	179.3	123.92
Stacked LSTMs	**121.46**	125.32
OOV	12.71%	

Table 2: Perplexities on the BSL test set after applying the transfer learning on FFNN and LSTMs

5.3   Discussion

The salient idea of this paper is whether transfer learning is a legitimate method for modelling one language with the knowledge of another, assuming the languages are different, but share some common properties, such as vocabulary. This theory is intuitive and has been discussed in linguistics for spoken languages (Kaivapalu and Martin, 2007). In our case, PTB corpus covers most of the vocabulary found in the BSL corpus (12.71% OOV) by the virtue of the gloss annotation of the BSL corpus (Schembri et al., 2013). However, the languages are assumed to be different as they evolved independently of one another (Brennan, 1992).

The results obtained are different from reported in similar research. For example, for the FFNN model, Audhkhasi et al. (2014) report 137.32 versus our achieved 190.46 perplexity and for the stacked LSTMs model, Merity et al. (2017) report 57.3 versus our achieved 65.91 perplexity. This can be explained by the fact that not all the regularisation techniques had been used in this research as in the past research and the model training had been restricted to 100 epochs. Further training may further reduce the perplexity to that reported in Merity et al. (2017).

From the results, we can see that the transfer learning leads to superior models than the models trained on the BSL directly (258.1 and 274.03 against 123.92 and 125.32). Since the quality of the trained models using either of the approaches is similar in case of the stacked LSTMs model (121.46 and 125.32), the choice between the fine-tuning and substitution can be guided based on the convergence speed. During the substitution, only one layer of the network is replaced with a new one and the rest of the weights in the network are locked, therefore, one set of weights will be optimized. This is in contrast to the fine-tuning method, which optimizes all of the weights, which may, in turn, require more interactions, depending on how different the new data is.

6 Conclusion

This paper shows how transfer learning techniques can be used to improve language modelling for the BSL language at the gloss level. Statistical modelling techniques are used to generate language models and to evaluate them using a perplexity measure.

The choice of the transfer learning technique is guided by the scarcity of available resources of the BSL language and the availability of the English language dataset that shares similar language modelling vocabulary with the annotated BSL. Feed-forward and recurrent neural models have been used to evaluate and compare generated language models. The results show that transfer learning can achieve superior quality of the generated language models. However, our pre-processed BSL corpus lacks constructs that are essential for a sign language, such as classifier signs and others. Nevertheless, transfer learning for modelling the BSL shows promising results and should be investigated further.

6.1 Future Work

Although this paper discusses the use of a model initially trained on English and presents promising preliminary results, the annotation of the BSL, used in this paper, is limited as this paper serves as a proof of concept. In particular, the annotation used is missing some of the grammatical aspects of the BSL, such as classifier signs and others. Inclusion of these into the BSL language modelling would increase the OOV count as the English language does not have equivalent language constructs. This raises a question whether a sign language can be modelled using other languages that may have these constructs. More generally, is it possible to model a language with transfer learning using other less-related languages? Similar questions have been partly answered for the written languages in the field of machine translation (Gu et al., 2018) by bringing words of different languages close to each other in the latent space. However, nothing similar has been done for the sign languages.

From the methodological side of the modelling, additional advanced state of the art techniques should be experimented with to achieve greater quality of the generated models, such as attention mechanism for the recurrent neural networks. Finally, this paper focuses on key techniques for sign processing, which could be part of a larger conversational system whereby signers could interact with computers and home devices through their natural communication medium of sign. Research in such end-to-end systems would include vision processing, segmentation, classification, and language modelling as well as language understanding and dialogue modelling, all tuned to sign language.

References

Kartik Audhkhasi, Abhinav Sethy, and Bhuvana Ramabhadran. 2014. Diverse embedding neural network language models. *arXiv preprint arXiv:1412.7063*, abs/1412.7063.

Yoshua Bengio, Réjean Ducharme, Pascal Vincent, and Christian Jauvin. 2003. A neural probabilistic language model. *Journal of machine learning research*, 3(Feb):1137–1155.

Mary Brennan. 1992. *The visual world of BSL: An introduction*. Faber and Faber. In David Brien (Ed.), Dictionary of British Sign Language/English.

Ivan Bulyko, Spyros Matsoukas, Richard Schwartz, Long Nguyen, and John Makhoul. 2007. Language model adaptation in machine translation from speech. In *Proceedings of the Acoustics, Speech and Signal Processing, 2007. ICASSP 2007. IEEE International Conference on*, volume 4, pages IV–117. IEEE.

Hardie Cate and Zeshan Hussain. 2017. Bidirectional american sign language to english translation. *arXiv preprint arXiv:1701.02795*, abs/1701.02795.

Belal Chaudhary. 2017. Real-time translation of sign language into text. Data Science Retreat. https://github.com/BelalC/sign2text, apr.

Stanley F Chen and Joshua Goodman. 1999. An empirical study of smoothing techniques for language modeling. *Computer Speech & Language*, 13(4):359–394.

Kearsy Cormier, Jordan Fenlon, Sannah Gulamani, and Sandra Smith. 2015. Bsl corpus annotation conventions.

Alexandre de Brébisson, Étienne Simon, Alex Auvolat, Pascal Vincent, and Yoshua Bengio. 2015. Artificial neural networks applied to taxi destination prediction. *arXiv preprint arXiv:1508.00021*, abs/1508.00021.

Salil Deena, Madina Hasan, Mortaza Doulaty, Oscar Saz, and Thomas Hain. 2016. Combining feature and model-based adaptation of rnnlms for multi-genre broadcast speech recognition. In *Proceedings of the Annual Conference of the International Speech Communication Association, INTERSPEECH*, pages 2343–2347. Sheffield.

Philippe Dreuw and Hermann Ney. 2008. Visual modeling and feature adaptation in sign language recognition. In *Voice Communication (SprachKommunikation), 2008 ITG Conference on*, pages 1–4. VDE.

Philippe Dreuw, Carol Neidle, Vassilis Athitsos, Stan Sclaroff, and Hermann Ney. 2008. Benchmark databases for video-based automatic sign language recognition. In *LREC*.

Jordan Fenlon, Adam Schembri, Ramas Rentelis, David Vinson, and Kearsy Cormier. 2014. Using conversational data to determine lexical frequency in British Sign Language: The influence of text type. *Lingua*, 143:187–202.

Denis Filimonov. 2011. *Decision tree-based syntactic language modeling*. University of Maryland, College Park.

Jens Forster, Christoph Schmidt, Thomas Hoyoux, Oscar Koller, Uwe Zelle, Justus H Piater, and Hermann Ney. 2012. Rwth-phoenix-weather: A large vocabulary sign language recognition and translation corpus. In *Proceedings of the 8th International Conference on Language Resources and Evaluation, LREC*.

Jens Forster, Oscar Koller, Christian Oberdörfer, Yannick Gweth, and Hermann Ney. 2013. Improving continuous sign language recognition: Speech recognition techniques and system design. In *Proceedings of the Fourth Workshop on Speech and Language Processing for Assistive Technologies*, pages 41–46.

Brandon Garcia and Sigberto Alarcon Viesca. 2016. Real-time american sign language recognition with convolutional neural networks. In *In Proceedings of Machine Learning Research, pp. 225-232.*

Srujana Gattupalli, Amir Ghaderi, and Vassilis Athitsos. 2016. Evaluation of deep learning based pose estimation for sign language. *arXiv preprint arXiv:1602.09065*, abs/1602.09065.

Jiatao Gu, Hany Hassan, Jacob Devlin, and Victor OK Li. 2018. Universal neural machine translation for extremely low resource languages. *arXiv preprint arXiv:1802.05368*.

David Guthrie, Ben Allison, Wei Liu, Louise Guthrie, and Yorick Wilks. 2006. A closer look at skip-gram modelling. In *Proceedings of the 5th international Conference on Language Resources and Evaluation (LREC-2006)*.

Thomas Hanke. 2004. Hamnosys-representing sign language data in language resources and language processing contexts.

Awni Y. Hannun, Carl Case, Jared Casper, Bryan Catanzaro, Greg Diamos, Erich Elsen, Ryan Prenger, Sanjeev Satheesh, Shubho Sengupta, Adam Coates, and Andrew Y. Ng. 2014. Deep speech: Scaling up end-to-end speech recognition. *CoRR*, abs/1412.5567.

Kazuki Irie, Zoltan Tuske, Tamer Alkhouli, Ralf Schluter, and Hermann Ney. 2016. LSTM, gru, highway and a bit of attention: an empirical overview for language modeling in speech recognition. Technical report, RWTH Aachen University Aachen Germany.

Annekatrin Kaivapalu and Maisa Martin. 2007. Morphology in Transition: Plural Inflection of Finnish nouns by Estonian and Russian Learners. *Acta Linguistica Hungarica*, 54(2):129–156.

Jayesh Kudase Karthick Arya. 2017. Convolutional neural networks based sign language recognition. *International Journal of Innovative Research in Computer and Communication Engineering*, 5(10), oct.

Hai-Son Le, Ilya Oparin, Alexandre Allauzen, Jean-Luc Gauvain, and François Yvon. 2013. Structured output layer neural network language models for speech recognition. *IEEE Transactions on Audio, Speech, and Language Processing*, 21(1):197–206.

Min Ma, Michael Nirschl, Fadi Biadsy, and Shankar Kumar. 2017. Approaches for neural-network language model adaptation. *Proc. Interspeech 2017*, pages 259–263.

Bill MacCartney. 2005. NLP lunch tutorial: Smoothing.

Guillem Massó and Toni Badia. 2010. Dealing with sign language morphemes in statistical machine translation. In *4th workshop on the representation and processing of sign languages: corpora and sign language technologies*.

Mike McTear. 2004. *Spoken Dialogue Technology: Toward the Conversational User Interface*. Springer, London.

Stephen Merity, Nitish Shirish Keskar, and Richard Socher. 2017. Regularizing and Optimizing LSTM Language Models. *arXiv preprint arXiv:1708.02182*.

Stephen Merity, Nitish Shirish Keskar, and Richard Socher. 2018. An Analysis of Neural Language Modeling at Multiple Scales. *arXiv preprint arXiv:1803.08240*.

T. Mikolov, J. Kopecky, L. Burget, O. Glembek, and J. Cernocky. 2009. Neural network based language models for highly inflective languages. In *2009 IEEE International Conference on Acoustics, Speech and Signal Processing*, pages 4725–4728, April.

Tomáš Mikolov, Martin Karafiát, Lukáš Burget, Jan Černocký, and Sanjeev Khudanpur. 2010. Recurrent neural network based language model. In *Eleventh Annual Conference of the International Speech Communication Association*.

Boris Mocialov, Patricia A Vargas, and Micael S Couceiro. 2016. Towards the evolution of indirect communication for social robots. In *Computational Intelligence (SSCI), 2016 IEEE Symposium Series on*, pages 1–8. IEEE.

Boris Mocialov, Graham Turner, Katrin Lohan, and Helen Hastie. 2017. Towards continuous sign language recognition with deep learning. In *Proc. of the Workshop on the Creating Meaning With Robot Assistants: The Gap Left by Smart Devices*.

Dr G.N. Rathna Muskan Dhiman. 2017. Sign language recognition. https://edu.authorcafe.com/academies/6813/sign-language-recognition.

Ronald Rosenfeld. 2000. Two decades of statistical language modeling: Where do we go from here? *Proceedings of the IEEE*, 88(8):1270–1278.

Rubén San-Segundo, José Manuel Pardo, Javier Ferreiros, Valentín Sama, Roberto Barra-Chicote, Juan Manuel Lucas, D Sánchez, and Antonio García. 2009. Spoken spanish generation from sign language. *Interacting with Computers*, 22(2):123–139.

Adam Schembri, Jordan Fenlon, Ramas Rentelis, Sally Reynolds, and Kearsy Cormier. 2013. Building the British Sign Language corpus. *Language Documentation and Conservation 7*.

Iulian Vlad Serban, Ryan Lowe, Laurent Charlin, and Joelle Pineau. 2016. Generative deep neural networks for dialogue: A short review. *arXiv preprint arXiv:1611.06216*.

Daniel Stein, Philippe Dreuw, Hermann Ney, Sara Morrissey, and Andy Way. 2007. Hand in hand: automatic sign language to english translation.

Andreas Stolcke. 2002. Srilm-an extensible language modeling toolkit. In *Proceedings of the Seventh international conference on spoken language processing*.

R. Sutton-Spence and B. Woll. 1999. *The Linguistics of British Sign Language: An Introduction*. The Linguistics of British Sign Language: An Introduction. Cambridge University Press.

Jason Yosinski, Jeff Clune, Yoshua Bengio, and Hod Lipson. 2014. How transferable are features in deep neural networks? In *Advances in neural information processing systems*, pages 3320–3328.

Liwei Zhao, Karin Kipper, William Schuler, Christian Vogler, Norman Badler, and Martha Palmer. 2000. A machine translation system from english to american sign language. In *Conference of the Association for Machine Translation in the Americas*, pages 54–67. Springer.

Paraphrastic Variance between European and Brazilian Portuguese

Anabela Barreiro
INESC-ID, Rua Alves Redol 9
1000-029 Lisboa, Portugal
anabela.barreiro@inesc-id.pt

Cristina Mota
INESC-ID, Rua Alves Redol 9
1000-029 Lisboa, Portugal
cristina.mota@inesc-id.pt

Abstract

This paper presents a methodology to extract a paraphrase database for the European and Brazilian varieties of Portuguese, and discusses a set of paraphrastic categories of multiwords and phrasal units, such as the compounds *toda a gente* vs *todo o mundo* "everybody" or the gerundive constructions [*estar a* + V-Inf] vs [*ficar* + V-Ger] (e.g., *estive a observar* vs *fiquei observando* "I was observing"), which are extremely relevant to high quality paraphrasing. The variants were manually aligned in the e-PACT corpus, using the CLUE-Aligner tool. The methodology, inspired in the Logos Model, focuses on a semantico-syntactic analysis of each paraphrastic unit and constitutes a subset of the Gold-CLUE-Paraphrases.[1] The construction of a larger dataset of paraphrastic contrasts among the distinct varieties of the Portuguese language is indispensable for variety adaptation, i.e., for dealing with the cultural, linguistic and stylistic differences between them, making it possible to convert texts (semi-)automatically from one variety into another, a key function in paraphrasing systems. This topic represents an interesting new line of research with valuable applications in language learning, language generation, question-answering, summarization, and machine translation, among others. The paraphrastic units are the first resource of its kind for Portuguese to become available to the scientific community for research purposes.

1 Introduction

Paraphrases are linguistic devices that allow to recognize and generate equivalent forms of expressing the same content, either oral or written, i.e., of saying and writing the same thing/idea using different wording or syntactic structure. Paraphrases are essential in human communication, both in language production and understanding. They can occur at various levels: multiword or phrasal unit, phrase, expression, sentence, paragraph, full text, etc.. Given the scale and nature of paraphrases, paraphrase research has become an activity of growing importance in natural language processing, and a vital and strategic area for future language technology industries, ranging from text production, language learning, dialogue systems and machine translation applications, among others. The work presented here lies within the scope of ongoing research activities of the eSPERTo project[2], which aims to develop an automated paraphraser to assist writers and language learners in text production and revision. eSPERTo has the challenging objectives of guaranteeing thorough knowledge of the context, fluency of language, appropriate style and consistent terminology. Within these objectives, eSPERTo is designed to enable the adaption of a text within the different varieties of the Portuguese language.

In order to enable variety adaptation, we have analyzed the contrastive pairs of paraphrastic units aligned and collected from the corpus e-PACT (eSPERTo Paraphrase Aligned Corpus of EN-EP/BP Translations), a parallel corpus of aligned paraphrases (Barreiro and Mota, 2017). One of the motivations behind the creation of this corpus was to contrast the European (EP) and Brazilian (BP) varieties

---

This work is licensed under a Creative Commons Attribution 4.0 International Licence. Licence details: http://creativecommons.org/licenses/by/4.0/

[1] An approach based on word-level alignment clues is often referred to as the "clue alignment approach" (Tiedemann, 2003) (Tiedemann, 2011)). In our approach, CLUE is an acronym that stands for "Cross-Language Unit Elicitation" that is based on manual alignments of multiwords and other phrasal units, which can be monolingual or bilingual.

[2] https://esperto.l2f.inesc-id.pt/esperto/esperto/demo.pl

Proceedings of the Fifth Workshop on NLP for Similar Languages, Varieties and Dialects, pages 111–121
Santa Fe, New Mexico, USA, August 20, 2018.

of Portuguese by exploring monolingual alignments taking into account both similar and differing forms of expression between them. This approach allows finding vocabulary and expressions common to both varieties, but also linguistic constructions that constitute lexico-syntactic and stylistic differences between EP and BP. Breaking away from ad-hoc and random alignment practices, our methodology centers around the Logos Model (cf. (Scott, 2003), (Barreiro et al., 2011), (Scott, 2018)) and its semantico-syntactic approach, which results from over 30 years of experience in successful commercial machine translation.

The paraphrastic units collected, which are common between the two language varieties, are useful to increase eSPERTo's paraphrasing capabilities, whereas the paraphrastic variants, i.e., multiwords, phrases or expressions not used in one of the varieties, are useful for variety adaptation. Variety adaptation allows, for example, the necessary amending proposals to ensure that eSPERTo's user text, ways of expression or style can add clarity to the text and improve its readability in the other Portuguese variety. Adaptation will also attempt to reduce communication barriers among the Portuguese varieties, and eventually, contribute to an international variety of Portuguese (cf. (Santos, 2014) and (Santos, 2015)).

The alignments were performed with the support of the CLUE-Aligner tool (Barreiro et al., 2016), developed to facilitate the alignment of both paraphrasing and translation units in monolingual and in bitexts, including the alignment of discontinuous multiwords and phrasal units, such as the support verb constructions *fazer* [] *caminhadas por* = *dar* [] *passeios por* "taking [] walks through", or *ficar contente* "be happy". Within this line of research, we have developed a set of guidelines – CLUE4Paraphrasing Alignment Guidelines – that use information about the syntactic and semantic properties of phrases to align paraphrastic correspondences in a monolingual EP–BP sentence pair. Our alignment research focuses mainly on lexical and semantico-syntactic phenomena that can be, to a greater or lesser extent, challenging to a paraphrasing system. As the paraphrastic database grows, our aim is to create an automated alignment model with pre-defined elements and concepts that can be used for future applications involving monolingual or bilingual alignment tasks.

2   Related Work on Alignments

Paraphrasing systems can be trained using similar methods to those used in machine translation systems[3], i.e., they can be trained with **paraphrastic alignments**[4], which are representations of semantically-equivalent words, phrases, expressions or sentences within the same language or language variety, such as EP and BP. The paraphrastic alignment process consists of identifying, analyzing and registering corresponding phrasal equivalents within pairs of parallel sentences, where the source and the target sentences correspond to the same language.

Paraphrastic alignments extracted from parallel corpora may be either of high quality or of questionable quality depending on the quality of those corpora or the quality of the work performed during the alignment task, respectively. For Portuguese, there is a lack of freely available parallel corpora that can be used to train and test paraphrasing systems. Linguistic knowledge-based alignments extracted from good quality corpora can contribute to increased precision and, subsequently, improve the quality of generated paraphrases. In particular, alignments of paraphrastic units can be extremely useful to collect data and obtain an adequate dimension of the work to be executed prior to linguistic validation and integration of good quality data into real-world systems.

Our alignment task consisted of identifying, aligning, and collecting paraphrastic equivalences, i.e., multiwords and phrasal units or expressions that represented semantic correspondences in the aligned sentence pairs of the EP–BP parallel text. The outcome of our alignment task contained a set of individual paraphrastic alignments between meaningful sequences of words, i.e., linguistically-motivated pairs of paraphrastic units.[5] From an applicational perspective for Portuguese, no research has been done at a

---

[3]In machine translation, several works have been published on alignment annotation guidelines or other aspects of alignment research (cf. (Och and Ney, 2000), (Lambert et al., 2005), (Graça et al., 2008), or (Tiedemann, 2011), among others)

[4]In comparison to *translation alignments*, which are representations of semantically-equivalent words, phrases, expressions or sentences within the source and target sentences of a bilingual or multilingual parallel corpus (Brown et al., 1990).

[5]In statistics, a sequence of more than one n-gram is commonly called "phrase". Our alignments do not contain statistical phrases, but linguistic phrases or other linguistic units. Alignments based on random n-grams or statistical phrases do not

level beyond the lexicon. Early work on EP–BP standard and technical language lexical distinctions has been compiled in a contrastive lexicon (Barreiro et al., 1996) that led to INESC's Lusolex and Brasilex dictionaries (Wittmann et al., 2000), but no alignment methods have been used. Despite meagre initial resources, manually annotated paraphrastic alignments represent an important step in the development of paraphrasing systems.

3 The eSPERTo Project

Variety adaptation is an important feature of the eSPERTo project, whose main focus is the development of a paraphrasing system with capacity to produce semantically equivalent sentences and ways of expression, also when these are contrasting, as in the case of varieties of the same language. Figure 1 illustrates the usefulness of paraphrases in eSPERTo's variety adaptation capability, where for a sentence written in EP, the system offers suggestions to paraphrase and rewrite it in BP (and vice-versa). For example, for the BP sentence *Todo mundo em Plotino tem a mesma vista* "Everybody in Plotinus has the same view", eSPERTo presents *toda a gente* as the EP suggestion for the BP phrase *todo mundo* and the EP suggestion *tem a mesma vista* for the BP phrase *tem vista igual*. This adaptation is extremely useful when the user wants to reach an audience that speaks the variety that he/she is less familiar with.

eSPERTo - System for Paraphrasing in Editing and Revision of Text

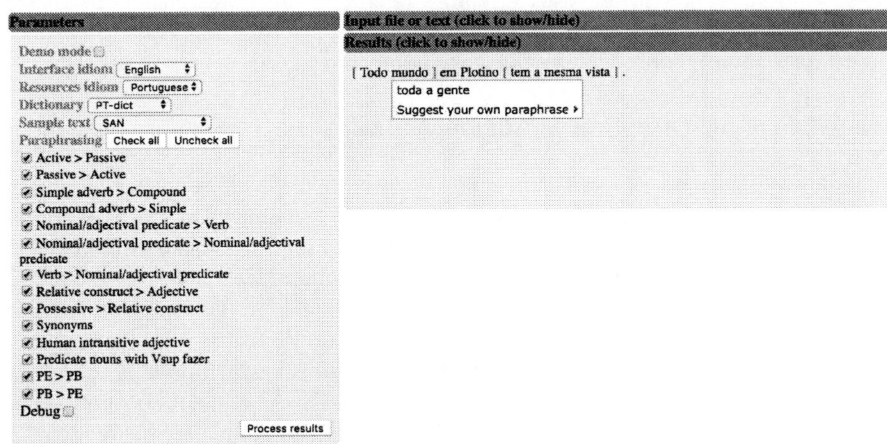

Figure 1: EP–BP paraphrastic variants *toda a gente* | *todo mundo* and *tem a mesma vista* | *tem vista igual*

eSPERTo uses semantico-syntactic knowledge to identify multiwords and other phrasal units, and applies local grammars to transform them into semantically equivalent phrases, expressions, or sentences. The quantity and quality of the resources have been increasing considerably with the integration of tables developed within the lexicon-grammar theoretical and methodological framework (cf. (Gross, 1984) and (Gross, 1987)), based on the transformational operator grammar (cf. (Harris, 1952), (Harris, 1965), (Harris, 1991), among others). Lexicon-grammar tables contain distributional and transformational properties of nominal predicates that can be used in paraphrasing tasks with successful results. Several lexicon-grammar research works have been describing these predicates in great detail, establishing relations between different types of predicate, and defining properties in tables that can be adapted and converted into dictionary entries, becoming a useful resource for paraphrasing. Predicates are not necessarily verbal, they can be nominal too, and they are often used interchangeably without any significant difference in meaning. There are nominal predicates, both nouns and adjectives, which, like verbs,

---

have a linguistic motivation or contrastive analysis lying behind them. Even though they represent an efficient intermediate representation developed for engineering purposes in natural language processing and machine translation systems, they present shortcomings from a linguistic point-of-view. In "n-grams in search of theories", (Maia et al., 2008) raised the question of the need to create linguistically more robust n-gram tools, which imply a supporting theoretical or practical framework for the research on word alignment.

have argumental selection properties. For example, there are adjectives that require complements (e.g., *ele está desejoso de ir à praia* "he is eager to go to the beach"), being classified as transitive adjectives, and there are adjectives that do not require any complement (e.g., *ele está doente* "he is sick"), classified as intransitive adjectives. In these cases, it is not the verb, which in both sentences is the same auxiliary, *está* "is", that imposes these argument restrictions, it is the adjective instead. The same can be said with regard to predicate nouns.

In our research work, three lexicon-grammar tables formalized for EP have recently been added to expand eSPERTo's paraphrastic capabilities: (i) the lexicon-grammar of human intransitive adjectives (Mota et al., 2015), (ii) the lexicon-grammar of predicate nouns co-occurring with the support verb *fazer* "do" or "make" (Mota et al., 2017), and (iii) the lexicon-grammar of predicate nouns which co-occur in constructions with the support verb *ser de* "be of" (Mota et al., 2018). These resources allow the generation of paraphrases such as *de origem portuguesa* "of Portuguese origin/roots" = *portugueses* "Portuguese" = *de Portugal* "from Portugal"; *fez uma classificação de NP* "made a classification of NP" = *classificou NP* "classified NP"; *é de uma certa cortesia* "is of a certain courtesy" = *é cortês* "is courteous". So far, we have not managed to integrate any lexicon-grammar tables for BP, but we would only need to formalize those entries which are exclusive or differ from the ones in EP.

Even though eSPERTo has been explored in a question-answering system and in a summarization tool (Mota et al., 2016), the lexicon-grammar integrated resources have not been tested in these applications. We envisage to test the new paraphrastic resources in an e-learning environment to assist Portuguese language learners with the editing and revision of texts. But, precise paraphrases can also be helpful in professional translation, editing, and proofreading, among other tasks.

4   Description of the Paraphrastic Alignment Task

Our paraphrastic alignment task was facilitated by the use of the CLUE-Aligner, an alignment tool that permits the alignment and storage of both continuous and discontinuous multiwords and other phrasal units to be used in paraphrasing (and also in translation), i.e., in monolingual or bilingual parallel sentences. Based on the CLUE4Paraphrasing Alignment Guidelines[6], we built a gold collection of pairs of EP–BP paraphrastic variants for the e-PACT corpus. The CLUE4Paraphrasing Alignment Guidelines summarize the most important recommendations and decisions for the alignment of multiwords and phrasal units found in monolingual parallel sentences corresponding to the EP and BP translations of two books by David Lodge, *Therapy* and *Changing Places*.[7] The initial e-PACT corpus contained 30% of the two novels extracted from the COMPARA English and Portuguese bidirectional parallel corpus. To create the initial corpus (Barreiro and Mota, 2017), we extracted the first 3 parallel sentences of each group of 10 parallel sentences, the EBDL1 batch contains 489 sentence alignments and the EBDL3 batch contains 313 sentence alignments, in a total of 802 parallel sentences. For the current work, we enlarged the original e-PACT with 10% more of the total number of sentences for the 2 novels, which correspond to the first 4 parallel sentences in each group of 10. This 10% increase corresponds to 163 sentence alignments in a first batch and 312 sentence alignments in a second batch. Therefore, so far, we manually annotated 40% of the total number of aligned sentences for both novels, in total 1,277 parallel sentences. From the enlarged e-PACT corpus, we have collected a few thousands of paraphrastic alignments that still need to be revised by a Portuguese and a Brazilian linguist before making them publicly available. From this collection, not all the paraphrastic alignments correspond to contrasts between the EP and BP varieties of Portuguese. Our goal in exploring monolingual alignments of two varieties of the same language was not only to capture differing forms of expression between these varieties, but also take into account paraphrases that can apply to one variety or the other. These variety-free/independent paraphrases can contribute to the development of the eSPERTo paraphrase acquisition system.

---

[6]The CLUE4Paraphrasing Alignment Guidelines are a set of CLUE Alignment Guidelines.

[7]We have used EP and BP translations of the same English novels as alignment data, because this is a popular and straightforward approach to gather parallel paraphrastic data. However, one drawback of this kind of corpora is that there may be a syntactic and lexical bias carrying over from the English original. It is possible that non-translation corpora may be less biased, but more difficult to find or prepare.

5 Examples of EP–BP Contrastive Paraphrasing Phenomena

In this Section, we will illustrate several types of EP–BP paraphrases, which constitute real examples from the e-PACT corpus. We provide the English source sentence for each EP–BP paraphrase case. Lack of space precludes a detailed description of most of the paraphrasing phenomena found in the corpus. We have selected a few examples of paraphrastic alignments. All multiwords, phrases and expressions, including discontinuous ones, have been aligned as illustrated in Figure 2. Due to space limitation we present only this illustrative image, which represents the paraphrastic alignment pair highlighted in example (1). The alignment refers to the EP–BP variety contrast between the discontinuous support verb construction *subiram [] em espiral*, literally "climbed [] in a spiral" in EP and the BP prepositional verb *espiralando* "spiraling up". In EP the predicate noun *espiral* "spiral" is placed apart from the support verb *subir* "climb". The direct object noun phrase insertion in the support verb construction, *o tronco* "the branch", aligns independently (not highlighted in this image).

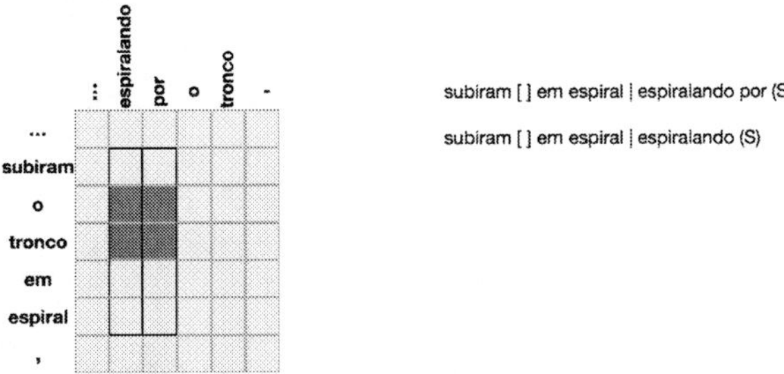

Figure 2: Paraphrastic S-alignment *EP - subiram [ ] em espiral* | *BP - espiralando (por)*

5.1 Verbal Constructions

5.1.1 Verbs and Support Verb Constructions

Verbs and support verb constructions are frequent in commutative conditions. Often paraphrastic variance between EP and BP results from the use of a support verb construction or of a verb, in one or another direction. There are cases where their respective use is simply related to an arbitrary decision by the translator. In other cases, the frontier between stylistic choice and variety adaptation is not straightforward. In example (1), EP and BP adopt different surface structures (i.e., syntax); EP uses a support verb construction, while BP uses a verb. These could be simply considered stylistic variants resulting from the fact that the BP translator translated less conventionally by using a new verb instead of the more conventional support verb construction, but in a sense there seems to be a more evident translation permissibly that is allowed or fostered in BP as far as new vocabulary is concerned.[8] A clear stylistic choice was the translation of the support verb into the past tense, *subiram*, by the EP translator who arbitrarily or voluntarily did not maintain the gerundive form used in the English source and in the BP translation.

(1) *EN - I watched two playing tag [...] just outside my study window:* **spiralling up a trunk**...
EP - Estive a observar da janela do meu escritório dois esquilos a brincarem à apanhada [...]: **subiram o tronco em espiral**...
BP - Fiquei observando os dois esquilos que brincavam de pegapega [...] em frente à janela do meu estúdio: **espiralando pelo tronco**...

5.1.2 EP [*estar a* + V–Inf] versus BP [*ficar* + V–Ger] Constructions

The use of progressive constructions when aligning EP–BP paraphrases is extremely frequent and there are many interesting cases that are worth analyzing. However, due to space limitations we focus on: (i)

---

[8] While this verb is rather far-fetched even for a Brazilian speaker, it is known that BP speakers are in general less conservative as far as the formation of new words is concerned. It appears less likely that the verb *espiralar* would be employed by a EP native speaker or translator. But, it is also possible that the English gerund *spiralling* induced a corresponding Portuguese form *espiralando* from a translator that would not otherwise have used it, because it is a lexeme less likely to cross someone's mind.

the gerundive infinitive, formed with the auxiliary verb *estar* "be" (or *ficar* "remain", or *ir* "go") plus the preposition *a* "at" plus the infinitive form of the main verb: [*estar a* + V–Inf] (e.g., *estar* + *a* + *trabalhar* = "to be + working"), used in written EP, and (ii) the gerundive construction made up of the auxiliary verb *estar* (or *ficar*, or *ir*) plus the present participle (gerundive) of the main verb, which ends with the suffix *-ndo* "-ing": [*ficar* + V–Ger] (e.g., *ficar/estar* + *trabalhando* = "to be + working), used in BP. Example (2) illustrates the contrast between the EP gerundive infinitive, which is formed with the verb *estar* in the past imperfect tense (*estive*) "(I) was", followed by the preposition *a*, and by the main verb in the infinitive form, *observar* "observe", and the BP gerundive form, which is formed with the auxiliary verb *ficar* in the preterit tense, *fiquei* ("(I) remained/stayed"), followed by the gerundive form of the main verb, *observando* "observing".

> (2) *EN* - ***I watched*** *two playing tag [...] just outside my study window:*
> *EP* - ***Estive a observar*** *da janela do meu escritório dois esquilos a brincarem à apanhada [...]:*
> *BP* - ***Fiquei observando*** *os dois esquilos que brincavam de pegapega [...] em frente à janela do meu estúdio:*

5.2 Word Order – Placement of Clitic Pronouns: V–Pro versus Pro V

The placement of the clitic pronoun is different in EP and BP. In EP, the normal position for the clitic is after the verb and connected to it by an hyphen[9] ([(Prep)V]–Pro), while in BP, the normal position for the clitic is before the verb with no attaching hyphen (Pro [(Prep)V]). As illustrated in example (3), the prepositional verb[10] *puseram-me em*, literally "(they) put me in", in the EP sentence is a paraphrastic variant of the prepositional verb *me mandaram para* "(they) sent me to" in the BP sentence. While there is a stylistic difference with regards to the translator's choice of the prepositional verb, the word order difference is a clear case of EP–BP paraphrastic variance.

> (3) *EN* - *My Mum and Dad **sent me to** Sunday school when I was a nipper...*
> *EP* - *Os meus pais **puseram-me** na [em + a] catequese quando ainda era pequeno...*
> *BP* - *Minha mãe e meu pai **me mandaram para** a Escola Dominical quando eu era pequeno...*

5.3 Lexical versus non-Lexical Realization in Nominal Constructions

Within noun phrases, it is common to find paraphrastic alignments where one element of the pair of paraphrases contains a lexically-realized determiner or a pronoun and the other element does not contain them. Section 5.3.1 discusses the alignment of phrases containing determiners with phrases containing what is known as *zero determiners*. Section 5.3.2 discusses the EP–BP variance cases involving subject pronouns, or lack of them, which is normally designated as *subject pronoun drop* or simply *pro-drop*.

5.3.1 Determiners and Zero Determiners

The presence of zero articles is common in BP, and less frequent in EP. Aligning a zero determiner with a lexically realized determiner implies association of the determiner to the noun. Determiners are aligned together with the noun (single or compound) when they do not appear in one of the varieties (mostly BP) of an alignment pair. When determiners appear in both variants of the alignment pair, they are also aligned individually. For example, the noun phrase *o Nizar* with the definite article *o* and the named entity *Nizar* in EP aligns with the single noun "Nizar" (no determiner) in BP, i.e., the alignment of *EP* - [DET N] | *BP* - [Ø-DET N]. The alignment of phrases with determiners with phrases with no determiners implies that the lexically realized determiner is associated to the phrase. In example (4), the noun phrase containing the definite article *os* in the noun phrase *os meus grupos* "my groups" in the EP sentence aligns with the noun phrase without a determiner *meus grupos* in the BP sentence.

> (4) *EN* - *I gather from Busby that you'll probably be taking over **my** tutorial **groups**.*
> *EP* - *Soube pelo Busby que vai ficar com **os meus grupos**.*
> *BP* - *Pelo que Busby me contou, o senhor vai ser o orientador de **meus grupos** de estudos.*

---

[9]Although in both EP and BP there are differences between written and spoken language (some correspond to regional differences), and also between verb tenses or antecedents in the sentence, we will not enter into any of these details here.

[10]Prepositional verbs are preposition-governing transitive verbs, where the preposition is at the right-hand side of the verb.

EP	BP	EN
braço de um gira-discos	*agulha de um toca-discos*	*the stylus arm of a [] record deck*
comboio	*trem*	*train*
revisor	*cobrador*	*ticket-collector*
serviço de mesas	*serviço de garçom*	*table-service*
fio do berbequim	*fio da furadeira*	*lead on [] Black and Decker*
maçã-de-adão	*pomo-de-adão*	*Adam's apple*
desporto	*esporte*	*sport*
fato	*terno*	*suit*
blusão de cabedal	*jaqueta de couro*	*leather jacket*

Table 1: EP–BP lexical contrasts

5.3.2 Subject Pronoun Drop

The contrast of overt pronouns with omitted or null pronouns is a recurring phenomenon in the alignment task (e.g., *Ø sugeri = Eu disse* "I said"). If a personal pronoun is overt in one of the varieties and omitted in the other variety, alignment should be made on a one-by-two basis. In example (5), the subject pronoun *Ele* "He" together with the verb *era* "was" of the adjectival support verb construction *era um desportista* "(he) was a sportsman" in BP aligns with its equivalent without the pronoun *Ele* in BP.

(5) *EN - **He** was in fact a keen sportsman*
    *EP - **Ø** Era de facto um desportista hábil*
    *BP - **Ele** era de fato um esportista aplicado*

5.4 Forms of Address – 2nd versus 3rd Person

EP and BP have different forms of addressing people and different forms of courtesy. In EP, the pronoun *tu* "you" is used as an informal way of addressing friends and family in casual situations. In formal situations, it is used the pronoun *você* (sometimes omitted) with the verb conjugated in the third person singular. In BP, the most common form of address is *você* in both formal and informal contexts.[11] For example, *tens a certeza* is used in EP, while *tem certeza* "you're sure" is used in BP. Similarly, *não te importas* is used in EP and *não se importa* "you don't mind" is used in BP. The form of address is a very frequent source of EP–BP paraphrastic variance.

(6) *EN - **You're sure** [Ø] **you don't mind**?*
    *EP - **Tens a certeza** de que **não te importas**?*
    *BP - **Tem certeza** de que **não se importa**?*

6 Variety Differences

The most important issue to be considered, at this particular point in our research, is to distinguish between those paraphrastic alignments that represent stylistic differences but that are natural and fluent multiwords, expressions or phrases in both the EP and BP varieties, and those paraphrastic alignments that represent contrastive variance between EP and BP and they cannot be used in commutative conditions in both varieties, i.e., they are exclusively used either in EP or in BP. In the list of contrasts, we have also registered lexical contrasts, illustrated in Table 1, even though they are not the focus of our discussion. Table 2 illustrates contrasts of a syntactic nature, i.e., multiwords expressions or phrases that are used only in EP or only in BP. Future work should focus on the categorization of each one of these syntactic phenomena, and the creation of grammars that can use these phenomena in more generalized contexts. This research needs to be deepened and sustained with validation of the contrasts by expert linguists on both varieties. Table 4 illustrates stylistic contrasts that correspond to valid paraphrases for both varieties of Portuguese.

Many of the EP–BP contrasts that we have collected have insertions, i.e., elements that are external to the multiword or phrasal unit, either in the English source or in any of the Portuguese varieties, such

---

[11]However, in BP, *você* can be combined both with the second and third person singular personal pronouns to distinguish between a more or less familiar person.

117

EP	BP	EN
viu-me vir <u>a correr</u> por [NP]	*me viu <u>correndo</u> por* [NP]	*saw me running down* [NP]
estaria <u>a querer dizer</u>	*estaria <u>insinuando</u>*	*What was he implying*
a brincarem à apanhada	*brincavam de pegapega*	*playing tag*
*A Alexandra **perguntou-me***	*Alexandra **me perguntou***	*Alexandra asked me*
***há pessoas** que*	***tem gente** que*	*people*
***pessoas** que só querem comprar <u>selos</u>*	***gente** que só quer comprar <u>selo</u>*	*people who just want to buy stamps*
*se **hei-de** acender* [NP]	*se **devo** acender* [NP]	*whether I should turn on* [NP]
Não gosto que	*não gosto **do jeito** que*	*I don't like **the way** that*
*Talvez seja altura de **acabar***	*Talvez devêssemos **dar um xeque-mate** em*	*Perhaps we should call it a day*
*campo de girassóis **de pernas para o ar***	*campo de girassóis **de ponta-cabeça***	*inverted field of sunflowers*
*Dá **que** pensar*	*Dá **o que** pensar*	*Makes you think*
*em que era **mergulhado** em*	*sobre ser **jogado** em*	*being dunked in*
***queres** ficar sozinho com* [NP]	***você quer** ficar sozinho com* [NP]	*you want to be alone with* [NP]

Table 2: Examples of EP–BP contrasts of a syntactic nature

EP	BP	EN
Estamos <u>a falar de</u>	*Estamos <u>falando de</u>*	*We're talking* [NP] *here*
nunca mais me obrigaram a ir a [NP]	*não me fizeram ir mais a* [NP]	*didn't make me go to* [NP] *any more*
vou de [N(CO-clothes)]	*estou usando / estou com* [N(CO-clothes)]	*I'm wearing / I'm in* [N(CO-clothes)]
Já contei a [NP]	*Já botei* [NP] *a par de*	*I've put* [NP] *in the picture about*
ir ocupar [PRO-Poss] *lugar em*	*tomar* [PRO-Poss] *lugar em*	*go take* [PRO-Poss] *place in*
há alturas em que	*Tem hora* [ADV] *que*	*There are times*
as mulheres [ADV] *fazem coisas estranhas*	*mulher faz coisa estranha*	*women do funny things*

Table 3: Examples of EP–BP contrasts with insertions or SAL categories

as *We're talking [sitcom] here, didn't make me go to [Sunday School] any more, as mulheres [às vezes] fazem coisas estranhas*, or *Já botei [Hal] a par do problema*. According to the methodology described in (Barreiro and Batista, 2016) for translation, we have extracted all these insertions from the paraphrastic alignments and subsequently have assigned generic categories to these insertions, such as [NP] for noun phrase, [ADV] for adverb, [PRO-Poss] for possessive pronoun, and so on and so forth. In the derived generic grammars, extracted alignments are generalized by replacing dependents words with constituent variables such as NP and ADV, etc., or SAL categories. The reason for this, is that we want grammars to apply independently of the word (noun, adverb, pronoun, etc.) inserted. So, for example, instead of the proper name *Hal*, the grammar would still be able to transform the expression no matter which proper name would appear as an insertion. In other cases, we have defined semantico-syntactic (SAL) categories so that grammars apply to a certain group of words (See (Scott, 2003; Barreiro et al., 2011; Scott, 2018) for a description of SAL). For example, the English expressions *I'm wearing a suit* and *I'm in jeans and leather jacket* were found in the same sentence illustrated in example (7) in the e-PACT corpus with the EP translations *vou de fato* and *vou de jeans e blusão de cabedal*, and with the BP translations *estou usando um terno* and *estou com jeans e jaqueta de couro*. The use of the SAL category [N(CO-clothes)] ([**CO**ncrete noun + **clothes** that one can wear/dress]) for the noun *suit* and the coordinated nouns *jeans and leather jacket* and their corresponding translations in both EP and BP allows the grammar to apply the paraphrases with any noun or coordinated nouns that are classified with the same SAL category (e.g., *pants, dress, sweatshirt*, etc.).

(7) EN - ***I'm wearing** a suit myself today [...], but sometimes, when **I'm in** jeans and leather jacket*
EP - *Hoje também **vou de** fato [...] mas, às vezes, quando **vou de** jeans e blusão de cabedal*
BP - *Hoje **estou usando** um terno [...], mas às vezes, **estou com** jeans e jaqueta de couro*

7 Conclusions and Future Work

This paper describes the methodology to build a new linguistic resource of manual paraphrastic alignments representing multiwords and phrasal units in EP and BP collected from the e-PACT corpus. The

EP	BP	EN
*todos os problemas **que já tenho***	*todos os **meus** problemas*	*all my other problems*
***era mais normal que** tivesse ido para*	***normalmente** teria ido para*	*I would normally have gone into*
*Vou **fazer** uma pequena **cirurgia***	*Vou **ser operado**. Uma operação simples*	*I'm having a minor operation*
*ficar **naquelas** filas intermináveis*	*ficar **numa dessas** longas filas*	*stand in one of those long [] queues*
*fazerem o seu trabalho **o melhor possível***	*produzirem **o melhor que puderem***	*make it as good as it possibly can be*
*discotecas **duvidosas***	*discotecas **de reputação duvidosa***	*dubious discos*
***perto** de*	***nas imediações** de*	*near*
***não me cruzei com** ninguém*	***não vi** ninguém*	*I haven't seen anybody*
***coloquei** esta questão*	***levantei** essa questão*	*I raised this question*
***tem disponibilidade** para*	***fica livre** para*	*free to*
***fazer** teatro*	***atuar em peças de** teatro*	*do live theatre*
*não me **importo** de*	*eu não me **importaria** de*	*I wouldn't mind*
***Parti do princípio de** que*	***Imaginei** que*	*I assumed*
***que nem** um doido*	***como** um louco*	*like a drain*
***a maior parte** deles*	***a maioria** deles*	*most of them*

Table 4: Examples of stylist variants = paraphrases both possible in EP and BP

paraphrastic alignment can provide a sort of contrastive dictionary function after validation. We have illustrated a few cases of paraphrasing phenomena, but many more could be brought for reflection. Our main goal was to show how short paraphrastic variants can contribute to the development of a paraphraser that handles variety adaptation. This is a fertile research field that still needs to mature in order to bear fruit to enrich technological applications for language learning, writing and editing, among others.

A first observation to be made concerns the validation of the words, multiwords, phrases, expressions, structures and sentences of each variety that are taken into consideration in the paraphrastic alignments. Some ways of expression may vary according to the translator, the translator's experience or professional performance and be less related to the variety itself. For example, the use of the word *estúdio* with the meaning of *office* is questionable (context-specific knowledge is important). Normally, it refers only to an artist's work place, not a regular office. While the kind of corpora used may be a rich source of paraphrases, not all paraphrases are reliable, and some of them are not indicative of language variance.

We have targeted several morpho-syntactic alignment problems that have not been consistently considered up to now, such as the alignment of articles together with the nouns with zero articles, a solution for a significant number of gender and number agreement problems between an article, and a noun, or the alignment of the preposition with a noun in noun adjunct cases. Due to the extent of the work at hand, a large amount of paraphrastic phenomena was left undiscussed. A detailed analysis of these phenomena is important for the improvement of alignment techniques and for the enhancement of the quality of paraphrasing. One of the phenomenon that we are currently revisiting is the alignment of multiwords when there are contracted forms involved (Barreiro and Batista, 2018). Another one is the alignment of verbal constructions involving clitic pronouns (Rebelo and Barreiro, 2018 forthcoming). As we move along the development process of a manually aligned dataset and definition of a typology of linguistic phenomena, we wish to attempt an automated alignment tool.

Finally, it is worth noting that the computational tools available for alignment also present shortcomings and limitations. The process of collecting paraphrastic alignments is a far-reaching work that is far from complete. In future work, we envisage to create grammars from many of these contrasts that will use semantico-syntactic knowledge and apply to a larger number of cases whenever that is possible.

Acknowledgements

This work was supported by Fundação para a Ciência e a Tecnologia under project eSPERTo, with references EXPL/MHC-LIN/2260/2013 and UID/CEC/50021/2013. Anabela Barreiro was also funded by FCT through post-doctoral grant SFRH/BPD/91446 /2012. We would like to thank Ida Rebelo-Arnold for her interest in our paper as well as for her helpful comments and suggestions that contributed to improving the quality of our study.

References

Anabela Barreiro and Fernando Batista. 2016. Machine Translation of Non-Contiguous Multiword Units. In Wolfgang Maier, Sandra Kübler, and Constantin Orasan, editors, *Proceedings of the Workshop on Discontinuous Structures in Natural Language Processing*, DiscoNLP 2016, pages 22–30, San Diego, California, June. Association for Computational Linguistics (ACL).

Anabela Barreiro and Fernando Batista. 2018. Contractions: to align or not to align, that is the question. In Anabela Barreiro, Kristina Kocijan, Peter Machonis, and Max Silberztein, editors, *Proceedings of the COLING-Workshop on Linguistic Resources for NLP, New Mexico, USA,*

Anabela Barreiro and Cristina Mota. 2017. e-PACT: eSPERTo Paraphrase Aligned Corpus of EN-EP/BP Translations. *Tradução em Revista*, 1(22):87–102.

Anabela Barreiro, Luzia Wittmann, and Maria Pereira. 1996. Lexical differences between European and Brazilian Portuguese. *INESC Journal of Research and Development*, 5(2):75–101.

Anabela Barreiro, Bernard Scott, Walter Kasper, and Bernd Kiefer. 2011. OpenLogos Rule-Based Machine Translation: Philosophy, Model, Resources and Customization. *Machine Translation*, 25(2):107–126.

Anabela Barreiro, Francisco Raposo, and Tiago Luís. 2016. CLUE-Aligner: An Alignment Tool to Annotate Pairs of Paraphrastic and Translation Units. In Nicoletta Calzolari, Khalid Choukri, Thierry Declerck, Sara Goggi, Marko Grobelnik, Bente Maegaard, Joseph Mariani, Hélène Mazo, Asunción Moreno, Jan Odijk, and Stelios Piperidis, editors, *Proceedings of the 10th Edition of the Language Resources and Evaluation Conference*, LREC 2016, pages 7–13. European Language Resources Association.

Peter F. Brown, John Cocke, Stephen Della Pietra, Vincent J. Della Pietra, Frederick Jelinek, John D. Lafferty, Robert L. Mercer, and Paul S. Roossin. 1990. A Statistical Approach to Machine Translation. *Computational Linguistics*, 16(2):79–85.

João Graça, Joana Paulo Pardal, Luísa Coheur, and Diamantino Caseiro. 2008. Building a Golden Collection of Parallel Multi-Language Word Alignment. In Nicoletta Calzolari, Khalid Choukri, Bente Maegaard, Joseph Mariani, Jan Odjik, Stelios Piperidis, and Daniel Tapias, editors, *Proceedings of the 6th International Conference on Language Resources and Evaluation*, LREC 2008, pages 986–993, Marrakech, Morocco, May. European Language Resources Association.

Maurice Gross. 1984. Lexicon-grammar and the syntactic analysis of French. In *Proceedings of the 10th International Conference on Computational Linguistics and 22nd Annual Meeting of the Association for Computational Linguistics*, COLING 1984, pages 275–282, Stroudsburg, PA, USA. Association for Computational Linguistics.

Maurice Gross. 1987. The use of finite automata in the lexical representation of natural language. In Maurice Gross and Dominique Perrin, editors, *Electronic Dictionaries and Automata in Computational Linguistics*, volume 377 of *Lecture Notes in Computer Science*, pages 34–50. Springer.

Zellig Sabettai Harris. 1952. Discourse analysis. *Language*, 1(28):1–30.

Zellig Sabettai Harris. 1965. Transformational Theory. *Language*, 41(3):363–401.

Zellig Sabettai Harris. 1991. *A Theory of Language and Information: A Mathematical Approach*. Clarendon Press, Oxford.

Patrik Lambert, Adrià De Gispert, Rafael Banchs, and José B. Mariño. 2005. Guidelines for Word Alignment Evaluation and Manual Alignment. *Language Resources and Evaluation*, 39(4):267–285.

Belinda Maia, Rui Sousa Silva, Anabela Barreiro, and Cecília Fróis. 2008. N-grams in search of theories. In Barbara Lewandowska-Tomaszczyk, editor, *Corpus Linguistics, Computer Tools, and Applications - State of the Art*, volume 17, pages 71–84. Peter Lang.

Cristina Mota, Paula Carvalho, Francisco Raposo, and Anabela Barreiro. 2015. Generating Paraphrases of Human Intransitive Adjective Constructions with Port4NooJ. In Tatsiana Okrut, Yuras Hetsevich, Max Silberztein, and Hanna Stanislavenka, editors, *Automatic Processing of Natural Language Electronic Texts with NooJ - Selected Papers of the 9th International Conference*, Communications in Computer and Information Science, pages 107–122, Cham. Springer International Publishing.

Cristina Mota, Anabela Barreiro, Francisco Raposo, Ricardo Ribeiro, Sérgio Curto, and Luísa Coheur. 2016. eSPERTo's Paraphrastic Knowledge Applied to Question-Answering and Summarization. In Linda Barone, Mario Monteleone, and Max Silberztein, editors, *Automatic Processing of Natural Language Electronic Texts with NooJ - Selected Papers of the 10th International NooJ Conference*, Communications in Computer and Information Science, pages 208–220, Cham. Springer International Publishing.

Cristina Mota, Lucília Chacoto, and Anabela Barreiro. 2017. Integrating the lexicon-grammar of predicate nouns with support verb fazer into port4nooj. In Samir Mbarki, Mohammed Mourchid, and Max Silberztein, editors, *Formalizing Natural Languages with NooJ and Its Natural Language Processing Applications - Selected Papers of the 11th International Conference*, Communications in Computer and Information Science, pages 29–39, Cham. Springer International Publishing.

Cristina Mota, Jorge Baptista, and Anabela Barreiro. 2018. The Lexicon-Grammar of Portuguese Predicate Nouns with *ser de* in Port4NooJ. In Anabela Barreiro, Kristina Kocijan, Peter Machonis, and Max Silberztein, editors, *Formalising Natural Languages With Nooj and Its Natural Language Processing Applications - Selected Papers of the 11th International Conference*, Communications in Computer and Information Science, pages –, Cham. Springer International Publishing.

Franz Josef Och and Hermann Ney. 2000. Improved Statistical Alignment Models. In *Proceedings of the 38th Annual Meeting on Association for Computational Linguistics*, ACL 2000, pages 440–447, Stroudsburg, PA, USA. Association for Computational Linguistics.

Ida Rebelo and Anabela Barreiro. 2018 (forthcoming). EP–BP Paraphrastic Alignments of Verbal Constructions Involving the Clitic Pronoun *lhe*. In *International Conference on Computational Processing of Portuguese*, PROPOR 2018. Springer.

Diana Santos. 2014. Como estudar variantes do português e, ao mesmo tempo, construir um português internacional? Presentation at Contact, Variation and Change: corpora development and analysis of Iberoromance language varieties workhop.

Diana Santos. 2015. Portuguese language identity in the world: adventures and misadventures of an international language. In Elizaveta Khachaturyan, editor, *Language - Nation - Identity: The questione della lingua in an Italian and non-Italian context*, pages 31–54. Cambridge Scholars Publishing.

Bernard Scott. 2003. The logos model: An historical perspective. *Machine Translation*, 18(1):1–72, March.

Bernard Scott. 2018. *Translation, Brains and the Computer: A Neurolinguistic Solution to Ambiguity and Complexity in Machine Translation*. Machine Translation: Technologies and Applications. Springer International Publishing.

Jörg Tiedemann. 2003. Combining Clues for Word Alignment. In Ann Copestake and Jan Hajic, editors, *Proceedings of the 10th Conference of the European Chapter of the Association for Computational Linguistics*, EACL 2003, pages 339–346, Budapest, Hungary.

Jörg Tiedemann. 2011. *Bitext Alignment*. Synthesis digital library of engineering and computer science. Morgan & Claypool.

Luzia Wittmann, Ricardo Ribeiro, Tânia Pêgo, and Fernando Batista. 2000. Some Language Resources and Tools for Computational Processing of Portuguese at INESC . In Maria Gavrilidou, George Carayannis, Stella Markantonatou, Stelios Piperidis, and Gregory Stainhauer, editors, *Proceedings of the Second International Conference on Language Resources and Evaluation*, LREC 2000, pages 347–350, Athens – Greece.

Character Level Convolutional Neural Network
for Arabic Dialect Identification

Mohamed Ali
Cairo University, Egypt
`mohamedali@aucegypt.edu`

Abstract

This paper presents the systems submitted by the safina team to the Arabic Dialect Identification (ADI) shared task at the VarDial Evaluation Campaign 2018. The ADI shared task included five Arabic dialects: Modern Standard Arabic (MSA), Egyptian, Gulf, Levantine, and North-African. The proposed approach is to use character-level convolution neural network in addition to dialect embedding vectors, a low dimensional representation extracted from linguistic features, to distinguish the 5 dialects. We submitted three models with the same architecture except for the first layer. The first system uses one-hot character representation as input to the convolution layer. The second system uses an embedding layer before the convolution layer. The third system uses a recurrent layer before the convolution layer. The best results were obtained using the third model achieving 57.6% F1-score, ranked the second among six teams.[1]

1   Introduction

In the Arab world, several varieties of the Arabic language are co-existing together. Those varieties include Modern Standard Arabic (MSA), and many regional dialects as Egyptian, Gulf, Levantine and North-African dialects . Arabic Dialect Identification task is concerned with identifying the specific Arabic dialect in spoken and written forms which is a crucial task in many Natural Language Processing (NLP) applications.

In this paper we present the safina team submission for the 2018 ADI shared task which was organized as a part of Vardial Evaluation Campaign 2018 (Zampieri et al., 2018). We have used character-level Convolutional Neural Network approach to identify Arabic dialects using both lexical and dialect embedding features. Our team ranked the second with F1-weighted score 57.59%.

2   Related Work

Research in Arabic Dialect Identification took two tracks: spoken dialect identification and written dialect identification. For spoken dialect identification, Biadsy et al. (2009) described a system that can identify the Arabic dialect from a spoken text using acoustic features. In a later research, authors examined the role of prosodic features in identifying the speaker dialect and reported that using prosodic features showed a significant improvement over using phonotatcic-approach alone.

On the other hand, more research took place for written text dialect identification. Elfardy and Diab (2013) used word level labels to derive sentence-level features then used those features to label the sentence with the appropriate dialect. Zaidan and Callison-Burch (2014) used an annotated dialectal data set called Arabic On-line Commentary (AOC) for training a system to identify the dialect of an Arabic sentence. Later and using the same data set, Tillmann et al. (2014) used word-based binary features to

---

[1]The code for our submissions is available at: https://github.com/bigoooh/adi

This work is licensed under a Creative Commons Attribution 4.0 International License. License details: http://creativecommons.org/licenses/by/4.0/.

Proceedings of the Fifth Workshop on NLP for Similar Languages, Varieties and Dialects, pages 122–127
Santa Fe, New Mexico, USA, August 20, 2018.

train a linear support vector machine classifier to distinguish between the Egyptian dialect and MSA. Darwish et al. (2014) showed that the data in AOC corpus has some homogeneity as it is drawn from singular sources. This homogeneity would prevent models trained on this data from generalizing to unseen topics. Darwish et al. (2014) found that character-based n-grams outperformed word-based n-grams to distinguish between Egyptian dialect and MSA.

Ali et al. (2016) combined acoustic features with lexical features obtained from a speech recognition system which yield to a classifier stronger than classifiers that use acoustic-only or lexical-only features. In 2016, ADI appeared as a subtask of the Discriminating between Similar Languages (DSL) shared task. The data set in this subtask was a transcribed speech in MSA and in four dialects (Ali et al., 2016): Egyptian (EGY), Gulf (GLF), Levantine (LAV), and North African (NOR). Most of the teams in this subtask used character n-grams and the best result achieved using the support vector machine classifier over character n-grams (1-7) (Çöltekin and Rama, 2016). Belinkov and Glass (2016) used character-level convolution neural network, the same approach we are using, but they only used the ASR transcripts of Arabic speech as the acoustic features were not available at that time. Also, they did not experiment using a recurrent layer as an embedding layer which showed an improvement in our system. In 2017 ADI Shared Task, data set contained the original audio files and some low-level audio features, called i-vectors, along with the ASR transcripts of Arabic speech collected from the Broadcast News domain. Best result in this subtask achieved using a Kernel Discriminant Analysis (KDA) classifier trained on multiple kernel functions over character n-grams and the i-vectors features (Ionescu and Butnaru, 2017).

3   Methodology and Data

3.1   Character-Level Convolutional Neural Network

Convolutional Neural Networks (CNN) were invented to deal with images and it have achieved excellent results in computer vision (Krizhevsky et al., 2012; Sermanet et al., 2013; Ji et al., 2013). Later, it have been applied in Natural Language Processing (NLP) tasks and outperformed traditional models such as bag of words, n-grams and their TFIDF variants (Collobert and Weston, 2008; Zhang et al., 2015). The architecture, shown in Figure 1, describes the character-level CNN model we have used in identifying the Arabic dialects. We formulate the task as a multi-class classification problem. Given the ASR transcript $t^{(i)}$, 600-dimensional dialect embedding feature vectors $v^{(i)}$ and the corresponding label $l^{(i)}$, we need to predict l using v and t. We designed a neural network classifier that takes as input both the transcript as one-hot encoded array of characters (padded or truncated to match a predefined maximum length) and the corresponding dialect embedding feature vector. As shown in Figure 1, the transcript text goes through the convolution layer then a softmax layer while the embedding vector goes directly to another softmax layer. The network final output is the average of the two softmax layers and it represents the probability distribution over the 5 Arabic dialects. The network layers are as follows:

- **Input Layer:** mapping each character to one-hot vector.

- Optional **Embedding or Recurrent Layer :** using embedding or GRU recurrent layer to capture the context of the character (Chung et al., 2014).

- **Convolutional Layer:** contains multiple filter widths and feature maps which is applied to a window of characters to produce new features. Each convolution is followed by a Rectified Linear Unit (ReLU) nonlinearity and batch-normalization layers (Glorot et al., 2011; Ioffe and Szegedy, 2015).

- **Max-Pooling Layer:** apply max-over-time pooling operation over the feature map of each filter and take the maximum value as a feature for this filter (Collobert et al., 2011). The max-pooling operation is followed by a dropout layer to prevent over-fitting (Srivastava et al., 2014).

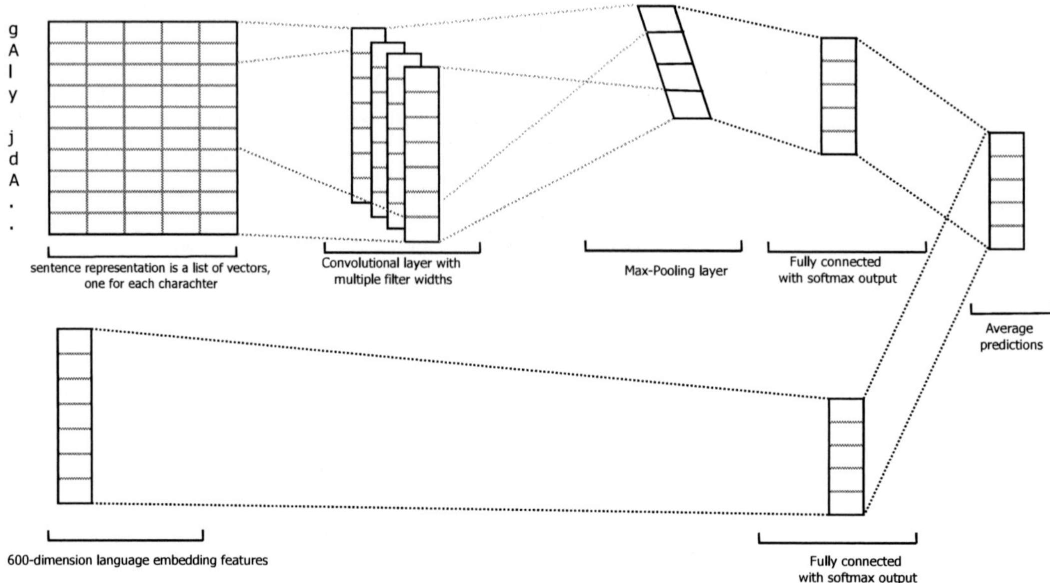

Figure 1: Character-level CNN architecture

- **Softmax Layers**: there are two softmax layers, one for lexical features and another for the embedding features.

- **Output Layer**:the final output is the average of the two softmax layers' output and it represents the probability distribution over the labels.

Depending on our cross-validation results we used the following parameters for the neural network architecture:

- **Sentence maximum length:** 256 characters

- **Embedding length:**128

- **GRU layer unites:**128 units

- **Convolution filters sizes:** from 2 to 8

- **Convolution filters feature maps:** 256 feature map for each filter

- **Dropout rate:** 0.2

In our implementation, we used Keras framework with TensorFlow as a backend (Chollet and others, 2015; Abadi et al., 2015).

3.2 Data

The ADI shared task data set contains four sets of features for 14591 utterances for training and 1566 utterances for validation (Ali et al., 2016):

- **Raw audio wave files:** contains the audio recordings at 16Khz segmented to remove speaker overlaps and non-speech parts as music or background noise

- **ASR transcripts:** generated by a multi-dialect Arabic Large Vocabulary Speech Recognition (LVCSR) system

- **Dialect Embedding Features:** 600-dimensional dialect embeddings for each utterance. These features were extracted from linguistic features using Siamese neural network approach (Shon et al., 2018).

- **Phonetic Features:** contains phoneme sequence as output of four different speech recognizers (Czech, Hungarian, Russian and English).

In our experiments, we have used only the ASR transcripts and the dialect embedding features.

4   Results

4.1   Cross-Validation Results

We combined the training data and the validation data provided by the shared task to apply 5-fold cross validation. We tested our three different configurations in addition to a TF-IDF features based classifier, Logistic Regression classifier implemented in scikit-learn toolkit (Pedregosa et al., 2011), as a baseline. Results are shown in Table 1.

System	Accuracy
Logistic Regression using TF-IDF features	0.5898
CNN with one-hot encoded input	0.9214
CNN with an embedding layer	0.9262
CNN with a GRU recurrent layer	**0.9264**

Table 1: Cross-validation results

4.2   Test Set Results

Our submission results are shown in Table 2. We have used the same configuration for three runs except for the input to the convolution layer. In the first run, we fed the one-hot encoded vectors for the sequence of characters directly to the convolution layer. In the second run, we fed the one-hot encoded vectors to an embedding layer before the convolution layer. In the third run, we fed the one-hot encoded vectors to a GRU recurrent layer before the convolution layer. As shown in the results, using a recurrent layer achieved a slightly better results than feeding the one-hot encoded representation directly to the convolution layer. However, the cost of this slight enhancement was huge in the training time as training the network with recurrent layers took about ten times the period of training the network without the recurrent layer. As shown in the confusion matrix in Figure 2 In the ADI shared task evaluation, the submitted systems were ranked according to it F1-weighted score. Our team ranked the second with F1-weighted score 57.59%. Figure 2 shows the confusion matrix for our best run. From the matrix, we can see that Gulf dialect is the most confusing one; it is highly recognized as Levantine dialect. Also, the Levantine dialect is highly recognized as North African dialect.

System	F1 (macro)
Random Baseline	0.1995
CNN with one-hot encoded input	0.5711
CNN with an embedding layer	0.5697
CNN with a GRU recurrent layer	**0.5759**

Table 2: Our three runs results, the best run in bold

5   Conclusion

In this work, we presented our team's three submissions for the ADI shared task. Our approach is to use Character level CNN as a feature extractor from text in addition to the dialect embedding features extracted from text. Our best submission achieved by using a GRU recurrent layer as an embedding

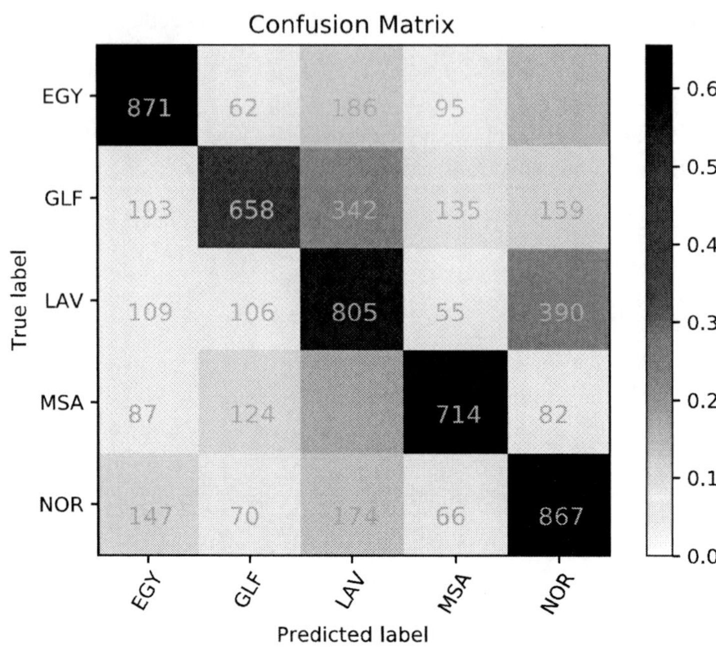

Figure 2: Confusion matrix for "CNN with a GRU recurrent layer" run

layer before the convolutional layer. However, the gain of using the recurrent layer was minor compared to the cost of the long time used for training a network with a recurrent layer compared to that for a network with a regular embedding layer.

References

Martín Abadi, Ashish Agarwal, Paul Barham, Eugene Brevdo, Zhifeng Chen, Craig Citro, Greg S. Corrado, Andy Davis, Jeffrey Dean, Matthieu Devin, Sanjay Ghemawat, Ian Goodfellow, Andrew Harp, Geoffrey Irving, Michael Isard, Yangqing Jia, Rafal Jozefowicz, Lukasz Kaiser, Manjunath Kudlur, Josh Levenberg, Dandelion Mané, Rajat Monga, Sherry Moore, Derek Murray, Chris Olah, Mike Schuster, Jonathon Shlens, Benoit Steiner, Ilya Sutskever, Kunal Talwar, Paul Tucker, Vincent Vanhoucke, Vijay Vasudevan, Fernanda Viégas, Oriol Vinyals, Pete Warden, Martin Wattenberg, Martin Wicke, Yuan Yu, and Xiaoqiang Zheng. 2015. Tensor-Flow: Large-scale machine learning on heterogeneous systems. Software available from tensorflow.org.

Ahmed Ali, Najim Dehak, Patrick Cardinal, Sameer Khurana, Sree Harsha Yella, James Glass, Peter Bell, and Steve Renals. 2016. Automatic Dialect Detection in Arabic Broadcast Speech. In *Proceedings of INTER-SPEECH*, pages 2934–2938.

Yonatan Belinkov and James Glass. 2016. A Character-level Convolutional Neural Network for Distinguishing Similar Languages and Dialects. In *Proceedings of the Third Workshop on NLP for Similar Languages, Varieties and Dialects (VarDial3)*, pages 145–152, Osaka, Japan.

Fadi Biadsy, Julia Hirschberg, and Nizar Habash. 2009. Spoken arabic dialect identification using phonotactic modeling. In *Proceedings of the eacl 2009 workshop on computational approaches to semitic languages*, pages 53–61. Association for Computational Linguistics.

Çağri Çöltekin and Taraka Rama. 2016. Discriminating Similar Languages with Linear SVMs and Neural Networks. In *Proceedings of the Third Workshop on NLP for Similar Languages, Varieties and Dialects (VarDial3)*, pages 15–24, Osaka, Japan.

François Chollet et al. 2015. Keras. https://keras.io.

Junyoung Chung, Caglar Gulcehre, KyungHyun Cho, and Yoshua Bengio. 2014. Empirical evaluation of gated recurrent neural networks on sequence modeling. *arXiv preprint arXiv:1412.3555*.

Ronan Collobert and Jason Weston. 2008. A unified architecture for natural language processing: Deep neural networks with multitask learning. In *Proceedings of the 25th international conference on Machine learning*, pages 160–167. ACM.

Ronan Collobert, Jason Weston, Léon Bottou, Michael Karlen, Koray Kavukcuoglu, and Pavel Kuksa. 2011. Natural language processing (almost) from scratch. *Journal of Machine Learning Research*, 12(Aug):2493–2537.

Kareem Darwish, Hassan Sajjad, and Hamdy Mubarak. 2014. Verifiably effective arabic dialect identification. In *Proceedings of the 2014 Conference on Empirical Methods in Natural Language Processing (EMNLP)*, pages 1465–1468.

Heba Elfardy and Mona Diab. 2013. Sentence level dialect identification in arabic. In *Proceedings of the 51st Annual Meeting of the Association for Computational Linguistics (Volume 2: Short Papers)*, volume 2, pages 456–461.

Xavier Glorot, Antoine Bordes, and Yoshua Bengio. 2011. Deep sparse rectifier neural networks. In *Proceedings of the Fourteenth International Conference on Artificial Intelligence and Statistics*, pages 315–323.

Sergey Ioffe and Christian Szegedy. 2015. Batch normalization: Accelerating deep network training by reducing internal covariate shift. *arXiv preprint arXiv:1502.03167*.

Radu Tudor Ionescu and Andrei Butnaru. 2017. Learning to identify arabic and german dialects using multiple kernels. In *Proceedings of the Fourth Workshop on NLP for Similar Languages, Varieties and Dialects (VarDial)*, pages 200–209, Valencia, Spain, April.

Shuiwang Ji, Wei Xu, Ming Yang, and Kai Yu. 2013. 3d convolutional neural networks for human action recognition. *IEEE transactions on pattern analysis and machine intelligence*, 35(1):221–231.

Alex Krizhevsky, Ilya Sutskever, and Geoffrey E Hinton. 2012. Imagenet classification with deep convolutional neural networks. In *Advances in neural information processing systems*, pages 1097–1105.

F. Pedregosa, G. Varoquaux, A. Gramfort, V. Michel, B. Thirion, O. Grisel, M. Blondel, P. Prettenhofer, R. Weiss, V. Dubourg, J. Vanderplas, A. Passos, D. Cournapeau, M. Brucher, M. Perrot, and E. Duchesnay. 2011. Scikit-learn: Machine learning in Python. *Journal of Machine Learning Research*, 12:2825–2830.

Pierre Sermanet, David Eigen, Xiang Zhang, Michaël Mathieu, Rob Fergus, and Yann LeCun. 2013. Overfeat: Integrated recognition, localization and detection using convolutional networks. *arXiv preprint arXiv:1312.6229*.

Suwon Shon, Ahmed Ali, and James Glass. 2018. Convolutional neural network and language embeddings for end-to-end dialect recognition. In *Proc. Odyssey 2018 The Speaker and Language Recognition Workshop*, pages 98–104.

Nitish Srivastava, Geoffrey Hinton, Alex Krizhevsky, Ilya Sutskever, and Ruslan Salakhutdinov. 2014. Dropout: A simple way to prevent neural networks from overfitting. *The Journal of Machine Learning Research*, 15(1):1929–1958.

Christoph Tillmann, Saab Mansour, and Yaser Al-Onaizan. 2014. Improved sentence-level arabic dialect classification. In *Proceedings of the First Workshop on Applying NLP Tools to Similar Languages, Varieties and Dialects*, pages 110–119.

Omar F Zaidan and Chris Callison-Burch. 2014. Arabic dialect identification. *Computational Linguistics*, 40(1):171–202.

Marcos Zampieri, Shervin Malmasi, Preslav Nakov, Ahmed Ali, Suwon Shon, James Glass, Yves Scherrer, Tanja Samardžić, Nikola Ljubešić, Jörg Tiedemann, Chris van der Lee, Stefan Grondelaers, Nelleke Oostdijk, Antal van den Bosch, Ritesh Kumar, Bornini Lahiri, and Mayank Jain. 2018. Language Identification and Morphosyntactic Tagging: The Second VarDial Evaluation Campaign. In *Proceedings of the Fifth Workshop on NLP for Similar Languages, Varieties and Dialects (VarDial)*, Santa Fe, USA.

Xiang Zhang, Junbo Zhao, and Yann LeCun. 2015. Character-level convolutional networks for text classification. In *Advances in neural information processing systems*, pages 649–657.

Neural Network Architectures for Arabic Dialect Identification

Elise Michon, Minh Quang Pham, Josep Crego, Jean Senellart

SYSTRAN / 5 rue Feydeau, 75002 Paris, France
`firstname.lastname@systrangroup.com`

Abstract

SYSTRAN competes this year for the first time to the DSL shared task, in the Arabic Dialect Identification subtask. We participate by training several Neural Network models showing that we can obtain competitive results despite the limited amount of training data available for learning. We report our experiments and detail the network architecture and parameters of our 3 runs: our best performing system consists in a Multi-Input CNN that learns separate embeddings for lexical, phonetic and acoustic input features (F1: 0.5289); we also built a CNN-biLSTM network aimed at capturing both spatial and sequential features directly from speech spectrograms (F1: 0.3894 at submission time, F1: 0.4235 with later found parameters); and finally a system relying on binary CNN-biLSTMs (F1: 0.4339).

1 Introduction

Dialect identification (DID) consists in automatically identifying the corresponding dialect of an utterance, either written or spoken. This task is a particularly challenging case of language identification since dialects are closely related languages. It is not only useful but often a requirement for various Natural Language Processing (NLP) tasks such as Machine Translation (MT) or Automatic Speech Recognition (ASR). In the context of the shared task *Discriminating between Similar Languages, Varieties and Dialects (DSL)*, dialect identification can be seen as a multi-class sentence classification problem, in which participants must predict a label for each sentence, given several features describing the sentence.

We present our results for the Arabic Dialect Identification (ADI) subtask, where the similar languages to discriminate are Modern Standard Arabic and four dialects of Arabic: Egyptian, Gulf, Levantine and North African. Given their high success in many other NLP tasks and lower cost in feature engineering compared to more traditional machine learning methods, in this paper we mostly focus on the design of suitable Neural Networks, knowing that the limited size of the training dataset is a well known handicap for such models as already pointed out in previous editions of the DSL workshop.

2 Related Work

Arabic speakers are used to write in Modern Standard Arabic and express orally with Arabic dialects. Although closely related, dialects differ lexically, morphologically, phonetically and prosodically. Recently, the increasing use of social media has seen the rise of spoken and written materials with Arabic dialects, which motivates related NLP tasks such as Arabic Dialect Identification (Zaidan and Callison-Burch, 2014). To tackle this challenge, from 2016 the DSL shared task has proposed an ADI subtask with multi-dialectal Arabic data based on audio files accompanied with dialect labels. Best performances have so far been reached by Support Vector Machine (SVM), Kernel Ridge Regression (KRR), and sophistications of these traditional classifiers like ensemble methods. However, in this section we focus on describing the performance of neural networks in previous editions.

In 2016 (Malmasi et al., 2016), the data represented each utterance using a transcription in words obtained using the ASR engine described in (Ali et al., 2014). The best performing systems obtained F1

This work is licensed under a Creative Commons Attribution 4.0 International Licence. Licence details: http://creativecommons.org/licenses/by/4.0/.

Proceedings of the Fifth Workshop on NLP for Similar Languages, Varieties and Dialects, pages 128–136
Santa Fe, New Mexico, USA, August 20, 2018.

scores ranging from 0.495 to 0.513. Three teams reported experiments with neural network architectures that were finally not submitted as their models following other machine learning methods obtained higher accuracy scores, QCRI (Eldesouki et al., 2016), GW_ LT3 (Zirikly et al., 2016) and tufbasfs (Çöltekin and Rama, 2016). Two teams submitted systems training neural networks: the team cgli competed using a character-level Convolutional Neural Network (CNN) with the combination of filters 3*128, 4*128, 5*128 (convention adopted throughout the whole article: filter size*number of filters) inspired from (Kim, 2014) which gave a macro F1 score of 0.433. They also reported in their paper a Long-Short Term Memory network (LSTM) with pre-compiled word embeddings giving as F1 score 0.423 after bug correction (Guggilla, 2016). The team mitsls used another character-level CNN architecture based on (Kim et al., 2016) using filters of increasing size 1*50, 2*50, 3*100, 4*100, 5*100, 6*100, 7*100 which gave a better F1 score 0.483 and ranked 2nd in the competition (Belinkov and Glass, 2016).

Character-level CNNs present the advantage to be fast and able to learn local representations, which can be likened to char n-grams features successfully used by SVMs. One reason advanced by (Sadat et al., 2014) for the efficiency of character-level representations for Arabic Dialect Identification in speech transcription is that a great part of the variation between Arabic dialects is based on their affixes. However, as noticed by the organisers, Arabic speakers distinguish Arabic dialects not only according to words but also on the basis of speech cues absent from written transcripts. So for the DSL shared task 2017 (Zampieri et al., 2017), the ADI dataset contained twice more utterances than in 2016 and not only speech transcriptions but also acoustic features corresponding to sentences, namely i-vectors modelled on bottleneck features extracted from an ASR-Deep Neural Network as described in (Ali et al., 2016). This time the only team submitting neural networks, deepCybErNetRun, competed with a bidirectional Long Short Term Memory network (biLSTM) on words (F1: 0.208) and a biLSTM on i-vectors (F1: 0.574) but did not publish any description paper. Their lower performance compared to the best system of the competition, achieving a F1 score of 0.763, in this subtask and other subtasks of the challenge led to the conclusion that the size of the DSL data was insufficient for tuning the numerous parameters of a neural network.

3 Methodology and Data

3.1 Data description

This 2018 edition saw the apparition of phonetic features in addition to lexical and acoustic features, to represent sentences with finer-grained information. Furthermore, end-to-end deep learning approaches based on Mel-Frequency Cepstrum Coefficients (MFCCs) or spectrograms recently proved to provide better acoustic representation for dialect identification than previously used i-vectors. Thus this year ADI's dataset contained: word transcripts in Buckwalter by an ASR system; phone transcripts according to 4 phoneme recognisers (Czech, English, Hungarian, Russian) from Brno University of Technology including phonemes and non-phonetic units (*int* for intermittent noise, *pau* for short pause and *spk* for non-speech speaker noise); and 600-size acoustic embeddings extracted as the last fully-connected layer before the softmax layer in an end-to-end CNN system trained for audio dialect identification, all detailed in (Shon et al., 2018).

Acoustic embeddings released for the challenge were trained only on the train set to enable participants to use the dev set for parameter tuning, while acoustic embeddings from the system reported in (Shon et al., 2018) were trained on the train and dev set, leading to an increase in performance, and were made available after submission date. Two test datasets were released as a single one during the testing phase, and were later made available separately: one is the test set from the MGB-3 challenge made of extracts of multi-domain Youtube videos (Ali et al., 2017), the other is a Youtube surprise test dataset. The distribution of the 5 dialects Egyptian (EGY), Gulf (GLF), Levantine (LAV), Modern Standard Arabic (MSA) and North African (NOR) in the datasets is shown in Table 1.

We note a few facts about word transcripts: first, transcription is empty for a significant proportion of the sentences as reported in Table 1. For some audio files, the sentence is truly barely intelligible whereas for others, the sentence is clear but the sound file seems to have a lower volume. Second, word transcripts tend to contain less unknown words compared to previous years but many words are missing from the

Dialect		EGY	GLF	LAV	MSA	NOR	Total
Number of utterances	train	3177	2873	3117	2219	3205	14591
	dev	315	265	348	238	355	1566
	MGB-3 test	302	250	334	262	344	1492
	Youtube test	1143	1147	1131	944	980	5345
Empty word transcripts (%)	train	2.90	5.78	5.68	0.50	10.58	5.38
	dev	5.71	2.26	6.03	1.06	2.54	3.64
	MGB-3 test	1.66	1.20	1.50	0.00	1.45	1.21
	Youtube test	4.37	2.09	12.82	1.06	8.47	5.84

Table 1: Distribution of dialects and percentage of empty word transcripts in 2018 ADI datasets.

transcription. Finally, transcriptions seem dominated by MSA, with some dialectal phrases transcribed as MSA sequences.

This encouraged us towards methods directly leveraging acoustic information. We considered log-amplitude mel-spectrograms as an alternative acoustic representation computed on audio files thanks to the python library Librosa (McFee et al., 2015), resulting in an input shape of sequence length x 40. Nevertheless, inspection of the audio data reveals some inconsistencies in the attribution of the labels, sometimes based on the speaker, sometimes on the spoken dialect: for instance, some extracts where an Egyptian speaker is speaking Modern Standard Arabic are categorised as EGY, other similar ones are categorised as MSA (e.g. interviewed speaker in the news). Code-switching between dialectal Arabic and Modern Standard Arabic is also found to be common, especially in the EGY, GLF and LAV dialects. We finally noticed that some of the audio files were duplicates (e.g. up to 6% of the train set for North African dialect).

3.2 System description

As already outlined, previous editions of the ADI subtask showed how more traditional classifiers, like SVM or KRR, outperformed neural network approaches. In this edition, SYSTRAN participates by training several neural network models to show that we can also obtain competitive results compared to such classifiers. We are mostly interested in how neural networks perform for this task, due to their ability to learn adequate representation for the data. Not only do we investigate multi-input systems making the most of the various features on the sentences given in the challenge, but also end-to-end systems directly working on acoustic representation of speech data.

3.2.1 SVM

In order to compare traditional machine learning and neural network approaches, we trained a multi-class Support Vector Machine (SVM) classifier using a radial basis function. We used the freely available LIBSVM[1] software (Chang and Lin, 2011).

3.2.2 Multi-Input CNN (run 1)

Our search for a simple and fast architecture to independently learn input embeddings of different type and combine them oriented us towards the Multi Group Convolutional Neural Network, also called Multi-Input CNN (Zhang et al., 2016). Initially designed to join different word embeddings, these models allow the input embeddings to come from various sources and not to share the same dimensionality.

Therefore, our first run is a Multi-Input CNN that we tailored to take as input the lexical, phonetic and acoustic data proposed for the challenge: it independently learns char embeddings and 4 phone embeddings by running convolutions with various filter sizes, respectively char-level convolutions on word transcripts and phone-level convolutions on phone transcripts. Then it concatenates the 5 resulting embeddings and the given acoustic embeddings for the sentences, adds fully-connected layers and finally predicts the dialect. We implemented the model in Keras (Chollet and others, 2015) with Tensorflow back-end and made the code freely available[2].

---

[1]https://www.csie.ntu.edu.tw/~cjlin/libsvm/
[2]https://github.com/elisemicho/multi_input_classification

3.2.3   CNN-biLSTM (run 2)

In an attempt to improve the classification by better controlling the extracted acoustic features, we also decided to design and test several configurations of end-to-end neural networks taking as input acoustic representations of audio files and as output the dialect label. Motivated by their good performance in Music Classification (Choi et al., 2017) and Language Identification (Ganapathy et al., 2014), we chose CNN to slide over the sequence and learn representations of the signal. CNN are efficient in terms of locally representing information, but speech data are also sequences where earlier or later information can provide context for the current window. Therefore the combination of a Recurrent Neural Network (RNN) such as LSTM or Gated Recurrent Units network (GRU) to summarise temporal patterns after a CNN enables to capture both spatial and sequential features: (Choi et al., 2017) outperformed several CNN-only architectures by using a 4-layer CNN with 2D filters of size [3,3] followed by a RNN with GRU. Similarly in (Bartz et al., 2017), a 2D CNN with filters of decreasing size in increasing number [7,7]*16, [5,5]*32, [3,3]*64, [3,3]*128, [3,3]*256 followed by a biLSTM led to promising improvement for smaller dataset compared to similar CNN.

Hence, our second run is a CNN-biLSTM neural network that we designed to take as input the log-amplitude mel-spectrograms obtained on the original audio files: layers of one-dimension convolutions with decreasing filter sizes but increasing number of filters compose the CNN part of the system. A bidirectional LSTM layer then takes its result and the initial sequence lengths of the signal to link the current window with previous and next windows in the sequence, and outputs a final prediction of the dialect. Our implementation used TensorFlow (Abadi et al., 2015) and its code is freely available[3].

3.2.4   Binary classification with CNN-biLSTM (run 3)

Our third run is a system using 5 CNN-biLSTM neural networks of the type previously described (run 2) that we adapted to perform binary classification (one dialect against the others). For each utterance, the network predicting that it belongs to its positive class with the highest probability wins the final decision:

$$class(utterance) = argmax_{i \in \{1,..,5\}} P(1|net_i, utterance)$$

4   Results

We present the results of our three runs in Table 2. Comparable to our SVM results (0.5270), our Multi-Input CNN achieves the highest F1 score of 0.5289, in line with other participants this year and ranking 3rd in the competition. Contrary to our expectations, our CNN-biLSTM directly operating on audio data failed to learn better acoustic representations for dialect identification with a F1 score of 0.3894. However, using CNN-biLSTMs for binary classification and taking the maximum probability improved the performance to 0.4339. Both test sets come from Youtube videos, but all our systems performed notably better on MGB-3 test set, which is of much smaller size. As for the classification results of our best run summarised in Figure 1, the biggest error rate is for Levantine utterances often predicted to belong to North African dialect, whereas these dialects are neither geographically nor typologically close.

System	F1 (macro) on test sets		
	MGB-3	Youtube	Total
Random Baseline			0.1995
SVM	**0.5632**	0.5143	0.5270
Multi-input CNN (run 1)	0.5552	**0.5186**	**0.5289**
CNN-biLSTM (run 2)	0.4380	0.3711	0.3894
Binary CNN-biLSTMs (run3)	0.4600	0.4241	0.4339

Table 2: Results for the ADI task (macro-averaged F1 scores).

In the following subsections, we report our tests to tune the different models, placing a greater emphasis on Neural Networks. We also examine how the provided features, the various refinements or the model elements perform separately and in combination.

---

[3]`https://github.com/elisemicho/escolta`

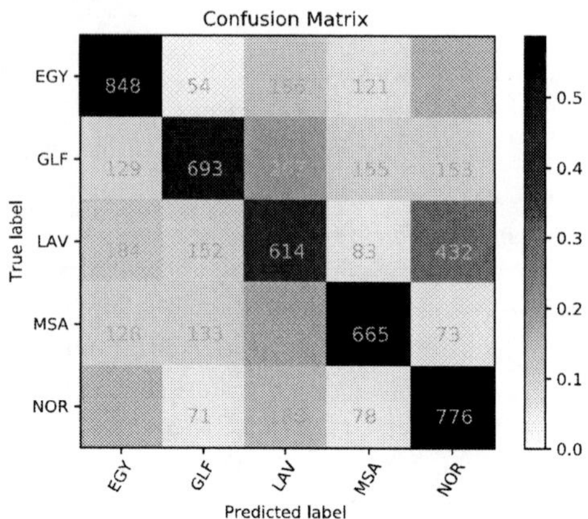

Figure 1: Confusion Matrix for Multi-Input CNN (run 1).

4.1 SVM

In Table 3 we present F1 scores we obtained with SVMs using only one or a combination of the features. Classification with lexical features gives better results (F1: 0.4502) than with phonetic features (F1: 0.2891), but classification with acoustic features only (F1: 0.5239) outperforms them both. Acoustic features therefore seem the most useful representation of the data for this dialect identification task. The combinations of features only achieve slightly higher results (F1: 0.5270), and not for the MGB-3 test set. The new acoustic embeddings trained on train and dev sets (released after submission date) further enhance performance up to 0.5905.

Model	Test sets		
	MGB-3	**Youtube**	**Total**
Only lexical features	0.4493	0.4494	0.4502
Only phonetic features	0.3035	0.2839	0.2891
Only acoustic features	**0.5656**	0.5097	0.5239
Lexical + acoustic features	0.5630	0.5138	0.5267
Lexical + phonetic + acoustic features	0.5632	**0.5143**	**0.5270**
Only new acoustic features	0.7334	0.5379	0.5823
Lexical + new acoustic features	0.7350	0.5439	0.5873
Lexical + phonetic + new acoustic features	**0.7376**	**0.5470**	**0.5905**

Table 3: Results of the SVM models (macro-averaged F1 scores).

4.2 Multi-Input CNN (run 1)

Model	Test sets		
	MGB-3	**Youtube**	**Total**
Only lexical features	0.2988	0.3635	0.3505
Only phonetic features	0.3347	0.3251	0.3307
Only acoustic features	0.5495	0.5100	0.5209
Lexical + acoustic features	0.5483	0.5075	0.5184
Lexical + phonetic + acoustic features (run 1)	**0.5552**	**0.5186**	**0.5289**
Only new acoustic features	**0.7260**	0.5363	**0.5791**
Lexical + new acoustic features	0.7105	**0.5374**	0.5767
Lexical + phonetic + new acoustic features	0.7212	0.5258	0.5697

Table 4: Results of the Multi-Input CNN models (macro-averaged F1 scores).

We selected as our best configuration for Multi-Input CNN char embeddings and phone embeddings of size 32, learnt separately through 1D convolutions with filters [5*8, 3*8] (filter size*number), *tanh* activation function, dropout 0.5 and global max-pooling; then once concatenated, one fully-connected layer of size 32, ReLu activation function, dropout 0.5. We achieve the best accuracy on dev set after 7 epochs, but we note that on the train set the loss is already very low and the accuracy very high from the beginning of the 2nd epoch, signalling probable overfitting. Our tests of higher (64) or lower (16, 8) size of embeddings, higher dropout (0.7), higher filter sizes [3, 5, 7], and two fully-connected layers of size 16 all led to comparable, slightly lower results. In Table 4 we present F1 scores we obtained with systems relying on this configuration, selectively using one, some or all of the features. Comparably with SVM, we notice that acoustic features alone achieve similar performance to the combination of features, suggesting that classification in our system mostly relies on acoustic information. We observe a clear jump in performance when using the new acoustic embeddings trained on train and dev sets, especially on MGB-3 test set.

4.3 CNN-biLSTM (run 2)

We built a CNN-biLSTM firstly with two layers of 1D convolutions using filters of decreasing size, each followed by ReLU activation function, dropout 0.5, and max-pooling, then a bi-LSTM of comparable hidden unit size with the number of filters in the last convolutional layer and finally a softmax layer. Both SGD with learning rate 0.001 and Adam with learning rate 0.0001 performed well. Dynamic padding was applied to batches to save computational resources. At the time of submission, we achieved our best score on the dev set with filters 8*200, 4*400, which yielded a F1 score of 0.3894 on the test set. After submission, we found that an earlier of our models, simply decreasing the number of filters to 8*64, 4*64, outperforms the previous configuration with an F1 score of 0.4235 on test set as shown in Table 5.

Conv	Filters and Options	Test sets		
		MGB-3	Youtube	Total
1D	8*200, 4*400 (run 2)	0.4380	0.3711	0.3894
1D	8*200, 4*400 with masking	0.3587	0.2843	0.3013
1D	8*200, 4*400 with masking + batch normalization	0.2506	0.1932	0.2062
1D	**8*64, 4*64**	**0.4614**	**0.4098**	**0.4235**
1D	8*64, 4*64 with masking + balanced batch	0.3542	0.3046	0.3174
1D	8*64, 4*64 with batch normalization	0.1421	0.1390	0.1398
1D	3*3, 3*3, 3*3, 3*3	0.0749	0.0620	0.0649
2D	[3x3]*3, [3x3]*3, [3x3]*3, [3x3]*3	0.0652	0.0620	0.0763
2D	[7x7]*16, [5x5]*32, [3x3]*64, [3x3]*128, [3x3]*256	0.2507	0.2771	0.2721

Table 5: Results for the CNN-biLSTM models (macro-averaged F1 scores). Layers are described with the convention filter size*number of filters.

Optimisation tricks such as masking (to compute the convolutions only on the signal and not on the padding), balancing the batch (so that it necessarily contains items from the 5 classes) or applying batch normalisation after convolutions, surprisingly all negatively impacted the performance. We found that 2D convolutions that could have learnt even more localised features in the spectrograms (Choi et al., 2017; Bartz et al., 2017), were computationally expensive, even when we reduced batch size to 5 instead of 10, and less successful than 1D convolutions in our case. We note that CNN alone and biLSTM alone perform at the random baseline (F1: 0.1995), suggesting that learning in our CNN-biLSTM comes from the combination of the two architectures.

4.4 Binary classification with CNN-biLSTM (run 3)

	F1 in binary systems		F1 in final system
	This dialect	Other dialects	This dialect
EGY	0.50	0.78	0.49
GLF	0.53	0.84	0.54
LAV	0.39	0.82	0.31
MSA	0.38	0.92	0.37
NOR	0.47	0.84	0.47
F1 (macro)			**0.43**

Table 6: Results by dialect in the 5 binary systems and final system (F1 scores).

Run 2 and Run 3 give similar error profiles, the latter of which is displayed in Figure 2: Egyptian, Gulf and North African dialects are in majority correctly classified, but what is striking is the high precision but poor recall in classification of Modern Standard Arabic and the high uncertainty of the model for Levantine. This suggests that our CNN-biLSTM can usefully recognise that the 4 dialects are different from MSA but fails to recognise Levantine or MSA utterances, assigning a label at chance level. A tentative explanation of this confusion is the high presence of MSA in utterances of other dialects, namely in the Egyptian, Gulf and Levantine audio files. As shown in Table 6, the F1 score of each dialect in our final system of CNN-biLSTMs is virtually identical with the F1 score in the binary systems, which entails no real benefit was gained from combining the binary classifiers. Thus, Levantine and MSA for which the system exhibits the highest confusion and that are actually typologically the closest dialects, present the lowest F1 score in binary systems.

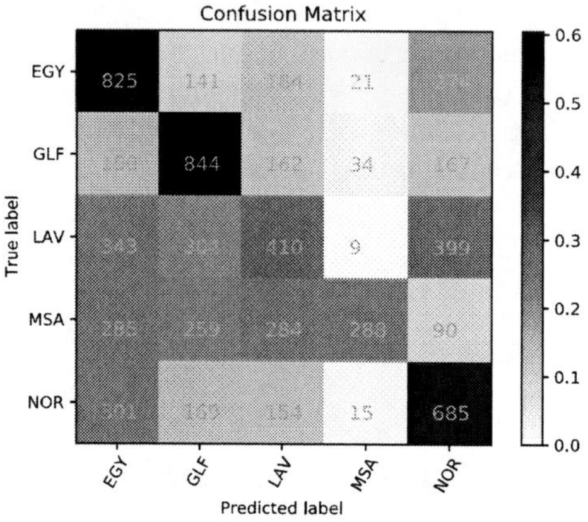

Figure 2: Confusion Matrix for binary CNN-biLSTMs (run 3).

5 Conclusion

In this paper we described our first contribution to the Arabic Dialect Identification subtask in the DSL shared task: our best run is a Multi-Input CNN, learning independent embeddings on lexical and phonetic features and concatenating them with the provided acoustic features to make a prediction. This architecture stays relatively simple yet highly parallel and comparable to more traditional machine learning methods as it ranked 3rd in the competition. Since most of the classification power of this system came from the acoustic features, we investigated end-to-end models directly operating on speech data and generating acoustic features, by means of a CNN-biLSTM and its use for binary classification. Even if these runs proved more informative than competitive, we would like to encourage research with neural networks in future DSL shared tasks despite of the limited size of datasets as it still seems embryonic and evolving at that stage. Furthermore, this approach follows the trend to leave dialect-specific or task-specific features and shift to simpler but powerful architectures, learning useful representations for Dialect Identification while optimising another task such as Automatic Speech Recognition (Li et al., 2017). We were actually led to VarDial DSL shared task by our research in written Arabic Dialect Identification. However, the relative scarcity of word transcripts and their discrepancy with human evaluation, especially for dialectal utterances, do not allow to consider them as realistic data. We advocate that the existence of a separate task for written Arabic Dialect Identification, as MGB challenge exists for spoken Arabic Dialect Identification, would be fruitful for the research community interested in ADI since text (either formal or informal) is a frequently encountered raw data type.

References

Martín Abadi, Ashish Agarwal, Paul Barham, Eugene Brevdo, Zhifeng Chen, Craig Citro, Greg S. Corrado, Andy Davis, Jeffrey Dean, Matthieu Devin, Sanjay Ghemawat, Ian Goodfellow, Andrew Harp, Geoffrey Irving, Michael Isard, Yangqing Jia, Rafal Jozefowicz, Lukasz Kaiser, Manjunath Kudlur, Josh Levenberg, Dandelion Mané, Rajat Monga, Sherry Moore, Derek Murray, Chris Olah, Mike Schuster, Jonathon Shlens, Benoit Steiner, Ilya Sutskever, Kunal Talwar, Paul Tucker, Vincent Vanhoucke, Vijay Vasudevan, Fernanda Viégas, Oriol Vinyals, Pete Warden, Martin Wattenberg, Martin Wicke, Yuan Yu, and Xiaoqiang Zheng. 2015. TensorFlow: Large-scale machine learning on heterogeneous systems. Software available from tensorflow.org.

Ahmed Ali, Yifan Zhang, Patrick Cardinal, Najim Dahak, Stephan Vogel, and James Glass. 2014. A complete kaldi recipe for building arabic speech recognition systems. In *Spoken Language Technology Workshop (SLT), 2014 IEEE*, pages 525–529. IEEE.

Ahmed Ali, Najim Dehak, Patrick Cardinal, Sameer Khurana, Sree Harsha Yella, James Glass, Peter Bell, and Steve Renals. 2016. Automatic Dialect Detection in Arabic Broadcast Speech. In *Proceedings of INTERSPEECH*, pages 2934–2938.

Ahmed Ali, Stephan Vogel, and Steve Renals. 2017. Speech Recognition Challenge in the Wild: Arabic MGB-3. *arXiv preprint arXiv:1709.07276*.

Christian Bartz, Tom Herold, Haojin Yang, and Christoph Meinel. 2017. Language identification using deep convolutional recurrent neural networks. In *International Conference on Neural Information Processing*, pages 880–889. Springer.

Yonatan Belinkov and James Glass. 2016. A Character-level Convolutional Neural Network for Distinguishing Similar Languages and Dialects. In *Proceedings of the Third Workshop on NLP for Similar Languages, Varieties and Dialects (VarDial3)*, pages 145–152, Osaka, Japan.

Çağri Çöltekin and Taraka Rama. 2016. Discriminating Similar Languages with Linear SVMs and Neural Networks. In *Proceedings of the Third Workshop on NLP for Similar Languages, Varieties and Dialects (VarDial3)*, pages 15–24, Osaka, Japan.

Chih-Chung Chang and Chih-Jen Lin. 2011. LIBSVM: A library for support vector machines. *ACM Transactions on Intelligent Systems and Technology*, 2:27:1–27:27.

Keunwoo Choi, György Fazekas, Mark Sandler, and Kyunghyun Cho. 2017. Convolutional recurrent networks for music classification. In *Acoustics, Speech and Signal Processing (ICASSP), 2017 IEEE International Conference on*, pages 2392–2396. IEEE.

François Chollet et al. 2015. Keras. https://keras.io.

Mohamed Eldesouki, Fahim Dalvi, Hassan Sajjad, and Kareem Darwish. 2016. QCRI @ DSL 2016: Spoken Arabic Dialect Identification Using Textual Features. In *Proceedings of the Third Workshop on NLP for Similar Languages, Varieties and Dialects (VarDial3)*, pages 221–226, Osaka, Japan.

Sriram Ganapathy, Kyu Han, Samuel Thomas, Mohamed Omar, Maarten Van Segbroeck, and Shrikanth S Narayanan. 2014. Robust language identification using convolutional neural network features. In *Fifteenth annual conference of the international speech communication association*.

Chinnappa Guggilla. 2016. Discrimination between Similar Languages, Varieties and Dialects using CNN- and LSTM-based Deep Neural Networks. In *Proceedings of the Third Workshop on NLP for Similar Languages, Varieties and Dialects (VarDial3)*, pages 185–194, Osaka, Japan.

Yoon Kim, Yacine Jernite, David Sontag, and Alexander M Rush. 2016. Character-aware neural language models. In *AAAI*, pages 2741–2749.

Yoon Kim. 2014. Convolutional neural networks for sentence classification. *arXiv preprint arXiv:1408.5882*.

Bo Li, Tara N Sainath, Khe Chai Sim, Michiel Bacchiani, Eugene Weinstein, Patrick Nguyen, Zhifeng Chen, Yonghui Wu, and Kanishka Rao. 2017. Multi-dialect speech recognition with a single sequence-to-sequence model. *arXiv preprint arXiv:1712.01541*.

Shervin Malmasi, Marcos Zampieri, Nikola Ljubešić, Preslav Nakov, Ahmed Ali, and Jörg Tiedemann. 2016. Discriminating between similar languages and arabic dialect identification: A report on the third dsl shared task. In *Proceedings of the 3rd Workshop on Language Technology for Closely Related Languages, Varieties and Dialects (VarDial)*, Osaka, Japan.

Brian McFee, Colin Raffel, Dawen Liang, Daniel PW Ellis, Matt McVicar, Eric Battenberg, and Oriol Nieto. 2015. librosa: Audio and music signal analysis in python. In *Proceedings of the 14th python in science conference*, pages 18–25.

Fatiha Sadat, Farnazeh Kazemi, and Atefeh Farzindar. 2014. Automatic identification of arabic dialects in social media. In *Proceedings of the first international workshop on Social media retrieval and analysis*, pages 35–40. ACM.

Suwon Shon, Ahmed Ali, and James Glass. 2018. Convolutional Neural Networks and Language Embeddings for End-to-End Dialect Recognition. *ArXiv e-prints arXiv:1803.04567*.

Omar F Zaidan and Chris Callison-Burch. 2014. Arabic dialect identification. *Computational Linguistics*, 40(1):171–202.

Marcos Zampieri, Shervin Malmasi, Nikola Ljubešić, Preslav Nakov, Ahmed Ali, Jörg Tiedemann, Yves Scherrer, and Noëmi Aepli. 2017. Findings of the VarDial Evaluation Campaign 2017. In *Proceedings of the Fourth Workshop on NLP for Similar Languages, Varieties and Dialects (VarDial)*, Valencia, Spain.

Ye Zhang, Stephen Roller, and Byron Wallace. 2016. Mgnc-cnn: A simple approach to exploiting multiple word embeddings for sentence classification. *arXiv preprint arXiv:1603.00968*.

Ayah Zirikly, Bart Desmet, and Mona Diab. 2016. The GW/LT3 VarDial 2016 Shared Task System for Dialects and Similar Languages Detection. In *Proceedings of the Third Workshop on NLP for Similar Languages, Varieties and Dialects (VarDial3)*, pages 33–41, Osaka, Japan.

HeLI-based Experiments in Discriminating Between Dutch and Flemish Subtitles

Tommi Jauhiainen
University of Helsinki
`@helsinki.fi`

Heidi Jauhiainen
University of Helsinki
`@helsinki.fi`

Krister Lindén
University of Helsinki
`@helsinki.fi`

Abstract

This paper presents the experiments and results obtained by the SUKI team in the *Discriminating between Dutch and Flemish in Subtitles* shared task of the VarDial 2018 Evaluation Campaign. Our best submission was ranked 8th, obtaining macro F1-score of 0.61. Our best results were produced by a language identifier implementing the HeLI method without any modifications. We describe, in addition to the best method we used, some of the experiments we did with unsupervised clustering.

1 Introduction

The four first VarDial workshops have hosted several shared tasks concentrating on language identification of close languages or language varieties. The fifth VarDial workshop (Zampieri et al., 2018) introduced a new shared task concentrating on finding differences between the subtitles written in Netherlandic Dutch and Flemish Dutch (DFS). Netherlandic Dutch and Flemish Dutch are considered the same language by the ISO-639-3 standard since the Belgian dialect (Flemish) is only slightly different from the Dutch used in the Netherlands (Lewis et al., 2013). We had never experimented with the language identification of Dutch varieties and we were interested to see how well it can be done with the methods we have used in the past.

For the past five years we have been developing a language identifying method, which we call HeLI, for the Finno-Ugric Languages and the Internet project (Jauhiainen et al., 2015a). The HeLI method is a general purpose language identification method relying on observations of word and character n-gram frequencies from a language labeled corpus. The method is similar to Naive Bayes when using only relative frequencies of words as probabilities. Unlike Naive Bayes, it uses a back-off scheme to calculate the probabilities of individual words if the words themselves are not found in the language models. The optimal combination of language models used with the back-off scheme depend on the situation and is determined empirically using a development set. The choice is affected for example by the number and type of languages and the amount of training material. The back-off scheme begins from the most rarely seen features and backs off to more common features. We have participated in the shared tasks of three previous VarDial workshops (Zampieri et al., 2015; Malmasi et al., 2016; Zampieri et al., 2017) with language identifiers using the HeLI method or its variations (Jauhiainen et al., 2015b; Jauhiainen et al., 2016; Jauhiainen et al., 2017a). The method has turned out to be robust and competitive with other state-of-the-art language identification methods. For the current workshop, we wanted to try out some more variations and possible improvements to the original method. In addition to the adaptive language models we experimented with unsupervised clustering.

2 Related Work

Language identification is a task related to general text categorization and many of the methods are the same or similar to those used in that field. For more information on language identification and the

This work is licensed under a Creative Commons Attribution 4.0 International Licence. Licence details: `http://creativecommons.org/licenses/by/4.0/`.

Proceedings of the Fifth Workshop on NLP for Similar Languages, Varieties and Dialects, pages 137–144
Santa Fe, New Mexico, USA, August 20, 2018.

methods used for it, see the recent survey by Jauhiainen et al. (2018).

The language identification of Dutch, its varieties and the languages close to it has been considered earlier outside the VarDial context. Trieschnigg et al. (2012) evaluated rank- and cosine-similarity (nearest neighbour and nearest prototype) based language identification methods on the Dutch Folktale Database (Meder, 2010). The version of the database they used contained 15 languages or dialects close to Dutch, as well as English. The best macro F-score for document size identifications, 0.63, was obtained by the nearest neighbor cosine similarity method trained on word unigrams. Tulkens et al. (2016) used word2vec word embeddings in dialect identification of Dutch varieties.

Afrikaans is a close language to Dutch spoken in South Africa. The language identification between Afrikaans and Dutch has been examined several times in the past. Cowie et al. (1999) evaluated the common word, minimal distance, rank distance (Cavnar and Trenkle, 1994), and their own LZC methods and note that all of them were able to distinguish relatively well between the two languages. When automatically creating language trees from the universal declarations of human rights, Benedetto et al. (2002) group Afrikaans and Dutch together, with both equally related to Frisian. Singh (Singh, 2006; Singh, 2010) lists Dutch and Afrikaans as confusable languages with each other and Lui (2014) noticed that Afrikaans was confused especially with West Frisian. The latest study on Dutch language identification by van der Lee and van den Bosch (2017) led to the current shared task.

2.1 Unsupervised clustering

Unsupervised clustering of text aims to form coherent groups by gathering similar texts together. One of the first unsupervised clustering approaches to language identification task was presented by Biemann and Teresniak (2005). They use the co-occurrences of words to group words together in order to form a vocabulary of a language. Their method was later evaluated by Shiells and Pham (2010).

3 Task setup and data

To prepare for the shared task, the participants were provided with training and development datasets. The training set consisted of 150,000 lines for each of the Dutch varieties. In the other shared tasks of the VarDial workshops, the datasets have mostly contained only one sentence per line. The dataset for Dutch varieties, however, usually contained several sentences per line. The development part was quite small compared with the training data, only 250 lines per variety. However, the test set was comparably large: 10,000 lines for each language. This subtitles dataset and the methods used for collecting it are described in detail by van der Lee and van den Bosch (2017).

Participants were allowed to submit three runs for the DFS task. We submitted two, one with the original HeLI method, and one using HeLI with language model adaptation.

4 HeLI method in Discriminating between Dutch and Flemish, run 1

The HeLI method was first presented by Jauhiainen (2010) and later more formally by Jauhiainen et al. (2016). The description presented below differs from the original mostly in that we are leaving out the cut-off value c for the size of the language models. In this years shared tasks we found, and have already noticed it earlier, that if the corpus used as the training material is of good quality it is generally advisable to use all the available material. Furthermore, the penalty value compensates for some of the possible impurities in the language models. Leaving out the cut-off value negates the need for using the derived corpus C' in the equations. We also use both the original and lowercased versions of the words and n-grams as different language models, as using the original words was clearly beneficial with the development set. We present the complete formulas here as used by the best submitted run in order to make this article as self contained as possible.

Description of the used version of the HeLI method The goal is to correctly guess the language $g \in G$ for each of the lines in the test set. In the HeLI method, each language g is represented by several different language models only one of which is used for every word t in the line M. The language models are: a model based on words and one or more models based on character n-grams from one to n_{max}. For the DFS task, we used n_{max} up to eight. When we encounter a word not found in the word-based language models, we back off to using the n-grams of the size n_{max}. If we are unable to apply the n-grams of the size n_{max}, we back off to lower order n-grams and, if needed, we continue backing off until character unigrams. As both original and lowercased models are used, the models with original words are used first. If the back-off function is needed, we back of to lowercased words, then to original n-grams and then to lowercased n-grams. When backing from original n-grams to lowercased n-grams, the current implementation first backs off all the way to unigrams of original characters before moving on to lowercased n-grams of the size n_{max}, practically dropping the lowercased n-grams out of the equation.

The training data is tokenized into words using non-alphabetic and non-ideographic characters as delimiters. If lowercased language models are being created, the data is lowercased. The relative frequencies of the words are calculated. Also the relative frequencies of character n-grams from 1 to n_{max} are calculated inside the words, so that the preceding and the following space-characters are included. The n-grams are overlapping, so that for example a word with three characters includes three character trigrams. Word n-grams were not used, so all subsequent references to n-grams in this article refer to n-grams of characters. Then we transform those relative frequencies into scores using 10-based logarithms. Among the language models generated from the DFS corpus, the largest model was for original (non-lowercased) character 7-grams, including 333,256 different 7-grams for Dutch.

$dom(O(C))$ is the set of all words found in the models of any language $g \in G$. For each word $t \in dom(O(C))$, the values $v_{C_g}(t)$ for each language g are calculated, as in Equation 1.

$$v_{C_g}(t) = \begin{cases} -\log_{10}\left(\frac{c(C_g,t)}{l_{C_g}}\right) & \text{, if } c(C_g,t) > 0 \\ p & \text{, if } c(C_g,t) = 0, \end{cases} \tag{1}$$

where $c(C_g,t)$ is the number of words t and l_{C_g} is the total number of all words in language g. If $c(C_g,t)$ is zero, then $v_{C_g}(t)$ gets the penalty value p. The penalty value has a smoothing effect in that it transfers some of the probability mass to unseen features in the language models.

The corpus containing only the n-grams in the language models is called C^n. The domain $dom(O(C^n))$ is the set of all character n-grams of length n found in the models of any language $g \in G$. The values $v_{C_g^n}(u)$ are calculated similarly for all n-grams $u \in dom(O(C^n))$ for each language g, as shown in Equation 2.

$$v_{C_g^n}(u) = \begin{cases} -\log_{10}\left(\frac{c(C_g^n,u)}{l_{C_g^n}}\right) & \text{, if } c(C_g^n,u) > 0 \\ p & \text{, if } c(C_g^n,u) = 0, \end{cases} \tag{2}$$

where $c(C_g^n,u)$ is the number of n-grams u found in the corpus of the language g and $l_{C_g^n}$ is the total number of the n-grams of length n in the derived corpus of language g. These values are used when scoring the words while identifying the language of a text.

When using n-grams, the word t is split into overlapping n-grams of characters u_i^n, where $i = 1, ..., l_t - n$, of the length n. Each of the n-grams u_i^n is then scored separately for each language g in the same way as the words.

If the n-gram u_i^n is found in $dom(O(C_g^n))$, the values in the models are used. If the n-gram u_i^n is not found in any of the models, it is simply discarded. We define the function $d_g(t,n)$ for counting n-grams in t found in a model in Equation 3.

$$d_g(t,n) = \sum_{i=1}^{l_t-n} \begin{cases} 1 & \text{, if } u_i^n \in dom(O(C^n)) \\ 0 & \text{, otherwise} \end{cases} \tag{3}$$

When all the n-grams of the size n in the word t have been processed, the word gets the value of the average of the scored n-grams u_i^n for each language, as in Equation 4.

$$v_g(t, n) = \begin{cases} \frac{1}{d_g(t,n)} \sum_{i=1}^{l_t-n} v_{C_g^n}(u_i^n) & \text{, if } d_g(t, n) > 0 \\ v_g(t, n-1) & \text{, otherwise,} \end{cases} \tag{4}$$

where $d_g(t, n)$ is the number of n-grams u_i^n found in the domain $dom(O(C_g^n))$. If all of the n-grams of the size n were discarded, $d_g(t, n) = 0$, the language identifier backs off to using n-grams of the size $n - 1$. If no values are found even for unigrams, a word gets the penalty value p for every language, as in Equation 5.

$$v_g(t, 0) = p \tag{5}$$

The mystery text is tokenized into words using the non-alphabetic and non-ideographic characters as delimiters. The words are lowercased when lowercased models are being used. After this, a score $v_g(t)$ is calculated for each word t in the mystery text for each language g. If the word t is found in the set of words $dom(O(C_g))$, the corresponding value $v_{C_g}(t)$ for each language g is assigned as the score $v_g(t)$, as shown in Equation 6.

$$v_g(t) = \begin{cases} v_{C_g}(t) & \text{, if } t \in dom(O(C_g)) \\ v_g(t, min(n_{max}, l_t + 2)) & \text{, if } t \notin dom(O(C_g)) \end{cases} \tag{6}$$

If a word t is not found in the set of words $dom(O(C_g))$ and the length of the word l_t is at least $n_{max} - 2$, the language identifier backs off to using character n-grams of the length n_{max}. In case the word t is shorter than $n_{max} - 2$ characters, $n = l_t + 2$.

The whole line M gets the score $R_g(M)$ equal to the average of the scores of the words $v_g(t)$ for each language g, as in Equation 7 .

$$R_g(M) = \frac{\sum_{i=1}^{l_{T(M)}} v_g(t_i)}{l_{T(M)}} \tag{7}$$

where $T(M)$ is the sequence of words and $l_{T(M)}$ is the number of words in the line M. Since we are using negative logarithms of probabilities, the language having the lowest score is returned as the language with the maximum probability for the mystery text.

Results of the run 1 on the development and the test sets   The development set was used for finding the best values for the parameters n_{max} and p. The recall-values for different combinations can be seen in Table 1.

Leaving out any of the models did not seem to move recall into a better direction from the 64.6% obtained when using all the available language models. We decided to use all the generated models with the penalty value of 7.7 for the first run. We included the development set in the training material to generate the final language models. The run on the test set reached the recall of 61.4%. The results on the test set are naturally somewhat worse than on the development set, as the parameters have not been optimized for it. The macro F1-score obtained was 0.61. The recall was clearly better for Flemish than for Dutch as can be seen in Table 2. The length of the lines to be identified ranged from 111 to 385 characters. The results indicate that the length of the sequence to be identified is not a major issue for the method as the average lengths were very similar for both correctly and incorrectly identified texts.

5   HeLI with adaptive language models, run 2

With adaptive language models, new information is introduced in the language models from unlabeled texts while they are being identified. Using adaptive language models with HeLI means that we first identify all the lines in the test corpus, then we determine which of our identifications is most probably correct. For guessing the correctness, we used the absolute difference between the scores of the two languages as given by the HeLI method. We then labeled the line with the largest difference as the winning

Original words	Original n_{max}	Lowercased words	Lowercased n_{max}	Penalty p	Recall
yes	8	yes	8	7.7	64.6%
yes	8	no	8	7.7	64.6%
yes	7	no	8	8.6	64.6%
yes	7	no	7	8.6	64.6%
yes	7	no	6	8.6	64.6%
yes	7	no	-	8.6	64.6%
yes	7	yes	8	8.5-8.6	64.4%
yes	8	yes	7	7.7	64.4%
yes	6	no	7	7.7-7.8/8.0-8.6	64.2%
yes	6	no	-	8.4	64.2%
yes	6	yes	8	7.7-7.8/8.0-8.6	64.0%
yes	7	no	-	8.5	64.0%
no	7	no	-	8.9	63.8%
no	8	yes	8	8.0	63.6%
no	-	yes	8	8.0	63.4%
no	6	no	-	8.4	63.0%
no	-	no	8	7.8-8.3/8.5-8.7/9.2-9.4	62.2%
no	5	no	-	8.9	61.8%
no	4	no	-	8.4	57.8%
no	-	no	4	7.9	55.0%

Table 1: Baseline HeLI recall in development data with different combinations of parameters.

Correct language	Identified language	Number	Average length in words	Average length in characters
DUT	DUT	5679	34	187
DUT	BEL	4321	34	178
BEL	BEL	6592	33	178
BEL	DUT	3408	34	185

Table 2: Baseline HeLI statistics for run 1.

language and added the words and character n-grams from that line to the corresponding language model. Then we used the adapted models to re-identify the remaining unlabeled lines and continued labeling one line at a time until all the lines were labeled. This method worked very well with German dialects and Indo-Aryan languages for the other two tasks we participated in the VarDial workshop. However, as can be seen in Table 3, using the adaptive language models did not change the results very much for the Dutch varieties.

Orig. words	Orig. n_{max}	Low. words	Low. n_{max}	Penalty p	Recall (dynamic)	Recall (original)
yes	8	yes	8	7.7	64.8%	64.6%
no	8	yes	8	8.0	63.6%	63.6%
no	-	no	4	7.9	54.8%	55.0%
no	-	no	8	7.8	61.6%	62.2%

Table 3: Recall in development with different combinations of language models.

We submitted the second, and our final run, to the DFS task using HeLI with adaptive language models and with the same parameters as for the first run. The recall on the test set was 61.15%, which did not improve on the first run. Similarly, the resulting F1-score of 0.6107 did not improve the score gained with the unmodified HeLI method.

6 Experiments with unsupervised clustering

We wanted to try out an idea that using unsupervised clustering on the test set before actual language identification might be beneficial. The idea is that the lines of the test set written in the same language might be more alike with each other than with the material used for training the language identifier. Grouping similar lines together would make it easier for the language identifier to identify the text as the length of the text to be identified is usually directly related to the accuracy of the identification (Jauhiainen et al., 2017b). To our knowledge, this strategy has not been used previously.

We decided to try clustering with an ad-hoc nearest neighbor clustering-method using the HeLI method as the similarity measure. In our nearest neighbor clustering each line is considered a separate language and language models are created for them. Each line is then scored using these models with the language model of the line itself omitted from the repertoire. After scoring, each line is grouped in the same group with the line whose model gave the best score. In this way each identified group would include at least two lines. We created a separate language model for each of the 500 lines in the development set. We tested clustering with lowercased character n-gram models. The results of the accuracy of any line being paired with a line from the same language can be seen in Table 4.

Lowercased n_{max}	Penalty p	Accuracy
1	5	55.8%
2	3	53.2%
3	6	59.0%
4	11	56.6%
5	11	57.0%
6	4	54.4%
7	4	55.0%
8	4	56.2%

Table 4: Clustering accuracy with different language models.

Character trigrams made the best clusters with accuracy of 59%. However, the grouping created by the unsupervised method seemed to be too random, so we concluded that identifying the groups would only make results worse and did not continue with these experiments.

7 Conclusions and future work

The non-discriminative nature of the HeLI method leaves it at a disadvantage against some of the more discriminative classification methods when the languages or dialects to be distinguished are extremely close. We did not use any discriminative features with the method for this shared task. In the future, we will continue experimenting with adding some discriminative elements to the HeLI method when dealing with very close languages.

Our adaptive language models fared very well in the two other tasks of this years evaluation campaign. We believe that the reasons the adaptive language models did not succeed so well in the DFS task are that the training corpus was already quite large and the test set was not from any one homogenous domain. If the mystery text would have been for example a set of subtitles for a single television series or a new movie, the adaptive language models could have learned the names used in the set from the more distinguishable lines and the names might have in turn helped with the more difficult lines.

The unsupervised clustering should be trialed on other datasets, and it might be applicable in an out-of-domain situation. We used only lowercased character n-grams for clustering and the effect of also using words should be verified. We, furthermore, experimented with only one unsupervised clustering method; it may not have been the best one and others should be evaluated.

Acknowledgments

This research was partly conducted with funding from the Kone Foundation Language Programme (Kone Foundation, 2012).

References

Dario Benedetto, Emanuele Caglioti, and Vittorio Loreto. 2002. Language Trees and Zipping. *Physical Review Letters*, 88(4).

Chris Biemann and Sven Teresniak. 2005. Disentangling from Babylonian confusion — Unsupervised Language Identification. In Alexander Gelbukh, editor, *Proceedings of the 6th International Conference on Intelligent Text Processing and Computational Linguistics (CICLing-2005)*, pages 773–784, Mexico City, Mexico. Springer.

William B. Cavnar and John M. Trenkle. 1994. N-Gram-Based Text Categorization. In *Proceedings of SDAIR-94, Third Annual Symposium on Document Analysis and Information Retrieval*, pages 161–175, Las Vegas, USA.

Jim Cowie, Yevgeny Ludovik, and Ron Zacharski. 1999. Language Recognition for Mono- and Multi-lingual Documents. In *Proceedings of the VexTal Conference*, pages 209–214, Venice, Italy.

Heidi Jauhiainen, Tommi Jauhiainen, and Krister Lindén. 2015a. The Finno-Ugric Languages and The Internet Project. *Septentrio Conference Series*, 0(2):87–98.

Tommi Jauhiainen, Heidi Jauhiainen, and Krister Lindén. 2015b. Discriminating Similar Languages with Token-Based Backoff. In *Proceedings of the Joint Workshop on Language Technology for Closely Related Languages, Varieties and Dialects (LT4VarDial)*, pages 44–51, Hissar, Bulgaria.

Tommi Jauhiainen, Krister Lindén, and Heidi Jauhiainen. 2016. HeLI, a Word-Based Backoff Method for Language Identification. In *Proceedings of the Third Workshop on NLP for Similar Languages, Varieties and Dialects (VarDial3)*, pages 153–162, Osaka, Japan.

Tommi Jauhiainen, Krister Lindén, and Heidi Jauhiainen. 2017a. Evaluating HeLI with Non-Linear Mappings. In *Proceedings of the Fourth Workshop on NLP for Similar Languages, Varieties and Dialects (VarDial)*, pages 102–108, Valencia, Spain, April.

Tommi Jauhiainen, Krister Lindén, and Heidi Jauhiainen. 2017b. Evaluation of Language Identification Methods Using 285 Languages. In *Proceedings of the 21st Nordic Conference on Computational Linguistics (NoDaLiDa 2017)*, pages 183–191, Gothenburg, Sweden. Linköping University Electronic Press.

Tommi Jauhiainen, Marco Lui, Marcos Zampieri, Timothy Baldwin, and Krister Lindén. 2018. Automatic Language Identification in Texts: A Survey. *arXiv preprint arXiv:1804.08186*.

Tommi Jauhiainen. 2010. Tekstin kielen automaattinen tunnistaminen. Master's thesis, University of Helsinki, Helsinki.

Kone Foundation. 2012. The language programme 2012-2016. http://www.koneensaatio.fi/en.

M. Paul Lewis, Gary F. Simons, and Charles D. Fennig, editors. 2013. *Ethnologue: Languages of the world, seventeenth edition*. SIL International, Dallas, Texas.

Marco Lui. 2014. *Generalized Language Identification*. Ph.D. thesis, The University of Melbourne.

Shervin Malmasi, Marcos Zampieri, Nikola Ljubešić, Preslav Nakov, Ahmed Ali, and Jörg Tiedemann. 2016. Discriminating between Similar Languages and Arabic Dialect Identification: A Report on the Third DSL Shared Task. In *Proceedings of the 3rd Workshop on Language Technology for Closely Related Languages, Varieties and Dialects (VarDial)*, Osaka, Japan.

Theo Meder. 2010. From a Dutch folktale database towards an international folktale database. *Fabula*, 51:6–22.

Karen Shiells and Peter Pham. 2010. Unsupervised Clustering for Language Identification. Project Report, Stanford University.

Anil Kumar Singh. 2006. Study of Some Distance Measures for Language and Encoding Identification. In *Proceedings of the Workshop on Linguistic Distances*, pages 63–72, Sydney, Australia.

Anil Kumar Singh. 2010. *Modeling and Application of Linguistic Similarity*. Ph.D. thesis, International Institute of Information Technology, Hyderabad.

Dolf Trieschnigg, Djoerd Hiemstra, Mariët Theune, Franciska de Jong, and Theo Meder. 2012. An Exploration of Language Identification Techniques for the Dutch Folktale Database. In *Proceedings of the LREC workshop Adaptation of Language Resources and Tools for Processing Cultural Heritage*, pages 47–51, Istanbul, Turkey.

Stéphan Tulkens, Chris Emmery, and Walter Daeleman. 2016. Evaluating Unsupervised Dutch Word Embeddings as a Linguistic Resource. In Nicoletta Calzolari (Conference Chair), Khalid Choukri, Thierry Declerck, Sara Goggi, Marko Grobelnik, Bente Maegaard, Joseph Mariani, Helene Mazo, Asuncion Moreno, Jan Odijk, and Stelios Piperidis, editors, *Proceedings of the Tenth International Conference on Language Resources and Evaluation (LREC 2016)*, pages 4130–4136. European Language Resources Association (ELRA).

Chris van der Lee and Antal van den Bosch. 2017. Exploring Lexical and Syntactic Features for Language Variety Identification. In *Proceedings of the Fourth Workshop on NLP for Similar Languages, Varieties and Dialects (VarDial)*, pages 190–199, Valencia, Spain.

Marcos Zampieri, Liling Tan, Nikola Ljubešić, Jörg Tiedemann, and Preslav Nakov. 2015. Overview of the DSL Shared Task 2015. In *Proceedings of the Joint Workshop on Language Technology for Closely Related Languages, Varieties and Dialects (LT4VarDial)*, pages 1–9, Hissar, Bulgaria.

Marcos Zampieri, Shervin Malmasi, Nikola Ljubešić, Preslav Nakov, Ahmed Ali, Jörg Tiedemann, Yves Scherrer, and Noëmi Aepli. 2017. Findings of the VarDial Evaluation Campaign 2017. In *Proceedings of the Fourth Workshop on NLP for Similar Languages, Varieties and Dialects (VarDial)*, Valencia, Spain.

Marcos Zampieri, Shervin Malmasi, Preslav Nakov, Ahmed Ali, Suwon Shon, James Glass, Yves Scherrer, Tanja Samardžić, Nikola Ljubešić, Jörg Tiedemann, Chris van der Lee, Stefan Grondelaers, Nelleke Oostdijk, Antal van den Bosch, Ritesh Kumar, Bornini Lahiri, and Mayank Jain. 2018. Language Identification and Morphosyntactic Tagging: The Second VarDial Evaluation Campaign. In *Proceedings of the Fifth Workshop on NLP for Similar Languages, Varieties and Dialects (VarDial)*, Santa Fe, USA.

Measuring language distance among historical varieties using perplexity. Application to European Portuguese.

Jose Ramom Pichel
imaxin|software,
Santiago de Compostela,
Galiza
jramompichel@imaxin.com

Pablo Gamallo
CiTIUS
Univ. of Santiago
de Compostela. Galiza
pablo.gamallo@usc.es

Iñaki Alegria
IXA group
Univ. of the Basque Country
UPV/EHU
i.alegria@ehu.eus

Abstract

The objective of this work is to quantify, with a simple and robust measure, the distance between historical varieties of a language. The measure will be inferred from text corpora corresponding to historical periods. Different approaches have been proposed for similar aims: Language Identification, Phylogenetics, Historical Linguistics or Dialectology. In our approach, we used a perplexity-based measure to calculate language distance between all the historical periods of that language: European Portuguese. Perplexity has already proven to be a robust metric to calculate distance between languages. However, this measure has not been tested yet to identify diachronic periods within the historical evolution of a specific language. For this purpose, a historical Portuguese corpus has been constructed from different open sources containing texts with spelling close to the original one. The results of our experiments show that Portuguese keeps an important degree of homogeneity over time. We anticipate this metric to be a starting point to be applied to other languages.

1 Introduction

In this article, we deal with the concept of diachronic language distance, which refers to how different one historical period of a language is from another. The prevailing view is that language distance between two languages cannot be measured appropriately by using a well-established score because they may differ in many complex linguistic aspects such as phonetics and phonology, lexicography, morphology, syntax, semantics, pragmatics, and so on. In addition, languages change internally as well as in relation to other languages throughout their history (Millar and Trask, 2015).

Quantifying all these aspects by reducing them to a single distance score between languages or between historical periods of a language is a difficult task which is far from being fulfilled or at least appropriately addressed, perhaps because it has not yet been a priority in natural language processing. Also, there is not any standard methodology to define a metric for language distance, even though there have been different attempts to obtain language distance measures, namely in phylogenetic studies within historical linguistics (Petroni and Serva, 2010), in dialectology (Nerbonne and Heeringa, 1997), in language identification (Malmasi et al., 2016), or in studies about learning additional languages within the field of second language acquisition (Chiswick and Miller, 2004).

In the present work, we consider that the concept of language distance is closely related to the process of language identification. Actually, the more difficult the identification of differences between two languages or language varieties is, the shorter the distance between them. Language identification was one of the first natural language processing problems for which a statistical and corpus-based approach was used.

The best language identification systems are based on n-gram models of characters extracted from textual corpora (Malmasi et al., 2016) . Thus, character n-grams not only encode lexical and

This work is licensed under a Creative Commons Attribution 4.0 International License. License details: http://creativecommons.org/licenses/by/4.0/.

Proceedings of the Fifth Workshop on NLP for Similar Languages, Varieties and Dialects, pages 145–155
Santa Fe, New Mexico, USA, August 20, 2018.

morphological information, but also phonological features since phonographic written systems are related to the way languages were pronounced in the past. In addition, long n-grams (>=5-grams) also encode syntactic and syntagmatic relations as they may represent the end of a word and the beginning of the next one in a sequence. For instance, the 7-gram ion#de# (where '#' represents a blank space) is a frequent sequence of letters shared by several Romance languages (e.g. French, Spanish, or Galician). This 7-gram might be considered as an instance of the generic pattern "noun-prep-noun" since "ion" (The stress accent (e.g. ión) has been removed to simplify language encoding) is a noun suffix and "de" a very frequent preposition, introducing prepositional phrases.

In our previous work, perplexity-based measures were used for language identification (Gamallo et al., 2016) and for measuring the distance between languages (Gamallo et al., 2017a). Now, the main objective of our current work is to extend this approach in order to measure distance between periods of the same language (diachronic language distance), also based on perplexity. This method has been applied to a case of study on European Portuguese from 12th to 20th century. Two experiments are reported: the first one uses our "perplexity-based" method in a historical corpus of Portuguese with an orthography closely related to that of the original texts, and the second experiment was applied using a transliterated corpus trying to use the same orthography for the whole corpus. The article is organized as follows: First, we will introduce some studies on language distance (Sec. 2). Then, our language distance measure is described in Section 3. In Section 4, we introduce the experimental method and finally, in Section 5, we describe the two above mentioned experiments and discuss the results. Conclusions are addressed in Section 6.

2   Related Work

Linguistic distance has been measured and defined from different perspectives using different methods. Many of the methods compare lists of words in order to find phylogenetic links or dialectological relations (Wieling and Nerbonne, 2015). According to Borin (2013), genetic linguistics (also known as "phylogenetics" or "comparative-historical linguistics") and dialectology are the most popular fields dealing with language distance. This author stated: (Borin, 2013, p. 7) "Traditionally, dialectological investigations have focused mainly on vocabulary and pronunciation, whereas comparative-historical linguists put much stock in grammatical features". However, "we would expect the same kind of methods to be useful in both cases" (Borin, 2013, p. 7).

Degaetano-Ortlieb et al. (2016) present an information-theoretic approach, based on entropy, to investigate diachronic change in scientific English.

In the following sections, we introduce some relevant work on phylogenetics and dialectology, but also on corpus-based approaches.

2.1   Phylogenetics

The objective of linguistic phylogenetics, a sub-field of historical and comparative linguistics, is to build a rooted tree describing the evolutionary history of a set of related languages or varieties. In order to automatically build phylogenetic trees, many researchers made use of a specific technique called *lexicostatistics*, which is an approach of comparative linguistics that involves quantitative comparison of lexical cognates, which are words with a common historical origin (Nakhleh et al., 2005; Holman et al., 2008; Bakker et al., 2009; Petroni and Serva, 2010; Barbançon et al., 2013). More precisely, lexicostatistics is based on cross-lingual word lists (e.g. Swadesh list (Swadesh, 1952) or ASJP database (Brown et al., 2008)) to automatically compute distances using the percentage of shared cognates. Levenshtein distance among words (Yujian and Bo, 2007) in a cross-lingual list is one the most common metrics used in this field (Petroni and Serva, 2010). Ellison and Kirby (2006) present a method, called PHILOLOGICON, for building language taxonomies comparing lexical forms. The method only compares words language-internally and never cross-linguistically.

Rama and Singh (2009) test four techniques for constructing phylogenetic trees from corpora: cross–entropy, cognate coverage distance, phonetic distance of cognates and feature N-Gram.

They conclude that these measures can be very useful for languages which do not have linguistically hand-crafted lists.

2.2 Dialectology

As in phylogenetics, Levenshtein distance among list of words is employed very often in dialectology (Nerbonne and Hinrichs, 2006; Nerbonne et al., 1999).

In addition to raw Levenshtein distance, (Nerbonne and Hinrichs, 2006) proceed to measuring pronunciation differences, focusing on differences in the pronunciation of the same words in different varieties. Results are validated using measurements based on the degree to which they correlate with dialect speakers' judgments about those differences. Also, Heeringa et al. (2006) evaluated several string distance algorithms for dialectology, but always based on pairs of words.

2.3 Corpus-Based Approaches

To measure language distances, very recent approaches construct complex language models not from word lists, but from large cross-lingual and parallel corpora. In these works, models are mainly built with distributional information on words, i.e., they are based on co-occurrences of words, and therefore languages are compared by computing cross-lingual similarity on the basis of word co-occurrences (Liu and Cong, 2013; Gao et al., 2014; Asgari and Mofrad, 2016).

It is worth noting that most techniques in language identification also use corpus-based approaches, mainly based on n-gram language models. Language identification is considered as being a pretty solved task (McNamee, 2005), specially for languages by distance, also called *Ausbau* languages (Kloss, 1967). However, there are already big challenges to classify some closely related varieties of the same language (e.g. Nicaraguan Spanish and Salvadoran Spanish) or *Abstand* languages (Kloss, 1967) (e.g. Czech and Slovak). Two specific tasks of language identification have attracted a lot of research attention in recent years, namely discriminating among closely related languages (Malmasi et al., 2016) and language detection on noisy short texts such as tweets (Gamallo et al., 2014; Zubiaga et al., 2015). Reasonable results have been achieved even for very closely related varieties using corpus-based strategies. For instance, Zampieri et al. (2013) reported an approach using a log-likelihood estimation method for language models built on orthographical (character n-grams), lexical (word unigrams) and lexico-syntactic (word bigrams) features. As a result, they reported a extremely high accuracy of 0.998 for distinguishing between European Portuguese and Brazilian Portuguese, and 0.990 for Mexican and Argentinian Spanish.

2.4 Historical Portuguese

Historical periods of the Portuguese language are reported in several language monographies: *História da Literatura Portuguesa* (History of Portuguese Literature) (Saraiva, 2001) and *História da Língua Portuguesa* (Portuguese Language History) (Teyssier, 1982), Historical Phonology and Morphology of the Portuguese Language (Williams, 1962), as well as in different books of History of Portugal: *História de Portugal em datas* (History of Portugal in a timeline) (Capelo et al., 1994), *História de Portugal* (History of Portugal) (Mattoso and Ramos, 1994) and *História concisa de Portugal* (Brief history of Portugal) (Saraiva, 1978).

3 Perplexity

Perplexity is a widely-used evaluation metric for language models. It has been used as a quality measure for language models built with n-grams extracted from text corpora. It has also been used in very specific tasks, such as to classify between formal and colloquial tweets (González, 2015), classification of related languages (Gamallo et al., 2016) and measuring distances among languages (Gamallo et al., 2017a).

3.1 Perplexity of a language model

Perplexity is frequently used as a quality measure for language models built with n-grams extracted from text corpora (Chen and Goodman, 1996; Sennrich, 2012). This is a metric about how well a language model is able to fit a text sample. A low perplexity indicates the language model is good at predicting the sample. On the contrary, a high perplexity shows the language model is not good to predict the given sample. It turns out that we could use perplexity to compare the quality of language models in relation to specific textual tests.

More formally, the perplexity (called PP for short) of a language model on a textual test is the inverse probability of the test. For a test of sequences of characters $CH = ch_1, ch_2, ..., ch_n$ and a language model LM with n-gram probabilities $P(\cdot)$ estimated on a training set, the perplexity PP of CH given a character-based n-gram model LM is computed as follows:

$$PP(CH, LM) = \sqrt[n]{\prod_i^n \frac{1}{P(ch_i|ch_1^{i-1})}} \tag{1}$$

where n-gram probabilities $P(\cdot)$ are defined in this way:

$$P(ch_n|ch_1^{n-1}) = \frac{C(ch_1^{n-1}ch_n)}{C(ch_1^{n-1})} \tag{2}$$

Equation 2 estimates the n-gram probability by dividing the observed frequency (C) of a particular sequence of characters by the observed frequency of the prefix, where the prefix stands for the same sequence without the last character. To take into account unseen n-grams, we use a smoothing technique based on linear interpolation.

3.2 Perplexity-Based Language Distance (PLD)

A Perplexity-based distance between two languages or two periods of the same language is defined by comparing the n-grams of a text in one language or period of language with the n-gram model trained for the other language or period of language. This comparison must be made in the two directions. Then, the perplexity of the test text CH in language $L2$, given the language model LM of language $L1$, as well as the perplexity of the test text in $L1$, given the language model of $L2$, are used to define the perplexity-based language distance, PLD, between $L1$ and $L2$ as follows:

$$PLD(L1, L2) = (PP(CH_{L2}, LM_{L1}) + PP(CH_{L1}, LM_{L2}))/2 \tag{3}$$

The lower the perplexity of both CH_{L2} given LM_{L1} and CH_{L1} given LM_{L2}, the lower the distance between languages (or language periods) $L1$ and $L2$. Notice that PLD is the symmetric mean derived from two asymmetric divergences: $PP(CH_{L2}, LM_{L1})$ and $PP(CH_{L1}, LM_{L2})$.

4 Methodology

Our methodology is based on applying PLD measure to a historical corpus of a language (also called "diachronic corpus"), in order to obtain a diachronic language distance between periods. A representative and balanced historical corpus is required. This corpus is divided into two parts: train and test corpora. Also, train and test must be divided into different language periods, which should be previously defined according to philological criteria. Finally, the test corpus should contain roughly 20% number of words with regard to the train corpus. It is worth mentioning that the train partitions are not manually annotated as our method is fully unsupervised.

More precisely, to apply PLD on diachronic corpora for computing the distance between periods, our method is divided into the following specific steps:

1. First, we need to define historical periods of a language. For this purpose, it will be necessary to take into account philological studies on the specific language at stake. For Portuguese,

the periods were defined according to the ideas reported in two pieces of work about, on the one hand, the History of Portuguese Language (Teyssier, 1982) and, on the other, about Historical Phonology and Morphology of the Portuguese Language (Williams, 1962). As a result of this philological research, Portuguese language may be divided into a medieval period (XII-XVth centuries), a renaissance period (XVI-XVIIth), XVIIIth, first half XIXth, second half XIXth, first half XXth, and second half XXth century. Yet, considering the lack of documents for some of these periods, we had to merge renaissance and XVIIIth into one single period. Thus, we have selected the following 6 periods: XII-XV, XVI-XVIII, XIX-1, XIX-2, XX-1, and XX-2.

2. In the second step, we select a representative and balanced historical corpus. For this purpose, texts from several genres must be retrieved. For our corpus, we collected texts from both non-fiction and literature. In addition, we consider that it is important to get documents with a spelling as close as possible to the original one. It is quite relevant to bear in mind that the oldest period (medieval) is where there are more differences between texts, since language was not standarized at that time. Unlike other historical Portuguese corpora (Galves and Faria, 2010), in the construction of the corpus we have paid special attention to maintain the original spelling for every text. Bearing this aim in mind, adapted or edited versions have been ruled out (for example, in the 19th century, the spelling "ph" was used for the phoneme /f/, and in many available digital versions the texts are adapted to modern spelling by replacing "ph" with "f", but we discarded these versions).

3. Then, text corpus is divided into both train and test partitions. As soon as we get documents in their original spelling and they are classified in the pre-defined historical periods, we must decide if these documents must belong to either the train or the test corpus, each one also divided in the same 6 periods. The size of each period of the test corpus is about 20% of the size of the corresponding period in the train corpus.

4. Finally, PLD is applied to the previously organized train/test dataset and results are evaluated. The results obtained by using PLD between periods are compared with those obtained between well-established languages and reported in Gamallo et al. (2017a), where the distance among more than 40 languages was analyzed. Considering that two historical periods belong to the same language, for Portuguese the PLD score between two periods should not be greater than the perplexity between two recognized languages. Therefore, given that the perplexity-based distance between Catalan and Spanish is about 8, the distance between two Portuguese periods should be lower than that value; otherwise we consider that there might be some problems with, at least, one aspect of our methodology: either the corpus or the measure.

5   Experiments

5.1   Corpus

As we aim to test our methodology on Portuguese, the language models were generated by making use of a collection of documents in several periods of Portuguese language. These documents are not translations of each other and are constituted by a balanced combination of genres (both literature and nonfiction) period by period. As a result, we collected comparable and balanced corpus from literature and nonfiction in six different periods of languages from different sources. Our method to compile the historical corpus was the following.

First, in order to know which were the most relevant nonfiction and literature documents in Portuguese for each historical period, we took into account information reported in historical work cited above in Sec. 2.4. As a result, we selected a set of relevant candidate documents to be part of our experiments.

Second, we searched for these candidate texts in open repositories such as *Corpus Informatizado do Português Medieval* (Digited Corpus of Medieval Corpus) (Xavier et al., 1994), Project

	XII-XV	XVI-XVIII	XIX-1	XIX-2	XX-1	XX-2
Train corpus (Words)	1,509,774	1,426,636	1,327,045	1,612,320	1,325,353	1,688,787
Test corpus (Words)	305,773	310,405	296,712	334,145	293,952	363,693
Proportion (Test/Train)	20.25%	21.75%	22.35%	20.72%	22.17%	21.53%

Table 1: Number of words using in Train and Test corpus

Gutenberg, specially for the XIX century[1], Wiki source[2], OpenLibrary [3], Tycho Brahe corpus[4] (Galves and Faria, 2010), Domínio Público[5], Arquivo Pessoa[6], Linguateca[7], *Corpus de Textos antigos* (Corpus of old texts)[8] and Colonia corpus[9] (Zampieri, 2017).

It is worth noting that the further back we go in historical texts (e.g.: renaissance, medieval), the more spelling differences between texts are found due to a lack of a stable spelling standard. Also, there were high rates of illiteracy since there was not any kind of public schools to learn how to read or write the language. Actually, the first relevant language standard for Portuguese is defined and applied at the end of XVIIIth century, as it also happened in other Romance languages such as French or Spanish. *Academia das Ciências de Lisboa* (Lisbon Academy of Sciences), one of the bodies that regulate the standardization of European Portuguese language, was created in 1779 in Lisbon.

Then, we checked whether the documents selected in the previous step were in the original spelling. If so, they were indexed and their OCR errors were cleaned; otherwise they were not considered.

All texts with original spelling were digitized and cleaned. It resulted in a new diachronic corpus, we call Diachronic Portuguese Corpus (DiaPT). To compute PLD measure between all periods, each period of DiaPT (i.e. XII-XV, XVI-XVIII, XIX-1, XIX-2, XX-1, XX-2) was divided into two partitions: train and test. As a result, each training partition is constituted by about 1,3/1.5M word tokens. Balanced train-test pairs allows us to compute PLD measure without bias.

5.2 Results

The objective of the current experiments is to compare six language periods of European Portuguese language using PLD. The specific implementation of PLD consists of 7-gram models and a smoothing technique based on linear interpolation. Two experiments have been performed. The first one consists of applying PLD measure on a Portuguese historical corpus keeping the original spelling. In the second experiment, we apply the same PLD measure to the same historical documents, but previously transcribed by means of a normalization process.

5.2.1 PLD with original spelling

In this experiment, we have developed a set of scripts (https://github.com/gamallo/Perplexity) to create a train 7-gram diachronic language model, period by period. As a result, six 7-gram diachronic language models are obtained. Then, we have generated 7-gram models from all test corpora. Once all models have been created, PLD is computed for each possible train-test pair of models. Table 2 shows the diachronic language distance between all historical Portuguese periods with original spelling using PLD. Some representative samples of these distances are depicted in Figure 1. More precisely, Figure 1(a) compares the distance evolution across all periods of the two

---

[1] https://www.gutenberg.org/browse/languages/pt
[2] https://en.wikisource.org/wiki/Category:Portuguese_authors
[3] https://openlibrary.org/
[4] http://www.tycho.iel.unicamp.br/corpus/index.html
[5] http://www.dominiopublico.gov.br/pesquisa/DetalheObraForm.do?select_action= &co_obra=16090
[6] http://arquivopessoa.net/textos/
[7] https://www.linguateca.pt/
[8] http://alfclul.clul.ul.pt/teitok/cta/index.php?action=textos
[9] http://corporavm.uni-koeln.de/colonia/

	XII-XV	XVI-XVIII	XIX-1	XIX-2	XX-1	XX-2
XII-XV	2.849	5.408	6.451	7.002	7.692	7.411
XVI-XVIII	5.408	3.745	6.373	6.633	6.785	7.128
XIX-1	6.451	6.373	2.990	4.081	3.965	4.972
XIX-2	7.002	6.633	4.081	3.037	3.937	4.698
XX-1	7.692	6.785	3.965	3.937	2.872	4.878
XX-2	7.411	7.129	4.972	4.698	4.878	3.013

Table 2: PLD diachronic measure in original spelling (DiaPT corpus)

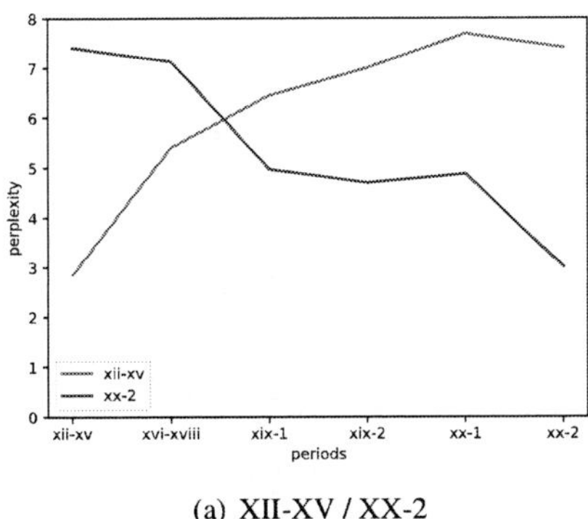

(a) XII-XV / XX-2

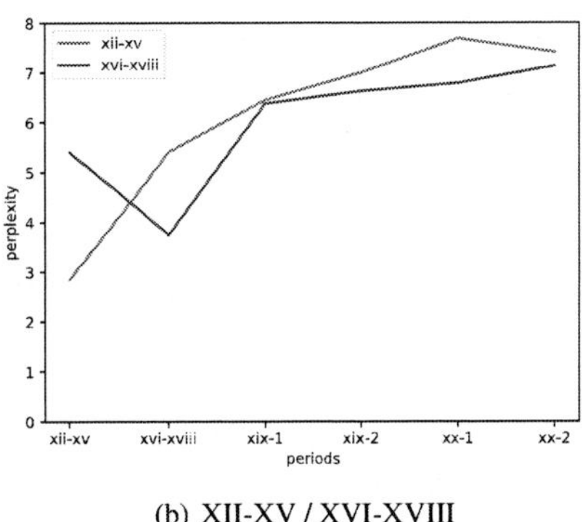

(b) XII-XV / XVI-XVIII

Figure 1: Original spelling. In (a) we compare the PLD distances of XII-XV and XX-2 across all periods. In (b) the same comparison is made between XII-XV and XVI-XVIII.

further away periods, namely medieval (XII-XV) and second half XXth period (XX-2), whereas Figure 1(b) compares two close historical periods: XII-XV and XV-XVIII.

Figure 1(a) plots how XII-XVth diverges from all the periods in a regular basis: there is an almost linear growth from 4.48 for XVI-XVIII (the closest PLD distance), up to 7.69 for XX-1 (the furthest one), even though the distance grows smoothly from XIX-1 and decreases slightly in XX-2. The same pattern can be observed for XX-2, but in the reverse direction: distance grows slightly until XIX-1, but there is a more pronounced divergence with regard to the furthest periods.

On the other hand, Figure 1(b) compares XII-XVth and XVI-XVIIIth periods. The most relevant information in this plot is the following: XVI-XVIII is more distant from the modern periods (6.37 with regard to XIX-1) than from the medieval period, (5.4 with regard to to XII-XV). In addition, as it was expected, the distance grows very slowly from XIX, in the same way as XII-XV with regard to the modern periods.

In general, distance between periods is correlated with chronology.

5.2.2 PLD with transcribed spelling

In a second experiment, we have converted DiaPT corpus into a new one in which documents of all periods share a common spelling: DiaPT_norm. To do so, all Portuguese historical periods were both transliterated into Latin script and normalized using a generic orthography closer to phonological issues. The encoding of the final spelling normalization consists of 34 symbols, representing 10 vowels and 24 consonants, designed to cover most of the commonly occurring sounds, including several consonant palatalizations and a variety of vowel articulation. As the encoding is close to a phonological one, the new spelling might be seen as a pointer to phonology. After this transformation we have carried out the same experiment as for DiaPT (described in the previous subsection).

151

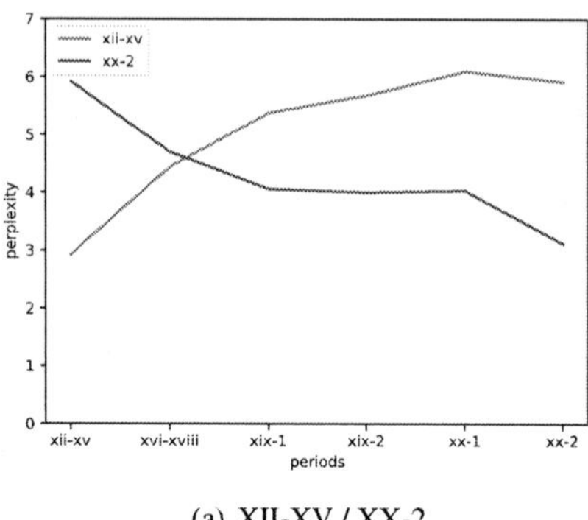

(a) XII-XV / XX-2

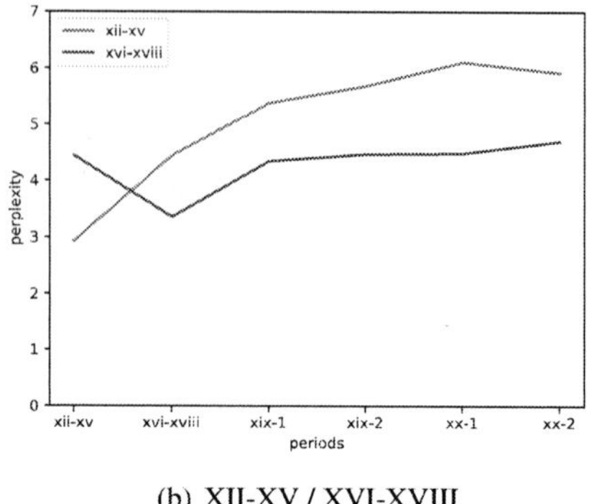

(b) XII-XV / XVI-XVIII

Figure 2: Transcribed spelling. In (a) we compare the PLD distances of XII-XV and XX-2 across all periods. In (b) the same comparison is made between XII-XV and XVI-XVIII.

	XII-XV	XVI-XVIII	XIX-1	XIX-2	XX-1	XX-2
XII-XV	2.937	4.443	5.386	5.689	6.106	5.925
XVI-XVIII	4.443	3.355	4.346	4.467	4.484	4.697
XIX-1	5.386	4.346	3.118	3.676	3.620	4.060
XIX-2	5.689	4.467	3.676	3.137	3.569	4.000
XX-1	6.106	4.484	3.620	3.569	2.997	4.036
XX-2	5.925	4.697	4.060	4.000	4.036	3.120

Table 3: PLD diachronic measure in a common transcribed spelling (DiaPT_norm corpus.)

In this new experiment on DiaPT_norm, the PLD distances shown in Table 3 are very similar to those of the previous experiment (Tab 2). The pattern of distances is the same in both experiments, even though in DiaPT_norm there is a closer approximation between periods since there is lower divergence in general as a result of using normalized orthography.

5.3 Discussion

The results obtained in our experiments allow us to conclude that there are only three clearly separated historical periods of Portuguese: XII-XV, XVI-XVIII and XIX-XX. If we look in depth our results, we can observe that the distance between the modern periods (from XIX to XX) could be too low to justify the existence of different periods in terms of language variation.

The results also lead us to observe that European Portuguese language is historically a compact language. There is not a large divergence within the different historical periods of European Portuguese language. The longest difference between XII-XV and XX-2 is over 6.19, which drops to 5.92 with a normalized orthography for all periods. By considering the results reported in (Gamallo et al., 2017b), this score is in the same range as the distance between diatopic varieties or *Ausbau* languages (e.g. Bosnian-Croatian, perplexity = 5.90), and is not larger than the distance between languages considered undoubtedly different but closely related (e.g. Spanish-Portuguese, perplexity=7.74).

6 Conclusions and Future Work
6.1 Conclusions

We have defined a new diachronic language distance measure, PLD, to identify the main evolution phases of a language and measure how much these phases differ from one another. Even though a similar measure was used to compute language distance in our previous work (Gamallo et al.,

2017b), as far as we know, this is the first attempt to use it for measuring distance between periods in a diachronic perspective. Its application to Portuguese language allows us to quantify its historical evolution as well as its main standarization changes over time.

Three main periods of Portuguese have been identified, and the distance between ancient periods and the modern ones is not bigger than the distance between language varieties from a diatopic perspective. So, Portuguese keeps an important degree of homogeneity over time.

Another contribution of our work is that a new diachronic Portuguese corpus in original spelling has been created: DiaPT. This corpus has been collected from different open historical corpora and texts repositories, priorizing those who have original spelling [10].

PLD is a robust measure since the transcription of the corpus with a shared ortography has not had any impact in changing the distance of Portuguese periods. On the contrary, this change has compacted the internal distance between language periods, but has not generated different relations between them.

6.2 Further work

Based on these results, we are planning to test diachronic distance on another languages and linguistic varieties. Also, we aim at using PLD with different language models: e.g. n-grams calculated from relevant linguistic words, phonological rules modifying the spelling, etc. Additionally we would like to test this technique for labeling undated texts. Finally, we will use PLD to enhance precision on other NLP tools, such as language identification, specially for *Ausbau* languages and closely related varieties.

Acknowledgments

The authors thanks the referees for thoughtful comments and helpful suggestions. We are very grateful to Marcos Garcia of the University of A Coruña for his contributions to the development of the experiments. Special acknowledgment is due José António Souto Cabo of the University of Santiago de Compostela for his expertise in medieval historical linguistics of Galician-Portuguese. This work has been partially supported by a 2016 BBVA Foundation Grant for Researchers and Cultural Creators, by TelePares (MINECO, ref:FFI2014-51978-C2-1-R) and TADeep (MINECO, ref: TIN2015-70214-P) projects. It also has received financial support from the Consellería de Cultura, Educación e Ordenación Universitaria (accreditation 2016-2019, ED431G/08) and the European Regional Development Fund (ERDF).

References

Ehsaneddin Asgari and Mohammad R. K. Mofrad. 2016. Comparing fifty natural languages and twelve genetic languages using word embedding language divergence (WELD) as a quantitative measure of language distance. In *Proceedings of the Workshop on Multilingual and Cross-lingual Methods in NLP*, pages 65–74, San Diego, California.

Dik Bakker, Andre Muller, Viveka Velupillai, Soren Wichmann, Cecil H. Brown, Pamela Brown, Dmitry Egorov, Robert Mailhammer, Anthony Grant, and Eric W. Holman. 2009. Adding typology to lexicostatistics: A combined approach to language classification. *Linguistic Typology*, 13(1):169–181.

F. Barbançon, S. Evans, L. Nakhleh, D. Ringe, and T. Warnow. 2013. An experimental study comparing linguistic phylogenetic reconstruction methods. *Diachronica*, 30:143–170.

Lars Borin. 2013. The why and how of measuring linguistic differences. *Approaches to measuring linguistic differences, Berlin, Mouton de Gruyter*, pages 3–25.

Cecil H. Brown, Eric W. Holman, Søren Wichmann, and Viveka Velupilla. 2008. Automated classification of the world's languages: a description of the method and preliminary results. *Language Typology and Universals*, 61(4).

---

[10] `https://github.com/gamallo/Perplexity/tree/master/resources/DiaPT`

Rui Grilo Capelo, A Monteiro, J Nunes, A Rodrigues, L Torgal, and F Vitorino. 1994. *História de Portugal em datas*. Círculo de Leitores, Lisboa.

Stanley F. Chen and Joshua Goodman. 1996. An empirical study of smoothing techniques for language modeling. In *Proceedings of the 34th Annual Meeting on Association for Computational Linguistics*, ACL '96, pages 310–318, Stroudsburg, PA, USA. Association for Computational Linguistics.

B.R. Chiswick and P.W. Miller. 2004. *Linguistic Distance: A Quantitative Measure of the Distance Between English and Other Languages*. Discussion papers. IZA.

Stefania Degaetano-Ortlieb, Hannah Kermes, Ashraf Khamis, and Elke Teich. 2016. An information-theoretic approach to modeling diachronic change in scientific english. *Selected Papers from Varieng-From Data to Evidence (d2e)*.

T Mark Ellison and Simon Kirby. 2006. Measuring language divergence by intra-lexical comparison. In *Proceedings of the 21st international conference on computational linguistics and 44th annual meeting of the association for computational linguistics*, pages 273–280.

Charlotte Galves and Pablo Faria. 2010. Tycho Brahe parsed corpus of historical Portuguese. *URL: http://www. tycho. iel. unicamp. br/~tycho/corpus/en/index. html*.

Pablo Gamallo, Susana Sotelo, and José Ramom Pichel. 2014. Comparing ranking-based and naive bayes approaches to language detection on tweets. In *Workshop TweetLID: Twitter Language Identification Workshop at SEPLN 2014*, Girona, Spain.

Pablo Gamallo, Inaki Alegria, José Ramom Pichel, and Manex Agirrezabal. 2016. Comparing two basic methods for discriminating between similar languages and varieties. In *Proceedings of the Third Workshop on NLP for Similar Languages, Varieties and Dialects (VarDial3)*, pages 170–177.

Pablo Gamallo, José Ramom Pichel, and Iñaki Alegria. 2017a. From language identification to language distance. *Physica A: Statistical Mechanics and its Applications*, 484:152–162.

Pablo Gamallo, Jose Ramom Pichel, Santiago de Compostela, and Inaki Alegria. 2017b. A perplexity-based method for similar languages discrimination. *VarDial 2017*, page 109.

Yuyang Gao, Wei Liang, Yuming Shi, and Qiuling Huang. 2014. Comparison of directed and weighted co-occurrence networks of six languages. *Physica A: Statistical Mechanics and its Applications*, 393(C):579–589.

Meritxell González. 2015. An analysis of twitter corpora and the differences between formal and colloquial tweets. In *Proceedings of the Tweet Translation Workshop 2015*, pages 1–7.

Wilbert Heeringa, Peter Kleiweg, Charlotte Gooskens, and John Nerbonne. 2006. Evaluation of string distance algorithms for dialectology. In *Proceedings of the workshop on linguistic distances*, pages 51–62. Association for Computational Linguistics.

E.W. Holman, S. Wichmann, C.H. Brown, V. Velupillai, A. Muller, and D. Bakker. 2008. Explorations in automated lexicostatistics. *Folia Linguistica*, 42(2):331–354.

Heinz Kloss. 1967. "Abstand languages" and "Ausbau languages". *Anthropological linguistics*, pages 29–41.

Haitao Liu and Jin Cong. 2013. Language clustering with word co-occurrence networks based on parallel texts. *Chinese Science Bulletin*, 58(10):1139–1144.

Shervin Malmasi, Marcos Zampieri, Nikola Ljubešić, Preslav Nakov, Ahmed Ali, and Jörg Tiedemann. 2016. Discriminating between similar languages and Arabic dialect identification: A report on the third DSL Shared Task. In *Proceedings of the 3rd Workshop on Language Technology for Closely Related Languages, Varieties and Dialects (VarDial)*, pages 1–14, Osaka, Japan.

José Mattoso and Rui Ramos. 1994. *História de Portugal*. Editorial Estampa.

Paul McNamee. 2005. Language identification: a solved problem suitable for undergraduate instruction. *Journal of Computing Sciences in Colleges*, 3:94–101.

Robert McColl Millar and Larry Trask. 2015. *Trask's historical linguistics*. Routledge.

Luay Nakhleh, Donald A Ringe, and Tandy Warnow. 2005. Perfect phylogenetic networks: A new methodology for reconstructing the evolutionary history of natural languages. *Language*, 81(2):382–420.

John Nerbonne and Wilbert Heeringa. 1997. Measuring dialect distance phonetically. In *Proceedings of the Third Meeting of the ACL Special Interest Group in Computational Phonology*, pages 11–18.

John Nerbonne and Erhard Hinrichs. 2006. Linguistic distances. In *Proceedings of the workshop on linguistic distances*, pages 1–6. Association for Computational Linguistics.

John Nerbonne, Wilbert Heeringa, and Peter Kleiweg. 1999. Edit distance and dialect proximity. *Time Warps, String Edits and Macromolecules: The theory and practice of sequence comparison*, 15.

Filippo Petroni and Maurizio Serva. 2010. Measures of lexical distance between languages. *Physica A: Statistical Mechanics and its Applications*, 389(11):2280–2283.

Taraka Rama and Anil Kumar Singh. 2009. From bag of languages to family trees from noisy corpus. In *Proceedings of the International Conference RANLP-2009*, pages 355–359.

José Hermano Saraiva. 1978. *História concisa de Portugal*. Publ. Europa-América.

António José Saraiva. 2001. *História da literatura portuguesa*. Porto: Porto Editora, 2001.

Rico Sennrich. 2012. Perplexity minimization for translation model domain adaptation in statistical machine translation. In *Proceedings of the 13th Conference of the European Chapter of the Association for Computational Linguistics*, EACL '12, pages 539–549, Stroudsburg, PA, USA. Association for Computational Linguistics.

M. Swadesh. 1952. Lexicostatistic dating of prehistoric ethnic contacts. In *Proceedings of the American Philosophical Society 96*, pages 452–463.

Paul Teyssier. 1982. *História da língua portuguesa*. Livraria Sá da Costa Editora.

Martijn Wieling and John Nerbonne. 2015. Advances in dialectometry.

Edwin Bucher Williams. 1962. *From Latin to Portuguese: Historical Phonology and Morphology of the Portugese Language*. Univ. Pennsylvania Press.

Maria Francisca Xavier, Maria Teresa Brocardo, and MG Vicente. 1994. CIPM–UM corpus informatizado do português medieval. *Actas do X Encontro da Associação Portuguesa de Linguística*, 2:599–612.

Li Yujian and Liu Bo. 2007. A normalized levenshtein distance metric. *IEEE transactions on pattern analysis and machine intelligence*, 29(6):1091–1095.

Marcos Zampieri, Binyam Gebrekidan Gebre, and Sascha Diwersy. 2013. N-gram language models and POS distribution for the identification of Spanish varieties. In *Proceedings of TALN*, volume 2, pages 580–587.

Marcos Zampieri. 2017. Compiling and processing historical and contemporary Portuguese corpora. *arXiv preprint arXiv:1710.00803*.

Arkaitz Zubiaga, Iñaki San Vicente, Pablo Gamallo, José Ramom Pichel, Iñaki Alegria, Nora Aranberri, Aitzol Ezeiza, and Víctor Fresno. 2015. Tweetlid: a benchmark for tweet language identification. *Language Resources and Evaluation*, pages 1–38.

Comparing CRF and LSTM performance on the task of morphosyntactic tagging of non-standard varieties of South Slavic languages

Nikola Ljubešić
Dept. of Knowledge Technologies
Jožef Stefan Institute
Jamova cesta 39
1000 Ljubljana, Slovenia
`nikola.ljubesic@ijs.si`

Abstract

This paper presents two systems taking part in the Morphosyntactic Tagging of Tweets shared task on Slovene, Croatian and Serbian data, organized inside the VarDial Evaluation Campaign. While one system relies on the traditional method for sequence labeling (conditional random fields), the other relies on its neural alternative (bidirectional long short-term memory). We investigate the similarities and differences of these two approaches, showing that both methods yield very good and quite similar results, with the neural model outperforming the traditional one more as the level of non-standardness of the text increases. Through an error analysis we show that the neural system is better at long-range dependencies, while the traditional system excels and slightly outperforms the neural system at the local ones. We present in the paper new state-of-the-art results in morphosyntactic annotation of non-standard text for Slovene, Croatian and Serbian.

1 Introduction

In this paper we present two systems taking part in the MTT (Morphosyntactic Tagging of Tweets) shared task, part of the VarDial Evaluation Campaign (Zampieri et al., 2018). In the task, general-domain and in-domain datasets with tokens manually annotated with morphosyntactic descriptions (MSDs), are given, together with large web-based datasets, for three South Slavic languages: Slovene, Croatian and Serbian. The challenge of the task is to exploit similarity of standard vs. non-standard variants, as well as the overall proximity of the three languages in question.

While the first system, JANES, relies on the traditional method for sequence labeling, namely conditional random fields (CRF), the second system, JSI, relies on the currently hugely popular neural networks, more precisely bidirectional long short-term memories (BiLSTM).

The contributions of this paper are the following: (1) a direct comparison of CRFs and BiLSTMs on a series of datasets, where CRFs are equipped with carefully engineered features, not generic ones, and (2) a new state-of-the-art in tagging non-standard varieties of the three languages in question.

2 System Descriptions

2.1 Datasets Distributed inside the Shared Task

Before we describe our two systems participating in the task, we quickly quantify the available resources through token number in Table 1 as these heavily influence our decisions in the system setup. The `twitter.*` datasets come from the Janes-Tag manually annotated dataset of Slovene computer-mediated communication (Erjavec et al., 2017) and the ReLDI-NormTagNER-* manually annotated datasets of Croatian (Ljubešić et al., 2017b) and Serbian (Ljubešić et al., 2017c) tweets. They are all similar in size, with cca. 40 thousand tokens available for training, 8 thousand for development and 20 thousand for testing.

This work is licensed under a Creative Commons Attribution 4.0 International Licence. Licence details: http://creativecommons.org/licenses/by/4.0/.

Proceedings of the Fifth Workshop on NLP for Similar Languages, Varieties and Dialects, pages 156–163
Santa Fe, New Mexico, USA, August 20, 2018.

The `standard.train` datasets mostly cover the general domain. While the Slovene and Croatian datasets are similar in size with around 500 thousand tokens, the Serbian dataset is significantly smaller with only 87 thousand tokens.

The `web.auto` datasets are large web-based datasets, slWac for Slovene (Erjavec et al., 2015), hrWaC for Croatian and srWaC for Serbian (Ljubešić and Klubička, 2014). These are automatically annotated with state-of-the-art taggers of standard language for Slovene (Ljubešić and Erjavec, 2016) and Croatian and Serbian (Ljubešić et al., 2016).

	twitter.train	twitter.dev	twitter.test	standard.train	web.auto
Slovene	37,756	7,056	19,296	586,248	895,875,492
Croatian	45,609	8,886	21,412	506,460	1,397,757,548
Serbian	45,708	9,581	23,327	86,765	554,627,647

Table 1: Size of datasets distributed through the MTT shared task. Sizes are in number of tokens.

2.2 The JANES System

The JANES system (the name of the system comes from the Slovene national project JANES inside which the system was developed[1]) is based on conditional random fields (CRFs) (Lafferty et al., 2001), exploiting the following handcrafted features:

- lowercased focus token (token for which features are being extracted)

- lowercased tokens in a window of $\{-3, -2, -1, 1, 2, 3\}$ form the focus token

- focus token suffixes of length $\{1, 2, 3, 4\}$

- features encoding whether the focus token starts with `http` (link), # (hashtag) or @ (mention)

- Brown cluster binary paths for the focus token, with the path length of $\{2, 4, 6, 8\}$

These features were proven to yield optimal results in our previous work on tagging non-standard Slovene (Ljubešić et al., 2017a).

The Brown clusters, the output of a method for context-dependent hierarchical word clustering (Brown et al., 1992), were calculated from the web data that were made available through the shared task, namely the slWaC web corpus of Slovene (Erjavec et al., 2015) and the hrWaC and srWaC corpora of Croatian and Serbian (Ljubešić and Klubička, 2014). We have used default parameters for calculating Brown clusters, except for the minimum occurrence parameter which was set to 5. The web text was previously lowercased and punctuations and newlines were removed from it.

For training the tagger, we exploited (1) the proximity of the Croatian and Serbian language, and (2) the fact that we have much more standard training data and much less Twitter training data. We sampled our final training data for each language in the following manner:

- for Slovene: we added to the Slovene standard training data ten times the available non-standard data, thereby reaching a similar amount of standard and non-standard data in our training set; from previous work we know that for CRFs oversampling in-domain data is the simplest and most effective method in merging out-domain and in-domain training data (Horsmann and Zesch, 2015; Ljubešić et al., 2017a)

- for Croatian: we merged the Croatian and the Serbian standard language training datasets, added to it ten copies of the Croatian Twitter training dataset and two copies of the Serbian training dataset, thereby putting emphasis on the Croatian training data, which is expected to be closer to the Croatian test data

---

[1] `http://nl.ijs.si/janes/english/`

- for Serbian: we merged the Croatian standard training data, two copies of the Serbian standard training data (as these are more than five times smaller than the Croatian ones), ten copies of non-standard Croatian training data, and four copies of non-standard Serbian training data, with the rationale that most non-standard elements in Croatian are present in non-standard Serbian as well, but with lower frequency; by oversampling non-standard Croatian in the Serbian dataset we emphasize the non-standard elements in the Croatian non-standard training data as the Serbian non-standard data is much closer to the standard language (Miličević and Ljubešić, 2016)

The system was implemented in CRFSuite (Okazaki, 2007), using the passive aggressive optimizer and 10 epochs, a setting which proved to yield best results in previous experiments (Ljubešić and Erjavec, 2016).

2.3 The JSI System

The JSI system (the name comes from the name of our current employer, the Jožef Stefan Institute) is an adaptation of the BiLSTM tagger written in pytorch[2], with some added modifications. The architecture of the submitted system is the following:

- a character-level subnetwork, consisting of a character embedding layer of 16 dimensions and a BiLSTM layer with 25 units

- the main network

    - concatenating the character-level representation of a word from the subnetwork described above (25*2, i.e., 50 dimensions), and the word embedding layer (100 dimensions)
    - feeding this concatenated 150-dimensional character- and word-level representation into a BiLSTM layer with 100 units
    - the per-token BiLSTM output being fed to a fully-connected layer with 256 units and a final softmax layer for prediction

While developing this architecture, we investigated the impact of various setups on the Slovene dataset. The results of experimenting with (1) different pretrained word embeddings, (2) the impact of adding different character-level representations, (3) fine-tuning the model on in-domain data and (4) pretraining the character-level encoder on a inflectional lexicon, are shown in Table 2. We performed our experiments on each of the above mentioned issues subsequently, always propagating to the next experiment set the setup achieving best results in the previous one. The setup we start with consists only of the main network, without the character-level subnetwork.

2.3.1 Word Embeddings

The first group of results considers different ways of pretraining word embeddings. The word embeddings were always pretrained on the web data available for each language.

We considered only two tools for pretraining word embeddings: word2vec (Mikolov et al., 2013) and fasttext (Bojanowski et al., 2017), and two architectures, CBOW and Skipgram. The results (*word2vec cbow* vs. *word2vec skipgram*) show for Skipgram to be significantly better suited for this task, which is in line with previous results (Reimers and Gurevych, 2017).

Comparing word2vec and fasttext (*word2vec skipgram* vs. *fasttext skipgram*), fasttext shows a slightly better performance, but the difference gets more obvious (almost half a point in token accuracy) once fasttext is used to generate representations for the words not present in the pretrained word embeddings (*fasttext skipgram generated*).[3]

---

[2]`https://github.com/neulab/dynet-benchmark/blob/master/pytorch/`
`bilstm-tagger-withchar.py`

[3]We would expect the positive impact of generating embeddings for out-of-vocabulary words to diminish once character-level representations are added to the model. However, we did not investigate this.

setup	token accuracy with stdev
word2vec cbow	0.8407 ± 0.0025
word2vec skipgram	0.8550 ± 0.0041
fasttext skipgram	0.8578 ± 0.0041
fasttext skipgram generated	$\mathbf{0.8596 \pm 0.0031}$
added character-level encoding	0.8780 ± 0.0030
added bidirectional encoding	$\mathbf{0.8790 \pm 0.0032}$
additionally tuned on in-domain data	$\mathbf{0.8836 \pm 0.0026}$
pretrained character-level encoder on web data	$\mathbf{0.8855 \pm 0.0015}$

Table 2: Initial experiments on the JSI system, performed on the Slovene dataset. The standard deviation is calculated from ten evaluations performed during the last epoch.

2.3.2 Character-level Representations

The second group of experiments considers the impact of adding character-level representations of each token to the word representation via a dedicated character-level BiLSTM. Adding the character-level representation has shown the biggest impact among all the experiments, with ~ 2 accuracy points increase, and a minor difference between encoding the character sequence with a single-direction or a bi-directional LSTM.

2.3.3 Fine-tuning on the In-Domain Dataset

The third experiment considers the impact of not training the network on a simple merge of all the available relevant training data, but also fine-tuning the network exclusively on in-domain data.

Running three epochs on the concatenation of all datasets, and then additional two epochs only on the in-domain Twitter data, consistently improved the results for around half an accuracy point.

This method is somewhat similar to the oversampling method applied on the JANES system. It is, however, more elegant as it gives greater control over the amount and order of data fed into the system.

2.3.4 Pretraining the Character-level BiLSTM

Finally, in the last set of experiments we investigated whether there is positive impact if the character-level encoder was pretrained on a inflectional-lexicon-like resource. In this shared task the web data were automatically tagged with a CRF tagger relying on a lexicon (Ljubešić et al., 2016; Ljubešić and Erjavec, 2016), therefore we transformed the automatically-tagged web data into a lexicon by (1) picking only token-tag pairs occurring at least 100 times in the web data and (2) selecting only the most frequent token-tag pair per token. With the second criterion we lost some information on homonymous words, but also got rid of a lot of wrong automatic annotations of frequent words.

The results on pretraining the character-level encoder show that the improvement lies below half an accuracy point, but this improvement showed to be consistent across all the three languages.[4]

3 Results

In this section we report the results of the final setups of the JANES and the JSI system and compare it to the HunPos baseline (Halácsy et al., 2007) defined by the shared task organizers.

Additionally, we report the results of the JANES system using an inflectional lexicon for the specific language, namely Sloleks for Slovene (Dobrovoljc et al., 2015), hrLex for Croatian (Ljubešić et al., 2016a) and srLex for Serbian (Ljubešić et al., 2016b). We call this system JANES-lex. We compare to this system as it is very straightforward to add information from an inflectional lexicon as additional features to a CRF-based system.

---

[4]On Croatian data we ran an additional experiment not with the noisy web data, but the manually constructed inflectional lexicon hrLex (Ljubešić et al., 2016a), improving additionally for almost half an accuracy point. However, in this shared task we decided not to use resources that were not shared by the organizers as we (correctly) assumed that other teams will not use additional resources neither and that we would lower the comparability of the obtained results.

	Slovene	Croatian	Serbian
HunPos baseline	0.832	0.834	0.832
JANES	0.871	0.893	0.900
JANES-lex	0.877	0.897	0.901
JSI	0.883	0.890	0.900
JSI-simpler	**0.891**	**0.898**	**0.903**

Table 3: Results of the two systems, their two adaptations and the baseline on the test data. Reported metric is token-level accuracy.

We also report a modification of the JSI system that we implemented after the shared task was already concluded. Namely, we removed the fully connected layer between the main BiLSTM and the softmax layer, which is actually the most frequent setup for sequence labeling. The removed layer in the JSI system is a residue from the tagger we based our implementation on[5]. We call the simplified tagger JSI-simpler.

The results of the two taggers and the two variants are given in Table 3. The reported results are those obtained on the test data.

We can first observe that (1) all the systems outperform the HunPos baseline by a wide margin and that (2) the results of the four remaining systems are rather close.

The largest difference that can be observed between the four systems are 2 accuracy points on Slovene between the basic CRF implementation (JANES) and the simplified BiLSTM implementation (JSI-simpler). The same difference is not to be observed on the other two languages, with the same systems having a difference of 0.5 points on Croatian and 0.3 points on Serbian. The reason for the larger difference on Slovene data lies in the fact that the Slovene data is least standard (17% tokens being non-standard), followed by Croatian (13% non-standard tokens), with Serbian data deviating the least from the norm (10% non-standard tokens) (Miličević et al., 2017) as more complex modeling techniques pay off more as the language deviates stronger from the norm.

Adding lexicon information to the JANES system (JANES vs. JANES-lex) improves the results on all three languages, but just slightly, between 0.1% and 0.6%. Previous work on the problem (Ljubešić et al., 2017a) has shown that Brown clusters already provide to a large extent the information that was traditionally obtained through inflectional lexicons.

Comparing the JANES and JSI results by using the McNemar's statistical test (McNemar, 1947), the difference on Slovene is statistically significant at the $p < 0.001$ level, with an absolute difference in 1.2 points and an relative error reduction of 9.3%. The differences on the remaining two languages are not statistically significant.

When comparing the JSI and JSI-simpler results, it becomes obvious that the additional layer in the JSI system actually deteriorates the results. On all the three languages, the differences are statistically significant, on Slovene and Croatian on the $p < 0.001$ level, while on Serbian it is on the $p < 0.05$ level. The level of significance of difference between the JANES and JSI-simpler systems is identical to that of between JSI and JSI-simpler.

The most interesting observation from the final evaluation of the submitted and modified systems is that the difference between the traditional CRFs and the (probably over-hyped?) BiLSTMs is actually quite small, with relative error reductions being 15% on Slovene, 5% on Croatian and only 3% on Serbian. These results, as well as some preliminary results on standard test sets, suggest that there would be no significant difference in the results between CRFs and BiLSTMs on standard training and test data.

---

[5] `https://github.com/neulab/dynet-benchmark/blob/master/pytorch/bilstm-tagger-withchar.py`

JANES			JSI-simpler		
pred	true	freq	pred	true	freq
Xf	Npmsn	74	Xf	Npmsn	55
Cc	Qo	59	Cc	Qo	55
Ncmsan	Ncmsn	46	Npmsn	Xf	40
Ncmsn	Ncmsan	34	Ncmsan	Ncmsn	34
Ncmsn	Npmsn	31	Rgp	Cs	23
Xf	Npmsan	23	Xf	Ncmsn	24
Rgp	Cs	23	Sl	Sa	23
Npmsn	Xf	23	Ncmsn	Ncmsan	23
Xf	Ncmsn	22	Agpnsny	Rgp	20
Cs	Rgp	20	Sa	Sl	19

Table 4: The ten most frequent confusion pairs for the JANES and the JSI-simpler systems.

4   Error analysis

In this section we perform an analysis of confusion matrices of the JANES and the JSI-simpler system. We perform the analysis on the output of the system on the Croatian test set. We analyze and compare the 10 most frequent confusions for each system, which covers roughly 20% of all errors done by each of the systems. The confusion pairs are given in Table 4. Both systems make similar most frequent mistakes, some of which are typical for morphosyntactic tagging of standard varieties of South Slavic languages, other being more specific for the Twitter variety.

The typical mistakes on the standard language include confusing nominative masculinum common nouns (Ncmsn) for accusative masculinum common nouns (Ncmsan) and vice versa, confusing the word "i" (English "and") in its coordinating conjunction (Cc) and particle (Qo) usage, confusing adverbs (Rgp) for adjectives (Agpnsny for instance) and confusing the word "kada" (English "when") in its subordinative conjunction (Cs) and adverbial (Rgp) usage.

The errors that are more due to the specificity of the Twitter variety are confusing proper names (Np.*) or common nouns (Nc.*) for foreign residuals (mostly foreign words or foreign sequences of words, Xf) and vice versa.

When comparing the most frequent errors between the two systems, the JANES CRF-based system seems to have more problems with the traditional discrimination between different context-dependent cases of nouns, which points to the direction that BiLSTMs are better at modeling long-range dependencies as discriminating between the nominative and the accusative case often requires a very wide context. On the other hand, what the BiLSTM system seems to be worse at is discriminating between different cases for prepositions, which heavily depends on the following adjective or noun. While confusing an accusative preposition (Sa) for a locative one (Sl) the BiLSTM system did 23 times, this happened to the CRF system 17 times. In the opposite direction, the BiLSTM system did 19 mistakes while the CRF system did one mistake less, namely 18 of them. While it is clear why CRFs excel at predicting prepositional cases correctly as this dependence is in the scope of the local features, it seems that the BiLSTMs trade more mistakes in the local context for less mistakes in a wider one.

5   Conclusion

In this paper we have compared two popular sequence labeling techniques: conditional random fields (CRFs) and bidirectional long short-term memories (BiLSTMs) on the task of morphosyntactic annotation of tweets written in three closely related South Slavic languages: Slovene, Croatian and Serbian.

We have shown that CRFs with well defined features come very close to the performance of the stronger BiLSTM models, the difference between those two being bigger as the data are more nonstandard. The relative error reduction between those two systems lies between 15% for Slovene, for which the Twitter variety deviates the most from the standard, and 3% for Serbian, for which the Twitter variety deviates the least.

For the CRF system, we have shown that using contextual, suffixal and distributional features gives very good results. The latter make an inflectional lexicon mostly obsolete, with just minor improvements in accuracy if features from large inflectional lexicons are added.

For the BiLSTM system, we have shown that encoding a character-level representation of a word is the single most useful intervention, with minor improvements obtained through proper word embedding pretraining, fine-tuning on in-domain data and pretraining the character-level encoder on pairs of words and MSD tags from a large automatically tagged web corpus.

With an error analysis we have shown that the types of error performed by each of the systems are actually very similar, most of them still being typical tagger errors for languages with a rich inflectional morphology. However, there is evidence that BiLSTMs resolve long-range dependencies much better, such as discriminating between masculinum nouns in nominative and accusative singular, but yielding slightly more mistakes in the close-range dependencies such as the case of prepositions.

Acknowledgements

The work presented in this paper has been funded by the Slovenian Research Agency national basic research project "Resources, methods and tools for the understanding, identification and classification of various forms of socially unacceptable discourse in the information society" (ARRS J7-8280, 2017-2020), and by the Slovenian research infrastructure CLARIN.SI.

References

Piotr Bojanowski, Edouard Grave, Armand Joulin, and Tomas Mikolov. 2017. Enriching word vectors with subword information. *Transactions of the Association for Computational Linguistics*, 5:135–146.

Peter F. Brown, Peter V. Desouza, Robert L. Mercer, Vincent J. Della Pietra, and Jenifer C. Lai. 1992. Class-based n-gram models of natural language. *Computational linguistics*, 18(4):467–479.

Kaja Dobrovoljc, Simon Krek, Peter Holozan, Tomaž Erjavec, and Miro Romih. 2015. Morphological lexicon sloleks 1.2. Slovenian language resource repository CLARIN.SI.

Tomaž Erjavec, Nikola Ljubešić, and Nataša Logar. 2015. The slWaC Corpus of the Slovene Web. *Informatica*, 39(1):35–42.

Tomaž Erjavec, Darja Fišer, Jaka Čibej, Špela Arhar Holdt, Nikola Ljubešić, and Katja Zupan. 2017. CMC training corpus Janes-Tag 2.0. Slovenian language resource repository CLARIN.SI.

Péter Halácsy, András Kornai, and Csaba Oravecz. 2007. HunPos: An open source trigram tagger. In *Proceedings of the 45th Annual Meeting of the ACL*, pages 209–212, Stroudsburg. Association for Computational Linguistics.

Tobias Horsmann and Torsten Zesch. 2015. Effectiveness of Domain Adaptation Approaches for Social Media PoS Tagging. *CLiC it*, page 166.

John D. Lafferty, Andrew McCallum, and Fernando C. N. Pereira. 2001. Conditional random fields: Probabilistic models for segmenting and labeling sequence data. In *Proceedings of the Eighteenth International Conference on Machine Learning*, ICML '01, pages 282–289, San Francisco, CA, USA. Morgan Kaufmann Publishers Inc.

Nikola Ljubešić and Filip Klubička. 2014. {bs,hr,sr}wac - web corpora of bosnian, croatian and serbian. In *Proceedings of the 9th Web as Corpus Workshop (WaC-9)*, pages 29–35. Association for Computational Linguistics.

Nikola Ljubešić, Filip Klubička, and Damir Boras. 2016a. Inflectional lexicon hrLex 1.2. Slovenian language resource repository CLARIN.SI.

Nikola Ljubešić, Filip Klubička, and Damir Boras. 2016b. Inflectional lexicon srLex 1.2. Slovenian language resource repository CLARIN.SI.

Nikola Ljubešić, Tomaž Erjavec, and Darja Fišer. 2017a. Adapting a state-of-the-art tagger for south slavic languages to non-standard text. In *Proceedings of the 6th Workshop on Balto-Slavic Natural Language Processing*, pages 60–68.

Nikola Ljubešić, Tomaž Erjavec, Maja Miličević, and Tanja Samardžić. 2017b. Croatian Twitter training corpus ReLDI-NormTagNER-hr 2.0. Slovenian language resource repository CLARIN.SI.

Nikola Ljubešić, Tomaž Erjavec, Maja Miličević, and Tanja Samardžić. 2017c. Serbian Twitter training corpus ReLDI-NormTagNER-sr 2.0. Slovenian language resource repository CLARIN.SI.

Nikola Ljubešić and Tomaž Erjavec. 2016. Corpus vs. Lexicon Supervision in Morphosyntactic Tagging: the Case of Slovene. In *Proceedings of the Tenth International Conference on Language Resources and Evaluation (LREC 2016)*, Paris, France. European Language Resources Association (ELRA).

Nikola Ljubešić, Filip Klubička, Željko Agić, and Ivo-Pavao Jazbec. 2016. New Inflectional Lexicons and Training Corpora for Improved Morphosyntactic Annotation of Croatian and Serbian. In *Proceedings of the Tenth International Conference on Language Resources and Evaluation (LREC 2016)*, Paris, France. European Language Resources Association (ELRA).

Quinn McNemar. 1947. Note on the sampling error of the difference between correlated proportions or percentages. *Psychometrika*, 12(2):153–157.

Tomas Mikolov, Kai Chen, Greg Corrado, and Jeffrey Dean. 2013. Efficient estimation of word representations in vector space. *CoRR*, abs/1301.3781.

Maja Miličević and Nikola Ljubešić. 2016. Tviterasi, tviteraši or twitteraši? Producing and analysing a normalised dataset of Croatian and Serbian tweets. *Slovenščina 2.0: empirical, applied and interdisciplinary research*, 4(2):156–188.

Maja Miličević, Nikola Ljubešić, and Darja Fišer. 2017. Birds of a feather don't quite tweet together: An analysis of spelling variation in Slovene, Croatian and Serbian Twitterese. In Darja Fišer and Michael Beisswenger, editors, *Investigating Computer-mediated Communication: Corpus-based Approaches to Language in the Digital World*, pages 14–43. Ljubljana University Press, Faculty of Arts.

Naoaki Okazaki. 2007. Crfsuite: a fast implementation of conditional random fields (crfs).

Nils Reimers and Iryna Gurevych. 2017. Optimal hyperparameters for deep lstm-networks for sequence labeling tasks. *CoRR*, abs/1707.06799.

Marcos Zampieri, Shervin Malmasi, Preslav Nakov, Ahmed Ali, Suwon Shon, James Glass, Yves Scherrer, Tanja Samardžić, Nikola Ljubešić, Jörg Tiedemann, Chris van der Lee, Stefan Grondelaers, Nelleke Oostdijk, Antal van den Bosch, Ritesh Kumar, Bornini Lahiri, and Mayank Jain. 2018. Language Identification and Morphosyntactic Tagging: The Second VarDial Evaluation Campaign. In *Proceedings of the Fifth Workshop on NLP for Similar Languages, Varieties and Dialects (VarDial)*, Santa Fe, USA.

Computationally efficient discrimination between language varieties with large feature vectors and regularized classifiers

Adrien Barbaresi
Austrian Academy of Sciences (ÖAW)
Berlin-Brandenburg Academy of Sciences and Humanities (BBAW)
`adrien.barbaresi@oeaw.ac.at`

Abstract

The present contribution revolves around efficient approaches to language classification which have been field-tested in the *Vardial* evaluation campaign. The methods used in several language identification tasks comprising different language types are presented and their results are discussed, giving insights on real-world application of regularization, linear classifiers and corresponding linguistic features. The use of a specially adapted Ridge classifier proved useful in 2 tasks out of 3. The overall approach (XAC) has slightly outperformed most of the other systems on the DFS task (Dutch and Flemish) and on the ILI task (Indo-Aryan languages), while its comparative performance was poorer in on the GDI task (Swiss German dialects).

1 Introduction

Language identification is the task of predicting the language(s) that a given document is written in. It can be seen as a text categorization task in which documents are assigned to pre-existing categories. This research field has found renewed interest in the 1990s due to advances in statistical approaches and it has been active ever since, particularly since the methods developed have also been deemed relevant for text categorization, native language identification, authorship attribution, text-based geolocation, and dialectal studies (Lui and Cook, 2013).

As of 2014 and the first Discriminating between Similar Languages (DSL) shared task, a unified dataset (Tan et al., 2014) comprising news texts of closely-related language varieties has been used to test and benchmark systems. The instances to be classified are quite short and may even be difficult to distinguish for human annotators, thus adding to the difficulty and the interest of the task. An analysis of recent developments can be found in Goutte el al. (2016), in the reports on previous shared tasks as well as in a recently published survey on language and dialect identification (Jauhiainen et al., 2018). In previous editions the shared tasks organized at VarDial included dialects of Arabic, German, and the DSL shared task which featured similar languages and language varieties (Zampieri et al., 2017; Malmasi et al., 2016; Zampieri et al., 2015; Zampieri et al., 2014). Other related shared tasks are the MGB challenge on Arabic (Ali et al., 2017), the PAN lab on author profiling which included dialects and language varieties (Rangel et al., 2017), and the TweetLID shared task which included similar languages (Zubiaga et al., 2016).

The present study was conducted on the occasion of the fifth VarDial workshop (Zampieri et al., 2018). It focuses on submissions to three different datasets: the first iteration of the Discriminating between Dutch and Flemish in Subtitles (DFS) task (van der Lee and van den Bosch, 2017), the second iteration of work on Swiss German dialects based on the GDI dataset as described in Samardžić et al. (2016), and the first iteration of the Indo-Aryan Language Identification (ILI) shared task, based on the compiled ILI dataset (Kumar et al., 2018). The peculiarities of the datasets include their diversity in terms of linguistic characteristics and their fluctuating difficulty, as most varieties can be mutually intelligible with diverging degrees of lexical and morphosyntactic variation. As in previous tasks, the number of instances is limited in size, the training and test sets are on the order of magnitude of thousands or tens

This work is licensed under a Creative Commons Attribution 4.0 International License. License details: `http://creativecommons.org/licenses/by/4.0/`.

Proceedings of the Fifth Workshop on NLP for Similar Languages, Varieties and Dialects, pages 164–171
Santa Fe, New Mexico, USA, August 20, 2018.

of thousands of instances, the latter being fairly small in size, with at most a sentence each time. As a consequence, a classifier constructed on small training sets may be biased and have a large variance, as the classifier parameters (coefficients) are poorly estimated. It is also unstable, as small changes in the training set may cause large changes in the classifier. A key component of winning systems is their capacity to make correct predictions on unseen data based on the trained model.

In this context, it has been shown that more conventional statistical methods can very well be more accurate than latest machine learning approaches (Barbaresi, 2017), resulting in a paradox common to a fair number of applications: "Knowing that a certain sophisticated method is not as accurate as a much simpler one is upsetting from a scientific point of view as the former requires a great deal of academic expertise and ample computer time to be applied." (Makridakis et al., 2018)

The remainder of this paper is organized as follows: in section 2 the preprocessing and feature extraction steps are presented, the classifiers follow in section 3, and three systems are then evaluated and discussed in section 4.

2 Large feature vectors

2.1 Preprocessing

Preliminary tests have shown that adding a custom linguistic preprocessing step could slightly improve the results. As such, instances are tokenized using the *SoMaJo* tokenizer (Proisl and Uhrig, 2016), which achieves state-of-the-art accuracies on both web and CMC data for German. As it is rule-based, it is supposed to be efficient enough for the languages of the shared task. No stop words are used since relevant cues are expected to be found automatically as explained below. Additionally, the text is converted to lowercase (if applicable) as it led to better results during tests on training data, mostly because of the potential noise induced by words at the beginning of a sentence.

2.2 Bag of n-grams approach

Statistical indicators such as character- and token-based language models have proven to be efficient on short text samples, especially character n-gram frequency profiles from length 1 to 5, whose interest is (*inter alia*) to perform indirect word stemming (Cavnar and Trenkle, 1994). In the context of the shared task, a simple approach using n-gram features and discriminative classification achieved competitive results (Purver, 2014). Although features relying on the output of annotation tools may yield useful information such as POS-features (Zampieri et al., 2013), the varieties to classify here are less-resourced in terms of tools, which calls for low-resource methods that can be trained and applied easily.

In view of this I document work on a refined version of the *Bayesline* (Tan et al., 2014) which has been referenced and used in previous editions (Barbaresi, 2016a; Barbaresi, 2017). After looking for linguistically relevant subword methods to overcome data sparsity, it became clear that taking frequency effects into consideration is paramount. As a consequence, the present method grounds on a bag-of-n-grams approach. It first proceeds by constructing a dictionary representation which is used to map words to indices. After turning the language samples into numerical feature vectors (a process also known as vectorization), the documents can be treated as a sparse matrix (one row per document, one column per n-gram).

2.3 Term-weighting

The next step resides in counting and normalizing, which implies to weight with diminishing importance tokens that occur in the majority of samples. The concept of term-weighting originates from the field of information retrieval (Luhn, 1957; Spärck Jones, 1972). The whole operation is performed using existing implementations by the *scikit-learn* toolkit (Pedregosa et al., 2011), which features an adapted version of the *tf-idf* (term-frequency/inverse document-frequency) term-weighting formula. Smooth *idf* weights are obtained by systematically adding one to document frequencies, as if an extra document was seen containing every term in the collection exactly once, which prevents zero divisions. In addition, the feature vectors have been normalized using L2-norm, which led to marginal improvements.

Overall, the feature vectors are typically large and lead to high-dimensional sparse datasets, so that computationally efficient methods are called for. An additional constraint resides in finding classifiers which work well with sparse matrices.

3 Classifiers

3.1 Naive Bayes classifier

All naive Bayes classifiers assume that the value of a particular feature is independent of the value of any other feature, given the class variable. The classifier used entails a conditional probability model where events represent the occurrence of a n-gram in a single document. In this context, a multinomial Bayesian classifier assigns a probability to each target language during test phase, as categorical and multinomial distributions are conflated. This approach performs well with comparatively small training data, as the estimate of the parameters necessary for classification is good enough to compete with more complex approaches. In the case of large-scale data, it is computationally very efficient as it allows for classification in near linear time, i.e. reading the training data once and then reading the instances of the test data.

It has been shown that Naive Bayes classifiers were not merely baselines for text classification tasks. They can compete with state-of-the-art classification algorithms such as support vector machines, especially when using approriate preprocessing concerning the distribution of event frequencies (Rennie et al., 2003); additionally they are robust enough for the task at hand, as their decisions may be correct even if their probability estimates are inaccurate (Rish, 2001).

3.2 "Bayesline" formula

The *Bayesline* formula used in the shared task grounds on existing code (Tan et al., 2014) and takes advantage of a comparable feature extraction technique and of a similar Bayesian classifier. This approach outperformed most systems in the previous edition of the shared task (Barbaresi, 2017). It has been refined for this year's edition concerning the vector representation and the parameters of classification. After cross-validation tests on the training data parameters have been added compared to the default procedure, most importantly a regularization parameter as described above and another parameter for additive smoothing, also known as Laplace or Lidstone smoothing, which has been set to 0.04 instead of 0.005. Additive smoothing allows the assignment of non-zero probabilities to features which have not been seen during training. Character n-grams from varying lengths are taken into account and then the classification takes place.[1]

One of the potential shortcomings of this approach is that it does not see the instance space as a high dimensional space, but just as a collection of frequencies from which it estimates the probability of each class using the Bayes theorem.

3.3 Regularized Linear Classifiers

Regression analysis consists in estimating the relationship between a dependant variable (here the target language) and a number of predictors (here the linguistic cues). During training, a function of the independent variables is estimated, the fitted model is then used on test data. Generalized Linear Models consist in a regression in which the target value is expected to be a linear combination of the input variables. They can for example be used to discriminate between web texts for inclusion into web corpora for linguistic research (Barbaresi, 2015).

Ridge is a regularization technique also known as Ridge regression or Tikhonov regularization (Tikhonov, 1943; Hoerl, 1962). It is particularly useful when the number of input variables greatly exceeds the number of observations and when there are many small to medium-sized effects, which is often the case for n-gram data. In such cases, the least square regression estimator may not uniquely exist, and although it uses a biased estimator Ridge regression can reduce the expected squared loss. This

---

[1] *TfidfVectorizer(analyzer='char', ngram_range=(2,6), strip_accents=None, lowercase=True, sublinear_tf=True, smooth_idf=False, use_idf=True, min_df=0, norm='l2')* followed by *MultinomialNB(alpha=0.04)*, adapted from https://web.archive.org/web/20180507114732/http://scikit-learn.org/stable/auto_examples/text/document_classification_20-newsgroups.html See also https://github.com/adbar/vardial-experiments

Classifier	F1 (macro)
Random Baseline	0.5000
Naive Bayes	0.6207
SGD	0.6134
Ridge	**0.6318**

Table 1: Results for DFS task, all classifiers used the same data preparation pipeline

Classifier	F1 (macro)
Random Baseline	0.2521
Naive Bayes	**0.6336**
SGD	0.6291
Ridge	0.6296

Table 2: Results for GDI task, all classifiers used the same data preparation pipeline

method also proves useful in the presence of multicollinearity, that is when the predictor variables used in a regression are highly correlated, which can be expected at least in some cases for natural language. In practice, it imposes a penalty on the size of coefficients so that they become more robust to collinearity. Moreover the ridge parameter allows a linear regression to work in cases that are not completely linearly separable. From an practical point of view, ridge regression can avoid overfit through regularization, as it shrinks the coefficients towards zero (but not exactly zero) to reduce variance. This step can minimize the impact of statistically irrelevant features on the trained model, in this regard it is bound to simplify the model. In the present case, it is expected to focus on salient features and lead to a faster, more clear-cut classification. However, ridge regression cannot perform variable selection directly, thus the potential increase in prediction accuracy cannot be immediately used for interpretation.

The method used for the task is close to linear least-squares Support Vector Machine (SVM) classification in terms of formulation but faster in practice. The implementation in the Python framework *scikit-learn* (Pedregosa et al., 2011) includes a stochastic average gradient descent solver which is known to work well with large-scale and sparse machine learning problems often encountered in text classification and natural language processing.

To provide a basis for comparison, further experiments have been conducted using a stochastic gradient descent (SGD) classifier, a method which aims at finding minima or maxima by iteration and is thus more computationally complex but still an efficient approach to fit linear models, useful when the number of samples (and the number of features) is very large. Consequently, SGD has been successfully applied to large-scale and sparse machine learning problems often encountered in text classification and natural language processing. In the implementation used here, the regularized linear model with stochastic gradient descent (SGD) learning is equivalent to a (soft-margin) linear Support Vector Machine (SVM), thus providing a comparison with a well-known classification technique. As SGD requires a number of hyperparameters, parameter tuning using grid search has been performed on the training data using k-fold cross-validation tests.

4 Evaluation

The results for the DFS task are summarized in Table 4. The chosen n-gram window was 2 to 6 characters, the feature extraction and classification processes have been conducted as described above. The classification methods used yield relatively low improvements with respect to the *Bayesline*, which shows this is a challenging task. The multinomial Naive Bayes (run 1) indeed outperformed the SGD classifier (run 2) although the latter had been optimized during training by using parameter tuning. The Ridge classifier was significantly more robust during training (higher cross-validation scores) and effectively reached a slightly higher score in the test run. This submission has been ranked 3rd out of 7. The confusion matrix shown in Figure 1 depicts a rather balanced mix of errors.

The same method has been tested with the same data preprocessing in the identification of Swiss

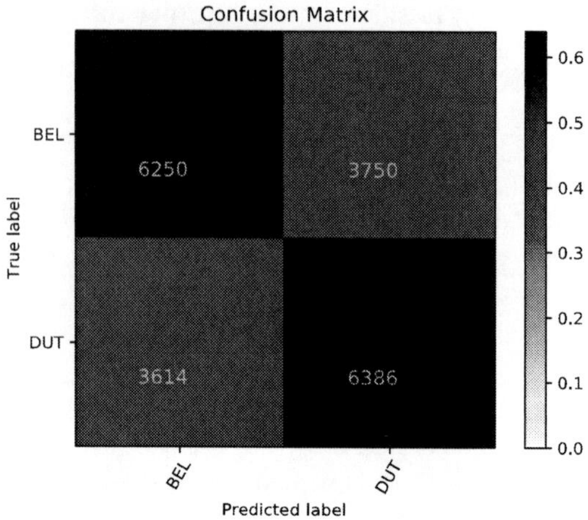

Figure 1: Confusion matrix for the Ridge classifier on the DFS task

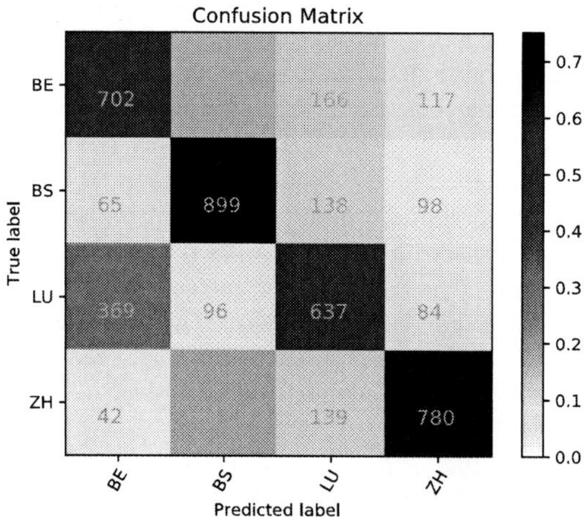

Figure 2: Confusion matrix for the Naive Bayes classifier on the GDI task

German varieties (GDI shared task), using only the training data from this year's edition. Contrarily to the other tasks, a larger N-Gram span has been selected (1 to 6) as this seemed to carry a little more useful information. The classifiers have been optimized during training in a similar way. The results are summarized in Table 2.

This task has seen the worst result compared to the other teams, with the best submission ranked 3rd out of 4. This result is in line with the fact that the Naive Bayes classifier outperformed more complex methods, which shows they could not gain more fine-grained information or generalize better on the test data. As in the last edition of the shared task, the classification of the Lucerne variant is more problematic than the other ones as shown in Figure 2, however the Ridge classifier is more robust so that the gap is closing. The F1 score is significantly higher than in the previous competition – 0.634 against 0.606 (Barbaresi, 2017). The improvements can be explained by potentially cleaner data, focus on F1 instead of accuracy during model selection and parameter tuning, whereas the comparatively low score can be explained by the nature of the occurrences to discriminate: they are much shorter and less regular than in the other tasks, orthographic normalization is a potential problem and the instances seem to be closer to speech corpora. Additionally, they had already been tokenized, so that the tokenization during

Classifier	F1 (macro)
Random Baseline	0.2024
Naive Bayes	0.8540
SGD	0.8833
Ridge	**0.8983**

Table 3: Results for the ILI task, all classifiers used the same data preparation pipeline

pre-processing is without effect here.

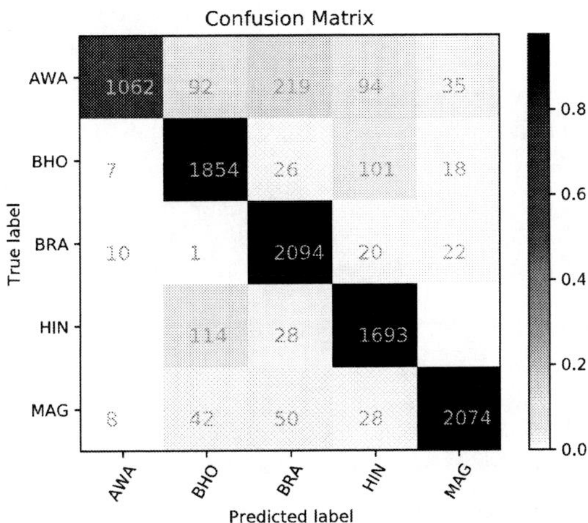

Figure 3: Confusion matrix for the Ridge classifier on the ILI task

Last, the Indo-Aryan varieties have seen the Naive Bayes classifier lead to a significantly lower score than the other methods, which highlights their comparatively good performance and also explains why the best submission (Ridge classifier) has been ranked 2nd out of 6 in the competition, which demonstrates empirically that the processing chain described here also works well for other alphabets. The results are summarized in Table 3, the finer discrimination using regularized classifiers can be explained by the morphological characteristics of Indo-Aryan languages and the subsequent necessity to better assess the statistical significance of the extracted n-grams. The confusion matrix in Figure 3 highlights the difficulty of the AWA variety, which has the worst recall whereas the BRA variety seems to be easier to discriminate from the rest.

5 Conclusion

The present contribution deals with computationally efficient discrimination between language varieties using large feature vectors and regularized classifiers. The methods described have been tested in the *VarDial* evaluation campaign. The characteristics of the shared tasks (most notably the limited training data and the relatively short length of instances) call for specially adapted solutions. Supervised optimization during the training phase shows that there is a major proportion of small to medium-sized effects, whereas the high-frequency spectrum could even be ignored without significantly impacting performance. This situation implies that it may be more difficult to avoid overfitting with more powerful methods, so that statistical models such as linear classifiers are not only computationally efficient but also lead to better results in practice because of their less precise modelization of phenomena. Moreover, as information in the low frequency spectrum is valuable, not performing feature selection and using regularization can often allow for better predictive performance. In a comparison of discriminative and generative learning as typified by logistic regression and naive Bayes, it has been shown that a generative classifier may also approach its (higher) asymptotic error much faster (Ng and Jordan, 2002) which partly explains why the classifier works better as training data is limited in size.

The *Bayesline* efficiency as well as the difficulty to reach higher scores in open training could be explained by these characteristics and also by artificial regularities in the test data. The conflict between in-vitro and real-world language identification has already been emphasized in the past (Baldwin and Lui, 2010), it calls for the inclusion of web texts (Barbaresi, 2016b) into the existing task reference.

Future work includes further refinements of classification methods. Reducing the dimensionality of datasets (for example by principal component analysis) can pave the way for more complex classifiers, however no performance improvement seems within easy reach so far. Another more promising option with respect to previous shared tasks could consist of bagging linear models, which may be a way to produce finer estimates without causing the models to overfit.

References

Ahmed Ali, Stephan Vogel, and Steve Renals. 2017. Speech Recognition Challenge in the Wild: Arabic MGB-3. *arXiv preprint arXiv:1709.07276.*

Timothy Baldwin and Marco Lui. 2010. Language Identification: The Long and the Short of the Matter. In *Human Language Technologies: The 2010 Annual Conference of the North American Chapter of the Association for Computational Linguistics*, pages 229–237. Association for Computational Linguistics.

Adrien Barbaresi. 2015. *Ad hoc and general-purpose corpus construction from web sources.* Ph.D. thesis, École Normale Supérieure de Lyon.

Adrien Barbaresi. 2016a. An Unsupervised Morphological Criterion for Discriminating Similar Languages. In *Proceedings of the Third Workshop on NLP for Similar Languages, Varieties and Dialects (VarDial3)*, pages 212–220, Osaka, Japan. The COLING 2016 Organizing Committee.

Adrien Barbaresi. 2016b. Efficient construction of metadata-enhanced web corpora. In *Proceedings of the 10th Web as Corpus Workshop*, pages 7–16. Association for Computational Linguistics.

Adrien Barbaresi. 2017. Discriminating between similar languages using weighted subword features. In *Proceedings of the Fourth Workshop on NLP for Similar Languages, Varieties and Dialects (VarDial)*, pages 184–189, Valencia, Spain, April.

William B. Cavnar and John M. Trenkle. 1994. N-Gram-Based Text Categorization. In *Proceedings of the 3rd Annual Symposium on Document Analysis and Information Retrieval*, pages 161–175.

Cyril Goutte, Serge Léger, Shervin Malmasi, and Marcos Zampieri. 2016. Discriminating Similar Languages: Evaluations and Explorations. In *Proceedings of the 10th International Conference on Language Resources and Evaluation (LREC 2016)*, pages 1800–1807. European Language Resources Association (ELRA).

Arthur E. Hoerl. 1962. Application of Ridge analysis to regression problems. *Chemical Engineering Progress*, 58:54–59.

Tommi Jauhiainen, Marco Lui, Marcos Zampieri, Timothy Baldwin, and Krister Lindén. 2018. Automatic language identification in texts: A survey. *arXiv preprint arXiv:1804.08186.*

Ritesh Kumar, Bornini Lahiri, Deepak Alok, Atul Kr. Ojha, Mayank Jain, Abdul Basit, and Yogesh Dawar. 2018. Automatic Identification of Closely-related Indian Languages: Resources and Experiments. In *Proceedings of the Eleventh International Conference on Language Resources and Evaluation (LREC)*.

Hans Peter Luhn. 1957. A Statistical Approach to Mechanized Encoding and Searching of Literary Information. *IBM Journal of research and development*, 1(4):309–317.

Marco Lui and Paul Cook. 2013. Classifying English Documents by National Dialect. In *Proceedings of the Australasian Language Technology Association Workshop*, pages 5–15.

Spyros Makridakis, Evangelos Spiliotis, and Vassilios Assimakopoulos. 2018. Statistical and Machine Learning forecasting methods: Concerns and ways forward. *PloS one*, 13(3):e0194889.

Shervin Malmasi, Marcos Zampieri, Nikola Ljubešić, Preslav Nakov, Ahmed Ali, and Jörg Tiedemann. 2016. Discriminating between Similar Languages and Arabic Dialect Identification: A Report on the Third DSL Shared Task. In *Proceedings of the 3rd Workshop on Language Technology for Closely Related Languages, Varieties and Dialects (VarDial)*, Osaka, Japan.

Andrew Y. Ng and Michael I. Jordan. 2002. On Discriminative vs. Generative Classifiers: A comparison of logistic regression and naive Bayes. In T. G. Dietterich, S. Becker, and Z. Ghahramani, editors, *Advances in Neural Information Processing Systems 14*, pages 841–848. MIT Press.

F. Pedregosa, G. Varoquaux, A. Gramfort, V. Michel, B. Thirion, O. Grisel, M. Blondel, P. Prettenhofer, R. Weiss, V. Dubourg, J. Vanderplas, A. Passos, D. Cournapeau, M. Brucher, M. Perrot, and E. Duchesnay. 2011. Scikit-learn: Machine learning in Python. *Journal of Machine Learning Research*, 12:2825–2830.

Thomas Proisl and Peter Uhrig. 2016. SoMaJo: State-of-the-art tokenization for German web and social media texts. In *Proceedings of the 10th Web as Corpus Workshop*, pages 57–62. Association for Computational Linguistics.

Matthew Purver. 2014. A Simple Baseline for Discriminating Similar Languages. In *Proceedings of the First Workshop on Applying NLP Tools to Similar Languages, Varieties and Dialects*, pages 155–160.

Francisco Rangel, Paolo Rosso, Martin Potthast, and Benno Stein. 2017. Overview of the 5th author profiling task at PAN 2017: Gender and language variety identification in Twitter. *Working Notes Papers of the CLEF*.

Jason D. Rennie, Lawrence Shih, Jaime Teevan, and David R. Karger. 2003. Tackling the Poor Assumptions of Naive Bayes Text Classifiers. In *Proceedings of the Twentieth International Conference on Machine Learning*, pages 616–623. ACM.

Irina Rish. 2001. An Empirical Study of the Naive Bayes Classifier. In *IJCAI 2001 workshop on empirical methods in artificial intelligence*, pages 41–46. IBM New York.

Tanja Samardžić, Yves Scherrer, and Elvira Glaser. 2016. ArchiMob–A corpus of spoken Swiss German. In *Proceedings of the Language Resources and Evaluation (LREC)*, pages 4061–4066, Portoroz, Slovenia).

Karen Spärck Jones. 1972. A Statistical Interpretation of Term Specificity and its Application in Retrieval. *Journal of Documentation*, 28(1):11–21.

Liling Tan, Marcos Zampieri, Nikola Ljubešić, and Jörg Tiedemann. 2014. Merging Comparable Data Sources for the Discrimination of Similar Languages: The DSL Corpus Collection. In *Proceedings of the 7th Workshop on Building and Using Comparable Corpora*, pages 11–15.

Andrey Nikolayevich Tikhonov. 1943. On the stability of inverse problems. *Doklady Akademii Nauk SSSR*, 39(5):195–198.

Chris van der Lee and Antal van den Bosch. 2017. Exploring Lexical and Syntactic Features for Language Variety Identification. In *Proceedings of the Fourth Workshop on NLP for Similar Languages, Varieties and Dialects (VarDial)*, pages 190–199, Valencia, Spain.

Marcos Zampieri, Binyam Gebrekidan Gebre, and Sascha Diwersy. 2013. N-gram language models and POS distribution for the identification of Spanish varieties. In *Proceedings of TALN 2013*, pages 580–587.

Marcos Zampieri, Liling Tan, Nikola Ljubešić, and Jörg Tiedemann. 2014. A Report on the DSL Shared Task 2014. In *Proceedings of the First Workshop on Applying NLP Tools to Similar Languages, Varieties and Dialects (VarDial)*, pages 58–67, Dublin, Ireland.

Marcos Zampieri, Liling Tan, Nikola Ljubešić, Jörg Tiedemann, and Preslav Nakov. 2015. Overview of the DSL Shared Task 2015. In *Proceedings of the Joint Workshop on Language Technology for Closely Related Languages, Varieties and Dialects (LT4VarDial)*, pages 1–9, Hissar, Bulgaria.

Marcos Zampieri, Shervin Malmasi, Nikola Ljubešić, Preslav Nakov, Ahmed Ali, Jörg Tiedemann, Yves Scherrer, and Noëmi Aepli. 2017. Findings of the VarDial Evaluation Campaign 2017. In *Proceedings of the Fourth Workshop on NLP for Similar Languages, Varieties and Dialects (VarDial)*, Valencia, Spain.

Marcos Zampieri, Shervin Malmasi, Preslav Nakov, Ahmed Ali, Suwon Shon, James Glass, Yves Scherrer, Tanja Samardžić, Nikola Ljubešić, Jörg Tiedemann, Chris van der Lee, Stefan Grondelaers, Nelleke Oostdijk, Antal van den Bosch, Ritesh Kumar, Bornini Lahiri, and Mayank Jain. 2018. Language Identification and Morphosyntactic Tagging: The Second VarDial Evaluation Campaign. In *Proceedings of the Fifth Workshop on NLP for Similar Languages, Varieties and Dialects (VarDial)*, Santa Fe, USA.

Arkaitz Zubiaga, Inaki San Vicente, Pablo Gamallo, José Ramom Pichel, Inaki Alegria, Nora Aranberri, Aitzol Ezeiza, and Víctor Fresno. 2016. TweetLID: a benchmark for tweet language identification. *Language Resources and Evaluation*, 50(4):729–766.

Character Level Convolutional Neural Network
for German Dialect Identification

Mohamed Ali
Cairo University, Egypt
`mohamedali@aucegypt.edu`

Abstract

This paper presents the systems submitted by the safina team to the German Dialect Identification (GDI) shared task at the VarDial Evaluation Campaign 2018. The GDI shared task included four German dialects: Basel, Bern, Lucerne and Zurich in addition to a fifth "surprise dialect" for which no training data is available. The proposed approach is to use character-level convolution neural network to distinguish the four dialects. We submitted three models with the same architecture except for the first layer. The first system uses one-hot character representation as input to the convolution layer. The second system uses an embedding layer before the convolution layer. The third system uses a recurrent layer before the convolution layer. The best results were obtained using the third model achieving 64.49% F1-score, ranked the second among eight teams.[1]

1 Introduction

German language has different national and regional variants. Standard national varieties spoken in Germany, Austria, and Switzerland co-exist with a number of dialects spoken in everyday communication. The German Dialect Identification task is concerned with identifying the specific German dialect in a written form. The German Dialect Identification was part of the VarDial Evaluation Campaign 2017 and it attracted many researchers, since 10 teams have participated in that task (Zampieri et al., 2017). That task included Swiss German dialects from four areas: Basel, Bern, Lucerne and Zurich and the goal was to train a model to detect the dialect using speech transcript.

In this paper we present the safina team's submissions for the 2018 GDI shared task which was organized as a part of Vardial Evaluation Campaign 2018 (Zampieri et al., 2018). In this year version, the organizers added a fifth "surprise dialect" for which no training data is available. The participants could take part in two sub-tracks: the four-way classification (without surprise dialect) and the five-way classification (with surprise dialect). We have participated in the four-way track only. We have used a Character-level Convolutional Neural Network approach to identify German dialects using lexical features. Our team ranked the second with F1-weighted score 64.49%.

2 Related Work

Dialect identification has two flavors: identifying dialect in spoken language and identifying dialect in written language. Research in German Dialect Identification took place in the two flavors. For spoken language, Schaeffler and Summers (1999) used prosodic features to discriminate between German dialects in spoken form.

For written language, Scherrer and Rambow (2010) used a bag-of-words approach to identify Germandialects in written-form. They were concerned with discriminating among six German dialects for

---

[1]The code for our submissions is available at: https://github.com/bigoooh/gdi

This work is licensed under a Creative Commons Attribution 4.0 International License. License details: http:// creativecommons.org/licenses/by/4.0/.

Proceedings of the Fifth Workshop on NLP for Similar Languages, Varieties and Dialects, pages 172–177
Santa Fe, New Mexico, USA, August 20, 2018.

six regions (known as Baseldytsch, Bärndütsch, Seislertütsch, Ostschwizertütsch, Wallisertiitsch and Züritüütsch). Hollenstein and Aepli (2015) developed a baseline for German Dialect Identification. They used character n-gram language model to build their system.

In 2017 GDI Shared Task, ten teams have participated (Zampieri et al., 2017); most of them used character n-grams for developing their models (Malmasi and Zampieri, 2017; Bestgen, 2017; Clematide and Makarov, 2017; Ionescu and Butnaru, 2017). Best result in this subtask achieved using a meta-classifier built on top of individual SVM classifiers using character n-grams (1-8) in addition to word-unigrams (Malmasi and Zampieri, 2017).

3 Methodology and Data

3.1 Character-Level Convolutional Neural Network

Convolutional Neural Networks (CNN) were invented to deal with images and they have achieved excellent results in computer vision (Krizhevsky et al., 2012; Sermanet et al., 2013; Ji et al., 2013). Later, it has been applied in Natural Language Processing (NLP) tasks and outperformed traditional models such as bag of words, n-grams and their TFIDF variants (Zhang et al., 2015). The architecture, shown in Figure 1, describes the character-level CNN model we have used in identifying the German dialects. We formulate the task as a multi-class classification problem. Given text transcript $t^{(i)}$ and the corresponding label $l^{(i)}$, we need to predict l using t. We designed a neural network classifier that takes as input the transcript as one-hot encoded array of characters (padded or truncated from the end to match a predefined maximum length). The network final output is the probability distribution over the 4 German dialects. The network layers are as follows:

- **Input Layer:** mapping each character to one-hot vector.

- Optional **Embedding or Recurrent Layer :** using embedding or GRU recurrent layer to capture the context of the character (Chung et al., 2014) .

- **Convolutional Layer:** contains multiple filter widths and feature maps which is applied to a window of characters to produce new features. Each convolution is followed by a Rectified Linear Unit (ReLU) nonlinearity and batch-normalization layers (Glorot et al., 2011; Ioffe and Szegedy, 2015).

- **Max-Pooling Layer:** apply max-over-time pooling operation over the feature map of each filter and take the maximum value as a feature for this filter (Collobert et al., 2011). The max-pooling operation is followed by a dropout layer to prevent over-fitting (Srivastava et al., 2014).

- **Softmax Layers**: represents the probability distribution over the labels.

Depending on our cross-validation results we used the following parameters for the neural network architecture:

- **Sentence maximum length:** 256 characters

- **Embedding length:**32

- **GRU layer units:**128

- **Convolution filters sizes:** from 2 to 8

- **Convolution filters feature maps:** 256 feature map for each filter

- **Dropout rate:** 0.2

In our implementation, we used Keras framework with TensorFlow as a backend (Chollet and others, 2015; Abadi et al., 2015).

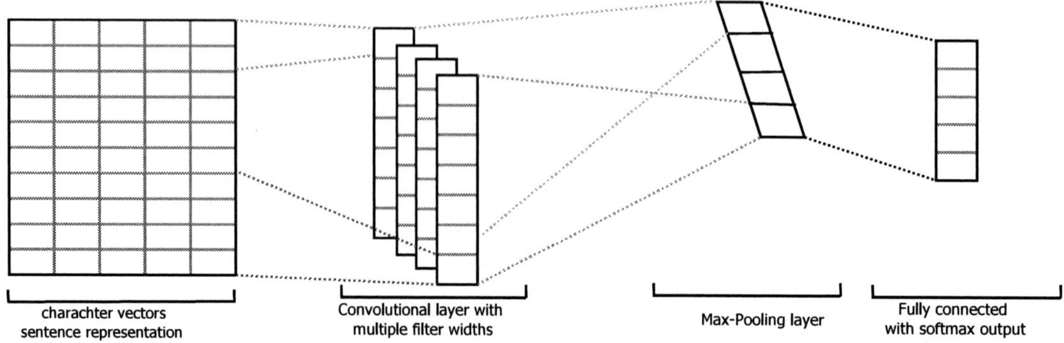

Figure 1: Character-level CNN architecture

3.2 Data

The GDI task data set contains transcriptions of video recordings collected by the ArchiMob association in the period 1999-2001 (Samardžić et al., 2016). This year's training set is an updated and expanded version of the 2017 training set. The data set contains utterances from four Swiss German dialects: Bern (BE), Basel (BS), Lucerne (LU) and Zurich (ZH). The training set contains transcripts for 14646 utterances, and the development set contains transcripts for 4658 utterances.

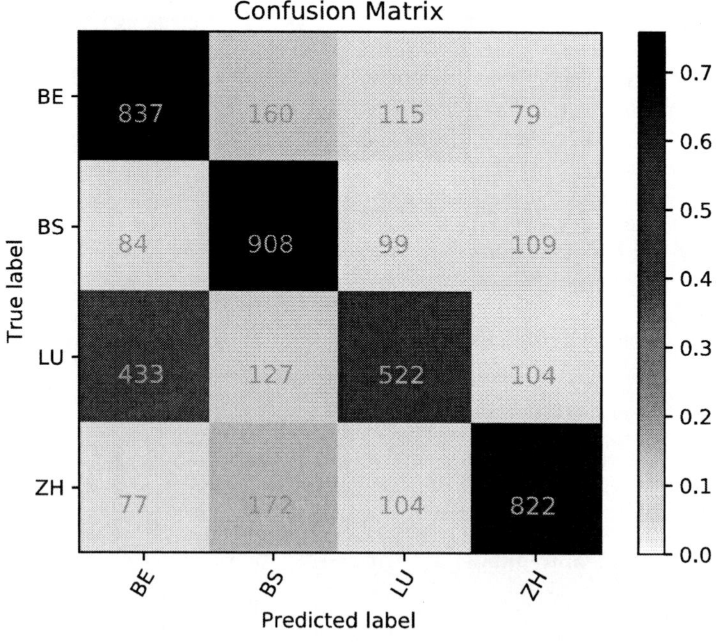

Figure 2: Confusion matrix for "CNN with a GRU recurrent layer" run

4 Results

4.1 Cross-Validation Results

We combined the training data and the validation data provided by the shared task to apply 10-fold cross validation. We tested our three different configurations in addition to a TF-IDF features based classifier, Logistic Regression classifier implemented in scikit-learn toolkit (Pedregosa et al., 2011), as a baseline. Results are shown in Table 1.

System	Accuracy
Logistic Regression using TF-IDF features	0.7714
CNN with one-hot encoded input	0.7821
CNN with an embedding layer	0.7802
CNN with a GRU recurrent layer	**0.7964**

Table 1: Cross-validation results

4.2 Test Set Results

Our three runs results are shown in Table 2. We have used the same configuration for three runs except for the input to the convolution layer. In the first run, we fed the one-hot encoded vectors for the sequence of characters directly to the convolution layer. In the second run, we fed the one-hot encoded vectors to an embedding layer before the convolution layer. In the third run, we fed the one-hot encoded vectors to a GRU recurrent layer before the convolution layer. As shown in the results, using a recurrent layer achieved better results than feeding the one-hot encoded representation directly to the convolution layer or using a regular embedding layer. However, the cost of this enhancement was huge in the training time as training the network with recurrent layers took about 5 times the period of training the network without the recurrent layer. In the GDI shared task evaluation, the submitted systems were ranked according to their F1-weighted score. Our team ranked the second with F1-weighted score 64.49%. Figure 2 shows the confusion matrix for our best run. From the matrix, we can see that the Lucerne dialect is the most confusing one; it is highly recognized as Bern dialect.

System	F1 (macro)
Random Baseline	0.2521
CNN with one-hot encoded input	0.6223
CNN with an embedding layer	0.6171
CNN with a GRU recurrent layer	**0.6449**

Table 2: Our three runs results, the best run in bold

5 Conclusion

In this work, we presented our team's three submissions for the GDI shared task. Our approach is to use Character level CNN as a feature extractor from text. Our best submission achieved by using a GRU recurrent layer as an embedding layer before the convolutional layer. However, the training of a network with a recurrent layer takes a much longer time than training a network with a regular embedding layer.

References

Martín Abadi, Ashish Agarwal, Paul Barham, Eugene Brevdo, Zhifeng Chen, Craig Citro, Greg S. Corrado, Andy Davis, Jeffrey Dean, Matthieu Devin, Sanjay Ghemawat, Ian Goodfellow, Andrew Harp, Geoffrey Irving, Michael Isard, Yangqing Jia, Rafal Jozefowicz, Lukasz Kaiser, Manjunath Kudlur, Josh Levenberg, Dandelion Mané, Rajat Monga, Sherry Moore, Derek Murray, Chris Olah, Mike Schuster, Jonathon Shlens, Benoit Steiner, Ilya Sutskever, Kunal Talwar, Paul Tucker, Vincent Vanhoucke, Vijay Vasudevan, Fernanda Viégas, Oriol Vinyals, Pete Warden, Martin Wattenberg, Martin Wicke, Yuan Yu, and Xiaoqiang Zheng. 2015. Tensor-Flow: Large-scale machine learning on heterogeneous systems. Software available from tensorflow.org.

Yves Bestgen. 2017. Improving the character ngram model for the dsl task with bm25 weighting and less frequently used feature sets. In *Proceedings of the Fourth Workshop on NLP for Similar Languages, Varieties and Dialects (VarDial)*, pages 115–123, Valencia, Spain, April.

François Chollet et al. 2015. Keras. https://keras.io.

Junyoung Chung, Caglar Gulcehre, KyungHyun Cho, and Yoshua Bengio. 2014. Empirical evaluation of gated recurrent neural networks on sequence modeling. *arXiv preprint arXiv:1412.3555*.

Simon Clematide and Peter Makarov. 2017. Cluzh at vardial gdi 2017: Testing a variety of machine learning tools for the classification of swiss german dialects. In *Proceedings of the Fourth Workshop on NLP for Similar Languages, Varieties and Dialects (VarDial)*, pages 170–177, Valencia, Spain, April.

Ronan Collobert, Jason Weston, Léon Bottou, Michael Karlen, Koray Kavukcuoglu, and Pavel Kuksa. 2011. Natural language processing (almost) from scratch. *Journal of Machine Learning Research*, 12(Aug):2493–2537.

Xavier Glorot, Antoine Bordes, and Yoshua Bengio. 2011. Deep sparse rectifier neural networks. In *Proceedings of the Fourteenth International Conference on Artificial Intelligence and Statistics*, pages 315–323.

Nora Hollenstein and Noëmi Aepli. 2015. A resource for natural language processing of swiss german dialects. In *GSCL*, pages 108–109.

Sergey Ioffe and Christian Szegedy. 2015. Batch normalization: Accelerating deep network training by reducing internal covariate shift. *arXiv preprint arXiv:1502.03167*.

Radu Tudor Ionescu and Andrei Butnaru. 2017. Learning to identify arabic and german dialects using multiple kernels. In *Proceedings of the Fourth Workshop on NLP for Similar Languages, Varieties and Dialects (VarDial)*, pages 200–209, Valencia, Spain, April.

Shuiwang Ji, Wei Xu, Ming Yang, and Kai Yu. 2013. 3d convolutional neural networks for human action recognition. *IEEE transactions on pattern analysis and machine intelligence*, 35(1):221–231.

Alex Krizhevsky, Ilya Sutskever, and Geoffrey E Hinton. 2012. Imagenet classification with deep convolutional neural networks. In *Advances in neural information processing systems*, pages 1097–1105.

Shervin Malmasi and Marcos Zampieri. 2017. Arabic dialect identification using ivectors and asr transcripts. In *Proceedings of the Fourth Workshop on NLP for Similar Languages, Varieties and Dialects (VarDial)*, pages 178–183, Valencia, Spain, April.

F. Pedregosa, G. Varoquaux, A. Gramfort, V. Michel, B. Thirion, O. Grisel, M. Blondel, P. Prettenhofer, R. Weiss, V. Dubourg, J. Vanderplas, A. Passos, D. Cournapeau, M. Brucher, M. Perrot, and E. Duchesnay. 2011. Scikit-learn: Machine learning in Python. *Journal of Machine Learning Research*, 12:2825–2830.

Tanja Samardžić, Yves Scherrer, and Elvira Glaser. 2016. ArchiMob–A corpus of spoken Swiss German. In *Proceedings of the Language Resources and Evaluation (LREC)*, pages 4061–4066, Portoroz, Slovenia).

Felix Schaeffler and Robert Summers. 1999. Recognizing german dialects by prosodic features alone. In *Proc. ICPhS*, volume 99, pages 2311–2314.

Yves Scherrer and Owen Rambow. 2010. Word-based dialect identification with georeferenced rules. In *Proceedings of the 2010 Conference on Empirical Methods in Natural Language Processing*, pages 1151–1161. Association for Computational Linguistics.

Pierre Sermanet, David Eigen, Xiang Zhang, Michaël Mathieu, Rob Fergus, and Yann LeCun. 2013. Overfeat: Integrated recognition, localization and detection using convolutional networks. *arXiv preprint arXiv:1312.6229*.

Nitish Srivastava, Geoffrey Hinton, Alex Krizhevsky, Ilya Sutskever, and Ruslan Salakhutdinov. 2014. Dropout: A simple way to prevent neural networks from overfitting. *The Journal of Machine Learning Research*, 15(1):1929–1958.

Marcos Zampieri, Shervin Malmasi, Nikola Ljubešić, Preslav Nakov, Ahmed Ali, Jörg Tiedemann, Yves Scherrer, and Noëmi Aepli. 2017. Findings of the VarDial Evaluation Campaign 2017. In *Proceedings of the Fourth Workshop on NLP for Similar Languages, Varieties and Dialects (VarDial)*, Valencia, Spain.

Marcos Zampieri, Shervin Malmasi, Preslav Nakov, Ahmed Ali, Suwon Shon, James Glass, Yves Scherrer, Tanja Samardžić, Nikola Ljubešić, Jörg Tiedemann, Chris van der Lee, Stefan Grondelaers, Nelleke Oostdijk, Antal van den Bosch, Ritesh Kumar, Bornini Lahiri, and Mayank Jain. 2018. Language Identification and Morphosyntactic Tagging: The Second VarDial Evaluation Campaign. In *Proceedings of the Fifth Workshop on NLP for Similar Languages, Varieties and Dialects (VarDial)*, Santa Fe, USA.

Xiang Zhang, Junbo Zhao, and Yann LeCun. 2015. Character-level convolutional networks for text classification. In *Advances in neural information processing systems*, pages 649–657.

Discriminating between Indo-Aryan Languages Using SVM Ensembles

Alina Maria Ciobanu[1], Marcos Zampieri[2], Shervin Malmasi[3]
Santanu Pal[4], Liviu P. Dinu[1]

[1]University of Bucharest, Romania, [2]University of Wolverhampton, United Kingdom
[3]Harvard Medical School, United States, [4]Saarland University, Germany
`alina.ciobanu@my.fmi.unibuc.ro`

Abstract

In this paper we present a system based on SVM ensembles trained on characters and words to discriminate between five similar languages of the Indo-Aryan family: Hindi, Braj Bhasha, Awadhi, Bhojpuri, and Magahi. We investigate the performance of individual features and combine the output of single classifiers to maximize performance. The system competed in the Indo-Aryan Language Identification (ILI) shared task organized within the VarDial Evaluation Campaign 2018. Our best entry in the competition, named ILIdentification, scored 88.95% F1 score and it was ranked 3rd out of 8 teams.

1 Introduction

As discussed in a recent survey (Jauhiainen et al., 2018) and in previous work (Tiedemann and Ljubešić, 2012; Goutte et al., 2016), discriminating between similar languages is one of the main challenges in automatic language identification. State-of-the-art n-gram-based language identification systems are able to discriminate between unrelated languages with very high performance but very often struggle to discriminate between similar languages. This challenge motivated the organization of recent evaluation campaigns such as the TweetLID (Zubiaga et al., 2016) which included languages spoken in the Iberian peninsula and the DSL shared tasks (Malmasi et al., 2016b; Zampieri et al., 2015) which included groups of similar languages such as Malay and Indonesian, Bulgarian and Macedonian, and Bosnian, Croatian, and Serbian as well as groups of language varieties such as Brazilian and European Portuguese.

In this paper we revisit the problem of discriminating between similar languages presenting a system to discriminate between five languages of the Indo-Aryan family: Hindi, Braj Bhasha, Awadhi, Bhojpuri, and Magahi. Inspired by systems that performed well in past editions of the DSL shared task such as the one by Malmasi and Dras (2015), we developed a system based on an ensemble of SVM classifiers trained on various groups of word and character features described in more detail in Section 4. Our system competed in the Indo-Aryan Language Identification (ILI) shared task (Zampieri et al., 2018) under the team name ILIdentification. Our best entry achieved performance of 88.95% weighted F1 score and ranked 3rd in the competition.

2 Related Work

While some studies focus on increasing the coverage of existing language identification systems by including more languages, as in Brown (2013) and Brown (2014) which include about 1,100 and 1,300 languages respectively, and for the purpose of corpus building (Scannell, 2007), other studies focus on training accurate methods to discriminate between groups of very similar languages such as Indonesian and Malay (Ranaivo-Malançon, 2006), Persian and Dari (Malmasi et al., 2015), and Bosnian, Croatian, Montenegrin, and Serbian (Ljubesic and Kranjcic, 2015).

This work is licensed under a Creative Commons Attribution 4.0 International License. License details: `http://creativecommons.org/licenses/by/4.0/`

Proceedings of the Fifth Workshop on NLP for Similar Languages, Varieties and Dialects, pages 178–184
Santa Fe, New Mexico, USA, August 20, 2018."

A first attempting of benchmarking the identification of very similar languages in multilingual settings are the aforementioned Discriminating between Similar Languages (DSL) shared tasks. The DSL tasks have been organized from 2014 (Zampieri et al., 2014) to 2017 (Zampieri et al., 2017b) within the scope of the VarDial workshop series. Four versions of the DSLCC dataset (Tan et al., 2014) have been released containing short excerpts of journalistic texts written in similar languages and language varieties. In the four editions of the DSL shared task a variety of computation methods have been tested. This includes Maximum Entropy (Porta and Sancho, 2014), Prediction by Partial Matching (PPM) (Bobicev, 2015), language model perplexity (Gamallo et al., 2017), SVMs (Purver, 2014), Convolution Neural Networks (CNNs) (Belinkov and Glass, 2016), word-based back-off models (Jauhiainen et al., 2015; Jauhiainen et al., 2016), and classifier ensembles (Malmasi and Dras, 2015), the approach we apply in this paper.

Classifier ensembles showed very good performance not only in language identification but also in similar tasks. Therefore, we build on the experience of our previous work and improve the system that we have previously applied to similar tasks, namely author profiling (Ciobanu et al., 2017) and native language identification (Zampieri et al., 2017a). A detailed description of our system is presented in Section 4.

3 Data

The dataset made available by the organizers of the Indo-Aryan Language Identification (ILI) task comprises five similar languages spoken in India: Hindi, Braj Bhasha, Awadhi, Bhojpuri, and Magahi. The process of data collection is described in detail in Kumar et al. (2018). In this paper the authors stress that available language resources are abundant for modern standard Hindi but not for the other four languages included in the dataset. To circumvent this limitation the dataset was compiled primarily by scanning novels, magazines, and newspapers articles using OCR with a subsequent proofreading step in which native speakers proofread the scanned texts to correct OCR mistakes. For Magahi and Bhojpuri texts retrieved from blogs were also included in the dataset.

Over 90,000 documents were made available and the dataset was split into three sets as follows: 70,306 documents were made available for training, 10,329 documents for development, and 9,692 documents for testing. We trained our system using only the data provided by the shared task organizers using no additional training material or external resource.

4 Methodology

Following our aforementioned previous work (Ciobanu et al., 2017), we built a classification system based on SVM ensembles using the same methodology proposed by Malmasi and Dras (2015).

The purpose of using classification ensembles is to improve the overall performance and robustness by combining the results of multiple classifiers. Such systems have proved successful not only in NLI and dialect identification, but also in various text classification tasks, such as complex word identification (Malmasi et al., 2016a) and grammatical error diagnosis (Xiang et al., 2015). The classifiers can differ in a wide range of aspects; for example, algorithms, training data, features or parameters.

We implemented our system using the Scikit-learn (Pedregosa et al., 2011) machine learning library, with each classifier in the ensemble using a different type of features. For the individual classifiers, we employed the SVM implementation based on the Liblinear library (Fan et al., 2008), LinearSVC[1], with a linear kernel. This implementation has the advantage of scaling well to large number of samples. For the ensemble, we employed the majority rule VotingClassifier[2], which chooses the label that is predicted by the majority of the classifiers. In case of ties,

---

[1]http://scikit-learn.org/stable/modules/generated/sklearn.svm.LinearSVC.html
[2]http://scikit-learn.org/stable/modules/generated/sklearn.ensemble.VotingClassifier.html

the ensemble chooses the label based on the ascending sort order of all labels. The individual classifiers were assigned uniform weights in the ensemble.

We employed the following features:

- Character n-grams, with n in $\{1, ..., 8\}$;

- Word n-grams, with n in $\{1, 2, 3\}$;

- Word k-skip bigrams, with k in $\{1, 2, 3\}$.

We used TF-IDF weighting for all features. In terms of preprocessing, we experimented with punctuation removal, but this did not improve performance.

We first trained a classifier for each type of feature. The individual performance of each classifier is listed in Table 1. The best performing classifier obtains 0.951 F1 score on the development dataset, using character 4-grams as features. Furthermore, we experimented with various ensembles (using various combinations of features) and performed a grid search to determine the optimal value for the SVM regularization parameter C, searching in $\{10^{-3}, ..., 10^3\}$. The optimal C value turned out to be 1, and the optimal feature combination was: character bigrams, character trigrams and character 4-grams. With this ensemble, we obtained 0.953 F1 score on the development dataset.

Feature	F1 (macro)
Character 1-grams	0.599
Character 2-grams	0.922
Character 3-grams	0.950
Character 4-grams	**0.951**
Character 5-grams	0.943
Character 6-grams	0.924
Character 7-grams	0.897
Character 8-grams	0.866
Word 1-grams	0.948
Word 2-grams	0.876
Word 3-grams	0.639
Word 1-skip bigrams	0.901
Word 2-skip bigrams	0.917
Word 3-skip bigrams	0.920

Table 1: Classification F1 score for individual classifiers on the development dataset.

5 Results

In this section we report the results obtained using the test set provided by the organizers. We submitted a single run for the ILI task, using the SVM ensemble that obtained the best performance on the development dataset. Our system was ranked 3rd, obtaining 0.8894 F1 score on the test set. In Table 2 we report the performance of our system and, for comparison, the performance of a random baseline provided by the organizers. Our system outperforms the baseline significantly.

System	F1 (macro)
Random Baseline	0.202
SVM Ensemble	**0.889**

Table 2: Results for the ILI task on the test dataset.

In Table 3 we present the results obtained by the eight entries that competed in the ILI shared task in terms of F1 score. Teams are ranked according to their performance taking statistical significance into account. ILIdentification was ranked third in the competition below the two teams that were tied in the second place, taraka_rama and XAC, and the best team, SUKI, which outperformed the other participants by a large margin. Team SUKI competed with a system based on the token-based back-off models mentioned in Section 2 (Jauhiainen et al., 2015; Jauhiainen et al., 2016).

Rank	Team	F1 (macro)
1	SUKI	0.958
2	taraka_rama	0.902
2	XAC	0.898
3	**ILIdentification**	**0.889**
4	safina	0.863
5	dkosmajac	0.847
5	we_are_indian	0.836
6	LaMa	0.819

Table 3: ILI shared task closed submission rank.

Finally, to better understand the performance of our system on the test set, in Figure 1, we render the confusion matrix of our system. Out of the five classes, BRA is identified correctly most often, while AWA is at the opposite end, with the lowest number of correctly classified instances. Out of the misclassified instances, most are considered to be AWA.

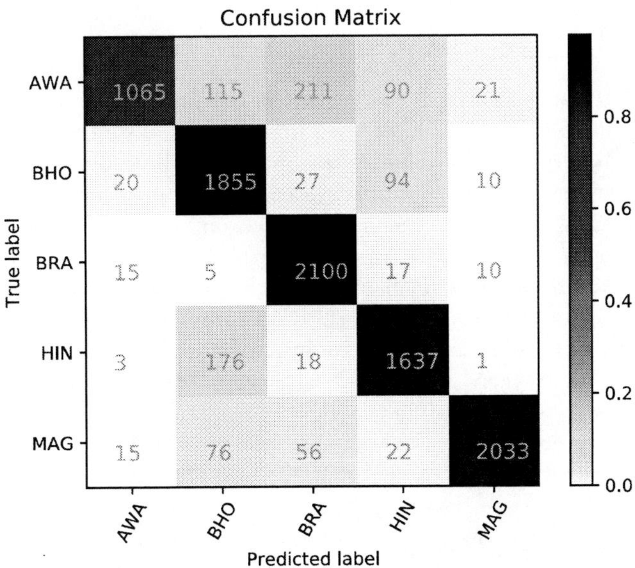

Figure 1: Confusion matrix for the SVM ensemble on ILI task. The languages codes are: Awadhi (AWA), Braj Bhasha (BRA), Bhojpuri (BHO), Hindi (HIN), and Magahi (MAG).

Based on these results, next we present an error analysis of the misclassified instances with the help of two Hindi speakers. This analysis identified a few interesting patterns in system performance and this information can be used to improve the performance of our system.

5.1 Error Analysis

In order to better understand the output of the classifiers, we carried out an analysis of the 484 misclassified instances of the development set with the help of two Hindi speakers with some knowledge of the other languages, in particular, of Bhojpuri.

Firstly, we observed that roughly 10% of the misclassified instances were too short containing only one, two or three words. Examples include:

(1) एल । (EN: Have it.)

(2) घर चल । (EN: Lets go home.)

Secondly, the speakers observed that some misclassified examples were named entities such as in the following example:

(3) इण्डियन इंस्टीच्यूट आफ साइन्स एण्ड इंजीनियरिंग न्यू दिल्ली । (EN: Indian Institute of Science and Engineering New Delhi)

Finally, the Hindi speakers observed that Magahi and Bhojpuri instances were very similar, or identical, to Hindi and vice-versa thus making it very challenging for classifiers to discriminate between them. This is particularly true for Bhojpurti, as the confusion matrix presented in Figure 1, shows that 94 Bhojpuri instances were labeled as Hindi and 176 Hindi instances were labeled as Bhojpuri.

One difference observed by the speakers is that Hindi instances often contains a support light verb whereas in Bhojpuri most sentences don't use light verbs. This includes the following example:

(4) सब लोग रामपेआरी के पुतोह समझथ । (EN: Everybody understands Rampyari as their daughter in law.)

6 Conclusion and Future Work

This paper presented our submission to the ILI shared task at VarDial 2018. Building on our previous work (Ciobanu et al., 2017), we used an ensemble system consisting of multiple SVM classifiers. Our system ranked third in the competition, obtaining 0.889 F1 score on the test dataset. The features used by the ensemble system were character bigrams, character trigrams, and character 4-grams. Based on the performance on the development dataset reported in Section 4, this was the optimal feature combination.

With the aid of Hindi speakers, in Section 5.1 we presented a concise error analysis of the misclassified instances of the development set. We observed a few interesting patterns in the misclassified instances, most notably that many of the misclassified sentences were too short, containing only one, two or three words, and that several of them contained only named entities. making it very challenging for classifiers to identify the language of these instances.

Another issue discussed in Section 5.1, is that some instances could not be discriminated by native speakers, as noted by Goutte et al. (2016). To cope with these instances one possible direction for future work is to allow a multi-label classification setup in which sentences could be assign to more than one category if annotators labeled them as such.

In future work we would like to explore and compare our methods to other high performance methods for this task. In particular, we would like to try an implementation of the token-based back-off method proposed by the SUKI team. As evidenced in Section 5, SUKI's system achieved substantially higher performance than the other methods in this competition.

Acknowledgements

We would like to thank the ILI organizers for organizing the shared task and for making the dataset available.

References

Yonatan Belinkov and James Glass. 2016. A Character-level Convolutional Neural Network for Distinguishing Similar Languages and Dialects. In *Proceedings of the Third Workshop on NLP for Similar Languages, Varieties and Dialects (VarDial3)*, pages 145–152, Osaka, Japan.

Victoria Bobicev. 2015. Discriminating between Similar Languages Using PPM. In *Proceedings of the Joint Workshop on Language Technology for Closely Related Languages, Varieties and Dialects (LT4VarDial)*, pages 59–65, Hissar, Bulgaria.

Ralf D Brown. 2013. Selecting and Weighting N-Grams to Identify 1100 Languages. In *Proceedings of the 16th International Conference on Text Speech and Dialogue (TSD2013), Lecture Notes in Artificial Intelligence (LNAI 8082)*, pages 519–526, Pilsen, Czech Republic. Springer.

Ralf D Brown. 2014. Non-linear Mapping for Improved Identification of 1300+ Languages. In *Proceedings of the Conference on Empirical Methods in Natural Language Processing (EMNLP)*, pages 627–623, Doha, Qatar.

Alina Maria Ciobanu, Marcos Zampieri, Shervin Malmasi, and Liviu P Dinu. 2017. Including Dialects and Language Varieties in Author Profiling. *Working Notes of CLEF*.

Rong-En Fan, Kai-Wei Chang, Cho-Jui Hsieh, Xiang-Rui Wang, and Chih-Jen Lin. 2008. LIBLINEAR: A Library for Large Linear Classification. *Journal of Machine Learning Research*, 9:1871–1874.

Pablo Gamallo, Jose Ramom Pichel, and Iñaki Alegria. 2017. A Perplexity-Based Method for Similar Languages Discrimination. In *Proceedings of the Fourth Workshop on NLP for Similar Languages, Varieties and Dialects (VarDial)*, pages 109–114, Valencia, Spain, April.

Cyril Goutte, Serge Léger, Shervin Malmasi, and Marcos Zampieri. 2016. Discriminating Similar Languages: Evaluations and Explorations. In *Proceedings of the Language Resources and Evaluation (LREC)*, Portoroz, Slovenia.

Tommi Jauhiainen, Heidi Jauhiainen, and Krister Lindén. 2015. Discriminating Similar Languages with Token-Based Backoff. In *Proceedings of the Joint Workshop on Language Technology for Closely Related Languages, Varieties and Dialects (LT4VarDial)*, pages 44–51, Hissar, Bulgaria.

Tommi Jauhiainen, Krister Lindén, and Heidi Jauhiainen. 2016. HeLI, a Word-Based Backoff Method for Language Identification. In *Proceedings of the Third Workshop on NLP for Similar Languages, Varieties and Dialects (VarDial3)*, pages 153–162, Osaka, Japan.

Tommi Jauhiainen, Marco Lui, Marcos Zampieri, Timothy Baldwin, and Krister Lindén. 2018. Automatic Language Identification in Texts: A Survey. *arXiv preprint arXiv:1804.08186*.

Ritesh Kumar, Bornini Lahiri, Deepak Alok, Atul Kr. Ojha, Mayank Jain, Abdul Basit, and Yogesh Dawar. 2018. Automatic Identification of Closely-related Indian Languages: Resources and Experiments. In *Proceedings of the Eleventh International Conference on Language Resources and Evaluation (LREC)*.

Nikola Ljubesic and Denis Kranjcic. 2015. Discriminating between Closely Related Languages on Twitter. *Informatica*, 39(1):1.

Shervin Malmasi and Mark Dras. 2015. Language Identification using Classifier Ensembles. In *Proceedings of the Joint Workshop on Language Technology for Closely Related Languages, Varieties and Dialects (LT4VarDial)*, pages 35–43, Hissar, Bulgaria.

Shervin Malmasi, Mark Dras, et al. 2015. Automatic Language Identification for Persian and Dari Texts. In *Proceedings of PACLING*, pages 59–64.

Shervin Malmasi, Mark Dras, and Marcos Zampieri. 2016a. LTG at SemEval-2016 Task 11: Complex Word Identification with Classifier Ensembles. In *Proceedings of SemEval*.

Shervin Malmasi, Marcos Zampieri, Nikola Ljubešić, Preslav Nakov, Ahmed Ali, and Jörg Tiedemann. 2016b. Discriminating between Similar Languages and Arabic Dialect Identification: A Report on the Third DSL Shared Task. In *Proceedings of the 3rd Workshop on Language Technology for Closely Related Languages, Varieties and Dialects (VarDial)*, Osaka, Japan.

Fabian Pedregosa, Gaël Varoquaux, Alexandre Gramfort, Vincent Michel, Bertrand Thirion, Olivier Grisel, Mathieu Blondel, Peter Prettenhofer, Ron Weiss, Vincent Dubourg, et al. 2011. Scikit-learn: Machine Learning in Python. *Journal of Machine Learning Research*, 12:2825–2830.

Jordi Porta and José-Luis Sancho. 2014. Using Maximum Entropy Models to Discriminate between Similar Languages and Varieties. In *Proceedings of the First Workshop on Applying NLP Tools to Similar Languages, Varieties and Dialects (VarDial)*, pages 120–128, Dublin, Ireland.

Matthew Purver. 2014. A Simple Baseline for Discriminating Similar Languages. In *Proceedings of the First Workshop on Applying NLP Tools to Similar Languages, Varieties and Dialects (VarDial)*, pages 155–160, Dublin, Ireland.

Bali Ranaivo-Malançon. 2006. Automatic Identification of Close Languages - Case study: Malay and Indonesian. *ECTI Transactions on Computer and Information Technology*, 2:126–134.

Kevin P Scannell. 2007. The Crúbadán Project: Corpus Building for Under-resourced Languages. In *Building and Exploring Web Corpora: Proceedings of the 3rd Web as Corpus Workshop*, volume 4, pages 5–15.

Liling Tan, Marcos Zampieri, Nikola Ljubešic, and Jörg Tiedemann. 2014. Merging Comparable Data Sources for the Discrimination of Similar Languages: The DSL Corpus Collection. In *Proceedings of the 7th Workshop on Building and Using Comparable Corpora*, pages 11–15, Reykjavik, Iceland.

Jörg Tiedemann and Nikola Ljubešić. 2012. Efficient Discrimination Between Closely Related Languages. *Proceedings of COLING 2012*, pages 2619–2634.

Yang Xiang, Xiaolong Wang, Wenying Han, and Qinghua Hong. 2015. Chinese Grammatical Error Diagnosis Using Ensemble Learning. In *Proceedings of the 2nd Workshop on Natural Language Processing Techniques for Educational Applications*, pages 99–104.

Marcos Zampieri, Liling Tan, Nikola Ljubešić, and Jörg Tiedemann. 2014. A Report on the DSL Shared Task 2014. In *Proceedings of the First Workshop on Applying NLP Tools to Similar Languages, Varieties and Dialects (VarDial)*, pages 58–67, Dublin, Ireland.

Marcos Zampieri, Liling Tan, Nikola Ljubešić, Jörg Tiedemann, and Preslav Nakov. 2015. Overview of the DSL Shared Task 2015. In *Proceedings of the Joint Workshop on Language Technology for Closely Related Languages, Varieties and Dialects (LT4VarDial)*, pages 1–9, Hissar, Bulgaria.

Marcos Zampieri, Alina Maria Ciobanu, and Liviu P. Dinu. 2017a. Native Language Identification on Text and Speech. In *Proceedings of the 12th Workshop on Innovative Use of NLP for Building Educational Applications*, pages 398–404, Copenhagen, Denmark, September. Association for Computational Linguistics.

Marcos Zampieri, Shervin Malmasi, Nikola Ljubešić, Preslav Nakov, Ahmed Ali, Jörg Tiedemann, Yves Scherrer, and Noëmi Aepli. 2017b. Findings of the VarDial Evaluation Campaign 2017. In *Proceedings of the Fourth Workshop on NLP for Similar Languages, Varieties and Dialects (VarDial)*, Valencia, Spain.

Marcos Zampieri, Shervin Malmasi, Preslav Nakov, Ahmed Ali, Suwon Shon, James Glass, Yves Scherrer, Tanja Samardžić, Nikola Ljubešić, Jörg Tiedemann, Chris van der Lee, Stefan Grondelaers, Nelleke Oostdijk, Antal van den Bosch, Ritesh Kumar, Bornini Lahiri, and Mayank Jain. 2018. Language Identification and Morphosyntactic Tagging: The Second VarDial Evaluation Campaign. In *Proceedings of the Fifth Workshop on NLP for Similar Languages, Varieties and Dialects (VarDial)*, Santa Fe, USA.

Arkaitz Zubiaga, Inaki San Vicente, Pablo Gamallo, José Ramom Pichel, Inaki Alegria, Nora Aranberri, Aitzol Ezeiza, and Víctor Fresno. 2016. Tweetlid: A Benchmark for Tweet Language Identification. *Language Resources and Evaluation*, 50(4):729–766.

IIT (BHU) System for Indo-Aryan Language Identification (ILI) at VarDial 2018

Divyanshu Gupta, Gourav Dhakad, Jayprakash Gupta and Anil Kumar Singh
Computer Science and Engineering
Indian Institute of Technology (Banaras Hindu University)
Varanasi-221005, India
{divyanshu.gupta.cse15, gourav.dhakad.cse15, jayprakash.gupta.cse15, aksingh.cse}@iitbhu.ac.in

Abstract

Text Language Identification is a Natural Language Processing (NLP) task of identifying and recognizing a given language out of many different languages from a piece of text. In the present scenario, this task has become the basis and beginning step of various other NLP tasks, for example, Machine Translation, improving search relevance for a multilingual query, processing code-switched data etc. The biggest limitation of many Language Identification systems is not being able to differentiate between closely related languages. This paper describes our submission to the ILI 2018 shared-task, which includes the identification of 5 closely related Indo-Aryan languages. We used a word-level LSTM (Long Short-Term Memory) model, a specific type of Recurrent Neural Network model, for this task. Given a sentence, our model embeds each word of the sentence and convert into its trainable word embedding, feeds them into our LSTM network and finally predict the language. We obtained an F1 macro score of 0.836, ranking 5th in the task.

1 Introduction

In the present scenario, Language Identification (LID) has become an important problem in the field of Natural Language Processing due to its wide range of applications. The Language Identification task has become an important step of various other NLP tasks, for example, Machine Translation, improving search relevance for a multilingual query, named entity recognition in code-switched data etc. The difficulty for Language Identification systems at present is that it is hard for them to differentiate between closely related languages. In this paper, we try out a language identification system that basically focuses on language identification of closely related Indian (Indo-Aryan) languages, i.e., Hindi, Awadhi, Magahi, Bhojpuri, and Braj. Language Identification is of special significance for multilingual countries like India.

The ILI shared task (Zampieri et al., 2018) focuses on identification of 5 closely related languages. The shared task also included an open track that allows additional resources, but we have only participated in the closed track that is, we performed closed training on the ILI dataset provided (Kumar et al., 2018).

The motivation behind our work is to find out how to build a system which can distinguish between closely related language over a domain. In the Indian context, it is a very important problem, since India has a large linguistic diversity, such that many of the languages/dialects/varieties are spoken by a large number of speakers. Many of these are closely related. There are also a large number of text documents which consist of a combination of two or more languages (due to code-switching or code-mixing). So, a system must be developed to serve the purpose. Even though language identification was one of the first NLP problems for which statistical techniques were applied, there is still a lot of scope for improvement in the performance of language identification systems for closely related languages. The shared task provided us a good opportunity to participate and find out the state-of-the-art for this problem. Due to the diversity in its languages, the given task could be an important step in bridging the digital divide between the Indian masses and the world.

This work is licensed under a Creative Commons Attribution 4.0 International Licence. Licence details: `http://creativecommons.org/licenses/by/4.0/`.

Proceedings of the Fifth Workshop on NLP for Similar Languages, Varieties and Dialects, pages 185–190
Santa Fe, New Mexico, USA, August 20, 2018.

For the shared task, we initially used character level n-gram based statistical approaches with various distance measures like mutual information (Zamora et al., 2014), out of place measure (Singh and Goyal, 2014) etc. But the result was not satisfactory for closely related languages in the task, although these approaches worked very well for distant languages. We then moved to an LSTM (Hochreiter and Schmidhuber, 1997) based word-level model which has improved our results. Generally, the traditional statistical approaches, which do not take sequences into account, are useful for distant languages, but in the case of closely related languages, sequence modelling approaches such as LSTM give better results, since these approaches effectively utilize the internal dependencies existing between words of sentences.

2   Related Work

Quite often, even human beings are unable to correctly identify similar languages. The accuracy attained by previous works on language identification is over 95 percent for distant languages, but for closely related language, the numbers are still significantly lower. In previous years' reports, there is available a detailed description of the methods, the datasets and their limitations. Here we briefly summarize these.

Most of the reports show that sequence modelling approaches are better than other classical approaches, such as n-gram (with distance metric as out of place measure (Singh and Goyal, 2014)), Support Vector Machines (Noor and Aronowitz, 2006), graph-based n-gram method (Tromp and Pechenizkiy, 2011), Naive Bayes Classifier (Peng et al., 2004) etc. for identifying the language. In some cases, where the task is mainly focused on short sentences, linear SVM and maximum entropy models (Lau et al., 1995) are performing better. It is also noted that Bhojpuri and Magahi are much more similar and too difficult to distinguish through the n-gram approach.

For distant languages, using an n-gram based approach, it was noted that character level n-grams are more appropriate than word-level n-grams. This may be due to the limitation caused by out of vocabulary words present in the given text document. It was also found that using a combination of six, seven and eight character n-grams to train the model gave better accuracy.

3   Methodology

We formulate the task as a multi-class classification problem where each language is a distinct class. So, for a given sentence, our task is to find the appropriate language class for that sentence. The prediction of language class is carried out with the help of Long Short-Term Memory (LSTM) network architecture (Gonzalez-Dominguez et al., 2014), which is a special kind of Recurrent Neural Networks (RNNs). We particularly, are using Bidirectional LSTMs, a variant of LSTMs, instead of unidirectional LSTMs, since they can see the past and future context of the words present in the sentences and are much better suited for our task. The overall description of our system is given in the following section.

Input
The input of the model is a sentence of words of an unknown language to be identified.

Output
The output will be a language class (the language name) corresponding to the given sentence. We will get a probability vector of $shape(1, 5)$ that we pass through an $argmax$ layer to extract the index of the most likely language label.

Steps Involved

1. The first step is to convert an input sentence into a word vector representation.

2. We train 50-dimensional GloVe (Pennington et al., 2014) word embedding during the training phase of LSTMs.

3. Finally, we feed GloVe representation of each word in a given sentence of unknown language label into the LSTM hidden layers and predict the most appropriate language label for the sentence.

Mini-batching

We are using Keras (Chollet and others, 2015) as the framework for implementing LSTM for our task. In our task, we will train LSTMs using mini-batches (Ioffe and Szegedy, 2015). The most basic requirement of a Deep Learning framework is that all sequences in the same mini-batch have the same length. If we had a five words sentence and, say, a seven words sentence, then the computations and calculations needed for them are quite different (one will take five steps of LSTMs, and other takes seven steps), so it is not possible for both to be processed in the same way.

The common solution for this problem is to use padding. We set a maximum limit on the sequence length and pad all the sentences to the same length. The padding could be done in two ways:

1. Forward padding
2. Backward padding

Forward padding is chosen over backward padding since forward padding does not face many problems of vanishing gradient problem as compared to Backward Padding. For example, if we set padding as 40 words, the sentence longer than 40 words will be truncated. In our task, we set the padding length to 40 words for each sentence.

Embedding Layer

In Keras, the embedding matrix is displayed as an embedding layer and maps word indices to their word embedding vectors. The main aim of this layer is to convert a matrix of indices of words of input sentences into their GloVe (Pennington et al., 2014) word embedding.

Building Model Architecture and Hyper-parameter Tuning

After creating embedding matrix, we need to decide on the architecture of our LSTM model. We choose some number of hidden layers, Dropout value (Srivastava et al., 2014), etc. to create the LSTM model. These details are given in Section 3.1.

After creating the architecture, we compile the model with loss function as **cross-entropy loss** (De Boer et al., 2005), optimizer as **Adam optimizer** and metrics as **accuracy**. The number of epochs and batch size are also tuned for getting improved results.

3.1 Training Details

We train the entire LSTM model jointly, including the embedding layers. We used Adam optimization (Kingma and Ba, 2014) with the original parameters that are the default, and the loss function used is cross-entropy. Our implementation is done with the help of Keras framework. The model is run with shuffled mini-batches of sizes 128 and the epochs were ended when the loss in the developmental set stopped improving.

We did hyperparameter tuning by trying out various values, and the best results were observed with following values of hyperparameters: Mini-batch size of 128, Number of hidden layers in LSTM cell to 128, Number of epochs used were 36 and dropout value is 0.45.

4 Results

The result of our system on various runs are described in Table 1. The scores of various metrics in the best run is also shown in the Table 2.

System	F1 (macro)
Random Baseline	0.2024
01	**0.8360**
02	0.7444
03	0.8269

Table 1: Results for the ILI task. Best results out of our runs are in bold.

Metric	Score
Accuracy	0.8478
F1-micro	0.8478
F1-macro	0.8360
F1-weighted	0.8442

Table 2: Table showing result of various metric in best run

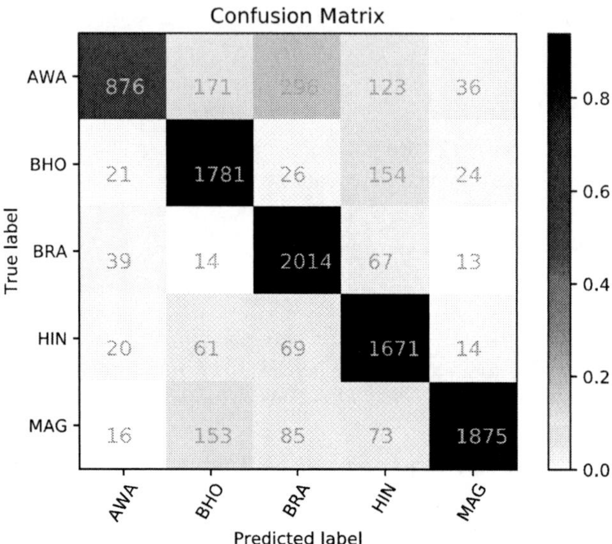

Figure 1: ILI task: Confusion Matrix of our best run

The confusion matrix for our best run is shown in Figure 1.

The results of different approaches used for implementing the task reveal that the best result is observed when we used sequence modelling approaches, i.e., by using the LSTM architecture, with which we achieved F1-macro score of 0.8360. In our second run, we used statistical n-gram approach with mutual information (Zamora et al., 2014) as the distance measure, in which we achieved F1-macro score of 0.7444. The reason for above result, could be the inability of n-gram approach to distinguish closely related languages, particularly, Bhojpuri and Magahi. The above method was unable to model the internal dependencies between the words of the sentence. So, we used sequence modelling approaches using LSTMs. The reason is that LSTMs can remember long-range dependencies among the words of the sentences.

5 Conclusion

The major conclusions which we can draw from our work in this shared task are:

1. In n-gram model, the result were improved when we increased the n-value. The combination of 6, 7 and 8-gram model yield the best result.

2. While tuning our n-gram model, we concluded that results of character-level n-gram model were much better than that of word-level n-gram model.

3. N-gram approach was not able to distinguish effectively between Bhojpuri and Magahi due to the high degree of similarity between them. So, the sequence modelling approach was implemented to

remember internal dependencies existing between words in the sentences.

4. The hyperparameter tuning was performed, and the best results were observed for LSTM model when mini-batch size was 128, the number of Hidden layers in LSTM was 128, with the dropout of 0.45 and number of epochs used were 36.

5. For smoothing the gradient descent, we used Adam optimization algorithm and the loss function used was the cross-entropy loss.

6 Future work

In future, we would like to apply our method to other natural language processing tasks such as multilingual search query, dialect identification, etc.

References

François Chollet et al. 2015. Keras.

Pieter-Tjerk De Boer, Dirk P Kroese, Shie Mannor, and Reuven Y Rubinstein. 2005. A tutorial on the cross-entropy method. *Annals of operations research*, 134(1):19–67.

Javier Gonzalez-Dominguez, Ignacio Lopez-Moreno, Haşim Sak, Joaquin Gonzalez-Rodriguez, and Pedro J Moreno. 2014. Automatic language identification using long short-term memory recurrent neural networks. In *Fifteenth Annual Conference of the International Speech Communication Association*.

Sepp Hochreiter and Jürgen Schmidhuber. 1997. Long short-term memory. *Neural computation*, 9(8):1735–1780.

Sergey Ioffe and Christian Szegedy. 2015. Batch normalization: Accelerating deep network training by reducing internal covariate shift. *arXiv preprint arXiv:1502.03167*.

Diederik P Kingma and Jimmy Ba. 2014. Adam: A method for stochastic optimization. *arXiv preprint arXiv:1412.6980*.

Ritesh Kumar, Bornini Lahiri, Deepak Alok, Atul Kr. Ojha, Mayank Jain, Abdul Basit, and Yogesh Dawar. 2018. Automatic Identification of Closely-related Indian Languages: Resources and Experiments. In *Proceedings of the Eleventh International Conference on Language Resources and Evaluation (LREC)*.

Raymond Lau, Ronald Rosenfeld, and Salim Roukos. 1995. Building scalable n-gram language models using maximum likelihood maximum entropy n-gram models, November 14. US Patent 5,467,425.

Elad Noor and Hagai Aronowitz. 2006. Efficient language identification using anchor models and support vector machines. In *Speaker and Language Recognition Workshop, 2006. IEEE Odyssey 2006: The*, pages 1–6. IEEE.

Fuchun Peng, Dale Schuurmans, and Shaojun Wang. 2004. Augmenting naive bayes classifiers with statistical language models. *Information Retrieval*, 7(3-4):317–345.

Jeffrey Pennington, Richard Socher, and Christopher Manning. 2014. Glove: Global vectors for word representation. In *Proceedings of the 2014 conference on empirical methods in natural language processing (EMNLP)*, pages 1532–1543.

Anil Kumar Singh and Pratya Goyal. 2014. A language identification method applied to twitter data. In *TweetLID@ SEPLN*, pages 26–29. Citeseer.

Nitish Srivastava, Geoffrey Hinton, Alex Krizhevsky, Ilya Sutskever, and Ruslan Salakhutdinov. 2014. Dropout: a simple way to prevent neural networks from overfitting. *The Journal of Machine Learning Research*, 15(1):1929–1958.

Erik Tromp and Mykola Pechenizkiy. 2011. Graph-based n-gram language identification on short texts. In *Proc. 20th Machine Learning conference of Belgium and The Netherlands*, pages 27–34.

Juglar Díaz Zamora, Adrian Fonseca Bruzón, and Reynier Ortega Bueno. 2014. Tweets language identification using feature weighting. In *TweetLID@ SEPLN*, pages 30–34. Citeseer.

Marcos Zampieri, Shervin Malmasi, Preslav Nakov, Ahmed Ali, Suwon Shuon, James Glass, Yves Scherrer, Tanja Samardžić, Nikola Ljubešić, Jörg Tiedemann, Chris van der Lee, Stefan Grondelaers, Nelleke Oostdijk, Antal van den Bosch, Ritesh Kumar, Bornini Lahiri, and Mayank Jain. 2018. Language Identification and Morphosyntactic Tagging: The Second VarDial Evaluation Campaign. In *Proceedings of the Fifth Workshop on NLP for Similar Languages, Varieties and Dialects (VarDial)*, Santa Fe, USA.

Exploring Classifier Combinations for Language Variety Identification

Tim Kreutz   **Walter Daelemans**
CLiPS - Computational Linguistics Group
Department of Linguistics
University of Antwerp
{tim.kreutz,walter.daelemans}@uantwerpen.be

Abstract

This paper describes CLiPS's submissions for the Discriminating between Dutch and Flemish in Subtitles (DFS) shared task at VarDial 2018. We explore different ways to combine classifiers trained on different feature groups. Our best system uses two Linear SVM classifiers; one trained on lexical features (word n-grams) and one trained on syntactic features (PoS n-grams). The final prediction for a document to be in Flemish Dutch or Netherlandic Dutch is made by the classifier that outputs the highest probability for one of the two labels. This confidence vote approach outperforms a meta-classifier on the development data and on the test data.

1 Introduction

Discriminating between Dutch and Flemish in Subtitles (DFS) is a shared task at the VarDial evaluation campaign 2018. The task aims at identifying language variety in written Dutch texts, specifically subtitles from movies and television, and classifying them as either Netherlandic Dutch or Flemish Dutch (Zampieri et al., 2018).

Although DFS is organized for the first time at VarDial, it adheres to the workshop's general themes of closely related languages and language varieties. The long-running discriminating between similar languages (DSL) shared task has been organized previously, and has yielded lessons about distinguishing similar languages and language varieties (Zampieri et al., 2017).

Since the Netherlands and Flanders adhere to the same standard language (Dutch), the task at hand is one of language variety identification rather than similar language identification. This distinction is important because differences between language varieties are often less obvious than differences between different languages, however related they are (Goutte et al., 2016). Still, native Dutch speakers from the Netherlands or Belgium mostly have no problem coming up with anecdotal or typical differences, and linguistic work has previously formulated the most important distinctions.

There are plenty of practical applications for identifying Dutch language variety. It can for example extend current work on Author Profiling (AP) for Dutch by estimating a speaker's origin. In data selection, researchers might only be interested in texts written by either Dutch or Belgian authors and use an automated system to make the distinction. For the purposes of theoretical linguists, a machine learning system that outputs feature weights might indicate differences between the language varieties that have not been systematically studied before.

This paper will describe the submissions of the Computational Linguistics & Psycholinguistics (CLiPS) research center of the University of Antwerpen to the DFS shared task for VarDial 2018. As we alluded to in the introduction we will draw lessons from previous work that aimed at discriminating similar languages and language varieties, and more theoretical linguistic work on differences between Netherlandic Dutch and Flemish Dutch.

This work is licensed under a Creative Commons Attribution 4.0 International Licence. Licence details: http://creativecommons.org/licenses/by/4.0/

Proceedings of the Fifth Workshop on NLP for Similar Languages, Varieties and Dialects, pages 191–198
Santa Fe, New Mexico, USA, August 20, 2018.

2   Related work

Eleven teams participated in the previous edition of the DSL shared task (Zampieri et al., 2017). The task involved determining the language or language variety for written news excerpts. It featured ten different languages with some having two or three varieties, making for a set of fourteen possible classes. For a multiclass classification problem with a random baseline at 10 percent, the performance of most systems was very good. The best system yielded a weighted F-score of .927 (Bestgen, 2017).

There are only slight differences with regards to performance and overall approach in the top-performing teams. One trend is the use of word and character n-grams as the most discriminating features, which is also commonly the case for the task of Native Language Identification (NLI) (Tetreault et al., 2017). In choosing a classification algorithm, four out of the five top teams opted to use linear support vector machines in their setup, which also echoes techniques used in NLI. The system paper describing the best submission (Bestgen, 2017) again underlines this methodological similarity, having drawn inspiration from entries in NLI shared tasks.

Alongside the main DSL task there were two specific tasks of language variety identification in 2017, namely Arabic Dialect Identification (ADI) and German Dialect Identification (GDI). The goal in both tasks is to identify a native language dialect in speech transcripts. For the Arabic variant, participants had access to transcripts and accompanying acoustic features from a multi-dialectal speech corpus and were tasked to discriminate between five Arabic dialects. A new dataset was developed specifically for the GDI task. The set contains transcribed interviews of one of four variants of Swiss German. The transcriptions use Schwyzertütschi Dialäktschrift which contains phonetic properties of language varieties (Tetreault et al., 2017).

The mentioned tasks on dialect identification are most closely related to the newly proposed DFS task, in that they deal with language variety, but the provided data in ADI and GDI is based on spoken data and provides some phonetic insight into these transcripts (either through separate acoustic Vectors or a rich phonetic transcript) whereas the DFS data does not.

We can, however, mention some promising approaches in the previous tasks using ensembles or meta-classifiers with a large variety of word and character n-gram features that yield top performances in ADI (Malmasi and Zampieri, 2017a) (second place) and GDI (Malmasi and Zampieri, 2017b) (first place). Malmasi and Zampieri use combinations of base classifiers to approach both tasks. In the first ensemble method, each base classifier votes for its most probable label output and the label with the most votes serves as the system's final output. The second ensemble method averages the probability outputs of all base classifiers and the class label with the highest averaged probability serves as the system's final output. The third variant, and most accurate approach, uses a Random Forest algorithm to meta-classify the probability distribution output of the base classifiers. The use of basic n-gram features with meta-methods seems to yield promising results regardless of the language varieties concerned.

The DFS data set and task are both closely related to and directly motivated by van der Lee and van den Bosch (2017), who offer the first comprehensive study of the automatic distinction between Dutch and Flemish. The authors explore lesser studied techniques, some of which apply specifically to the distinction between Netherlandic Dutch and Flemish Dutch. Syntactic features, of which part-of-speech n-grams yield the most important patterns, perform well even without combining them with word n-grams. Another important takeaway is that for their dataset, different feature groups are best combined using a meta-classifier. The configuration which combines all feature groups and trains a separate classification on their output probability distribution yields the highest F-score at 92 percent.

3   Data and methodology

In this section, we describe the characteristics of the provided data set and how this influences our methodology. We further select features and techniques that we deem important to try for the proposed task on the basis of the work discussed in the previous section.

Translation	Word form	Language variety	Occurrences in BEL	Occurrences in DUT
Onion	Ajuin	Flemish	6	0
	Ui	Netherlandic	46	53
Misery	Miserie	Flemish	12	0
	Ellende	Netherlandic	138	170
Microwave	Microgolf	Flemish	1	0
	Magnetron	Netherlandic	6	25
Cell phone	Gsm	Flemish	112	30
	Mobieltje	Netherlandic	15	51

Table 1: Excerpt of the lists of typical Flemish words and typical Dutch words with similar meanings. The frequencies of the words in the provided training set indicate the usefulness of the word list features over word n-grams because some words are very uncommon. This table somewhat overstates the differences between the Flemish and Netherlandic synonyms. For some words with similar meaning in the Wikipedia list there were no evident occurrence differences.

3.1 Data

The provided training data consists of 300,000 Dutch subtitles of which half were produced for Dutch television and half were produced for Flemish television (receiving the labels DUT and BEL respectively). A development set which contained 250 DUT-documents and 250 BEL-documents was also provided.

The subtitles originate from movies, television programs and documentaries but unlike the SUBTIEL corpus used in van der Lee and van den Bosch (2017), a single document does not represent as single movie or a single episode of a series. Rather, a document contains several (varying from one to thirty) lines and between thirty to 150 words.

We note two important implications from this prior data limitation: there is an expected performance drop compared to the work done by van der Lee and van den Bosch (2017) since each document contains fewer words, and some macro-features, notably document length features should not capture much in terms of language variety.

3.2 Features

We consider a top-down approach for our selection of features. Commonly stated language differences between Netherlandic Dutch and Flemish Dutch are in specific word choices (see Table 1) and word order choices. The latter is often a difference in placing finite verbs before versus after auxiliary verbs.

To see how word occurrence may differ we take an excerpt from the list of differences between Dutch and Flemish from Wikipedia (2018) and count occurrences of words in the training documents (Table 1). Using word n-grams with tf-idf weighting should let the classifier capture these and more subtle differences in occurrence patterns. We use unigrams up to trigrams to partly learn distinctive patterns of word order.

We also try lemma 1-3 grams. These features should be less important for capturing word order since removing inflection also means losing most morpho-syntactical information of the patterns. However, they can be useful for grouping words with diverse inflectional forms. We use Frog (van den Bosch et al., 2007) for finding the lemma of a given word.

Frog was also used to give detailed part-of-speech tags for our PoS n-gram features. We are interested in finding patterns of three or more words to capture distinctions in word type order between the target language varieties. Frog tags adhere to the CGN tagset (Van Eynde, 2004) and display a wide array of morpho-syntactic information. Verbs receive tags for their tense, whether it is singular or plural, finite or an infinitive, for example. We experimented with the level of detail in tagging to find the optimal configuration, but we found that more detailed tags consistently boost performance and pattern scarcity does not occur until we extend to 7-grams. Our final implementation relies on PoS patterns from trigrams up to 6-grams.

For our last group of features we were informed by work in Native Language Identification (Malmasi and Dras, 2017; Tetreault et al., 2017). Function words can feed important (and currently missing) stylometric information to our classifier. For our implementation of function word trigrams we remove words that are neither articles, pronouns, conjunctions or auxiliary verbs and construct patterns for the remaining words (regardless of the number of gap words). As with the other n-gram feature sets we apply tf-idf weighting on the word counts.

3.3 Classification methods

As a simplification we only consider the Linear Support Vector Machine (SVM) as a base classifier. The consideration is that SVMs have been shown to work well when using large feature sets and when making binary distinctions in the data. The algorithm is also fast to train and accurate in its default configuration, at least in its scikit-learn (Pedregosa et al., 2011) implementation, which further allows us to focus more on combining feature sets than finding optimal algorithms and parameters.

We consider three combination approaches:

1. **Default**. We combine the feature vectors and use only one SVM to find optimal separation in the feature space.

2. **Highest confidence vote**. Each of the feature vectors is fed into their own base classifier. Since each feature group is intended to capture a separate quality of the language varieties, which might be present or absent in the document, the classifier which outputs the highest probability for a certain label decides the final label.

3. **Meta-classifier**. Probability outputs of each of the base-classifiers serve as input for a meta-classifier. The meta-classifier should learn regularities in probability distribution such as in-balance between the labels and which of the feature sets makes less accurate predictions. We use Linear Discriminant Analysis as our meta-classifier here, which worked best in the case of NLI (Malmasi and Dras, 2017).

4 Results

Each of the feature groups are first tested separately on the development set to see their individual contribution to the classification results. We then test combinations of feature groups in each of the meta-classifier setups and motivate our selection of the three entries submitted to the shared task evaluation.

4.1 Feature group performance

Table 2 shows the F-scores of the individual feature groups. Although the linguistic information captured in the feature groups is different, performance of the feature groups is mostly similar. Only the function word n-grams perform very poorly with 55 percent F-score. We think this partly pertains to our operationalization of this feature set. It would be better to use stricter checks on what composes a function word, and to use placeholders to signal presence of other words. There can also be a limit on the number of words that may be skipped to form function word n-grams. Two function words that appear in separate sentences are not suited to be used as a bigram compared to two function words that have only one word between them. For further tests, we left out the function word n-grams because we expect them to harm performance in any configuration.

Feature group	N-gram range	F-score
Words	1-3	0.689
Lemmas	1-3	0.672
PoS	1-6	0.688
Function words	1-3	0.552

Table 2: Performance of individual features on the development set.

The content features (word n-grams) perform the best, but this is closely followed by the syntactic features (PoS n-grams). This again stresses the need for a suitable method to combine classifiers. Lemma n-grams perform slightly worse than word n-grams and since the feature groups capture somewhat similar language variety, it is important to consider if this feature group really contributes anything.

4.2 Combining feature groups

Table 3 compares the proposed classification combinations. A combination of the word and PoS n-grams features outperforms other combinations in the confidence vote and meta-classifier setting. No single classification combination consistently outperforms the others, which motivated us to make a submission for each of the proposed classification combinations.

Feature groups	Classification combination		
	Default	Confidence vote	Meta-classifier
Words + Lemmas	0.689	0.672	0.684
Words + PoS	0.693	**0.710**	**0.706**
Lemmas + PoS	0.680	0.694	0.684
All groups	**0.698**	0.697	0.692

Table 3: Combinations of feature groups using one of the three proposed methods. Meta-classification boosts performance in cases when the PoS feature group is included. The best combination of feature groups corresponds to individual feature group testing and our motivation to have features capture linguistic information. Confidence voting works best in this case, yielding 71 percent F-score on the development set.

4.3 Test set performance

The performances of our submissions show the same slight differences on the test data (see Table 4) as on the development data. Confidence voting again outperforms the others combination methods, followed by the meta-classifier and default vector combinations. Overall, the results on the test set are a lot lower than on the development set. There is no obvious way in which the test documents differ from those in the training or development set. The length of the documents is similar, and the distribution of the labels remained the same. In future attempts, it would be an improvement to evaluate the system during development using (embedded) cross-validation to better predict results on unseen data.

5 Discussion and Conclusion

In the following section we do a more in-depth discussion of the results and the different submissions. We first show which patterns in the features were captured by the system and why we believe they are distinctive for the two varieties of Dutch. We then critically discuss the submitted system and which improvements could be made.

5.1 Feature importance

Tables 5 and 6 show the most important features for both Flemish and Netherlandic Dutch by feature group as learnt by the base classifiers. The lexical differences contain mostly frequent interjections. This also explains why this table only shows unigrams.

Some unexpected results are 'ele', 'enten', 'ent' and 'ine' for Flemish Dutch. It turns out that these are suffixes that follow the special 'ë' or 'ï' characters. These characters were not processed correctly in the provided data, leaving a whitespace in their stead. Words containing these character and these suffixes such as 'financiële', 'cliënten', 'patiënt' or 'cocaïne' were more common in Flemish subtitles.

Submission no.	Class. combination	F-score
#1	Meta-classifier	0.629
#2	Confidence vote	**0.636**
#3	Default	0.627

Table 4: Test scores show the same pattern observed in the development set but our performance is consistently lower on the test set.

No.	BEL	DUT
1.	ele	oke.
2.	enten	oke,
3.	da's	he?
4.	ent	masterchef
5.	allee,	text
6.	komaan,	he.
7.	ine	grayson.
8.	vanop	eh,
9.	sami	eh.
10.	amai,	he,

No.	BEL	DUT
1.	IN NP SYM	VVZ VV PP
2.	NP PP$ N	VVD VVD PP
3.	NP SYM SENT	PP('Er') PP(fin) SENT
4.	SENT NP PP$	VV PP('ie') SENT
5.	SENT PP('U') IN	VVD VVN VVD
6.	IN NP PP$	FW SENT SENT
7.	PP$ NNS SENT	IN PP SENT
8.	SENT SYM('Da's') JJ	UH('O') UH('Ja')
9.	IN NP SYM SENT	RB('Zo') UH('Ja') SENT
10.	IN PP('dat') SENT	NN NN VV

Table 5: Most important word n-gram features. We find expected values and some that are particular to the subtitle data set. Future work could use intensive preprocessing to limit observed artifacts such as misformatting and genre-specific information.

Table 6: Most important part-of-speech n-gram features. Since we start with trigrams, these are more informative for analysing specific word orders. They are expressed in the Penn Treebank tagset to promote reader comprehensibility, but direct translations were not always possible. In cases where a tag referred to mostly one specific word, this word is included in brackets. We find new distinctive linguistic patterns that were not expected a priori.

'Sami' for Flemish and 'Masterchef' and 'Grayson' are also surprising terms in the list of top most distinctive features. These artifacts of the training data indicate that some television content was more common for one of the language varieties. For any shared task such artifacts pose a dilemma as removing them, for example through named entity recognition, would be more faithful to the task of language variety identification, but could potentially harm the competitive performance. We decided to use any information available in the subtitles to train a competitive system.

The part-of-speech n-grams (Table 6) are also interesting to analyze and contain some new patterns that we did not expect a priori. In section 3.2 we mentioned the order of finite and auxiliary verbs but we do not find this as one of the most important features. Instead, a common pattern in Flemish Dutch (in features 2, 4, 6 and 7) is using possessive pronouns after proper nouns whereas Netherlandic Dutch tends to use a possessive 's' in such cases. This was also found in van der Lee and van den Bosch (2017). Examples from the training set include 'Coryn haar moeder' and 'Tom zijn karakter' for Flemish versus 'Henry's auto' and 'Anne's verdwijning' for Netherlandic.

Our findings also echo some lexical characteristics for Flemish. The specific proper noun 'U' is more common, as well as two-word contraction 'Da's' which is tagged as a special 'incomplete' sign in our tagset (Van Eynde, 2004). The Netherlandic features show similar findings. Multiword interjections such as 'Oh ja', 'Zo ja' and 'Maar ja' are strong indicators for the label, but are sometimes mistagged. The personal pronoun 'ie' is indicative for Netherlandic as is 'er'.

On a syntactic level we find an interesting use of verbs in features 1, 2 and 5 for Netherlandic Dutch. It is not uncommon to see three consecutive verbs such as in the training sentence:

> *"Na alle verderf die ik had veroorzaakt was Lana mijn hoop op verlossing."*
> ('After all the misery I had caused her, Lana was my hope for salvation.')

In Flemish Dutch, commas are regularly placed before the last verb making this construction less common. This may be part or all of the reason why van der Lee and van den Bosch (2017) find the use of commas to be indicative of Flemish Dutch. An example training sentence is:

> *"De priester die me had opgeleid, was teleurgesteld."*
> ('The priest who trained me was dissapointed.').

The syntactic patterns we extracted from just the top ten most distinctive features show interesting differences between Flemish Dutch and Netherlandic Dutch. In future work these differences could be explicitely modelled for the task of NLI. We generally see that the tags that we used and the range of our n-grams are sometimes too detailed to capture the differences we found upon later inspection. Future work could benefit from an iterative approach to its feature design.

5.2 Conclusion

Our second submission, which implemented the confidence vote combination of classifiers, yielded the best results. Overall it achieved third place out of twelve at the DFS shared task. The first place submission achieved an f-score of 66 percent, which is considerably higher than our own result.

In this particular task setup, we think the confidence vote outperformed the meta-classifier because clues of language variety can vary greatly between the short documents in the data set. One document may contain a syntactic pattern typical of Flemish Dutch whilst containing words that are predominantly used in Netherlandic Dutch. A meta-classifier can learn that the probabilities that are output by the word n-gram classifier are generally more accurate than those output by the PoS n-gram classifier. The confidence vote approach allows this general logic to be overruled in cases that are easier to predict for one of either classifier; the n-gram classifier is ignored in documents with distinctive syntactic patterns.

Our n-gram feature groups performed well on this task but could further be improved. In any n-gram configuration, performance can be boosted by leaving very common or very uncommon patterns out of the feature. Very common uni and bigrams may not be informative and needlessly influence the classification while very uncommon patterns are hard to generalize and may lead to overfitting on the training set.

The part-of-speech n-grams were a useful feature group for discriminating Flemish Dutch from Netherlandic Dutch. The level of detail in the part-of-speech tags is something to critically analyze in future work. As we showed with a manual inspection of the most import PoS-patterns, the important differences between the language varieties on a syntactic level did not require as much detail in the tags to be captured. Because of the specificity of the tags, some of the found patterns also overlap with the lexical features. The pattern 'SENT SYM(incomplete) JJ' (PoS feature eight for Flemish) almost always refers to 'Da's' which was already captured using the word n-grams.

The function words for modelling stylometric aspects did not work with our operationalization. As noted, our implementation which skipped over arbitrarily long sequences of words to form function word n-grams was not optimal. It can be interesting to use function word co-occurrence as a feature, but different distances between these words should not be treated as the same pattern. We suggest the use of placeholders to signal the number of skips, or to limit the length of the skipped sequence.

Given time we would have used cross-validation. It would have given us more accurate performance assessments during development and would have allowed optimization of hyperparameters.

We only tried Linear Discriminant Analysis for the meta-classifier due to time constraints, but other options are available and might have performed better. Our result, which shows confidence voting outperforming the meta-classifier consistently should always be seen in the context of this specific task and with the specific meta-classifier we used. There are several other ways to combine classifiers using some form of averaging or voting that can also be explored.

In conclusion, we used a very directed approach to test features based on linguistic knowledge of both language varieties and found that these features added important discriminating information to the system. We also tried several classifier combinations, and found that a confidence voting algorithm outperformed a meta classifier in this specific task.

This project further yields a number of directions for future work to be explored for similar tasks or for providing a more extensive analysis of the differences between Dutch language varieties. We encourage such work to use our system, which is available from the CLiPS GitHub [1].

---

[1] https://github.com/clips/vardial-dfs

References

Yves Bestgen. 2017. Improving the character ngram model for the dsl task with bm25 weighting and less frequently used feature sets. In *Proceedings of the Fourth Workshop on NLP for Similar Languages, Varieties and Dialects (VarDial)*, pages 115–123.

Cyril Goutte, Serge Léger, Shervin Malmasi, and Marcos Zampieri. 2016. Discriminating similar languages: Evaluations and explorations. *arXiv preprint arXiv:1610.00031*.

Shervin Malmasi and Mark Dras. 2017. Native language identification using stacked generalization. *arXiv preprint arXiv:1703.06541*.

Shervin Malmasi and Marcos Zampieri. 2017a. Arabic dialect identification using ivectors and asr transcripts. In *Proceedings of the Fourth Workshop on NLP for Similar Languages, Varieties and Dialects (VarDial)*, pages 178–183.

Shervin Malmasi and Marcos Zampieri. 2017b. German dialect identification in interview transcriptions. In *Proceedings of the Fourth Workshop on NLP for Similar Languages, Varieties and Dialects (VarDial)*, pages 164–169.

Fabian Pedregosa, Gael Varoquaux, Alexandre Gramfort, Vincent Michel, Bertrand Thirion, Olivier Grisel, Mathieu Blondel, Peter Prettenhofer, Ron Weiss, Vincent Dubourg, Jake Vanderplas, Alexandre Passos, David Cournapeau, Matthieu Brucher, Matthieu Perrot, and Edouard Duchesnay. 2011. Scikit-learn: Machine learning in Python. *Journal of Machine Learning Research*, 12:2825–2830.

Joel Tetreault, Jill Burstein, Claudia Leacock, and Helen Yannakoudakis. 2017. Proceedings of the 12th workshop on innovative use of nlp for building educational applications. In *Proceedings of the 12th Workshop on Innovative Use of NLP for Building Educational Applications*.

Antal van den Bosch, Bertjan Busser, Sander Canisius, and Walter Daelemans. 2007. An efficient memory-based morphosyntactic tagger and parser for dutch. *LOT Occasional Series*, 7:191–206.

Chris van der Lee and Antal van den Bosch. 2017. Exploring lexical and syntactic features for language variety identification. In *Proceedings of the Fourth Workshop on NLP for Similar Languages, Varieties and Dialects (VarDial)*, pages 190–199, 4.

Frank Van Eynde. 2004. Part of speech tagging en lemmatisering van het corpus gesproken nederlands. *KU Leuven*.

Wikipedia. 2018. Lijst van verschillen tussen het nederlands in nederland, suriname en vlaanderen — Wikipedia, the free encyclopedia. [Online; accessed 03-May-2018].

Marcos Zampieri, Shervin Malmasi, Nikola Ljubešić, Preslav Nakov, Ahmed Ali, Jörg Tiedemann, Yves Scherrer, and Noëmi Aepli. 2017. Findings of the vardial evaluation campaign 2017. In *Proceedings of the Fourth Workshop on NLP for Similar Languages, Varieties and Dialects (VarDial)*, pages 1–15, Valencia, Spain, April. Association for Computational Linguistics.

Marcos Zampieri, Shervin Malmasi, Preslav Nakov, Ahmed Ali, Suwon Shon, James Glass, Yves Scherrer, Tanja Samardžić, Nikola Ljubešić, Jörg Tiedemann, Chris van der Lee, Stefan Grondelaers, Nelleke Oostdijk, Antal van den Bosch, Ritesh Kumar, Bornini Lahiri, and Mayank Jain. 2018. Language Identification and Morphosyntactic Tagging: The Second VarDial Evaluation Campaign. In *Proceedings of the Fifth Workshop on NLP for Similar Languages, Varieties and Dialects (VarDial)*, Santa Fe, USA.

Identification of Differences between Dutch Language Varieties with the VarDial2018 Dutch-Flemish Subtitle Data

Hans van Halteren
Centre for Language Studies
Radboud University Nijmegen
P.O. Box 9103, 6500-HD Nijmegen
The Netherlands
hvh@let.ru.nl

Nelleke Oostdijk
Centre for Language Studies
Radboud University Nijmegen
P.O. Box 9103, 6500-HD Nijmegen
The Netherlands
N.Oostdijk@let.ru.nl

Abstract

With the goal of discovering differences between Belgian and Netherlandic Dutch, we participated as Team Taurus in the Dutch-Flemish Subtitles task of VarDial2018. We used a rather simple marker-based method, but with a wide range of features, including lexical, lexico-syntactic and syntactic ones, and achieved a second position in the ranking. Inspection of highly distinguishing features did point towards differences between the two language varieties, but because of the nature of the experimental data, we have to treat our observations as very tentative and in need of further investigation.

1 Introduction

The main area where the Dutch Language is spoken is in The Netherlands and the Northern part of Belgium (Flanders). Although there are quite strong dialects in regions in both countries, the standard version of Dutch is shared. In fact, there is a joint Dutch Language Union that promotes and supports standard Dutch. Still, many native speakers have the feeling that there are subtle differences between the Northern and the Southern variety of standard Dutch, and that these differences are not limited to just pronunciation. We would like to verify whether this intuition is correct, by investigating (qualitatively and quantitatively) the language use in corpus material that is meant to represent standard Dutch (and not, e.g., the language used on social media as that tends to contain high levels of dialect in various regions) and that is balanced in all factors apart from the language variety. However, such a corpus is hard to come by. The Spoken Dutch Corpus (Oostdijk et al., 2000) contains both varieties, but the content is necessarily biased by location. The same can be said about SoNaR (Stevin Dutch Reference Corpus; Oostdijk et al., 2013). We were therefore pleased to find that one of the tasks of VarDial 2018 (Zampieri et al., 2018), namely Discriminating between Dutch and Flemish in Subtitles (DFS), appeared to provide exactly what we were looking for: a corpus of subtitles of international movies and tv shows, produced by the Dutch and Belgian branches of Broadcast Text International (BTI Studios) and decided to participate, as Team Taurus.

As can be deduced from the introduction above, our main goal is not the highest possible recognition score; rather, we want to establish if the two varieties differ from each other and if so, in what respect. Of course, a score higher than chance is required to show that indeed there are differences between the varieties, but mostly we are interested in which features are apparently used in distinguishing between Northern and Southern Dutch. This means that we are limited in our choice of recognition methods. For example Support Vector Machines, although very strong in recognition quality, are not suited for our purpose as the transformation of the feature space makes evaluation per feature impossible. Instead, we chose a very simple marker-based method, which allows us to see directly how much each feature contributes. As for recognition features, our main interest lies in syntax, even for text classification already more than two decades (Baayen et al., 1996). Still, we chose as wide a range as we could extract in the time allotted to this project, ranging from character n-grams to syntactic rewrites.

This work is licensed under a Creative Commons Attribution 4.0 International License. License details: http://crea-tivecommons.org/licenses/by/4.0/.

Proceedings of the Fifth Workshop on NLP for Similar Languages, Varieties and Dialects, pages 199–209
Santa Fe, New Mexico, USA, August 20, 2018.

In the sections below we will first describe some related work (Section 2) and then the experimental data and our preprocessing (Section 3). Next we describe our features in more detail (Section 4). Then we proceed with the recognition method and the recognition quality (Section 5). Our investigation on variety-distinguishing features in this paper will be restricted to token unigrams (Section 6) and syntactic features (Section 7). We conclude with a more general discussion of the results (Section 8).

2   Related Work

Existing work that is related to this paper can belong to several classes. Seeing the volume that this paper is published in, the most obvious class is also the one that needs least discussion: dialect recognition in general. Overviews of the field can be found in the VarDial reports (Zampieri et al., 2017; Zampieri et al., 2018). The field is dominated by text classification methods using knowledge-poor features, namely character n-grams and word n-grams. Differences are generally present in the choice of machine learning method and tuning approaches. Van der Lee and van den Bosch (2017) deserve a special mention, on various grounds. They compare Belgian and Netherlandic Dutch, using the SUBTIEL corpus from which the VarDial2018-DFS data has also been extracted. Furthermore, they explore a wide range of machine learning methods, as well as features based on POS-tagging (which they call 'syntactic features', whereas we reserve this term for features based on full syntactic analysis).

An entirely different field is that of linguistic studies into language variation, within which we now want to focus on differences between the Belgian and Netherlandic varieties of Standard Dutch (ignoring the many regional and local dialects that exist). Although many people seem to think that the two varieties are virtually identical in word use, and merely differ in pronunciation, native speakers do "feel" differences even in written texts. These intuitions also made their way into NLP, e.g. Despres et al. (2009) decided for their speech recognition of broadcast news not only to make specific acoustic models for the Dutch and Flemish datasets, but also separate lexicons and language models. Specific data for a more targeted study into lexical differences was provided by Keuleers et al. (2015). They conducted a large crowd-sourcing experiment, in which test subjects had to indicate for Dutch words and pseudowords whether or not they recognized the presented forms as Dutch words. On the basis of the collected data, they could study the influence of factors like age, education level and proficiency in other languages on vocabulary size. However, they also compiled a table which reports for each word which percentage of participants in Belgium and the Netherlands recognized the word, something they called *prevalence*. They pose that prevalence is complementary to corpus-based word frequency counts for the prediction of word occurrence. For more rare words, prevalence should be better, as these words will likely be absent, or show very low counts, in corpora. They prove their point by using both prevalence and frequency data (from SUBTLEX-NL; Keuleers et al, 2010) to predict reaction times from a lexical decision task. For the words for which both measures are present, prevalence and frequency have only a correlation of 0.35, showing they are really different. Log frequency predicted 36% of the variance in the reaction times, prevalence 33%, and jointly they predicted 51%. Whereas their analyses were conducted on the full set of measurements, the prevalence table contains separate values for Belgian and Netherlandic Dutch, which we will use below.

Studies investigating syntactic differences between Belgian and Netherlandic Dutch generally focus on specific constructions. The differences that are observed seldom concern constructions that are unique to either language variety. Mostly constructions are found to occur in both varieties with a preference for one construction over another, often under specific conditions and in specific contexts. This requires intricate analyses to bring to light the complexes of syntactic and semantic/pragmatic factors that can explain the subtle differences in the way the constructions are used. Examples are the studies by Grondelaers and Speelman (2007) on presentative sentences, Boogaart (2007) on conditional clauses with *moest(en)* and *mocht(en)*, Barbiers and Bennis (2010) on constituent ordering in the clause-final verb group and Gyselinck and Colleman (2016) on the intensifying use of the fake reflexive resultative construction.

3   Experimental Data

The data for the DFS shared task of VarDial2018 (Zampieri et al., 2018) originate from the SUBTIEL Corpus (van der Lee, 2017; van der Lee and van den Bosch, 2017). They consist of Dutch subtitles for movies and tv shows, produced by the Dutch and the Belgian branch of the company Broadcast Text

Feature type	Example	Total number	Number with odds ≥ 2
Char 1-gram	`C1_;`	70	2
Char 2-gram	`C2_ZE`	2,249	647
Char 3-gram	`C3_op!`	19,868	5,631
Char 4-gram	`C4_DiMe`	90,880	27,497
Char 5-gram	`C5_Sami#`	242,637	77,472
Token 1-gram	`T1_W_Text`	47,272	19,222
Token 2-gram	`T2_WW_#_Oke`	202,681	78,682
Token 3-gram	`T3_WWW_de_dingen_des`	264,367	107,595

Table 1: Lexical features

International (BTI Studios). For the shared task, the subtitles have been marked as either Belgian or Netherlandic Dutch depending on the market for which they were prepared. This is likely, but not guaranteed, to correspond to subtitling in the corresponding branch by a native speaker of the corresponding variety.

Sequences of subtitles comprising a number of full subtitles and containing about 30-35 words were selected randomly from the whole data set to be used as task items. 150,000 training items and 250 development items for each variety were provided beforehand, and 20,000 test items a few days before the submission deadline. As we did not use a tuning step in our training, we merged the development data with the training data. The training and test data were both selected completely randomly from the full data set. There was no overlap in items, but it was possible that there were test items belonging to the same movies or tv shows as training items. As we will see below, this had a substantial influence on the nature of the task.

When inspecting the data, we found several artefacts of earlier preprocessing steps. Most notably, all characters with diacritics were removed (e.g. *één* ("a") became *n*), or alternatively the diacritic was removed but also a space was inserted (e.g. *ruïne* ("ruin") became *ru ine*). Furthermore, periods in numbers had spaces inserted next to them (e.g. *20.000* ("20,000") became *20. 000*). Also apostrophes in words like *z'n* (*zijn*, "his") were removed; apparently, some correction had already been applied, but this also produced non-existing forms like *zeen*.

Now, these artefacts would not be a problem for character or token n-gram recognition. However, we were planning to use POS tagging and syntactic parsing, for which these artefacts would most certainly lead to errors. We therefore decided to include a preprocessing step in which we tried to correct most of these artefacts. For the diacritics, it would have been easiest to compare to a Dutch word list in which diacritics were included, but we did not manage to acquire such a resource quickly enough. Instead, we inspected derived word counts and the text itself manually, and build a list of about 270 regular expression substitutes, such as

```
s/\([Gg]e\) dealiseerde /\1idealiseerde /g
s/i re /iere /g
s/\([0-9]\)\([,.]\)  *\([0-9]\)/\1\2\3/g
```

As we spent only limited time on this, we missed cases, even (in retrospect) obvious ones like *financi ele* (*financiële*, "financial"), leading to non-words like *ele* in the observations below.

4 Recognition Features

As stated above, our main goal was to find differences between the Northern and Southern varieties of standard Dutch, both lexical and syntactic. To be able to extract features needed for this goal, we analysed the text with a combination of Frog (van den Bosch et al., 2007) and Alpino (Bouma et al., 2001). However, we also took the recognition task seriously, and included more traditional character and token n-gram features (Stamatatos, 2009). In the actual recognition we only used features with odds higher or equal to 2 in favour of either variety (see Section 5).

The character and token n-gram features (below called *lexical features*) were extracted from the original (but cleaned up) data. Hash characters (#) were inserted before and after each sentence for the extraction of begin/end n-grams. For character n-grams, n ranged from 1 to 5, for token n-grams from 1 to 3. Table 1 shows some examples and statistics for the lexical features.

```
Voor          VZ(init)
vandaag       BW()
had           WW(pv,verl,ev)
ik            VNW(pers,pron,nomin,vol,1,ev)
al            BW()
een           LID(onbep,stan,agr)
maand         N(soort,ev,basis,zijd,stan)
geen          VNW(onbep,det,stan,prenom,zonder,agr)
stem          N(soort,ev,basis,zijd,stan)
meer          VNW(onbep,grad,stan,vrij,zonder,comp)
gekregen      WW(vd,vrij,zonder)
.             LET()
```

Figure 1: POS tagging example.

Feature type	Example	Total number	Number with odds ≥ 2
Tagging 1-gram	`T1_P_WW(inf,prenom,zonder)`	34,771	14,527
Tagging 2-gram	`T2_GL_LID(bep)_redder`	1,320,282	497,488
Tagging 3-gram	`T3_GWG_TW(hoofd)_a_TW(hoofd)`	11,640,773	4,379,149

Table 2: Tagging features

The next level of features are those which can be extracted after POS tagging (below called *tagging features*). Frog yields an annotation with the tagset created for the Spoken Dutch Corpus (Oostdijk et al., 2000). An example is shown in Figure 1. We used the POS tags by themselves, but also in broader POS groups, retaining only the first attribute, leading to groups like *WW(inf)* and *N(soort)*. Also, apart from the POS tags, the tagging process provides us with lemmas, or rather stems as e.g. for *was* ("was"), we find the first person singular *ben* ("am"). From this annotation we derived unigrams, bigrams and trigrams. In each of the positions of the n-grams, we put one of the following: the word (W), the lemma (L), the full POS tag (P), or the POS group (G). As an example, `T3_GLP_LID(bep)_`
`ding_LID(bep,gen,evmo)` is the trigram built with a POS group, a lemma and a POS, that corresponds to the example *de dingen des* ("the things of") in Table 1. Table 2 shows some examples and statistics for the tagging features. Here the pure word combinations are excluded as they have been counted as lexical features.

The final group of features (below called *syntactic features*) have been derived from the syntactic parse produced by Frog and Alpino. However, since the dependency structure is less amenable to variation studies than a constituency structure, we first transformed the trees. We started with the 'surfacing' procedure developed by Erwin Komen (2015), and followed it up with a few more transformations, especially around the verb phrase. Furthermore, the analyses were lexicalized by percolating the head words upwards. As an example the parse of the sentence in Figure 1 is shown in Figure 2. From the trees we derived two types of features. We built a kind of syntactic n-grams by taking subtrees such as a functional constituent (F) realized by syntactic category (C) containing a functional constituent realized by syntactic category (e.g. `SFCFC_mod_WHREL_obj1_TW`, a modifier realized by a *wh*-relative clause (WHREL) containing a direct object (obj1) realized by a cardinal numeral (TW); or `SCFF-`
`CCL_NP_hd_N(ding)_mod_NP(leven)`, a noun phrase (NP) containing both a head (hd) realized by a noun (N) with lemma *ding* and a modifier (mod) realized by a noun phrase (NP) with a head *leven*, which corresponds to the example *de dingen des levens* ("the things of life") which we already saw above. The second type of feature are the full rewrites at all positions in the tree, e.g. `SRFC_WHQ_whd_VNW_hd_WWlex_obj1_TW_<NOFUN>_.` (a *wh-* question realized by a interrogative pronoun, a verb, and a direct object realized by a cardinal numeral, ending with a sentence closing

```
<NOFUN>:SMAIN(krijg) ->       [ mod auxv su mod obj1 mod lexv <NOFUN> ]
      mod:PP(voor|vandaag) ->       [ hd obj1 ]
          hd:VZ(voor) -> voor
          obj1:BW(vandaag) -> vandaag
      auxv:WWaux(heb) -> heb
      su:VNW(ik) -> ik
      mod:NP(maand) ->       [ mod det hd ]
          mod:BW(al) -> al
          det:LID(een) -> een
          hd:N(maand) -> maand
      obj1:NP(stem) ->       [ det hd ]
          det:VNW(geen) -> geen
          hd:N(stem) -> stem
      mod:VNW(meer) -> meer
      lexv:WWlex(krijg) -> krijg
      <NOFUN>:.(.) -> .
```

Figure 2: Syntactic analysis example

Feature type	Example	Total number	Number odds ≥ 2
Subtree (not lexicalized)	SCFCFC_NP_mod_REL_predc_PPRES	189,411	46,853
Subtree (lexicalized)	SCFFCCL_CP_cmp_VG(als)_ lexv_WWlex(overlijd)	630,926	242,976
Rewrite (to functions only)	SRF_SMAIN_su_auxv_lexv_predc	12,746	3,594
Rewrite to functions and categories	SRFC_NP_det_LID_hd_N_ mod_PP_mod_PP_mod_PP	36,545	11,756

Table 3: Syntactic features

punctuation mark (even the question mark has the category label .). Table 3 shows some examples and statistics for the syntactic features.

5   Recognition System and Results

Our choice of recognition system as well was influenced by our goal of finding differences between the two language varieties. After successful recognition, we wanted to be able to identify which features contributed to the success. For this experiment, we chose a very simple algorithm. We counted the occurrences of each feature in the Netherlandic and Belgian training items and compared the two counts to derive odds. For example, the word bigram *Komaan_,* ("Come on ,") was found 209 times in the Belgian items and 4 times in the Netherlandic items, leading to odds of 52.25 in favour of Belgian Dutch.

If a feature was not seen in one of the varieties, its count was set to 1 for the calculation of odds, e.g. the name *Sami* was found 275 times in the Belgian items and never in the Netherlandic items, leading to odds of 275. For the actual recognition, we only used features that had odds higher than or equal to 2 in either direction. In the numerical representations below, odds in favour of Netherlandic are shown as negative and in favour of Belgian as positive.

In the test phase, all features present in an item were taken and their odds contributed directly to the item score. In the simplest version, all odds were simply added, after which a positive total indicated

Method/features	Accuracy	F1micro	F1macro	F1weighted
Simple/all	0.6406	0.6406	0.6403	0.6403
Voted/lexical	0.6344	0.6344	0.6342	0.6342
Voted/tagging	0.6343	0.6343	0.6341	0.6341
Voted/syntactic	0.6142	0.6142	0.6134	0.6134
Voted/lexical+tagging+syntactic	0.6458	0.6458	0.6456	0.6456

Table 4: VarDial2018-DFS scores for various approaches

Word (Netherlandic)	Training data odds	#correct/ wrong in test		Word (Belgian)	Training data odds	#correct/ wrong in test
!	-13.19	59/4		da's	8.83	68/5
EEN	-264.00	22/0		Hope	4.52	30/1
MUZIEK	-482.00	26/2		Shawn	9.28	28/2
Oke	-228.00	19/0		Sami	289.00	21/0
gerecht	-2.750	48/11		Bo	6.51	24/1
MasterChef	-55.00	14/0		Lucas	3.72	22/1
inmiddels	-2.66	18/2		komaan	49.71	21/1
namelijk	-2.030	20/3		amuseren	5.51	24/2
melding	-2.68	11/0		plots	8.97	19/1
Foreman	-18.00	11/0		aanvaarden	3.16	19/1

Table 5: Top distinctive words for test set

Belgian and a negative total Netherlandic. Based on experience in other projects, we expected an increase in recognition quality when taking several feature classes and then combining the results. For such an approach, we split the features split into 15 classes. The lexical features `C1, C2, C3, C4, C5, T1_W, T2_WW` and `T3_WWW` each formed their own class. N-grams built purely from POS tags formed classes `T1_tag, T2_tag` and `T3_tag`. N-grams built with other component mixes formed classes `T2_mix` and `T3_mix`. Syntactic features were split into `Spure` and `Slexical`, depending on whether they contained references to lexical items. The odds addition was done per feature class, leading to a vote for Belgian or Netherlandic, or no vote if no features of the class were present. The 15 votes were combined without weighting and the variety with most votes was selected as final result. If the varieties had an equal number of votes, Belgian was selected, a heuristic based on some experiments within the training data.

The results of various settings are shown in Table 4. Looking at the processing needed for specific features, and taking the overall groups lexical features, tagging features and syntactic features, we see that all three groups perform worse than the simple odds addition of all features together. Voting with all features, however, outperforms the simple addition. Syntactic features by themselves perform quite poorly, and would have ended up at rank 5 in the shared task; lexical and tagging features by themselves at rank 3. However, their combination and the addition of the syntactic features pushes the result significantly higher, to rank 2, demonstrating the value of both system combination (widely accepted) and syntactic information (not widely accepted). Still, despite access to more informative features, we must admit defeat to team Tübingen-Oslo (Çöltekin et al., 2018), who reach a score of 0.6600 using an SVM classifier based on character and word n-grams. This we attribute to our choice of recognition method, which as already mentioned was based on explanatory power more than recognition power.

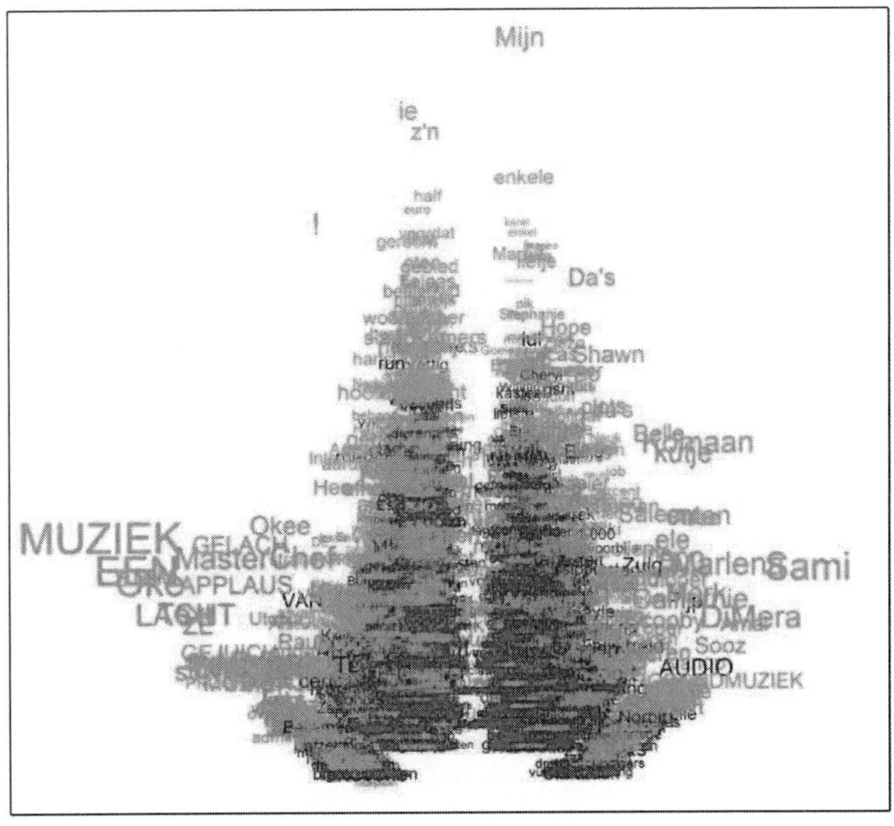

Figure 3: Word bias in training and test set. The horizontal position represents bias, with bias towards Netherlandic on the left and bias towards Belgian on the right. The vertical position represents the frequency in the training data (on a log scale). The colour represents whether the bias was the same in the test data (green) or not (red). Finally, the size represents how useful the feature proved in judging the test set (calculated as $(\#correct - 3*\#incorrect) * odds$).

6   Distinction Power of Individual Tokens

Seeing that the Southern and Northern varieties of Dutch can apparently be distinguished to some degree, we would like to know which features contribute to this distinction, in other words what the actual differences between the varieties are. In this section, we focus on individual tokens. Not only is this a stated focus of the VarDial workshop, but we can also compare the results with our intuitions. The observations for tokens can later on help in the examination of syntactic features (Section 7).

Table 5 shows the most useful features for the test set (here correlated features are ignored) and Figure 3 visually represents the usefulness of all features applied for the test set.[1] In both we see that it is

---

[1] The sources files for Figures 3 and 4, as well as the underlying data, can be found at https://cls.ru.nl/staff/hvhalteren/VarDial2018_DFS_Taurus_Support.zip

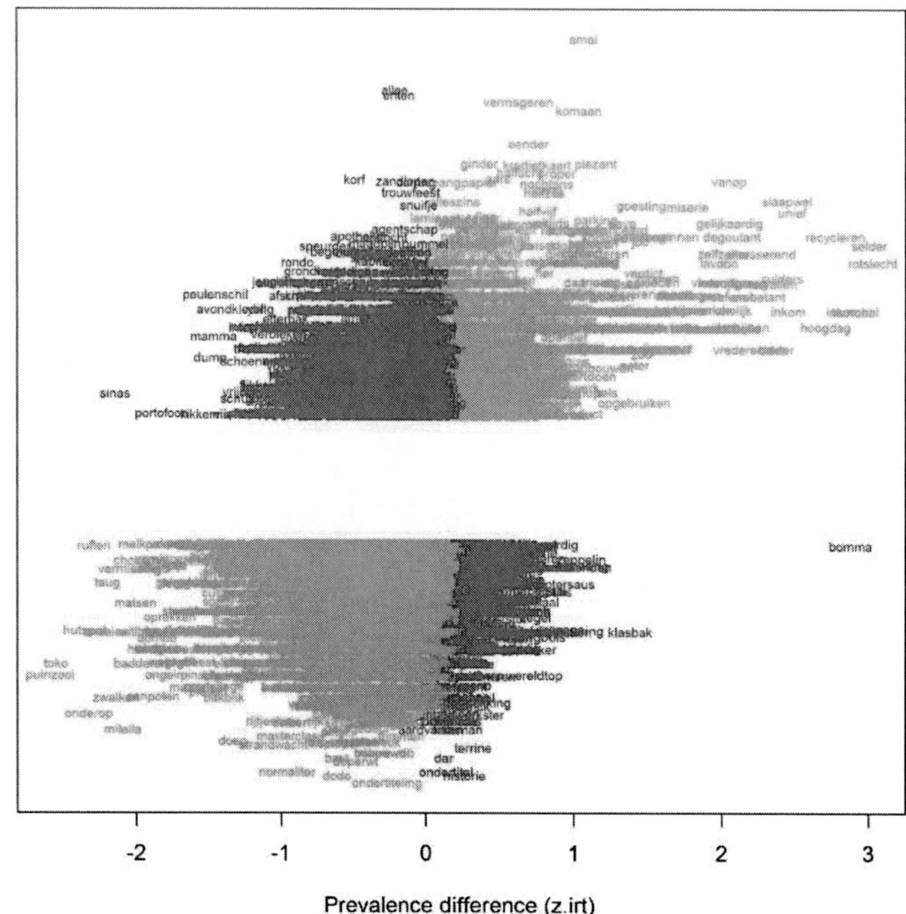

Figure 4: DFS bias compared to prevalence (Keuleers at al., 2015) for words present in both data sets. The horizontal position represents prevalence (z-scores) and the vertical positions odds in the DFS training data (log scale). The colour again indicates whether the two measurements agree on assigning the corresponding language variety.

certainly not only differences in language variety that we are measuring. First of all, we see many proper names, with as most striking example *Sami*, not the Finnish people, but a character from the soap series Days of our Lives. She occurs 289 times in the training set and 21 times in the test set, always on the Belgian side. On the Netherlandic side, we find the tv show *MasterChef*, complemented by the word *gerecht* ("dish"). Other words might also be linked to specific content: a remarkable number of police-connected words, such as *melding* ("report"), *bekeuring* ("traffic ticket") and *bestuurder* ("driver") occur on the Netherlandic side. Next we have a cluster of all-capital words, such as *MUZIEK* ("MUSIC"). These appear to be descriptions of background noises. They occur mostly on the Netherlandic side, with a few exceptions, e.g. *ACHTERGRONDMUZIEK* ("BACKGROUND MUSIC") on the Belgian side. This too is not related to language variety but more likely to the nature of subtitling in the two branches of BTI. The same might be true for the exclamation mark, which together with the semicolon are the only C1 features with odds greater than 2 (13.19 and 18.00).

Still, we also observe words which do seem linked to a specific language variety. Interjections like *komaan* ("come on") and *Oke* ("Right") also intuitively belong to Belgian and Netherlandic Dutch, respectively. The same can be said for *da's* ("that's"; Belgian, but probably extending into the South of The Netherlands), *ie* ("he"; Netherlandic) and *plots* ("suddenly"; Belgian). For the other visible words, we do not have clear intuitions. Most of them we will therefore check against another resource in the next paragraph. Before that, we want to mention the capitalized *Mijn* ("my"), which might have a stylistic rather than a lexical cause.

As mentioned in Section 2, Keuleers et al. (2015) provided prevalence measurements for (about 54,000) Dutch words (downloadable through http://crr.ugent.be/archives/1796). Figure 4 shows the relation between the difference in prevalence in Belgium and The Netherlands (using the irt z-scores also preferred by Keuleers et al.; for an explanation, see there) and the odds from our own training data. We include all lemmas which a) occur in the prevalence table and b) have odds higher than 2 in our measurements. The visual impression that the two resources agree more often than they disagree is correct: they agree 3,717 times (2,628 Netherlandic and 1,089 Belgian) while they disagree 2,060 times. Still, they disagree often enough to conclude that, if we accept prevalence as a good indicator of language variety bias, the DFS data is inadequate for proper identification of that bias. Furthermore, even high odds do not guarantee proper attribution. On the other hand, highly prevalent words do appear to be recognized also with the DFS data. Although we did not measure the exact same thing (difference versus sum), these observations are consistent with the findings by Keuleers et al. (2015) about the complementary nature of prevalence and corpus-based frequency counts.

7   Distinction Power of Syntactic Features

Our special interest in this experiment lay in syntactic differences between Northern and Southern Dutch. Ideally any different uses of syntax would be found by way of highly distinguishing syntactic features. However, our observations for the lexical features made us less optimistic. Trying at least to avoid syntactic features that were shadows of lexical ones, we filtered the set of syntactic features that we would examine: we used only rewrite features appearing in test items where the lexical features led to a wrong attribution but the tagging and syntactic features attributed correctly, and from the resulting feature list we then removed all syntactic features that were correlated to any lexical features. Upon manual inspection of the selected features we found various syntactic constructions that at least in these data point to Belgian or Netherlandic authorship. They give us a first handle as regards the potential syntactic differences that exist between the two varieties. Further research is needed to establish whether these are not just an artefact of the data. Below we present and discuss some of the constructions that were identified.

The use of constructions with anticipatory *het* were found to be associated with Belgian authorship. An example is *En het is vanwege jou dat ze deze sessies hebben georganiseerd.* ("And it is because of you that they have organised these sessions."). What is striking in the instances that we come across is that in all of them the subject complement (here: *vanwege jou*) is an adverb (*wel, niet, dus*) or, as in the example, a prepositional phrase.

Coordinations in which *dus* ("so") appears in the function of coordinator joining main clauses were associated with Netherlandic authorship. An example is *er gebeurde niks dus is ze dood.* ("nothing happened so now she is dead."). All cases share the same structure where a cause, circumstance or reason is given in the first conjoin of the coordination and the second conjoin introduced by *dus* relates the consequence(s), result, or the thing(s) that happened next.

As an apparent feature of Netherlandic Dutch we found that the final conjoin in a coordination is a word or phrase equivalent to *etcetera*. For Dutch we came across *enzovoort, et cetera*, but also *noem maar op*, as in for example *hij weet wel alles over de vissen in de zee over bomen en planten, noem maar op.* ("he knows everything about the fish in the sea about trees and plants, and what have you").

Then there are adverbial clauses in sentence-initial position in monotransitive declarative sentences. In standard Dutch in regular declarative sentences with unmarked word order, the subject precedes the verb operator. However, when an adverbial occurs sentence-initially, subject and verb operator are inverted. For Netherlandic Dutch the occurrence of monotransitive sentences with sentence-initial adverbial clauses was found to be a distinctive feature. These initial adverbial clauses included both conditional clauses (typically introduced by *als* ("if") as well as temporal adverbial clauses (for example introduced by *nadat* ("after"), *terwijl* ('while"), or *toen* ("when"), as in *Toen we gingen dansen speelden ze dit liedje.* ("When we went dancing they played this song.").

Another feature associated with Netherlandic Dutch was the use of *wh*-clauses as direct object. For example, *U weet dus wat er in zit.* ("You know what is in there.").

Finally, one more feature typically associated with Belgian Dutch was the use of an imperative clause followed by a form of address as for example in *Geef hier dat geld, vuile hufter.* ("Hand over that money, you bastard.").

8   Conclusion

We built a recognition system to distinguish between Belgian and Netherlandic Dutch subtitles, as provided for the DFS shared task at VarDial2018. We used a wide range of features, spanning from character n-grams to syntactic rewrites. As our primary goal was to identify features which differed between the two language varieties, we used a simple marker-based recognition method, with which we could measure directly how informative each feature was for the test data.

As for the participation in the shared task, we can judge our results to be positive. Achieving the second place in the ranking shows that even a simple marker-based method can hold its own in a competition which we expected to be dominated by more intricate machine learning methods. We can only assume that our wide range of knowledge-inspired features, including fully syntactic ones, made up for the weaker method.

However, as for identifying differences between Belgian and Netherlandic Dutch, we have to view our current results as merely a first step. We did manage to identify some features that appear to be biased towards either Belgian or Netherlandic Dutch, but it is as yet unclear if this is because of the language variety of the source text. There were too many interfering factors to be sure, such as topic (the movie or show the subtitles were from), differing genres (subtitling conventions in the local branches of BTI), and processing difficulties (not quite optimally appropriate software, run on not quite clean text). Still, we did manage to identify some potential syntactic differences between Belgian and Netherlandic Dutch, our main goal, while taking precautions to avoid interference from these factors. As a result, we do have a basis for research on further data, in which we can try to confirm our findings.

Acknowledgements

We thank Erwin Komen and Micha Hulsbosch for preparing a script for the analysis of the text with Frog, Alpino and the surfacing software.

Reference

R. Harald Baayen, Hans van Halteren, and Fiona Tweedie. 1996. Outside the cave of shadows: Using syntactic annotation to enhance authorship attribution. *Literary and Linguistic Computing*, 11(3), 121-131.

Sjef Barbiers and Hans Bennis. 2010. De plaats van het werkwoord in zuid en noord. In: Barbiers, S., H. Bennis, J. De Caluwe & J. Van Keymeulen (red.). *Voor Magda. Artikelen voor Magda Devos bij haar afscheid van de Universiteit Gent*. Gent: Academia Press, 25-42.

Ronny Boogaart. 2007. Conditionele constructies met *moest(en)* en *mocht(en)* in Belgisch-Nederlands en Nederlands-Nederlands. *Neerlandistiek.nl*. 07.05

Gosse Bouma, Gertjan Van Noord, and Robert Malouf. 2001. Alpino: Wide-coverage computational analysis of Dutch. *Language and Computers*, 37 (2001): 45-59.

Çağrı Çöltekin, Taraka Rama, and Verena Blaschke. 2018. Tübingen-Oslo Team at the VarDial 2018 Evaluation Campaign: An Analysis of N-gram Features in Language Variety Identification. In *Proceedings of the Fifth Workshop on NLP for Similar Languages, Varieties and Dialects (VarDial), Santa Fe, USA*.

Julien Despres, Petr Fousek, Jean-Luc Gauvain, Sandrine Gay, Yvan Josse, Lori Lamel, and Abdel Messaoudi. 2009. Modeling Northern and Southern varieties of Dutch for STT. *Tenth Annual Conference of the International Speech Communication Association*.

Stefan Grondelaers and Dirk. Speelman. 2007. A Variationist Account of Constituent Ordering in Presentative Sentences in Belgian Dutch. *Corpus Linguistics and Linguistic Theory*, 3(2): 161-193.

Emmeline Gyselinck and Timothy Colleman. 2016. Je dood vervelen of je te pletter amuseren? Het intensiverende gebruik van de pseudoreflexieve resultatiefconstructie in hedendaags Belgisch en Nederlands Nederlands. HANDELINGEN: KONINKLIJKE ZUID-NEDERLANDSE MAATSCHAPPIJ VOOR TAAL-EN LETTERKUNDE EN GESCHIEDENIS 69 (2016): 103-136.

Emmanuel Keuleers, Kevin Diependaele, and Marc Brysbaert. 2010. Practice Effects in Large-Scale Visual Word Recognition Studies: A Lexical Decision Study on 14,000 Dutch Mono- and Disyllabic Words and Nonwords. *Frontiers in Psychology*, 1.

Emmanual Keuleers, Michaël Stevens, Paweł Mandera, and Marc Brysbaert. 2015. Word knowledge in the crowd: Measuring vocabulary size and word prevalence in a massive online experiment. *Quarterly Journal of Experimental Psychology*, 68, 1665-1692.

Erwin Komen. 2015. Surfacing Dutch syntactic parses. Presentation at Computational Linguistics in the Netherlands (CLIN26), Amsterdam, 2015. http://wordpress.let.vupr.nl/clin26/abstracts/

Nelleke Oostdijk. 2000. The Spoken Dutch Corpus: Overview and first evaluation, *Proceedings of the Second International Conference on Language Resources and Evaluation (LREC)*, 887–894.

Nelleke Oostdijk, Martin Reynaert, Veronique Hoste, and Ineke Schuurman. 2013. The construction of a 500-million-word reference corpus of contemporary written Dutch. In *Essential speech and language technology for Dutch*. Springer, Berlin, Heidelberg. 219-247.

Efstathios Stamatatos. 2009. A Survey of Modern Authorship Attribution Methods. *Journal of the American Society for Information Science and Technology*. Volume 60 Issue 3, March 2009. 538-556.

Antal van den Bosch, Bertjan Busser, Walter Daelemans, and Sander Canisius. 2007. An efficient memory-based morphosyntactic tagger and parser for Dutch, In F. van Eynde, P. Dirix, I. Schuurman, and V. Vandeghinste (Eds.), *Selected Papers of the 17th Computational Linguistics in the Netherlands Meeting*, Leuven, Belgium, 99-114.

Chris van der Lee. 2017. *Text-based video genre classification using multiple feature categories and categorization methods*. Master's Thesis. Tilburg University.

Chris van der Lee and Antal van den Bosch. 2017. Exploring Lexical and Syntactic Features for Language Variety Identification. In *Proceedings of the Fourth Workshop on NLP for Similar Languages, Varieties and Dialects (VarDial)*, pages 190–199, Valencia, Spain.

Marcos Zampieri, Shervin Malmasi, Nikola Ljubešić, Preslav Nakov, Ahmed Ali, Jörg Tiedemann, Yves Scherrer, and Noëmi Aepli. 2017. Findings of the VarDial Evaluation Campaign 2017. *Proceedings of the Fourth Workshop on NLP for Similar Languages, Varieties and Dialects (VarDial)*. Valencia, Spain.

Marcos Zampieri, Shervin Malmasi, Preslav Nakov, Ahmed Ali, Suwon Shon, James Glass, Yves Scherrer, Tanja Samardžić, Nikola Ljubešić, Jörg Tiedemann, Chris van der Lee, Stefan Grondelaers, Nelleke Oostdijk, Antal van den Bosch, Ritesh Kumar, Bornini Lahiri and Mayank Jain. 2018. Language Identification and Morphosyntactic Tagging: The Second VarDial Evaluation Campaign. *Proceedings of the Fifth Workshop on NLP for Similar Languages, Varieties and Dialects (VarDial)*. Santa Fe, USA.

Birzeit Arabic Dialect Identification System for the 2018 VarDial Challenge

Rabee Naser
Electrical & Computer Engineering Dept
Birzeit University
West Bank, Palestine
rabinasser@gmail.com

Abualsoud Hanani
Electrical & Computer Engineering Dept
Birzeit University
West Bank, Palestine
ahanani@birzeit.edu

Abstract

This paper describes our Automatic Dialect Recognition (ADI) system for the VarDial 2018 challenge, with the goal of distinguishing four major Arabic dialects, as well as Modern Standard Arabic (MSA). The training and development ADI VarDial 2018 data consists of 16,157 utterances, their words transcription, their phonetic transcriptions obtained with four non-Arabic phoneme recognizers and acoustic embedding data. Our overall system is a combination of four different systems. One system uses the words transcriptions and tries to recognize the speaker dialect by modeling the sequence of words for each dialect. Another system tries to recognize the dialect by modeling the phone sequences produced by non-Arabic phone recognizers, whereas, the other two systems use GMM trained on the acoustic features for recognizing the dialect. The best performance was achieved by the fused system which combines four systems together, with F1 micro of 68.77%.

1 Introduction

Work on accent and dialect recognition in the literature is still traditionally split into acoustic-only, acoustic-lexical and acoustic-phonetic classification systems. Most of the state-of-the-art systems focus on acoustic methods. In the past work on the VarDial 2017/2016 (Zampieri et al., 2017)(Malmasi et al., 2016) shared tasks, the presented work capitalized on the combination of i-vector technique, which represents each utterance by a low-dimensional vector estimated from the variability subspace (DeMarco and COX, 2013), and lexical word sequence extracted by Arabic ASR. Deep Neural Networks (DNN) has been successfully used for modelling both the acoustic features and the lexical features extracted from the words sequences. (Ionescu and Butnaru, 2017) got the first rank on the ADI shared task with F1 score of 76.32% in the last year challenge (Zampieri et al., 2017) . They used multiple kernel approach for this task. Our previous work on the same task (Hanani et al., 2017) ranked in the fourth place with our fused system that combines word-entropy and character-string entropy with the acoustic i-vector system. The best F1 (micro) score we had achieved was 62.87%.

The VarDial 2018 (Zampieri et al., 2018) consists of the same five shared tasks of the last year edition. One of these tasks is the Arabic Dialect Identification (ADI) which addresses the multi-dialectal challenge in spoken Arabic in broadcast news domain. Previously, organizers of the ADI shared acoustic features and lexical word sequence extracted from large-vocabulary speech recognition (LVCSR). This year, they add phonetic features, which allow the use of both acoustic and phonetic features, which are helpful for distinguishing between different dialects. In the previous work, the most successful ADI systems that combine acoustic with lexical features. With the added phonetic features, the Phonotactic systems such as Phone Recognizer followed by Language Model (PRLM) is investigated and compared with the lexical and acoustic based systems.

This work is licensed under a Creative Commons Attribution 4.0 International License. License details: http://creativecommons.org/licenses/by/4.0/

Proceedings of the Fifth Workshop on NLP for Similar Languages, Varieties and Dialects, pages 210–217
Santa Fe, New Mexico, USA, August 20, 2018.

2   Data Description

The training data presented by the organizers of the ADI shared task contained embedding acoustic features, lexical words recognized by an Arabic Automatic Speech Recognition (AASR) system, and phonemes recognized by four non-Arabic (Czech,English,Hungarian and Russian) phone recognizers. A list of the WAV files with links was also provided. The dataset is already divided into three subsets; train, dev and test. The train subset consists of 14591 utterances, dev subset consists of 1566 utterances, whereas test subset consists of 6837 utterances. Each utterance was labeled with one of the five target Arabic dialects (Egyptian, Levantine, Gulf, North Africa, MSA). 5435 testing utterances were added to the original 1492 testing utterances from the mgb_3 dataset .

Dialect	Training	Development	Testing
Egyptian	3177	315	1445
Gulf	2873	265	1397
Levantine	3117	348	1465
North African	3205	355	1324
MSA	2219	283	1206
Total	14591	1566	6837

Table 1: The ADI Data for VarDial 2018 shared task

3   Systems Description

Our overall system consists of multiple systems. Some of them use acoustic features for modeling target dialects, some use lexical features extracted from the words sequence and some use phonetic features extracted from phones and GMM tokens sequences. The main difference from the last year systems is the deep neural networks incorporation in the acoustic and words/phones sequences.

Multiple Systems were investigated for the purpose of participation in the ADI shared task, we had the results of only one system ready at the the submission deadline.

We will first introduce the participating system. And then we will state the other systems that were prepared for the shared task and we will discuss their results. We will show also potential candidate systems that could have raised the rank of our team.

3.1   Embedding Features SVM

SVM models have shown in (Hanani et al., 2017) that it is a good classifier with low dimension interpretation of the data files. We have chosen to train two separate SVM models for the training and development data instead of using one model. The chosen SVM model is a multiclass SVM that predicts the class of the utterance instead of the traditional 2 class SVM. We have presented the 600 embedding features directly as inputs to the models. And the predicted classes of each model was recorded.

3.2   Feed Forward Neural Network

We have trained two separate feed-forward DNN models with multiple layers each. The inputs of the DNN models were once again the acoustic embedding features. The output of the DNNs is a layer of five values, each value represents the probability that a given utterance belongs to the corresponding dialect. The dialect that corresponds to the output with highest value is recorded as the predicted dialect of the model.

3.3   ADI Run

As stated before, we had only one valid run in the shared task and it was a combination of the previous systems. Every test file has four predictions, these predictions were gathered in one vector. Then we have used a voting technique to specify the final predicted dialect. This system will serve as the baseline to our post shared task work. We have completed our proposed systems and proposed new systems that have shown encouraging results. The following systems are the systems that we continued our work on after the official ADI run.

3.4 SVM Baseline

We reconfigured and tuned the SVM model. The training and development data was concatenated, and the system performed slightly better than the original system scoring up to 53.82%.

3.5 WAV Fles Processing

We used the wav files to extract acoustic features. The files were divided into frames by the length of 25ms. 19 Mel-Scale Cepstral Coefcients (MFCC) was extracted, then we applied the Rasta Filtration. we appended the Shifted-Delta Cepstra to each frame features, resulting in 38 features per frame. These feature were used in the acoustic based models.

3.6 GMM-UBM Model

we have built different Gaussian mixture models with different number of Gaussian mixtures. A GMM-UBM model for each number of Gaussian mixtures was built. we used all of the training and development data to build one Universal Background GMM (referred as UBM). We used a K-means algorithm to initialize the model parameters. We then ran the expectation maximization algorithm for four iterations to estimate the UBM model parameters.

we adapted the UBM to every dialect using dialect specific data and MAP adaptation technique. The resulting GMM models then was used for predicting the labels of the testing data. The class model with maximum score determines the predicted dialect. The GMM-UBM model performed poorly comparing to the embedding features result scoring only 35.1% for 2048 mixtures.

3.7 GMM Tokenizer

We used the UBM model described above as a tokenizer, that converts a sequence of acoustic features into a sequence of the gaussian components which gives the highest probability for each frame. Comparing with phonotactic system, the Gaussian component with the highest probability is recognized as the phoneme of the frame. A vector of the recognized phonemes is extracted for each file.

N-gram vector is extracted for each utterance by counting the occurrences of each n-gram. The n-gram vectors are then fed to a Multiclass SVM model. Uni-gram and bi-gram vectors of 128 mixtures models was applied, and only uni-gram vectors was tested for the 2048 mixtures due to memory limitation. The systems resulted in 40.28%, 46.18%, 47.86% respectively.

3.8 Word TF-IDF Model

We gathered all the word files from training and development data to extract a vocabulary of 68707 unique words. Then we provided the word files to a tf-idf vector extractor, which takes the utterances as an input and then produces a vector of 68707 features, each feature represents the term frequency-inverse document frequency of a single word in the vocabulary.

The term frequency represents how frequent the word is in the text, the word which occurred the most will have the highest score. But the words that are frequent in all the documents will have little information for the classifier. The Inverse Document Frequency is used to reduce the score of the words that are frequent in most of the documents.

The term frequency and inverse-document frequency are calculated by the following equations:

$$tf_t = 1 + \log(count_t) \tag{1}$$

$$idf_t = 1 + \log(\frac{N}{d_t}) \tag{2}$$

$count_t$ represents the count of term t in the document while N represents the total number of utterances and d_t is the number of documents that contains the word t, then the $tf - idf$ is calculated by the following equation:

$$tfidf_t = tf_t \times idf_t \tag{3}$$

A Multiclass SVM model was used to train and test the tf-idf vectors, the result was 51.47% accuracy.

3.9 Sentence Similarity Model

In this system for each utterance the similarity to all the sentences in the training and development data is calculated resulting in a vector of 16157 features which is the number of training and development data files.

We used the Jaccard similarity algorithm to find the similarity between the utterances. The Jaccard algorithm is also known as intersection over union. The Jaccard similarity between sentences A and B is shown in the following equation:

$$J(A, B) = \frac{A \cap B}{A \cup B} \tag{4}$$

The similarity index varies from 0 to 1. The similarity index of 1 means that the two sentences are actually one sentence, while 0 similarity means no similarity. Using the similarity coefficients for the purpose of classification can be justified because sentences are likely to be more similar to sentences from their own dialect than to sentences from other dialects.

An application was developed to produce the similarity vectors, and the 16157 vectors of 16157 features of training and development were used to train an SVM model. The model was used to predict the dialect of the testing data, and the system has 51.89% accuracy.

3.10 PRLM Model

We have used the phonemes of the Czech phoneme recognizer to build a Phonotactic Phone Recognizer followed by Language Model (PRLM). Three separate PRLM models for uni-gram, uni+bi-gram and uni+bi+tri-gram sequences were trained. The sequences were used as inputs to SVM models. We used the development data for testing and our results were 37.04%, 38.9% and 38.76%, respectively. We used these results as baseline to test our proposed tf-idf approach on the phoneme level.

3.11 Phoneme TF-IDF Model

We have adopted the same system used in the word tf-idf system in the phoneme level. First we developed a system to extract uni-grams and bi-grams and concatenate them in one sentence. Then the sentences were introduced to the word tf-idf vector extractor. An SVM was built to test the performance of the new features, and it scored 41.12% accuracy in identifying development data.

3.12 Bottleneck Features

Neural networks had been lately used extensively in machine learning problems. The deep neural networks which consists of multiple interconnected layers between the input and output layers was used in speech recognition tasks(Najafian et al., 2018). DNNs had not been used just as classifiers but they were also used as feature extractors(Ali et al., 2016). Neural networks can be configured to have multiple layers with big numbers of neurons, and between these layers a much smaller layer can be added as illustrated in Figure 1 . The state of this layer can be used as feature vector to represent the original data. The bottleneck features can be used to feed another learning model or another DNN.

In the embedding acoustic features system and the sentence similarity system a total of 16757 features were used to train the SVM models. Bottleneck features were extracted to reduce dimensionality and combine both systems.

A Neural network was built for the embedding features system, and the similarity system with multiple hidden layers, each one of them contained a bottleneck layer of 30 neurons, the DNNs were trained and the state of the 30 neurons was recorded for each of the dataset files.

The bottleneck features were combined for each utterance into 60 features long vectors. The vectors then were used to train an SVM model, the system scored 61.3% F1 macro which outperformed any score presented by any team in this year ADI competition.

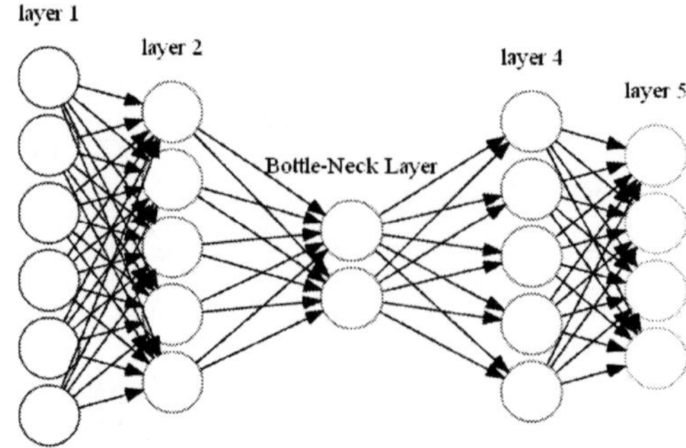

Figure 1: Bottleneck features

3.13 Systems Fusing

A fusing system was introduced to fuse the results of all the previously described systems. The raw output of each of the previous models is a vector of 5 features that represents the scores of the dialect specific models for each utterance. The vectors of the testing data were recorded and concatenated.

Seven fold cross validation was applied on the fused vectors by dividing the testing data into seven segments, leaving one segment at a time for testing and the six other segments for training fusion SVM model.

4 Results and Discussion

The results of the ADI shared task of this year are much worse than the results of the 2017 shared task. This was expected since this year's testing data was much bigger than previous year's. 6837 test files were used in 2018 instead of 1492 files in 2017. The number of the files was not the only cause but as it was stated by the organizers this years testing data contained files obtained from YouTube, in addition to the original files used in the previous year.

Six teams participated in the ADI Shared Task. Only the baseline system results were ready at the submission due date. It ranked third as shown in Table 2 and its confusion matrix is shown in Figure 2. The work continued on other systems and models as well as on the baseline model to improve accuracy.

Team Name	Score
UnibucKernel	0.5892
safina	0.5759
BZU	0.5338
SystranLabs	0.5289
taraka_rama	0.5140
Arabic_Identification	0.4997

Table 2: Shared Task Results.

The traditional baseline GMM system performed below last year's result in (Hanani et al., 2017) (35.1% compared to 40.16%). This can be related to the additional testing data coming from different environment. It can be also related to the reduced choice of the MFCC features extracted this year (38 instead of 68 in 2017). Interestingly, the GMM tokenizer performed slightly better than last year in (Hanani et al., 2017) with this year best result of 47.86% in contrast to 46.85% in 2017.

The tf-idf model was a replacement of traditional uni-gram model. It scored 51.47% better than we would have expected and relatively close to the submitted result. It is interesting to compare this system's score to what would a uni-gram word count model score.

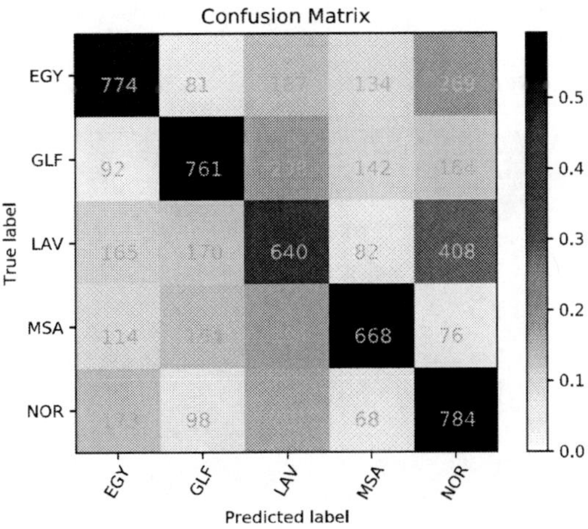

Figure 2: ADI task, RUN1 (Baseline results)

The tf-idf model showed promising results when compared to the PRLM model on czech phone recognizer data. By testing with the testing data, it only scored 35.79%, due to time limitation no further phone recognizer's data or setups were tested.

The result of the sentence similarity system with 51.89% accuracy was slightly better than that of the tf-idf; but the idea of using 16157 features instead of 68707 and getting better results led to further investigation of the use of smaller vectors.

After analyzing the results of each system, it was apparent that different systems predicted different correct utterances. Only 30% of the testing files were predicted correctly by both of the similarity model and the embedding feature SVM model. And 40% of the data was correctly identified only by one of them. That showed us that there is room for improvement by fusing the systems together.

The use of bottleneck features improved the performance of the system to 61.3%. The fact that the systems don't need the labels of the testing data, means that it could have been presented to the shared task and it would have easily ranked the first with 2.5% improvement over the best score. The confusion matrix of the best system is shown in Figure 3

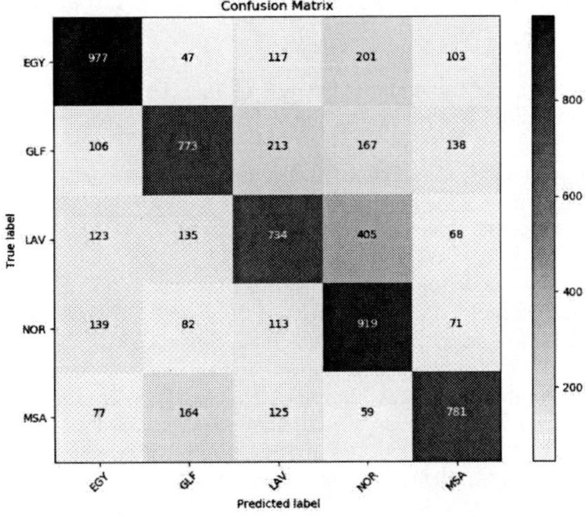

Figure 3: Bottleneck features results

The overall fused system scored 68.77% F1 micro. The confusion matrix of this system is shown in Figure 4

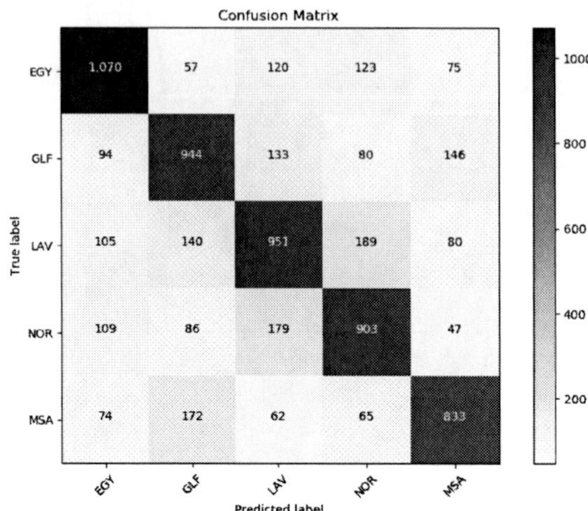

Figure 4: fusing results

5   Conclusions and Future Work

In this paper we presented some of the techniques we intended to use for the the shared task. We are looking forward to further investigate the bottleneck features on the word and phoneme level and to study the sentence similarity approach looking into other sentence to sentence relation models. we have used deep learning in different techniques and we have tried to use Long Short Term Memory models that didn't converge in the learning process, so they weren't described in the paper. It would be interesting to analyze the reasons behind that. we would like to divide the data in other ways to include the new testing data in training to examine the effect of the difference of recording environment if it exists.

References

[Ali et al.2016] Ahmed Ali, Najim Dehak, Patrick Cardinal, Sameer Khurana, Sree Harsha Yella, James Glass, Peter Bell, and Steve Renals. 2016. Automatic Dialect Detection in Arabic Broadcast Speech. In *Proceedings of INTERSPEECH*, pages 2934–2938.

[DeMarco and COX2013] Andrea DeMarco and Stephen J. COX. 2013. Native accent classification via i-vectors and speaker compensation fusion. In *Proceedings of INTERSPEECH*, pages 1472–1476.

[Hanani et al.2017] Abualsoud Hanani, Aziz Qaroush, and Stephen Taylor. 2017. Identifying dialects with textual and acoustic cues. In *Proceedings of the Fourth Workshop on NLP for Similar Languages, Varieties and Dialects (VarDial)*, pages 93–101, Valencia, Spain, April.

[Ionescu and Butnaru2017] Radu Tudor Ionescu and Andrei Butnaru. 2017. Learning to identify arabic and german dialects using multiple kernels. In *Proceedings of the Fourth Workshop on NLP for Similar Languages, Varieties and Dialects (VarDial)*, pages 200–209, Valencia, Spain, April.

[Malmasi et al.2016] Shervin Malmasi, Marcos Zampieri, Nikola Ljubešić, Preslav Nakov, Ahmed Ali, and Jörg Tiedemann. 2016. Discriminating between similar languages and arabic dialect identification: A report on the third dsl shared task. In *Proceedings of the 3rd Workshop on Language Technology for Closely Related Languages, Varieties and Dialects (VarDial)*, Osaka, Japan.

[Najafian et al.2018] Maryam Najafian, Sameer Khurana, Suwon Shon, Ahmed Ali, and James Glass. 2018. Exploiting convolutional neural networks for phonotactic based dialect identification. In *ICASSP*.

[Zampieri et al.2017] Marcos Zampieri, Shervin Malmasi, Nikola Ljubešić, Preslav Nakov, Ahmed Ali, Jörg Tiedemann, Yves Scherrer, and Noëmi Aepli. 2017. Findings of the VarDial Evaluation Campaign 2017. In *Proceedings of the Fourth Workshop on NLP for Similar Languages, Varieties and Dialects (VarDial)*, Valencia, Spain.

[Zampieri et al.2018] Marcos Zampieri, Shervin Malmasi, Preslav Nakov, Ahmed Ali, Suwon Shuon, James Glass, Yves Scherrer, Tanja Samardžić, Nikola Ljubešić, Jörg Tiedemann, Chris van der Lee, Stefan Grondelaers, Nelleke Oostdijk, Antal van den Bosch, Ritesh Kumar, Bornini Lahiri, and Mayank Jain. 2018. Language Identification and Morphosyntactic Tagging: The Second VarDial Evaluation Campaign. In *Proceedings of the Fifth Workshop on NLP for Similar Languages, Varieties and Dialects (VarDial)*, Santa Fe, USA.

Twist Bytes - German Dialect Identification with Data Mining Optimization

Fernando Benites[1], Ralf Grubenmann[2], Pius von Däniken[2], Dirk von Grünigen[1],
Jan Deriu[1], and Mark Cieliebak[1]

[1]Zurich University of Applied Sciences, Switzerland
[2]SpinningBytes AG, Switzerland
benf@zhaw.ch, rg@spinningbytes.com, pvd@spinningbytes.com,
vogr@zhaw.ch, deri@zhaw.ch, ciel@zhaw.ch

Abstract

We describe our approaches used in the German Dialect Identification (GDI) task at the VarDial Evaluation Campaign 2018. The goal was to identify to which out of four dialects spoken in German speaking part of Switzerland a sentence belonged to. We adopted two different meta-classifier approaches and used some data mining insights to improve the preprocessing and the meta-classifier parameters. Especially, we focused on using different feature extraction methods and how to combine them, since they influenced the performance very differently of the system. Our system achieved second place out of 8 teams, with a macro averaged F-1 of 64.6%. We also participated on the surprise dialect task with a multi-label approach.

1 Introduction

The German Dialect Identification (GDI) task (Zampieri et al., 2018), organized by the VarDial Evaluation Campaign 2018, was a continuation of last year's competitions (Zampieri et al., 2017). It consisted in classifying sentences into classes corresponding to different selected dialects.

In the German speaking part of Switzerland, there are many dialects which are quite different, and speakers of one dialect might even have difficulty understanding other dialects of regions not far away. The selected dialects were roughly represented by cantons Bern, Basel (Basel-Stadt and Baselland), Luzern (Luzern and Nidwalden) and Zurich. Geographically speaking, the cantons chosen to represent the dialects create roughly a square with each side of 100 kilometers. Each sentence was transcribed and annotated with the canton of the speaker.

The identification of dialect based on the script for non-standardized dialects is a difficult task. Not only it is difficult to transcribe the dialects (although there are guidelines), but the annotation process can be very subjective. This subjectivity of the annotation manifests in similar tasks such as in labelling multi-label samples (Benites, 2017). A good example, found in this competition's dataset, was "schön" and "schöön", both meaning beautiful and both labelled with Luzern dialect. An interesting restriction was that no additional information than the task data should be used (closed submission).

Notably this year's competition had a special task, to predict a surprise dialect in the test set. Thus, the training data had no data on that new dialect (training set data 4 classes, test set data 5 classes). Such a task is particularly difficult because of the small amount of training data.

We describe here the approaches taken by our team Twist Bytes. We achieved second place[1] with one of our approaches. The key feature of the approaches is based on the fact that we investigated the data set using data mining methods and applied feature optimization to build two different meta-classifiers.

2 Related Work

One of the focuses of VarDial has been the challenge of dialect identification. Especially important for our study are the previous and current GDI tasks (VarDial competition reports: Zampieri et al. (2017;

This work is licensed under a Creative Commons Attribution 4.0 International License. License details: `http://creativecommons.org/licenses/by/4.0/`.

[1]The ranking proposed by the organizers was more broad, since many systems achieved similar results. We achieved second rank with three other systems.

Proceedings of the Fifth Workshop on NLP for Similar Languages, Varieties and Dialects, pages 218–227
Santa Fe, New Mexico, USA, August 20, 2018.

Set	BE	BS	LU	ZH	XY
Train	3547	3109	3262	3577	
Dev	985	1297	965	909	
Test	1191	1200	1186	1175	790
sentences removed for RTS					
Train	342	240	252	317	
Dev	0	0	0	0	

Table 1: Number of instances by Canton and Set

Zampieri et al. (2018)). Solving this problem can have a positive impact on many tasks, e.g. POS-tagging of dialectal data (Hollenstein and Aepli, 2014) and on compilation of German dialect corpora (Hollenstein and Aepli, 2015). Many studies engaged the problem in the GDI tasks, creating already a noticeable amount of related work, described in short in the competition reports. Predominantly, SVMs with different feature extraction methods performed very well.

Our approach is most similar to MAZA (Malmasi and Zampieri, 2017). MAZA uses Term Frequency on n-grams for character and unigrams for word features to train SVMs. Then it uses a Random Forest meta-classifier with 10-fold crossvalidation on the predictions of the SVMs. We additionally used Term Frequency-Inverse Document Frequency on word and, uncommonly used, on character level. We also used an SVM as meta-classifier and did not concatenate the output of the base classifiers but summed them, as will be explained in the next sections.

For the surprise task, we used a global confidence threshold which is usually a good baseline for such tasks. See (Benites, 2017) for a review on multi-label threshold strategies.

3 Methodology and Data

3.1 Task Definition

The task of GDI is, simply speaking, to classify a transcribed sentence from the ArchiMob data set (Samardžić et al., 2016) into one of four classes. Each class stands for a different canton[2] (Bern (BE), Basel (BS), Luzern (LU) and Zurich (ZH)), where a different German dialect is spoken. Since the dialects are very different from standard high German, the sentences are transcribed using the guideline by Dieth (Dieth and Schmid-Cadalbert, 1986). It is a phonetics oriented transcription method but it is orthographic and partially adapted to standard German spelling habits. It uses the standard German alphabet and therefore loses some of the precision and expliciteness of phonetic transcription methods suchs as the International Phonetic Alphabet. Thus, it is not phonetic (which could give more hints about the canton) but uses a standard German script. We expect therefore that character-based and error tolerant methods will perform best, since different spellings of the same word might occur.

Although the number of speakers is clearly defined in training set (3-7 per dialect) and development set (one per dialect). There were one (BE, BS, XY) or two (LU, ZH) speakers per dialect in the test set[3].

Table 1 shows the number of sentences in the training set, the development set, and test set per canton. The training set was slightly changed in comparison to the one from last year. The development set was the test set of last year's GDI competition. The sentence distribution is almost evenly balanced over all cantons. The XY column will be discussed in Section 3.2.6 and RTS in Section 3.2.5.

3.2 System Definition

In this section, we describe our approach in detail. One part (meta crossvalidation) is based on the system from (Malmasi and Zampieri, 2017) but extended in several ways. The key improvements were focused on the data mining, specifically, the optimization of the preprocessing and feature extraction plus a preprocessing step between base classifier and meta-classifier.

---

[2] A canton is a national state in Switzerland.

[3] We could only find information about the number of speakers in the test set, after the competition.

We observed that much of the recognition can be performed on a character-base level, where character bigrams can provide a key insight, while demonstrating a high efficiency. The four processing steps of the system are: a) to preprocess the sentences, b) extract features from them, c) classify with a base classifier and d) pass the predictions to a meta-classifier which, in turn, provides the final prediction.

3.2.1 Preprocessing

The basic preprocessing step was to split the sentences in words by using white-spaces and convert them to lower case. No stopword removal or lemmatization was performed since these steps might erase any traces of key features for differentiating between the dialects (see (Maharjan et al., 2014)). Afterwards multiple feature extraction methods were applied.

3.2.2 Feature Extraction

We used feature extraction methods similar to (Malmasi and Zampieri, 2017), which we extended in several ways. Term Frequency (TF) with n-grams for characters and words was used for n ranging from 1 to 7. An additional preprocessing for the classifiers employed (see next section) is to normalize the TF values, at least per sentence, which in some cases can improve prediction quality. Also, we calculated the TF-IDF (Manning et al., 2008), which usually gives the best single feature set for prediction quality.

For the feature extraction we mainly used the scikit-learn[4] package with one modification: We also used a custom character bigram analyzer (referred to later as CB) in order to produce character bigrams without spaces, since the standard implementation considers all characters in the text including the spaces, especially at the beginning and end of a word. We employed TF-IDF not only on word level but also on character level.

The bm-25 measure (Jones et al., 2000) was not implemented in scikit-learn 0.19.1, therefore we used our own implementation[5] with the key parameter set to b=0.5.

Each of the feature extraction methods served as a separate feature set which was processed by a base classifier. The entire list: TF word n-grams (TF-W), TF character n-grams (TF-C), TF-IDF words (TF-IDF-W), customed bigrams analyzer (CB-C), TF-C normalized to 0 and 1 (TF-C-N) and TF-IDF character n-grams (TF-IDF-C).

3.2.3 Classifiers

We employed a meta classification process, where the same base classifier was trained on multiple tasks. We assessed several standard classifiers as base and meta-classifiers such as Random Forest, extreme Gradient Boosting and ARAM (Tan, 1995), and we achieved the best results with SVMs. We chose the standard implementation of scikit-learn for linear Support Vector Machines (SVMs)(Fan et al., 2008) as base classifier. It performs particularly well on large sparse feature sets, such as text classification with TF-IDF.

We tried concatenating all extracted features into one feature vector for a single SVM classifier, however, the performance decreased in this setting (see Section 4.1 for more information). Instead, we used the *sum of the scores* assigned by each SVM (trained on separate feature sets) to each sample, and then using the maximum score per class to chose the predicted class (referred to as S-Classifier in Figure 1). This lead to an large increase in prediction quality (as discussed in Section 4.1). The possibility of weighting this sum will be explained in the next section.

3.2.4 Meta-Classifiers

We explored various ensemble architectures, and finally implemented two approaches: a meta-classifier trained on the predictions of the base classifier through crossvalidation, and a hierarchical (divide and conquer) classifier.

---

[4]http://scikit-learn.org

[5]The implementation was used as in https://nlp.stanford.edu/IR-book/html/htmledition/okapi-bm25-a-non-binary-model-1.html .

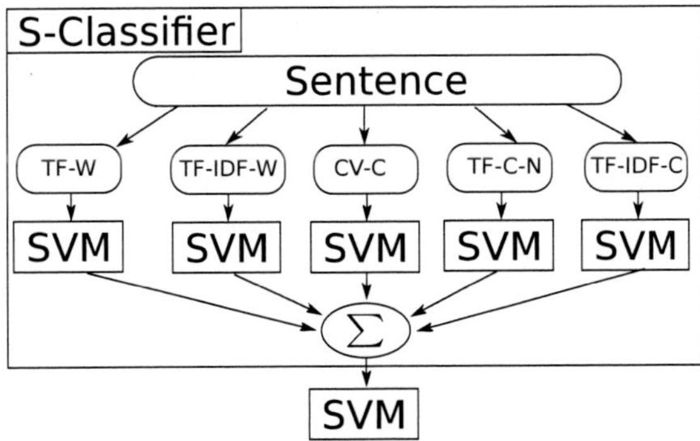

Figure 1: TB-Meta Classifier Workflow, with S-Classifier

Meta Crossvalidation Classifier We experimented with a two-tier meta-classifier bottom-up with crossvalidation (referred as TB-Meta) to eliminate the need for parameter/weighting search. The workflow of the system is depicted in Figure 1. First an input sentence is preprocessed, then the features are extracted it and passed to the base classifiers, one classifier per feature set. The predictions of the classifiers are summed (until now it is an S-Classifier), and a last classifier (meta-classifier) decides about the final label. The key challenge is how to train the meta-classifier. The system is trained in three passes. First a 10-fold crossvalidation is generated and each base classifier is trained on all four classes for each single feature set. The per-class predictions are summed (output of S-Classifier). This sum is saved for each sample of the training set.[6]

After the crossvalidation with the S-Classifier generated predictions for all samples of the training set, these predictions together with the true labels are used to train a new linear SVM classifier, the meta-classifier. This classifier has four input features and four classes as output. Afterwards, the base classifiers are again trained with the whole training set. The idea is to grasp which predictions are likely to be a misprediction and which class should be used instead. This is practically a counter measure to solve problems with the confusion matrix.

The second level of the procedure also ensures that the class interdiscrimination is improved. Further, each base classifier prediction is then weighted by the classifier itself. That means a weighting scheme and time-consuming parameter search is not needed anymore.

Hierarchical Classifier In cases where a confusion between two classes is frequent, one can also apply divide and conquer approaches, especially in a binary fashion. We used a meta-label hierarchical approach (referred to as TB-Hierarchical). First an S-classifier selects between two clusters of classes (which it was trained on), and then this procedure is re-applied on the predicted cluster of classes until there is only one class left. In the four classes case of GDI 2018, there are only three possible balanced binary trees as depicted in Figure 2, referred to as H1, H2 and H3. More specifically, first the S-Classifier (with all base classifiers per feature set and summation) decides between which pair the sentence is more likely to belong to. That means the target classes of this classifier are meta classes (e.g. BS+LU). Afterwards a second S-Classifier decides which of the two cantons the sample belongs to (i.e. target classes are the actual cantons). This is a top-down approach.

In addition, we introduced an important processing step, modifying the S-Classifier. When summing the prediction of the single base classifiers, we weighted them with different values between 0 and 1 (choosing the values using a grid-search approach). For example, the prediction scores of the base classifier using TF-matrix as input feature were weighted with 0.5. We used in the competition the following weights: (TF-W:0.5, TF-IDF-W:1, CB-C:1, TF-IDF-C:0.5, TF-C:0.2).

---

[6]Although a sum is counter-intuitive, since the linear meta SVM should learn a simple summation, it seems to overfit, and the sum counteracts this process. We consistently achieved better results with the summation in all sets used.

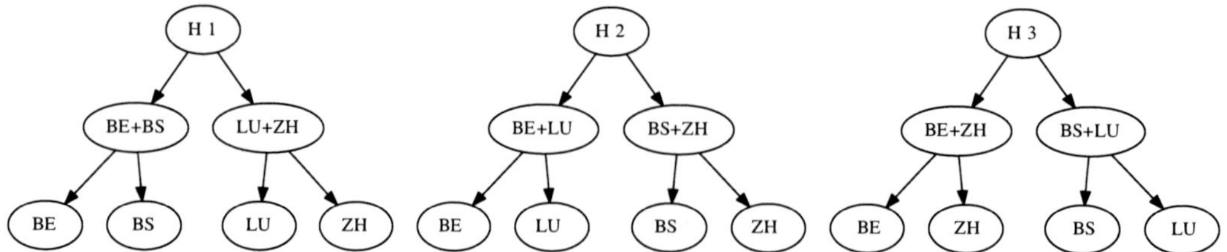

Figure 2: Different combinations by divide and conquer of the labelset

3.2.5 Data Mining Optimization

Preliminary experiments showed that many errors come from the fact that many two-word sentences had different class assignments. This is not a real error as different dialects can share words and expressions. For example, the sample "ja ja" ("yes, yes") occurred twice, and was once assigned to Zurich dialect and once to Bern. These inconsistencies make the classification more difficult, i.e. to generate a consistent model from this ambiguous data.

As a consequence, we removed one and two-word sentences from the training set, since they might decrease the performance of the model. This is the standard preprocessing of the approaches employed in this study. We will show in the experiments the impact of that step, referred to as Reduced Training Set (RTS), and differentiate to the case where all sentences are included, referred to as Complete Training Set (CTS). The affected number of sentences can be seen in Table 1. They are between 240 and 342, depending on the canton.

3.2.6 Handling Unknown Dialects

The "Surprise Task" at GDI was to detect a previously unknown dialect. No training examples were given for this new dialect. One challenge was the small amount of training data, which makes it difficult to generate a model-discriminator for untypical samples. Number of samples of the unknown class is depicted in Table 1, referred to as XY. It has a little less samples than the other cantons.

This task is similar to multi-label problems, where a threshold must be defined up to which the confidence score of the classifier can be used to predict a certain label. We did a standard threshold based post-processing approach on the predictions of the meta S-Classifier. If the prediction score for every known class was too low, i.e. below the threshold, the sample belongs to the surprise dialect. The threshold was set a little lower than indecision where it was 0. We also assessed the mean and standard deviation in the development set of the prediction scores in order to make a more precise estimation.

4 Results

4.1 Performance on Development Set

We tested different combinations of the feature sets to build base classifiers, despite expecting the character based feature extraction methods to perform best. We believed that because the data was relatively scarce, a multi-perspective/ensemble model was, in our view, a promising choice. Hence we trained classifiers for different feature sets and combinations. Since the number of combinations increases exponentially, we limited ourselves to what we expected to be the most promising combinations. The results are shown in Table 2. Basically, in the table, a base system is extended in every new line with an additional feature. The measures used are weighted and macro F-1. We also compare between RTS and CTS. In italics are those approaches that we implemented only after the competition. Marked in bold are the 6 best results, fifth and sixth best were submitted to the competition. We describe below each line in detail:

We start (#0) with a linear SVM with TF (not normalized) as feature input. Afterwards we tested instead TF-IDF (#1). Because of the No Free Lunch assumption[7], we compared these two approaches

---

[7] In that context that means that no classifier is apt to perform best in every problem.

Nr/#	System	RTS		CTS	
		Weighted F-1	**Macro F-1**	**Weighted F-1**	**Macro F-1**
-	Random Baseline Dev	≈ 0.2500			
0	SVM TF-W	0.6438	0.6524	0.6422	0.6350
1	SVM TF-IDF-W	0.6592	0.6515	0.6566	0.6497
2	RF TF-W	0.4885	0.4250	0.5100	0.4261
3	RF TF-IDF-W	0.4894	0.4228	0.5071	0.4238
4	SVM CB-C bigrams	0.6773	0.6700	0.6823	0.6739
5	same as #4 + with TF-IDF-W	0.6785	0.6687	0.6837	0.6733
6	same as #5 but CB-C n-grams 1-7	0.6785	0.6687	0.6837	0.6733
7	same as #6 + TF-IDF-C	0.6808	0.6709	0.6812	0.6713
8	same as #7 + TF-C	0.6817	0.6725	0.6830	0.6730
9	same as #8 as S-Classifier	0.6923	0.6811	0.6931	0.6829
10	same as #9 but with TF-W	0.6971	0.6878	0.6974	0.6884
11	*same as #9 but with TF-W-N*	**0.7027**	0.6929	**0.7026**	0.6930
12	same as #10 + bm25	0.6830	0.6751	0.6853	0.6774
13	same as #11 + bm25	0.6872	0.6786	0.6903	0.6818
14	TB-Meta	**0.7010**	0.6907	0.6979	0.6878
15	*TB-Meta + TF-W*	**0.7037**	0.6938	**0.7015**	0.6918
16	TB-Meta + bm25	0.6984	0.6904	0.6894	0.6792
17	TB-Meta + bm25 + TF-W	0.6951	0.6871	0.6932	0.6833
18	TB-Hierarchical	**0.7012**	0.6931	0.6976	0.6880
19	MAZA VarDial 2017 GDI winner	-	-	0.662	-

Table 2: Per Feature System Results for the GDI Task from 2017 (using dev set). TB-Meta is Twist Bytes Meta classifier and TB-Hierarchical is Twist Bytes Hierarchical one. RF stands for random forests. CB stands for CounterVectorizer (scikit-learn TF with analyzer). Baseline random assignment (over 10 runs): weighted F-1 0.246 ± 0.003, macro F-1 0.250 ± 0.005

with when switching to a classifier Random Forest instead of SVM(#2-3). Then, we used the module CountVectorizer, which generates a TF matrix. However, we passed our analyzer to count character bigrams without considering white-spaces (#4). This increased F-1 scores by about 0.02. Next, method #4 was used for concatenation of TF and TF-IDF feature set but also combined with word n-grams in range 1-7 for the TF-IDF (#5). In the next line, we extended the n-grams also to the character analyzer (#6). This caused no improvement. An additional character analyzer with n-grams (range 1-7), term-weighted with TF-IDF (#7) produced a small increase. Concatenating a TF analyzer of character ngrams (range 1-7) helped to increase a little more (#8). The next line presents a considerable increase. Here, we applied the summation method and not concatenation (S-Classifier) (#9). In #10 we used TF with word n-grams in range 1-7. Since SVMs cope better with normalized values in range of [0,1], we normalized the TF values, which further increased the prediction quality (#11). Unfortunately, we did not have time to discover this until after the competition. Still, we will see that this was not best approach on the test set (but it was in the dev). We also employed bm-25, which last year's second place was based also because it takes into account the document length. Unfortunately, this weighting scheme did not produce better results on this set (#12-13).

The next line is the submitted Twist Bytes Meta (crossvalidation) system (#14), see 3.2.4. Using normalized TF increased again the prediction quality on the development set (#15). The hierarchical performed best out among all approaches that we implemented before the competition. The H3 constellation, depicted in Figure 2, consistently achieved the best results in the development set and H1 the worst ones. A possible reason for H3 achieving best results can be assessed by the confusion matrix, where LU was often mistaken for BE, as can be seen from Figure 3. Although maybe H2 could be seen as a better solution, the confusion is not symmetric (as can be seen from the confusion matrix), and it seems differentiating with the help of the other classes is easier. Yet, H1 did not work as good as H3, so this seems to be a specific solution for this case. The hierarchical classification had performed best in the

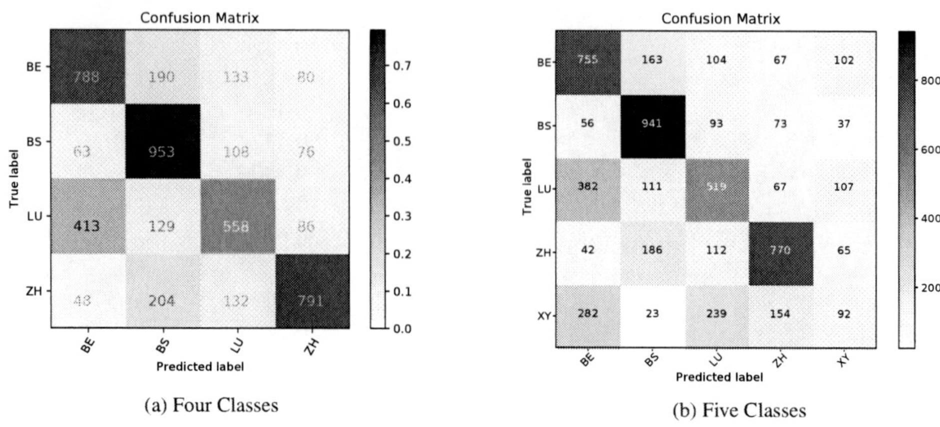

(a) Four Classes   (b) Five Classes

Figure 3: TB-Meta Confusion Matrices for GDI and Surprise Task

dev set. Notably, we see that the RTS preprocessing step consistently improved the performance of the meta-classifiers. The approaches using the CB-C always outperformed the MAZA performance of 2017.

4.2 Competition Results

There were only 3 possible runs/submissions for each task in this year's VarDial. This limited the number of approaches and the parameter optimization that could be done on the actual test set before the final submission. We therefore submitted the best systems from the previous section without any further optimization to the competition, i.e., the meta-classifier and the hierarchical classifier with the best features. The results are depicted in Table 3. The system SUKI outperforms the second best system, our TB-Meta, by around 0.04 macro F-1. We also compared in that table the approaches/parameters we optimized and investigated in depth for this study, but marked them in the column competition as N (not submitted to the competition).

From the systems not submitted, we can also see that the bm-25 feature extraction was helpful for the TB-Meta in the actual test set. It was only surpassed by controlling the maximum number of features per feature set, namely 50k features, which will be discussed in Section 4.2.1. Interestingly, using the TF features decreased the quality of the predictions.

Contrary to the previous section, TB-Hierarchical performed much worse than TB-Meta on the test set. One explanation would be that the weighting was overfitted to the development set. We did not explore all the possibilities on the test set (grid search).

The difference between RTS and CTS produced only a 0.02 points improvement in the test set; however, this was enough to beat the third place by a scant. A further development was to remove all ambiguities in the training data (i.e. not only the limited by the number of words, since RTS regards only one and two word sentences). Unfortunately, this degrades the score by 0.004. This points to the fact that the ambiguities obeys a distribution for large sentences differently, decreasing the performance of the classifier.

4.2.1 Feature Number Dependency

For the competition, we used a maximum of 20000 features per subclassifier/feature set. This decision was made quite early in the process and only questioned again after the competition.

For this reason, we tested with the gold standard the dependency between maximum number of features and macro F1-score. The results are depicted in Figure 4. We selected multiple values for the maximum number of features for each feature extraction method, and we used the TB-Meta classifier on this year's test set. The submission can be seen at 20k features (macro F-1 of 0.646, as in the competition results). Interestingly, using 50k features increased the macro F-1 score to 0.6511. Also there was no clear trend between 20k and 300k. After 300k it seems to not change anymore (no more features

224

System	macro F-1	Submitted	Place
SUKI	0.6857	Y	1
TB-Meta 50k features	0.6511	N	
TB-Meta-all + bm25	0.6485	N	
TB-Meta + bm25	0.6479	N	
TB-Meta-all + bm25 + TF	0.6468	N	
TB-Meta	**0.6464**	Y	2
safina	0.6448	Y	3
TB-Meta + TF	0.6445	N	
TB-Meta-all	0.6440	N	
TB-Meta-all + TF	0.6439	N	
taraka_rama	0.6398	Y	4
LaMa	0.6374	Y	5
XAC	0.6336	Y	6
TB-Hierarchical	0.6280	Y	-
GDI_classification	0.6203	Y	7
dkosmajac	0.5909	Y	8
Random Baseline	0.2521	-	-

Table 3: Results for the GDI task. TB-Meta is Twist Bytes Meta classifier and TB-Hierarchical is Twist Bytes Hierarchical classifier. TB-Meta-all is TB-Meta with Complete Training Set. Best TB-system in competition marked in bold. Submitted column states if system was actually submitted to the competition. Only best submissions were placed.

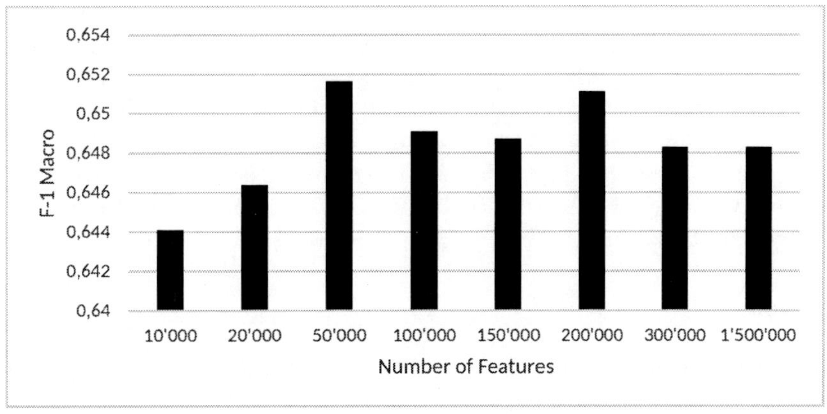

Figure 4: Macro F-1 versus the maximum number of allowed features per subclassifier on test set

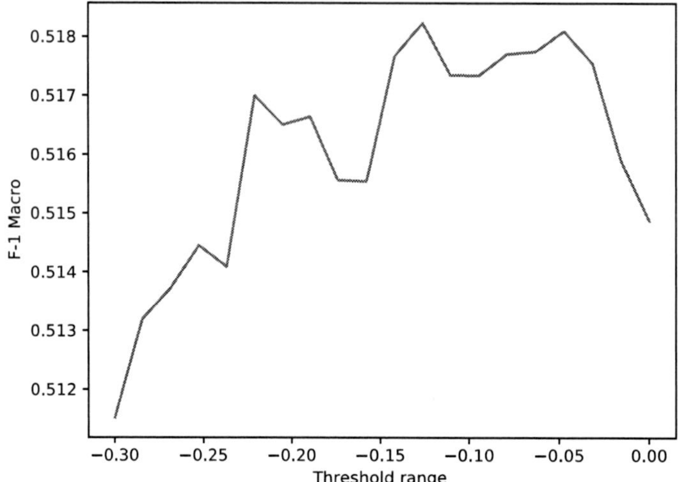

Figure 5: Variations of threshold value for the confidence score to detect one of the 4 known dialects, measured in macro F-1

extracted or at least without any noticeable effect). The huge number of features comes from the fact that the analyzers using many n-grams create so many features.

4.3 Handling Unknown Dialects

The surprise task is similar to the multi-label problems, where a threshold must be defined up to which the confidence/score of the classifier can be used to predict a certain label. We did a standard threshold based approach, i.e. we trained an SVM and when, during prediction, none of the class score exceeded the threshold, we predicted the surprise dialect. We set this threshold for the competition to -0.3 for all classes based on our qualitative assessment on the prediction of the development set. The result was a macro F-1 of 0.5115 and weighted F-1 of 0.5373. With the gold standard we investigated how the macro F-1 score varies with the threshold. The results can be seen in Figure 5 and show that a peek of 0.518 occurs around -0.12.

As can be seen from Figure 3b class XY was often mispredicted. Especially BE and LU were predicted when the true class was the XY. The difference to Figure 3b is small showing that the procedure mostly conserved the predictions. It penalized uncertain predictions, so that XY is distributed similarly as the prediction error: The good predicted class BS had small confusion with XY, where the highest confusion was with LU which had also the most predictions errors.

Also a per class optimization can be employed in this setup. Using a gridsearch over the interval -0.4 and 0.1, we achieve a macro F-1 score of 0.5230 with the following values: BE:-0.2143, BS:-0.2571, LU:-0.1286 and ZH:-0.0429.

5   Conclusion

We described our dialect identification systems that were submitted to the VarDial GDI competition. We achieved second place among 8 teams with the TB-Meta classifier system, using linear SVM as base, meta crossvalidation training, multiple word and character features. A further preprocess improved slightly the prediction quality, producing a final macro-averaged F1-score of 0.646.

We also submitted for the surprise task, where it was the sole submission. Our system achieved an F1-score of 0.5115. We hope that our system can serve as a baseline for next year's competition.

References

Fernando Benites. 2017. *Multi-label Classification with Multiple Class Ontologies*. Ph.D. thesis, University of Konstanz, Konstanz.

E. Dieth and C. Schmid-Cadalbert. 1986. *Schwyzertütschi Dialäktschrift: Dieth-Schreibung*. Lebendige Mundart. Sauerländer.

Rong-En Fan, Kai-Wei Chang, Cho-Jui Hsieh, Xiang-Rui Wang, and Chih-Jen Lin. 2008. Liblinear: A library for large linear classification. *J. Mach. Learn. Res.*, 9:1871–1874, June.

Nora Hollenstein and Noëmi Aepli. 2014. Compilation of a Swiss German dialect corpus and its application to pos tagging. In *Proceedings of the First Workshop on Applying NLP Tools to Similar Languages, Varieties and Dialects*, pages 85–94.

Nora Hollenstein and Noëmi Aepli. 2015. A resource for natural language processing of Swiss German dialects.

K Sparck Jones, Steve Walker, and Stephen E. Robertson. 2000. A probabilistic model of information retrieval: development and comparative experiments: Part 2. *Information processing & management*, 36(6):809–840.

Suraj Maharjan, Prasha Shrestha, and Thamar Solorio. 2014. A simple approach to author profiling in mapreduce. In *CLEF*.

Shervin Malmasi and Marcos Zampieri. 2017. German dialect identification in interview transcriptions. In *Proceedings of the Fourth Workshop on NLP for Similar Languages, Varieties and Dialects (VarDial)*, pages 164–169, Valencia, Spain, April.

Christopher D. Manning, Prabhakar Raghavan, and Hinrich Schütze. 2008. *Introduction to Information Retrieval*. Cambridge University Press, New York, NY, USA.

Tanja Samardžić, Yves Scherrer, and Elvira Glaser. 2016. ArchiMob–A corpus of spoken Swiss German. In *Proceedings of the Language Resources and Evaluation (LREC)*, pages 4061–4066, Portoroz, Slovenia).

Ah-Hwee Tan. 1995. Adaptive resonance associative map. *Neural Networks*, 8(3):437–446.

Marcos Zampieri, Shervin Malmasi, Nikola Ljubešić, Preslav Nakov, Ahmed Ali, Jörg Tiedemann, Yves Scherrer, and Noëmi Aepli. 2017. Findings of the VarDial Evaluation Campaign 2017. In *Proceedings of the Fourth Workshop on NLP for Similar Languages, Varieties and Dialects (VarDial)*, Valencia, Spain.

Marcos Zampieri, Shervin Malmasi, Preslav Nakov, Ahmed Ali, Suwon Shon, James Glass, Yves Scherrer, Tanja Samardžić, Nikola Ljubešić, Jörg Tiedemann, Chris van der Lee, Stefan Grondelaers, Nelleke Oostdijk, Antal van den Bosch, Ritesh Kumar, Bornini Lahiri, and Mayank Jain. 2018. Language Identification and Morphosyntactic Tagging: The Second VarDial Evaluation Campaign. In *Proceedings of the Fifth Workshop on NLP for Similar Languages, Varieties and Dialects (VarDial)*, Santa Fe, USA.

STEVENDU2018's system in VarDial 2018: Discriminating between Dutch and Flemish in Subtitles

Steven Du

stevenlol@qq.com

Yuan Yuan Wang

circlea@sina.com

Abstract

This paper introduces the submitted system for team STEVENDU2018 during VarDial 2018 (Zampieri et al., 2018) Discriminating between Dutch and Flemish in Subtitles(DFS). Post evaluation analyses are also presented. The results obtained indicate that it is a challenging task to discriminate between Dutch and Flemish.

1 Introduction

The DFS task is a supervised learning task to classify text into Dutch or Flemish. Dutch is the language spoken in the Netherlands and Flemish is a variant of Dutch language and also known as Belgian Dutch. There are 300000 labeled training data, 500 labeled development data, 20000 on-hold test data (van der Lee and van den Bosch, 2017). DUT in training data denotes Dutch, and BEL is the label for Flemish. F1 score is the evaluation metric.

This paper is structured as follows: first, a brief training data analysis will be given. Then systems trained during the evaluation will be introduced. Finally more systems will be explored for post evaluation analysis.

2 Data analysis

The training data set consists of 300000 labeled sentences. After being lower cased and tokenized, the average sentence length in characters and number of words for both DUT and BEL is nearly the same. As showed in Table 1, it is a well balanced data set. It is worth to note that the two languages share 57.2% of vocabulary.

Dialect	DUT	BEL
Number of samples	150000	150000
Average sentence length in characters	187.86	187.90
Average number of words per sentence	40.36	40.35
Unique words	115560	115442
Shared words	66142	
Percentage of shared words	57.2%	57.2%

Table 1: Statistics for the training data set.

One interesting finding is that the use of punctuation is a little bit different. BEL has more commas, periods and question marks but less exclamation marks than DUT as showed in Table 2.

3 Systems trained during evaluation

There are two systems trained during evaluation: a bag-of-ngram model and dual convolutional neural network model.

This work is licensed under a Creative Commons Attribution 4.0 International License. License details: http://creativecommons.org/licenses/by/4.0/

Proceedings of the Fifth Workshop on NLP for Similar Languages, Varieties and Dialects, pages 228–234
Santa Fe, New Mexico, USA, August 20, 2018.

Dialect	DUT	BEL
,	157725	183736
.	690629	708076
?	118236	136742
!	1450	110

Table 2: Statistics for the punctuation in training data set.

3.1 Bag-of-ngram

Conventional methods for text classification apply common features such as bag-of-words, n-grams, and their TF-IDF (Zhang et al., 2008) as input of machine learning algorithms, such as support vector machine (SVM) (Joachims, 1998), logistic regression (Genkin et al., 2007), naive Bayes (NB) (Mccallum, 1998) for classification.

In this work, the bag-of-ngram system and Linear SVM are used as the baseline system. First the text is lower-cased and converted to n-gram word tokens (n is from 1 to 3), then filtered by TF-IDF with minimal document frequency of 5. Extracted features are utilized to train Linear SVM classifier. A 20 folds cross validation is performed on the training set, the average F1 score is 0.63. This system obtains 0.69 on development set.

3.2 Dual-CNN

This approach builds simple CNN model (with pre-trained embedding) for each language. The input text will pass through these CNNs separately. Outputs of two CNN networks are then concatenated together. This is followed by a fully connected layer for classification task. Detail of this network can be found in Figure 1, in which we limit the length of input word tokens to 60. During evaluation the proposed Dual-CNN network obtained 0.62 through cross validation and 0.61 on the development set. The final

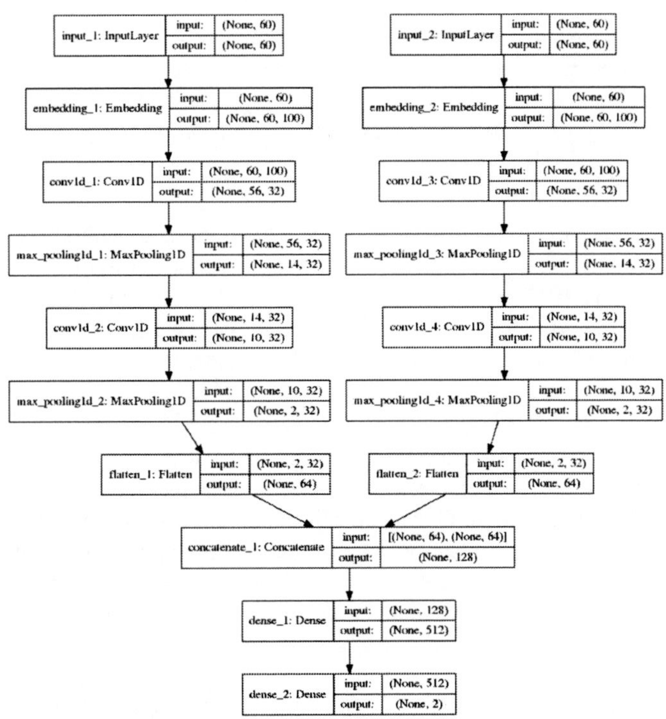

Figure 1: Proposed Dual-CNN architecture

submitted system is only a bag-of-ngram model which has better performance than Dual-CNN.

3.3 Evaluation results

The score on the released test set range from 0.55 to 0.66 in Table 3, our bag-of-ngram, the most simple approach yields 0.623. On the other hand the proposed Dual-CNN yields 0.621. The test score correlated well with the local cross validation score, development set is not the right choice for model selection. The best score is just 0.66, which implies that the DFS task is challenging.

Rank	Team	Run	F1 (macro)
1	Tübingen-Oslo	3	0.6600474291
2	Taurus	4	0.6455823383
3	clips	2	0.6357352338
3	LaMa	3	0.6325606971
3	XAC	3	0.6317829736
3	safina	0	0.6308914957
4	**STEVENDU2018**	2	**0.6230923676**
4	mskroon	5	0.6201248435
5	SUKI	1	0.6127429864
6	DFSlangid	3	0.5961836466
7	dkosmajac	1	0.5674320041
7	benf	2	0.5582862249

Table 3: Evaluation results

4 Post evaluation systems

Since the bag-of-ngram system only scores 0.623 on test set, to achieve better result a series of studies had been carry out after the evaluation. These can be broadly divided into three groups: one group focus on finding the vector representation for the given text data, another group focus on deep learning approaches, third group utilize existing text classification framework.

4.1 Vector representation based approach

Vector representation approach intends to convert text data in variable-length pieces of text into a fixed-length low dimension vector. There are many works have been done in this direction (Kim, 2014; Wieting et al., 2015; Kusner et al., 2015; Kenter et al., 2016; Ye et al., 2017), only two basic approaches are investigated here: by taking mean value of word vectors and through doc2vec from the work in distributed representation of sentences and documents (Le and Mikolov, 2014).

4.1.1 Mean word vector system

A popular idea in modern machine learning is to represent words by vectors. These vectors capture hidden information about a language, like word analogies or semantics. Commonly used word vectors are word2vec (Mikolov et al., 2013), Glove (Pennington et al., 2014) and fastText (Bojanowski et al., 2017). FastText is capable to capture sub-word information, thus in this study, we use FastText to train word vectors. Skip-gram, window size of 5 and minimal word count of 5, 5 negative samples, sub-word range is between 3 and 6 characters are the default training parameters. After training, for each sentence, the mean value of its word vectors is used as feature, Linear Discriminant Analysis classifier[1] is selected as the learning algorithm.

Table 4 shows F1 score for the mean word vector system. With increase in the number of dimensions, the system performance improved.

---

[1] `http://scikit-learn.org/stable/modules/lda_qda.html`

Word vector dimension	40	100	250	300	400
Test F1 Score		0.5642	0.5848	0.5922	0.598	0.6024

Table 4: F1 scores for mean word vector system

4.1.2 Doc2vec

In this study we use the doc2vec (Le and Mikolov, 2014) from gensim[2]. The doc2vec model is trained on training data set with minimal word occurrence of 5 and window size of 8. Table 5 shows the best score is 0.5308, which is slightly better than random guess.

Sentence vector dimension	100	200	300
Test F1 Score	0.5282	0.5246	0.5308

Table 5: F1 scores for Doc2vec

Two sets of sentence vector have been evaluated in this study. The average word vector approach is better than doc2vec. In the following experiment, 400 is used as the default size of word embedding.

4.2 Deep learning based approaches

Our proposed Dual-CNN didn't beat the conventional bag-of-ngram model. This motivated us to examine the performance of deep learning approaches. Five types of deep learning based approaches are investigated (all of them use word level embeddings), starting from the most basic architecture, they are:

4.2.1 MLP

The MLP system is built by an embedding layer, one flatten layer and fully connected layer as illustrated in Figure 2 . Please also refer to system diagrams in github repository[3].

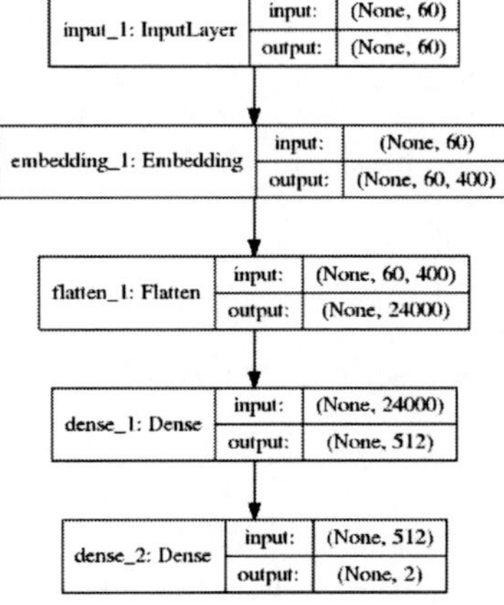

Figure 2: MLP architecture

4.2.2 AVERAGE

The AVERAGE system is similar to MLP system but the flatten layer is replaced by an average pooling layer. It is also known as neural bag-of-word model and being surprisingly effective for many tasks (Iyyer et al., 2015).

[2]https://radimrehurek.com/gensim/index.html
[3]https://github.com/StevenLOL/vardial2018_dfs_stevendu2018

4.2.3 GRU

The GRU system is similar to AVERAGE system but the average pooling layer is replaced by a bidirectional GRU layer.

4.2.4 CNN-LSTM

The CNN-LSTM system is built by an embedding layer followed by two convolution-max pooling layers and one bidirectional GRU layer.

These four deep approaches are indeed the most fundamental networks in NLP research. Incorporating language model fine-tunning (Howard and Ruder, 2018) and attention mechanism (Vaswani et al., 2017) are the recent trends, which we leave them for further exploration.

Word Embedding	D20 Random	D400 Random	D400 pre-trained
MLP	0.6350	**0.6365**	0.6334
AVERAGE	0.6352	0.6356	**0.6402**
GRU	0.6299	0.6388	**0.6413**
CNN-LSTM	0.6352	**0.6421**	0.6399

Table 6: F1 scores for popular deep learning based approaches

Table 6 presents results for four popular deep learning based approaches. D20 Random denotes randomized word embedding of 20 dimensions. D400 pre-trained denotes embedding layer is pre-trained with word vector size of 400 dimensions. These results confirm the observation in 4.1.1, that the 400 dimension word vectors is a good choice for this task. Three out of four systems are higher than 0.64 which are significantly better than submitted baseline system.

4.2.5 CapsuleNet

Capsules with transformation matrices allowed networks to automatically learn part-whole relationships. Consequently, (Sabour et al., 2017) proposed capsule networks that replaced the scalar-output feature detectors of CNNs with vector-output capsules and max-pooling with routing-by-agreement. The capsule network has shown its potential by achieving a state-of-the-art result on highly overlapping digit parts in MutiMNIST data set. The PrimaryCapsule employed in that paper is a convolutional capsule layer with 32 channels of convolutional 8D capsules. We increase the number of channels from 32 to 320 in this study, the assumption is that there are more part-whole relations in the language than those in MNIST digit images.

Number of Channels	32	320	320
Output dimension	1	1	2
Test F1 Score	0.5992	0.6076	**0.6206**

Table 7: CapsuleNet classification results.

Table 7 introduces F1 score of CapsuleNet on the test data set. The results indicate that with the increase of number of channels and thus the number of capsules, the system performed better. When changing the binary classification problem to two class classification problem, the capsule net yielded comparable result to the bag-of-ngram baseline. Work by (Zhao et al., 2018) also shows significant improvement when transferring single-label to multi-label text classifications.

4.3 Text Classification Framework

FastText (Joulin et al., 2016) is a library for efficient learning of word representations and sentence classification[4]. It uses vectors to represent word n-grams to take into account local word order, which is important for many text classification problems. Following Table 8 shows fastText classification results. The 0.6476 is the highest score achieved.

---

[4] `https://github.com/facebookresearch/fastText`

Word n-gram	1	2	3
Test F1 Score	0.6318	**0.6476**	0.6377

Table 8: FastText classification results.

5 Conclusion

In this paper, a wide range of systems have been evaluated for the VarDial 2018 DFS task. A bag-of-ngram system score 0.6230 and serves as the baseline. Complex systems such as Dual-CNN and CapusleNet have competitive score to baseline system. Four simple deep learning based methods outperform baseline, three of them are higher than 0.64. FastText is identified as the best single system, yielded a F1 score of 0.6476.

References

Piotr Bojanowski, Edouard Grave, Armand Joulin, and Tomas Mikolov. 2017. Enriching word vectors with subword information. *Transactions of the Association for Computational Linguistics*, 5:135–146.

Alexander Genkin, David D Lewis, and David Madigan. 2007. Large-scale bayesian logistic regression for text categorization. *Technometrics*, 49(3):291–304.

J. Howard and S. Ruder. 2018. Universal Language Model Fine-tuning for Text Classification. *ArXiv e-prints*, January.

Mohit Iyyer, Varun Manjunatha, Jordan Boyd-Graber, and Hal Daumé Iii. 2015. Deep unordered composition rivals syntactic methods for text classification. In *Meeting of the Association for Computational Linguistics and the International Joint Conference on Natural Language Processing*, pages 1681–1691.

Thorsten Joachims. 1998. Text categorization with support vector machines: Learning with many relevant features. In Claire Nédellec and Céline Rouveirol, editors, *Machine Learning: ECML-98*, pages 137–142, Berlin, Heidelberg. Springer Berlin Heidelberg.

Armand Joulin, Edouard Grave, Piotr Bojanowski, and Tomas Mikolov. 2016. Bag of tricks for efficient text classification. *arXiv preprint arXiv:1607.01759*.

Tom Kenter, Alexey Borisov, and Maarten De Rijke. 2016. Siamese cbow: Optimizing word embeddings for sentence representations. In *Meeting of the Association for Computational Linguistics*, pages 941–951.

Y. Kim. 2014. Convolutional Neural Networks for Sentence Classification. *ArXiv e-prints*, August.

Matt J. Kusner, Yu Sun, Nicholas I. Kolkin, and Kilian Q. Weinberger. 2015. From word embeddings to document distances. In *International Conference on International Conference on Machine Learning*, pages 957–966.

Quoc V Le and Tomas Mikolov. 2014. Distributed representations of sentences and documents. 4:II–1188.

A Mccallum. 1998. A comparison of event models for naive bayes text classification. *IN AAAI-98 WORKSHOP ON LEARNING FOR TEXT CATEGORIZATION*, pages 41–48.

Tomas Mikolov, Ilya Sutskever, Kai Chen, Greg Corrado, and Jeffrey Dean. 2013. Distributed representations of words and phrases and their compositionality. *Advances in Neural Information Processing Systems*, 26:3111–3119.

Jeffrey Pennington, Richard Socher, and Christopher Manning. 2014. Glove: Global vectors for word representation. In *Conference on Empirical Methods in Natural Language Processing*, pages 1532–1543.

S. Sabour, N. Frosst, and G. E Hinton. 2017. Dynamic Routing Between Capsules. *ArXiv e-prints*, October.

Chris van der Lee and Antal van den Bosch. 2017. Exploring Lexical and Syntactic Features for Language Variety Identification. In *Proceedings of the Fourth Workshop on NLP for Similar Languages, Varieties and Dialects (VarDial)*, Valencia, Spain.

Ashish Vaswani, Noam Shazeer, Niki Parmar, Jakob Uszkoreit, Llion Jones, Aidan N Gomez, Lukasz Kaiser, and Illia Polosukhin. 2017. Attention is all you need.

J. Wieting, M. Bansal, K. Gimpel, and K. Livescu. 2015. Towards Universal Paraphrastic Sentence Embeddings. *ArXiv e-prints*, November.

Jianbo Ye, Yanran Li, Zhaohui Wu, James Z. Wang, Wenjie Li, Jia Li, Jianbo Ye, Yanran Li, Zhaohui Wu, and James Z. Wang. 2017. Determining gains acquired from word embedding quantitatively using discrete distribution clustering. In *Meeting of the Association for Computational Linguistics*, pages 1847–1856.

Marcos Zampieri, Shervin Malmasi, Preslav Nakov, Ahmed Ali, Suwon Shuon, James Glass, Yves Scherrer, Tanja Samardžić, Nikola Ljubešić, Jörg Tiedemann, Chris van der Lee, Stefan Grondelaers, Nelleke Oostdijk, Antal van den Bosch, Ritesh Kumar, Bornini Lahiri, and Mayank Jain. 2018. Language Identification and Morphosyntactic Tagging: The Second VarDial Evaluation Campaign. In *Proceedings of the Fifth Workshop on NLP for Similar Languages, Varieties and Dialects (VarDial)*, Santa Fe, USA.

W. Zhang, T. Yoshida, and X. Tang. 2008. Tfidf, lsi and multi-word in information retrieval and text categorization. In *2008 IEEE International Conference on Systems, Man and Cybernetics*, pages 108–113, Oct.

W. Zhao, J. Ye, M. Yang, Z. Lei, S. Zhang, and Z. Zhao. 2018. Investigating Capsule Networks with Dynamic Routing for Text Classification. *ArXiv e-prints*, March.

Using Neural Transfer Learning for Morpho-syntactic Tagging of South-Slavic Languages Tweets

Sara Meftah[*], Nasredine Semmar[*], Fatiha Sadat[+], Stephan Raaijmakers[∓]

[*]CEA, LIST, LVIC, F-91191, Gif-sur-Yvette, France
{sara.meftah, nasredine.semmar}@cea.fr
[+]UQÀM, Montréal, Canada
sadat.fatiha@uqam.ca
[∓]TNO, The Hague, The Netherlands
stephan.raaijmakers@tno.nl

Abstract

In this paper, we describe a morpho-syntactic tagger of tweets, an important component of the CEA List DeepLIMA tool which is a multilingual text analysis platform based on deep learning. This tagger is built for the Morpho-syntactic Tagging of Tweets (MTT) Shared task of the 2018 VarDial Evaluation Campaign. The MTT task focuses on morpho-syntactic annotation of non-canonical Twitter varieties of three South-Slavic languages: Slovene, Croatian and Serbian. We propose to use a neural network model trained in an end-to-end manner for the three languages without any need for task or domain specific features engineering. The proposed approach combines both character and word level representations. Considering the lack of annotated data in the social media domain for South-Slavic languages, we have also implemented a cross-domain Transfer Learning (TL) approach to exploit any available related out-of-domain annotated data.

1 Introduction

Part-of-Speech (POS) tagging is one of the basic and indispensable tasks in any Natural Language Processing (NLP) pipeline; it consists of assigning adequate and unique grammatical categories (Part-of-Speech tags) to words in the sentence. When POS tags are enriched by Morpho-Syntactic Descriptions (MSDs), such as gender, case, tenses, etc. the task is called Morpho-Syntactic Tagging (MST) (Agić et al., 2013). As an example, we provide a Slovene sentence with its MS tags in Figure 1.

MST is a challenging task especially for languages with rich word inflections and free word order like South-Slavic languages. In addition, MST of informal text like social media content of these languages is a more complex task, especially conversational texts. This is due to the conversational nature of the text, the lack of conventional orthography, the noise, linguistic errors, spelling inconsistencies, informal abbreviations and the idiosyncratic style. Also, social media platforms such as Twitter pose an additional issue by imposing 280 characters limit for each tweet.

While recent approaches based on end-to-end Deep Neural Networks (DNNs) have shown promising results for sequence tagging in many languages such as English, much less work has been done on neural models for MST of Slavic languages. In this paper, we evaluate the effect of using neural networks techniques for MST of South-Slavic tweets, where we are faced with a large number of possible word-class tags and only a small hand-tagged in-domain dataset.

NLP neural models with high performance often require huge volumes of annotated data to produce powerful models and prevent over-fitting. Consequently, in the case of social media content, it is difficult to achieve the performances of state-of-the-art models based on hand-crafted features by applying neural models trained on small amounts of annotated data. For this reason, Transfer Learning (TL) was proposed to exploit annotated out-of-domain data-sets. TL aims at performing a task on a target dataset using features learned from a source dataset (Pan and Yang, 2010).

The method presented in this work aims to overcome the problem of the lack of annotated data by significantly limiting the necessary data and instead extrapolating the relevant knowledge from another, related domain. This contribution generalizes previous results for POS tagging of user generated content

This work is licensed under a Creative Commons Attribution 4.0 International License. License details: http://
creativecommons.org/licenses/by/4.0/.

Proceedings of the Fifth Workshop on NLP for Similar Languages, Varieties and Dialects, pages 235–243
Santa Fe, New Mexico, USA, August 20, 2018.

in social media for five languages: English, French, Italian, German and Spanish (Meftah et al., 2018), by applying our approach on three Twitter corpora of South-Slavic languages: Slovene, Croatian, and Serbian.

POS = pronoun Type = demonstrative Gender = neuter Number= singular Case = nominative	POS = verb Type = auxiliary Vform = present Person = third Number= singular Negative = yes	POS = pronoun Type = negative Gender = feminine Number = singular Case = nominative	POS = noun Type = common Gender = feminine Number= singular Case = nominative	POS = Punctuation
MS tag = Pd-nsn	Va-r3s-y	Pz-fsn	Ncfsn	z
To	**ni**	**nobena**	**novost**	**.**

Figure 1: Example of a morphologically-tagged sentence in Slovene: *To ni nobena novost* ("This is not a novelty" in English) .

2 The Model

In this section, we introduce the model we experimented for MS tagging of South-Slavic languages. The model takes as input a tweet T, separated into a succession of n tokens w_i, such as $T = \{w_1, w_2, ..., w_n\}$. The objective is to predict the morpho-syntactic tag $\hat{y}_i$ for each token w_i of the tweet.

2.1 System Architecture

We use a similar architecture to that used in (Meftah et al., 2018) for English, French, Spanish, Italian and German Social Media content's POS tagging, we propose to use a bi-GRU (bidirectional Gated Recurrent Unit) sequence labelling model, preceded by a hybrid word representation. The model architecture is the same among all languages and tasks (Figure 3).

2.1.1 Words Representation

The model learns word-level we_i and character-level ce_i representations respectively for each token x_i, and combines them to get the final representation x_i.

Character level embedding: To capture morphological features, instead of Convolutional Neural Networks (CNNs) used in our previous work (Meftah et al., 2018), we apply in this work a bi-GRU encoder on all characters of each token to induce fully context sensitive character level embedding.

Figure 2 shows the character-level embedding model, a word w_i is divided into a succession of l characters c_i, each defined as a one-hot vector, with value 1 at index c_i and 0 in all other dimensionality, such as w_i will be represented with a $v \times l$ dimensional matrix. Next it's embedded into a $d \times l$ dimensional matrix, where v is the character's vocabulary size of the training set, l is the maximal length of words and d is the character embedding's dimension. Next, a forward GRUs model reads the character vectors from left to right and a backward GRUs model reads characters from right to left. The combination between the last hidden state of the forward GRUs and the last hidden state of the backward GRUs represents ce_i: the character level embedding for the word w_i.

Word-level embedding: we initialize words vectors we_i with FastText (Bojanowski et al., 2016) word embeddings to accurately capture words' semantics.

The combination between character-level embedding and word-level embedding x_i is fed into the bi-GRUs layer.

2.1.2 Bidirectional Gated Recurrent Units

Word vectors $\{x_1, x_2, ..., x_n\}$, which are constructed as a combination of word-level embeddings and character-based representations, are given as input to a 100-dimension bi-GRUs layer which iteratively passes through the sentence in both directions. Let $\overrightarrow{h_t}$ be the GRUs hidden state at time-step t. Formally, a forward GRUs model's unit at a time-step t takes x_t and the previous hidden state $\overrightarrow{h_{t-1}}$ as input, and outputs the current hidden state $\overrightarrow{h_t}$. Each GRUs apply the following transformations:

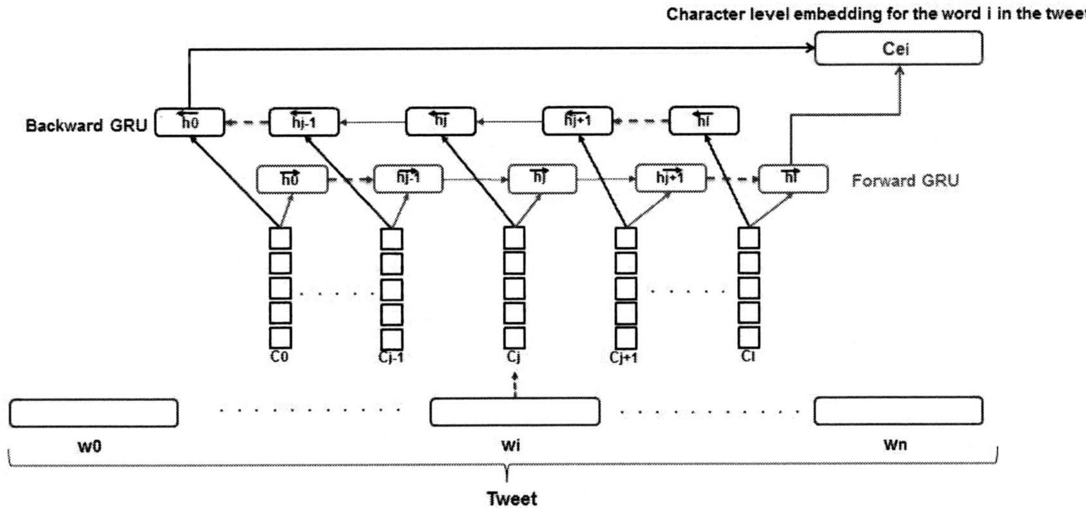

Figure 2: Bi-GRUs layer for character-level embedding.

$$\overrightarrow{r_t} = \sigma(W_{rx}x_t + W_{rh}\overrightarrow{h_{t-1}}) \tag{1}$$

$$\overrightarrow{z_t} = \sigma(W_{zx}x_t + W_{zh}\overrightarrow{h_{t-1}}) \tag{2}$$

$$\overrightarrow{\hat{h}_t} = \tanh(W_{hx}x_t + W_{hh}(\overrightarrow{r_t} \otimes \overrightarrow{h_{t-1}})) \tag{3}$$

$$\overrightarrow{h_t} = \overrightarrow{z_t} \otimes \overrightarrow{h_{t-1}} + (1 - \overrightarrow{z_t}) \otimes \overrightarrow{\hat{h}_t} \tag{4}$$

Here, W's are model parameters of each unit, $\hat{h}_t$ is a candidate hidden state that is used to compute h_t, σ is an element-wise sigmoid logistic function defined as $\sigma(x) = 1/(1 + e^{-x})$, and $\otimes$ denotes element-wise multiplication of two vectors. The update gate z_t controls how much the unit updates its hidden state, and the reset gate r_t determines how much information from the previous hidden state needs to be reset.

In order to take into account the context on both sides of that word, hidden representations $\overrightarrow{h_t}$ and $\overleftarrow{h_t}$ from forward and backward units, respectively, are concatenated at every token position, resulting h_t vectors.

$$h_t = [\overrightarrow{h_t}; \overleftarrow{h_t}] \tag{5}$$

2.1.3 Sequence Labelling

Hidden representations at each time-step are fed through a 80 dimension Fully Connected Layer (FCL) with a ReLU activation, followed by a final dense layer with a softmax activation to generate a probability distribution over the output classes at each time-step.

3 Neural Transfer Learning Methodology

Neural transfer learning is applied to address the problem of the need for annotated data for morphosyntactic tagging of social media texts. It consists of learning a parent neural network on a source problem with enough data, then transferring a part of its weights to represent data of a target problem with few training examples.

In this work, we experiment with cross-domain transfer; knowledge is transferred from a source domain to a target domain. In our case, the source domain is a standard text corpus of a language and the

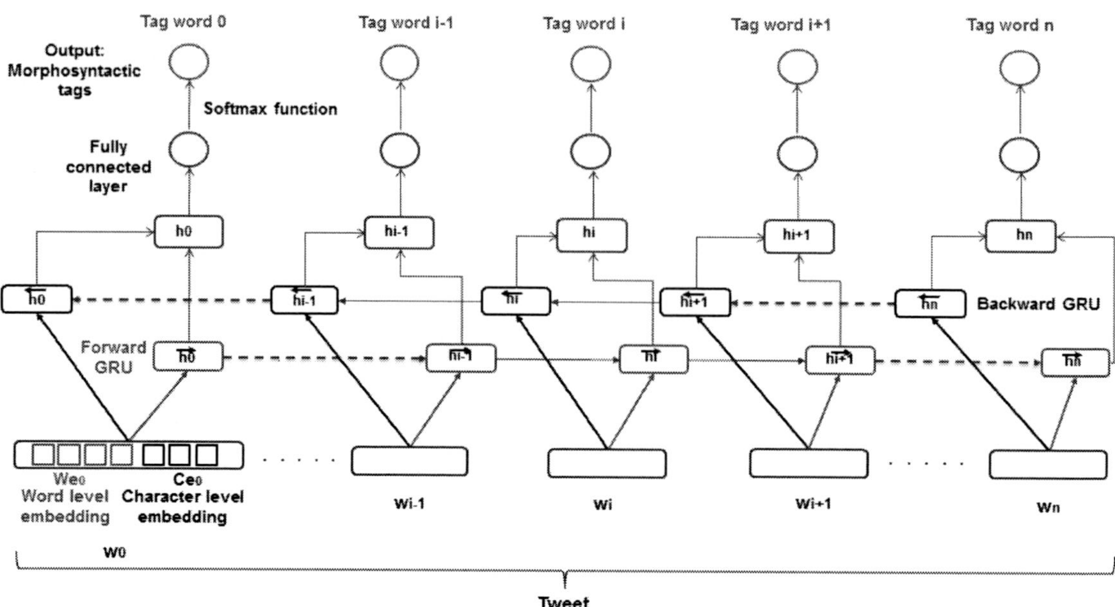

Figure 3: Overall system architecture. First, the system embeds each word of the current sentence into two representations: a character-level representation using bi-GRUs and a word-level representation. Then, the two representations are combined and fed into a bi-GRUs layer, the resulting vector is fed to a fully connected layer and finally a softmax layer to perform MS tagging.

target domain is the Twitter text of the same language. The source and the target problems are trained for the same task (MST), even if source and target data-sets do not share the same tag-set.

As illustrated in Figure 4, we have a parent neural network N_p with a set of parameters θ_p split into two sets: $\theta_p = (\theta_p^1, \theta_p^2)$, and a child network N_c with a set of parameters θ_c split into two sets: $\theta_c = (\theta_c^1, \theta_c^2)$.

(1) We learn the parent network on annotated data from the source problem on a source dataset D_s.

(2) We transfer weights of the first set of parameters of the parent network N_p to the child network N_c: $\theta_c^1 = \theta_p^1$.

(3) Then, the child network is fine-tuned to the target problem by training it on the target data-set D_c.

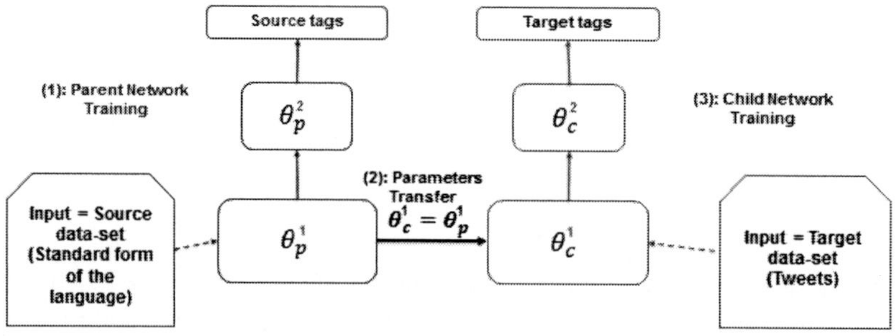

Figure 4: Cross-domain transfer learning scheme for morpho-syntactic tagging.

Language	Domain	Corpus	Tag-set size	# Sentences	# Tokens
Slovene	Out of domain	All	1,304	27,829	586,248
	In domain	Train	758	3,934	37,756
		Dev	422	713	7,056
		Test	598	2023	19,296
Croatian	Out of domain	All	772	24,611	506,460
	In domain	Train	580	4,089	45,609
		Dev	363	791	8,886
		Test	487	1,883	21412
Serbian	Out of domain	All	557	3891	86765
	In domain	Train	575	3463	45,708
		Dev	385	737	9581
		Test	498	1,684	23327

Table 1: Statistics of the different source and target data-sets.

4 Experiments Setup

4.1 Task and Data Description

Two types of data-sets were provided in the MTT shared task (Zampieri et al., 2018) for each language: (1) a small manually annotated Twitter data-set (in-domain data) (Erjavec et al., 2017; Ljubešić et al., 2017a; Ljubešić et al., 2017b); (2) a large manually annotated raw canonical data-set (out-of-domain data) (Erjavec et al., 2015; Ljubešić and Klubička, 2014)[1].

The statistics of the data-sets are described in table 1. All corpora are in the CoNLL format. They are already tokenized. Each token in a tweet is associated with a single morpho-syntactic tag using different alphabetical characters for denoting different category values. The first letter represents POS tag, while other tag positions represent morpho-syntactic categories like case, genre, etc. For instance, the MS tag *Ncfsn* of the word *novost* in the example, provided in figure 1, would denote a noun, common, feminine, singular, nominative token.

4.2 Transfer Learning Experiments

Cross-domain TL is evaluated on the three languages: Slovene, Serbian and Croatian, following three main phases: (1) training the parent network on the source problem on rich out-of-domain data, (2) transferring weights of the first set of parameters to the target problem (these weights are used to initialize the child model's first set of parameters, rather than starting from a random position[2]), and finally (3) fine-tuning the child network on low-resource in-domain data.

Our experiments have shown that using a smaller learning rate for weights that will be fine-tuned (first set of weights), in comparison to the randomly initialized weights (second set of weights) leads to slightly improvements.

4.3 Implementation Details

All experiments described in this section are implemented using the PyTorch deep learning library. We use the Stochastic Gradient Descent (SGD) optimizer with momentum of Nesterov (Sutskever et al., 2013) in all experiments. We set the character embedding dimension at 50, the dimension of hidden states of the character level embeddings GRUs layer at 80, 100 for sequence labelling GRUs layer and FCL dimension at 80. We use dropout training with probability 0.3 before the input to GRUs and FCL layers in order to avoid overfitting.

Tokens are lowercased while the character-level component still retains access to the capitalization information. Word embeddings were set to size 300, pre-loaded from publicly available FastText pre-trained vectors on common crawl[3]. Word level embeddings are fine-tuned during training. The training was performed in batches of 64 sentences for parent models training and 32 sentences for child networks

---

[1] A large automatically annotated web data was also provided by the shared task organizers, but we did not make use of it in this work.

[2] The weights of the second set of parameters of the child model are randomly initialized.

[3] https://github.com/facebookresearch/fastText/blob/master/docs/crawl-vectors.md

training, and was stopped if development set accuracy did not improve for 4 epochs. The best overall model on the development set was then used to report performance on the test data.

5 Results

In this section, we report the results of our system described in section 3. Firstly, we report the results of our system submitted to the MTT shared task. Thereafter, we present some improvements done on our model after the submission of the results for this task.

Language	Slovene	Croatian	Serbian
Acc. without transfer learning (%)	79.8	80.3	81.2
Acc. with transfer learning - A (%)	82.6	82.9	82.1
Acc. with transfer learning - B (%)	**83.36**	**83.87**	**82.54**

Table 2: Our system accuracy (acc.) with and without cross-domain transfer learning (A represents the results of the system submitted to the shared task, and B an improved performance after the submission).

In Table 2, we compare the performances of the neural network model described in section 3 trained only on target data-set (first line) against the neural network trained with TL (second line). We can see that the TL method significantly improves results on all languages. Table 2 further shows that the improvements made by cross-domain TL for Slovene and Croatian (+2.8% , +2.7%) are more important than improvements made by cross-domain TL for Serbian (+0.9%). This phenomenon can be explained by the fact that as illustrated in Table 1, the source data-set for Serbian experiments is very small compared to source data-sets for Slovene and Croatian, hence the improvement is less substantial.

In the above experiments submitted to the MTT shared task, we transfer the parameters of the parent network when they achieve the highest performance on development set of the out-of-domain data-set. However, as shown in previous studies on TL (Mou et al., 2016), the parameters perfectly trained on a source data-set may be too specific to it, hence, the model may underfit on the target data-set. We therefore made more experiments to pick the parent model trained on the ideal epoch for the target data-sets for further fine-tuning. In the third line in table 2, we give the highest performance of TL on target data-sets.

6 Discussion

6.1 Ablation Study

In order to assess the importance of embeddings to handle the problem of Out Of Vocabulary words (OOVs), we have conducted a series of experiments through ablating one layer each time, character-level embedding and word-level embedding and observing how that affects the performance.

For these experiments, we use the neural model described in section 2 without TL technique (i.e., only in-domain data).

In table 3, we report the results of our experiments on Slovene data-set. In each column, we provide the results on a different set of tokens. In the first, we used all tokens of the test set, in the second, only In Training Vocabulary words (ITVs), i.e words that have been seen in the training set, in the third, Out Of Training vocabulary words (OOTVs), in the fourth, In Embedding Vocabulary words (IEVs), i.e words that have been found in the FastText pre-trained words vectors, and in the fifth, Out Of Embedding Vocabulary words (OOEVs).

We provide for each set of tokens, the number of tokens in the first line, the vocabulary size in the second, the simple neural model's accuracy in the third, the accuracy of the neural network without character-level embedding in the fourth and the accuracy of the neural network without pretrained word-level embedding (i.e, words embeddings are randomly initialized) in the fifth.

We notice in table 3 a significant gap between the overall accuracy on ITVs (89.78%) and the accuracy on OOTVs (45.92%). We can also see that removing character-level embedding drops significantly the overall accuracy (-7%). However, the accuracy on OOTVs drops by 27% (33.40% error reduction) while the one for ITVs drops only by 1.5% (13.7% error reduction), which confirms the effectiveness of character-level embedding on OOTVs.

	All tokens	ITVs	OOTVs	IEVs	OOEVs
# tokens	19,296	14,828	4.468	17,045	2,251
Vocabulary size	6,538	2,400	4,138	4,850	1,688
Neural model (NM) acc. (%)	79.8	89.78	45.92	80.86	70.27
NM without character embedding acc. (%)	72.16	88.23	18.80	74.23	56.46
NM without pre-trained words embedding acc. (%)	76.42	88.67	36.05	77.88	65.97

Table 3: Ablation study on character-level embedding and pre-trained words embedding for Slovene tweets MS tagging.

6.2 Impact of Transfer Learning

In the experiments below, we are interested on the impact of using TL on Slovene data-set. In table 4, we compare the performance of our model on the full MSD features and the performance on only POS tags. The first two columns give token-level and the sentence-level accuracy without using TL, and the second two columns give token-level and the sentence-level accuracy using TL. The first line shows the accuracies on all MSD features (the overall accuracy), the second one gives the accuracies on only POS tags.

Table 4 shows that POS accuracy is quite high compared to the full accuracy, this is due to the small POS tag-set (13 POS tags). In addition to that, POS ambiguity of Slovene words is relatively low conversely to the other MSD features. We can observe an improvement of 4.56% brought by TL on the token-level full accuracy, and 2.16% on POS tags. This means that 50% of the error reduction made by TL was on POS tags.

	Without transfer learning		With transfer learning	
	Token acc. (%)	Sentence acc. (%)	Token acc. (%)	Sentence acc. (%)
All MSD features	79.8	27.92	83.36	33.61
Only POS Tags	89.55	45.72	91.71	53.97

Table 4: Comparison between our model accuracy on Slovene on the full MSD features and on POS tags.

Table 5 gives the results for the Slovene data-set first tagged without TL and then using TL. The first two columns give the numbers and the percentage of tokens that have their POS tags changed by the model using TL compared to the model without TL, and the second two columns give the numbers and the percentage of tokens with changed morpho-syntactic tags (including POS tags). The first line shows the tags that were wrong, but the TL changed to the correct ones, the second gives the numbers of those tokens which the standard neural network tagged correctly, but the TL technique falsified. The third line shows those instances where the tag was not changed by the TL technique. The last line shows the number of tokens that have tag assigned that was subsequently changed by the TL technique into a wrong tag.

	POS tags		Morphosyntactic descriptions	
	# Token	Percentage (%)	# Token	Percentage (%)
Corrected	949	4.91	1,402	7.26
Falsified	532	2.75	682	3.53
Identical	17,459	9047	15,789	81.82
Confused	356	1.84	1,423	7.37

Table 5: Modifications made by transfer learning on Slovene data-set.

We can observe that 7.26% of MSD tags were corrected by the TL technique and 3.53% were falsified. In table 6, we investigate which POS tags have benefited the most from the cross-domain TL technique. The first column presents the number of tokens of each POS tag on the test-set, the second (the third) set of columns gives the accuracy, number of true positives (TP), number of false negatives (FN) and false positives without using TL (with TL). We can observe a significant accuracy improvement on adjectives (+10%), nouns (+6%) and adverbs (+2%), with a drop of accuracy on abbreviations and interjections (-8%).

POS tags	# tokens	Without transfer learning				With transfer learning			
		Accuracy (%)	# TP	# FN	# FP	Accuracy (%)	# TP	# FN	# FP
X (Residual)	1782	88.10	1570	212	150	90.62+	1615	167	217
Q (Particle)	1011	89.02	900	111	78	89.61+	906	105	88
R (Adverb)	1548	85.01	1316	232	265	87.33+	1352	196	211
Z (Punctuation)	2872	99.68	2863	9	6	99.75+	2865	7	5
N (Noun)	2808	79.98	2246	562	551	86.36+	2425	383	379
V (Verb)	3427	92.64	3175	252	357	94.28+	3231	196	245
P (Pronoun)	1652	88.68	1465	187	149	90.25+	1491	161	129
C (Conjunction)	1571	96.37	1514	57	59	96.05-	1509	62	49
A (Adjective)	852	69.71	594	258	281	79.34+	676	176	151
S (Adposition)	1096	96.98	1063	33	33	97.71+	1071	25	25
Y (Abbreviation)	107	87.85	94	13	23	86.91-	93	14	30
M (Numeral)	334	89.82	300	34	22	90.41+	302	32	34
I (Interjection)	236	76.69	181	55	41	68.64-	162	74	35

Table 6: The impact of transfer learning on POS tags prediction on Slovene data-set.

6.3 Improvements when Using Conditional Random Fields

In this section, we report new improvements of the performance of our model after the submission to the MTT shared task. Instead of using a softmax function in the topmost of the model for inference (MS tagging), as described in the section 2, we use Conditional Random Fields (CRFs) (Lafferty et al., 2001) layer to decode the best tag sequence from all possible tag sequences with consideration of outputs from bi-GRUs layer and correlations between surroundings labels.

Indeed, it has been shown that CRFs are more appropriate for sequence labelling tasks and can produce higher performances (Huang et al., 2015; Ma and Hovy, 2016). Table 7 shows a significant improvement on the performances of our system for all languages, by replacing the softmax function by a CRFs layer (Ma and Hovy, 2016).

	Slovene	Croatian	Serbian
Model + softmax acc. (%)	83.36	83.87	82.54
Model + CRFs acc. (%)	**86.23**	**87.47**	**86.4**

Table 7: Comparison between the model's performances using Softmax and CRFs layers.

7 Conclusion

In this paper, we have presented a neural network model using Transfer Learning (TL) for Morphosyntactic (MS) tagging of Twitter texts. In particular, we have conducted experiments on tweets for three South-Slavic languages: Slovene, Croatian and Serbian. We have more specifically used an approach which combines both character and word level representations. The obtained results show that TL improves the performance of the MS tagging task for the three involved languages.

This work leaves two important open issues, which certainly deserve further research. First, we intend to apply our model to other morphologically rich languages like MSA and its dialects. The second perspective consists in modelling the lexical and syntactic similarities between the source and target languages (domains) in order to incorporate this external linguistic knowledge in the neural network model.

8 Acknowledgments

This research work is supported by the ASGARD project. This project has received funding from the European Unions Horizon 2020 research and innovation programme under grant agreement No 700381.

References

Željko Agić, Nikola Ljubešić, and Danijela Merkler. 2013. Lemmatization and morphosyntactic tagging of croatian and serbian. In *Proceedings of the 4th Biennial International Workshop on Balto-Slavic Natural Language Processing*, pages 48–57.

Piotr Bojanowski, Edouard Grave, Armand Joulin, and Tomas Mikolov. 2016. Enriching word vectors with subword information. *arXiv preprint arXiv:1607.04606*.

Tomaž Erjavec, Nikola Ljubešić, and Nataša Logar. 2015. The slWaC Corpus of the Slovene Web. *Informatica*, 39(1):35–42.

Tomaž Erjavec, Darja Fišer, Jaka Čibej, Špela Arhar Holdt, Nikola Ljubešić, and Katja Zupan. 2017. CMC training corpus janes-tag 2.0. Slovenian language resource repository CLARIN.SI.

Zhiheng Huang, Wei Xu, and Kai Yu. 2015. Bidirectional lstm-crf models for sequence tagging. *arXiv preprint arXiv:1508.01991*.

John Lafferty, Andrew McCallum, and Fernando CN Pereira. 2001. Conditional random fields: Probabilistic models for segmenting and labeling sequence data.

Nikola Ljubešić and Filip Klubička. 2014. {bs,hr,sr}wac - web corpora of bosnian, croatian and serbian. In *Proceedings of the 9th Web as Corpus Workshop (WaC-9)*, pages 29–35. Association for Computational Linguistics.

Nikola Ljubešić, Tomaž Erjavec, Maja Miličević, and Tanja Samardžić. 2017a. Croatian twitter training corpus ReLDI-NormTagNER-hr 2.0. Slovenian language resource repository CLARIN.SI.

Nikola Ljubešić, Tomaž Erjavec, Maja Miličević, and Tanja Samardžić. 2017b. Serbian twitter training corpus ReLDI-NormTagNER-sr 2.0. Slovenian language resource repository CLARIN.SI.

Xuezhe Ma and Eduard Hovy. 2016. End-to-end sequence labeling via bi-directional lstm-cnns-crf. *arXiv preprint arXiv:1603.01354*.

Sara Meftah, Nasredine Semmar, and F Sadat. 2018. A neural network model for part-of-speech tagging of social media texts. In *Proceedings of the Eleventh International Conference on Language Resources and Evaluation, LREC 2018, Miyazaki, Japan, May 7-12, 2018*.

Lili Mou, Zhao Meng, Rui Yan, Ge Li, Yan Xu, Lu Zhang, and Zhi Jin. 2016. How transferable are neural networks in nlp applications? *arXiv preprint arXiv:1603.06111*.

Sinno Jialin Pan and Qiang Yang. 2010. A survey on transfer learning. *IEEE Transactions on knowledge and data engineering*, 22(10):1345–1359.

Ilya Sutskever, James Martens, George Dahl, and Geoffrey Hinton. 2013. On the importance of initialization and momentum in deep learning. In *International conference on machine learning*, pages 1139–1147.

Marcos Zampieri, Shervin Malmasi, Preslav Nakov, Ahmed Ali, Suwon Shon, James Glass, Yves Scherrer, Tanja Samardžić, Nikola Ljubešić, Jörg Tiedemann, Chris van der Lee, Stefan Grondelaers, Nelleke Oostdijk, Antal van den Bosch, Ritesh Kumar, Bornini Lahiri, and Mayank Jain. 2018. Language Identification and Morphosyntactic Tagging: The Second VarDial Evaluation Campaign. In *Proceedings of the Fifth Workshop on NLP for Similar Languages, Varieties and Dialects (VarDial)*, Santa Fe, USA.

When Simple n-gram Models Outperform Syntactic Approaches: Discriminating between Dutch and Flemish

Martin Kroon
Leiden University Centre for Linguistics
Leiden University
The Netherlands
m.s.kroon@hum.leidenuniv.nl

Masha Medvedeva
Center for Language and Cognition
University of Groningen
The Netherlands
m.medvedeva@rug.nl

Barbara Plank
Department of Computer Science
IT University of Copenhagen
Denmark
bplank@itu.dk

Abstract

In this paper we present the results of our participation in the *Discriminating between Dutch and Flemish in Subtitles* VarDial 2018 shared task. We try techniques proven to work well for discriminating between language varieties as well as explore the potential of using syntactic features, i.e. hierarchical syntactic subtrees. We experiment with different combinations of features. Discriminating between these two languages turned out to be a very hard task, not only for a machine: human performance is only around 0.51 F_1 score; our best system is still a simple Naive Bayes model with word unigrams and bigrams. The system achieved an F_1 score (macro) of 0.62, which ranked us 4th in the shared task.

1 Introduction

The Dutch language is regulated by the Dutch Language Union. The varieties of Dutch spoken in the Netherlands and spoken in Belgium are both subject to this regulation. Despite this, there are still differences to be found between Netherlandic Dutch and Flemish Dutch, most clearly in phonology and pronunciation, but also in terms of word use and word order. Nevertheless, there is little to no work on automatic classification to distinguish between the two varieties. A first attempt was made by van der Lee and van den Bosch (2017), in light of whose work this year's iteration of the annual Workshop on NLP for Similar Languages, Varieties and Dialects (VarDial) took on *Discriminating between Dutch and Flemish in Subtitles* (DFS) as one of their evaluation campaigns (Zampieri et al., 2018).[1]

For the DFS 2018 shared task, our team (mmb_lct), built a model that discriminates between the two varieties. The model achieved the fourth place out of seven in the ranking of the results – statistical significance of the differences between the F_1 scores of the submissions was taken into account, such that the third place was shared by four teams and we shared our fourth place with STEVENDU2018 (even though their model performed slightly better).

As mentioned, the difference between Dutch and Flemish is most noticeable in spoken language. As we are not dealing with spoken language in this shared task, we are left only with lexical differences and syntactic differences, making the task significantly harder. A problem is that most variety-characterizing words are not all that common. An example would be Dutch *slager* vs. Flemish *beenhouwer* 'butcher' or Dutch *punaise* vs. Flemish *duimnagel* 'thumbtack'. More frequent lexical differences can have another

---

This work is licensed under a Creative Commons Attribution 4.0 International Licence. Licence details: http://creativecommons.org/licenses/by/4.0/.

[1] As the shared task is called *Discriminating between Dutch and Flemish in Subtitles*, we shall refer to Netherlandic Dutch and Flemish Dutch as Dutch and Flemish, respectively. It should be noted that, in this task, Dutch and Flemish are both the standard varieties, as regulated by the Dutch Language Union, and not dialects.

Proceedings of the Fifth Workshop on NLP for Similar Languages, Varieties and Dialects, pages 244–253
Santa Fe, New Mexico, USA, August 20, 2018.

problem, where the words occur in both varieties, but are used differently: Dutch *mooi* vs. Flemish *schoon* 'beautiful' are more frequent, but *schoon* also occurs in Dutch, meaning 'clean'.

Syntactic differences are found mostly in verbal clusters, where the two varieties show different word orders – or at least, a preference for certain word orders. For example, in Flemish the word order in sentence-final verbal clusters is modal–main verb–perfective auxiliary (*moet gemaakt hebben* lit. 'must made have'), while in Dutch the orders modal–perfective auxiliary–main verb and main verb–modal–perfective auxiliary are both widespread (*moet hebben gemaakt* 'must have made' and *gemaakt moet hebben* lit. 'made must have', respectively). Flemish also, for example, allows for the interruption of these types of verbal clusters by adpositions, adverbs or even nominal objects, whereas Dutch is much less likely to exhibit this syntactic behaviour (Barbiers et al., 2005; Barbiers et al., 2008).

In order to quantify these syntactic differences, we used syntactic subtrees of dependency parses to distinguish between the two varieties, which is, to the best of our knowledge, a novel approach in language identification (Jauhiainen et al., 2018). As opposed to n-grams, dependency subtrees allow us to detect non-contiguous patterns of words as well as to determine syntactic relations between the words. This is useful as this also, for example, allows us to quantify whether one of the two varieties is more inclined to topicalize the object of a verb.

We decided to approach the DFS 2018 shared task by mainly focusing on the use of linear classification algorithms, as they steadily seem to outperform neural approaches in the task of language identification (Zampieri et al., 2017; Malmasi et al., 2016; Zampieri et al., 2015; Zampieri et al., 2014). In the next Section we discuss relevant previous research in the discrimination between similar languages. In Section 3 we describe the data released for the DFS shared task, the features we used as well as our system submissions. Section 4 follows with the results, which are discussed in Section 5.

2   Related Work

Although this year is already VarDial's fifth anniversary (Zampieri et al., 2018; Zampieri et al., 2017; Malmasi et al., 2016; Zampieri et al., 2015; Zampieri et al., 2014), it is the first time that the DFS shared task was organized. Previous iterations of VarDial saw shared tasks concerning Arabic dialect identification, German dialect identification, cross-lingual dependency parsing, and discrimination between similar languages (DSL).

Last year our team participated in the DSL shared task (Medvedeva et al., 2017), where it ranked second with an F_1 score of 0.925. Bestgen (2017) won by 0.002 points. Both systems used a two-layer classification, comparable to Goutte et al. (2014): the first layer identified the language group, the second layer trained multiple classifiers to identify language varieties within the groups.

However, while we only used word and character n-grams in both classification layers, the winning team, Bestgen (2017), also used POS-tags n-grams (the POS tags were obtained using language-group specific POS taggers) and some global statistics, such as proportion of capital letters and punctuation marks, as features in the second layer. This is in line with van der Lee and van den Bosch (2017), who, next to word n-grams, use global statistics and POS-tag n-grams in the classification of Dutch vs. Flemish subtitles, achieving an F_1 score of 0.92. For this task we depart from our earlier system but explore alternatives, in particular one based on using syntactic information.

Even though POS-tagging is a challenging method to use for language identification due to its language-dependent nature, it has often been explored for distinguishing between language varieties (Martinc et al., 2017; Adouane and Dobnik, 2017, among others). To add to previous experiments that exploited POS-tag n-grams and thus retaining the linear structure of the text, we explore the possibilities of using hierarchical subtrees to allow for non-contiguous groups of POS tags as well as to exploit the syntactic relations between them.

3   Methodology and Data

In this section we describe the DFS data as it was released to participants, the features we used in our approaches, and our three system submissions.

FLEMISH	DUTCH
Sami, DiMera, Amai, Sooz, interesseerd, Kenshee, Moz, vanop, AUDIO, Megatron, Shishio, enant, ACHTERGRONDMUZIEK, Celeste, ente, komaan, Jumanji, Kiriakis, yardlijn, Breanna	MUZIEK, EEN, Oke, STEM, Text, LACHT, ZE, GEJUICH, LACHEN, AFV, SPANNENDE, Broadcast, Funniest, Brainiac, Piha, surveillanten, BEAU, oke, Biaggi, MUZIEKJE

Table 1: Most frequent words in each language variety.

3.1 Data

The data consisted of professionally produced subtitles for Dutch and Flemish television. The gold label – i.e. whether the fragment was Dutch or Flemish – was based on the country for which the subtitles were created. If the subtitles were shown on a Dutch TV network, it was labelled Dutch; if they were shown on a Flemish TV network, it was labelled Flemish. As for distribution of genres between Dutch and Flemish in this dataset, it is fairly similar (van der Lee and van den Bosch, 2017).

In particular, the training set consisted of 300,000 fragments with an average length of 40.62 tokens, including punctuation. The set was evenly balanced, such that 150,000 fragments were Dutch and 150,000 fragments were Flemish (with an average of 40.69 and 40.56 tokens per fragment, respectively). A fragment may contain multiple sentences, averaging at 5.52 sentences per fragment. The vocabulary for Dutch consisted of 127,546 tokens, for Flemish it consisted of 120,050 tokens. Out of those, 62,758 Dutch tokens only occurred in Dutch, while 55,262 tokens in the Flemish vocabulary only occurred in Flemish fragments. The 20 most frequent words in the training data that only occurred in one language variety are shown in Table 1. The development set was significantly smaller, consisting of only 500 fragments (on average 40.58 tokens and 5.64 sentences per fragment).

The test set, which was withheld, consisted of an evenly balanced set of 20,000 fragments. In terms of average number of tokens and sentences, the test set is very similar to the training an development sets: 40.60 and 5.54, respectively.

It was noted, however, that the training set and the development set contained several encoding errors. For example, the third fragment of the training set contained *financi le*, where an *ë* is missing (intended was *financiële* 'financial'), leading to two non-existing words *financi* and *le*. Although this might not be of much influence when using character n-grams, it will be of influence when using word n-grams, when POS-tagging or when parsing syntactically. Our team made no attempt, though, to mitigate these encoding errors by, for example, using a spell checker to fill in the missing characters.

The first author of this work, as a native speaker of (Netherlandic) Dutch, also noted how hard it was in this particular data set to manually classify the subtitles. Very few specifically Dutch and Flemish words were used (although there were plenty of words that were only used in Dutch or only in Flemish, most of these words are not necessarily characterizing for Dutch or Flemish – this is illustrated in Table 1, where only *komaan* 'come on' is typically Flemish; most Dutch-only words are commentary for the hearing-impaired (written in capitals), such as *MUZIEK* 'music'), nor were there many specifically Dutch or Flemish syntactic constructions that the first author recognized. As a test on 25 randomly selected fragments from the training data, the first author performed on chance level with an F_1 score of only 0.51. This difficult character of the task was also reflected in the results of the DFS shared task: the system of the winning team achieved an F_1 score of 0.66.

3.2 Features

As features we mostly resorted to word and character n-grams, as motivated by our submission to last year's DSL shared task. We also present a novel approach to language classification which relies on subtrees of dependency parses as features. This was motivated by the fact that we can use one Dutch parser model, since standard Dutch and standard Flemish are sufficiently similar. Of course, when one needs to classify between two languages (as opposed to two – very similar – varieties), one cannot easily

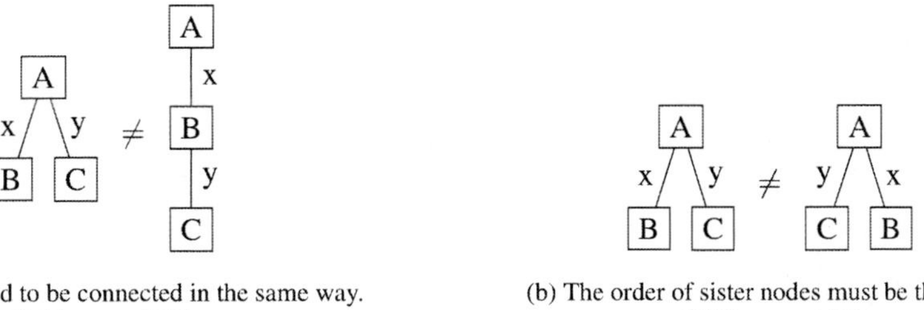

(a) Nodes need to be connected in the same way.   (b) The order of sister nodes must be the same.

(c) Labels of corresponding edges need to be the same.   (d) Corresponding nodes need to have the same label.

Figure 1: Isomorphism constraints of subtrees.

use parsers, since the parser models are language-specific.

In order to use subtree features, we parsed the data using a Universal Dependencies parser implemented in UDPipe (Straka and Straková, 2017), specifically using the CoNLL17 Shared Task Baseline UD 2.0 Model for Dutch.[2] Dependency parses of fragments were represented as a directed acyclic graph in the Python package `networkx` (Hagberg et al., 2008), with every sentence in the fragment being its own connected component in the graph. Graphs were also ordered, meaning that the linear order of sister nodes was retained. The order of words relative to their head was not necessarily retained: verbs with a direct object to their left were not automatically distinct from verbs with a direct object to their right – we experimented with the option of retaining this relative order of words to their heads. From these graphs, subtrees were extracted, counting for every fragment which subtrees occurred in them and how often.

A subtree was defined as any combination of n nodes in the dependency tree that form a connected component. Nodes (that is, words) were represented as POS tags. Therefore, these subtrees can be considered hierarchical POS-tag n-grams containing syntactic relations; whereas normal n-grams are contiguous sequences, these subtrees are not necessarily.

Two subtrees were considered to be isomorphic if they contained the same amount of words, the words were connected in the same way with the same syntactic relation, the corresponding words between the two subtrees had the same POS tags, and the order of sister nodes was the same. This is illustrated in Figure 1.

Bare POS tags in Universal Dependencies (which are 17 coarse-grained categories) can be quite unspecific: there is no distinction between finite verbs and past participles. Therefore we experimented with using morphological features (as tagged by UDPipe) as well, effectively adding another isomorphism constraint that requires all morphological features of corresponding nodes to be the same as well (making that infinitives are not considered the same as third person verbs, for example).

3.3 Systems

We submitted three runs with different classifiers and features. We only focused on linear classifiers, specifically, Support Vector Machines with a linear kernel (LinearSVC) and a Naive Bayes classifier.[3] We chose which systems to submit based on cross-validation and evaluation on the development set.

3.4 Run 1

For the first run we used a linear SVM with word and character n-grams, which has been proven to work for language identification between similar languages before (Medvedeva et al., 2017; Rama and

---

[2]`http://ufal.mff.cuni.cz/udpipe/users-manual`
[3]As implemented in `scikit-learn` (Pedregosa et al., 2011).

Çöltekin, 2017). We use the same features as in our earlier participation in a related VarDial shared task: word uni- and bigrams and character n-grams with 1 to 6 characters. As opposed to last year, we have though not used tf-idf weighting, as it has shown to yield lower results. Regarding preprocessing, we split the data into tokens with a simple multilingual tokenizer[4] that uses whitespaces as the main reference point. Punctuation was not separated from the words, nor have we lowercased the text.

We found it performed with mean 62.1% accuracy using 3-fold cross-validation and 69% accuracy on the development set. Despite being very similar to the system used in Medvedeva et al. (2017), which is seemingly language-independent and performed very well in the task of distinguishing between Bosnian, Croatian and Serbian, these results indicate that distinguishing between Flemish and Dutch is a much harder task. A confusion matrix can be found in Table 2.

	predicted: BEL	predicted: DUT
true: BEL	93291	56709
true: DUT	56948	93052

Table 2: Confusion matrix for 3-fold cross-validation for Run 1 - Linear SVM.

Additionally, we have plotted the top coefficients for both classes in Figure 2. The coefficients show once again that the data hardly contain any characterizing words for the two varieties: only Flemish interjections such as *Allee*, 'come on', *Komaan*, 'come on' and *Wel*, 'well' are very characterizing, as is the bigram *naar hier* 'to here'. Other predictors are not as typical: for example, although Dutch *MasterChef* has 114 instances in the training data for Dutch and 2 for Flemish, that only suggests that a MasterChef TV-show was included in the Dutch part of the dataset.

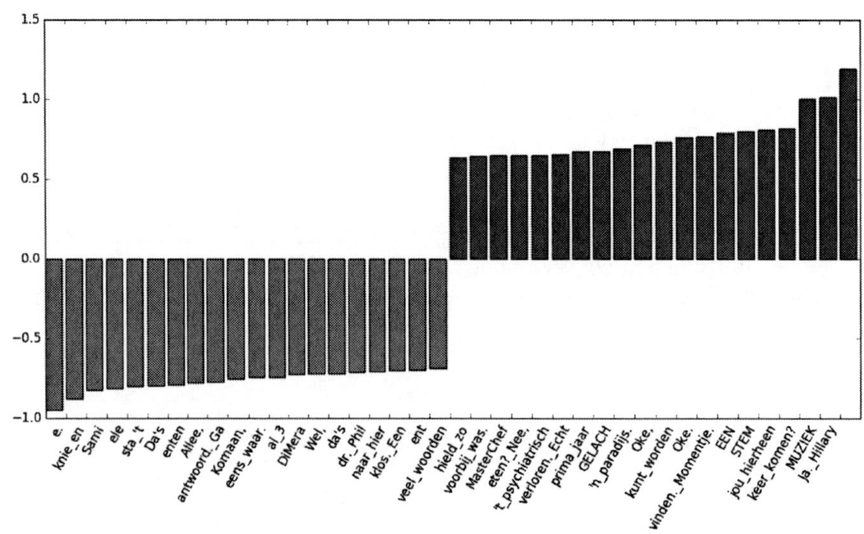

Figure 2: Coefficients (weights) as assigned by the first run's SVM to the two varieties. The top 20 predictors for Flemish are on the left (red) and the top 20 predictors for Dutch are on the right (blue).

---

[4] https://github.com/bplank/multilingualtokenizer

3.5 Run 2

For the second run we also used a linear SVM, with hierarchical POS-tag subtrees, as decribed in Section 3.2. We used ordered subtrees of sizes 1 and 2, retaining the relative position of words to their head, but ignoring morphology. Including larger subtrees showed lower results (i.e. 55% vs. 57% accuracy on the development set). We also experimented with using tf-idf weighting, but this also resulted in a worse performance. Using cross-validation, the system achieved 55% accuracy. A confusion matrix for the run can be found in Table 3.

	predicted: BEL	predicted: DUT
true: BEL	95161	54839
true: DUT	80045	69955

Table 3: Confusion matrix for 3-fold cross-validation for Run 2 - Syntactic Subtrees.

Since these features didn't include any information on the words themselves, but only on the POS tags, our hope was that if we combine the syntactic information with the features from the first run, we will be able to pick up on much more differences between the dialects. However, the results showed the opposite. With a combination run we achieved an accuracy of only 54%, which means that adding syntactic information only hurts performance.

3.6 Run 3

Our third run was a simple Naive Bayes system that used word uni- and bigrams. In this model we lowered case and used a built-in `scikit-learn` tokenizer (Pedregosa et al., 2011).

The model achieved 63% accuracy when evaluated using 3-fold cross-validation. From the confusion matrix for cross-validation results in Table 4 we can see that Dutch is confused more often than Flemish. Moreover, on the development set this classifier performed with a 68% accuracy. This made it a good contender for our first run, which got 69%.

	predicted: BEL	predicted: DUT
true: BEL	101993	48007
true: DUT	62672	87328

Table 4: Confusion matrix for 3-fold cross-validation for Run 3 - Naive Bayes.

4 Results

The results on the official evaluation data are shown in Table 5 and confirm our findings on the development data. Our best system is the simple Naive Bayes classifier, reaching an F_1 score of 0.62. It is closely followed by the our first run (0.61). Our syntactic subtrees reached a much lower F_1 score of 0.49. Our results corroborate earlier findings where a Naive Bayes outperformed alternative approaches (Tiedemann and Ljubešić, 2012). We also investigated their blacklist approach, but in preliminary experiments on the development data it resulted in below-chance performance. The Naive Bayes approach is slightly more robust on this task, as shown by comparing a cross-validation to a single official dev split setup, on which the Naive Bayes dropped less than the more overfitting-prone higher capacity SVM approach.

Overall our approach ranked 4th in the shared task, with most systems ranking around 0.63, and the winning system reaching a top performance of 0.66.

We also saw that Dutch is more often wrongly classified as Flemish than Flemish as Dutch by our best system, suggesting that, based on our features, it is harder to correctly classify Dutch than Flemish.

System	F1 (macro)
Random Baseline	0.5000
NAIVE BAYES	**0.6201**
SVM	0.6105
SYNTACTIC SUBTREES	0.4895

Table 5: Results of our submissions on the official DFS task test data.

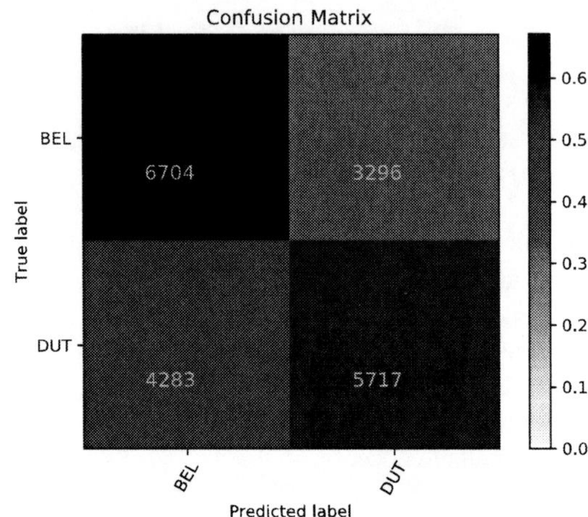

Figure 3: Confusion matrix of our best system (run 3) on the test data provided by the organisers.

This is shown in the confusion matrix in Figure 3. This is contrary to what van der Lee and van den Bosch (2017) found, who found that Flemish was harder to classify. They had though a different setup, in particular an imbalanced data set, which surely had an influence on the results.

5 Discussion

The use of ordered syntactic subtrees (hierarchical POS-tag n-grams containing syntactic relations, if you will) in the automatic identification between Dutch and Flemish, then, does not seem to help – in fact, it influences results negatively: a classifier that uses word and character n-grams alone performs significantly better than one that uses a feature union between n-grams and syntactic subtrees. There are several possible explanations for this.

A first explanation can be the performance of UDPipe in general. The labelled attachment score (LAS)[5] of Dutch parses is about 70% to 80% (Straka and Straková, 2017). Errors in the parses may have led to noisy features. Additionally, the already addressed encoding errors in the data as well as the frequent commentary for the hearing-impaired will have led to more incorrect parses, leading to more noisy features.

Secondly, it may be the case that (standard) Dutch and (standard) Flemish are simply not sufficiently distinct syntactically in terms of simple POS tags. As described above, we did try using morphological features, such that finite verbs can be distinguished from infinitives or participles. However, using morphological features resulted in lower performance. It may be that using morphological features made the POS tags too specific, as it also distinguishes singular nouns from plural nouns, for example. It was not tested in this work if perhaps using certain combinations of morphological features (as opposed to using all or none) do yield better results. This is certainly worth looking into in future research.

---

[5]The LAS measures the percentage of words that are assigned both the correct syntactic head and the correct dependency label, i.e. syntactic relation. Unlabelled attachment scores, where the correct head is assigned though with a wrong label, are usually somewhat higher (about 5%), but because our isomorphism constraints require all edge labels to be identical, we need the LAS.

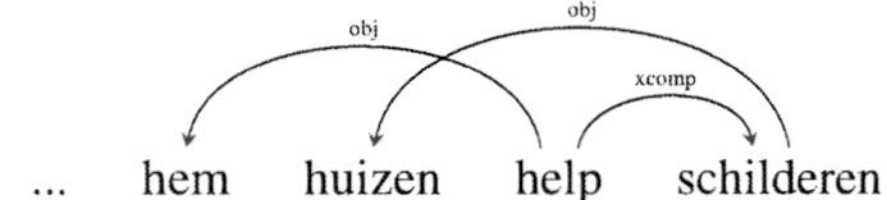

(a) A sentence fragment with a cross-serial dependency relation.

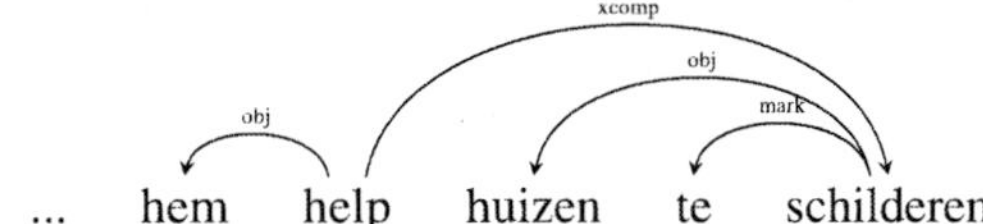

(b) A sentence fragment without a cross-serial dependency relation.

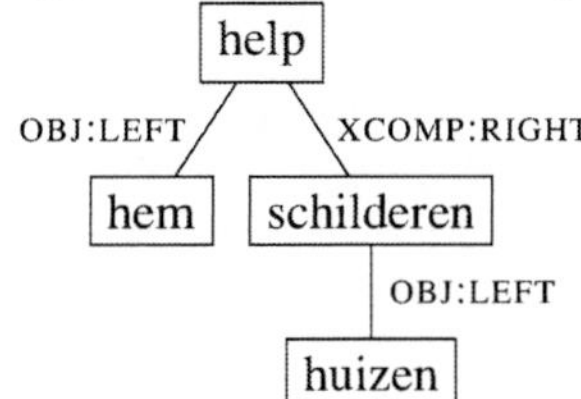

(c) The `networkx` representation of Figures 4a and 4b, ignoring the presence of *te* 'to'.

Figure 4: An illustration of how the presence of cross-serial dependency relations in a fragment is lost when converting to `networkx` subtrees. The relative order of sister nodes is retained, as is the relative order of words to their head using a tag on the syntactic relations. Because the relative order of nodes to the head of their head is not retained, we can no longer distinguish between 4a and 4b. The fragment means '... help him paint the house'.

Lastly, the size of the subtrees that we extracted could also be of influence. Having looked only at subtrees with one, two or three words in them, we ignored larger subtrees that may in fact be more informative in the task of automatic classification of Dutch vs. Flemish. We deem this unlikely, though, given that the frequencies of subtrees plummet as the size increases – comparable to n-grams. At the same time the amount of possible subtrees of size n that can be extracted from a fragment increases faster than the amount of possible n-grams (of size n) due to a multitude of distinct dependency labels, in addition to the fact that the words in a subtree need not be string-adjacent but only need to form a connected component. This decreases the average frequency of subtrees even further as the amount of words in them grows.

On a different note concerning parses, the way syntactic subtrees are represented in `networkx` in this work, does not support for cross-serial dependency relations, which are prevalent in Dutch (Bresnan et al., 1982): although it does retain the relative order of sister nodes and optionally of nodes to their mothers, it never retains the relative order of nodes to their grandmothers (i.e. the head of its head). This results in the impossibility to distinguish between the construction in Figure 4a, which shows a cross-serial dependency relation, and the construction in Figure 4b, which does not. In this work Figure 4a and Figure 4b yield identical subtrees, ignoring the presence of *te* 'to' in Figure 4b; this is illustrated in Figure 4c. If the relative order of *huizen* to *help*, which is its grandmother node, were retained, the subtrees would have been distinct, as *help* is on the left of *huizen* in 4a, whereas in 4b it is on its right. When there is, then, a strong difference in the usage of these two constructions between Dutch and Flemish, this information is lost. It will be interesting for future research to see if adequately representing cross-serial dependency relations in subtrees will influence the performance of a Dutch-Flemish classifier.

The use of feature selection in our subtree approach should certainly be explored in future work. As mentioned before, the amount of noisy subtree features was probably quite high. By reducing these noisy features, the weight assignment to more informative features can thus be boosted, yielding better predictors. Setting a simple minimum-frequency constraint for features, for example, could improve results, in line with Bestgen (2017), who only uses character n-grams that occur at least 100 times.

We also did not explore the use of subtrees with algorithms other than linear SVMs. It would be interesting to see if different results can be achieved with a non-linear SVM, a neural approach or a decision tree. It would also be interesting to experiment with a blacklist approach (Tiedemann and Ljubešić, 2012) applied to subtrees.

Although the dependency-subtree approach as proposed in this work is outperformed by traditional n-gram models, there are still many options to try and improve its performance, such as morphological fine-tuning, using words instead of POS tags, changing the isomorphism constraints, implementing support for cross-serial dependency relations, feature selection and different classification algorithms. We leave these suggestions to future research.

As a final note, we had a few concerns about the data: van der Lee and van den Bosch (2017) mention that the gold labels were based on the country where the program was broadcast, but whether subtitles are broadcast in the Netherlands or in Belgium does not necessarily imply that they were produced by a Dutchman or a Fleming. Moreover, professional subtitlers often try to avoid specifically Dutch or specifically Flemish language (which is also supported by the words that occur only in one variety; see Table 1), making the task particularly hard for subtitles. Nevertheless, it was shown by van der Lee and van den Bosch (2017) as well that the task can be done with a high performance, despite the subtitular nature of their data. In fact, this DFS shared task uses another distribution of their data, however it is unclear what exactly causes such a vast difference between their performance and the performances in this shared task.

6   Conclusion

We presented our participation in the VarDial 2018 shared task on discriminating between Dutch and Flemish in subtitles. We investigated both traditional n-gram based models and a syntactic approach. Our results show that the simplest model with the simplest feature set (Naive Bayes with word n-grams) outperforms more involved approaches, in particular our dependency-tree approach, which only performed around chance level. The task turns out to be rather difficult, as shown by the relatively low results among all participating teams in the DFS shared task and the difficulty in a preliminary manual investigation.

References

Wafia Adouane and Simon Dobnik. 2017. Identification of languages in Algerian Arabic multilingual documents. In *Proceedings of the Third Arabic Natural Language Processing Workshop*, pages 1–8.

Sjef Barbiers, Hans Bennis, Gunther De Vogelaer, Magda Devos, and Margreet van der Ham. 2005. *Syntactische Atlas van de Nederlandse Dialecten Deel I / Syntactic Atlas of the Dutch Dialects Volume I*. Amsterdam University Press.

Sjef Barbiers, Johan van der Auwera, Hans Bennis, Eefje Boef, Gunther De Vogelaer, and Margreet van der Ham. 2008. *Syntactische Atlas van de Nederlandse Dialecten Deel II / Syntactic Atlas of the Dutch Dialects Volume II*. Amsterdam University Press.

Yves Bestgen. 2017. Improving the character ngram model for the DSL task with BM25 weighting and less frequently used feature sets. In *Proceedings of the Fourth Workshop on NLP for Similar Languages, Varieties and Dialects (VarDial)*, pages 115–123, Valencia, Spain, April.

Joan Bresnan, Ronald M. Kaplan, Stanley Peters, and Annie Zaenen. 1982. Cross-serial dependencies in Dutch. In *The formal complexity of natural language*, pages 286–319. Springer.

Cyril Goutte, Serge Léger, and Marine Carpuat. 2014. The NRC system for discriminating similar languages. In *Proceedings of the First Workshop on Applying NLP Tools to Similar Languages, Varieties and Dialects (VarDial)*, pages 139–145, Dublin, Ireland.

Aric A. Hagberg, Daniel A. Schult, and Pieter J. Swart. 2008. Exploring network structure, dynamics, and function using NetworkX. In Gäel Varoquaux, Travis Vaught, and Jarrod Millman, editors, *Proceedings of the 7th Python in Science Conference (SciPy2008)*, pages 11–15, Pasadena, CA USA, August.

Tommi Jauhiainen, Marco Lui, Marcos Zampieri, Timothy Baldwin, and Krister Lindén. 2018. Automatic language identification in texts: A survey. *arXiv preprint arXiv:1804.08186*.

Shervin Malmasi, Marcos Zampieri, Nikola Ljubešić, Preslav Nakov, Ahmed Ali, and Jörg Tiedemann. 2016. Discriminating between similar languages and Arabic dialect identification: A report on the third DSL shared task. In *Proceedings of the 3rd Workshop on Language Technology for Closely Related Languages, Varieties and Dialects (VarDial)*, Osaka, Japan.

Matej Martinc, Iza Škrjanec, Katja Zupan, and Senja Pollak. 2017. PAN 2017: Author profiling – gender and language variety prediction. In *Working Notes of CLEF*, CEUR Workshop Proceedings. CEUR-WS.org.

Maria Medvedeva, Martin Kroon, and Barbara Plank. 2017. When sparse traditional models outperform dense neural networks: the curious case of discriminating between similar languages. In *Proceedings of the Fourth Workshop on NLP for Similar Languages, Varieties and Dialects (VarDial)*, pages 156–163, Valencia, Spain, April.

Fabian Pedregosa, Gaël Varoquaux, Alexandre Gramfort, Vincent Michel, Bertrand Thirion, Olivier Grisel, Mathieu Blondel, Peter Prettenhofer, Ron Weiss, Vincent Dubourg, et al. 2011. Scikit-learn: Machine learning in Python. *Journal of machine learning research*, 12(Oct):2825–2830.

Taraka Rama and Çağrı Çöltekin. 2017. Fewer features perform well at native language identification task. In *Proceedings of the 12th Workshop on Innovative Use of NLP for Building Educational Applications*, pages 255–260, Copenhagen, Denmark.

Milan Straka and Jana Straková. 2017. Tokenizing, POS tagging, lemmatizing and parsing UD 2.0 with UDPipe. In *Proceedings of the CoNLL 2017 Shared Task: Multilingual Parsing from Raw Text to Universal Dependencies*, pages 88–99, Vancouver, Canada, August. Association for Computational Linguistics.

Jörg Tiedemann and Nikola Ljubešić. 2012. Efficient discrimination between closely related languages. *Proceedings of COLING 2012*, pages 2619–2634.

Chris van der Lee and Antal van den Bosch. 2017. Exploring Lexical and Syntactic Features for Language Variety Identification. In *Proceedings of the Fourth Workshop on NLP for Similar Languages, Varieties and Dialects (VarDial)*, pages 190–199, Valencia, Spain.

Marcos Zampieri, Liling Tan, Nikola Ljubešić, and Jörg Tiedemann. 2014. A report on the DSL shared task 2014. In *Proceedings of the First Workshop on Applying NLP Tools to Similar Languages, Varieties and Dialects (VarDial)*, pages 58–67, Dublin, Ireland.

Marcos Zampieri, Liling Tan, Nikola Ljubešić, Jörg Tiedemann, and Preslav Nakov. 2015. Overview of the DSL shared task 2015. In *Proceedings of the Joint Workshop on Language Technology for Closely Related Languages, Varieties and Dialects (LT4VarDial)*, pages 1–9, Hissar, Bulgaria.

Marcos Zampieri, Shervin Malmasi, Nikola Ljubešić, Preslav Nakov, Ahmed Ali, Jörg Tiedemann, Yves Scherrer, and Noëmi Aepli. 2017. Findings of the VarDial Evaluation Campaign 2017. In *Proceedings of the Fourth Workshop on NLP for Similar Languages, Varieties and Dialects (VarDial)*, Valencia, Spain.

Marcos Zampieri, Shervin Malmasi, Preslav Nakov, Ahmed Ali, Suwon Shon, James Glass, Yves Scherrer, Tanja Samardžić, Nikola Ljubešić, Jörg Tiedemann, Chris van der Lee, Stefan Grondelaers, Nelleke Oostdijk, Antal van den Bosch, Ritesh Kumar, Bornini Lahiri, and Mayank Jain. 2018. Language Identification and Morphosyntactic Tagging: The Second VarDial Evaluation Campaign. In *Proceedings of the Fifth Workshop on NLP for Similar Languages, Varieties and Dialects (VarDial)*, Santa Fe, USA.

HeLI-based Experiments in Swiss German Dialect Identification

Tommi Jauhiainen
University of Helsinki
@helsinki.fi

Heidi Jauhiainen
University of Helsinki
@helsinki.fi

Krister Lindén
University of Helsinki
@helsinki.fi

Abstract

In this paper we present the experiments and results by the SUKI team in the German Dialect Identification shared task of the VarDial 2018 Evaluation Campaign. Our submission using HeLI with adaptive language models obtained the best results in the shared task with a macro F1-score of 0.686, which is clearly higher than the other submitted results. Without some form of unsupervised adaptation on the test set, it might not be possible to reach as high an F1-score with the level of domain difference between the datasets of the shared task. We describe the methods used in detail, as well as some additional experiments carried out during the shared task.

1 Introduction

The fifth VarDial workshop (Zampieri et al., 2018) included for the second time a shared task for German Dialect Identification (GDI). The varieties of German were from the areas of Basel, Bern, Lucerne, and Zurich. These varieties are considered dialects of Swiss German (gsw) by the ISO-639-3 standard (Lewis et al., 2013). For the first time the GDI shared task included a separate track for unknown language detection.

We have used the HeLI method and its variations in the shared tasks of the three previous VarDial workshops (Jauhiainen et al., 2015a; Jauhiainen et al., 2016; Jauhiainen et al., 2017a). The HeLI method is robust and competes with the other state-of-the-art language identification methods. For the current workshop we wanted to try out some variations and possible improvements to the original method. We submitted two different runs on the four-way classification track and in the end we did not submit any runs on the unknown language detection track.

2 Related Work

The differences between definitions of dialects and languages are not usually clearly defined, at least not in terms which would be able to help us automatically decide whether we are dealing with languages or dialects. Also the methods used for dialect identification are most of the time exactly the same as for general language identification. Language identification of close languages and dialects is one of the remaining challenges of language identification research. For a recent survey on language identification and the methods used in the field, the reader is referred to an article by Jauhiainen et al. (2018).

2.1 German dialect identification

The German dialect identification has earlier been considered by Scherrer and Rambow (2010), who used a lexicon of dialectal words. Hollenstein and Aepli (2015) experimented with a perplexity based language identifier using character trigrams. They reached an average F-score of 0.66 on sentence level between 5 German dialects.

The results of the first shared task on German dialect identification are described by Zampieri et al. (2017). Ten teams submitted results on the task utilizing a variety of machine learning methods used

This work is licensed under a Creative Commons Attribution 4.0 International Licence. Licence details: http://creativecommons.org/licenses/by/4.0/.

Proceedings of the Fifth Workshop on NLP for Similar Languages, Varieties and Dialects, pages 254–262
Santa Fe, New Mexico, USA, August 20, 2018.

for language identification. We report the results in Table 1. The methods used are listed in the first column, used features in the second column, best reached weighted F1-score in the third column, and the describing article in the fourth column.

Method	Features used	Weighted F1	Reference
Ensemble of 9 individual SVMs	char. n-grams 1-8 and words	0.662	(Malmasi and Zampieri, 2017)
BM25 weighted SVM	char. n-grams 1-5	0.661	(Bestgen, 2017)
Conditional Random Fields	char. n-grams, prefixes, suffixes...	0.653	(Clematide and Makarov, 2017)
SVM + SGD ensemble	n-grams 1-8	0.639	
Kernel Ridge Regression	n-grams 3-6	0.637	(Ionescu and Butnaru, 2017)
Linear SVM	char. n-grams and words	0.626	(Çöltekin and Rama, 2017)
Cross Entropy	char. n-grams up to 25 bytes	0.614	(Hanani et al., 2017)
Perplexity	words	0.612	(Gamallo et al., 2017)
Naive Bayes with TF-IDF		0.605	(Barbaresi, 2017)
LSTM NN	characters or words	0.263	

Table 1: The weighted F1-scores using different methods on the 2017 GDI test set.

2.2 Unknown language detection

Unknown languages are languages with which the language identifier has not been trained. Especially in a real-world situation it is always possible to encounter unknown languages. If the language identification method used produces a comparable score for different texts, it is possible to try thresholding. In thresholding, we find a score under (or over) which our prediction of the language is so poor, that we label it as unknown. Suzuki et al. (2002) describes a language identification method which was originally designed for identifying the language of web pages crawled from the internet. They had a predetermined threshold for each language known by the identifier and if the threshold was not reached the web page was categorized as junk. In the Finno-Ugric Languages and the Internet project (Jauhiainen et al., 2017b), we have also experimented with unknown language (or just junk) detection in order to cope with pages written in languages not known to our identifier. The method we use in production is based on a language set identification method (Jauhiainen et al., 2015b), which determines the languages used on a page. The method is simply a threshold for the number of languages: if too many languages are found in a piece of text, the text is categorized as junk. In the production environment our threshold is currently 10 languages on one web page. The production threshold has been empirically determined for the parameters used with the language set identification method and for the number of languages known by the identifier.

2.3 Language model adaptation

Language model adaptation was used by Chen and Liu (2005) for identifying the language of speech. In the system built by Chen and Liu (2005), the speech is first run through Hidden Markov Model-based phone recognizers (one for each language), which tokenize the speech into sequences of phones. The probabilities of those sequences are calculated using corresponding language models and the most probable language is selected. An adaptation routine is then used so that each of the phonetic transcriptions of the individual speech utterances is used to calculate probabilities for words t, given a word n-gram history of h as in Equation 1.

$$P_a(t|h) = \lambda P_o(t|h) + (1 - \lambda)P_n(t|h),\tag{1}$$

where P_o is the original probability calculated from the training material, P_n the probability calculated from the data being identified, and P_a the new adapted probability. λ is the weight given to original probabilities. This adaptation method resulted in decreasing the error rate in a three-way identification between Chinese, English, and Russian by 2.88% and 3.84% on an out-of-domain (different channels) data, and by 0.44% on in-domain (same channel) data.

Zhong et al. (2007) also used language model adaptation with language adaptation of speech. They evaluated three different confidence measures and the best faring measure is defined as follows:

$$C(g_i, M) = \frac{1}{n}[\log(P(M|g_i)) - \log(P(M|g_j))], \tag{2}$$

where M is the sequence to be identified, n the number of frames in the utterance, g_i the best identified language, and g_j the second best identified language. The two other evaluated confidence measures were clearly inferior. Although the $C(g_i, M)$ measure performed the best of the individual measures, a Bayesian classifier based ensemble using all the three measures gave slightly higher results. Zhong et al. (2007) use the same language adaptation method as Chen and Liu (2005), using the confidence measures to set the λ for each utterance.

3 Test setup

The dataset used in the shared task consists of manual transcriptions of speech utterances by speakers from different areas: Bern, Basel, Lucerne, and Zurich. The transcriptions are written entirely in lower-cased letters. Samardžić et al. (2016) describe the ArchiMob corpus, which is the source for the shared task dataset. Zampieri et al. (2017) describe how the training and test sets were extracted from the Archi-Mob corpus for the 2017 shared task. The sizes of the training and development sets can be seen in Table 2. The first track of the shared task was a standard four-way language identification between the four German dialects present in the training set.

Variety	Training	Development
Bern (BE)	32,447	8,471
Basel (BS)	30,770	11,116
Lucerne (LU)	32,955	9,966
Zurich (ZH)	32,714	9,039

Table 2: The sizes in words of the datasets distributed for the 2018 GDI shared task.

This year the GDI task also included a second track for unknown dialect detection. The unknown dialect was not included in the training or the development sets, but it was present in the test set. The test set was identical for both tracks, but the lines containing unknown dialect were ignored when calculating the scores for the first track.

4 Basic HeLI method, run 1 on track 1

We first presented the HeLI method, originally published by Jauhiainen (2010), at the VarDial 2016 (Jauhiainen et al., 2016). To make this article more self-contained, we present the full description of the method as it is used in the best submitted run for the GDI shared task. The survey by Jauhiainen et al. (2018) uses the same unified notation to define the features and methods used for language identification. This description differs from the original mostly in that we are leaving out the cut-off value c for the size of the language models as using all the available material was always the best option. When we are not using the cut-off value, no derived corpus C' consisting of the used features is generated. The final submissions were done with a system using only lowercased character 4-grams, so we present the method without the back-off function. For the complete description of the HeLI method see our VarDial 2016 article (Jauhiainen et al., 2016).

4.1 Description of the HeLI method using only 4-grams of characters

The goal is to correctly guess the language $g \in G$ for each of the lines in the test set. In the method, each language g is represented by a lowercased character 4-gram language model. The training data is tokenized into words using non-alphabetic and non-ideographic characters as delimiters and the words are lowercased. The relative frequencies of character 4-grams are calculated inside the words, so that the preceding and the following space-characters are included. The 4-grams are overlapping, so that for example a word with three characters include two character 4-grams. Then we transform the relative frequencies into scores using 10-based logarithms.

The corpus containing only the n-grams of the length 4 in the language models is called C'^4. The domain $dom(O(C'^4))$ is the set of all character n-grams of length 4 found in the models of any language $g \in G$. The values $v_{C_g^4}(u)$ are calculated similarly for all n-grams $u \in dom(O(C'^4))$ for each language g, as shown in Equation 3.

$$v_{C_g^4}(u) = \begin{cases} -\log_{10}\left(\frac{c(C_g^4, u)}{l_{C_g^4}}\right) & \text{, if } c(C_g^4, u) > 0 \\ p & \text{, if } c(C_g^4, u) = 0, \end{cases} \tag{3}$$

where $c(C_g^4, u)$ is the number of n-grams u found in the corpus of the language g and $l_{C_g^4}$ is the total number of the n-grams of length 4 in the corpus of language g. These values are used when scoring the words while identifying the language of a text. The word t is split into overlapping 4-grams of characters u_i^4, where $i = 1, ..., l_t - 4$. l_t is the length of the word in characters, including the preceding and the following space-characters. Each of the n-grams u_i^4 is then scored separately for each language g.

If the n-gram u_i^4 is found in $dom(O(C_g^4))$, the values in the models are used. If the n-gram u_i^4 is not found in any of the models, it is simply discarded. We define the function $d_g(t, 4)$ for counting n-grams in t found in a model in Equation 4.

$$d_g(t, 4) = \sum_{i=1}^{l_t-4} \begin{cases} 1 & \text{, if } u_i^4 \in dom(O(C^4)) \\ 0 & \text{, otherwise.} \end{cases} \tag{4}$$

When all the n-grams of the size 4 in the word t have been processed, the word gets the value of the average of the scored n-grams u_i^4 for each language, as in Equation 5.

$$v_g(t, 4) = \frac{1}{d_g(t, 4)} \sum_{i=1}^{l_t-4} v_{C_g^4}(u_i^4) \quad \text{, if } d_g(t, 4) > 0, \tag{5}$$

where $d_g(t, 4)$ is the number of n-grams u_i^4 found in the domain $dom(O(C_g^4))$. If all of the n-grams of the size 4 were discarded, $d_g(t, 4) = 0$, a word gets the penalty value p for every language, as in Equation 6.

$$v_g(t, 0) = p \tag{6}$$

The mystery text is tokenized into words using the non-alphabetic and non-ideographic characters as delimiters. The words are lowercased. After this, a score $v_g(t, 4)$ is calculated for each word t in the mystery text for each language g. The whole line M gets the score $R_g(M)$ equal to the average of the scores of the words $v_g(t, 4)$ for each language g, as in Equation 7.

$$R_g(M) = \frac{\sum_{i=1}^{l_{T(M)}} v_g(t_i, 4)}{l_{T(M)}} \tag{7}$$

where $T(M)$ is the sequence of words and $l_{T(M)}$ is the number of words in the line M. Since we are using negative logarithms of probabilities, the language having the lowest score is returned as the language with the maximum probability for the mystery text.

4.2 Experiments on the development set and results on the test set

The training dataset was completely written in lowercase so we used only lowercased versions of the language models. First we tested the effect of not using all the data in the language models with varying the cut-off parameter c on the development set. The largest language model was the character 6-gram model for the Basel-area dialect with 16,947 different 6-grams. The results using optimized penalty values for each c are presented in Table 3. The results would seem to indicate that the recall starts to decline in an increasing manner as soon as some of the material from the language models is left out. This is something we have noticed before in settings where the training data is of very good quality. If we are using the identifier in a production setting with, for example, Wikipedia-derived language models, some of the models include so much noice that not using the complete models improves the results (Jauhiainen et al., 2017b). The optimal penalty value is also clearly tied to the maximum size of the used language models.

Lowercased words	Lowercased n_{max}	Penalty p	Cut-off c	Recall
yes	8	5.1	16,947	64.47%
yes	8	4.9	15,000	64.41%
yes	8	4.8	10,000	64.19%

Table 3: Basic HeLI method results on the development set with varying c.

We decided to use all the available data and then optimized the used language models and the penalty value p. The results on the development set with different model combinations can be seen in Table 4. The penalty value p presented in the third column was the optimal one for each configuration. The HeLI method using character n-grams from one to four attained the best recall 65.97%.

Lowercased words	Lowercased n_{max}	Penalty p	Recall
no	4	5.8	65.97%
no	5	5.4	65.39%
no	6	5.3	64.79%
no	8	5.4	64.56%
no	7	5.1	64.51%
yes	8	5.1	64.47%
no	3	5.7	62.80%
no	2	5.7	53.43%
no	1	5.6	33.13%

Table 4: Basic HeLI method results on the development set using different language model combinations.

We also experimented with leaving out the lower order n-grams. The results of these experiments on the development set can be seen in Table 5. To our surprise, the best results were attained using only the 4-grams of characters, which means that the backoff function of the HeLI method is not used at all. The recall on the development set was 66.10%. We also re-tested using lower cut-offs c, but leaving off any material in the language models only made the results worse again.

Lowercased words	Lowercased n-gram range	Penalty p	Recall
not used	4 - 4	5.8	66.10%
not used	1 - 4	5.8	65.97%
not used	2 - 4	5.8	65.97%
not used	3 - 4	5.8	65.97%

Table 5: Basic HeLI method results on the development set with different n-gram ranges.

We decided to use the character 4-grams and the penalty value of 5.8 for the first run. We added the development data to the training data and generated new models. The system attained a recall of 63.97% on the test set, which was somewhat less than what we had seen with the development set.

5   HeLI with language model adaptation, run 2 on track 1

While experimenting with the basic HeLI method we created a test setting to detect the difference of using out-of-domain and in-domain training data. For each language, we divided the development set in two halves. We experimented with adding the first half of the development data (we call it *dv-dv*) to the training data (*tr*) of each language, creating new language models and testing them on the second half of the development data (*dv-tst*). The recalls on the second half of the development set (*dv-tst*) using the combined *tr* and *dv-dv* for training were much better than the recalls on the first half (*dv-dv*) using just *tr* for training. The recalls can be seen in the fourth column of Table 6. In the heading of the table, the training data used is indicated in parenthesis after the test data. We decided to try to test *dv-tst* also without including *dv-dv* in the training set in order to see if *dv-tst* was for some reason generally easier to identify than *dv-dv*. The second half of the development data, *dv-tst*, turned out to be a little bit easier to identify than the first half, *dv-dv*, using the original models generated from just the training data as can be seen in the fifth column of Table 6. Another hypothesis is that the development data is from an another source than the training data and the first half introduces a great number of new words which are relevant to the second half. Also we wanted to know if just 15.9% increase in training text amount could generate this much better recall. In order to test this hypothesis we removed the same amount of lines as was in *dv-dv* from the training data, marked as *tr-sz(dv-dv)* in the table, and inserted the *dv-dv* lines instead. The recall percentages from those tests are in the final column of Table 6 and they suggest that the development data is indeed from a somewhat different domain than the training data and the identifier actually performs better when some of the original training data is removed.

It can also be seen from the results of the experiments that the best models for in-domain experiments were word and character *n*-grams from one to five and for the out-of-domain they were character *n*-grams from one to four or just 4-grams. This would then indicate that if the domain of the language to be tested is the same or similar to the one that the models have been created from, the models could use longer character *n*-grams and words, if not, then using just character *n*-grams is a better strategy.

n-gram range	Words	dv-dv (tr)	dv-tst (tr+dv-dv)	dv-tst (tr)	dv-tst (tr-sz(dv-dv)+dv-dv)
1 - 8	yes	63.65%	78.65%	65.46%	79.55%
1 - 7	yes	63.82%	78.95%	65.89%	79.68%
1 - 6	yes	64.16%	78.91%	66.02%	79.90%
1 - 5	yes	64.59%	79.55%	65.98%	80.41%
1 - 4	yes	64.76%	79.25%	66.07%	79.94%
1 - 3	yes	65.28%	78.74%	66.67%	79.77%
1 - 2	yes	65.11%	78.35%	66.37%	79.17%
1	yes	63.95%	78.01%	65.29%	78.57%
-	yes	63.61%	77.53%	64.86%	78.01%
1 - 8	no	63.65%	78.74%	65.59%	79.47%
1 - 7	no	63.73%	78.91%	65.42%	79.51%
1 - 6	no	64.21%	78.95%	65.21%	79.55%
1 - 5	no	65.15%	79.21%	65.76%	79.94%
1 - 4	no	65.45%	78.35%	66.58%	79.25%
4	no	65.28%	78.14%	67.35%	78.57%
1 - 3	no	61.89%	73.20%	63.70%	73.97%
1 - 2	no	52.88%	60.87%	54.08%	61.60%
1	no	33.18%	36.34%	33.08%	37.5%

Table 6: Baseline HeLI recalls using different combinations of training and development sets.

What we learned from these experiments with the basic HeLI method is that, if we would be able to somehow incorporate well identified sentences into the original models it might introduce crucial new word or character *n*-gram vocabulary. We decided to try always adding the character 4-grams from the most confidently identified sentence to the language model of the respective language and re-identifying the rest, always marking the best identified sentence as not needing to be identified again. This process is recursive and it runs until all the sentences except the last one are used for language modelling. In order to decide which sentence is most confidently identified, we need a confidence score. As a confidence measure CM, we used the difference between the scores of the best $R_g(M)$ and the second best $R_h(M)$ identified language for each line. Later we found that basically the same confidence measure was earlier proposed by Zhong et al. (2007). In our case it is calculated using the Equation 8:

$$CM(C_g, M) = R_h(M) - R_g(M) \qquad (8)$$

where M is the line containing the mystery text. It could be beneficial to end the recursive adaptation before all the sentences are exhausted, if the confidence score is reliable enough. However, we did not have time to experiment with a cut-off value for the confidence score before the submissions were due.

The identifier with language model adaptation reached 77.99% recall on the development set with the same language models (character 4-gram) and penalty value (5.8) which we used with the basic HeLI method in run 1. It was an increase of 12.71% on top of the recall of the basic HeLI method.

We suspected that using higher order n-grams or words could produce even better results, but we did not have time to test this theory. We added the development data to the training data, generated new language models and submitted our run 2. The second run reached a recall of 69.19% on the test set, an increase of 5.22%. The macro F1-score attained on the run 2 was 0.6857. The results are very good considering that there was an unknown dialect within the actual test set and all the lines in the unknown dialect were incorrectly incorporated into some of the language models. The final results compared with the best results submitted by other teams are shown in Table 7.

System	F1 (macro)
HeLI with adaptive language models, run 2	**0.6857**
benf	0.6464
safina	0.6449
taraka_rama	0.6398
The basic HeLI method, run 1	**0.6386**
LaMa	0.6374
XAC	0.6336
GDI_classification	0.6203
dkosmajac	0.5909
Random Baseline	0.2521

Table 7: Results compared with the other submitted runs. Our submitted results are bolded.

6 Experiments with unknown language detection, track 2

The basic HeLI method always maps the mystery text M into one of the languages it has been trained with. The 2015 Discriminating Between Similar Languages shared task included an unknown category which contained several a priori unknown languages. One of the methods we used in 2015 was using a threshold for the score $R_g(M)$ to detect the unknown language. In order to assess the suitability of using the threshold score with the German dialects, we compared the range of the scores when g was correctly or incorrectly identified using the character 4-gram language models on the development set. The score ranges can be seen in Table 8, where the line with correct identifications is bolded. The lower the score, the better the mystery text fits the language. The scores ranged from 1.28 to 4.56 when the dialect was correctly identified, with most of the scores higher than the lower ranges of the incorrect identifications. The fact that the worst absolute score (4.56) was attained with a correct identification drove us to the conclusion that simply using the score as a cut-off would not be a quick solution to the unseen language problem. Due to time restrictions, we did not pursue this investigation further. We were also unable to test the language set based thresholding method we are using in the production environment. In the end, we did not submit any results to the unknown language detection track.

Correct language	Identified language	Lowest score	Highest score
ZH	**ZH**	**1.28**	**4.56**
ZH	LU	2.37	4.23
ZH	BS	1.71	4.21
ZH	BE	2.26	3.95

Table 8: Score ranges when trying to identify the dialect from Zurich area.

7 Conclusions

The macro F1-score attained by the basic HeLI method is within 0.0078 score difference to the best five results submitted by the other teams. Unsupervised language model adaptation improved on the recall of the basic HeLI-method by 5.22%. The score difference between our run using the adaptive language models and the second best submitted run is 0.0393. Language model adaptation would seem to be especially usable in situations where the training material can be expected to be from a different domain than the material to be identified. The adaptation method proved to be very robust as it performed well even with the unknown language present in the test set.

Acknowledgments

This research was partly conducted with funding from the Kone Foundation Language Programme (Kone Foundation, 2012).

References

Adrien Barbaresi. 2017. Discriminating between Similar Languages using Weighted Subword Features. In *Proceedings of the Fourth Workshop on NLP for Similar Languages, Varieties and Dialects (VarDial)*, pages 184–189, Valencia, Spain.

Yves Bestgen. 2017. Improving the Character Ngram Model for the DSL Task with BM25 Weighting and Less Frequently Used Feature Sets. In *Proceedings of the Fourth Workshop on NLP for Similar Languages, Varieties and Dialects (VarDial)*, pages 115–123, Valencia, Spain.

Çağri Çöltekin and Taraka Rama. 2017. Tübingen system in VarDial 2017 shared task: experiments with language identification and cross-lingual parsing. In *Proceedings of the Fourth Workshop on NLP for Similar Languages, Varieties and Dialects (VarDial)*, pages 146–155, Valencia, Spain.

Yingna Chen and Jia Liu. 2005. Language Model Adaptation and Confidence Measure for Robust Language Identification. In *Proceedings of International Symposium on Communications and Information Technologies 2005 (ISCIT 2005)*, volume 1, pages 270–273, Beijing, China.

Simon Clematide and Peter Makarov. 2017. CLUZH at VarDial GDI 2017: Testing a Variety of Machine Learning Tools for the Classification of Swiss German Dialects. In *Proceedings of the Fourth Workshop on NLP for Similar Languages, Varieties and Dialects (VarDial)*, pages 170–177, Valencia, Spain.

Pablo Gamallo, Jose Ramom Pichel, and Iñaki Alegria. 2017. A Perplexity-Based Method for Similar Languages Discrimination. In *Proceedings of the Fourth Workshop on NLP for Similar Languages, Varieties and Dialects (VarDial)*, pages 109–114, Valencia, Spain.

Abualsoud Hanani, Aziz Qaroush, and Stephen Taylor. 2017. Identifying dialects with textual and acoustic cues. In *Proceedings of the Fourth Workshop on NLP for Similar Languages, Varieties and Dialects (VarDial)*, pages 93–101, Valencia, Spain.

Nora Hollenstein and Noëmi Aepli. 2015. A Resource for Natural Language Processing of Swiss German Dialects. In *Proceedings of the International Conference of the German Society for Computational Linguistics and Language Technology (GSCL 2015)*, pages 108–109, University of Duisburg-Essen, Germany.

Radu Tudor Ionescu and Andrei Butnaru. 2017. Learning to Identify Arabic and German Dialects using Multiple Kernels. In *Proceedings of the Fourth Workshop on NLP for Similar Languages, Varieties and Dialects (VarDial)*, pages 200–209, Valencia, Spain.

Tommi Jauhiainen, Heidi Jauhiainen, and Krister Lindén. 2015a. Discriminating Similar Languages with Token-Based Backoff. In *Proceedings of the Joint Workshop on Language Technology for Closely Related Languages, Varieties and Dialects (LT4VarDial)*, pages 44–51, Hissar, Bulgaria.

Tommi Jauhiainen, Krister Lindén, and Heidi Jauhiainen. 2015b. Language Set Identification in Noisy Synthetic Multilingual Documents. In *Proceedings of the Computational Linguistics and Intelligent Text Processing 16th International Conference, CICLing 2015*, pages 633–643, Cairo, Egypt.

Tommi Jauhiainen, Krister Lindén, and Heidi Jauhiainen. 2016. HeLI, a Word-Based Backoff Method for Language Identification. In *Proceedings of the Third Workshop on NLP for Similar Languages, Varieties and Dialects (VarDial3)*, pages 153–162, Osaka, Japan.

Tommi Jauhiainen, Krister Lindén, and Heidi Jauhiainen. 2017a. Evaluating HeLI with Non-Linear Mappings. In *Proceedings of the Fourth Workshop on NLP for Similar Languages, Varieties and Dialects (VarDial)*, pages 102–108, Valencia, Spain.

Tommi Jauhiainen, Krister Lindén, and Heidi Jauhiainen. 2017b. Evaluation of Language Identification Methods Using 285 Languages. In *Proceedings of the 21st Nordic Conference on Computational Linguistics (NoDaLiDa 2017)*, pages 183–191, Gothenburg, Sweden. Linköping University Electronic Press.

Tommi Jauhiainen, Marco Lui, Marcos Zampieri, Timothy Baldwin, and Krister Lindén. 2018. Automatic Language Identification in Texts: A Survey. *arXiv preprint arXiv:1804.08186.*

Tommi Jauhiainen. 2010. Tekstin kielen automaattinen tunnistaminen. Master's thesis, University of Helsinki, Helsinki.

Kone Foundation. 2012. The Language Programme 2012-2016. http://www.koneensaatio.fi/en.

M. Paul Lewis, Gary F. Simons, and Charles D. Fennig, editors. 2013. *Ethnologue: Languages of the world, seventeenth edition*. SIL International, Dallas, Texas.

Shervin Malmasi and Marcos Zampieri. 2017. German Dialect Identification in Interview Transcriptions. In *Proceedings of the Fourth Workshop on NLP for Similar Languages, Varieties and Dialects (VarDial)*, pages 164–169, Valencia, Spain.

Tanja Samardžić, Yves Scherrer, and Elvira Glaser. 2016. ArchiMob–A corpus of spoken Swiss German. In *Proceedings of the Language Resources and Evaluation (LREC)*, pages 4061–4066, Portoroz, Slovenia.

Yves Scherrer and Owen Rambow. 2010. Word-based Dialect Identification with Georeferenced Rules. In *Proceedings of the 2010 Conference on Empirical Methods in Natural Language Processing (EMNLP 2010)*, pages 1151–1161, Massachusetts, USA. Association for Computational Linguistics.

Izumi Suzuki, Yoshiki Mikami, Ario Ohsato, and Yoshihide Chubachi. 2002. A Language and Character Set Determination Method Based on ngram Statistics. *ACM Transactions on Asian Language Information Processing (TALIP)*, 1(3):269–278.

Marcos Zampieri, Shervin Malmasi, Nikola Ljubešić, Preslav Nakov, Ahmed Ali, Jörg Tiedemann, Yves Scherrer, and Noëmi Aepli. 2017. Findings of the VarDial Evaluation Campaign 2017. In *Proceedings of the Fourth Workshop on NLP for Similar Languages, Varieties and Dialects (VarDial)*, Valencia, Spain.

Marcos Zampieri, Shervin Malmasi, Preslav Nakov, Ahmed Ali, Suwon Shon, James Glass, Yves Scherrer, Tanja Samardžić, Nikola Ljubešić, Jörg Tiedemann, Chris van der Lee, Stefan Grondelaers, Nelleke Oostdijk, Antal van den Bosch, Ritesh Kumar, Bornini Lahiri, and Mayank Jain. 2018. Language Identification and Morphosyntactic Tagging: The Second VarDial Evaluation Campaign. In *Proceedings of the Fifth Workshop on NLP for Similar Languages, Varieties and Dialects (VarDial)*, Santa Fe, USA.

Shan Zhong, Yingna Chen, Chunyi Zhu, and Jia Liu. 2007. Confidence measure based incremental adaptation for online language identification. In *Proceedings of International Conference on Human-Computer Interaction (HCI 2007)*, pages 535–543, Beijing, China.

Deep Models for Arabic Dialect Identification on Benchmarked Data

Mohamed Elaraby   **Muhammad Abdul-Mageed**
Natural Language Processing Lab
University of British Columbia
`mohamed.elaraby@alumni.ubc.ca,muhammad.mageeed@ubc.ca`

Abstract

The Arabic Online Commentary (AOC) (Zaidan and Callison-Burch, 2011) is a large-scale repository of Arabic dialects with manual labels for 4 varieties of the language. Existing dialect identification models exploiting the dataset pre-date the recent boost deep learning brought to NLP and hence the data are not benchmarked for use with deep learning, nor is it clear how much neural networks can help tease the categories in the data apart. We treat these two limitations: We (1) benchmark the data, and (2) empirically test 6 different deep learning methods on the task, comparing peformance to several classical machine learning models under different conditions (i.e., both binary and multi-way classification). Our experimental results show that variants of (attention-based) bidirectional recurrent neural networks achieve best accuracy (acc) on the task, significantly outperforming all competitive baselines. On blind test data, our models reach 87.65% acc on the binary task (MSA vs. dialects), 87.4% acc on the 3-way dialect task (Egyptian vs. Gulf vs. Levantine), and 82.45% acc on the 4-way variants task (MSA vs. Egyptian vs. Gulf vs. Levantine). We release our benchmark for future work on the dataset.

1 Introduction

Dialect identification is a special type of language identification where the goal is to distinguish closely related languages. Explosion of communication technologies and the accompanying pervasive use of social media strongly motivates need for technologies like language, and dialect, identification. These technologies are useful for applications ranging from monitoring health and well-being (Yepes et al., 2015; Nguyen et al., 2016; Nguyen et al., 2017; Abdul-Mageed et al., 2017), to real-time disaster operation management (Sakaki et al., 2010; Palen and Hughes, 2018), and analysis of human mobility (Hawelka et al., 2014; Jurdak et al., 2015; Louail et al., 2014). Language identification is also an enabling technology that can help automatically filter foreign text in some tasks (Lui and Baldwin, 2012), acquire multilingual data (e.g., from the web) (Abney and Bird, 2010), including to enhance tasks like machine translation (Ling et al., 2013).

Arabic. In this paper our focus is on *Arabic*, a term that refers to a wide collection of varieties. These varieties are the result of the interweave between the native languages of the Middle East and North Africa and Arabic itself. Modern Standard Arabic (MSA), the modern variety of the language used in pan-Arab news outlets like AlJazeera and in educational circles in the Arab world, differs phonetically, phonologically, lexically, and syntactically from the varieties spoken in everyday communication by native speakers of the language (Diab et al., 2010; Habash, 2010; Abdul-Mageed, 2015; Abdul-Mageed, 2017). These 'everyday' varieties constitute the *dialects* of Arabic. Examples of these are Egyptian (EGY), Gulf (GLF), Levantine (LEV), and Moroccan (MOR). In addition to MSA and dialects, Classical Arabic also exists and is the variety of historical literary texts and religious discourse.

Arabic Dialects. Language varieties, including those of Arabic, can be categorized based on shared linguistic features. For Arabic, one classical categorization is based on geographical locations. For example, in addition to MSA, Habash et al. (2012), provides 5 main categories, as shown in Figure 1. This same classification is also common in the literature, and includes:

This work is licensed under a Creative Commons Attribution 4.0 International Licence. Licence details: `http://creativecommons.org/licenses/by/4.0/`.

Proceedings of the Fifth Workshop on NLP for Similar Languages, Varieties and Dialects, pages 263–274
Santa Fe, New Mexico, USA, August 20, 2018.

- **Egyptian:** The variety spoken in Egypt, which is widely spread due to the historical impact of Egyptian media

- **Gulf:** A variety spoken primarily in Saudi Arabia, UAE, Kuwait and Qatar

- **Iraqi:** The variety spoken by the people of Iraq

- **Levantine:** The variety spoken primarily by the Levant (i.e., people of Syria, Lebanon, and Palestine)

- **Maghrebi:** The variety spoken by people of North Africa, excluding Egypt

Figure 1: One categorization of Arabic dialects (Zaidan and Callison-Burch, 2011)

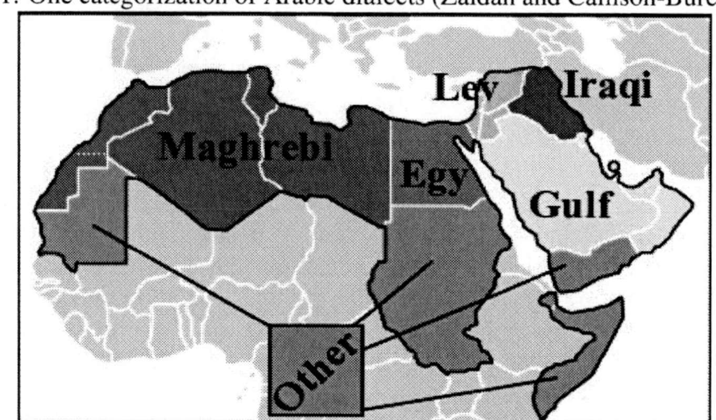

Arabic dialectal data. For a long time, Arabic dialects remained mostly spoken. Dialects started to find their way in written form with the spread of social media, thus affording an opportunity for researchers to use these data for NLP. This motivated Zaidan and Callison-Burch (2014) to create a large-scale repository of Arabic texts, the Arabic Online Commentary (AOC). The resource is composed of $\sim$ 3M MSA and dialectal comments on a number of Arabic news sites. A portion of the data ($>$ 108K comments) is manually annotated via crowdsourcing. The dataset was exploited for dialect identification in Zaidan and Callison-Burch (2014) and later in Cotterell and Callison-Burch (2014). These works, however, pre-date the current boom in NLP where deep neural networks enable better learning (given sufficiently large training data). Cotterell and Callison-Burch (2014) use n-fold cross validation in their work, thus making it costly to adopt the same data split procedure to develop deep learning models. This is the case since deep models can take long times to train and optimize. For this reason, it is desirable to benchmark the AOC dataset for deep learning research. This motivates our work. We also ask the empirical question: To what extent can we tease apart the Arabic varieties in AOC using neural networks. Especially given (a) the morphological richness of Arabic and (b) the inter-relatedness (e.g., lexical overlap) between Arabic varieties, it is not clear how accurately these varieties can be automatically categorized (using deep learning methods). To answer these important questions, we investigate the utility of several traditional machine learning classifiers and 6 different deep learning models on the task. Our deep models are based on both recurrent neural networks and convolutional neural networks, as well as combinations (and variations) of these.

Overall, we offer the following contributions: (1) We benchmark the AOC dataset, especially for deep learning work, (2) we perform extensive experiments based on deep neural networks for identifying the 4 Arabic varieties in AOC under various classification conditions, allowing us to perform well on the task, and (3) we carry out an analysis to uncover how the varieties in the data relate to one another based on shared lexica. The rest of the paper is organized as follows: In Section 2 we review related work, in Section 3 we briefly describe the AOC dataset. In Section 4 we describe our models, Section 5 is

Variety	Example
MSA	شدوا الهمة يا منتخبنا ، انتم لا تسيرون وحدكم (1) Go, go, our team; you've our passionate support. بصراحة لقد عجزت عن الكلام فلا الجهل يبرر هذه الفعلة ولا حتى اي سبب اخر (2) Frankly, I'm speechless. Neither ignorance nor any other reason justify this action.
EGY	بتقولوا ان اعلامنا وفضائيتنا فجروا الازمة وكانوا مجرمين في نظركم (3) You say our media and satellite channels initiated the crisis and were criminals in your review. قمر صناعي ولا قمر ١٤، في الشمش لو عرف القمر يلف في الجو (3) Either its a satellite or a full moon [playful for "beautiful female"], it will never rotate in its orbit correctly.
GLF	يعطي العافية على من اقترح هذا القرار ومن ساهم في تطبيقه (5) Healthy be the one who proposed this decision, and those who contributed in applying it. عندنا بعض الناس ما يرضيهم شيء ولا يكفيهم ولا يبغون يشتغلون شيء، (6) Nothing would please nor be enough for some of these people; they don't even want to put any efforts.
LEV	وانا كمان لا بصلح سيارتي ولا على بالي وابوي واخوي بيتكفلوا فيها (7) And I also won't repair my car, nor do I care. My brother and dad will take care of it. لان مو معقول توصل الامور لهلدرجة وكانت رح تصير مليون مشكلة بسبب اشاعاتهم لطلب الجامعة (8) Because it isn't reasonable for things to get to that bad. There is a million problems college students have because of their rumors.

Table 1: Example comments from the 4 varieties in the AOC dataset

where we describe our experimental set up, Section 6 provides our experimentation results. Section 7 is a visualization-based analysis of our results. Section 8 is where we conclude our work and overview future directions.

2   Related work

Work on Arabic dialect identification has focused on both spoken (Ali et al., 2015; Belinkov and Glass, 2016; Najafian et al., 2018; Shon et al., 2018; Shon et al., 2017; Najafian et al., 2018) and written form (Elfardy and Diab, 2013; Zaidan and Callison-Burch, 2014; Cotterell and Callison-Burch, 2014; Darwish et al., 2014; Abdul-Mageed et al., 2018). Early works have focused on distinguishing between MSA and EGY. For example, Elfardy and Diab (2013) propose a supervised method for sentence-level MSA-EGY categorization, exploiting a subset of the AOC dataset (12, 160 MSA sentences and 11, 274 of user commentaries on Egyptian news articles). The authors study the effect of pre-processing on classifier performance, which they find to be useful under certain conditions. Elfardy and Diab (2013) report 85.5% accuracy using 10-fold cross-validation with an SVM classifier, compared to the 80.9% accuracy reported by Zaidan and Callison-Burch (2011). Similarly, Tillmann et al. (2014) exploit the same portion of the AOC data Elfardy and Diab (2013) worked on, to build an MSA-EGY classifier. The authors report an improvement of 1.3% over results acquired by Zaidan and Callison-Burch (2014) using a linear classifier utilizing an expanded feature set. Their features include n-grams defined via part of speech tags and lexical features based on the AIDA toolkit (Elfardy et al., 2014). The work of Darwish et al. (2014) is also similar to these works in that it also focuses on the binary MSA-EGY classification task, but the authors exploit Twitter data. More specifically, Darwish et al. (2014) collected a dataset of 880K tweets on which they train their system, while testing on 700 tweets they labeled for the task. The authors explore a range of lexical and morphological features and report a 10% absolute gain over models trained with n-grams only. Our work is similar to these works in that we exploit the AOC dataset and develop MSA-EGY, binary classifiers. However, we model the task at more fine-grained levels as well (i.e., 3-way and 4-way classification).

Huang (2015) focus on the 4-way classification task using the AOC categories (MSA, EGY, GLF, LEV). The authors report improved classification accuracy using a simple word-level n-gram model trained on the manually annotated portion of AOC as well as unannotated Facebook data. The authors employ an ensemble of co-training and self-training semi-supervised learning methods exploiting 165M data points from Facebook posts. Huang (2015) report an accuracy of 87.8% on 10% of the manually annotated AOC dataset. Our work is similar to Huang (2015) in that we consider the 4-way classification task, but we do not exploit any external data. In addition, Huang (2015) did not release their data splits, nor benchmark the task on AOC. Their results are not directly comparable to our work for these reasons.

Finally, our work has some similarity to general works on language detection (Jurgens et al., 2017; Jauhiainen et al., 2017; Kocmi and Bojar, 2017; Jauhiainen et al., 2018) and geographical location (Rahimi et al., 2018; Mahmud et al., 2014; Rahimi et al., 2017).

3 Dataset: Arabic Online Commentary (AOC)

As we mentioned earlier, our work is based on the AOC dataset. AOC is composed of 3M MSA and dialectal comments, of which $108,173$ comments are labeled via crowdsourcing. For our experiments, we randomly shuffle the dataset and split it into 80% training (*Train*), 10% validation (*Dev*), and 10% test (*Test*). Table 2 shows the distribution of the data across the different splits. We were interested in identifying how the 4 varieties relate to one another in terms of their shared vocabulary, and so we performed an analysis on the training split (*Train*) as shown in the heat map in Figure 2. The Figure presents the percentages of shared vocabulary between the different varieties after normalizing for the number of data points in each class. As the Figure shows, both the GLF and LEV dialects are lexically closer to (i.e., share more vocabulary with) MSA than EGY is (does). This finding is aligned with the intuition of native speakers of Arabic that EGY diverges more from MSA than the GLF and LEV varieties. This empirical finding lends some credibility to this intuition.

Table 2: Distribution of classes in our AOC *Train* split

Variety	MSA	EGY	GLF	LEV	ALL
Train	50,845	10,022	16,593	9,081	86,541
Dev	6,357	1,253	2,075	1,136	10,821
Test	6,353	1,252	2,073	1,133	10,812

Figure 2: Heat map for shared vocabulary between different data variants

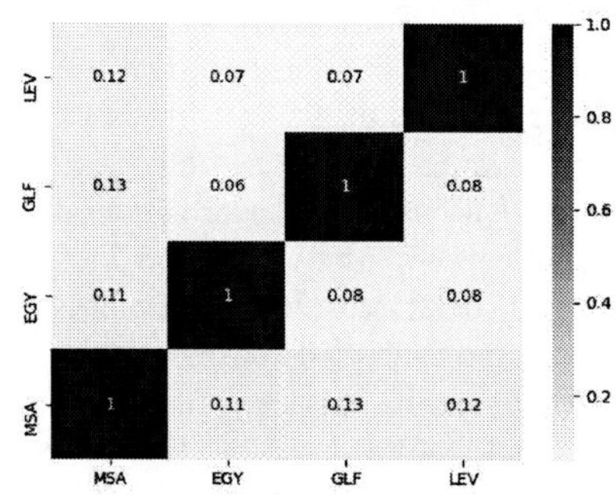

4 Models

4.1 Traditional models

Traditional models refer to models based on feature engineering methods with linear and probabilistic classifiers. In our experiments, we use (1) logistic regression, (2) multinomial Naive Bayes, and (3) support vector machines (SVM) classifiers.

4.2 Deep Learning Models

Recently, deep learning models have been successfully applied to the tasks of language modeling and text classification. For these reasons, we experiment with a number of popular models, as follows: (1) convolutional neural networks (CNN), (2) long-short term memory (LSTM), (3) convolutional LSTM (CLSTM), (4) bidirectional LSTM (BiLSTM), (5) bidirectional gated recurrent units (BiGRU), and (6)

BiLSTM with attention. While there are other variations of how some of these models learn (Vaswani et al., 2017), we believe these models with the variations we exploit form a strong basis for our benchmarking objective. In all our models, we use pre-trained word vectors based on word2vec to initialize the networks. We then fine-tune weights during learning.

Word-based Convolutional Neural Network (CNN): This model is conceptually similar to the one described in Kim (2014), and has the following architecture:

- *Input layer:* an input layer to map word sequence w into a sequence vector $\mathbf{x}$ where x_w is a real-valued vector ($x_w \in \mathbb{R}^{d_{emb}}$, with $d_{emb} = 300$ in all our models) initialized from external embedding model and tuned during training. The embedding layer is followed by a dropout rate of 0.5 for regularization (in this case to prevent co-adaptation between hidden units).

- *Convolution layer:* Two 1-D convolution operations are applied in parallel to the input layer to map input sequence $\mathbf{x}$ into a hidden sequence $\mathbf{h}$. A filter $k \in \mathbb{R}^{wd_{emb}}$ is applied to a window of concatenated word embedding of size w to produce a new feature c_i . Where $c_i \in \mathbb{R}$, $c_i = k \odot x_{i:i+w-1} + b$, b is the bias $b \in \mathbb{R}$, and $x_{i:i+w-1}$ is a concatenation of $x_i, ...x_{i+w1}$. The filter sizes used are 3 and 8 and the number of filters used is 10. After each convolution operation a non-linear activation of type Rectifier Linear Unit (ReLU) (Nair and Hinton, 2010) is applied. Finally different convolution outputs (the two convolutional maps in our case) are concatenated into a sequence $\mathbf{c} \in \mathbb{R}^{n-h+1}$ (where n is the number of filters and h is the dimensionality of the hidden sequence) and passed to a pooling layer.

- *Maxpooling:* Temporal max-pooling, which is the 1-D version of pooling, is applied over the concatenated output of the multiple convolutions $\mathbf{c}$, as mentioned above. The sequence $\mathbf{c}$ is converted into a single hidden vector $\mathbf{c}'$ by taking the maximum values of extracted feature map $\mathbf{c}' = max\{\mathbf{c}\}$. The size of $\mathbf{c}'$ is $\Sigma_i n_i w_i$ where n_i is the number of filters and w_i the width of these filters.

- *Dense layer:* A 100 dimension fully-connected layer with a ReLU non-linear activation is added to map vector $\mathbf{c}'$ into a final vector $\mathbf{c}''$. For regularization, we employ a dropout rate of 0.8 and an l2-norm.

- *Softmax layer:* Finally, the hidden units $\mathbf{c}''$ is converted into probability distribution over l via softmax function, where l is the number of classes.

Long-Short Term Memory (LSTM): In our experiments, we use different variations of recurrent neural networks. The first one is LSTM (Hochreiter and Schmidhuber, 1997). We use a word-based LSTM, with the following architecture:

- *Input layer:* The input layer is exactly the same as the one described in the CNN model above.

- *LSTM layer:* We use a vanilla LSTM architecture consisting of 100 dimensions hidden units. The LSTM is designed to capture long-term dependencies via augmenting a standard RNN with a memory state C_t, with $C_t \in \mathbb{R}$ at time step t. The LSTM takes in a previous state h_{t-1} and input x_t, to calculate the hidden state h_t as follows:

$$
\begin{aligned}
i_t &= \sigma(W_i.[h_{t-1}, x_t] + b_i) \\
f_t &= \sigma(W_f.[h_{t-1}, x_t] + b_f) \\
\tilde{C}_t &= tanh(W_C.[h_{t-1}, x_t] + b_C) \\
C_t &= f_t \odot C_{t-1} + i_t \odot \tilde{C} \\
o_t &= \sigma(W_o[h_{t-1}, x_t] + b_o) \\
h_t &= o_t \odot tanh(C_t)
\end{aligned}
\tag{1}
$$

where σ is the sigmoid, $tanh$ is the hyperpolic tangent function, and $\odot$ is the dot product between two vectors. The i_t, f_t, o_t are the *input, forget,* and *output* gates, and the $\tilde{C}_t$ is a new memory cell vector with candidates that could be added to the state. We use the same regularization as we apply on the dense layer in the CNN model mentioned above.

- *Softmax layer:* Similar to that of the CNN above as well.

Convolution LSTM (CLSTM): This model is described in Zhou et al. (2015). The model architecture is similar to the CNN described earlier, but the fully-connected (dense) layer is replaced by an LSTM layer. The intuition behind the CLSTM is to use the CNN layer as a feature extractor, and directly feed the convolution output to the LSTM layer (which can capture long-term dependencies).

Bidirectional LSTM (BiLSTM): One limitation of conventional RNNs is that they are able to make predictions based on previously seen content only. Another variant of RNNs that addresses this problem is Bidirectional RNNs (BRNNs), which process the data in both directions in two separate hidden layers. These two hidden layers are then fed forward to the same output layer. BRNNs compute three sequences; a forward hidden sequence $\overrightarrow{h}$, a backward hidden sequence $\overleftarrow{h}$, and the output sequence y. The model transition equations are as below:

$$\overrightarrow{h} = \mathcal{H}(W_{x\overrightarrow{h}}x_t + W_{\overrightarrow{h}\overrightarrow{h}}\overrightarrow{h}_{t+1} + b_{\overrightarrow{h}})$$
$$\overleftarrow{h} = \mathcal{H}(W_{x\overleftarrow{h}}x_t + W_{\overleftarrow{h}\overleftarrow{h}}\overleftarrow{h}_{t+1} + b_{\overleftarrow{h}}) \tag{2}$$
$$y_t = W_{\overrightarrow{h}y}\overrightarrow{h}_t + W_{\overleftarrow{h}y}\overleftarrow{h}_t + b_y$$

Where $\mathcal{H}$ can be any activation function. Combining BRNN and LSTM gives the BiLSTM model. In our experiments we use a 100 hidden units dimension to ensure a fair comparison with LSTM's results. We apply the same regularization techniques applied for the LSTM layer described above.

Bidirectional Gated Recurrent Units (BiGRU): Gated Recurrent Unit (GRU) (Chung et al., 2014) is a variant of LSTMs that combines the *forget* and *input* gates into a single update gate z_t by primarily merging the *cell* state and *hidden* state. This results in a simpler model composed of an *update* state z_t, a *reset* state r_t, and a new simpler *hidden* state h_t. The model transition equations are as follows:

$$z_t = \sigma(W_z.[h_{t-1}, x_t])$$
$$r_t = \sigma(W_r.[h_{t-1}, x_t])$$
$$\tilde{h}_t = tanh(W.[r_t * h_{t-1}, x_t]) \tag{3}$$
$$h_t = (1 - z_t) * h_{t-1} + z_t * \tilde{h}_t$$

The Bidirectional GRU (BiGRUs) can be obtained by combining two GRUs, each looking at a different direction similar to the case of BiLSTMs above. We employ the same regularization techniques applied to the LSTM and BiLSTM networks.

Attention-based BiLSTM

Recently, using an attention mechanism with a neural networks has resulted in notable success in a wide range of NLP tasks, such as machine translation, speech recognition, and image captioning (Bahdanau et al., 2014; Xu et al., 2015; Chorowski et al., 2015). In this section, we describe an attention mechanism that we employ in one of our models (BiLSTM) that turned out to perform well without attention, hoping the mechanism will further improve model performance. We use a simple implementation inspired by Zhou et al. (2016) where attention is applied to the output vector of the LSTM layer. If H is a matrix consisting of output vectors $[h_1, h_2, ..h_T]$ (where T is the sentence length), we can compute the attention vector α of the sequence as follows:

$$\mathbf{e}_t = tanh(h_t)$$
$$\alpha_t = \frac{exp(e_t)}{\Sigma_{i=1}^{T}exp(e_i)} \tag{4}$$

Finally, the representation vector for input text $\mathbf{v}$ is computed by a weighted summation over all the time steps, using obtained attention scores as weights.

$$\mathbf{v} = \Sigma_{i=1}^{T} \alpha_i h_i \tag{5}$$

The vector $\mathbf{v}$ is an encoded representation of the whole input text. This representation is passed to the $softmax$ layer for classification.

5 Experiments

We perform 3 different classification tasks: (A) *binary classification*, where we tease apart the MSA and the dialectal data, (B) *3-way dialects*, where we attempt to distinguish between EGY, GLF, and LEV; and (C) *4-way variants* (i.e., MSA vs. EGY vs. GLF vs. LEV). Since our goal in this work is to explore how several popular traditional settings and deep learning model architectures fare on the dialect identification task, we use classifiers with pre-defined hyper-parameters inspired by previous works as described in Section 4. As we mention in Section 3, we split the data into 80% *Train*, 10% *Dev*, and 10% *Test*. While we train on *Train* and report results on both the *Dev* and *Test* sets in the current work, our goal is to invest on hyper-parameter tuning based on the development set in the future. Benchmarking the data is thus helpful as it facilitates comparisons in future works. [1]

5.1 Pre-processing

We process our data the same way across all our traditional and deep learning experiments, as follows:

- **Tokenization and normalization:** We tokenize our data based on white space, excluding all non-unicode characters. We then normalize *Alif maksura* to *Ya*, reduce all *hamzated Alif* to plain *Alif*, and remove all non-Arabic characters/words (e.g., "very", "50$").

- **Input sequence quantization:** In our experiments, we fix the vocabulary at the most frequent 50K words. The input tokens are then converted into indices ranging from 1 to 50K based on our look-up vocabulary.

- **Padding:** For the deep learning classifiers, all input sequences are truncated to arbitrary maximum sequence length of 30 words per comment. Comments of length < 30 are zero-padded. This number can be tuned in future work.

5.2 Traditional Classifier Experiments

We have two settings for the traditional classifiers: (1) presence vs. absence (0 vs. 1) vectors based on combinations of unigrams, bigrams, and trigrams; and (2) term-frequency inverse-document-frequency (TF-IDF) vectors based on combinations of unigrams, bigrams, and trigrams (Sparck Jones, 1972). We use scikit-learn's (Pedregosa et al., 2011) implementation of these classifiers.

5.3 Deep Learning Experiments

All our deep models are trained for 10 epochs using the RMSprop optimizer. The model's weights W are initialized from a normal distribution $W \sim N$ with a small standard deviation of $\sigma = 0.05$. Our models are trained using the Keras (Chollet and others, 2015) library with a Tensorflow (Abadi et al., 2016) backend. We train each of our 6 deep learning classifiers across 3 different settings pertaining the way we initialize the embeddings for the input layer in each network. The three embedding settings are:

1. **Random embeddings:** Where we initialize the input layer randomly.

2. **AOC-based embeddings:** We make use of the $\sim$ 3M unlabeled comments in AOC by training a "continuous bag of words" (CBOW) (Mikolov et al., 2013) model exploiting them. We adopt the settings in Abdul-Mageed et al. (2018) for training our model to acquire 300 dimensional word vectors.

---

[1] The benchmarked data can be obtained by emailing the authors. See also project repository at: `https://github.com/UBC-NLP/aoc_id`.

Method	Binary		Three-way		Four-way	
	Dev	*Test*	*Dev*	*Test*	*Dev*	*Test*
Traditional Classifiers						
Baseline (majority class in *Train*)	58.75	58.75	58.75	58.75	46.49	46.49
Logistic Regression (1+2+3 grams)	84.18	83.71	86.91	85.75	75.75	78.24
Naive Bayes (1+2+3 grams)	84.97	84.53	87.51	**87.81**	80.15	77.75
SVM (1+2+3 grams)	82.79	82.41	85.51	84.27	74.5	75.82
Logistic Regression (1+2+3 grams TF-IDF)	83.96	83.24	86.71	85.51	75.81	78.24
Naive Bayes (1+2+3 grams TF-IDF)	83.52	82.91	86.61	86.87	73.21	75.81
SVM (1+2+3 grams TF-IDF)	84.07	83.61	86.76	85.93	76.65	78.61
Deep Learning - Random Embeddings						
CNN (Kim, 2014)	85.69	85.16	81.63	81.11	66.34	68.86
CLSTM (Zhou et al., 2015)	84.73	84.17	78.91	78.32	64.58	65.25
LSTM	85.41	85.28	78.61	78.51	70.21	68.71
BiLSTM	84.11	83.77	85.82	84.99	75.94	77.55
BiGRU	82.81	82.77	84.88	84.45	74.56	76.51
Attention-BiLSTM	85.5	85.23	86.12	85.93	79.97	80.21
Deep Learning - AOC Embeddings						
CNN (Kim, 2014)	85.02	84.51	76.81	76.53	64.23	64.17
CLSTM (Zhou et al., 2015)	85.17	84.73	76.81	75.71	64.61	63.89
LSTM	85.04	84.07	83.89	82.67	70.01	68.91
BiLSTM	85.33	84.88	86.21	86.01	76.12	78.35
BiGRU	85.39	85.27	86.92	86.57	79.61	80.11
Attention-BiLSTM	85.77	85.71	87.01	86.93	80.25	81.12
Deep Learning - Twitter-City Embeddings (Abdul-Mageed et al., 2018)						
CNN (Kim, 2014)	86.68	86.26	85.51	85.36	74.13	75.61
CLSTM (Zhou et al., 2015)	86.61	86.28	82.77	82.56	79.41	77.51
LSTM	85.52	85.07	84.41	84.61	75.21	78.53
BiLSTM	87.16	86.99	87.31	87.11	82.81	81.93
BiGRU	**87.65**	**87.23**	87.11	86.18	83.25	82.21
Attention BiLSTM	87.61	87.21	**87.81**	87.41	**83.49**	**82.45**

Table 3: Experimental results, in accuracy, on our *Dev* and *Test* AOC splits

3. **Twitter-City embeddings:** This is based on the CBOW word2vec model released by Abdul-Mageed et al. (2018). The authors train their models on a $\frac{1}{4}$ billion tweets dataset collected from 29 different cities from 10 Arab countries. The authors use a window of size 5 words, minimal word frequency set at 100 words, and 300 dimensional word vectors to train this model.

6   Results

Table 3 shows our results in accuracy across the three classification tasks (i.e., *binary, 3-way,* and *4-way*), as described in Section 5. Our baseline in each task is the majority class in the respective *Train* set. As Table 6 shows, among traditional models, the Naive Bayes classifier achieves the best performance across all three tasks both on *Dev* and *Test* data. As a sole exception, SVMs outperforms Naive Bayes on the *Test* set for the 4-way classification task. As best accuracy, traditional classifiers yield 84.53 (*binary*), 87.81 (*3-way*), and 78.61 (*4-way*) on the *Test* splits.

As Table 3 shows, across the different classification tasks, models initialized with the Twitter-City embeddings (Abdul-Mageed et al., 2018) perform best on the task compared to those initialized randomly or with the AOC embeddings. We also observe that AOC embeddings are better than random initialization. For ***binary classification***, as Table 6 shows, BiGRU obtains the best accuracy on both *Dev* (87.65) and *Test* (87.23), with attention-BiLSTM performing quite closely. For the ***3-way classification*** task (dialect only classifier), while attention-BiLSTM obtains the best result on the *Dev* (87.81), it is slightly outperformed by the Naive Bayes classifier on *Test* (also 87.81). For ***4-way classification***, attention-BiLSTM obtained best accuracy on both *Dev* (83.49) and *Test* (82.42).

Aligned with knowledge about deep models, we note the positive effect of larger training data on classification. For example, when we reduce the size of *Train* by excluding the MSA comments (58% of the manually annotated data), traditional classifiers outperform most of the deep learning classifiers on 3-way classification. Similarly, results drop when we thinly spread the data across the 4 categories for 4-way classification.

7 Analysis

Figure 3 is a visualization of classification errors acquired with attention-BiLSTM results (best accuracy in the multi-class tasks). The *left-side (3-way/dialects)* matrix shows how LEV is confused 20% of the time with GLF, directly reflecting the closer lexical distance between the two varieties compared to the distance of either of them to EGY. The *right-side (4-way)* matrix shows that 23% of the GLF errors are confused with MSA, followed by LEV errors (confused with MSA 20% of the time). This is a result of the higher lexical overlap between the two dialects and MSA, as we described in our observations around Figure 2. As Table 2 shows, MSA also dominates *Train* and hence these confusions with MSA are expected.

Figure 3: Analysis of Attention-BiLSTM results. **Left:** Confusion matrix for *3-way* predictions. **Right:** Confusion matrix for *4-way* classification.

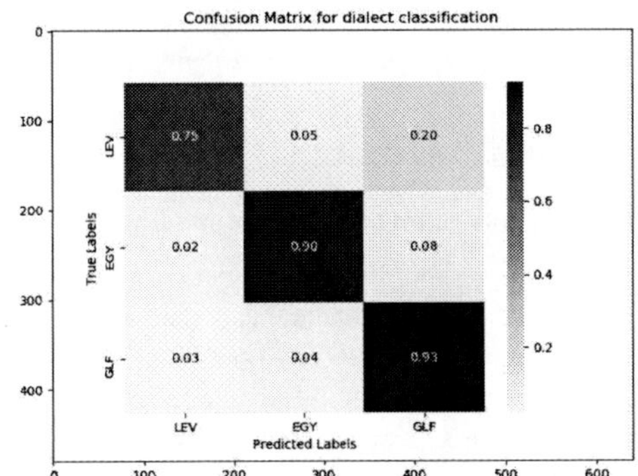
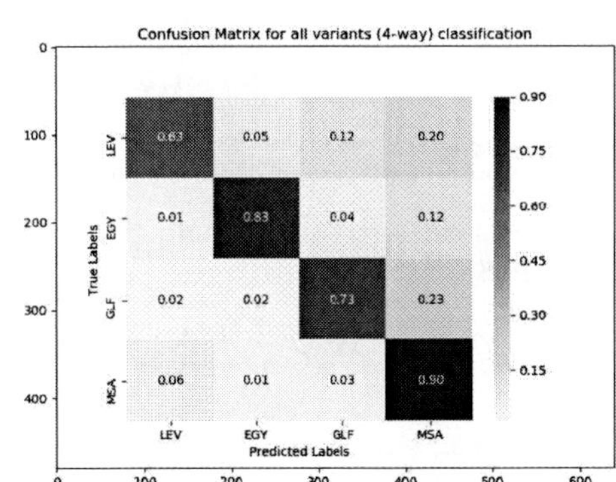

8 Conclusion

We benchmarked the AOC dataset, a popular dataset of Arabic online comments, for deep learning work focused at dialect identification. We also developed 12 different classifiers (6 traditional and 6 based on deep learning) to offer strong baselines for the task. Results show attention-based BiLSTMs to work well on this task, especially when initialized using a large dialect specific word embeddings model. In the future, we plan to exploit sub-word and further tune hyper-parameters of our models.

9 Acknowledgement

We acknowledge the support of the Natural Sciences and Engineering Research Council of Canada (NSERC). This research was also supported by the Social Sciences and Humanities Research Council of Canada (SSHRC).The research was enabled in part by support provided by WestGrid (https://www.westgrid.ca/) and Compute Canada (www.computecanada.ca). We thank Omar Zaidan and Chris Callison-Burch for sharing the AOC data.

References

Martín Abadi, Paul Barham, Jianmin Chen, Zhifeng Chen, Andy Davis, Jeffrey Dean, Matthieu Devin, Sanjay Ghemawat, Geoffrey Irving, Michael Isard, et al. 2016. Tensorflow: A system for large-scale machine learning. In *OSDI*, volume 16, pages 265–283.

Muhammad Abdul-Mageed, Anneke Buffone, Hao Peng, Johannes C Eichstaedt, and Lyle H Ungar. 2017. Recognizing pathogenic empathy in social media. In *ICWSM*, pages 448–451.

Muhammad Abdul-Mageed, Hassan Alhuzali, and Mohamed Elaraby. 2018. You tweet what you speak: A city-level dataset of arabic dialects. In *LREC*, pages 3653–3659.

Muhammad Abdul-Mageed. 2015. *Subjectivity and sentiment analysis of Arabic as a morophologically-rich language*. Ph.D. thesis, Indiana University.

Muhammad Abdul-Mageed. 2017. Modeling arabic subjectivity and sentiment in lexical space. *Information Processing & Management*.

Steven Abney and Steven Bird. 2010. The human language project: building a universal corpus of the world's languages. In *Proceedings of the 48th annual meeting of the association for computational linguistics*, pages 88–97. Association for Computational Linguistics.

Ahmed Ali, Najim Dehak, Patrick Cardinal, Sameer Khurana, Sree Harsha Yella, James Glass, Peter Bell, and Steve Renals. 2015. Automatic dialect detection in arabic broadcast speech. *arXiv preprint arXiv:1509.06928*.

Dzmitry Bahdanau, Kyunghyun Cho, and Yoshua Bengio. 2014. Neural machine translation by jointly learning to align and translate. *arXiv preprint arXiv:1409.0473*.

Yonatan Belinkov and James Glass. 2016. A character-level convolutional neural network for distinguishing similar languages and dialects. *arXiv preprint arXiv:1609.07568*.

François Chollet et al. 2015. Keras.

Jan K Chorowski, Dzmitry Bahdanau, Dmitriy Serdyuk, Kyunghyun Cho, and Yoshua Bengio. 2015. Attention-based models for speech recognition. In *Advances in neural information processing systems*, pages 577–585.

Junyoung Chung, Caglar Gulcehre, KyungHyun Cho, and Yoshua Bengio. 2014. Empirical evaluation of gated recurrent neural networks on sequence modeling. *arXiv preprint arXiv:1412.3555*.

Ryan Cotterell and Chris Callison-Burch. 2014. A multi-dialect, multi-genre corpus of informal written arabic. In *LREC*, pages 241–245.

Kareem Darwish, Hassan Sajjad, and Hamdy Mubarak. 2014. Verifiably effective arabic dialect identification. In *Proceedings of the 2014 Conference on Empirical Methods in Natural Language Processing (EMNLP)*, pages 1465–1468.

Mona Diab, Nizar Habash, Owen Rambow, Mohamed Altantawy, and Yassine Benajiba. 2010. Colaba: Arabic dialect annotation and processing. In *Lrec workshop on semitic language processing*, pages 66–74.

Heba Elfardy and Mona Diab. 2013. Sentence level dialect identification in arabic. In *Proceedings of the 51st Annual Meeting of the Association for Computational Linguistics (Volume 2: Short Papers)*, volume 2, pages 456–461.

Heba Elfardy, Mohamed Al-Badrashiny, and Mona Diab. 2014. Aida: Identifying code switching in informal arabic text. In *Proceedings of The First Workshop on Computational Approaches to Code Switching*, pages 94–101.

Nizar Habash, Mona T Diab, and Owen Rambow. 2012. Conventional orthography for dialectal arabic. In *LREC*, pages 711–718.

Nizar Y Habash. 2010. Introduction to arabic natural language processing. *Synthesis Lectures on Human Language Technologies*, 3(1):1–187.

Bartosz Hawelka, Izabela Sitko, Euro Beinat, Stanislav Sobolevsky, Pavlos Kazakopoulos, and Carlo Ratti. 2014. Geo-located twitter as proxy for global mobility patterns. *Cartography and Geographic Information Science*, 41(3):260–271.

Sepp Hochreiter and Jürgen Schmidhuber. 1997. Long short-term memory. *Neural computation*, 9(8):1735–1780.

Fei Huang. 2015. Improved arabic dialect classification with social media data. In *Proceedings of the 2015 Conference on Empirical Methods in Natural Language Processing*, pages 2118–2126.

Tommi Jauhiainen, Krister Lindén, and Heidi Jauhiainen. 2017. Evaluation of language identification methods using 285 languages. In *Proceedings of the 21st Nordic Conference on Computational Linguistics*, pages 183–191.

Tommi Jauhiainen, Marco Lui, Marcos Zampieri, Timothy Baldwin, and Krister Lindén. 2018. Automatic language identification in texts: A survey. *arXiv preprint arXiv:1804.08186*.

Raja Jurdak, Kun Zhao, Jiajun Liu, Maurice AbouJaoude, Mark Cameron, and David Newth. 2015. Understanding human mobility from twitter. *PloS one*, 10(7):e0131469.

David Jurgens, Yulia Tsvetkov, and Dan Jurafsky. 2017. Incorporating dialectal variability for socially equitable language identification. In *Proceedings of the 55th Annual Meeting of the Association for Computational Linguistics (Volume 2: Short Papers)*, volume 2, pages 51–57.

Yoon Kim. 2014. Convolutional neural networks for sentence classification. *arXiv preprint arXiv:1408.5882*.

Tom Kocmi and Ondřej Bojar. 2017. Lanidenn: Multilingual language identification on character window. *arXiv preprint arXiv:1701.03338*.

Wang Ling, Guang Xiang, Chris Dyer, Alan Black, and Isabel Trancoso. 2013. Microblogs as parallel corpora. In *Proceedings of the 51st Annual Meeting of the Association for Computational Linguistics (Volume 1: Long Papers)*, volume 1, pages 176–186.

Thomas Louail, Maxime Lenormand, Oliva G Cantu Ros, Miguel Picornell, Ricardo Herranz, Enrique Frias-Martinez, José J Ramasco, and Marc Barthelemy. 2014. From mobile phone data to the spatial structure of cities. *Scientific reports*, 4:5276.

Marco Lui and Timothy Baldwin. 2012. langid. py: An off-the-shelf language identification tool. In *Proceedings of the ACL 2012 system demonstrations*, pages 25–30. Association for Computational Linguistics.

Jalal Mahmud, Jeffrey Nichols, and Clemens Drews. 2014. Home location identification of twitter users. *ACM Transactions on Intelligent Systems and Technology (TIST)*, 5(3):47.

Tomas Mikolov, Kai Chen, Greg Corrado, and Jeffrey Dean. 2013. Efficient estimation of word representations in vector space. *arXiv preprint arXiv:1301.3781*.

Vinod Nair and Geoffrey E Hinton. 2010. Rectified linear units improve restricted boltzmann machines. In *Proceedings of the 27th international conference on machine learning (ICML-10)*, pages 807–814.

Maryam Najafian, Sameer Khurana, Suwon Shon, Ahmed Ali, and James Glass. 2018. Exploiting convolutional neural networks for phonotactic based dialect identification. ICASSP.

Quynh C Nguyen, Dapeng Li, Hsien-Wen Meng, Suraj Kath, Elaine Nsoesie, Feifei Li, and Ming Wen. 2016. Building a national neighborhood dataset from geotagged twitter data for indicators of happiness, diet, and physical activity. *JMIR public health and surveillance*, 2(2).

Quynh C Nguyen, Kimberly D Brunisholz, Weijun Yu, Matt McCullough, Heidi A Hanson, Michelle L Litchman, Feifei Li, Yuan Wan, James A VanDerslice, Ming Wen, et al. 2017. Twitter-derived neighborhood characteristics associated with obesity and diabetes. *Scientific reports*, 7(1):16425.

Leysia Palen and Amanda L Hughes. 2018. Social media in disaster communication. In *Handbook of Disaster Research*, pages 497–518. Springer.

Fabian Pedregosa, Gaël Varoquaux, Alexandre Gramfort, Vincent Michel, Bertrand Thirion, Olivier Grisel, Mathieu Blondel, Peter Prettenhofer, Ron Weiss, Vincent Dubourg, et al. 2011. Scikit-learn: Machine learning in python. *Journal of machine learning research*, 12(Oct):2825–2830.

Afshin Rahimi, Trevor Cohn, and Timothy Baldwin. 2017. A neural model for user geolocation and lexical dialectology. *arXiv preprint arXiv:1704.04008*.

Afshin Rahimi, Trevor Cohn, and Tim Baldwin. 2018. Semi-supervised user geolocation via graph convolutional networks. *arXiv preprint arXiv:1804.08049*.

Takeshi Sakaki, Makoto Okazaki, and Yutaka Matsuo. 2010. Earthquake shakes twitter users: real-time event detection by social sensors. In *Proceedings of the 19th international conference on World wide web*, pages 851–860. ACM.

Suwon Shon, Ahmed Ali, and James Glass. 2017. Mit-qcri arabic dialect identification system for the 2017 multi-genre broadcast challenge. *arXiv preprint arXiv:1709.00387*.

Suwon Shon, Ahmed Ali, and James Glass. 2018. Convolutional neural networks and language embeddings for end-to-end dialect recognition. *arXiv preprint arXiv:1803.04567*.

Karen Sparck Jones. 1972. A statistical interpretation of term specificity and its application in retrieval. *Journal of documentation*, 28(1):11–21.

Christoph Tillmann, Saab Mansour, and Yaser Al-Onaizan. 2014. Improved sentence-level arabic dialect classification. In *Proceedings of the First Workshop on Applying NLP Tools to Similar Languages, Varieties and Dialects*, pages 110–119.

Ashish Vaswani, Noam Shazeer, Niki Parmar, Jakob Uszkoreit, Llion Jones, Aidan N Gomez, ukasz Kaiser, and Illia Polosukhin. 2017. Attention is all you need. In *Advances in Neural Information Processing Systems*, pages 6000–6010.

Yan Xu, Lili Mou, Ge Li, Yunchuan Chen, Hao Peng, and Zhi Jin. 2015. Classifying relations via long short term memory networks along shortest dependency paths. In *Proceedings of the 2015 Conference on Empirical Methods in Natural Language Processing*, pages 1785–1794.

Antonio Jimeno Yepes, Andrew MacKinlay, and Bo Han. 2015. Investigating public health surveillance using twitter. *Proceedings of BioNLP 15*, pages 164–170.

Omar F Zaidan and Chris Callison-Burch. 2011. The arabic online commentary dataset: an annotated dataset of informal arabic with high dialectal content. In *Proceedings of the 49th Annual Meeting of the Association for Computational Linguistics: Human Language Technologies: short papers-Volume 2*, pages 37–41. Association for Computational Linguistics.

Omar F Zaidan and Chris Callison-Burch. 2014. Arabic dialect identification. *Computational Linguistics*, 40(1):171–202.

Chunting Zhou, Chonglin Sun, Zhiyuan Liu, and Francis Lau. 2015. A c-lstm neural network for text classification. *arXiv preprint arXiv:1511.08630*.

Peng Zhou, Wei Shi, Jun Tian, Zhenyu Qi, Bingchen Li, Hongwei Hao, and Bo Xu. 2016. Attention-based bidirectional long short-term memory networks for relation classification. In *Proceedings of the 54th Annual Meeting of the Association for Computational Linguistics (Volume 2: Short Papers)*, volume 2, pages 207–212.

A Neural Approach to Language Variety Translation

Marta R. Costa-jussà[1], Marcos Zampieri[2], Santanu Pal[3]
[1]TALP Research Center, Universitat Politècnica de Catalunya, Barcelona, Spain
[2]Research Group in Computational Linguistics, University of Wolverhampton, U.K.
[3]Department of Language Science and Technology, Saarland University, Germany
`marta.ruiz@upc.edu`

Abstract

In this paper we present the first neural-based machine translation system trained to translate between standard national varieties of the same language. We take the pair Brazilian - European Portuguese as an example and compare the performance of this method to a phrase-based statistical machine translation system. We report a performance improvement of 0.9 BLEU points in translating from European to Brazilian Portuguese and 0.2 BLEU points when translating in the opposite direction. We also carried out a human evaluation experiment with native speakers of Brazilian Portuguese which indicates that humans prefer the output produced by the neural-based system in comparison to the statistical system.

1 Introduction

In the last five years Neural Machine Translation (NMT) has evolved from a new and promising paradigm in Machine Translation (MT) to an established state-of-the-art technology. A few studies pose that performance difference between Statistical Machine Translation (SMT) and NMT is not as a great as one could imagine (Castilho et al., 2017) while others show interesting challenges for NMT (compared to SMT) such as learning with limited amount of data, out-of-domain, long sentences, low frequency words or lack of word alignment model (Koehn and Knowles, 2017). Even so, NMT systems have constantly ranked in the top positions in the competitions held in MT conferences and workshops such as WMT (Bojar et al., 2016) and WAT (Nakazawa et al., 2016). They have also been achieving commercial success (e.g. Google's GNMT (Wu et al., 2016)).

Far from being settled, the architecture of NMT systems is constantly evolving. Given the youth of the paradigm and while the main structure of encoder-decoder is still maintained, the implementation of such is done either using recurrent neural networks (RNN) with attention mechanisms (Bahdanau et al., 2015), to convolutional neural networks (CNN) (Gehring et al., 2017) and to only attention mechanisms (Vaswani et al., 2017). For the same reason, research in NMT goes in many directions, including minimal units (Sennrich et al., 2016), unsupervised training and low resources (Artetxe et al., 2018) or transfer learning (Zoph et al., 2016), to name and cite just a few.

In this paper we tackle an under-explored problem and apply NMT techniques to translate between language varieties. In previous work (Costa-jussà, 2017), NMT has been used to translate between Spanish and Catalan, two closely-related Romance languages from the Iberian peninsula, outperforming phrase-based SMT approaches. In this paper we test whether this is also true for national varieties of the same language taking Brazilian and European Portuguese as a case study. To the best of our knowledge the use of NMT to translate between national language varieties has not yet been studied and this paper contributes to opening new avenues for future research.

This work is licensed under a Creative Commons Attribution 4.0 International License. License details: `http://creativecommons.org/licenses/by/4.0/`

Proceedings of the Fifth Workshop on NLP for Similar Languages, Varieties and Dialects, pages 275–282
Santa Fe, New Mexico, USA, August 20, 2018.

1.1 Linguistic Motivation

Translating[1] between varieties of pluricentric languages such as French, Portuguese, and Spanish is an important task carried out in localization companies and language service providers. In the case of Portuguese, although mutually intelligible, the varieties spoken in Brazil and Portugal differ substantially in terms of phonetics, syntax, and lexicon. In previous work, researchers have shown that texts from these two varieties can be discriminated using word and character n-gram-based models with 99% accuracy (Zampieri and Gebre, 2012).

Books written in Brazil are often edited when published in Portugal and vice-versa. Many companies adapt content, product instructions, and user manuals from one country to the other to meet the expectations of costumers and readers of the target country. Brazilian and European Portuguese – henceforth BP and EP – is therefore a particularly relevant and interesting language variety pair to investigate the use of NMT approaches.

A few of the most distinctive characteristics of these two language varieties are summarized next:

- **Orthographic differences:**[2] In the European variety muted consonants such as in *acto, baptismo* (EP) for *act, baptism* (EN) continue to be written whereas in the Brazilian variety for many decades speakers no longer write them *ato, batismo* (BP).

- **Verb tenses:** When expressing progressive events (e.g. *I am running* (EN)), the Brazilian variety prefers the gerund form *correndo* (BP) whereas the European one typically favors the use of the infinitive form *a correr* (EP).

- **Clitics:** Personal pronouns are used in different positions in the two varieties. European Portuguese speakers prefer the use of enclitic personal pronouns, that is after the verb, such as in *Ele viu-me* (EP) whereas Brazilian speakers would typically prefer to use personal pronouns in a proclitic position, before the verb, as in *Ele me viu* (BP) (*He saw me* (EN)).

- **Use of pronouns:** The use of the second person singular pronoun *tu* (*you* (EN)), is only restricted to regional use in Brazil but widespread in Portugal. BP speakers use *você* in most contexts whereas this form is considered to be a formal register in Portugal used only in specific formal contexts similar to the use of *tu - usted* in Spanish and *du - Sie* in German.

Apart from the aforementioned differences, lexical variation is abundant between these two varieties. Examples of these are preferences such as *nomeadamente* which is rare in BP and very frequent in EP and false cognates such as the word *propina*. Its most frequent sense in BP is *bribe* and in EP is *fee*.

2 Related Work

There have been a few papers published on translating texts between Brazilian and European Portuguese. One example is the work by Marujo et al. (2011) which proposed a rule-based system to adapt texts from BP to EP. Marujo et al. (2011) used comparable journalistic corpora available at Linguateca (Santos, 2014), namely CETEMPublico and CETEMFolha, a collection of texts collected from the Brazilian newspaper *Zero Hora*, and Ted Talks to evaluate their method.

Another example of a system developed to translate between Brazilian and European Portuguese is the one by Fancellu et al. (2014) who presented and SMT system trained on a parallel collection from Intel translation memories. The authors report 0.589 BLEU score using a Moses baseline system.

Apart from the two aforementioned studies on translating between Portuguese varieties there have been a few studies published on translating between similar languages, language varieties, and dialects of other languages. Examples of such studies include Zhang (1998) on Mandarin and Cantonese Chinese, Scannell (2006) on Irish and Scottish Gaelic, (Goyal and Lehal, 2010) on Hindi and Punjabi, a few studies

---

[1] In this paper, when talking about language varieties, we use the verbs *adapt, edit,* and *translate* interchangeably. In previous work Marujo et al. (2011) used the word *adaptation* whereas Fancellu et al. (2014) used the word *conversion*. We consider it, however, as a full-fledged translation task and approach the task as such.

[2] The 1990 orthographic agreement has been recently introduced in both countries diminishing these differences.

on Afrikaans and Dutch (Van Huyssteen and Pilon, 2009; Otte and Tyers, 2011), and Hassani (2017) on Kurdish dialects.

To the best of our knowledge, however, the use of NMT is under-explored in these tasks and no language variety translation system has been developed using NMT. The most similar study is the one by (Costa-jussà et al., 2017) who developed a neural-based MT system to translate between Catalan and Spanish. The use of NMT to translate between language varieties is the main contribution of our work.

3   Methods

To be able to compare MT approaches, we trained SMT and NMT systems using the same dataset described in Section 3.1. The two systems are described in detail in Section 3.2.

Systems within the SMT category use statistical techniques to compose the final translation. There are a variety of alternatives that are state-of-the art, including: n-gram (Mariño et al., 2006), syntax (Yamada and Knight, 2001) or hierarchical to name a few. In this paper, we are using the popular phrase-based system (Koehn et al., 2003).

Systems within the NMT category use a machine learning architecture based on neural networks to compose the final translation. As mentioned, there are several architectures which have been proven state-of-the-art, all of them based on an encoder-decoder schema but using either recurrent neural networks (Cho et al., 2014), convolutional neural networks (Gehring et al., 2017) or the transformer architecture based only on attention-based mechanisms (Vaswani et al., 2017). These architectures can be adapted to deal with different input representations either words, subwords (Sennrich et al., 2016), characters (Costa-jussà and Fonollosa, 2016; Lee et al., 2017) or bytes (Costa-jussà et al., 2017).

In this paper, we are using the first option of recurrent neural networks with an added attention-based mechanism (Bahdanau et al., 2015) and bytes as input representations (Costa-jussà et al., 2017).

3.1   Data

Compiling suitable parallel language variety corpora for NLP tasks is not trivial. Popular and freely available data sources (e.g. Wikipedia) used in NLP do not account for regional variation. One possible data source that includes national varieties of the same language are technical user manuals which are often localized between countries. However, user manuals contain a very specific technical language with short and idiomatic sentences representing commands.

We searched for suitable datasets and we acquired an aligned Brazilian - European Portuguese parallel corpus of film subtitle dialogues from Open Subtitles available at Opus[3] (Tiedemann, 2012). We removed all XML tags available in the data. The cleaned corpus, which we will be making available for the community as another contribution of our work[4], comprises 4.3 million sentences in each language for training, with over 33 million tokens for BP and over 34 million tokens for EP. Finally, 2,000 parallel sentences were kept for development and another 2,000 sentences for testing.

3.2   Systems

Statistical-based.   In a phrase-based system, the main model, which is the translation model, is extracted by statistical co-occurrences from a parallel corpus at the level of sentences. This translation model is combined in the decoder with other models to compose the most probable translation given a source input. We built a standard phrase-based system with Moses open source toolkit (Koehn et al., 2007). The main parameters of our implementation include: grow-diagonal-final-and word alignment symmetrization, lexicalized reordering, relative frequencies (conditional and posterior probabilities) with phrase discounting, lexical weights, phrase bonus, accepting phrases up to length 10, 5-gram language model with Kneser-Ney smoothing, word bonus and MERT (Minimum Error Rate Training) optimisation. These parameters are taken from previous work (Costa-jussà et al., 2017).

---

[3] http://opus.lingfil.uu.se/
[4] The clean version of the corpus is available upon request.

Neural-based. Specifically, neural MT computes the conditional probability of the target sentence given the source sentence by means of an encoder-decoder or sequence-to-sequence (seq2seq) architecture, where the encoder reads the source sentence, does a word embedding, and encodes it into an intermediate representation using a bidirectional recurrent neural network with Long Short Term Memory units (LSTM) as activation functions. Then, the decoder, which is also a recurrent neural network, generates translation based on this intermediate representation. This baseline seq2seq architecture is improved with an attention-based mechanism (Bahdanau et al., 2015) which allows for the introduction of contextual information while decoding. This architecture is extended to deal with bytes (Costa-jussà et al., 2017) to overcome unknown words. We are adopting the same parameters as set in mentioned previous work. We use an in-house Theano implementation based on code available[5]. We use a bidirectional LSTM of 512 units for encoding, a batch size of 32, no dropout and ADAM optimization. For more details about the architecture refer to previous work (Costa-jussà et al., 2017).

3.3 Human Evaluation

To validate the results obtained with the automatic evaluation metrics, we used the ranking and rating features available in CATaLog online (Pal et al., 2016a; Pal et al., 2016b), a web-based CAT tool developed for translation process research. We ask native speakers of Brazilian Portuguese first to compare segments translated by NMT and SMT, choosing the best output, and subsequently to rate translations taking both fluency and adequacy into account using a 1 to 7 Likert scale. More information and the results of these experiments are presented in Section 4.2.

4 Results

4.1 Automatic Metrics

In this section we present the results obtained by the statistical-based system based of phrases and the neural-based system based on seq2seq with attention and bytes in terms of BLEU score (Papineni et al., 2002). Table 1 presents the results obtained by the three systems when translating from EP to BP and Table 2 presents results obtained from BP to EP. The best results for each setting are presented in bold.

System	BLEU Score
Phrase-based SMT	47.68
Neural MT	**48.58**

Table 1: European to Brazilian Portuguese translation results in terms of BLEU score.

System	BLEU Score
Phrase-based SMT	47.34
Neural MT	**47.54**

Table 2: Brazilian to European Portuguese translation results in terms of BLEU score.

We observed that in both directions the NMT system outperformed the SMT approach. The neural system obtained the best performance translating from European to Brazilian Portuguese achieving 48.58 BLEU points on average, and from Brazilian to European Portuguese achieving 47.54 BLEU points on average. This performance was 0.9 and 0.2 BLEU points better than the average performance obtained by the SMT system.

---

[5]`https://github.com/nyu-dl/dl4mt-c2c`

4.2   Human Evaluation

Following the best practice in translation evaluation, as observed in the WMT shared tasks (Bojar et al., 2016; Bojar et al., 2017), we present two human evaluation experiments to validate the results obtained with the automatic evaluation metrics. The first one is a ranking experiment in which participants were asked to choose which translation of a given segment they preferred without knowing which system produced the translations. The second one is a pilot rating experiment in which participants were asked to rate translations using a 1 to 7 Likert scale.

We start by reporting the results obtained in the ranking experiment. We evaluated the quality of the EP-BP translation direction asking a group of seven native speakers of BP to rank sentences produced by the SMT system and by the NMT system. We presented native speakers with the source segment in EP and two translations in BP. Their task was to select the best output (ties were allowed). The decision to use only BP native speakers was motivated by the findings reported in (Goutte et al., 2016) which indicate that speakers of BP are generally not familiar with what is acceptable in the European variety and vice-versa.

We considered the full set of 2,000 test sentences and disregard sentences where 1) no transformation has been made (the source, outputs, and the reference are the same), and 2) transformations have been made but NMT and SMT outputs are the same. After filtering, 679 distinct segments were left for the human evaluation. We randomly selected 20% of these segments 679 (136 sentences) and presented them to two annotators to calculate inter-annotator agreement. Finally, the set of 815 segments, 679 segments plus 136 segments (20% redundancy), divided into 23 sub-sets and presented to each of the annotators. Each annotator evaluated between three and four sub-sets.

To assess the reliability of the rankings, we first compute the agreement between the annotators. We report substantial inter-annotator agreement achieving 0.88 pairwise Kappa score. We present the results obtained by the ranking experiment in terms of the percentage of segments in which 1) NMT was preferred by the annotator, 2) the two segments were consider the same, 3) SMT was preferred by the annotator. Results are summarized in Table 3. We observed that the NMT output was judged to be equal or better the SMT output in 57.81% of the cases. The NMT output was preferred in 48.43% of the rankings and judged to be of same quality as SMT in 9.38% of the cases.

Outcome	Percentage of Cases
NMT preferred	48.43%
Ties	9.38%
SMT preferred	42.19%

Table 3: Human evaluation scores - Raking experiment.

To further investigate how humans perceive the quality of the EP-BP translations, we carry out a pilot rating experiment with two of the aforementioned annotators. From the 679 segments included in the ranking experiment, we randomly selected 100 segments and create two sub-sets of 50 segments each. We provide each annotator with a sub-set and ask them to rate the translations taking both fluency and adequacy into account using a Likert scale of 1 to 7. The average results obtained by each system in the pilot rating experiment are presented in Table 4.

Outcome	Average Score
Neural MT	5.4
Phrase-based SMT	5.1

Table 4: Human evaluation scores - Ranking pilot experiment.

The average results suggest that humans have a rather positive opinion about the translations produced by both systems. The average score obtained by the NMT system was 5.4 whereas the SMT obtained 5.1. The outcomes of both the ranking and the rating experiments confirm that the NMT system produces a higher quality output than SMT for this task and that the improvement in BLEU score is indeed perceived by humans. We are currently replicating this pilot experiment with more annotators.

4.3 Discussion

We observed several interesting patterns in the NMT and SMT outputs and here we present a brief linguistic analysis of the output of both systems.

In our analysis, we observed that NMT was generally better in handling the transformation from the proclitic pronominal position generally used in BP to the enclitic pronominal position generally preferred in EP as shown in Example 1. This is just true for declarative-affirmative main clauses (other syntactic contexts involve proclisis).

(1) **SOURCE (EP)**: Fizeste-me chorar
    SMT: Fez chorar.
    NMT: Você me fez chorar.
    REFERENCE (BP): Me fez chorar.
    EN: You made me cry.

In Example 1 NMT produces the correct translation in a particularly challenging case in which *tu* was omitted in the source segment. Even when this re-ordering operation had to occur in the opposite direction, EP enclitic and BP proclitic, NMT was able to handle it better than SMT as demonstrated in Example 2.

(2) **SOURCE (EP)**: Nem me estás a ouvir, querido.
    SMT: Nem me está a ouvir, querido.
    NMT: Nem está me ouvindo, querido.
    REFERENCE (BP): Nem está me ouvindo, querido.
    EN: You are not even hearing me, honey.

NMT also proved to be better in translating the infinitive form used in EP *a ouvir* to the gerund preferred in BP *ouvindo* (EN: *doing*). Example 2 is a good example in which NMT produced a better output than SMT handling both pronominal positions and verb form correctly.

In Example 1 both systems translated *fizeste* from the second person singular *tu* preferred in EP to the third person singular *fez* as in *você fez* (EN: *you did*) preferred in BP. However, we observed a wide variation when handling the forms *tu* and *você* and their respective verbs. We spotted several translations in which SMT handled this phenomenon better than the NMT system as in Example 3.

(3) **SOURCE (EP)**: Tu não pedes nada a ninguém.
    SMT: Você não pede nada a ninguém.
    NMT: Tu não pedes nada a ninguém.
    REFERENCE (BP): E você jamais pediria nada, não é?
    EN: You don't ask anything to anyone.

Finally, it is important to note that, as evidenced in Example 3, in many cases the reference BP translation was substantially or completely different from the EP source. This is probably related to the data domain, movie subtitles, which presents a great deal of variability and encourages creative translations, in this case from the language of the movie to the respective variety of Portuguese. This variability certainly led both systems to obtain lower BLEU scores. Nevertheless, the results of the pilot rating experiment indicate that humans have a rather positive opinion about both systems' output and that NMT is preferred.

5 Conclusion and Future Work

This paper presented the first NMT system trained to translate between national language varieties. We used the language variety pair Brazilian and European Portuguese as an example and a parallel corpus of subtitles to train the NMT system.

Compared to an SMT system trained on the same data, we report a performance improvement of 0.9 BLEU points in translating from European to Brazilian Portuguese and 0.2 BLEU points when translating in the opposite direction. Our results indicate that the NMT system produces better translations than the SMT system not only in terms of BLEU scores but also according to the judgments of seven native speakers. The human evaluation experiments contribute to recent empirical evaluations on the quality of NMT output beyond automatic metrics (Castilho et al., 2017).

We would like to carry out a more comprehensive human evaluation experiment in future work. This includes a rating experiment with more annotators and replicating the EP to BP evaluation to the BP to EP translations. A pilot experiment with EP speakers indicates that NMT output is also preferred. We would like to measure the cognitive effort and post-editing time for both SMT and NMT outputs. This could provide valuable information for translation and localization companies about translation productivity. Finally, and since NMT is progressing fast, future comparisons will be built with other NMT architectures like (Vaswani et al., 2017).

Acknowledgments

We would like to thank the annotators who helped us with the human evaluation experiments. This work is supported in part by the Spanish Ministerio de Economía y Competitividad, the European Regional Development Fund and the Agencia Estatal de Investigación, through the postdoctoral senior grant Ramón y Cajal, the contract TEC2015-69266-P (MINECO/FEDER,EU) and the contract PCIN-2017-079 (AEI/MINECO).

References

Mikel Artetxe, Gorka Labaka, Eneko Agirre, and Kyunghyun Cho. 2018. Unsupervised neural machine translation. In *Proceedings of ICLR*.

Dzmitry Bahdanau, Kyunghyun Cho, and Yoshua Bengio. 2015. Neural machine translation by jointly learning to align and tran slate. *CoRR*, abs/1409.0473.

Ondrej Bojar, Rajen Chatterjee, Christian Federmann, Yvette Graham, Barry Haddow, Matthias Huck, Antonio Jimeno Yepes, Philipp Koehn, Varvara Logacheva, Christof Monz, et al. 2016. Findings of the 2016 Conference on Machine Translation (WMT16). In *Proceedings of WMT*.

Ondřej Bojar, Rajen Chatterjee, Christian Federmann, Yvette Graham, Barry Haddow, Shujian Huang, Matthias Huck, Philipp Koehn, Qun Liu, Varvara Logacheva, et al. 2017. Findings of the 2017 Conference on Machine Translation (WMT17). In *Proceedings of WMT*.

Sheila Castilho, Joss Moorkens, Federico Gaspari, Iacer Calixto, John Tinsley, and Andy Way. 2017. Is Neural Machine Translation the New State of the Art? *The Prague Bulletin of Mathematical Linguistics*, 108(1):109–120.

Kyunghyun Cho, Bart van Merrienboer, Dzmitry Bahdanau, and Yoshua Bengio. 2014. On the properties of neural machine translation: Encoder–decoder approaches. In *Proceedings of SSST*.

Marta R. Costa-jussà and José A. R. Fonollosa. 2016. Character-based Neural Machine Translation. In *Proceedings of ACL*.

Marta R. Costa-jussà, Carlos Escolano, and José A. R. Fonollosa. 2017. Byte-based neural machine translation. In *Proceedings of the First Workshop on Subword and Character Level Models in NLP*.

Marta R. Costa-jussà. 2017. Why Catalan-Spanish Neural Machine Translation? Analysis, Comparison and Combination with Standard Rule and Phrase-based Technologies. In *Proceedings of VarDial*.

Federico Fancellu, Andy Way, and Morgan O'Brien. 2014. Standard Language Variety Conversion for Content Localisation via SMT. In *Proceedings of EAMT*.

Jonas Gehring, Michael Auli, David Grangier, Denis Yarats, and Yann N Dauphin. 2017. Convolutional sequence to sequence learning. *arXiv preprint arXiv:1705.03122*.

Cyril Goutte, Serge Léger, Shervin Malmasi, and Marcos Zampieri. 2016. Discriminating Similar Languages: Evaluations and Explorations. *Proceedings of LREC*.

Vishal Goyal and Gurpreet Singh Lehal. 2010. Web based Hindi to Punjabi Machine Translation System. *Journal of Emerging Technologies in Web Intelligence*, 2(2):148–151.

Hossein Hassani. 2017. Kurdish Interdialect Machine Translation. *Proceedings of VarDial*.

Philipp Koehn and Rebecca Knowles. 2017. Six challenges for neural machine translation. In *Proceedings of the NMT Workshop*, pages 28–39, Vancouver.

Philipp Koehn, Franz Josef Och, and Daniel Marcu. 2003. Statistical phrase-based translation. In *Proceedings of NAACL-HLT*.

Philipp Koehn, Hieu Hoang, Alexandra Birch, Chris Callison-Burch, Marcello Federico, Nicola Bertoldi, Brooke Cowan, Wade Shen, Christine Moran, Richard Zens, Chris Dyer, Ondřej Bojar, Alexandra Constantin, and Evan Herbst. 2007. Moses: Open source toolkit for statistical machine translation. In *Proceedings of ACL*.

Jason Lee, Kyunghyun Cho, and Thomas Hofmann. 2017. Fully character-level neural machine translation without explicit segmentation. *Transactions of the Association for Computational Linguistics*, 5:365–378.

José B. Mariño, Rafael E. Banchs, Adrià Crego, Josep M. an d de Gispert, Patrik Lambert, José A. R. Fonollosa, and Marta R. Cõsta jussà. 2006. N-gram-based machine translation. *Computational Linguistics*, 32(4):527–549, December.

Luıs Marujo, Nuno Grazina, Tiago Luıs, Wang Ling, Luısa Coheur, and Isabel Trancoso. 2011. BP2EP–Adaptation of Brazilian Portuguese texts to European Portuguese. In *Proceedings of EAMT*.

Toshiaki Nakazawa, Hideya Mino, Chenchen Ding, Isao Goto, Graham Neubig, Sadao Kurohashi, and Eiichiro Sumita. 2016. Overview of the 3rd Workshop on Asian Translation. *Proceedings of WAT*.

Pim Otte and Francis M Tyers. 2011. Rapid Rule-based Machine Translation between Dutch and Afrikaans. In *Proceedings of EAMT*.

Santanu Pal, Sudip Kumar Naskar, Marcos Zampieri, Tapas Nayak, and Josef van Genabith. 2016a. CATaLog Online: A Web-based CAT Tool for Distributed Translation with Data Capture for APE and Translation Process Research. In *Proceedings of COLING*.

Santanu Pal, Marcos Zampieri, Sudip Kumar Naskar, Tapas Nayak, Mihaela Vela, and Josef van Genabith. 2016b. CATaLog Online: Porting a Post-editing Tool to the Web. In *Proceedings of LREC*.

Kishore Papineni, Salim Roukos, Todd Ward, and Wei-Jing Zhu. 2002. BLEU: A Method for Automatic Evaluation of Machine Translation. In *Proceedings of ACL*.

Diana Santos. 2014. Corpora at Linguateca: Vision and Roads Taken. *Working with Portuguese Corpora*, pages 219–236.

Kevin P. Scannell. 2006. Machine Translation for Closely Related Language Pairs. In *Proceedings of the Workshop Strategies for Developing Machine Translation for Minority Languages*.

Rico Sennrich, Barry Haddow, and Alexandra Birch. 2016. Neural machine translation of rare words with subword units. In *Proceedings of ACL*.

Jörg Tiedemann. 2012. Parallel Data, Tools and Interfaces in OPUS. In *Proceedings of LREC*.

Gerhard B Van Huyssteen and Suléne Pilon. 2009. Rule-based Conversion of Closely-related Languages: a Dutch-to-Afrikaans Convertor.

Ashish Vaswani, Noam Shazeer, Niki Parmar, Jakob Uszkoreit, Llion Jones, Aidan N. Gomez, Lukasz Kaiser, and Illia Polosukhin. 2017. Attention is all you need. *CoRR*, abs/1706.03762.

Yonghui Wu, Mike Schuster, Zhifeng Chen, Quoc V Le, Mohammad Norouzi, Wolfgang Macherey, Maxim Krikun, Yuan Cao, Qin Gao, Klaus Macherey, et al. 2016. Google's Neural Machine Translation System: Bridging the Gap Between Human and Machine Translation. *arXiv preprint arXiv:1609.08144*.

Kenji Yamada and Kevin Knight. 2001. A syntax-based statistical translation model. In *Proceedings of ACL*.

Marcos Zampieri and Binyam Gebrekidan Gebre. 2012. Automatic Identification of Language Varieties: The Case of Portuguese. In *Proceedings of KONVENS*.

Xiaoheng Zhang. 1998. Dialect MT: A Case Study Between Cantonese and Mandarin. In *Proceedings of ACL*.

Barret Zoph, Deniz Yuret, Jonathan May, and Kevin Knight. 2016. Transfer Learning for Low-Resource Neural Machine Translation. In *Proceedings of EMNLP*.

Character Level Convolutional Neural Network
for Indo-Aryan Language Identification

Mohamed Ali
Cairo University, Egypt
mohamedali@aucegypt.edu

Abstract

This paper presents the systems submitted by the safina team to the Indo-Aryan Language Identification (ILI) shared task at the VarDial Evaluation Campaign 2018. The ILI shared task included
5 closely-related languages of Indo-Aryan language family: Hindi (also known as Khari Boli),
Braj Bhasha, Awadhi, Bhojpuri and Magahi. The proposed approach is to use character-level
convolution neural network to distinguish the four dialects. We submitted three models with the
same architecture except for the first layer. The first system uses one-hot char representation as
input to the convolution layer. The second system uses an embedding layer before the convolution layer. The third system uses a recurrent layer before the convolution layer. The best results
were obtained using the first model achieving 86.27% F1-score, ranked the fourth among eight
teams.[1]

1 Introduction

Indo-Aryan is the largest and the dominant language families in the Indian subcontinent. There is no
single classification of these languages. Indo-Aryan Language Identification shared task concerned with
identifying 5 closely-related languages of Indo-Aryan language family: Hindi (also known as Khari
Boli), Braj Bhasha, Awadhi, Bhojpuri and Magahi. This is the first iteration of the ILI shared task at
VarDial.

In this paper we present the safina team's submissions for the 2018 ILI shared task which was
organized as a part of Vardial Evaluation Campaign 2018 (Zampieri et al., 2018). We have used
Char-level Convolutional Neural Network approach to identify Indo-Aryan languages using lexical
features. Our team ranked the fourth with F1-weighted score 86.27%.

2 Related Work

Language identification has two flavors: identifying language in spoken text and identifying language
in written text. Research in Indo-Aryan Language Identification took place in the two flavors. For the
spoken form, Rao et al. (2010) developed Auto Associative Neural Network (AANN) model to identify
five prominent dialects of Hindi: Chattisgharhi (spoken in central India), Bengali (Bengali accented
Hindi spoken in Eastern region), Marathi (Marathi accented Hindi spoken in Western region), General
(Hindi spoken in Northern region) and Telugu (Telugu accented Hindi spoken in Southern region). They
examined using spectral and prosodic features to distinguish among those dialects and their best results
using a combination of both the spectral and prosodic features. Rao and Koolagudi (2011) explored
using Support Vector Machines algorithm which performed poorly compared to AANN. Sinha et al.
(2014) used a fully connected Feed Forward Neural Network model four dialects of Hindi: Khariboli,

---

[1]The code for our submissions is available at: https://github.com/bigooooh/ili

This work is licensed under a Creative Commons Attribution 4.0 International License. License details: http://
creativecommons.org/licenses/by/4.0/.

Proceedings of the Fifth Workshop on NLP for Similar Languages, Varieties and Dialects, pages 283–287
Santa Fe, New Mexico, USA, August 20, 2018.

Bhojpuri, Haryanvi and Bagheli. They also used spectral and prosodic features to train their classifier.

For the written form, Indhuja et al. (2014) examined using word and character n-grams to discriminate among five languages used in India (Hindi, Sanskrit, Marathi, Nepali and Bhojpuri). They reported that using word unigrams achieved the best results then character trigrams. However, their findings conflicted with Kumar et al. (2018) who found that using character n-grams significantly out performed using word n-grams in discriminating the same five languages.

3   Methodology and Data

3.1   Character-Level Convolutional Neural Network

Convolutional Neural Networks (CNN) were invented to deal with images and it have achieved excellent results in computer vision (Krizhevsky et al., 2012; Sermanet et al., 2013; Ji et al., 2013). Later, it have been applied in Natural Language Processing (NLP) tasks and outperformed traditional models such as bag of words, n-grams and their TFIDF variants (Zhang et al., 2015). The architecture, shown in Figure 1, describes the character-level CNN model we have used in identifying the Indo-Aryan languages. We formulate the task as a multi-class classification problem. Given text transcript $t^{(i)}$ and the corresponding label $l^{(i)}$, we need to predict l using t. We designed a neural network classifier that takes as input the transcript as one-hot encoded array of characters (padded or truncated from the end to match a predefined maximum length corresponding to the length of the network input layer). The network final output is the probability distribution over the 5 Indo-Aryan languages. The network layers are as follows:

- **Input Layer:** mapping each character to one-hot vector.

- Optional **Embedding or Recurrent Layer :** using embedding or GRU recurrent layer to capture the context of the character (Chung et al., 2014). In the embedding layer case, a list of embedded vectors, one for each character, will fed into the convolutional layer. In the recurrent layer case, using the "return sequences" option will allow it to return one hidden state output vector for each input character. The list of the hidden state output vectors will be fed into the convolutional layer.

- **Convolutional Layer:** contains multiple filter widths and feature maps which is applied to window of characters to produce new features. Each convolution is followed by a Rectified Linear Unit (ReLU) nonlinearity and batch-normalization layers (Glorot et al., 2011; Ioffe and Szegedy, 2015) .

- **Max-Pooling Layer:** apply max-over-time pooling operation over the feature map of each filter and take the maximum value as a feature for this filter (Collobert et al., 2011). The max-pooling operation is followed by a dropout layer to prevent over-fitting (Srivastava et al., 2014).

- **Softmax Layers**: represents the probability distribution over the labels.

Depending on our cross-validation results we used the following parameters for the neural network architecture:

- **Sentence maximum length:** 256 characters

- **Embedding length:**32

- **GRU layer unites:**128

- **Convolution filters sizes:** from 2 to 8

- **Convolution filters feature maps:** 256 feature map for each filter

- **Dropout rate:** 0.2

In our implementation, we used Keras framework with TensorFlow as a backend (Chollet and others, 2015; Abadi et al., 2015).

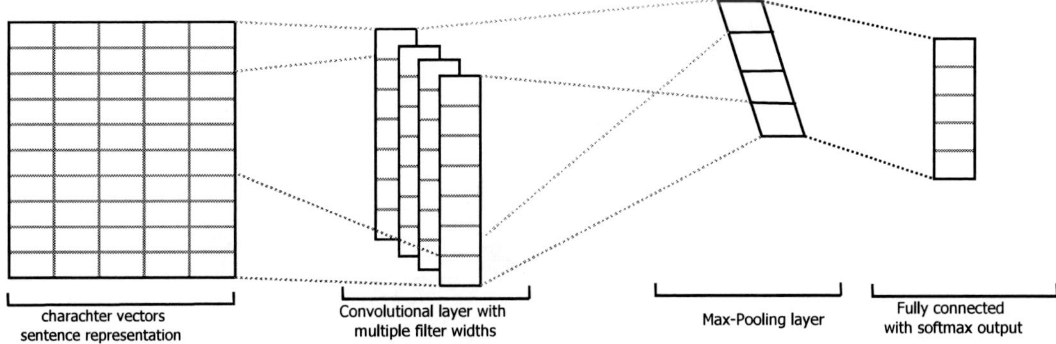

Figure 1: Character-level CNN architecture

3.2 Data

(Kumar et al., 2018) collected a corpus for the five Indo-Aryan languages. The corpus contains about 50,000 sentences distributed over the five languages as shown in Table 1. The authors divided the dataset into: 80% for training and 20% for testing.

Language	number of sentences
Hindi	10,000
Braj	10,000
Bhojpuri	10,000
Magahi	10,000
Awadhi	9,744

Table 1: Number of sentences for each language in the dataset

4 Results

4.1 Cross-Validation Results

We combined the training data and the validation data provided by the shared task to apply 5-fold cross validation. We tested our three different configurations in addition to a TF-IDF features based classifier, Logistic Regression classifier implemented in scikit-learn toolkit (Pedregosa et al., 2011), as a baseline. Results are shown in Table 2.

System	Accuracy
Logistic Regression using TF-IDF features	0.7946
CNN with one-hot encoded input	0.9722
CNN with an embedding layer	0.9718
CNN with a GRU recurrent layer	**0.9774**

Table 2: Cross-validation results

4.2 Test Set Results

Our three runs results are shown in Table 4. We have used the same configuration for three runs except for the input to the convolution layer. In the first run, we fed the one-hot encoded vectors for the sequence of characters directly to the convolution layer. In the second run, we fed the one-hot encoded

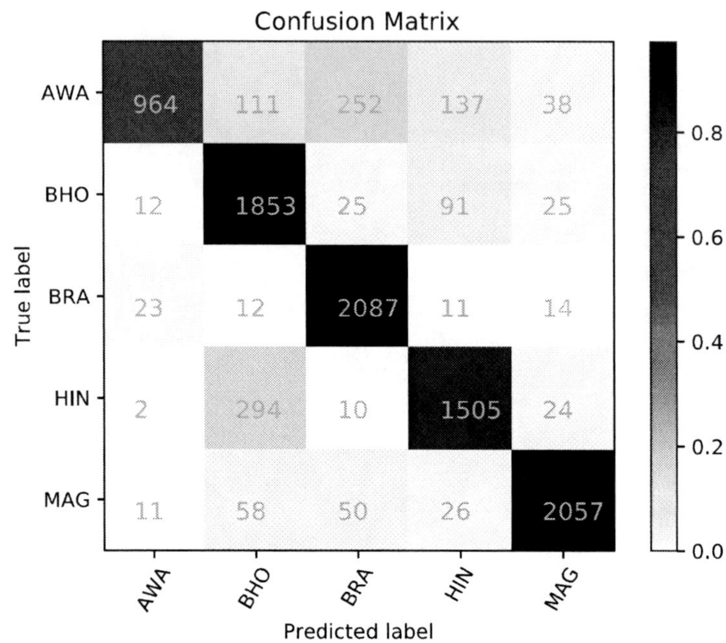

Figure 2: Confusion matrix for our ILI best run

vectors to an embedding layer before the convolution layer. In the third run, we fed the one-hot encoded vectors to a GRU recurrent layer before the convolution layer. As shown in the results, feeding the one-hot encoded representation directly to the convolution layer achieved the best results. This was a surprise for us as it conflicts with our results in the German and Arabic Dialect Identification sub-tasks where using a GRU recurrent layer outperformed feeding one-hot encoded directly to the convolution layer. This may be happened as result of using a large size dataset in the ILI sub-task compared to the ADI and the GDI sub-tasks. In the ILI shared task evaluation, the submitted systems were ranked according to its F1-weighted score. Our team ranked the fourth with F1-weighted score 86.27%. Figure 2 shows the confusion matrix for our best run. From the matrix, we can see that Awadhi and Hindi languages are a little bit confused with the Braj Bhasha and Bhojpuri languages respectively.

System	F1 (macro)
Random Baseline	0.2024
CNN with one-hot encoded input	**0.8627**
CNN with an embedding layer	0.8435
CNN with a GRU recurrent layer	0.8260

Table 3: Our three runs results, the best run in bold

5 Conclusion

In this work, we presented our team's three submissions for the ILI shared task. Our approach is to use Character level CNN as a feature extractor from text. Our best submission achieved by feeding the one-hot vector representation of the text as a list of characters directly to the convolution layer without an embedding layer. This abnormal results, compared to our submissions to the the ADI and GDI shared tasks, may be a consequence of using a larger data set in the ILI task.

References

Martín Abadi, Ashish Agarwal, Paul Barham, Eugene Brevdo, Zhifeng Chen, Craig Citro, Greg S. Corrado, Andy Davis, Jeffrey Dean, Matthieu Devin, Sanjay Ghemawat, Ian Goodfellow, Andrew Harp, Geoffrey Irving, Michael Isard, Yangqing Jia, Rafal Jozefowicz, Lukasz Kaiser, Manjunath Kudlur, Josh Levenberg, Dandelion Mané, Rajat Monga, Sherry Moore, Derek Murray, Chris Olah, Mike Schuster, Jonathon Shlens, Benoit Steiner, Ilya Sutskever, Kunal Talwar, Paul Tucker, Vincent Vanhoucke, Vijay Vasudevan, Fernanda Viégas, Oriol Vinyals, Pete Warden, Martin Wattenberg, Martin Wicke, Yuan Yu, and Xiaoqiang Zheng. 2015. TensorFlow: Large-scale machine learning on heterogeneous systems. Software available from tensorflow.org.

François Chollet et al. 2015. Keras. `https://keras.io`.

Junyoung Chung, Caglar Gulcehre, KyungHyun Cho, and Yoshua Bengio. 2014. Empirical evaluation of gated recurrent neural networks on sequence modeling. *arXiv preprint arXiv:1412.3555*.

Ronan Collobert, Jason Weston, Léon Bottou, Michael Karlen, Koray Kavukcuoglu, and Pavel Kuksa. 2011. Natural language processing (almost) from scratch. *Journal of Machine Learning Research*, 12(Aug):2493–2537.

Xavier Glorot, Antoine Bordes, and Yoshua Bengio. 2011. Deep sparse rectifier neural networks. In *Proceedings of the Fourteenth International Conference on Artificial Intelligence and Statistics*, pages 315–323.

K Indhuja, M Indu, C Sreejith, Palakkad Sreekrishnapuram, and PC Reghu Raj. 2014. Text based language identification system for indian languages following devanagiri script. *International Journal of Engineering*, 3(4).

Sergey Ioffe and Christian Szegedy. 2015. Batch normalization: Accelerating deep network training by reducing internal covariate shift. *arXiv preprint arXiv:1502.03167*.

Shuiwang Ji, Wei Xu, Ming Yang, and Kai Yu. 2013. 3d convolutional neural networks for human action recognition. *IEEE transactions on pattern analysis and machine intelligence*, 35(1):221–231.

Alex Krizhevsky, Ilya Sutskever, and Geoffrey E Hinton. 2012. Imagenet classification with deep convolutional neural networks. In *Advances in neural information processing systems*, pages 1097–1105.

Ritesh Kumar, Bornini Lahiri, Deepak Alok, Atul Kr. Ojha, Mayank Jain, Abdul Basit, and Yogesh Dawar. 2018. Automatic Identification of Closely-related Indian Languages: Resources and Experiments. In *Proceedings of the Eleventh International Conference on Language Resources and Evaluation (LREC)*.

F. Pedregosa, G. Varoquaux, A. Gramfort, V. Michel, B. Thirion, O. Grisel, M. Blondel, P. Prettenhofer, R. Weiss, V. Dubourg, J. Vanderplas, A. Passos, D. Cournapeau, M. Brucher, M. Perrot, and E. Duchesnay. 2011. Scikit-learn: Machine learning in Python. *Journal of Machine Learning Research*, 12:2825–2830.

K Sreenivasa Rao and Shashidhar G Koolagudi. 2011. Identification of hindi dialects and emotions using spectral and prosodic features of speech. *IJSCI: International Journal of Systemics, Cybernetics and Informatics*, 9(4):24–33.

K Sreenivasa Rao, Sourav Nandy, and Shashidhar G Koolagudi. 2010. Identification of hindi dialects using speech. *WMSCI-2010*.

Pierre Sermanet, David Eigen, Xiang Zhang, Michaël Mathieu, Rob Fergus, and Yann LeCun. 2013. Overfeat: Integrated recognition, localization and detection using convolutional networks. *arXiv preprint arXiv:1312.6229*.

Shweta Sinha, Aruna Jain, and Shyam S Agrawal. 2014. Speech processing for hindi dialect recognition. In *Advances in Signal Processing and Intelligent Recognition Systems*, pages 161–169. Springer.

Nitish Srivastava, Geoffrey Hinton, Alex Krizhevsky, Ilya Sutskever, and Ruslan Salakhutdinov. 2014. Dropout: A simple way to prevent neural networks from overfitting. *The Journal of Machine Learning Research*, 15(1):1929–1958.

Marcos Zampieri, Shervin Malmasi, Preslav Nakov, Ahmed Ali, Suwon Shon, James Glass, Yves Scherrer, Tanja Samardžić, Nikola Ljubešić, Jörg Tiedemann, Chris van der Lee, Stefan Grondelaers, Nelleke Oostdijk, Antal van den Bosch, Ritesh Kumar, Bornini Lahiri, and Mayank Jain. 2018. Language Identification and Morphosyntactic Tagging: The Second VarDial Evaluation Campaign. In *Proceedings of the Fifth Workshop on NLP for Similar Languages, Varieties and Dialects (VarDial)*, Santa Fe, USA.

Xiang Zhang, Junbo Zhao, and Yann LeCun. 2015. Character-level convolutional networks for text classification. In *Advances in neural information processing systems*, pages 649–657.

German Dialect Identification Using Classifier Ensembles

Alina Maria Ciobanu[1], Shervin Malmasi[2], Liviu P. Dinu[1]
[1]University of Bucharest, Romania
[2]Harvard Medical School, United States
`alina.ciobanu@my.fmi.unibuc.ro`

Abstract

In this paper we present the GDI_classification entry to the second German Dialect Identification (GDI) shared task organized within the scope of the VarDial Evaluation Campaign 2018. We present a system based on SVM classifier ensembles trained on characters and words. The system was trained on a collection of speech transcripts of five Swiss-German dialects provided by the organizers. The transcripts included in the dataset contained speakers from Basel, Bern, Lucerne, and Zurich. Our entry in the challenge reached 62.03% F1 score and was ranked third out of eight teams.

1 Introduction

Discriminating between dialects and language varieties is a challenging aspect of language identification that sparked interest in the NLP community in the past few years. As evidenced in a recent survey (Jauhiainen et al., 2018), a number of papers have been published on this topic on dialects of Arabic (Tillmann et al., 2014) and Romanian (Ciobanu and Dinu, 2016), and language varieties of English (Lui and Cook, 2013) and Portuguese (Zampieri et al., 2016).

This challenge motivated the organization of a number of competitions such as the Discriminating between Similar Languages (DSL) shared tasks which included language varieties and similar languages (Zampieri et al., 2014; Zampieri et al., 2015; Malmasi et al., 2016b), the MGB challenge 2017 (Ali et al., 2017) on Arabic, the PAN lab on author profiling, which in 2017 included varieties and dialects (Rangel et al., 2017), and finally the first German Dialect Identification (GDI) shard task in 2017 (Zampieri et al., 2017). The GDI shared task 2017 preceded the second GDI shared task (Zampieri et al., 2018) in which our team, GDI_classification, participated.

In this paper we describe the GDI_classification system trained to identify four dialects of (Swiss) German. The GDI dataset included speech transcripts from speakers from Basel, Bern, Lucerne, and Zurich. The system is based on an ensemble of multiple SVM classifiers trained on words and characters as features. Our approach is inspired by the approach of Malmasi and Zampieri (2017b), which was ranked first in the first edition of the GDI task and also performed well on identifying dialects of Arabic (Malmasi and Zampieri, 2017a). We build on the experience of previous work of members of the GDI_classification team improving a system that we have previously applied to a similar classification task, namely author profiling (Ciobanu et al., 2017).

2 Related Work: The First GDI Shared Task

There have been a few studies on German dialect identification published before the first GDI shared task, using different corpora and evaluation methods (Scherrer and Rambow, 2010; Hollenstein and Aepli, 2015). To the best of our knowledge, the first GDI shared task organized in 2017 was the first attempt to provide a benchmark for this task.

This work is licensed under a Creative Commons Attribution 4.0 International License. License details: `http://creativecommons.org/licenses/by/4.0/`

Proceedings of the Fifth Workshop on NLP for Similar Languages, Varieties and Dialects, pages 288–294
Santa Fe, New Mexico, USA, August 20, 2018.

The GDI shared task 2017 setup and dataset were similar to those of the 2018 edition presented in more detail in Section 3. The results of the 2017 edition along with a reference to each system description paper are presented in Table 1.

Rank	Team	F1 (weighted)	Reference
1	MAZA	0.662	(Malmasi and Zampieri, 2017b)
2	CECL	0.661	(Bestgen, 2017)
3	CLUZH	0.653	(Clematide and Makarov, 2017)
4	qcri_mit	0.639	-
5	unibuckernel	0.637	(Ionescu and Butnaru, 2017)
6	tubasfs	0.626	(Çöltekin and Rama, 2017)
7	ahaqst	0.614	(Hanani et al., 2017)
8	Citius_Ixa_Imaxin	0.612	(Gamallo et al., 2017)
9	XAC_Bayesline	0.605	(Barbaresi, 2017)
10	deepCybErNet	0.263	-

Table 1: GDI shared task 2017: Closed submission results.

The ten teams who competed in the first GDI challenge applied different computational methods to approach the task. These include linear SVM classifiers (Çöltekin and Rama, 2017; Bestgen, 2017), string kernels (Ionescu and Butnaru, 2017), Naive Bayes classifiers (Barbaresi, 2017), and SVM ensembles (Malmasi and Zampieri, 2017b), which achieved the first place in 2017. For this reason, this is the approach we apply in our GDI_identification system.

3 Data

In this paper we used only the dataset provided by the GDI organizers. The dataset is part of the ArchiMob corpus (Samardžić et al., 2016).[1] It contains transcripts of interviews with speakers from Basel (BS), Bern (BE), Lucerne (LU), and Zurich (ZH). The interviews have been transcribed using the 'Schwyzertütschi Dialäktschrift' system (Dieth, 1986).

The evaluation was divided into two tracks. In the first of them organizers provided participants with a test set containing the four aforementioned dialects included in the training set. In the second track they provided a test set containing the four dialects plus a 'surprise' dialect not included in the training set. We opted to participate only in the first track which contained only previously 'seen' dialects.

The dataset comprise nearly 25,000 instances divided in training, development, and test partitions as presented in Table 2.

Partition	Instances
Training	14,647
Development	4,659
Test	5,543
Total	**24,849**

Table 2: Instances in the GDI dataset 2018.

4 Methodology

The system that we propose for the GDI shared task consists of an ensemble of classifiers, namely SVMs. In this approach, we employ the methodology proposed by Malmasi and Dras (2015).

Ensembles of classifiers are deemed useful when there are disagreements between the comprising classifiers, which can use different features, training data, algorithms or parameters. The scope of the ensemble is to combine the results of the classifiers in such a way that the overall performance is improved

---

[1]http://www.spur.uzh.ch/en/departments/research/textgroup/ArchiMob.html

over the individual performances of the classifiers. Ensembles have proven useful in various tasks, such as complex word identification (Malmasi et al., 2016a) and grammatical error diagnosis (Xiang et al., 2015).

To distinguish the classifiers, we employ a different type of features for each of them. After obtaining predictions from each classifier, they need to be combined, to obtain the final predictions of the ensemble. To implement this system we used the Scikit-learn (Pedregosa et al., 2011) library. For the individual classifiers, we used LinearSVC,[2] an SVM implementation based on the Liblinear library (Fan et al., 2008), with a linear kernel. For the ensemble, we used the VotingClassifier,[3] with a majority rule fusion method: for each instance, the class that has been predicted by the majority of the classifiers is considered the final prediction of the ensemble. When there are ties, this implementation chooses the final prediction based on the ascending sort order of all labels.

4.1 Features

Each classifier from the ensemble uses one of the following features with TF-IDF weighting:

- Character n-grams, with n in $\{1, ..., 8\}$;

- Word n-grams, with n in $\{1, 2, 3\}$;

- Word k-skip bigrams, with k in $\{1, 2, 3\}$.

We obtain, thus, 14 classifiers. Training the individual classifiers, we achieve the results reported in Table 3. The features that lead to the best results are character 4-grams. The SVM using these features obtains 0.621 F1 score during our evaluation on the development dataset. In Table 4 we report the most informative character 4-grams for each class.

Feature	F1 (macro)
Character 1-grams	0.349
Character 2-grams	0.569
Character 3-grams	0.618
Character 4-grams	**0.621**
Character 5-grams	0.604
Character 6-grams	0.583
Character 7-grams	0.555
Character 8-grams	0.509
Word 1-grams	0.617
Word 2-grams	0.529
Word 3-grams	0.381
Word 1-skip bigrams	0.532
Word 2-skip bigrams	0.541
Word 3-skip bigrams	0.544

Table 3: Classification F1 score for individual classifiers on the development dataset.

To improve the performance of the SVM classifier using character 4-grams as features, we built various ensembles and performed a grid search with the purpose of determining the optimal value for the SVM regularization parameter C. We searched in $\{10^{-3}, ..., 10^{3}\}$ and obtained the optimal value 1. Experimenting with different classifiers as part of the ensemble, we determined the optimal feature combination to be character n-grams with n in $\{2, 3, 4, 5\}$. This ensemble obtained 0.638 F1 score on the development dataset.

---

[2]http://scikit-learn.org/stable/modules/generated/sklearn.svm.LinearSVC.html
[3]http://scikit-learn.org/stable/modules/generated/sklearn.ensemble.VotingClassifier.html

Class	Most Informative Features
BE	| näc| aus |seit|nei |gsee| ein| ds | aus|hei | hei|
BS	| uns|aabe| kha|rlig| kho| äu | häi| dr |häi | net|
LU	| sen| hem| gch|ech | oü | hai|gcha|hend|ond | hen|
ZH	|maal|zwäi|deet|änn |dän | dän| hät|dänn|hät | näd|

Table 4: Top 10 most informative character 4-grams for each class.

5 Results

We submitted a single run for the GDI task for the official evaluation. The results of our system and of a random baseline (provided by the organizers) on the test dataset are reported in Table 5. The run that we submitted corresponds to our best performing SVM ensemble, comprising 4 classifiers, each using one of the following features: character n-grams with n in $\{2, 3, 4, 5\}$. Our system was ranked third, obtaining 0.6203 F1 score on the test set, significantly outperforming the random baseline, which obtained 0.2521 F1 score on the test set.

In the official evaluation, the ranking was made taking statistical significance into account, and thus our team ranked third. The best performing team obtained 0.685 F1 score on the test dataset.

System	F1 (macro)
Random Baseline	0.2521
SVM Ensemble	**0.6203**

Table 5: Results for the GDI shared task on the test dataset.

Looking at the confusion matrix of our system (see Figure 1), we notice that BS is identified correctly most often, while LU is at the opposite end, with the lowest number of correctly classified instances. Out of the misclassified instances, we noticed that LU sentences are very often identified as BE.

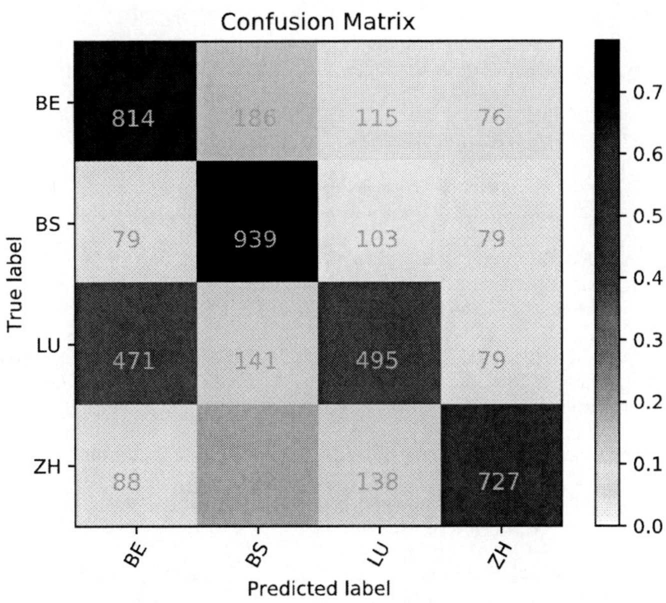

Figure 1: Confusion matrix for the SVM ensemble on the GDI shared task. The four Swiss German dialects are abbreviated as follows: Bern (BE), Basel (BS), Lucerne (LU) and Zurich (ZH).

6 Conclusion

In this paper we presented the GDI_identification entry for the GDI shared task at VarDial 2018. We employed an ensemble of SVM classifiers, continuing our previous work in this direction (Ciobanu et al., 2017). We obtained 0.6203 F1 score on the test dataset, ranking third in the competition. We experimented with various character and word n-gram features, and obtained our best performance with an ensemble of four classifiers, each using a different group of features. A variation of this system has been submitted for the Indo-Aryan language identification (ILI) shared task at VarDial 2018 (Ciobanu et al., 2018), achieving good performance, ranking third out of eight teams.

As future work, we intend to improve our ensemble implementation and to experiment with other features as well as in Bestgen (2017), in order to improve the performance of our system.

Acknowledgements

We would like to thank the GDI organizers, Yves Scherrer and Tanja Samardžić, for organizing the shared task and for replying promptly to our questions.

We further thank the anonymous reviewers and Marcos Zampieri for the feedback and suggestions provided.

References

Ahmed Ali, Stephan Vogel, and Steve Renals. 2017. Speech Recognition Challenge in the Wild: Arabic MGB-3. *arXiv preprint arXiv:1709.07276*.

Adrien Barbaresi. 2017. Discriminating between Similar Languages using Weighted Subword Features. In *Proceedings of the Fourth Workshop on NLP for Similar Languages, Varieties and Dialects (VarDial)*, pages 184–189, Valencia, Spain, April.

Yves Bestgen. 2017. Improving the Character Ngram Model for the DSL Task with BM25 Weighting and Less Frequently Used Feature Sets. In *Proceedings of the Fourth Workshop on NLP for Similar Languages, Varieties and Dialects (VarDial)*, pages 115–123, Valencia, Spain, April.

Çağrı Çöltekin and Taraka Rama. 2017. Tübingen System in VarDial 2017 Shared Task: Experiments with Language Identification and Cross-lingual Parsing. In *Proceedings of the Fourth Workshop on NLP for Similar Languages, Varieties and Dialects (VarDial)*, pages 146–155, Valencia, Spain, April.

Alina Maria Ciobanu and Liviu P Dinu. 2016. A Computational Perspective on the Romanian Dialects. In *Proceedings of Language Resources and Evalution (LREC)*.

Alina Maria Ciobanu, Marcos Zampieri, Shervin Malmasi, and Liviu P Dinu. 2017. Including Dialects and Language Varieties in Author Profiling. *Working Notes of CLEF*.

Alina Maria Ciobanu, Marcos Zampieri, Shervin Malmasi, Santanu Pal, and Liviu P. Dinu. 2018. Discriminating between Indo-Aryan Languages Using SVM Ensembles. In *Proceedings of the Fifth Workshop on NLP for Similar Languages, Varieties and Dialects (VarDial)*, Santa Fe, USA.

Simon Clematide and Peter Makarov. 2017. CLUZH at VarDial GDI 2017: Testing a Variety of Machine Learning Tools for the Classification of Swiss German Dialects. In *Proceedings of the Fourth Workshop on NLP for Similar Languages, Varieties and Dialects (VarDial)*, pages 170–177, Valencia, Spain, April.

Eugen Dieth. 1986. *Schwyzertütschi Dialäktschrift*. Sauerländer, Aarau, 2 edition.

Rong-En Fan, Kai-Wei Chang, Cho-Jui Hsieh, Xiang-Rui Wang, and Chih-Jen Lin. 2008. LIBLINEAR: A Library for Large Linear Classification. *Journal of Machine Learning Research*, 9:1871–1874.

Pablo Gamallo, Jose Ramom Pichel, and Iñaki Alegria. 2017. A Perplexity-Based Method for Similar Languages Discrimination. In *Proceedings of the Fourth Workshop on NLP for Similar Languages, Varieties and Dialects (VarDial)*, pages 109–114, Valencia, Spain, April.

Abualsoud Hanani, Aziz Qaroush, and Stephen Taylor. 2017. Identifying Dialects with Textual and Acoustic Cues. In *Proceedings of the Fourth Workshop on NLP for Similar Languages, Varieties and Dialects (VarDial)*, pages 93–101, Valencia, Spain, April.

Nora Hollenstein and Noëmi Aepli. 2015. A Resource for Natural Language Processing of Swiss German Dialects. In *Proceedings of GSCL*.

Radu Tudor Ionescu and Andrei Butnaru. 2017. Learning to Identify Arabic and German Dialects using Multiple Kernels. In *Proceedings of the Fourth Workshop on NLP for Similar Languages, Varieties and Dialects (VarDial)*, pages 200–209, Valencia, Spain, April.

Tommi Jauhiainen, Marco Lui, Marcos Zampieri, Timothy Baldwin, and Krister Lindén. 2018. Automatic Language Identification in Texts: A Survey. *arXiv preprint arXiv:1804.08186*.

Marco Lui and Paul Cook. 2013. Classifying English Documents by National Dialect. In *Proceedings of the Australasian Language Technology Association Workshop 2013 (ALTA)*, pages 5–15.

Shervin Malmasi and Mark Dras. 2015. Language Identification using Classifier Ensembles. In *Proceedings of the Joint Workshop on Language Technology for Closely Related Languages, Varieties and Dialects (LT4VarDial)*, pages 35–43, Hissar, Bulgaria.

Shervin Malmasi and Marcos Zampieri. 2017a. Arabic Dialect Identification Using iVectors and ASR Transcripts. In *Proceedings of the Fourth Workshop on NLP for Similar Languages, Varieties and Dialects (VarDial)*, pages 178–183, Valencia, Spain, April.

Shervin Malmasi and Marcos Zampieri. 2017b. German Dialect Identification in Interview Transcriptions. In *Proceedings of the Fourth Workshop on NLP for Similar Languages, Varieties and Dialects (VarDial)*, pages 164–169, Valencia, Spain, April.

Shervin Malmasi, Mark Dras, and Marcos Zampieri. 2016a. LTG at SemEval-2016 Task 11: Complex Word Identification with Classifier Ensembles. In *Proceedings of SemEval*.

Shervin Malmasi, Marcos Zampieri, Nikola Ljubešić, Preslav Nakov, Ahmed Ali, and Jörg Tiedemann. 2016b. Discriminating between Similar Languages and Arabic Dialect Identification: A Report on the Third DSL Shared Task. In *Proceedings of the 3rd Workshop on Language Technology for Closely Related Languages, Varieties and Dialects (VarDial)*, Osaka, Japan.

Fabian Pedregosa, Gaël Varoquaux, Alexandre Gramfort, Vincent Michel, Bertrand Thirion, Olivier Grisel, Mathieu Blondel, Peter Prettenhofer, Ron Weiss, Vincent Dubourg, et al. 2011. Scikit-learn: Machine Learning in Python. *Journal of Machine Learning Research*, 12:2825–2830.

Francisco Rangel, Paolo Rosso, Martin Potthast, and Benno Stein. 2017. Overview of the 5th Author Profiling Task at PAN 2017: Gender and Language Variety Identification in Twitter. *Working Notes Papers of the CLEF*.

Tanja Samardžić, Yves Scherrer, and Elvira Glaser. 2016. ArchiMob–A Corpus of Spoken Swiss German. In *Proceedings of the Language Resources and Evaluation (LREC)*, pages 4061–4066, Portoroz, Slovenia).

Yves Scherrer and Owen Rambow. 2010. Word-based Dialect Identification with Georeferenced Rules. In *Proceedings of EMNLP*.

Christoph Tillmann, Saab Mansour, and Yaser Al-Onaizan. 2014. Improved Sentence-level Arabic Dialect Classification. In *Proceedings of the First Workshop on Applying NLP Tools to Similar Languages, Varieties and Dialects (VarDial)*, pages 110–119.

Yang Xiang, Xiaolong Wang, Wenying Han, and Qinghua Hong. 2015. Chinese Grammatical Error Diagnosis Using Ensemble Learning. In *Proceedings of the 2nd Workshop on Natural Language Processing Techniques for Educational Applications*, pages 99–104.

Marcos Zampieri, Liling Tan, Nikola Ljubešić, and Jörg Tiedemann. 2014. A Report on the DSL Shared Task 2014. In *Proceedings of the First Workshop on Applying NLP Tools to Similar Languages, Varieties and Dialects (VarDial)*, pages 58–67, Dublin, Ireland.

Marcos Zampieri, Liling Tan, Nikola Ljubešić, Jörg Tiedemann, and Preslav Nakov. 2015. Overview of the DSL Shared Task 2015. In *Proceedings of the Joint Workshop on Language Technology for Closely Related Languages, Varieties and Dialects (LT4VarDial)*, pages 1–9, Hissar, Bulgaria.

Marcos Zampieri, Shervin Malmasi, Octavia-Maria Sulea, and Liviu P Dinu. 2016. A Computational Approach to the Study of Portuguese Newspapers Published in Macau. In *Proceedings of Workshop on Natural Language Processing Meets Journalism (NLPMJ)*.

Marcos Zampieri, Shervin Malmasi, Nikola Ljubešić, Preslav Nakov, Ahmed Ali, Jörg Tiedemann, Yves Scherrer, and Noëmi Aepli. 2017. Findings of the VarDial Evaluation Campaign 2017. In *Proceedings of the Fourth Workshop on NLP for Similar Languages, Varieties and Dialects (VarDial)*, Valencia, Spain.

Marcos Zampieri, Shervin Malmasi, Preslav Nakov, Ahmed Ali, Suwon Shon, James Glass, Yves Scherrer, Tanja Samardžić, Nikola Ljubešić, Jörg Tiedemann, Chris van der Lee, Stefan Grondelaers, Nelleke Oostdijk, Antal van den Bosch, Ritesh Kumar, Bornini Lahiri, and Mayank Jain. 2018. Language Identification and Morphosyntactic Tagging: The Second VarDial Evaluation Campaign. In *Proceedings of the Fifth Workshop on NLP for Similar Languages, Varieties and Dialects (VarDial)*, Santa Fe, USA.

Author Index

Association for Computational Linguistics
209 N. Eighth Street
Stroudsburg, Pennsylvania 18360

ISBN 978-1-5108-6916-5